T0137410

The Springer Series on Challenges in Machine Learning

Series editors

Hugo Jair Escalante, Astrofisica Optica y Electronica, INAOE, Puebla, Mexico

Isabelle Guyon, ChaLearn, Berkeley, CA, USA

Sergio Escalera ⓘ , University of Barcelona, Barcelona, Spain

The books in this innovative series collect papers written in the context of successful competitions in machine learning. They also include analyses of the challenges, tutorial material, dataset descriptions, and pointers to data and software. Together with the websites of the challenge competitions, they offer a complete teaching toolkit and a valuable resource for engineers and scientists.

More information about this series at http://www.springer.com/series/15602

Isabelle Guyon • Alexander Statnikov
Berna Bakir Batu

Editors

Cause Effect Pairs in Machine Learning

 Springer

Editors
Isabelle Guyon
Team TAU - CNRS, INRIA
Université Paris Sud
Université Paris Saclay
Orsay France

ChaLearn, Berkeley
CA, USA

Berna Bakir Batu
University of Paris-Sud
Paris-Saclay, Paris, France

Alexander Statnikov
SoFi
San Francisco, CA, USA

ISSN 2520-131X   ISSN 2520-1328   (electronic)
The Springer Series on Challenges in Machine Learning
ISBN 978-3-030-21812-6   ISBN 978-3-030-21810-2   (eBook)
https://doi.org/10.1007/978-3-030-21810-2

This Springer imprint is published by the registered company Springer Nature Switzerland AG.
The registered company address is: Gewerbestrasse 11, 6330 Cham, Switzerland

Foreword

The problem of distinguishing cause from effect caught my attention, thanks to the *ChaLearn Cause-Effect Pairs Challenge* organized by Isabelle Guyon and her collaborators in 2013. The seminal contribution of this competition was casting the cause-effect problem ("Does altitude cause a change in atmospheric pressure, or vice versa?") as a binary classification problem, to be tackled by machine learning algorithms. By having access to enough pairs of variables labeled with their causal relation, participants designed distributional features and algorithms able to reveal "causal footprints" from observational data. This was a striking realization: Had we discovered some sort of "lost causal signal" lurking in data so far ignored in machine learning practice?

Although limited in scope, the cause-effect problem sparked significant interest in the machine learning community. The use of machine learning techniques to discover causality synergized these two research areas, which historically struggled to get along, and while the cause-effect problem exemplified "machine learning helping causality," we are now facing the pressing need for having "causality help machine learning." Indeed, current machine learning models are untrustworthy when dealing with data obtained under test conditions (or interventions) that differ from those seen during training. Examples of these problematic situations include domain adaptation, learning under multiple environments, reinforcement learning, and adversarial learning. Fortunately, the long sought-after partnership between machine learning and causality continues to forge slowly but steadily, as can be seen from the bar graph below illustrating the frequency of submissions related to causality at the NeurIPS conference (a premier machine learning conference).

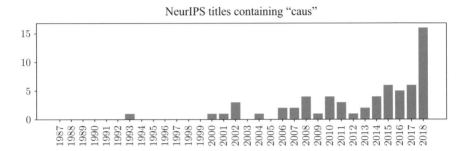

NeurIPS titles containing "caus"

This book is a great reference for those interested in the cause-effect problem. Chapter 1 by Dominik Janzing is an excellent motivation that borrows ideas and intuitions matured over a decade of expertise. Chapter 2 by Isabelle Guyon deepens into the conundrum of evaluating causal hypotheses from observational data. Chapters 3 and 4, led by Olivier Goudet and Diviyan Kalainathan, are fantastic surveys on cause-effect methods, divided into generative and discriminative models, respectively. The first part of this book closes with two important extensions of the cause-effect problem: Nicolas Doremus et al. discuss time series in Chap. 5, while Frederick Eberhardt explores the multivariable case in Chap. 6. The second part of the book, *Selected Readings*, discusses the results of the cause-effect pairs competitions (Chap. 6), as well as a selection of algorithms to address this problem (Chaps. 8–14).

I believe that the robustness and invariance properties of causation will be key to remove the elephant from the room (the "identically and independently distributed" assumption) and move towards a new generation of causal machine learning algorithms. This quest begins in the following pages.

Paris, France   David Lopez-Paz
April 2019

Preface

Discovering causal relationships from observational data will become increasingly important in data science with the increasing amount of available data, as a means of detecting the potential triggers in epidemiology, social sciences, economy, biology, medicine, and other sciences. Although causal hypotheses made from observations need further evaluation by experiments, they are still very important to reduce costs and burden by guiding large-scale experimental designs. In 2013, we conducted a challenge on the problem of cause-effect pairs, which pushed the state-of-the-art considerably, revealing that the joint distribution of two variables can be scrutinized by machine learning algorithms to reveal the possible existence of a "causal mechanism," in the sense that the values of one variable may have been generated from the values of the other. This milestone event has stimulated a lot of research in this area for the past few years. The ambition of this book is to provide both tutorial material on the state-of-the-art on cause-effect pairs and expose the reader to more advanced material, with a collection of selected papers, some of which are reprinted from the JMLR special topic on "large-scale experimental design and the inference of causal mechanisms." Supplemental material includes videos, slides, and code that can be found on the workshop website.

In the first part of this book, six tutorial chapters are provided. In Chap. 1, an introduction to the cause-effect problem is given for the simplest but nontrivial case where the causal relationships are predicted from the observations of only two variables. In this chapter, the reader gains a better understanding of the causal discovery problem as well as an intuition about its complexity. Common methods and recent achievements are explored besides pointing out some misconceptions. In Chap. 2, the benchmarking problem of causal inference from observational data is discussed, and a methodology is provided. In this chapter, the focus is the methods that produce a coefficient, called causation coefficient, that is used to decide direction of causal relationship. By this way, the cause-effect problem becomes a usual classification problem, which can be evaluated by classification accuracy metrics. A new notion of "identifiability," which defines a particular data generation process by bounding type I and type II errors, is also proposed as a validation metric. In Chap. 3, the reader dives into algorithms that solve the cause-effect pair problem by modeling the data generating process. Such methods allow gaining not only a clue about the causal direction but also information about the mechanism itself, making causal discovery less of a black box decision process. In Chap. 4, discriminative algorithms are explored. A contrario, such algorithms do not attempt to reverse engineer the data generating process; they merely classify the empirical joint distribution of two variables X and Y (a scatter plot) as being and X cause Y or a Y cause X (or neither). While throughout Chaps. 1–4, the emphasis is on cross-sectional data (without explicit reference to time), in Chap. 5, the authors investigate the causal discovery methods for time series. One interesting contribution compared to the older approaches of Granger causality is the introduction of instantaneous causal relationships. Finally, in Chap. 6, the authors present research going beyond the treatment of two variables, including triplet and more. This put in perspective the effort of the rest of the book, which focuses on two variables only, and reminds the reader of the limitations of the analyses limited to two variables, particularly when it comes to the treatment of the problem of confounding.

In the second part of the book, we compile articles related to the 2013 ChaLearn Cause-Effect Pairs challenges[1] including articles that were part of the proceedings of the NIPS 2013 workshop on causality and the JMLR special topic on large-scale experimental design and the inference of causal mechanisms. The cause-effect pairs challenge, described in Chap. 7, provided a new point of view to the problem of causal modeling by reformulating it as a classification problem. Its purpose was attributing causes to effects by defining a causation coefficient between variables such that positive and negative large values indicate causal relation in one or the other direction, whereas the values close to zero indicates no causal relationship. The participants were provided with hundreds of pairs from different domains, such as ecology, medicine, climatology, engineering, etc., as well as artificial data for all of which the ground truth is known (causally related, dependent but not causally related or independent pairs). Because of problem setting, the methods based on conditional independence tests were not applicable. Inspired by the starting kit provided by Ben Hamner at Kaggle, the majority of the participants engineered features of the joint empirical distribution of pairs of variables then applied standard classification methods, such as gradient boosting.

From Chap. 8, the approaches used by the top participants of the challenges and their results are given in the second part as selected readings. In Chap. 8, the authors perform an extensive comparison of methods on data of the challenge, including a method that they propose based on Gaussianity measures that fare well. The winner of the challenge, the team *ProtoML* (Chap. 10), proposes a feature extraction method which takes extensive number of algorithms and functions as an input parameters to build many models and extracts features by computing their goodness of fit in many different ways. The method achieves 0.84 accuracy for artificial data and 0.70 accuracy for real data. If the features are extracted without human intervention, the method is prone to create redundant features. It

---

[1] http://www.causality.inf.ethz.ch/cause-effect.php.

also increases computational time since about 9000 features are calculated from the input parameters. There is a trade-off between computational time/complexity and automated feature extraction. The second ranked participant, *jarfo* (Chap. 12), concentrates on conditional distributions of pairs of random variables, without enforcing a strict independence between the cause and the conditional distribution of effect. He defines a Conditional Distribution Score (CDS) measuring variability, based on the assumption that for a given mechanism, there should be a similarity among the conditional distributions of effect, regardless of causal distributions. Other features of *jarfo* are based on information theoretic measures (e.g., entropy, mutual information, etc.) and variability measures (e.g., standard deviation, skewness, kurtosis, etc.). The algorithm achieves 0.83 and 0.69 accuracy for artificial and real data, respectively. It has comparable results with the algorithm proposed by the winner in terms of predictive performance, with a better run time. It also performs better on novel data, based on post-challenge analyses we report in Chap. 7. The team *HiDLoN*, having the third place in the challenge (Chap. 11), defines a causation coefficient as the difference in (estimated) probability of either causal direction. They consider two binary classifiers using information theoretic features, each classifying one causal direction versus all other relations. By this way, a score representing a causation coefficient can be defined by taking the difference of the probabilities for each sample to be belonging to a certain class. Using one classifier for each causal direction makes possible to evaluate feature importance for each case. Another participant, *mouse*, having fifth place, evaluates how features are ranked based on the variable types by using different subsets of training data (Chap. 13). He defines 13 groups of features resulting in 211 features in total and determine their importance to estimate causal relation. Polynomial regression and information theoretical features are the most important features for all cases; in particular polynomial regression is the best feature to predict causal direction when the type of variables is both numerical, whereas it is information theoretical features if the cause is categorical and the effect is numerical variables. Similarly, the method proposed by Bontempi (Chap. 9) defines features based on some statistical dependency, such as quantiles of marginal and conditional distributions and learn mapping from features to causal directions. In addition to having only pairs of variables to predict their causal structure, He also extends his solution for n-variate distributions. In this case, features are defined as a set of descriptors to define dependency between the variables, which are the elements of Markov blankets of two variables of interest. Finally, the last chapter (Chap. 14) provides a complementary perspective opening up to the treatment of more than two variables with a more conventional Markov blanket approach.

Berkeley, CA, USA   Isabelle Guyon
San Francisco, CA, USA   Alexander Statnikov
Paris, France   Berna Bakir Batu
January 2019

Acknowledgments

The initial impulse of the cause-effect pair challenge came from the cause-effect pair task proposed in the causality "potluck" challenge by Joris Mooij, Dominik Janzing, and Bernhard Schölkopf, from the Max Planck Institute for Intelligent Systems, who contributed an initial dataset and several algorithms. Alexander Statnikov and Mikael Henaff of New York University provided additional data and baseline software. The challenge was organized by ChaLearn and coordinated by Isabelle Guyon. The first round of the challenge was hosted by Kaggle, and we received a lot of help from Ben Hamner. The second round of the challenge (with code submission) was sponsored by Microsoft and hosted on the Codalab platform, with the help of Evelyne Viegas and her team. Many people who reviewed protocols, tested the sample code, and challenged the website are gratefully acknowledged: Marc Boullé (Orange, France), Léon Bottou (Facebook), Hugo Jair Escalante (IANOE, Mexico), Frederick Eberhardt (WUSL, USA), Seth Flaxman (Carnegie Mellon University, USA), Mikael Henaff (New York University, USA), Patrick Hoyer (University of Helsinki, Finland), Dominik Janzing (Max Planck Institute for Intelligent Systems, Germany), Richard Kennaway (University of East Anglia, UK), Vincent Lemaire (Orange, France), Joris Mooij (Faculty of Science, Nijmegen, Netherlands), Jonas Peters (ETH Zuerich, Switzerland), Florin Popescu (Fraunhofer Institute, Berlin, Germany), Bernhard Schölkopf (Max Planck Institute for Intelligent Systems, Germany), Peter Spirtes (Carnegie Mellon University, USA), Alexander Statnikov (New York University, USA), Ioannis Tsamardinos (University of Crete, Greece), Jianxin Yin (University of Pennsylvania, USA), and Kun Zhang (Max Planck Institute for Intelligent Systems, Germany). We would also like to thank the authors of software made publicly available that were included in the sample code: Povilas Daniušis, Arthur Gretton, Patrik O. Hoyer, Dominik Janzing, Antti Kerminen, Joris Mooij, Jonas Peters, Bernhard Schölkopf, Shohei Shimizu, Oliver Stegle, and Kun Zhang. We also thank the co-organizers of the NIPS 2013 workshop on causality (Large-Scale Experiment Design and Inference of Causal Mechanisms): Léon Bottou (Microsoft, USA), Isabelle Guyon (ChaLearn, USA), Bernhard Schölkopf (Max Planck Institute for Intelligent Systems, Germany), Alexander Statnikov (New York University, USA), and Evelyne Viegas (Microsoft, USA).

Contents

Contributors

Gianluca Bontempi Machine Learning Group, Computer Science Department, ULB, Université Libre de Bruxelles, Brussels, Belgium

Sebastiano Cattaruzzo Rovira i Virgili University, Tarragona, Spain

Diogo Moitinho de Almeida Google, Menlo Park, CA, USA

Nicolas Doremus IUSS Pavia, Pavia, Italy

Frederick Eberhardt Caltech, Pasadena, CA, USA

Maxime Flauder Machine Learning Group, Computer Science Department, ULB, Université Libre de Bruxelles, Brussels, Belgium

Josè A. R. Fonollosa Universitat Politécnica de Catalunya, Barcelona Tech. c/ Jordi Girona 1-3, Barcelona, Spain

Olivier Goudet Team TAU - CNRS, INRIA, Université Paris Sud, Université Paris Saclay, Orsay, France

Isabelle Guyon Team TAU - CNRS, INRIA, Université Paris Sud, Université Paris Saclay, Orsay, France

ChaLearn, Berkeley, CA, USA

Daniel Hernández-Lobato Universidad Autónoma de Madrid, Madrid, Spain

Dominik Janzing Amazon Development Center, Tübingen, Germany

Diviyan Kalainathan Team TAU - CNRS, INRIA, Université Paris Sud, Université Paris Saclay, Orsay, France

David Lopez-Paz Facebook AI Research, Paris, France

Simon Lucas University of Essex, Wivenhoe Park, Colchester, Essex, UK

School of Electronic Engineering and Computer Science, Queen Mary University of London, London, UK

Bram Minnaert ArcelorMittal, Ghent, Belgium

Alessio Moneta Sant'Anna School of Advanced Studies, Pisa, Italy

Pablo Morales-Mombiela Quantitative Risk Research, Madrid, Spain

Diego Perez University of Essex, Wivenhoe Park, Colchester, Essex, UK

School of Electronic Engineering and Computer Science, Queen Mary University of London, London, UK

Spyridon Samothrakis University of Essex, Wivenhoe Park, Colchester, Essex, UK

Michèle Sebag Team TAU – CNRS, INRIA, Université Paris Sud, Université Paris Saclay, Orsay, France

Alexander Statnikov SoFi, San Francisco, CA, USA

Eric V. Strobl Department of Biomedical Informatics, University of Pittsburgh School of Medicine, Pittsburgh, PA, USA

Alberto Suárez Universidad Autónoma de Madrid, Madrid, Spain

Shyam Visweswaran Department of Biomedical Informatics, University of Pittsburgh School of Medicine, Pittsburgh, PA, USA

Part I
Fundamentals

Chapter 1
The Cause-Effect Problem: Motivation, Ideas, and Popular Misconceptions

Dominik Janzing

1.1 The Cause-Effect Problem: Notation and Introduction

Telling cause from effect from purely observational data has been a challenge at the NIPS 2008 workshop on Causality. Let me first describe the scenario as follows:

> Given observations $(x_1, y_1), \ldots, (x_k, y_k)$ iid drawn from some distribution $P_{X,Y}$, infer whether X causes Y or Y causes X, given the promise that exactly one of these alternatives is true.

Here it is implicitly understood that there is no significant confounding, that is, that the observed statistical dependences between X and Y are due to the influence of one of the variables on the other one and not due to a third variable influencing both.[1] Assuming such a strict restriction for valid cause-effect pairs (which is certainly only approximately satisfied for empirical data) we can write structural

---

The major part of this work has been done in the author's spare time before he joined Amazon.

---

[1] If there is a known common cause Z that is observed, conditioning on fixed values of Z can in principle control for confounding, but if Z is high-dimensional there are serious limitation because the required sample size is exploding. Note that Chap. 2 of this book also considers the case of pure confounding as a third alternative (certainly for good reasons). Nevertheless I will later argue why I want to focus on the simple binary classification problem.

D. Janzing (✉)
Amazon Development Center, Tübingen, Germany
e-mail: janzind@amazon.com

© Springer Nature Switzerland AG 2019
I. Guyon et al. (eds.), *Cause Effect Pairs in Machine Learning*,
The Springer Series on Challenges in Machine Learning,
https://doi.org/10.1007/978-3-030-21810-2_1

equations (SEs), also called functional causal models (FCMs) [1] as follows. If the causal relation reads $X \to Y$, there exists an 'assignment' [2]

$$Y := f_Y(X, N_Y) \quad \text{with } N_Y \perp\!\!\!\perp X, \tag{1.1}$$

where N_Y is an unobserved noise term. Likewise, if the causal relation reads $Y \to X$, there exists an assignment

$$X := f_X(Y, N_X) \quad \text{with } N_X \perp\!\!\!\perp Y, \tag{1.2}$$

where N_X is an unobserved noise term. The fact that Eqs. (1.1) and (1.2) are structural equations, implies that they formalize causal relations rather than only describing a model that reproduces the observed joint probability distribution correctly. After all, any joint distribution $P_{X,Y}$ can be generated either way, via a model of the form Eqs. (1.1) and (1.2), see Proposition 4.1 in [2].

To be more explicit, reading (1.1) as *structural equation* implies that the value Y would have attained, if X were set to x by an external intervention, is given by the variable

$$Y^{do(X=x)} = f(x, N_Y). \tag{1.3}$$

Since the right hand sides of (1.1) and (1.2) also describe the observational conditionals, they imply

$$P_Y^{do(X=x)} = P_{Y|X=x}, \tag{1.4}$$

and

$$P_X^{do(Y=y)} = P_{X|Y=y}, \tag{1.5}$$

respectively. Hence, interventional probabilities can be computed from the joint distribution once the causal direction is known. In contrast, the structural equations (1.1) and (1.2) are not uniquely determined by joint distribution and causal direction. They entail additional *counterfactual* statements about which value Y or X, respectively, would have attained in every *particular instance* for which the values of the noise are known, given that X or Y (respectively) had been set to some specific value (see, e.g., [1] and 3.3 in [2]). Although the cause-effect problem, as it has usually been phrased, does not entail the harder task of inferring the structural equations (1.1) and (1.2), several approaches to cause-effect inference are based on fitting structural equations. Additive noise based causal inference [3, 4], for instance, amounts to fitting regressions

$$\hat{f}_Y(x) := \mathbf{E}[Y|x] \tag{1.6}$$

and

$$\hat{f}_X(Y) := \mathbf{E}[X|y] \qquad (1.7)$$

and deciding $X \to Y$ whenever the regression residual $Y - \hat{f}_Y(X)$ is independent of X, provided that the regression residual $X - \hat{f}_X(Y)$ for the converse direction is not independent of Y. Then, (1.1) turns into

$$Y = \hat{f}_Y(X) + N_Y \quad \text{with } N_Y \perp\!\!\!\perp X. \qquad (1.8)$$

Consequently, for each particular instance, the value n_Y of N_Y can be easily computed from the observed pair (x, y) due to

$$n_Y = y - \hat{f}_Y(x). \qquad (1.9)$$

This entails the counterfactual statement 'Y would have attained the value $y' := y + \hat{f}_Y(x') - \hat{f}_Y(x)$ instead of y if an intervention had changed X from x to x'. The inference method 'additive noise' thus provides counterfactual statements for free—regardless of whether one is interested in them or not. Similar statements also hold for the post-nonlinear model [5], which reads $Y = g_Y(\hat{f}_Y(X) + N_Y)$ with some possibly non-linear function g_Y.

The chapter is structured as follows. Section 1.2 motivates the cause-effect problem in the context of tasks that may occur more often in practice. Section 1.3 briefly reviews the principles behind common approaches. Section 1.4 provides a critical discussion of human intuition about the cause-effect problem. Finally, Sect. 1.5 sketches the relation to the thermodynamic arrow of time to argue for accepting the cause-effect problem also as a *physics* problem.

Note that finite sample issues are not in the focus of any of the sections. This should by no means mistaken as ignoring their importance. I just wanted to avoid that problems that are unique to *causal* learning gets hidden behind problems that occur everywhere in statistics and machine learning.

1.2   Why Looking at This "Toy Problem"?

In the era of 'Big Data' one would rather expect challenges that address problems related with high dimensions, that is, a large number of variables. It thus seems surprising to put so much focus on a causal inference problem that focuses on two variables only. One reason is that for causality it can sometimes be helpful to look at a domain where the fundamental problem of inferring causality does not interfere too much with purely *statistical* problems that dominate high dimensional problems. 'Small data' problems show more clearly how much remains to be explored even regarding simple questions on causality.

1.2.1 Easier to Handle Than Detection of Confounders

The cause-effect problem became surprisingly popular after 2008, e.g., [3, 5–9]. Nevertheless, the majority of causal problems I have seen from applications are *not* cause-effect problems (although cause-effect problems do also occur in practice). After all, for two statistically dependent variables X, Y, Reichenbach's Principle of Common Cause describes *three* possible scenarios (which may also interfere) in Fig. 1.1.

(1) X causes Y, (3) Y causes X, or (2) there is a third variable Z causing X and Y. If X precedes Y in time, (3) can be excluded and the distinction between (1) and (2) remains to be made. Probably the most important case in practice, however, is the case where X is causing Y and in addition there is a large number of confounding variables Z_j (or one high-dimensional variable Z if this view is preferred) of which only some are observed. Consider, for instance, the statistical relation between genotype and phenotype in biology: It is known that Single Nucleotid Polymorphisms (SNPs) influence the phenotypes of plant and animals, but given the correlation between a SNP and a phenotype, it is unclear whether the SNP at hand influences the respective phenotype or whether it is only correlated with another SNP causing the phenotype.

Even the toy problem of distinguishing between case (1) and (2), given that they don't interfere, seems harder than the cause-effect problem. Although there are also some ideas to address this task [10–13], the following fundamental problem should be mentioned. Consider a scenario where the hidden common cause Z influences X by a mechanism where X becomes just a copy of Z with some small error probability. In the limit of zero error probability, $P_{X,Y}$ and $P_{Z,Y}$ have the same distribution, although X, Y are related by $X \leftarrow \cdot \rightarrow Y$ (even in the limit of zero error probability, interventions on X have no effect on Y) while Z and Y are related by $Z \rightarrow Y$. One may object that also $X \rightarrow Y$ and $Y \rightarrow X$ become indistinguishable when the causal mechanism is just a copy operation. However, in the later case, observing $P_{X,Y}$ already tells us that the causal relation is deterministic, while the deterministic relation between Z and X cannot be detected from $P_{X,Y}$. It is then impossible to distinguish between the cases (1) and (2) in Reichenbach's principle. In the following scenario it is even pointless: if Z is some physical quantity and X the value obtained in a measurement of Z (with some measurement error) one would certainly identify X with the quantity Z itself and consider it as the cause of Y—in contradiction to the outcome of a hypothetical powerful causal inference algorithm

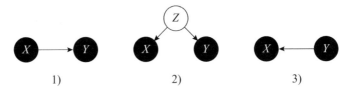

Fig. 1.1 The three types of causal explanations of observed dependences between X and Y in Reichenbach's principle

that recognizes $P_{X,Y}$ as obtained by a common-cause scenario. Due to all these obstacles, it seems reasonable to start with the cause-effect problem as a challenging toy problem, being aware of the fact that it is not the most common problem that data science needs to address in applications (although it does, of course, also occur in practice).

1.2.2   Falsifiable Causal Statements Are Needed

Accounting for the fact that the three types of causal relations in Reichenbach's Principle typically interfere in practice, one could argue that a more useful causal inference task consists in the distinction between the five possible acyclic graphs shown in Fig. 1.2 (formally, there are, more possible DAGs, but they are irrelevant for our purpose. We only care about Z if it influences both observed variables X and Y).

Thinking about which of the alternatives most often occur in practice one may speculate that (2), (4), and (5) are the main candidates because entirely unconfounded relations are probably rare. A causal inference algorithm that always infers the existence of a hidden common cause is maybe never wrong—it is just useless unless it further specifies *to what extent* the dependences between X and Y can be attributed to the common cause and to what extent there is a causal influence from X to Y or from Y to X that explains part of the dependences. The DAGs (1), (2), and (3), imply the following post-interventional distributions

$$
\begin{array}{llll}
1) & P_Y^{do(X=x)} = P_{Y|X=x} & \text{and} & P_X^{do(Y=y)} = P_X \\
2) & P_Y^{do(X=x)} = P_Y & \text{and} & P_X^{do(Y=y)} = P_X \\
3) & P_Y^{do(X=x)} = P_Y & \text{and} & P_X^{do(Y=Y)} = P_{X|Y=y}.
\end{array}
\tag{1.10}
$$

In contrast, the DAGs (4) and (5) do not imply any equations for any interventional conditionals without further specification of structural equations or the joint distribution $P_{X,Y,Z}$. This raises the question of how to construct an experiment that could disprove these hypotheses. After all, falsifiability of causal hypotheses is, according to Karl Popper [14], a necessary criterion for their scientific content. Accordingly, one can argue that (4) and (5) only define causal hypotheses with scientific content when these DAGs come with further specifications of parameters, while the DAGs (1)–(3) are causal hypotheses in their own right due to their strong implications

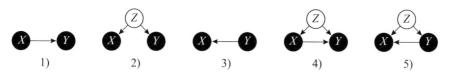

1)   2)   3)   4)   5)

Fig. 1.2   Five acyclic causal structures obtained by combining the three cases in Reichenbach's principle

for interventional probabilities. Maybe discussions about which causal DAG is 'the true causal structure' in the past have sometimes blurred the fact that scientific hypotheses need to be specific enough to entail falsifiable consequences (at the cost of being oversimplified) rather than insisting in finding 'the true' causal graph.

1.2.3 Binary Classification Problems Admit Simple Benchmarking

Evaluating causal discovery methods is a non-trivial challenge in particular if the task is—as it traditionally was the case since the 1990s—to infer a causal DAG with n nodes. On the one hand, it is hard to find data sets with generally accepted DAGs as ground truth. Despite the abundance of interesting data sets from economy, biology, psychology, etc, discussions of the underlying causal structure usually requires domain knowledge of experts, and then these experts need not agree. Further, even worse, given the 'true' DAG, it remains unclear how to assess the performance if the inferred DAG coincides with the 'true' DAG with respect to some arrows, but disagrees regarding other edges: Should one count an arrow $X_i \to X_j$ as wrong if 'the true DAG' contains no edge between X_i and X_j—without asking whether the inferred arrow describes a weak or strong influence?[2] The cause-effect problem does not suffer from these problems because the two options read: the statistical dependences between X and Y are either entirely due to the influence of X on Y or entirely due to the influence of Y on X. In Sect. 1.2.2 we have already explained that both hypotheses are easy to test if interventions can be made. Assessing the performance in a binary classification problem amounts to a straightforward counting of errors. The problem of finding data sets where the ground truth does not require expert knowledge remains non-trivial. However, discussing ground truth for the causal relation between just two variables is much easier than for more complex causal relations and Ref. [17] is an example on how to perform extensive evaluations of cause effect inference algorithms using empirical data from the database [18] as well as simulated data.

1.2.4 Relations to Recent Foundational Questions in Theoretical Physics

Since causes precede there effects it is natural to conjecture that statistical asymmetries between cause and effect [19] are related to asymmetries between past and

---

[2]Of course, causal inference algorithms like PC [15] do not infer the strength of the arrow. However, given a hypothetical causal DAG on the nodes $X_1, \ldots, X_n$, the influence of X_i on X_j is determined by the joint distribution $P_{X_1,\ldots,X_n}$ and the strength of this influence becomes just a matter of definition [16].

Fig. 1.3 There exist statistical dependences between two quantum systems A, B that uniquely indicate whether they were obtained by the influence of one on the other (left) or by a common cause (right). In the latter case, the joint statistics of the two systems is described by a positive operator on the joint Hilbert space, while the former case is described by an operator whose *partial transpose* is positive [26, 27]

future, which is one of the main subjects of statistical physics and thermodynamics. Understanding why processes can be irreversible—despite the invertibility of elementary physical laws—has bothered physicists since a long time [20, 21]. In Sect. 1.5 we will briefly sketch how the cause-effect problem is related to the standard arrow of time in physics. This is worth pointing out in particular because the scientific content of the concept of causality has been denied for a long time, in tradition of Russel's famous quote [22]:

> The law of causality, I believe, like much that passes muster among philosophers, is a relic of a bygone age, surviving, like the monarchy, only because it is erroneously supposed to do no harm.

In stark contrast to this attitude, there is a recent tendency (apart from the above link to thermodynamics) to consider causality as crucial for a better understanding of physics: in exploring the foundations of quantum theory, researchers have adopted framework and ideas from causal inference [23], including Pearl's framework, and even tried to derive parts of the axioms of quantum theory from causal concepts [24, 25]. In some of this recent work on causality in theoretical physics, toy problems similar to the cause-effect problem occur. Reference [26], for instance, shows that there exist statistical dependences between two quantum systems A and B that uniquely indicate whether one is the cause of the other or whether there is a common cause of both, see Fig. 1.3. This kind of recent advances in better understanding physics by rephrasing simple scenarios in a causal language [28] can be seen as a general tendency to accept the scientific content of causality.

1.2.5   Impact for General Machine Learning Tasks

The fact that it makes a difference in machine learning whether a learning algorithms infers the effect from its cause ('causal learning scenario') or a cause from its effect ('anticausal scenario') has been explained in [29]. The idea is that P_{cause} and $P_{\text{effect|cause}}$ usually correspond to independent mechanisms of nature. This should entail, among others, the following consequences for machine learning: First, P_{cause} and $P_{\text{effect|cause}}$ contain no information about each other and therefore semi-supervised learning only works in anticausal direction (for a more precise statement see [2, Section 5.1.2]). To sketch the argument, recall the standard semi-supervised learning scenario where X is the predictor variable and Y is supposed to be predicted from X. Given some (x, y)-pairs, additional unpaired x-values provide additional information about P_X. A priori, there is no reason why knowing more about P_X should help in better predicting Y from X since the latter requires information about $P_{Y|X}$. However, if Y is the cause and X the effect, P_X may contain information about $P_{Y|X}$, while [29] assumes that the insights about P_X do not help if X is the cause and Y the effect.

A second reason why causal directions can be important for machine learning is that the independence of the objects P_{cause} and $P_{effect|cause}$ can be seen as implying that they change independently across data sets [29]. This matters for important problems such as *domain adaptation* and *transfer learning*, see e.g. [30]: whenever $P_{cause,effect}$ changed it may often be the case that only P_{cause} *or* $P_{effect|cause}$ changed. Therefore, optimal machine learning algorithms that combine data from different distributions should account for whether the scenario is causal or anticausal. Of course, the causal structure matters also in the multi-variate scenario, but many ideas can already be explained for just two variables [2].

1.2.6 Solving a So-Called 'Unsolvable' Problem

One of the fascination of the cause-effect problem comes from the fact that it has been considered unsolvable for many years. Although most authors have been cautious enough not to state this explicitly, one could hear this general belief often in private communication and read in anonymous referee reports during the previous decade. The reason is that the causal inference community has largely focused on conditional independence based methods [1, 31], which is only able to infer the direction of an arrow if the variable pair is part of a causal DAG with at least three variables.

The cause-effect problem has stimulated a discussion about what properties of distributions other than conditional independences contain information on the underlying causal structure, with significant impact for the multivariate scenario [32, 33] where causal inference algorithms that only employ the Markov condition and causal faithfulness suffer from many weaknesses, for instance because of the difficulty of conditional independence testing for non-linear dependences.

1.3 Current Approaches

The cause-effect problem has meanwhile been tackled by a broad variety of approaches, e.g., [3, 7, 8, 17, 34–37]. Note, however, that these references are only restricted to the case where both X and Y are scalar random variables. When X

and Y are vector-valued, there are other methods e.g., [38, 39]. If X and Y are time-series, there exist well-known approaches like Granger-causality [40], but also novel approaches, e.g. [41]. For an overview of assumptions see [2]. The underlying principles may roughly be classified into the three categories in Sects. 1.3.1, 1.3.2, and 1.3.4. Section 1.3.3 explains why Sects. 1.3.1 and 1.3.2 are so closely linked that it is hard to tell them apart.

1.3.1   Complexity of Marginal and Conditional

Several approaches to cause-effect inference are more or less based on the idea to look at the factorization of $P_{X,Y}$ into

$$P_X P_{Y|X} \qquad \text{and} \qquad P_Y P_{X|Y} \qquad\qquad (1.11)$$

and compare the complexities of the terms with respect to some appropriate notion of complexity. In a Bayesian approach, the decision on which model is 'more simple' could also be based on a likelihood with respect to some prior on the parameter spaces for P_X, $P_{Y|X}$ and, accordingly for P_Y, $P_{X|Y}$ [36]. Other practical approaches are based on description length [7] or regression error [8]. Some approaches infer the direction by just defining a class of 'simple' marginals and conditionals [42–44], other define only classes of conditionals, such as, for instance, additive noise models [3], or post-nonlinear models [5]. The problem of whether a set of marginals and conditionals is small enough to fit the joint distribution in at most one direction is often referred to as *identifiability*.

1.3.2   Independent Mechanisms

The postulate reads that P_{cause} and $P_{\text{effect}|\text{cause}}$ contain no information about each other, in a sense that needs to be further specified. In [45, 46], for instance, this has been formalized as *algorithmic independence* meaning that knowing P_{cause} does not enable a shorter description of $P_{\text{effect}|\text{cause}}$ and vice versa. Reference [29] phrased independence as the hypothesis that semi-supervised learning does not work in a scenario where the effect is predicted from the cause.

Depending on the formalization of the independence principle, it yet needs to be explored to what extent the independence can be confirmed for real data. In biological systems, for instance, evolution may have developed dependences between mechanisms when creatures adapt to their environment. This limitation of the independence idea has already been pointed out in the case of causal faithfulness [31] (which can be seen as a special kind of independence of mechanisms for the multi-variate case), see also the example in Fig. 5 in [46].

To understand further possible limitations of the independence principle note that there is some 'dependence of scales' due to the following 'attention bias'. Assume, for instance, a causal relation between X and Y given by

$$Y = f_Y + N_Y, \tag{1.12}$$

where N_Y is some, not necessarily independent noise term and $f_Y : \mathbb{R} \to \mathbb{R}$ a function that shows some kind of saturation for $x \to \pm\infty$. Just as an example, consider the function

$$f_Y(x) := \tanh x, \tag{1.13}$$

which satisfies

$$\lim_{x \to \pm\infty} f_Y(x) = \pm 1, \tag{1.14}$$

see Fig. 1.4. Whenever the distribution P_X is mainly located at small or at large x-values, the function f_X does not generate any significant dependences between X and Y. Given some 'interesting' cause-effect pair, that is, where X and Y are reasonably dependent, P_X must have significant probability mass around $x = 0$. In this sense, P_X and $P_{Y|X}$ are not entirely 'independent'. Despite these limitations, independence can be a guiding principle for developing new approaches to cause-effect inference.

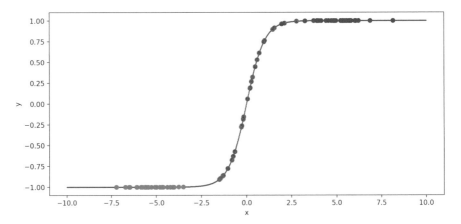

Fig. 1.4 Toy example of a functional relation between X and Y that becomes only apparent when the x-values are in a certain range (here: the red points). The green and the blue points correspond to data sets for which X and Y look unrelated. By focusing only on 'interesting' data sets for which the relation becomes apparent (red points), researchers observe that P_X and $P_{Y|X}$ are not 'independent' in the sense that P_X is typically localised in the region with large slope

1.3.3 Relations Between Independence and Complexity

The two types of postulates described in Sects. 1.3.1 and 1.3.2 are closely related. To provide an idea of this relation, I show two instructive examples.

Algorithmic Information Theory Independence can be formalized as *algorithmic independence* [45], that is,

$$I(P_{\text{cause}} : P_{\text{effect}|\text{cause}}) = 0, \tag{1.15}$$

approximately, where I denotes algorithmic mutual information. It is defined by the description length (in the sense of Kolmogorov complexity K) of P_{cause} plus the description length of $P_{\text{effect}|\text{cause}}$ minus the joint description length [45]. Hence, independence amounts to the statement that the description of P_{cause} does not get shorter when $P_{\text{effect}|\text{cause}}$ is known. Equivalently, the description of $P_{\text{effect}|\text{cause}}$ does not get shorter when P_{cause} is known.[3]

One can show [2] that (1.15) implies

$$K(P_{\text{cause}}) + K(P_{\text{effect}|\text{cause}}) \overset{+}{\leq} K(P_{\text{effect}}) + K(P_{\text{cause}|\text{effect}}), \tag{1.16}$$

where the symbol $\overset{+}{<}$ means that the inequality only holds up to a constant error (uniformly over all possible choices of the joint distribution $P_{\text{cause, effect}}$. Inequality (1.16), on the other hand, can be seen as a possible formalization of the principle in Sect. 1.3.1 to prefer the direction that yields less complex terms.

Additive Noise Based Inference To see another relation between the postulates described in Sects. 1.3.1 and 1.3.2, recall that Ref. [3] infer $X \rightarrow Y$ if there is an additive noise model from X to Y as in (1.8), but not from Y to X. It is an easy exercise [48] to show that the differential Shannon entropies H satisfy

$$H(X) + H(Y - \tilde{f}_Y(X)) < H(Y) + H(X - \tilde{f}_X(Y)), \tag{1.17}$$

if $\tilde{f}_Y$ is chosen such that $Y - \tilde{f}_Y(X)$ is independent of X and $\tilde{f}_X$ is arbitrary. Taking those marginal entropies as complexity measure, the description is less complex in causal direction whenever the independence of the input and noise holds in causal direction but not in anticausal direction.

---

[3]It is not obvious at all that these two statements are equivalent, but this is a deep result from algorithmic information theory [47].

1.3.4   Supervised Learning

Despite intense research one has to admit that cause-effect inference is still a challenging task[4] and that at least most of the approaches are based on too specific assumptions. It is therefore instructive to explore whether machine learning methods are able to learn the classification task by standard supervised learning techniques [6] rather than by hand-designing features that contain information about the causal direction. The idea is to represent the distributions P_X, $P_{Y|X}$, P_Y, $P_{X|Y}$ as vectors in a so called Reproducing Kernel Hilbert Space (RKHS) and consider the cause-effect inference problem as standard binary classification task (in such a scenario, arguments from statistical learning theory can even provide generalization bounds [6]). Approaches of this kind may be useful to understand the limits of cause-effect inference in empirical data.

1.4   Human Intuition About the Cause-Effect Problem

1.4.1   Examples Where Our Intuition Seems Right

Ideas for the cause-effect problem can already be found in earlier work before the problem was explicitly phrased as problem of causal inference. Whenever one defines classes of 'generating models' for distributions $P_{X,Y}$ for which generating X first and generating Y from X later yields a different class than starting from Y, one has already defined an approach to causal inference [42] even if the word 'causality' does not appear explicitly.

There are quite intriguing toy examples where either of one direction is considerably more plausible as generating model than the other direction. This phenomenon occurs in particular when discrete and continuous variables are combined. Then, describing distributions generated by quite natural conditionals yield rather strange conditionals when described in the wrong causal direction. In other words, combining discrete and continuous variables yield scenarios where complexity of conditionals vary particularly strongly in different causal directions. This has been observed already in [49] for causal structures with 2–4 variables. Here, complexity of conditionals is meant in a purely intuitive sense without any formalization. Among the most obvious examples we should mention the cases where one of the variables is binary and the other is real-valued, as illustrated by the Gaussian mixture model displayed in Fig. 1.5. Although most people would agree that $X \rightarrow Y$ is more plausible than $Y \rightarrow X$ in this simple toy scenario, it is not that clear how to justify this statement. One may argue that $X \rightarrow Y$ is plausible [43, 44] because one yields 'simple' marginal $p(x)$ and conditionals $p(y|x)$: after all, $p(x)$ is just a binary distribution and each $p(y|X = 0)$ and $p(y|X = 1)$ is a Gaussian with

---

[4]See, for instance, the challenge http://www.causality.inf.ethz.ch/cause-effect.php.

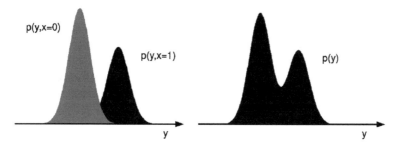

Fig. 1.5 Left: joint distribution p_{XY} of a binary variable X and a real-valued variable Y that strongly suggests that X causes Y and not vice versa: Then, X is simply shifting the mean of the Gaussian, see Fig. 5.4 in [2]. Right: the marginal distribution of Y (mixture of two Gaussians) already suggests a joint distribution where each Gaussian corresponds to a different x-value

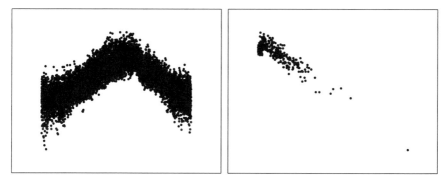

Fig. 1.6 Scatter plots from two cause-effect pairs in our benchmark data base [18]. Left: day of the year (x-axis) vs. temperature (y-axis). Right: altitude of some places in Germany (x-axis) vs. long-term average temperature (y-axis). In both cases I have repeatedly observed that humans tend to correctly infer that X is the cause and Y the effect

different expectation. The decomposition for the converse causal statement, on the other hand, yields more complex terms: $p(y)$ is a mixture of Gaussians and the conditional $p(y|x)$ is given by

$$p(X = 1|y) = \frac{p(X = 1)e^{-(y-c)^2}}{p(X = 0)e^{-y^2} + p(X = 1)e^{-(y-c)^2}}, \tag{1.18}$$

where we have assumed standardized Gaussians with mean 0 and c, respectively. It is hard to find examples in real data that are as nice as this toy example, but our cause-effect data base[5] http://webdav.tuebingen.mpg.de/cause-effect/ contains scatter plots where many humans indeed guessed the correct causal direction, see Fig. 1.6. In both cases, the idea is that Y is basically given by a function of X up

---

[5] See also http://www.causality.inf.ethz.ch/cause-effect.php.

to some noise, while a hypothetical causal model from Y to X does not admit any functional form since there are y-values for which there are *two clusters* of x-values. These and further examples that I have discussed with the audience in many talks suggest that humans do have a reasonable intuition about cause-effect asymmetries for many cases—even for those where formalizing the asymmetry seems difficult. On the other hand, I have heard a large number of ideas for cause-effect inference about which I have some doubts. This will be discussed in the following section.

1.4.2 Be Aware of Too Simple Approaches: Some Misconceptions

On the one hand, the simple examples in Sect. 1.4 are inspiring. On the other hand, there is some danger of generating ideas that are conceptually flawed. After more than one decade of research, one should admit that telling cause from effect from purely observational data remains a challenging enterprise [17] and one should be skeptical about too simple proposals.

Preferring the Deterministic Direction
The real-world examples in Fig. 1.6 and the remarks at the end of Sect. 1.4 may suggest to consider bijectivity or not as a criterion for inferring the causal direction. In other words, if $Y = f(X)$ where f is not injective, one may prefer $X \to Y$ as the causal direction. Although the relation in Fig. 1.6 is noisy, one can easily think of an underlying deterministic mechanism: After all, seasons are just a result of the change of the incident angle of the solar radiation. To think of a deterministic dependence on the season, one could put a planar surface, parallel to the surface of the earth, above the atmosphere (without disturbing weather exposure) and look at the solar radiation at 12pm, see Fig. 1.7. Then the solar radiation will periodically depend on the season and be close to a sine function of the day of the year after

Fig. 1.7 Seasonal change of the solar radiation at some point on the earth in non-equatorial position. Angle of the earth is the cause of the radiation strength, not vice versa

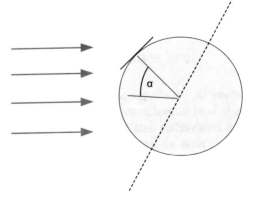

removing the offset. Clearly, the season is the cause of the strength of the solar radiation and not vice versa.

Examples like the above seem to confirm the intuition that the causal direction is the one that admits a functional relation $Y = f(X)$ if the converse direction is non-deterministic, that is, X is not a function of Y. Maybe this intuition is in fact more often true than it fails. Nevertheless it is worth describing a (more or less) natural scenario where this intuition fails, just to inspire thoughts about less superficial criteria. To this end, Fig. 1.8 shows a scenario with a causal relation that is deterministic in anticausal direction: A ball at position $x_0 \in (-\infty, c]$ flies with velocity v towards the point $c \in \mathbb{R}$, where a wall appears ($N = 1$) or not ($N = 0$) with probability $P(N = 1) = q$. After some fixed time t, the ball is at position $y = y_0$ if the wall didn't appear and at $y = y_0'$ if it did. We then obtain

$$ y = \begin{cases} x + vt & \text{for } N = 0 \\ 2c - x - vt & \text{for } N = 1 \end{cases} \tag{1.19} $$

Equation (1.19) can be read as structural equation of the form

$$ Y = f(X, N), \tag{1.20} $$

with the binary noise N. On the other hand, we have

$$ X = g(Y) = |Y - c| + c - vt, \tag{1.21} $$

that is, the cause X is a deterministic function of the effect Y contrary to the belief that the deterministic direction is the causal one.

To point out that even this contrived example does reveal the causal direction we should mention that there is a criterium other than determinism that indicates the causal direction: the 'independence of cause and mechanism', which appears

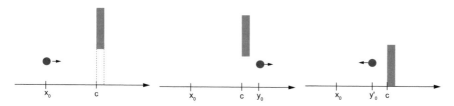

Fig. 1.8   Causal relation that is deterministic in *anti-causal* direction: A ball initially at position $x \in (-\infty, c]$ flies with velocity v towards the point c (left), where a binary random variable N controls whether a wall appears ($N = 1$) or not. For $N = 0$ (middle), the ball passes the point c, while it is reflected for $N = 1$. If y denotes the position at some later time after the potential reflection, the map $x \mapsto y$ depends on N and is thus non-deterministic. The relation is deterministic in anticausal direction because the initial position is uniquely determined by the final position without prior knowledge of N (the value of N can be seen from the final position anyway)

with different formalizations and names as 'algorithmic independence of P_{cause} and $P_{\text{effect|cause}}$' in [45, 46], as independence of 'input and mechanism' in [29], as 'independence of mechanisms' in [2]. Assume, for simplicity, that P_X is a Gaussian with mean μ_X and variance σ. Then P_Y is a mixture of two Gaussians at positions

$$\mu_Y := \mu + vt \quad \text{and} \quad \mu'_Y := -(\mu - c + vt) + c. \tag{1.22}$$

Then the independence of cause and mechanism is violated for $Y \rightarrow X$ because the position c of the wall can be reconstructed from both P_Y and g. This is seen as follows. On the one hand, c is the average of both means:

$$c = \frac{1}{2}(\mu_Y - \mu'_Y). \tag{1.23}$$

On the other hand, for each point $y \in (-\infty, c]$, there is a second point $y' := y + 2c$ for which $g(y) = g(y')$. For this reason, P_Y is not a *typical* input for the function g: Replacing P_Y with a Gaussian mixture with $c' \neq c$ does not yield a Gaussian P_X, but mixtures of two Gaussians, hence P_Y and g (which describes $P_{X|Y}$) are dependent. Therefore, we can reject the causal hypothesis $Y \rightarrow X$.

1.4.3   Abusing the Second Law: Superficial Entropy Arguments

As mentioned, there are good reasons to believe that asymmetries between cause and effect are related to asymmetries between past and future—which inevitably leads to the arrow of time, one of the big questions of theoretical physics [20, 21, 50]. Section 1.5 argues that this link is helpful for understanding the foundations of causal inference. There is, however, one idea that I have heard repeatedly of which I believe that it is a dead end: The decisive feature of physical processes whose time inversion is impossible, so called irreversible processes is the *increase of entropy*. It is therefore tempting to conjecture that effects have more entropy than causes. The idea is that the latter precede the former, thus the conjecture seems to be in agreement with the general law that physical systems can generate, but not annihilate, entropy.

The simplest argument disproving this conjecture is a cause-effect relation where the effect is binary and the cause real-valued with some probability density. The entropy of a continuous variable depends on the discretization, but one can hardly argue that it is smaller than the entropy of a simple binary since reasonable discretization yields entropy values that significantly exceed 1 bit.

The reason why simple entropy arguments of this kind fail is that, even if X and Y can be assigned to observables of physical systems, they will in general only describe a small parts of the system. The entropies of X and Y thus do not reveal anything about the entropy of the entire physical system. In fact, in Information Geometric Causal Inference (IGCI) [34, 35] the cause is the variable with *larger* entropy. This is because IGCI assumes a deterministic invertible function whose output is typically less uniform since it generically tends to *add peaks* to a distribution instead of *smoothing* peaks. This conclusion, however, heavily depends on the assumption of a deterministic relation and one can easily construct an example where the effect has larger entropy that the cause: Let C be a continuous variable and $E = C + N$ where N is some independent noise. Then the differential entropy $H(P_X) := -\int p(x) \log p(x) dx$ satisfies $H(P_E) > H(P_C)$ due to

$$H(P_E)=H\left(\int P_{C+n} p(n)dn\right) \geq \int H(P_{C+n})\, p(n)dn = \int H(P_C)p(n)dn = H(P_C).$$

$$(1.24)$$

If P_C and P_N are uniform distributions on some intervals, for instance, the entropy of the convolution is larger although it is no longer uniform (which is possible only because it is spread over a larger interval). Roughly speaking one can say: whether entropy decreases or increases from cause to effect for two real-valued variables depends on whether the entropy decrease due to non-linearity or the increase due to noise is more relevant. In both cases, however, entropy depends on the scaling of the variables—an issue that the idea of comparing entropies ignores anyway. IGCI, for instance, uses the convention that either both variables are scaled to have unit variance or scaled to have 0 and 1 as smallest and largest values, respectively. In the first case, comparing entropies amounts to comparing the relative *entropy distance* to the closest Gaussian, while scaling to the unit interval amounts to comparing relative *entropy distance* to the uniform distribution.

A related dead end is given by the claim that the distribution of the effect should usually be 'more complex' than the distribution of the cause with respect to whatever notion of complexity. The intuition is that the effect inherits complexity from both the mechanism relating cause and effect and the distribution of the cause. Indeed, the deterministic scenario in [34] confirms this idea, but once the causal relation is noisy the noise can also make the distribution of the effect smoother than the cause distribution, as mentioned above. Then the effect distribution can be arbitrarily simple (in the sense, for instance, of being close to a Gaussian).

1.4.4   Comparing Only Conditionals

An intuitive approach that many people come up with as first guess is to compare the conditionals $P_{Y|X}$ and $P_{X|Y}$ and prefer the direction with the 'less complex' conditional with respect to whatever notion of complexity. It is hard to argue against *postulates* of causal inference, but the following remarks may explain my concerns about this approach. Assume that X and Y are discrete variables attaining n_X and

n_Y different values, respectively. The space of joint distributions has a natural parameterization in terms of a vector in $\mathbb{R}^{n_X n_Y - 1}$. A model from X to Y can be parameterized by a vector in $\mathbb{R}^{n_X - 1}$ for P_X and a vector in $\mathbb{R}^{n_X(n_Y - 1)}$ for $P_{Y|X}$. Hence, the dimensions of the parameterizations add up to $n_X - 1 + n_X(n_Y - 1) = n_X n_Y - 1$, a value that is symmetric in X and Y, in agreement with the fact that we have parameterized the full set of joint distributions. In other words, the parameter space of P_X and $P_{Y|X}$ together is equally large as the space of P_Y and $P_{X|Y}$ together, no matter whether n_X and n_Y are similar or not. If we compare only complexities $P_{Y|X}$ and $P_{X|Y}$ we compare objects from the parameter spaces $\mathbb{R}^{n_X(n_Y - 1)}$ to objects described by a vector in $\mathbb{R}^{n_Y(n_X - 1)}$. If $n_X \gg n_Y$, the former space is much larger, which probably introduces bias towards $P_{Y|X}$ being more complex than $P_{X|Y}$ for many notions of complexity. This would result in preferring the variable with the smaller range as cause, which would be an undesired bias. In Sect. 1.3.3 we will explain that the postulate of independence of P_{cause} and $P_{\text{effect|cause}}$ also suggests to consider the *sum* of marginal and conditional complexities when complexities are quantified via Kolmogorov complexity. The following argument shows that the algorithmic independence of P_{cause} and $P_{\text{effect|cause}}$ does *not* imply

$$K(P_{\text{effect|cause}}) \overset{+}{\leq} K(P_{\text{cause|effect}}). \tag{1.25}$$

First, we simply consider the trivial case where X and Y are statistically independent and assume $K(P_X) < K(P_Y)$. Let us further assume the algorithmic independence $I(P_X : P_{Y|X}) \overset{+}{=} 0$ (which simply amounts to the algorithmic independence of P_X and P_Y here). Due to $P_Y = P_{Y|X}$ and $P_X = P_{X|Y}$ we have $K(P_{Y|X}) > K(P_{X|Y})$. The trivial case may not be convincing by itself, but it can be modified to making the case more convincingly: assume, in some causal model, an arbitrary distribution P_X is combined with some independent conditional $P_{Y|X}$ that is highly complex. Then the complexity of $P_{Y|X}$ does not necessarily result in a *complex relation* between X and Y. Instead, it could also result in P_Y being complex, as the limiting case of independent X and Y shows.

Despite these arguments it should be emphasized that several existing cause-effect approaches (e.g. additive noise) are based on the conditional only without accounting for the marginal of the hypothetical cause. There are, however, justifications (e.g. [51] for additive noise) that do not rely on the belief that $P_{\text{effect|cause}}$ is less complex than $P_{\text{cause|effect}}$.

To summarize this subsection in particular as well as the whole section in general, my main point is that there is meanwhile a large number of proposals for inferring causal directions by comparing model complexities (here I count entropies also as 'complexities'). One should always keep in mind, however, that different ranges and scaling of variables render the task of getting *comparable* complexity measures is non-trivial.

1.5   Where Does the Asymmetry Come From? A Detour to Physical Toy Models

On an abstract level it is not surprising that the asymmetry between cause and effect is somehow related to the asymmetry between past and future, but fortunately this link can be made more explicit. To this end, I consider a joint distribution of cause and effect for which a simple causal inference method works, namely the method 'Linear non-Gaussian Acyclic Models' (LiNGAM) [52]. The method infers that X_0 is the cause of X_1 whenever there is a linear model with independent additive noise from X_0 to X_1, that is

$$X_1 = \alpha X_0 + \beta N_0 \quad \text{with } X_0 \perp\!\!\!\perp N_0, \tag{1.26}$$

where $\alpha, \beta \in \mathbb{R}$ and N_0 is an unobserved noise term[6] provided that there is no additive noise model from X_1 to X_0. Unless the joint distribution of X_0, X_1 is bivariate Gaussian, an additive noise model can exist in at most one direction. Hence,

$$X_0 \neq \gamma X_1 + \delta N_1 \quad \text{with } X_1 \perp\!\!\!\perp N_1, \tag{1.27}$$

for all choices of γ, δ, N_1. Certainly, not every cause-effect relation can be described by an additive noise model, but if an additive noise model fits in either direction, it is unlikely not to be the causal direction, as argued via algorithmic information theory in [51]. To understand the asymmetry between cause and effect given by (1.26) and (1.27) from an underlying physical toy model, we assume that X_0 and N_0 are states of two physical systems S_X and S_N, respectively, before S_X and S_N are subjected to an interaction. Further, let X_1 and N_1 describe the states of S_X and S_N after they have interacted. Figure 1.9 shows the different levels of describing the system: The figure on the left hand side shows just the DAG with two nodes visualizing the cause-effect relation.

The figure in the middle visualizes the corresponding functional causal model showing not only the observed variables but also the unobserved noise term N_0 that renders the relation between cause and effect probabilistic. Finally, the figure on the right hand side shows the physical description level where X_0, N_0 are initial states and X_1, N_1 are final states of interacting physical systems S_X and S_N. More explicitly, let the interaction between S_X and S_N be given by the rotation

$$\begin{pmatrix} X_1 \\ N_1 \end{pmatrix} = R_\phi \begin{pmatrix} X_0 \\ N_0 \end{pmatrix}, \tag{1.28}$$

---

[6]The scaling factor β in front of the noise term is uncommon, but makes the argument below more concise.

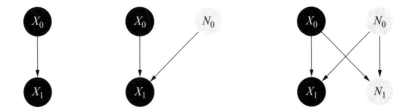

Fig. 1.9 Different description levels of the causal relation between the observed variables X_0 and X_1. Left: The DAG visualizing that X_0 is the cause and X_1 the effect. Middle: Functional causal model where X_1 is a deterministic function of X_0 and an independent unobserved noise variable N_0. Right: Underlying physical model where X_0, X_1 are initial and final state of an observed system S_X and N_0, N_1 initial and final state of an unobserved system S_N. If we assume that the dynamics defines a bijective map from (X_0, N_0) to (X_1, N_1), the only asymmetry of the scenario with respect to time inversion consists in the assumption that X_0 and N_0 are independent while X_1 and N_1 will then be dependent for typical maps (see text)

where R_ϕ is the rotation matrix

$$R_\phi := \begin{pmatrix} \cos\phi & \sin\phi \\ -\sin\phi & \cos\phi \end{pmatrix}, \tag{1.29}$$

with some angle ϕ. Assuming that S_X and S_N have never been interacting before, we necessarily have

$$X_0 \perp\!\!\!\perp N_0, \tag{1.30}$$

because any statistical dependence is due to some interaction according to Reichenbach's principle of the common cause [53]. Hence, the physical model indeed induces the additive noise model (1.26) with $\alpha = \cos\phi$ and $\beta = \sin\phi$. For our argument later it is crucial to mention that R_ϕ generates dependences between X_1 and N_1 unless ϕ is a multiple of $\pi/2$ since the resulting linear combinations of the non-Gaussian variables X_0 and N_0 cannot be statistically independent due to the Theorem of Darmoir-Skitovic [54].

Since R_ϕ is invertible, one may think that an interaction given by the inverse rotation $R_{-\phi}$ would induce an additive noise model from the effect X_1 to the cause X_0—which would mislead the causal inference algorithm LiNGAM. This would, however, require $X_1 \perp\!\!\!\perp N_1$, that is, the systems S_X, S_N would be independent *after* they have interacted, but dependent *before* the interaction. This is in contradiction to the obvious arrow of time in every-day experience: the fact that photographic images show the past and not the future is due to the fact that the light particles ('photons') contain information about an object *after* it has interacted with it, not *before* the interaction. As argued in [55], this asymmetry can be seen as a part of a more general independence principle stating that the initial state of a physical system does not contain information about the dynamics it is subjected to. Reference [55] further argues that this principle reproduces the standard thermodynamic arrow of time by implying that bijective dynamics can only increase physical entropy, but not decrease it, which implies that heat can only flow from the hot to the cold reservoir, but not vice versa. This way, the asymmetry between cause and effect is closely linked to known aspects of the thermodynamic arrow of time. In the above toy scenario, the arrow of time in physics provides some justification for the causal inference method LiNGAM.

On the other hand, causal inference can help to discover aspects of the arrow of time that have not been described before: Reference [56] directly infers the time direction of empirical time series using a modification of LiNGAM for time series and Ref. [41] distinguishes an acoustic signal from its echo using a new causal inference method for time-series.

To learn a more general lesson from the above toy model, note that the *causal* conditional $P_{X_1|X_0}$ inherits *linearity* from the underlying physical process R_ϕ, while the *anticausal* conditional $P_{X_0|X_1}$ does not admit a linear model although $R_{-\phi}$ is certainly also linear. The reason is, as stated before, that we would need independence of X_1 and N_1 to obtain an additive noise model for $P_{X_0|X_1}$. More generally speaking, this suggests that causal conditionals 'inherit' the simplicity of the underlying physical laws, while anticausal conditionals do not inherit the simplicity of the time-inverted physical law because the statistical dependences between the system under consideration and the system providing the noise destroys the simplicity [57, 58]. This way, the cause-effect problem can also refresh discussions on the right view on Occam's Razor, which nicely shows the philosophical dimension of this little toy problem.

References

1. J. Pearl. *Causality*. Cambridge University Press, 2000.
2. J. Peters, D. Janzing, and B. Schölkopf. *Elements of Causal Inference – Foundations and Learning Algorithms*. MIT Press, 2017.
3. P. Hoyer, D. Janzing, J. Mooij, J. Peters, and B Schölkopf. Nonlinear causal discovery with additive noise models. In D. Koller, D. Schuurmans, Y. Bengio, and L. Bottou, editors, *Proceedings of the conference Neural Information Processing Systems (NIPS) 2008*, Vancouver, Canada, 2009. MIT Press.
4. J. Peters, D. Janzing, and B. Schölkopf. Identifying cause and effect on discrete data using additive noise models. In *Proceedings of The Thirteenth International Conference on Artificial Intelligence and Statistics (AISTATS), JMLR: W&CP 9*, Chia Laguna, Sardinia, Italy, 2010.
5. K. Zhang and A. Hyvärinen. On the identifiability of the post-nonlinear causal model. In *Proceedings of the Twenty-Fifth Conference on Uncertainty in Artificial Intelligence*, UAI '09, pages 647–655, Arlington, Virginia, United States, 2009. AUAI Press.
6. D. Lopez-Paz, K. Muandet, B. Schölkopf, and I. Tolstikhin. Towards a learning theory of cause-effect inference. In *Proceedings of the 32nd International Conference on Machine Learning*, volume 37 of *JMLR Workshop and Conference Proceedings*, page 1452–1461. JMLR, 2015.
7. A. Marx and J. Vreeken. Telling cause from effect using MDL-based local and global regression. In *2017 IEEE International Conference on Data Mining, ICDM 2017, New Orleans, LA, USA, November 18–21, 2017*, pages 307–316, 2017.

8. P. Bloebaum, D. Janzing, T. Washio, S. Shmimizu, and B. Schölkopf. Cause-effect inference by comparing regression errors. In A. Storkey and F. Perez-Cruz, editors, *Proceedings of the 21th International Conference on Artificial Intelligence and Statistics (AISTATS)*, volume 84, pages 900–909. PMLR, 2018.
9. J. Song, S. Oyama, and M. Kurihara. Tell cause from effect: models and evaluation. *International Journal of Data Science and Analytics*, 2017.
10. D. Janzing, J. Peters, J. Mooij, and B. Schölkopf. Identifying latent confounders using additive noise models. In *Proceedings of the 25th Conference on Uncertainty in Artificial Intelligence (UAI 2009), 249–257. (Eds.) A. Ng and J. Bilmes, AUAI Press, Corvallis, OR, USA*, 2009.
11. D. Janzing, E. Sgouritsa, O. Stegle, P. Peters, and B. Schölkopf. Detecting low-complexity unobserved causes. In *Proceedings of the 27th Conference on Uncertainty in Artificial Intelligence (UAI 2011)*. http://uai.sis.pitt.edu/papers/11/p383-janzing.pdf.
12. D. Janzing and B. Schölkopf. Detecting confounding in multivariate linear models. *Journal of Causal Inference*, 6(1), 2017.
13. D. Janzing and B. Schölkopf. Detecting non-causal artifacts in multivariate linear regression models. In Jennifer Dy and Andreas Krause, editors, *Proceedings of the 35th International Conference on Machine Learning*, volume 80, pages 2245–2253. PMLR, 2018. http://proceedings.mlr.press/v80/janzing18a/janzing18a.pdf.
14. K. Popper. *The logic of scientific discovery*. Routledge, London, 1959.
15. TETRAD. The tetrad homepage. http://www.phil.cmu.edu/projects/tetrad/.
16. D. Janzing, D. Balduzzi, M. Grosse-Wentrup, and B. Schölkopf. Quantifying causal influences. *Annals of Statistics*, 41(5):2324–2358, 2013.
17. J. Mooij, J. Peters, D. Janzing, J. Zscheischler, and B. Schölkopf. Distinguishing cause from effect using observational data: methods and benchmarks. *Journal of Machine Learning Research*, 17(32):1–102, 2016.
18. Database with cause-effect pairs. https://webdav.tuebingen.mpg.de/cause-effect/. Copyright information for each cause-effect pair is contained in the respective description file.
19. D. Janzing. Statistical assymmeries between cause and effect. In R. Renner and S. Stupar, editors, *Time in physics*, volume Tutorials, Schools, and Workshops in the Mathematical Sciences. Birkhäuser, Cham, pages 129–139. Springer, 2017.
20. R. Balian. *From microphysics to macrophysics*, volume 1. Springer, 2007.
21. R. Balian. *From microphysics to macrophysics*, volume 2. Springer, 1991.
22. B. Russell. On the notion of cause. *Proceedings of the Aristotelian Society*, 3:1–26, 1912–1913.
23. C. Wood and R. Spekkens. The lesson of causal discovery algorithms for quantum correlations: causal explanations of Bell-inequality violations require fine-tuning. *New Journal of Physics*, 17(3):033002, 2015.
24. M. Pawlowski and V. Scarani. Information causality. In G. Chiribella and R. Spekkens, editors, *Quantum Theory: Informational Foundations and Foils*, pages 423–438. Springer, 2016.
25. H. Barnum and A. Wilce. Post-classical probability theory. In R. Spekkens and G. Chiribella, editors, *Quantum Theory: Informational Foundations and Foils*, pages 367–420. Springer, 2016.
26. K. Ried, M. Agnew, L. Vermeyden, D. Janzing, R. Spekkens, and K. Resch. A quantum advantage for inferring causal structure. *Nature Physics*, 11(5):414–420, 05 2015.
27. M. Leifer and R. Spekkens. Towards a formulation of quantum theory as a causally neutral theory of Bayesian inference. *Phys Rev*, A(88):052130, 2013.
28. D. Schmied, K. Ried, and R. Spekkens. Why initial system-environment correlations do not imply the failure of complete positivity: a causal perspective. *preprint*, arXiv:1806.02381, 2018.
29. B. Schölkopf, D. Janzing, J. Peters, E. Sgouritsa, K. Zhang, and J. Mooij. On causal and anticausal learning. In Langford J. and J. Pineau, editors, *Proceedings of the 29th International Conference on Machine Learning (ICML)*, pages 1255–1262. ACM, 2012.

30. K Zhang, B Schölkopf, Krikamol Muandet, and Z Wang. Domain adaptation under target and conditional shift. *30th International Conference on Machine Learning, ICML 2013*, pages 1856–1864, 01 2013.
31. P. Spirtes, C. Glymour, and R. Scheines. *Causation, Prediction, and Search (Lecture notes in statistics)*. Springer-Verlag, New York, NY, 1993.
32. J. Peters, J. Mooij, D. Janzing, and B. Schölkopf. Identifiability of causal graphs using functional models. In *Proceedings of the 27th Conference on Uncertainty in Artificial Intelligence (UAI 2011)*. http://uai.sis.pitt.edu/papers/11/p589-peters.pdf.
33. C. Nowzohour and P. Bühlmann. Score-based causal learning in additive noise models. *Statistics*, 50(3):471–485, 2016.
34. P. Daniusis, D. Janzing, J. M. Mooij, J. Zscheischler, B. Steudel, K. Zhang, and B. Schölkopf. Inferring deterministic causal relations. In *Proceedings of the 26th Annual Conference on Uncertainty in Artificial Intelligence (UAI)*, pages 143–150. AUAI Press, 2010.
35. D. Janzing, J. Mooij, K. Zhang, J. Lemeire, J. Zscheischler, P. Daniušis, B. Steudel, and B. Schölkopf. Information-geometric approach to inferring causal directions. *Artificial Intelligence*, 182–183:1–31, 2012.
36. J. Mooij, O. Stegle, D. Janzing, K. Zhang, and B. Schölkopf. Probabilistic latent variable models for distinguishing between cause and effect. In *Advances in Neural Information Processing Systems 23 (NIPS*2010)*, pages 1687–1695, 2011.
37. E. Sgouritsa, D. Janzing, P. Hennig, and B. Schölkopf. Inference of cause and effect with unsupervised inverse regression. In G. Lebanon and S. Vishwanathan, editors, *Proceedings of the 18th International Conference on Artificial Intelligence and Statistics (AISTATS)*, JMLR Workshop and Conference Proceedings, 2015.
38. D. Janzing, P. Hoyer, and B. Schölkopf. Telling cause from effect based on high-dimensional observations. *Proceedings of the 27th International Conference on Machine Learning (ICML 2010), Haifa, Israel*, 06:479–486, 2010.
39. J. Zscheischler, D. Janzing, and K. Zhang. Testing whether linear equations are causal: A free probability theory approach. In *Proceedings of the 27th Conference on Uncertainty in Artificial Intelligence (UAI 2011)*, 2011. http://uai.sis.pitt.edu/papers/11/p839-zscheischler.pdf.
40. C. W. J. Granger. Investigating causal relations by econometric models and cross-spectral methods. *Econometrica*, 37(3):424–38, July 1969.
41. N. Shajarisales, D. Janzing, B. Schölkopf, and M. Besserve. Telling cause from effect in deterministic linear dynamical systems. In *Proceedings of the 32th International Conference on Machine Learning (ICML)*, pages 285–294. Journal of Machine Learning Reach, 2015.
42. J. W. Comley and D. L. Dowe. General Bayesian networks and asymmetric languages. In *Proceedings of the Hawaii International Conference on Statistics and Related fields*, June 2003.
43. X. Sun, D. Janzing, and B. Schölkopf. Causal inference by choosing graphs with most plausible Markov kernels. In *Proceedings of the 9th International Symposium on Artificial Intelligence and Mathematics*, pages 1–11, Fort Lauderdale, FL, 2006.
44. D. Janzing, X. Sun, and B. Schölkopf. Distinguishing cause and effect via second order exponential models. http://arxiv.org/abs/0910.5561, 2009.
45. D. Janzing and B. Schölkopf. Causal inference using the algorithmic Markov condition. *IEEE Transactions on Information Theory*, 56(10):5168–5194, 2010.
46. J. Lemeire and D. Janzing. Replacing causal faithfulness with algorithmic independence of conditionals. *Minds and Machines*, 23(2):227–249, 7 2012.
47. G. Chaitin. A theory of program size formally identical to information theory. *J. Assoc. Comput. Mach.*, 22(3):329–340, 1975.
48. S. Kpotufe, E. Sgouritsa, D. Janzing, and B. Schölkopf. Consistency of causal inference under the additive noise model. In Eric P. Xing and Tony Jebara, editors, *Proceedings of the 31st International Conference on Machine Learning (ICML), W&CP 32 (1)*, pages 478–495. JMLR, 2014.

49. X. Sun. Schätzen von Kausalstrukturen anhand der Plausibilität ihrer Markoff-Kerne, 2004. Diploma thesis (in German), Universität Karlsruhe (TH).
50. S. Hawking. *A brief history of time*. Bantam, 1990.
51. D. Janzing and B. Steudel. Justifying additive-noise-based causal discovery via algorithmic information theory. *Open Systems and Information Dynamics*, 17(2):189–212, 2010.
52. Y. Kano and S. Shimizu. Causal inference using nonnormality. In *Proceedings of the International Symposium on Science of Modeling, the 30th Anniversary of the Information Criterion*, pages 261–270, Tokyo, Japan, 2003.
53. H. Reichenbach. *The direction of time*. University of California Press, Berkeley, 1956.
54. V. Skitovic. Linear combinations of independent random variables and the normal distribution law. *Select. Transl. Math. Stat. Probab.*, (2):211–228, 1962.
55. D. Janzing, R. Chaves, and B. Schölkopf. Algorithmic independence of initial condition and dynamical law in thermodynamics and causal inference. *New Journal of Physics*, 18(093052):1–13, 2016.
56. J. Peters, D. Janzing, A. Gretton, and B. Schölkopf. Detecting the direction of causal time series. In A Danyluk, L Bottou, and ML Littman, editors, *Proceedings of the 26th International Conference on Machine Learning*, pages 801–808, New York, NY, USA, 2009. ACM Press.
57. D. Janzing. On causally asymmetric versions of Occam's Razor and their relation to thermodynamics. http://arxiv.org/abs/0708.3411v2, 2008.
58. D. Janzing. On the entropy production of time series with unidirectional linearity. *Journ. Stat. Phys.*, 138:767–779, 2010.

Chapter 2
Evaluation Methods of Cause-Effect Pairs

Isabelle Guyon, Olivier Goudet, and Diviyan Kalainathan

2.1 Introduction and Motivations

The field of causal discovery from observational data has traditionally been divided into several schools of thought, including the "potential outcome" [53, 54], and the "graphical model" [47, 57] schools. The former (potential outcomes) focus on $(X = treatment, Y = outcome)$ pairs in the context case-control studies, when there is a strong enough dependency between X and Y to warrant an investigation of a possible causal effect $X \rightarrow Y$. In that context, the context, the direction $X \rightarrow Y$ of the putative causal relation is not questioned, but the "intensity" of the causal effect must be evaluated. This intensity can eventually be zero, if the observed dependency between X and Y solely results from one or several common cause(s) or confounding factor(s). Specifically, the data include "observations" of (X, Y) pairs for a number of patients together with jointly observed covariates $\mathbf{Z}$ (such as age, gender, origin, etc.), which are possible confounding factors. The hypothesis $X \rightarrow Y$ is tested against $X \leftarrow \mathbf{Z} \rightarrow Y$. The latter school of thoughts (graphical models) seek to recover a full causal graph from the joint observation of many variables $(X_1, X_2, \cdots)$, generally up to an equivalence class of graphs, using conditional independence between variables (Markov properties). Such methods do not allow us to orient pairs of variables taken in isolation, since $X \rightarrow Y$ and $X \leftarrow Y$

I. Guyon
Team TAU - CNRS, INRIA, Université Paris Sud, Université Paris Saclay, Orsay France

ChaLearn, Berkeley, CA, USA
e-mail: guyon@chalearn.org

O. Goudet · D. Kalainathan
Team TAU - CNRS, INRIA, Université Paris Sud, Université Paris Saclay, Orsay, France
e-mail: olivier.goudet@inria.fr; Diviyan.kalainathan@lri.fr

© Springer Nature Switzerland AG 2019   27
I. Guyon et al. (eds.), *Cause Effect Pairs in Machine Learning*,
The Springer Series on Challenges in Machine Learning,
https://doi.org/10.1007/978-3-030-21810-2_2

are Markov equivalent. In the past few years, new approaches have emerged, which have started to constitute a third school of thoughts [9, 33, 35, 46]: focus on orienting pairs (X, Y) of variables, i.e. determine whether $X \rightarrow Y$ or $X \leftarrow Y$.

Limiting ourselves to pairs of variables, rather than addressing the muti-variate case is a deliberate choice. At first sight, focusing on pairs seems easier. However, researchers versed in causal discovery know all-too-well the difficulty of distinguishing between a causal effect and a spurious dependency due to confounding. In layman terms, "correlation is not causation". This problem is even harder when potential confounding factors are hidden variables. Furthermore, observing additional variables may help orienting causal edges, e.g. using colliders or V-structures [47]. This is not possible when only pairs of variables are given. So why making things potentially more complicated than they already are by considering only pairs of variables?

There are multiple justifications to embrace the cause-effect pair setting. The primary justification is **practical**: cause-effect pair methods might extend the potential outcome framework to resolve cases with no a priori on causal direction $X \rightarrow Y$ or $X \leftarrow Y$. All is needed is to first condition $P(X, Y)$ on *known* potential confounders $\mathbf{Z}$ (e.g. age, gender, etc.) or adjust with a propensity score [53] to get $P(X, Y|\mathbf{Z})$, then address edge orientation as a cause-effect pair problem. The setting of cause-effect pairs, making no a priori assumption on causal orientation nor on the presence of hidden confounders, lends itself to applications in areas like epidemiology, when it is unclear which variable is the "treatment" and which one is the "outcome", e.g. $X = diabetes\_consumption$ and $Y = drinking\_diet\_soda$ [15]. Other justification have been invoked. One may argue that the cause-effect pair problem is of fundamental **scientific** interest. Indeed, it is the smallest problem addressing the issue of finding *asymmetries* in joint distributions of variables that are potentially revealing of causal relationships, and it cannot be resolved using Markov properties (conditional independence testing). Another argument is that basing causal discovery on cause-effect pairs may help fighting against the "curse of dimensionality" by avoiding to perform extensive conditional independence tests, which are very data hungry. However, what is gained on one side might be lost on another and ultimately, the effect of multiple testing might be the same. So it is better to think of pairwise methods as complements to multi-variate graphical model methods that help orienting edges left un-oriented in Markov equivalence classes.

This chapter introduces methodology to address both the problems of validating *methods*, validating *discoveries*, and *benchmarking*.

In Sect. 2.2, we describe the problem setting. In this section, we formulate the problem of cause-effect pairs as a "classical" machine learning problem in which we want to classify "objects". In this case, objects are pairs of variables (X, Y), or more concretely, jointly drawn samples of two variables, which can be viewed as a two-dimensional scatter plot representing an empirical joint distribution (see examples in Table 2.1). A theoretical framework around this setting was proposed in [43], replacing miscellaneous data generative hypotheses outlined in Chap. 1, deemed necessary to infer causal relationships, by a unified notion of **mother distribution**. A mother distribution is a distribution over input/output samples $\{(X, Y), G\}$, where

Table 2.1 Mini artificial examples

	Generative model	Scatter plot	C_{R2}	C_{IR}	C_H	C_S	C_{CDS}
1	$X \sim N(0, 1)$. $Z \sim N(0, 0.5)$. $Y = X + Z$.		✓			✓	
2	$X \sim U(-1, 1)$. $Z \sim U(-0.5, 0.5)$. $Y = X + Z$.			✓	✓		✓
3	$X \sim U(0, 1)$. $Z \sim U(0, 1)$. $Y = ZX$.				✓	✓	✓
4	$X \sim N(0, 1)$. $Z \sim N(0, 0.1)$. $Y = \tanh(X) + Z$.		✓	✓		✓	✓
5	$X \sim U(-1, 1)$. $Y = X^2$.		✓	✓	✓		✓
6	$X \sim U(0, 1)$. $Z \sim B(-1, 1)$. $Y = Z\sqrt{X}$.				✓	✓	

All pairs are $X \to Y$. The last columns indicate the success of simple causation coefficients (see Sect. 2.3.1), which give inconsistent results

G is the "ground truth" (causal graph). We consider **four** possible ground truth categories (as opposed to just two, in Chaps. 1 and 3):

1. $X \to Y$ (X causes Y)
2. $X \leftarrow Y$ (Y causes X)
3. $X \leftrightarrow Y$ (X and Y are dependent but neither causes the other)
4. $X \perp Y$ (X and Y are independent)

Chapter 6 refines ground truth categories to the case of partial confounding, i.e. classes 1 and 2 are subdivided depending on whether the dependency between X

and Y is partially explained by common causes $\mathbf{Z}$. The *mother distribution* fully describes the data generative process of cause-effect pairs: it can be endowed by any explicit data generative model, but can also represent unknown distributions of real (X, Y) pairs, eventually labeled by experts.

In Sect. 2.3 we then introduce a notion of **causation coefficient** $C(X, Y)$, which is a discriminant value in the problem of classifying $X \rightarrow Y$ *vs.* all other cases. Because of the symmetry of the problem, $C(X, Y)$ can also be used to separate $X \leftarrow Y$ *vs.* all other cases: small negative values of $C(X, Y)$ mean $X \leftarrow Y$, large positive values mean $X \rightarrow Y$, and middle values mean either $X \leftrightarrow Y$, $X \perp Y$, or "inconclusive result".

In Sect. 2.4, we tackle the problem of validating *methods*, from the point of view of algorithm developers. Since we bring the problem back to a two-class classification problem, usual metrics of classification accuracy may be used (such as accuracy, balanced accuracy, area under the ROC curve, area under the precision-recall curve, etc.). We propose a new notion of (α, β)-**identifiability**, in terms of tolerances on Type I and Type II errors for a given *mother distribution*, replacing classical notions of identifiability [33, 46, 66, 67], which refer to a particular data generative process (i.e. the existence of a functional causal model in one direction but not in the other). We demonstrate that our framework extends to the finite sample case.

In Sect. 2.5, we shift our attention to the problem of **validating discoveries**, i.e. evaluating the significance of given putative causal relationships for particular pairs of variables in the context of an application. We thus take the point of view of *practitioners* deploying causal discovery methods in their day to day work. Finally, in Sect. 2.6, we turn to the problem of **benchmarking** causal discovery algorithms and comparing their relative merits. This is the problem of *algorithm developers* and *benchmark* or *challenge organizers*. One central difficulty in causal discovery is gaining access to "ground truth" (or causal graph) G, necessary to validate either *methods* or *discoveries*. Building on prior work to create datasets of real and artificial data, such as the Tuebingen dataset [46], and expanding on earlier work we did on assessing causal discovery methods in the context of challenges [26], we describe in some details the dataset of the cause-effect pair challenges we organized in 2013–2014 [31] and explain the efforts we made to avoid common pitfalls biasing data.

Most of this chapter focuses on problems in which independently and identically drawn samples of the joint distribution of X and Y are given, as opposed to joint time series. The latter problem will be addressed in more details in Chap. 5.

2.2 Problem Setting

2.2.1 Definition of Causality and Ground Truth of Causal Relationships

In what follows, we consider a notion of **causality between pairs random variables** (denoted by capital letters X and Y), as opposed to causality between events or objects. Such random variables generally result from physical measurements (e.g. temperature, blood pressure, compressive strength) or surveys (e.g. age, income, number of children); they can be **binary, categorical, or continuous** (see Fig. 2.1), though most of our illustrative examples use continuous variables (e.g. Tables 2.1 and 2.2). For the most part, we consider a notion of **"instantaneous" causality**, for which effects are supposed to propagate instantaneously (from X to Y or Y to X or from a common cause). This allows us to consider that pairs $\{(x_1, y_1), (x_2, y_2), \cdots, (x_i, y_i), \cdots, (x_n, y_n)\}$ of joint observations of X and Y are drawn *i.i.d.* from a distribution $P(X, Y)$. However, in some cases, we extend the discussion to time series: the index i then represents the time ordering of the samples, and the samples are supposed to have been drawn from a dynamic system.

Many definitions of causality have been proposed in the scientific and philosophy literature [34, 47]. Some of the commonly used definitions include:

- **Counterfactuals:** X is a cause of Y if we observed $X = x$ and $Y = y$, but, had X been different, Y would have been different. For instance, the heat wave caused the thermometer needle to rise to a reading of 45°C. Had the temperature remained mild, the thermometer needle would not have risen that high. Note that we cannot go back in time and change the climate settings from "heat wave" to

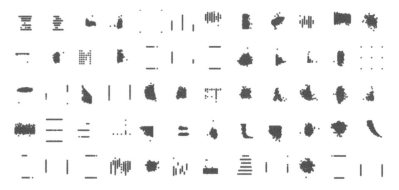

Fig. 2.1 Scatter plots of pairs of variables. Each little group of points represents a two-dimensional scatter plot of a pair of variables (X, Y) from the cause-effect pair challenge. The variables can be continuous, binary, or categorical. Each pair (X, Y) is labeled with a ground truth $G \in \{X \to Y, X \leftarrow Y, X \leftrightarrow Y, X \perp Y\}$

Table 2.2 Comparison of real and artificial examples

	Generative model	Graph	C_{R2}	C_{IR}	C_H	C_S	C_{CDS}
1	$X = log(altitude)$. $Y = temperature$.		✓		✓		
2	$X = N(9, 1.5)$. $Z \sim N(0, 1000)$. $Y = 14 \exp(0.75X) - \exp(X) + Z$.		✓	✓	✓		✓
3	$X = age$. $Y = weight$.				✓		
4	$X \sim N(0.8, 0.3)$. $Z \sim N(0, 0.2)$. $Y = (-(X-1)^2 + 1) + ZX$.		✓		✓		
5	$X = aspect$. $Y = hillshade3pm$.			✓	✓		✓
6	$X \sim U(-\pi, \pi)$. $Z \sim \exp(U(-1, 1))$. $Y = Z \sin(X)$.			✓	✓		✓

Each real pair is compared with a simple data generative model providing a similar-looking scatter plot, but not always the same causation coefficient results

"not heat wave": a counterfactual is different from an experiment. It can, at best, be a "thought experiment".

- **Interventions or experiments:** X is a cause of Y if, given *forced* assignments of X to values $X = do(x)$ (as opposed to naturally observed values $X = x$), $P(Y|X = do(x)) = P(Y|X = x)$ holds while $P(X|Y = do(y)) = P(X|Y = y)$ does not hold. For instance, temperature in a room causes the temperature value indicated by a thermometer's needle. So, forcing the room temperature to change to T should result in the same thermometer readings than letting the temperature change on its own to T, however manually moving the needle of the thermometer should not change the room temperature.

- **Mechanisms:** X is a cause of Y if there exists a mechanism f such that $Y :=$ $f(X, N)$, which generated Y from X and some noise N (summarizing the effect of other unknown variables). For instance, we can open the thermometer's box and observe that there is a coil spring whose dilatation increases with temperature and drives the motion of the needle. This is the mechanism by which the position of the needle is obtained from the temperature.

In Chap. 1, we saw that these three notions of causality are inter-related and practically we expect that, if one definition holds, the others are true too. For example, in medicine, if we establish with a randomized controlled trial (an **experiment**) [16] that a given drug is effective against a given disease, we assume that there is a **mechanism** that explains the effect and that, if a patient is cured after taking the medicine, he would not have been cured had he not taken it (a **counterfactual**). However, clearly these three definitions are not equivalent. Intuitively, we might think that mechanisms are the most fundamental way of evidencing causal relationships. But *the existence of a mechanism does not imply the existence of a measurable effect* that can be experimentally evidenced and, likewise, does not necessarily imply counterfactuals. In medicine, the gold standard of establishing causal relationships remains randomized controlled trials [19, 56, 62]. According to these sources, the use of a controlled study is the most effective way of establishing causality between variables. In a controlled study, the sample or population is split in two groups, comparable in almost every way. The two groups then receive different treatments, and the outcomes of each group are assessed. For example, in medical research, one group may receive a placebo while the other group is given a new type of medication. If the two groups have noticeably different outcomes, the different experiences may have caused the different outcomes. Due to ethical reasons, there are limits to the use of controlled studies; it would not be appropriate to use two comparable groups and have one of them undergo a harmful activity while the other does not. To overcome this situation, observational studies are often used to investigate correlation and causation for the population of interest. The studies can look at the groups' behaviors and outcomes and observe any changes over time. The objective of these studies is to provide statistical information to add to the other sources of information that would be required for the process of establishing whether or not causality exists between two variables.

In this chapter however, we focus on a definition of causality stemming from structural equation models, based on "mechanisms". We assume that if $X \rightarrow Y$, then there exists a mechanism that produced Y from X and that this mechanism can be mathematically represented by a functional relationship, called Structural Equation Model—SRM—or Functional Causal Model—FCM [47, 48]). Using informal mathematical notations, the "mechanical" definition of causality is:

$$G = [X \rightarrow Y] \quad \overset{def}{=} \quad \exists f \wedge \exists N \; s.t. \; Y := f(X, N) \Rightarrow P(Y|X) \qquad (2.1)$$

The symbol := should be thought of as an assignment, not an equality: Y was obtained from $f(X, N)$. Such mechanisms underlie our notion of ground truth, both for real and artificial data. We show examples of pairs in Tables 2.1 and 2.2.

Definition 2.1 (Pairwise Causal and Non-causal Relationships) We consider that pairs of variables X and Y can be in one of four types of relationships: X causes Y ($X \rightarrow Y$), Y causes X ($X \leftarrow Y$), X and Y are dependent, but not in a causal relationship ($X \leftrightarrow Y$) or X and Y are independent ($X \perp Y$). Any pair of variables (X, Y) is associated with one and only one such relationships, called "ground truth" G. By definition, we have:

$$\begin{cases} G = [X \rightarrow Y] \Rightarrow \exists f \wedge \exists N_y \; s.t. \; Y := f(X, N_y) \\ G = [X \leftarrow Y] \Rightarrow \exists f \wedge \exists N_x \; s.t. \; X := f(Y, N_x) \\ G = [X \leftrightarrow Y] \Rightarrow \exists f, g \wedge \exists N_x, N_y, Z \; s.t. \; X := f(Z, N_x) \wedge Y := g(Z, N_y) \\ G = [X \perp Y] \qquad \text{X and Y are independent, no functional relationship} \end{cases}$$

$$(2.2)$$

We do not necessarily assume that $(X \perp N_y)$ nor that $(Y \perp N_x)$, thus there can be additional latent confounders in the first two cases $X \rightarrow Y$ and $X \leftarrow Y$. In practice, variables X and Y are known to us through samples drawn according to a distribution $P(X, Y)$. For instance, if $G = [X \rightarrow Y]$, x samples are first drawn according to $P(X)$, then y samples are drawn according to $P(Y|X)$ using a "mechanism" $Y := f(X, N)$. Thus, the various data generative processes are the following:

$$\begin{cases} G = [X \rightarrow Y] : \; x \sim P(X), n_y \sim P(N_y) \qquad\qquad y := f(x, n_y) \\ G = [X \leftarrow Y] : \; y \sim P(Y), n_x \sim P(N_x) \qquad\qquad x := f(y, n_x) \\ G = [X \leftrightarrow Y] : \; z \sim P(Z), n_x \sim P(N_x), n_y \sim P(N_y) \; x := f(z, n_x), y := g(z, n_y) \\ G = [X \perp Y] : x \sim P(X), y \sim P(Y) \end{cases}$$

$$(2.3)$$

Thus, the structural equations entail a definition of causality and data generative processes. A graphical representation of the various cases is given in Fig. 2.2.

Let us make a few remarks:

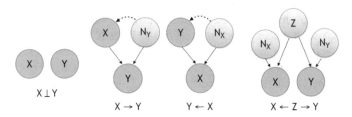

Fig. 2.2 Graphical representation of causal graphs considered in this chapter: the full edges represent necessary causal links. The dashed edges represents optional links

- The existence quantifier $\exists$ from the mechanistic definition of causality lets us understand that a mechanistic explanation of a causal relationship may not be unique. In particular, our explanation is limited to what we can apprehend of X and Y. For example, if $G = [X \to Y]$ and all we can "see" of X and Y is a sample of $P(X, Y)$ (even infinite), we will never be able to evaluate the difference between two explanations $Y := f^1(X, N_y^1)$ and $Y := f^2(X, N_y^2)$, yielding the same $P(Y|X)$ on the support of $P(X)$.
- The definition involves an implication $\Rightarrow$, not an equivalence. The existence of a function $Y := f(X, N_y)$ allowing us to predict Y from X (to the extent that we faithfully reproduce the joint distribution $P(X, Y)$, which assumes of course that we have also identified $P(X)$ and $P(N_y)$), does NOT imply that $X \to Y$. This is our dilemma: we will have to determine under which conditions finding an explanation of $P(X, Y)$ in terms of $P(X)$, $P(N_y)$, and $Y := f(X, N_y)$ allows us to prefer the hypothesis that $X \to Y$ over alternative hypotheses. It can even be shown, under some assumptions, that there always exists X, N_y, Y, N_x, f, g such that $Y := f(X, N_y)$ **and** $X := g(Y, N_x)$ (see [67]).
- For simplicity, in *artificially generated data*, we imposed that $(X \perp N_y)$ and $(Y \perp N_x)$. However, this is not necessarily the case in *real data* (partial confounding/dashed lines in Fig. 2.2). See Chap. 6 for extensions of this framework.
- The case $G = [X \leftrightarrow Y]$ represents a dependency between two variables, which is NOT causal. When we generate simulated data, we bring this case back to the existence of one or several common cause(s) **Z** (following Reichenbach's common cause principle [52]). In real data, there may be violations to the common cause principle: cases of inter-dependences between variables may be explained by constraints, equilibria, or cycles. However, for simplicity, we will not further discuss the mechanisms underlying non causal dependencies and we will model them all via the existence of a common cause.
- For real data, we are relying on "expert opinion" to determine ground truth. In the medical domain, this is considered a very low level of evidence, lower than randomized controlled trials (experiments) and even case-control studies (observational studies) [7]. We will see in Sect. 2.6 how we ensure the quality of real data labels.

2.2.2 Mathematical Statement of the Problem

We can cast the cause-effect pair problem as a regular machine learning classification problem in which input-output pairs $\left(P_{\Pi=\pi}(X, Y), G = g \right)$ are drawn randomly and independently from a "mother distribution" $P_{\mathcal{M}}\left(P_{\Pi}(X, Y), G \right)$ [43], then divided into training and test sets. The problem is to "classify" distributions $P_{\Pi=\pi}(X, Y)$ into one of four classes $g \in \{ X \to Y, X \leftarrow Y, X \leftrightarrow Y, X \perp Y \}$. The "mother distribution" $P_{\mathcal{M}}$ is a distribution over distributions $P_{\Pi}(X, Y)$, where the index Π is itself a random variable, identifying a particular joint distribution over X and Y. Practically, $P_{\Pi=\pi}(X, Y)$ is only known through a finite sample $S_{\Pi=\pi}(X, Y) = \{(x_1, y_1), (x_2, y_2), \cdots, (x_n, y_n)\}$ (a **scatter plot**). Hence, we have a **double random process**:

1. Draw pair $\left(P_{\Pi=\pi}(X, Y), G = g \right)$ from mother distrib. $P_{\mathscr{M}}\left(P_\Pi(X, Y), G \right)$.
2. Draw n samples from $P_{\Pi=\pi}(X, Y)$:
   $S_{\Pi=\pi}(X, Y) = \{(x_1, y_1), (x_2, y_2), \cdots, (x_n, y_n)\}$.
3. Repeat the process to obtain enough training and/or test examples:
   $\{(S_1(X, Y), g_1), (S_2(X, Y), g_2), \cdots, (S_N(X, Y), g_N)\}$.

$$(2.4)$$

Therefore the mother distribution is a distribution over join distributions of pairs of variables.[1] In what follows, we adopt the following definition of a "mother distribution":

Definition 2.2 (Mother Distribution) A mother distribution $P_{\mathscr{M}}\left(P_\Pi(X, Y), G \right)$ is a distribution over pairs $\left(P_{\Pi=\pi}(X, Y), G = g \right)$, where Π and G are random variables:

- $\Pi = \pi$ indexes distribution $P_{\Pi=\pi}(X, Y)$ over random variables X and Y; π may possibly take an infinite number of values (e.g. parameters of a generative process);
- $G = g$ labels causal relationship, $g \in \{X \to Y, X \leftarrow Y, X \leftrightarrow Y, X \perp Y\}$.

The meaning of this "mother distribution" may seem mysterious. However, let us consider a few examples of causal discovery problems, which could clarify this notion. For notational simplicity we sometimes reformulate $P_{\Pi=\pi}(X, Y)$ as $P(X_\pi, Y_\pi)$, the distribution over two random variables indexed by π. In our examples, π is just a discrete index k.

Example 1: **Genomics.**   Pharmaceutical companies are interested in determining the influence of genes on each other [58]. A dataset may consist of jointly recorded gene activities for N pairs of genes (X_k, Y_k), $k = 1, \cdots N$ and for n patients $S_k = \{(x_{k1}, y_{k1}), \cdots, (x_{kn}, y_{kn}\}$. Determining which gene influences which other gene is a costly experimental process, so only a subset of pairs of genes are generally labeled with ground truth of causal relationship $G = g_k$. The labeled dataset $\{(S_1, g_1), \cdots, (S_k, g_k), \cdots\}$, $k = 1 \cdots N$, is an empirical sample of the "mother distribution" over pairs of genes and their causal labels, which may be used as training data to obtain a classifier, such that predictions of unknown causal labels can be made on new pairs of genes.

Example 2: **Ecology.**   A study is conducted to understand better an ecosystem in a forest area and preserve biodiversity [3]. The question is to determine which factor influences which other factor. The dataset consists of n jointly recorded values of many variables (X_k, Y_k), $k = 1, \cdots N$, in different locations,

---

[1]In case of time series, $\{(x_1, y_1), (x_2, y_2), \cdots, (x_n, y_n)\}$ are time ordered and not drawn *i.i.d.*.

such as soil, humidity, lighting, presence of certain plants or animals, etc., resulting in samples $S_k = \{(x_{k1}, y_{k1}), \cdots, (x_{kn}, y_{kn}\}$. Determining which factor influences which other factor is a complicated process, however, prior knowledge of physics and biology may allow us to label some pairs with ground truth $G = g_k$ (for example the aspect of a slope can influence hill shade and not vice-versa, see example 5 in Table 2.2). The labeled dataset thus obtained $\{(S_1, g_1), \cdots, (S_k, g_k), \cdots\}, k = 1 \cdots N$, is an empirical sample of the "mother distribution". It is hoped that we can label automatically more pairs with a classifier trained on such data, if the mechanisms of the other pairs bear some similarity.

Example 3: **Social sciences.** A country conducts a census survey, including socio-demographic questions (age, gender, education, profession, number of children, salary, etc.), e.g. [39]. The question is to determine which factor influences which other factor. The dataset consists of joint answers from n citizens for factor pairs $(X_k, Y_k), k = 1, \cdots N$: $S_k = \{(x_{k1}, y_{k1}), \cdots, (x_{kn}, y_{kn}\}$. Prior knowledge allows us to determine the ground truth for a few pairs (X_k, Y_k) (for example age can influence wages and not vice-versa). This constitutes an empirical "mother distribution" of pairs $\{(S_1, g_1), \cdots, (S_k, g_k), \cdots, (S_N, g_N)\}$ from which we might train a classifier to label other similar pairs with their causal direction.

A mother distribution may be endowed with an explicit **data generative process** $\mathcal{P}_\Pi(X, Y)$ underlying $P_\Pi(X, Y)$, for example, an Additive Noise Model (ANM) [33, 49][2]:

$$\mathcal{P}_{\Pi=\pi}^{ANM}(X, Y) \begin{cases} g = [X \to Y] : x \sim P(X), n \sim P(N), X \perp N, \quad y := f(x)+n \\ g = [X \leftarrow Y] : \text{Reverse the role of } X \text{ and } Y. \end{cases}$$

(2.5)

The data generative process $\mathcal{P}_{\Pi=\pi}^{ANM}$ is parameterized by π, which includes the choice of ground truth (or causal graph) g, input distribution $P(X)$, noise distribution $P(N)$, and function f. Pairs (x, y) drawn according to $\mathcal{P}_{\Pi=\pi}^{ANM}(X, Y)$ are (by definition) distributed according to $P_{\Pi=\pi}^{ANM}(X, Y)$.[3] We will use the shorthand notation: $P_{\mathcal{M}}\left(\mathcal{P}_\Pi(X, Y), G\right)$. $P_{\mathcal{M}}$ provides a distribution over choices of parameters π of the generative process.

In what follows, we assume that the training and test sets are drawn from the same distribution $P_{\mathcal{M}}\left(P_\Pi(X, Y), G\right)$ or $P_{\mathcal{M}}\left(\mathcal{P}_\Pi(X, Y), G\right)$, leaving for further study problems of domain adaptation or transfer learning [64, 65]. Even though we cast our problem as a learning problem, we do not exclude approaches not involving any learning (see examples in Sect. 2.3). In that case, the training set is just unused.

---

[2]The difference with the general case is outlined in blue: the noise is additive. It is usually assumed that the noise and the input are independent in the ANM (noted $X \perp N$).

[3]However, we remind the reader that several data generative processes may generate the same data distribution.

Table 2.3 Comparing two pattern recognition problems

Attribute	Handwritten digits	Cause-effect pairs
Patterns "M"	Pixel maps	Scatter plots
Pattern resolution	Number of pixels	Number of sampled $\{x, y\}$ points
Generating process	Handwriting	SRM/FCM data generative process: points in scatter plot obtained from Eq. (2.15)
Ground truth "G"	$\{One, Two, Three, \cdots, Nine\}$	$\{X \to Y, X \leftarrow Y, X \leftrightarrow Y, X \perp Y\}$
Mother distribution $P_{\mathcal{M}}(M, G)$	Join distribution of images of digits (pixel maps "M") and labels $G \in \{One, Two, \cdots\}$	Join distribution of scatter plots (sample "M" of $P(X, Y)$) and labels $G \in \{X \to Y, \cdots\}$
Methods to obtain labeled data	(1) Generate artificial digits from handwriting models (2) Ask humans to handwrite given digits (3) Collect examples of digits e.g. from zip codes and have human experts labels them	(1) Generate artificial scatter plots from a causal model (2) Use a real causal system to generate data (3) Use real pairs of variables with known causal directions
Data split	Training, validation, and test sets	Training, validation, and test sets
Reduction to binary classification	Separate one class *vs.* the rest	Separate $[X \to Y]$ *vs.* the rest
Discriminant functions	One function $D_i(M; \mathbf{w}, \boldsymbol{\theta})$ per class	A "causation coefficient" $C(M; \mathbf{w}, \boldsymbol{\theta}) \simeq C(X, Y; \mathbf{w}, \boldsymbol{\theta})$
Classification method	$\hat{G} = \text{argmax}_i D_i(M; \mathbf{w}, \boldsymbol{\theta})$	$\hat{G} = [X \to Y] \; iff \, C(M; \mathbf{w}, \boldsymbol{\theta}) > 0$
Training	Adjust $\mathbf{w}$ of $D_i(M; \mathbf{w}, \boldsymbol{\theta})$ using training data and $\boldsymbol{\theta}$ using validation data	Adjust $\mathbf{w}$ of $C(M; \mathbf{w}, \boldsymbol{\theta})$ using training data and $\boldsymbol{\theta}$ using validation data
Evaluation	Error rate, BER (balanced error rate), etc., on test data	Error rate, BER= 0.5(FPR+FNR), AUC, etc., on test data
Overfitting avoidance	Don't use test data to select parameters, hyper-parameters or models	Don't use test data to select parameters, hyper-parameters or models

2.2.3   Causal Discovery as a Pattern Recognition Problem

In our setting, causal discovery is nothing but a regular pattern recognition problem. To gain further intuition, we compare the cause-effect pair problem with the well-known handwritten digit recognition problem (Table 2.3). Some parallels are interesting: First, digit resolution (number of pixels) and the number of points n in scatter plot, play a similar role. Second, in "on-line" character recognition, points are sampled with a touch sensitive pad, resulting in ordered samples $\{(x_1, y_1), (x_2, y_2), \cdots, (x_n, y_n)\}$. Similarly time-ordered (x, y) pairs may be obtained from a dynamic causal process. Even though handwritten characters are always the result of a sequential dynamic process, we often ignore time ordering and perform pattern recognition from pixel maps. Likewise, when we consider causal discovery from scatter plots, we ignore time dependencies. Even though we know that causes precede their effects, we assume instantaneous propagation of causal effects. Finally, overfitting may be an issue for causal discovery as in every pattern recognition problem. Until recently, many papers in causal discovery have been published with no data split: models were selected and evaluated using a single dataset (de facto serving both as training and test set), thus making error bars much worse than advertised. For a review on performance bounds, see [41].

2.3   Causation Coefficients

Once our problem has been formulated as a learning problem, we need to build a classifier (eventually using training data) to predict the ground truth of causal relationships as accurately as possible. For practical reasons, we find it convenient to recast the problem as a two-class classification problem separating $X \rightarrow Y$ from all other cases. We propose to construct a causation coefficient, which is a discriminant function in this two-class classification problem.

2.3.1   Definition

We consider a pair of random variables (X, Y) with ground truth $G \in \{X \rightarrow Y, X \leftarrow Y, X \leftrightarrow Y, X \perp Y\}$, drawn from an unknown mother distribution. We call $\hat{G}$ an estimator of G based on (X, Y). We define a causation coefficient for, as follows:

Definition 2.3 (Causation Coefficient) A causation coefficient $C(X, Y)$ is a real scalar value, such that the larger $C(X, Y)$, the more confident we are that $G = X \rightarrow Y$.

A causation coefficient must have the following desired properties:

1. $C(X, Y) = -C(Y, X)$ [Anti-symmetry]
2. $C(X, Y) > \theta \geq 0 \Rightarrow \hat{\mathbf{G}} = [X \rightarrow Y]$
   (and $\hat{\mathbf{G}} \neq [X \rightarrow Y]$ otherwise)   [Discriminant]
3. $C(aX + b, cY + d) = C(X, Y);\ a, b, c, d \in \mathbb{R}, a \neq 0, c \neq 0$ [Arbitrary units]

Several *cause-effect pair filters* (not involving any learning) have been proposed as causation coefficients, based on various data generative assumptions. Examples in Tables 2.1 and 2.2 show the result of applying some filters defined below to *continuous* variables:

- C_{R2}=**R-squared:** The difference between the R-square statistic measuring goodness of fit in both direction: $C_{R2} = R_y^2 - R_x^2$ [4, 33, 49].[4]
- C_{IR}=**Input/Residual Independence:** The difference between statistics of independence between input and residual: $C_{IR} = I(R_y, X) - I(R_x, Y)$ [33, 49].[5]
- C_H=**Entropy:** The difference in (discretized) entropy of the marginal distributions: $C_H = H_x - H_y$, with $H_x = \sum_{k=1}^{m} p_k \log p_k$; using $m = 20$ bins [36].[6]
- C_S=**Slope:** The difference in average slope in both direction: $C_S = S_y - S_x$, with $S_y = \sum_{k=1}^{m-1} p_k\ \Delta y_k / \Delta x_k$; using $m = 20$ intervals [36].[7]
- C_{CDS}: **Conditional Distribution Standard deviation:** The difference between conditional distributions average standard deviation, in both directions [18]: $C_{CDS} = CDS(X|Y) - CDS(Y|X)$.[8]

We give in Fig. 2.3 an example of cause-effect pair in which all causation coefficient filters agree and give the correct causal direction! This example was generated as follows:

---

[4]In our examples, we perform a piece-wise constant fit using $m = 20$ equally spaced points. If we believe that the fit should be better in the "causal direction", then $R^2 = R_y^2 - R_x^2$ should be positive if $X \rightarrow Y$), since R_y^2 is the residual of the fit $\hat{y} = f(x)$.

[5]Using an ANM model (Eq. (2.5)), we expect that input and residual of regression (our estimation of the noise) are independent, i.e. if $X \rightarrow Y$, $R_y \perp X$. We use a kernel independence test statistic [25] to calculate $I(X, Y)$; larger values of $I(X, Y)$ mean a greater confidence that X and Y are independent. For example, $I(.,.)$ can be the HSIC statistic.

[6]According to the Information Geometry Causal Inference (IGCI) principle, if $(X \rightarrow Y)$ and there is independence between "causal mechanism" and $P(X)$, then, under some conditions (e.g. no noise and invertible mechanism), $H_x \geq H_y$ [36].

[7]According to IGCI principle again, if $X \rightarrow Y$, under the same conditions as for the entropy criterion, $S_y \geq S_x$ [36].

[8]CDS measures variations in conditional distribution. The idea is that, for $X \rightarrow Y$, if X is independent of the noise, then, after normalizing the support $P(Y|X)$ should not vary a lot. For additive noise models, C_{CDS} should be similar to C_{IR} (but not always, because of support normalization). In the case of multiplicative noise, C_{CDS} should capture the independence of noise and input, where C_{IR} usually fails.

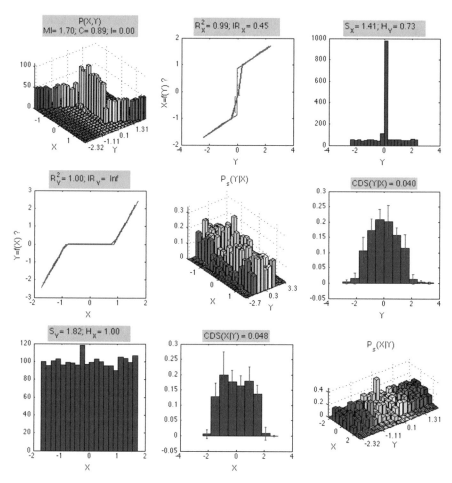

Fig. 2.3 Example of pair for which all causation coefficient filters agree. $P_s(Y|X)$ is the conditional distribution of Y given X with re-normalized support. Values of the statistics R_Y^2, IR_Y, S_Y, H_X, and $CDS(X|Y)$ (on top of in the lower left plots) are larger than those of R_X^2, IR_X, S_X, H_Y, and $CDS(Y|X)$ (on top of the upper right plots). Thus all corresponding causation coefficients agree that $X \to Y$

$$g = [X \to Y] : x \sim U(-1, 1), n \sim N(0, 0.001),$$

$$\begin{cases} x \leq -0.5, & y := x + 0.5 + n \\ -0.5 < x < 0.5, & y := n \\ x \geq 0.5, & y := x - 0.5 + n \end{cases}$$

But, don't be too hopeful. Causation coefficient filters succeed or fail depending on the validity of assumptions made, details of implementation, and sample variance, as can be seen in Tables 2.1 and 2.2 (all examples shown are of type

$X \to Y$ and the check marks indicate a correct prediction of the causal relationship; graphical representations such as Fig. 2.3 are provided in Appendix 3 for all example pairs.). Rather than making a wrong decision, if no hypothesis is significantly better supported than others, it is preferable to reject them all (see Sect. 2.5). Several authors, e.g. [58], have attempted to use ensemble methods to combine various causation coefficients proposed in the literature, reporting increased performance. The participants of the cause-effect pair challenge 2013–2014 [31] used them as features to train predictive models, in combination with other engineered features [6, 10, 17, 45, 55] (see Chap. 4). Other methods have emerged that will be described in Chap. 3 and 4 for the *i.i.d.* case, and in Chap. 5 for time series.

2.3.2 Bayes Optimal Causation Coefficients

In this section, we apply **Bayesian decision theory** to define several theoretically optimal causation coefficients. We make the following assumptions: (a) Data are drawn from a mother distribution $P_{\mathscr{M}}\Big(P_\Pi(X, Y), G\Big)$. (b) We treat the **asymptotic case** of perfect knowledge of $P_\Pi(X, Y)$ (i.e. we classify pairs (X, Y) given an infinite size sample). However, extending results to the finite sample case is trivial, by replacing $P_\Pi(X, Y)$ by $S_\Pi(X, Y)$, (see Sect. 2.4.2). (c) To ensure that property 3 in the definition of a causation coefficient holds (see Sect. 2.3), all variables X and Y are first **standardized** (subtract mean and divide by standard deviation). (d) The **ground truth** G belongs to $\{X \to Y, X \leftarrow Y, X \leftrightarrow Y, X \perp Y\}$. (e) The mother distribution is perfectly symmetrical and unbiased towards a particular causal direction: $P_{\mathscr{M}}\Big(G = [X \to Y]\Big) = P_{\mathscr{M}}\Big(G = [Y \to X]\Big)$; for the case of $X \leftrightarrow Y$ we also postulate that the mother distribution generates models and their swap (exchanging X and Y) with the same probability. A *causation coefficient* is a *discriminant function* (Property 2 in the definition of a causation coefficient, Sect. 2.4.2). Bayesian decision theory allows us to define optimal discriminant functions. Bayes' rule applied to the mother distribution yields,[9]

$$P_{\mathscr{M}}\Big(P_\Pi(X, Y), G\Big) = P_{\mathscr{M}}\Big(P_\Pi(X, Y) \mid G\Big) P_{\mathscr{M}}\Big(G\Big)$$
$$= P_{\mathscr{M}}\Big(G \mid P_\Pi(X, Y)\Big) P_{\mathscr{M}}\Big(P_\Pi(X, Y)\Big).$$

As per Bayesian decision theory [12], the largest attainable classification accuracy is:

---

[9]If Π takes continuous values, $P_{\mathscr{M}}\Big(P_\Pi(X, Y)\Big)$ and $P_{\mathscr{M}}\Big(P_\Pi(X, Y) \mid G\Big)$ should be understood as densities rather than a distributions.

$$\text{BayesAccuracy} = E\left[\max_j P_{\mathcal{M}}\big(G = j \mid P_\Pi(X, Y)\big)\right], \tag{2.6}$$

where the expectation $E[.]$ is taken over the randomness of Π. This is attainable with:

Classify pair (X_π, Y_π) as $[X \to Y]$ iff
$$P_{\mathcal{M}}\big(G = [X \to Y] \mid (X_\pi, Y_\pi)\big) > \quad P_{\mathcal{M}}\big(G \neq [X \to Y] \mid (X_\pi, Y_\pi)\big). \tag{2.7}$$

where we use the notation shorthand $P_{\Pi=\pi}(X, Y) = P(X_\pi, Y_\pi)$.

We show in Appendix 2 that the following causation coefficients are Bayes optimal:

$$
\begin{aligned}
C_{\mathcal{B}1}(X_\pi, Y_\pi) &= \Phi\Big(P_{\mathcal{M}}\big(G = [X \to Y]\big|(X_\pi, Y_\pi)\big)\Big) \\
&\quad - \Phi\Big(P_{\mathcal{M}}\big(G = [X \leftarrow Y]|(X_\pi, Y_\pi)\big)\Big) \\
C_{\mathcal{B}2}(X_\pi, Y_\pi) &= \Phi\Big(P_{\mathcal{M}}\big((X_\pi, Y_\pi)|G = [X \to Y]\big)\Big) \\
&\quad - \Phi\Big(P_{\mathcal{M}}\big((X_\pi, Y_\pi)|G = [Y \to X]\big)\Big)
\end{aligned} \tag{2.8}
$$

where the function $\Phi(.)$ is any convenient strictly monotonically increasing function, such as $\Phi(.) = log(.)$, introduced to make the formulas more general.

For $C_{\mathcal{B}1}$, $P_{\mathcal{M}}\big(G = [X \to Y]|(X_\pi, Y_\pi)\big)$ is **NOT** equal to $(1 - P_{\mathcal{M}}\big(G = [X \leftarrow Y]|(X_\pi, Y_\pi)\big)$, because we consider four possible truth values $G \in \{X \to Y, X \leftarrow Y, X \leftrightarrow Y, X \perp Y\}$.

For $C_{\mathcal{B}2}$, remarkably, even though we consider four possible truth values for G, this causation coefficient involves only two data generative processes, for $[X \to Y]$ and $[X \leftarrow Y]$. We remind the reader that (X_π, Y_π) is a shorthand for $P_\Pi(X, Y)$ and we denote by $\mathcal{P}_\Pi(X, Y)$ any data generative process yielding to a distribution identical to $P_\Pi(X, Y)$. Thus $C_{\mathcal{B}2}$ compares two data generative models:

$$\mathcal{P}_\Pi(X, Y) \mid G = [X \to Y]$$

and

$$\mathcal{P}_\Pi(X, Y) \mid G = [Y \to X].$$

This is similar to what is usually done in the literature of cause-effect pair generative models (see Chap. 3), except that we do NOT limit ourselves to just two classes $G = [X \to Y]$ or $G = [Y \to X]$. More about this in Sect. 2.4.1.

2.4   The Point of View of Algorithm Developers

In this section and in the following ones, we will talk about methods of evaluation of cause-effect pair algorithms. We take **three points of view**: that of **algorithm developers** in need to characterize their new algorithms both theoretically and empirically, that of **practitioners** who want to ensure the validity of a potential discovery, and that of **benchmark organizers** who want to make fair comparisons.

We begin in this section with the point of view of algorithm developers. We first discuss the problem of backing algorithms with theoretical justifications, then review empirical assessment methods.

2.4.1   Identifiability of Cause-Effect Pairs

One central question investigated in many causality papers is that of "identifiability". Identifiability refers to the feasibility of solving the inverse problem: given (X, Y) pairs having been generated by a given causal mechanism, recover the correct causal relationships unambiguously. In this section, we begin by defining the classical notion of identifiability considering that the (data generative) model class is the same as the hypothesis class, i.e. the method consists in fitting models belonging to the class of models that generated data. We then move to a generic machine learning approach in which no assumption is made about data generative models; rather, data are supposed to have been drawn from an unknown "mother distribution" and causation coefficients predict causal relationships without necessarily fitting a generative model or making assumptions about how data were generated.

The literature on identifiability of cause-effect pair mechanisms [33, 46, 66, 67] focuses for the most part only two class labels $g \in \mathcal{G} = \{X \to Y, X \leftarrow Y\}$, considering that only pairs that are significantly dependent should be tested for causal orientation and excluding the case of "confounding" (presence of a common cause). We call $\mathcal{B}_\Pi$ such a binary cause-effect pair data generative process:

Definition 2.4 (Binary Cause-Effect Pair Data Generative Process)

$$\mathcal{B}_\Pi(X, Y) \begin{cases} g = [X \to Y] : x \sim P(X), n \sim P(N) \quad y := f(x, n) \\ g = [X \leftarrow Y] : \text{Reverse the role of } X \text{ and } Y. \end{cases} \quad (2.9)$$

$\mathcal{B}_\Pi(X, Y)$ is parameterized by Π, which includes the choice of ground truth (causal graph) $g \in \mathcal{G}$, input distribution $P(X) \in \mathcal{X}$, noise distribution $P(N) \in \mathcal{N}$, and function $f \in \mathcal{F}$. Pairs (x, y) drawn according to $\mathcal{B}_\Pi(X, Y)$ are distributed according to $P_\Pi(X, Y)$.

This definition yield a first definition of "identifiability":

Definition 2.5 ($\mathscr{B}$-Identifiability) Given a cause-effect pair (X, Y) obtained from a data generative process $\mathcal{B}_\Pi(X, Y)$, its causal direction is $\mathscr{B}$-identifiable *iff*:

$$G = [X \to Y] \Rightarrow \begin{cases} \exists (f \in \mathcal{F} \wedge P(N) \in \mathcal{N}) \text{ s.t. } Y := f(X, N) \\ \nexists (f \in \mathcal{F} \wedge P(N) \in \mathcal{N}) \text{ s.t. } X := f(Y, N). \end{cases}$$

and vice versa if we reverse the roles of X and Y.
$\mathcal{B}_\Pi(X, Y)$ is $\mathscr{B}$-identifiable *iff* the causal direction of all possible generated pairs are $\mathscr{B}$-identifiable.[10]

Typically $\mathscr{B}$-identifiability is obtained by making restrictive assumptions on $\mathcal{F}$ (such as surjectivity, strict monotonicity/invertibility, continuity, derivability, smoothness) and on $\mathcal{X}$ and $\mathcal{N}$ (such as Gaussianity or non-Gaussianity, uniformity, etc.). Additionally, it is usually assumed that $X \perp N$ (X and N are independent). Also $\mathcal{G}$ excludes $X \perp Y$ on the grounds that independence can easily be tested, thus we can focus on dependent pairs. Less justifiably, $X \leftrightarrow Y$ is also excluded from $\mathcal{G}$, for simplicity.

As a particular case, if $P(X, Y)$ is symmetric, the pair (X, Y) is not identifiable. By symmetric, we mean that $P(X = x, Y = y) = P(X = y, Y = x)$ once the support of X and Y have been standardized. Data generated with a linear additive noise model with Gaussian input and Gaussian noise (Case 1 in Table 2.1) is a particular case if symmetric distribution. The more general the family of data generative models (i.e. the less restrictive the assumptions made), the larger the set of non-identifiable cases. It can be shown [67] that if no restrictions are placed, it is always possible to find a function f and noise N such that $Y := f(X, N)$ and another function f and noise N such that $X := f(Y, N)$. Thus it is essential to make some assumptions or place some restrictions on the data generative process. Notice that the notion of $\mathscr{B}$-identifiability is an asymptotic property: a perfect knowledge of $P(X, Y)$ is assumed. The finite sample case is addressed in Sect. 2.4.2.

A greater level of generality in the definition of identifiability is obtained by considering the notion of "mother distribution" $P_{\mathcal{M}}$. By definition (See Sect. 2.2.2), a mother distribution $P_{\mathcal{M}}\left(P_\Pi(X, Y), G\right)$ is a distribution over pairs $\left(P_{\Pi=\pi}(X, Y), G = g\right)$, where Π and G are random variables: $\Pi = \pi$ indexes distribution $P_{\Pi=\pi}(X, Y)$ over random variables X and Y and may include the parameters of a generative process; $G = g$ labels causal relationship, $g \in \mathcal{G} = \{X \to Y, X \leftarrow Y, X \leftrightarrow Y, X \perp Y\}$. Note that, even though there is an implicit data generative process underlying a mother distribution, the definition does not preclude of any particular data generative process and thus applies to synthetic/artificial data (for which the generative process is known) as well as to real data (for which mechanisms may be unknown). If we want to assume that a given data generative $\mathcal{P}_\Pi(X, Y)$ underlies $P_\Pi(X, Y)$ process, we can use the notation $P_{\mathcal{M}}\left(\mathcal{P}_\Pi(X, Y), G\right)$ instead of $P_{\mathcal{M}}\left(P_\Pi(X, Y), G\right)$.

---

[10]Except possibly for a finite subset or a subset of measure 0.

From the notion of mother distribution and of causation coefficient, we derive a more general notion of identifiability (see Fig. 2.4 for a schematic illustration the distribution of a hypothetical causation coefficient):

Definition 2.6 ((α, β)-Identifiability) Assume that pairs $\left(P_{\Pi=\pi}(X,Y), G = g\right)$ are drawn according to a given "mother distribution" $P_{\mathcal{M}}\left(P_{\Pi}(X,Y), G\right)$ or $P_{\mathcal{M}}\left(\mathcal{P}_{\Pi}(X,Y), G\right)$. The causal direction of a given pair (X,Y) with $G = X \to Y$ is (α, β)-identifiable for $P_{\mathcal{M}}$ (with $0 \leq \alpha \leq 1, 0 \leq \beta \leq 1$) *iff* there exist a causation coefficient $C(X,Y)$ and a threshold $\theta > 0$ such that:

$$Pr(C(X,Y) > \theta \mid G \neq [X \to Y]) \leq \alpha. \quad \text{(Type I errors)}$$

$$Pr(C(X,Y) < \theta \mid G = [X \to Y]) \leq \beta. \quad \text{(Type II errors)}$$

where the probability is taken over the randomness of Π. $P_{\mathcal{M}}$ is (α, β)-identifiable *iff* the causal direction of all possible pairs is (α, β)-identifiable.

This definition seeks to bound simultaneously Type I and Type II errors. Alternative definitions of identifiability using a "mother distribution" are possible. For example, one could set a threshold on the area under the ROC curve (plotting True Positive Rate as a function of False Positive Rate) obtained by varying θ.

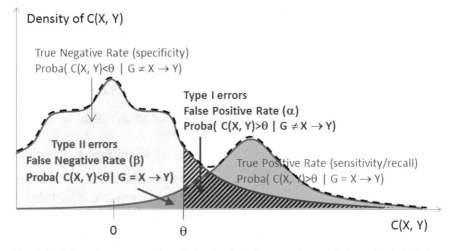

Fig. 2.4 Schematic representation of the density of a causation coefficient: the dashed line represents the density of a hypothetical causation coefficient C(X, Y). The blue shaded area represents the density of the negative class $G \in \{X \leftarrow Y, X \leftrightarrow Y, X \perp Y\}$ (multiplied by the prior probability of the negative class) and the red shaded area the density of the positive class $G = X \to Y$ (multiplied by the prior probability of the positive class). For a given threshold θ we have a given fraction of false positive (shaded area), corresponding to a p-value (called α in the text)

Yet another possibility would be to use the area under the precision-recall curve (precision is the number of true positive over (true positive + false positive) and recall is the sensitivity. For concreteness, we show in Fig. 2.5 examples of empirical densities (histograms) of the causation coefficients of three top ranking participants of the cause-effect pair challenge [29]. The data of the challenge constitutes an empirical "mother distribution"; it is described in Sect. 2.6.

In the definition of (α, β)-identifiability, we require the existence of a causation coefficient. This is not a restriction, since there exists several optimal Bayesian causation coefficients (see Sect. 2.3.2), which can be used to derive theoretical bounds of identifiability. Using the optimal Bayesian causation coefficient of Eq. (2.30), we can prove that $\mathscr{B}$-identifiability implies (α, β)-identifiability.

Theorem 2.1 ($\mathscr{B}$-Identifiability Implies (α, β)-Identifiability) *Given a mother distribution* $P_{\mathscr{M}}\Big(\mathcal{B}_\Pi(X, Y), G\Big)$ *endowed by a binary cause-effect pair data generative process* $\mathcal{B}_\Pi(X, Y)$ *with identical class priors* $P_{\mathscr{M}}\Big(G = [X \to Y]\Big) =$

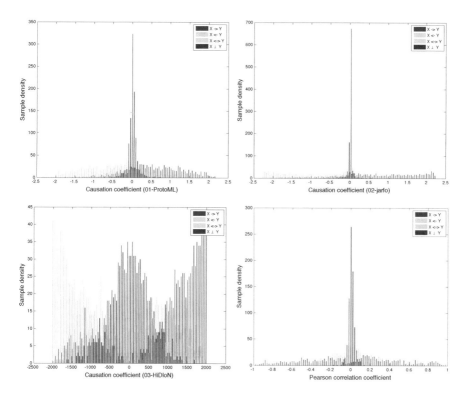

Fig. 2.5 Density of causation coefficients. We show the empirical density (histogram) of causation coefficients for the top three ranking participants of the cause-effect pair challenge [29]. For comparison we show the distribution of the Pearson correlation coefficient (excluding categorical variables)

$P_{\mathcal{M}}\Big(G = [X \leftarrow Y]\Big)$, if $\mathcal{B}_{\Pi}(X, Y)$ is $\mathcal{B}$-identifiable then $P_{\mathcal{M}}$ is (α, β)-identifiable, with $\alpha = \beta = \theta = 0$. Reciprocally, (α, β)-identifiability, with $\alpha = \beta = \theta = 0$ implies $\mathcal{B}$-identifiability.

Proof of the theorem is given in Appendix 2.

The definition of (α, β)-identifiability rests upon likelihoods $P(C \mid G)$ rather than posterior probabilities $P(G \mid C)$. It is useful to build bridges with statistical testing (Sect. 2.5.3). However, it may be impractical for empirical evaluations (Sect. 2.4.3). By using Bayes inversion $P(G \mid C \lesseqgtr \theta) = P(C \lesseqgtr \theta \mid G)P(G)/P(C \lesseqgtr \theta)$, we propose another notion of identifiability.

Definition 2.7 ((a, p)-Identifiability) Assume that pairs $\Big((X, Y), G = g\Big)$ are drawn according to a given "mother distribution" $P_{\mathcal{M}}$. $P_{\mathcal{M}}$ is said to be (a, p)-identifiable, for $0 \leq a \leq 1$ and $0 \leq p \leq 1$, *iff* there exist a causation coefficient $C(X, Y)$ and a threshold $\theta > 0$ such that:

$$Accuracy(\theta) = Pr\,(G{=}X{\rightarrow}Y|C(X, Y){>}\theta \ \vee \ G{=}X{\leftarrow}Y|C(X, Y){<} -\theta) \geq a$$

$$DecisionRate(\theta) = Pr = (\,|C(X, Y)| > \theta\,) \geq p$$

where the probability "Pr" means probability taken over the randomness of $P_{\mathcal{M}}$.

Finally, it is useful to specialize (a, p)-identifiability to the case when $a = 1$, namely 100% accuracy, no Type I error, i.e. no false causal discovery.

Definition 2.8 (p-Identifiability) Assume that pairs $\Big((X, Y), G = g\Big)$ are drawn according to a given "mother distribution" $P_{\mathcal{M}}$. $P_{\mathcal{M}}$ is said to be p-identifiable *iff* there exist a causation coefficient $C(X, Y)$ and a threshold $\theta^* > 0$ such that:

$$Accuracy(\theta) = Pr\,(G{=}X{\rightarrow}Y \mid C(X, Y){>}\theta \ \vee \ G = X \leftarrow Y \mid C(X, Y) < -\theta)$$

$$\theta^* = \text{argmax}_{\theta}\,[Accuracy(\theta) = 1] \quad (No\ Type\ I\ error)$$

$$p = Pr\,\Big(\,|C(X, Y)| > \theta^*\,\Big) \qquad (DecisionRate(\theta*))$$

where the probability "Pr" is taken over the randomness of $P_{\mathcal{M}}$.

For the definitions of (α, p)-identifiability and p-identifiability, we have symmetrized the roles of $X \rightarrow Y$ and $X \leftarrow Y$. If we compare with the definition of (α, β)-identifiability, a plays the role of $(1 - \alpha)$ and p plays the role of $(1 - \beta)$. Similarly, (α, p)-identifiability (and p-identifiability) is equivalent to $\mathcal{B}$-identifiability if the mother distribution is endowed by a binary cause-effect pair data generative process, in the case $a = p = 1$ and $\theta = 0$. This corresponds to 100%-identifiability. Note that (α, β)-identifiability, (α, p)-identifiability, and p-

identifiability are **intrinsic properties of the mother distribution**, NOT of any causal discovery algorithm. They are linked to the Bayes optimal classification accuracy and its associated Bayes optimal causation coefficients.

2.4.2 Finite Sample Case, Consistency, and Rates of Convergence

In the previous subsection, we only considered asymptotic properties, in the sense that we assumed that, for each pair (X_π, Y_π), its distribution $P_\Pi(X, Y)$ was perfectly known. In practice only samples $S_\Pi(X, Y)$ are given, i.e. scatter plots.

However, all the notions introduced before can be extended to empirical distributions. The only thing we have to do is to replace $P_\Pi(X, Y)$ by $S_\Pi(X, Y)$. This is totally justified by the fact that $S_\Pi(X, Y)$ is an empirical distribution (hence a distribution). Therefore we can define a mother distribution $P_\mathscr{M}\Big(S_\Pi(X, Y), G\Big)$ directly on empirical distributions $S_\Pi(X, Y)$, bypassing the notion of double random process of Eq. (2.4). For convenience, we repeat the definition of (α, β)-*identifiability* in the finite sample case, but it is exactly the same.

Definition 2.9 ((α, β)-Identifiability (Finite Sample Case)) Assume that pairs $\Big(S_{\Pi=\pi}(X, Y), G = g\Big)$ are drawn according to a given *mother distribution* $P_\mathscr{M}\Big(S_\Pi(X, Y), G\Big)$. The causal direction of a given pair (X, Y) with $G = X \to Y$ is (α, β)-identifiable for $P_\mathscr{M}$ (with $0 \leq \alpha \leq 1, 0 \leq \beta \leq 1$) *iff* there exist a causation coefficient $C\ (S_{\Pi=\pi}(X, Y))$ and a threshold $\theta > 0$ such that:

$$Pr(C\ (S_{\Pi=\pi}(X, Y)) > \theta \mid G \neq [X \to Y]) \leq \alpha. \quad \text{(Type I errors)}$$

$$Pr(C\ (S_{\Pi=\pi}(X, Y)) < \theta \mid G = [X \to Y]) \leq \beta. \quad \text{(Type II errors)}$$

where the probability is taken over the randomness of Π, which includes the drawing of scatter-plot samples. $P_\mathscr{M}$ is (α, β)-identifiable *iff* the causal direction of all pairs is (α, β)-identifiable.

The randomness of the finite sample in lumped into Π. If we want to consider empirical distributions with a variety of number of samples n, we can impose a prior distribution on n and lump it into Π. We can similarly define notions of empirical (a, p)-identifiability or p-identifiability.

The identifiability problem remains the same in the finite sample case, except that it becomes more difficult because empirical distributions are (presumably) harder to classify. From the theoretical point of view, it is useful to derive rates of convergence (learning curves), providing the speed at which asymptotic identifiability is reached from a finite sample (consistency). Some authors have started working on this subject in the context of the Additive Noise Model (ANM; Eq. (2.16)) [40, 46], but much remains to be done.

For simplicity, when there in no ambiguity, we will replace $C(S_{\Pi=\pi}(X, Y))$ with the simpler notation $\hat{C}(X, Y)$ in what follows.

2.4.3 Empirical Evaluations

In previous sections, we have adopted a framework in which the notion of **mother distribution** and (α, β)**-identifiability** (or p-identifiability) generalizes previous frameworks of binary cause-effect pair data generative process and $\mathscr{B}$-identifiability. Determining (α, β)-identifiability (or p-identifiability) only requires providing a *causation coefficient*, NOT a data generative model faithfully reproducing the data. In machine learning jargon: the hypothesis class does not need to be the same as the model class. The definition of (α, β)-identifiability provides a statistical notion of identifiability more general and flexible than $\mathscr{B}$-identifiability. It allows us to authorize a certain fraction of Type I and Type II errors. It does not require finding a generative model faithfully reproducing the data.

Few papers have explicitly adopted this framework pioneered in [43], but empirical evaluations are implicitly using it. Indeed, testing causation coefficients on empirical data, treating the problem as a classification problem while using a variety of datasets achieves essentially the same purpose as verifying (α, β)-*identifiability* empirically. In Sect. 2.6, we present several datasets that are suitable for that purpose.

The definition of (α, β)-*identifiability* is not necessarily practical for empirical evaluations. We review several alternatives:

Bi-Directional AUC In the cause-effect-pair challenge [29, 30], for instance, the metric of evaluation was the average of two Area under ROC curve (AUC). Let $\hat{C}(X, Y)$ be the predicted score and G the target values $G \in \{X \to Y, X \leftarrow Y, X \leftrightarrow Y, X \perp Y\}$. We define target values C_1 and C_2 as follows: $C_1 = 1$, if $X \to Y$ and -1 otherwise. $C_2 = -1$, if $X \leftarrow Y$ and 1 otherwise. Then, the score of the challenge is defined as:

$$\text{Score} = \text{Bidirectional AUC} = 0.5 \left(AUC(\hat{C}(X, Y), C_1) + AUC(\hat{C}(X, Y), C_2) \right) \tag{2.10}$$

Multi-Class Metrics Another related approach is to consider a four class classification problem (see e.g. [8]) and use classical multi-class classification metrics (for instance, error rate or balanced error rate). This requires defining multiple discriminant functions.

But, using a single causation coefficient, the problem could also be turned into a ternary classification problem, with target values $C_1 = 1$, if $X \to Y$, $C_2 = -1$, if $X \leftarrow Y$ and $C_3 = 0$ otherwise. Setting thresholds $\pm\theta$ allows you to make decisions $\hat{C}(X, Y) > \theta$, decide $X \to Y$, $\hat{C}(X, Y) < -\theta$ decide $X \leftarrow Y$, and decide $X \leftrightarrow Y$, or $X \perp Y$ otherwise.

Empirical p-Identifiability Even in the case of a simple binary classification problem $G \in \{X \rightarrow Y, X \leftarrow Y\}$, setting two thresholds can be advantageous to reserve
a region of rejection $-\theta \leq \hat{C}(X, Y) \leq \theta$. In [36], the authors use this approach.
They then plot the classification *Accuracy* as a function of *Decision Rate*, i.e. the
fraction of pairs on which a decision was taken $|\hat{C}(X, Y)| > \theta$. In Fig. 2.6 we show
an example of curves of *Accuracy vs. Decision Rate*, from [42].

We can view the curves plotting empirical *Accuracy vs. Decision Rate* as
a way of visualizing empirical p-indentifiability (Sect. 2.4.1). The largest value
of the *Decision Rate* such that *Accuracy* $= 1$ provides the value of p in p-
identifiability. For example, in Fig. 2.6, one would say that the Tuebingen dataset
is roughly 30%-identifiable (based on the best causation coefficient RCC). We
remind that p-indentifiability is a property of mother distributions (in this case the
Tuebingen dataset) and requires a (hopefully good) causation coefficient. Obviously,
if 100% accuracy cannot be attained, one can resort to reporting a weaker (a, p)-
indentifiability.

Statistical Significance and Machine Learning "Hygiene" As usual in any
machine learning problem, if learning is performed to tune parameters or hyper-
parameters of $\hat{C}(X, Y)$ or if model selection is performed, it is important to set
aside a test set to carry out evaluations, not to be used until the very final testing. It is
advisable to perform a three-way split of data into a training set to tune parameters of
$C(X, Y)$, a validation set to carry out hyper-parameter selection or model selection,

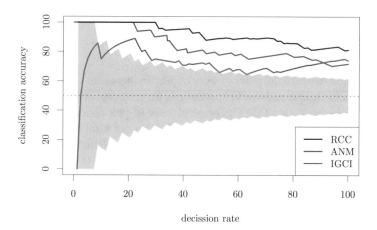

Fig. 2.6 Comparison of causation coefficient accuracies: three coefficients are compared: RCC
[42], ANM [33], and IGCI[36] on the 82 scalar pairs of the Tuebingen dataset [46] (see also
Sect. 2.6). For each decision rate, the authors indicated the 95% confidence interval that the
accuracy is not significantly different from 50% by a grey area (not corrected for multiple testing).
According to this figure (reprinted from [42]), the Tuebingen dataset is approximately 30%
identifiable, based on the RCC coefficient

and a final test set, which in theory should be used only once for final testing. In practice, most algorithm developers abuse their test set (i.e. use it many times). It is important to be aware that error bars reported should, in principle, be multiplied by the square root of the number of models compared (or ideas tried), to account for "multiple testing" [28]. If this discipline was really enforced, most of the results reported in the literature would be found not significant.

If results are mediocre, one might settle for showing that they are better than chance. This is the intention of the grey area in Fig. 2.6: results outside of the grey area are "statistically significantly" better than chance, i.e. they are in the rejection region of a statistical test whose null hypothesis is: decisions were made at random. Since we have a binary classification problem, the expected accuracy of a random decision is 50%. Decision follow a Bernoulli process with probability A of being correct $(1 - A)$ of being wrong (A being the classification accuracy). For n cause-effect pairs, the standard error is $\sqrt{A(1 - A)/n}$. A 95% confidence interval is approximately obtained for two times the standard error, defining the grey area in the figure: $0.5 \pm 1/\sqrt{n}$. Equivalently, for a decision rate d and a total number of available pairs N, since $n = d.N$, the gray area as a function of d is $0.5 \pm 1/\sqrt{d.N}$. For instance, since we have a total of $N = 82$ pairs available, for a decision rate of $d = 0.2$, the grey area is $0.5 \pm 1/\sqrt{d.N} = 0.5 \pm 0.25$. The method also work if the dataset includes $X \leftrightarrow Y$ and $X \perp Y$ pairs, and accuracy is defined as the average of the accuracy of classifying correctly pairs of class $X \rightarrow Y$ vs. the rest and the accuracy of classifying correctly pairs of class $X \leftarrow Y$ vs. the rest.

2.5 The Point of View of Practitioners

In this section, we take the point of view of practitioners who want to use causation coefficients in various real-world applications (in medicine or epidemiology, social sciences, econometrics, etc.). The point of view of practitioners differs from that of benchmark organizers (Sect. 2.6) in that they do not want to *evaluate* methods, they want to *use* them to identify potential cause-effect relationships in pairs of real variables. Thus, for practitioners, "evaluation" (the theme of this chapter) means assessing the reliability of given putative cause-effect relationship "discoveries" inferred from observational data.

2.5.1 Wish List

If practitioners are provided with a causation coefficient, what do they expect? Here is our tentative list, based on discussions with various practitioners:

1. **Prerequisites:**

   - **Reproducibility**: getting open source code and data, to inspect and re-run benchmarks demonstrating the validity of the approach.
   - **Speed:** getting results in reasonable time.
   - **Prior knowledge:** possibility of incorporating prior knowledge, such as model structure (including type of function, noise, potential confounders).
   - **Testability of assumptions:** if assumptions are made, e.g. additive noise, being able to test their validity.
   - **Flexibility:** being able to handle mixed data with binary, categorical, and continuous variables; not needing to make assumptions on the type of function, input, or noise distributions.

2. **Efficacy:**

   - **Theoretical groundings:** proofs of identifiability and consistency; rate of convergence as a function of sample size.
   - **Testability of hypothesis:** method for testing the validity of the presumed causal relationship, computing a confidence interval, a p-value or false positive rate (FPR) or a false discovery rate (FDR).
   - **Robustness:** method and/or guarantee of getting correct results even in the presence of outliers.
   - **Stability:** method and/or guarantee of getting the same results with multiple samples of the same size.

3. **Post-hoc evaluation:**

   - **Strength of effect:** obtaining a degree of influence or a signal to noise ratio.
   - **Direction of effect:** obtaining an indication of whether the effect is positive or negative.
   - **Explainability:** understanding why the causal direction decision was made.
   - **Mechanism:** obtaining a data generative model easily interpretable.
   - **Transfer:** obtaining a mechanism that explains other datasets, collected in different conditions.

Well... this is a long list, hopefully we did not forget anything! We hope it will be useful to researchers who design new algorithms. Let us make a few comments because some of these requirements conflict with one another and practitioners might need to be ready to make compromises.

2.5.2 Prerequisites

Regarding **Reproducibility**, we evidently encourage researchers to accompany publications with source code and data; luckily this is becoming a standard practice.

The **Speed** requirement is less obvious, because there may be speed-accuracy tradeoffs. However, if only a few pairs must be evaluated, speed is not such a critical aspect. In a past competition, we forced the participants to produce causation coefficients that ran relatively fast, by testing them in limited time on a large dataset,[11] leading to method that can rate a pair in less than a tenth of a second on a standard CPU [42].

As for **Prior knowledge**, being able to include prior knowledge is always nice, we will come back to it in Sect. 2.7.

Prior knowledge may be linked to **Testability** if it is uncertain whether some assumptions made hold in data. Those may include assumptions on (1) possible confounders used as conditioning set to "adjust" the data, e.g., with respect to age, gender, origin, (2) distribution of inputs, or noise, and (3) types of functions of the data generative process. Unfortunately, if we use available data to test our assumptions, we weaken further use of such data to test causal relationship, based on those assumptions. So it is better to only use "sure" prior knowledge and otherwise avoid making assumptions: this bring us to the need of **Flexibility**, i.e. providing methods not specific of certain kinds of data.

Flexibility is maybe best understood by making a comparison between "causation coefficients" and "correlation coefficients". Correlation coefficients are widely used indicators of dependencies between variables. Wouldn't is be nice to have a **universal correlation coefficient** that allows us to test (simply) whether two variables are dependent (not talking about causality, just dependence)? Does this exist? Here is a brief discussion of the subject [11, 24, 63]:

Is there a one-size-fit-all correlation coefficient?

The Pearson correlation coefficient is the most commonly used method; however, it is only sensitive to linear correlations. Spearman's correlation coefficient and Kendall's tau correlation coefficient are the two most common non-linear rank based correlation coefficients but they are limited to monotonic functional dependencies. Other commonly used methods measuring the correlation between random variables include distance correlation, Hoeffding's independence test, Maximal information coefficient (MIC), Hilbert-Schmidt Information Criterion (HSIC) and Heller Heller Gorfine distance (HHG). But none of those methods handle categorical (nominal) variables. Methods to handle categorical variables include the χ^2 statistic and the G-statistic (directly related to mutual information). If you have one continuous variable and one binary you may want to use the T-statistic or the AUC (are under ROC curve) and if one variable is continuous and the other categorical, an ANOVA statistic. But, what if you have several pairs (X, Y) and want to compare them with one another using the SAME metric of dependence? It seems to be that mutual information is the smallest common denominator. But, why then is not everybody just using mutual information? One aspect is the computational complexity of evaluating mutual information for continuous variables (often bypassed by binning). Another aspect is the statistical complexity and the risk of overfitting: detecting dependencies that do not exist. IF we know that dependencies are only linear with Gaussian noise, we are better off using Pearson correlation (less risk of false positive).

Likewise, the ambition of the cause-effect pair challenge [31] was to provide a one-size-fit-all causation coefficient. The following three chapters (Chaps. 3, 4, and 5) review and compare the properties of various causation coefficients. As convenient as a **universal causation coefficient** might be, we have to realize that

---

[11] https://competitions.codalab.org/competitions/1381.

the more universal a coefficient (less assumptions made), the larger the false positive (FPR) rate may be. Conversely, the more restrictive the assumptions made, the larger the false negative rate (FNR) may be. This is analogous to the common "bias-variance" tradeoff known to statistics and machine learning researchers [20]: large modeling spaces yield high variance and small modeling spaces large bias. This naturally leads us to **Efficacy** properties.

2.5.3   Efficacy and Confirmatory Analysis

We have already touched upon **theoretical foundations** in Sects. 2.4.1 and 2.4.2. Providing such a theoretical grounding is key to reassure practitioners. However, it is insufficient. Practitioners are looking for means of evaluating the "statistical significance" of their findings, in the finite sample case, for *particular observations* of a *given putative cause-effect pair*. They are accustomed to using statistical tests and p-values. Thus algorithm designers have been trying to provide **statistical tests** together with their *causation coefficient* to provide means of validating a given causal hypothesis, in the finite sample case.

Testing Causation Coefficients   In our framework, we have two sources of randomness: drawing the data generative process and drawing samples from that process. We take the angle of Sect. 2.4.2 in which we consider a mother distribution $P_{\mathcal{M}}$ from which we draw directly scatter plots $(\mathbf{x}, \mathbf{y}) = \{(x_1, y_1), (x_2, y_2), \cdots, (x_n, y_n)\}$ and their associated ground truth $g \in \{X \to Y, X \leftarrow Y, X \leftrightarrow Y, X \perp Y\}$, lumping together all factors of randomness, including the choice of ground truth (causal graph), input distribution, noise or hidden variable distribution(s), mechanisms, and number of examples n in the scatter plot.[12]

The **test statistic is the causation coefficient** $\hat{C}(X, Y)$. The null hypothesis is $H_0 : \neg\ X \to Y$ and the alternative hypothesis is $H_1 : X \to Y$. Given a *null distribution* for $\hat{C}(X, Y)$ (derived from prior knowledge we have of $P_{\mathcal{M}}$), a test can be conducted as follows:

1. Choose a significance level α, e.g. $\alpha = 0.05$.
2. Compute (empirically or analytically) the cumulative distribution of $\hat{C}(X, Y)$ under the null hypothesis $Pr(\hat{C}(X, Y) > \theta \mid H = H_0)$, where "Pr" is taken over the randomness of $P_{\mathcal{M}}$.
3. Determine the threshold θ_α, such that $Pr(\hat{C}(X, Y) > \theta_\alpha \mid H = H_0) = \alpha$.
4. For our given empirical sample $(\mathbf{x}, \mathbf{y})$, if $\hat{C}(\mathbf{x}, \mathbf{y}) > \theta_\alpha$, then reject H_0 (in the favor of H_1).

---

[12]This could easily be refined in a number of ways, including restricting the mother distribution $P_{\mathcal{M}}$ to scatter plots with the exact same number of samples as the pairs to be tested. In the dataset of the cause-effect pair challenge that we use as $P_{\mathcal{M}}$, the number of samples vary between 500 and 5000.

Table 2.4 Two-part tests: for each test result, 1 means the H_0 is rejected in the favor of H_1; 0 means that H_0 is not rejected

	Test 1	Test 2		
H_0	$\neg (X \rightarrow Y)$	$\neg (X \leftarrow Y)$	Test statistic	Conclusion
H_1	$X \rightarrow Y$	$X \leftarrow Y$		
One rejected in	1	0	$\hat{C}(X, Y) \geq \theta_\alpha$	$X \rightarrow Y$
favor of the other	0	1	$\hat{C}(X, Y) \leq -\theta_\alpha$	$X \leftarrow Y$
Neither rejected	0	0	$-\theta_\alpha < \hat{C}(X, Y) < \theta_\alpha$	?

At significance level α, pairs that have a causation coefficient $\hat{C}(X, Y) \geq \theta_\alpha$ are $X \rightarrow Y$ and those with $\hat{C}(X, Y) \leq -\theta_\alpha$ are $X \leftarrow Y$. The question mark means that there is no conclusive result

Two tests must be conducted, one for $H_0 : \neg X \rightarrow Y$ and $H_1 : X \rightarrow Y$, and one for $H_0 : \neg X \leftarrow Y$ and $H_1 : X \leftarrow Y$. It is not good enough to set a threshold on $|\hat{C}(X, Y)|$ and conduct a two-tailed test with null hypothesis $H_0 : X \leftrightarrow Y \vee X \perp Y$ and alternative hypotheses $H_1 : X \rightarrow Y$ and $H_2 : X \leftarrow Y$. This is because the distributions of $X \rightarrow Y$ and $X \leftarrow Y$ may overlap and therefore must each be taken into account in the null distribution of the other. The overall procedure is recapitulated in Table 2.4.

The big question is how to compute the cumulative distribution of $\hat{C}(X, Y)$ under the null hypothesis $Pr(\hat{C}(X, Y) > \theta \mid H = H_0)$. We propose to use a large dataset of pairs including many scatter plots of real and artificial pairs, which are "representative" of the pairs we are interested in testing. This is no unlike parametric tests, in which specific assumptions are made about the null distribution. In Fig. 2.7, we illustrate this procedure from the causation coefficient produced by Domcastro and Sayani in the first cause-effect pair challenge [29]. We use the test data of the cause-effect pair challenge to provide a null distribution for the tests. Using these data, we could determine the threshold $\theta_\alpha = 1.7$, for $\alpha = 0.05$.

This proposed method bears similarity with the "probe" method used in feature selection, allowing practitioners to use any feature selection criterion as a test statistic to evaluate the "significance" of the dependence between a feature and a target value (See [32], Chapter 2). These p-values must be taken with a grain of salt because they heavily on assumptions underlying $P_\mathcal{M}$, but, at the very least, they allow us to calibrate causation coefficients.

Obtaining p-values for causation coefficients can be done as follows:

$$\text{If } C(\mathbf{x}, \mathbf{y}) > \theta_\alpha, \; p\text{-value}_1(\mathbf{x}, \mathbf{y}) = Pr(\hat{C}(X, Y) > \hat{C}(\mathbf{x}, \mathbf{y}) \mid G \neq X \rightarrow Y),$$
$$\text{If } C(\mathbf{x}, \mathbf{y}) < -\theta_\alpha, \; p\text{-value}_2(\mathbf{x}, \mathbf{y}) = Pr(\hat{C}(X, Y) < \hat{C}(\mathbf{x}, \mathbf{y}) \mid G \neq X \leftarrow Y).$$
$$(2.11)$$

Those can be tabulated once and for all using $P_\mathcal{M}$ (e.g. estimated empirically with the dataset of the cause-effect pair challenge) for each causation coefficient.

Statistical Power We also represented in Fig. 2.7 the distributions of H_1 (alternative distributions) for the two tests considered, based on P_M (the distribution of the cause-effect pair challenge examples in this case). Those can be used to compute the

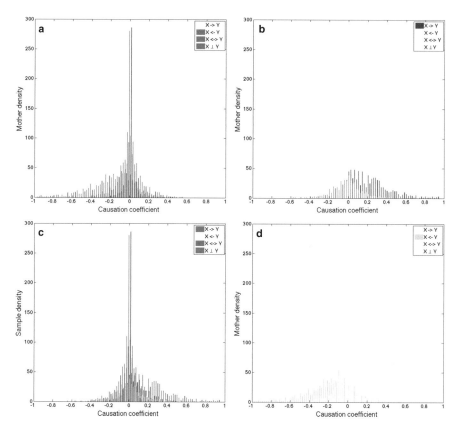

Fig. 2.7 Two-part test. We show the empirical density (histogram) of a mother distribution (cause-effect pair challenge dataset [29]) for the Domcasto-Sayani causation coefficient. Only 5% of pairs that are NOT $X \rightarrow Y$ have a causation coefficient $\hat{C}(X, Y) > 0.17$. Hence, at confidence level $\alpha = 0.05$, if $\hat{C}(X, Y) > \theta_\alpha = 0.17$, the null hypothesis of Test 1 is rejected, in favor of $H_1 : X \rightarrow Y$. Likewise, only 5% of pairs that are NOT $X \leftarrow Y$ have a causation coefficient $\hat{C}(X, Y) < -0.17$. Hence, at confidence level $\alpha = 0.05$, if $\hat{C}(X, Y) < -\theta_\alpha = -0.17$, the null hypothesis of Test 2 is rejected, in favor of $H_1 : X \leftarrow Y$. If $-\theta_\alpha < \hat{C}(X, Y) < \theta_\alpha$, no hypothesis, including $X \rightarrow Y$, $X \leftarrow Y$, $X \leftrightarrow Y$ or $X \perp Y$ can be rejected. In fact, there are quite a few pairs of all types in that region. (**a**) Test 1: $H_0 : X \leftarrow Y \vee X \leftrightarrow Y \vee X \perp Y$. (**b**) Test 1: $H_1 : X \rightarrow Y$. (**c**) Test 2: $H_0 : X \leftrightarrow Y \vee X \perp Y \vee X \rightarrow Y$. (**d**) Test 2: $H_1 : X \leftarrow Y$

power of the tests, i.e. $Pr(\text{reject } H_0 | H_1 \text{ is true})$, for a given level of significance α.

$$
\begin{aligned}
\text{If } C(\mathbf{x}, \mathbf{y}) &> \theta_\alpha, \ \text{power}_1 = Pr(\hat{C}(X, Y) > \theta_\alpha \mid G = X \rightarrow Y), \\
\text{If } C(\mathbf{x}, \mathbf{y}) &< -\theta_\alpha, \ \text{power}_2 = Pr(\hat{C}(X, Y) < -\theta_\alpha \mid G = X \leftarrow Y).
\end{aligned} \tag{2.12}
$$

Using a significance level $\alpha = 0.05$, in our example of Fig. 2.7, 44% of the $X \rightarrow Y$ pairs are found significant and 46% of the $X \leftarrow Y$ pairs. This evaluates the power of the test based on the Domcastro & Sayani causation coefficient. We show in

Table 2.5 the statistical power of tests based on the causation coefficients of the top ranking participants of the cause-effect pair challenge [31], for various levels of significance. The ranking of participants by statistical power is not quite the same as the ranking by the score of the challenge (see Table 2.11), but similar. The statistical power is not excellent: 0.8 is usually what is commonly sought.

Multiple Testing Instead of testing just one pair, practitioners may want to test n_c pairs simultaneously. As is known, p-values (or equivalently confidence intervals) then degrade. If we follow the Bonferroni correction [5], the p-value should be multiplied by n_c. However, this correction can be too conservative, particularly if the number of candidates n_c is large.

Another approach to multiple testing is to bound the False Discovery Rate (FDR):

$$FDR = \frac{FP}{FP + TP} = \frac{FP}{n_{sc}}$$

where FP is the number of pairs wrongly called significant, and TP the number of pairs correctly called significant, and $n_{sc} = FP + TP$ is the number of *selected candidates*. Of course, we have no way of knowing which pairs are correctly or not identified since the ground truth of pairs being tested is unknown. We can only compute a bound on the FDR. The total number of candidates to be tested $n_c = FP + TN + TP + FN$ can be bounded as $n_c \leq FP + TN$. We thus obtain:

$$FDR = \frac{FP}{n_c} \frac{n_c}{n_{sc}} \lesssim \frac{FP}{FP + TN} \frac{n_c}{n_{sc}} = FPR \frac{n_c}{n_{sc}}.$$

The bound is tight if $TP + FN \ll FP + TN$ that is if there are very few good candidates in the pairs tested, which is often the case for example in genomic applications. The next step is to estimate the false positive rate $FPR = \frac{FP}{FP+TN}$ by assuming that *the fraction of false positive in the set of candidates considered is the same as in the mother distribution*, for a given threshold on the causation coefficient. The FPR for the mother distribution corresponds to the p-values of Eq. (2.11). With this assumption, we get:

$$\begin{aligned} \text{If } C(\mathbf{x}, \mathbf{y}) &> \theta_\alpha, \quad FDR_1(\mathbf{x}, \mathbf{y}) \lesssim \text{p-value}_1. \, n_c/n_{sc}, \\ \text{If } C(\mathbf{x}, \mathbf{y}) &< -\theta_\alpha, \quad FDR_2(\mathbf{x}, \mathbf{y}) \lesssim \text{p-value}_2. \, n_c/n_{sc}. \end{aligned} \tag{2.13}$$

The FDR multiple testing method consists in setting a threshold of significance to bound FDR_1 and FDR_2, e.g. $FDR \lesssim$ p-value. $n_c/n_{sc} < 0.05$. This is more lenient than the Bonferroni correction, which boils down to setting a threshold of significance on the corrected p-value = p-value. n_c.

Tests for Binary Generative Processes Several authors have derived causation coefficients based on binary generative processes, which assume only two types of ground truth: $g \in \{X \rightarrow Y, X \leftarrow Y\}$. The most commonly used paradigm in that

Table 2.5 Power of tests based on causation coefficients of the cause-effect pair challenge, for various significance levels

Team	$\alpha = 0.1$				$\alpha = 0.05$				$\alpha = 0.01$			
	Test 1		Test 2		Test 1		Test 2		Test 1		Test 2	
	θ_α	Pow	θ_α	Pow	θ_α	Pow	θ_α	Pow	θ_α	Pow	θ_α	Pow
1. ProtoML	0.38	0.62	−0.40	0.62	0.60	0.50	−0.62	0.50	1.15	0.26	−1.12	0.27
2. Jarfo	0.40	0.64	−0.37	0.66	0.81	0.51	−0.78	0.54	1.58	0.27	−1.60	0.29
3. HiDIoN	1093	0.63	−1134	0.59	1417	0.45	−1417	0.46	1741	0.25	−1741	0.25
4. FirfiD	0.20	0.63	−0.22	0.61	0.44	0.47	−0.39	0.50	0.72	0.27	−0.67	0.28
5. Mouse	0.32	0.55	−0.31	0.56	0.47	0.43	−0.47	0.44	0.90	0.21	−0.90	0.23
6. Domcasto and Sayani	0.10	0.56	−0.12	0.54	0.18	0.43	−0.18	0.44	0.34	0.19	−0.34	0.21

We consider the two tests of Table 2.4

case is to use is a two-level test, testing **first for dependency** and **second for causal orientation**.

Methods based on binary generative processes compare the likelihood that an observed pair $(\mathbf{x}, \mathbf{y})$ was produced by a model generating $X \to Y$ pairs *vs.* a model generating $X \leftarrow Y$ pairs. Both models are tested separately. We call $C^+(X, Y)$ and $C^-(X, Y)$ the test statistics to test the adequacy of $(\mathbf{x}, \mathbf{y})$ to $X \to Y$ and $X \leftarrow Y$ models, respectively (satisfying $C^+(X, Y) = C^-(Y, X)$). A causation coefficient can be defined based on such statistics, here are a few examples, already provided in Sect. 2.3:

$$
\begin{aligned}
C(X, Y) &= C^+(X, Y) & &- C^-(X, Y) \\
C_{\mathcal{B}}(X, Y) &= P_{\mathcal{B}}\Big(G = [X \to Y] \mid (X, Y)\Big) - P_{\mathcal{B}}\Big(G = [X \leftarrow Y] \mid (X, Y)\Big) \\
C_{R2}(X, Y) &= R_y^2 & &- R_x^2 \\
C_{IR}(X, Y) &= HSIC(R_y, X) & &- HSIC(R_x, Y)
\end{aligned}
$$

$$(2.14)$$

As far as we know, this idea was first exploited for the additive noise models (ANM) [33, 49]. According to [46], one of the most effective cause-effect pair method is ANM-HSIC, namely the Additive Noise Model (Eq. (2.9)), equipped with the HSIC independence test [24], corresponding to the causation coefficient $C_{IR}(X, Y)$. The CDS method [17, 18] can be thought of as a generalization of this method to non additive noise models. The $C_{R2}(X, Y)$ simply comparing the residuals of fits was recently rejuvenated [4] and seems to be doing quite well under certain conditions. Chapter 3 gives many methods which use directly $C_{\mathcal{B}}(X, Y)$, i.e. exploit the likelihoods of the two alternative models.

The procedure to conduct the tests and conclude about the causal relationships is outlined in Table 2.6. Several hypotheses are being tested. First the independence between X and Y is tested (e.g. using the HSIC independence test [24]). If the hypothesis $H_0 : X \perp Y$ is rejected, then **two** other tests are conducted testing $H_0 : X \to Y$ (with alternative hypothesis $H_1 : X \leftarrow Y$) and $H_0 : X \leftarrow Y$ (with alternative hypothesis $H_1 : X \to Y$). The first one uses $C^+(X, Y)$ as test statistic and the second one $C^-(X, Y)$. The conclusions drawn depending on the results of the tests are shown in Table 2.6.

Note that, all causation coefficients can be expressed as the difference of two statistics $C^+(X, Y)$ and $C^-(X, Y)$ such that $C^+(X, Y) = C^-(Y, X)$, by virtue of the fact that they are anti-symmetric, i.e. $C(X, Y) = -C(Y, X)$. One trivial case is $C^+ = C$ and $C^- = -C$. This brings us back to the kind of test we were conducting in the previous section. However, not decompositions into $C^+(X, Y)$ and $C^-(X, Y)$ lend themselves to conduct two separate tests. Consider for instance the case of $C_H(X, Y) = H_x - H_y$. It would not make sense to use $C^+(X, Y) = H_x$ and $C^-(X, Y) = H_y$.

Although this chapter has seldom talked about time series, which will be covered in Chap. 5, is worth noting that the well known Granger causality test follows a similar two-part paradigm [23]. The test seeks to determine whether one time series is useful in forecasting another. There are many variants, but, for instance, an auto-

Table 2.6 Multi-level tests: for each test result, 1 means the H_0 is rejected in the favor of H_1; 0 means that H_0 is not rejected

Level 1					
	$X \perp Y$				Conclusion
H_0	0				$X \perp Y$?
1	Level 2				
		Test 1	Test 2		
	H_0	$X \leftarrow Y$	$X \rightarrow Y$	Test statistics	Conclusion
	H_1	$X \rightarrow Y$	$X \leftarrow Y$		
	One rejected in favor of the other	1	0	$\hat{C}^+(X, Y) \geq \theta_\alpha$ $\hat{C}^-(X, Y) < \theta_\alpha$	$X \rightarrow Y$
		0	1	$\hat{C}^+(X, Y) < \theta_\alpha$ $\hat{C}^-(X, Y) \geq \theta_\alpha$	$X \leftarrow Y$
	Neither rejected	0	0	$\hat{C}^+(X, Y) < \theta_\alpha$ $\hat{C}^-(X, Y) < \theta_\alpha$	$X \leftrightarrow Y$?
	Both rejected	1	1	$\hat{C}^+(X, Y) \geq \theta_\alpha$ $\hat{C}^-(X, Y) \geq \theta_\alpha$	$X \rightleftharpoons Y$?

First independence is tested (Level 1). If independence is rejected, causal direction is tested in both directions separately (Level 2, Test 1 and Test 2). Question marks indicate that the result is inconclusive or inconsistent with the modeling hypotheses (e.g. that there cannot be two-cycles or dependencies not explained by a causal relationship)

regressive model predicting X from past values of X and Y might provide a better fit than one based on past values of X only (and vice versa). A Granger causation coefficient can be defined as $C_G(X, Y) = R_{xy}/R_{xx} - R_{yx}/R_{yy}$, where R_{xy} is the residual of the model predicting X from past values of X and Y (supporting $X \leftarrow Y$), R_{xx} of an auto-regressive model for X (predicting X from past values of X), R_{yx} is the residual of the model predicting Y from past values of X and Y (supporting $X \rightarrow Y$), and R_{yy} of an auto-regressive model for Y. Thus larger values of $G(X, Y)$ support the hypothesis $X \rightarrow Y$. To conduct a two-part test, one defines $C^+(X, Y) = R_{xy}/R_{xx}$ and $C^-(X, Y) = R_{yx}/R_{yy}$, both of which lend themselves to conducting F-tests.

Two other desirable properties of "causation coefficients" are **Robustness** and **Stability**. Regarding **Robustness** to outliers, it is again useful to make a parallel with correlation coefficients. The issue of robustness has been extensively studied in that context. To avoid that large outlying value may result in a spurious high correlation, a standard technique is to repeat the computation of the correlation coefficient M times, each time removing one value, then averaging the results. The result is called "Jack-knife correlation coefficient" [13]. This procedure can easily be used for "causation coefficients" as well. The issue of **Stability** is tightly related to that of **Robustness**. Stability concerns the property of a "causation coefficients" to deliver values in the finite sample case that have a small variance, i.e. vary little across drawing of samples $S_n(X, Y) = \{(x_1^T, y_1^T), (x_2^T, y_2^T), \cdots, (x_n^T, y_n^T)\}$ of the same size n. Since in practice we only have a single sample of size n, a common way to estimate the variance is to resample the data, for instance using the bootstrap method [14]. The bootstrap method is a method of resampling with replacement. A large number of samples of size n are drawn form $S_n(X, Y)$, with replacement. This results in new samples of the same size, in which some samples are repeated, and which contain on average approximately 2/3 of the observations. It is then possible to compute $C(X, Y)$ for each bootstrap sample and compute an average and a variance. The variance obtained is an indicator of stability and it should decrease with n. The average provides a causation coefficient, which is more stable. This is analogous to ensemble methods such as "bagging" in machine learning, commonly used by Random Forests. Notice that the "Jack-knife" method is a resampling method that is an ancestor of the bootstrap method. Using a "bagged" causation coefficient adds both stability and robustness.

2.5.4 Post-hoc Evaluation

Assuming all previous steps went well and we have found one (or several) pairs that we believe have a statistically significant relationship of type $X \rightarrow Y$. Before engaging in possibly costly experimental verifications or basing decisions on this hypothetical causal relationship, we might want to consolidate our findings. Causation coefficients provide us with which we believe that $X \rightarrow Y$, but does not let us know about the **Strength** or **Direction** of effect. Strength measures the degree of influence of X on Y, e.g. how much change in Y would be obtained by doubling X. Direction measures whether the effect is positive or negative, for instance, does a certain substance cure a patient of disease or make him sicker.

For linear dependencies, the Pearson correlation coefficient $c(X, Y)$ provides us with both a Strength=abs($c(X, Y)$) and Direction=sign($c(X, Y)$). For monotonic (or quasi-monotonic) relationships, Spearman's and Kendall's tau correlation coefficients can be used in a similar way. For non monotonic relationships, it may be more meaningful to split the dependency into monotonic sub-domains.

Many practitioners may rightfully want to understand better why a certain causal relationship was unveiled by a given causation coefficient. **Explainability** is key for the adoption of the new methodology by practitioners. There is not just one way of making the decision of a causation coefficient explainable. This may include identifying the most prominent features, and, of course, exhibiting a plausible **Mechanism** i.e. a data generative model easily interpretable.

Finally, if such a mechanism is exhibited, one last way of verifying that the causal relationship is plausible before carrying out experiments is to use it as a predictive model to explains other datasets, collected in different conditions.

2.6 The Point of View of Benchmark Organizers

In this section, we investigate how algorithms to discover cause-effect pair relationships from observational data can be quantitatively evaluated in the context of a benchmark. Until the years 2000, most efforts to evaluate causal discovery methods in benchmarks were limited to generating data with Bayesian networks. One well-known source of data was the Bayesian Network repository,[13] last updated in 1998. A first departure from that limited paradigm stemmed from genomic studies and, in particular, the work of Aliferis and his collaborators [1] and the DREAM challenges.[14] Recognizing the need to evaluate causal discovery methods systematically, the Causality Workbench consortium started in 2007.[15] Its activities included the organization of several challenges. The 2008 a "Pot-luck challenge" allowed participants to propose their own tasks. Dominik Janzing and his collaborators of the Max Plank Institute for Intelligent Systems (from the lab of Bernhard Schoelkopf[16]) proposed the cause-effect pair task (with only eight pairs at the time). This kick-started research in that domain for the past decade, ultimately leading to this book.

We dwelled in previous sections on theoretical guaranties and confirmatory analysis (statistical tests). But the growing number of alternative methods, all having different assumptions, advantages and disadvantages, leaves practitioners with a choice dilemma. This prompted us in 2013 and 2014 to organize a large scale evaluation of cause-effect pair methods. The goal was to discover whether the data supports the hypothesis that $Y = f(X, noise)$, which for the purpose of this challenge was our definition of causality $X \rightarrow Y$, vs. other hypotheses: $X \leftarrow Y$, $X \leftrightarrow Y$, $X \perp Y$. Our objective was to scale up the Tuebingen dataset collected in the Schoelkopf lab [46]. Initially we only thought of providing test pairs. As we were brainstorming on the challenge design with Ben Hamner from Kaggle, it became clear that we should also provide training data. This led to the new Machine Learning statement of the cause-effect pair problem, which we described in Sect. 2.2, and was later more formalized mathematically by David Lopez Paz and collaborators [43]. This opened new horizons both in causality research and in benchmarking causal models. As in many other scientific domains, the **metric of success shapes the problem**. In this particular case, framing causal discovery as a pattern recognition problem, completely changed the way in which researchers thought about causality, moving a way from the necessity of uncovering the data

---

[13]http://www.cs.huji.ac.il/~galel/Repository/.

[14]http://dreamchallenges.org.

[15]Causality workbench: http://www.causality.inf.ethz.ch/. Founding members: Constantin F. Aliferis (Vanderbilt University, Tennessee), Gregory F. Cooper (University of Pittsburgh, Pennsylvania), André Elisseeff (IBM Research, Switzerland), Jean-Philippe Pellet (IBM Research, Switzerland), Alexander Statnikov (Vanderbilt University, Tennessee), Peter Spirtes (Carnegie Mellon University, Pennsylvania).

[16]https://ei.is.tuebingen.mpg.de/.

generative model (or at least its structure) and beginning to simply build predictive models to classify scatter plots as belonging to various ground truth classes of causal relationships. Implicitly, **the mother distribution "defines" the particular notion of causality we are interested in**. This section presents the efforts that the community has been making over the past few years to create good benchmark datasets and discusses various hurtles that must be overcome.

2.6.1 Benchmark Design

Prior to the cause-effect pair challenge, benchmarks in causal modeling required possessing a causal DAG representing the "True" causal structure. This blurred the fact that, in scientific modeling, *no model is ever "True"*: it is only "not rejected yet", based on empirical evidence accumulated thus far [51]. In machine learning, we are accustomed to the fact that the accuracy of classifiers is upper bounded by the Bayes optimal accuracy, which accounts for the fact that the ground truth may be partially wrong or uncertain. The Bayes optimal accuracy sets a limit on the accuracy that the best model can achieve. In causality, up until the cause-effect pair challenge, causal relationships needed to be either right or wrong. We changed that concept: the labeling of causal relationships can be uncertain and contain a certain fraction of errors.

This new "lenient" way of establishing ground truth, accepting noisy labels, facilitates the collection of real data. Establishing causal relationships is notoriously difficult, and requires (see Sect. 2.2) either identifying mechanisms or conducting randomized controlled experiments. Accepting possible errors makes it possible to rely on human judgement/prior knowledge to establish ground truth, as proposed first by the authors of the Tuebingen dataset [46]. For example, age causes how much you sleep and not the opposite. Determining from human expertise whether there is (some amount of) confounding is much harder though. We dealt with that in Sect. 2.6.6 by introducing semi-artificial pairs that were dependent but not causally related. One shortcoming of collecting real pairs in this way is that data usually comes with incomplete information about the data collection procedure. Some pairs may be purely observational, others may come from designed experiments. This may introduce a pernicious form of data leakage [38]: input variables in experimental data often have easily identifiable distributions, with quantized regularly spaced points, as opposed to output variables, which are continuous. Hence it is possible to distinguish causes from effects based on this artifact of marginal distributions. See Sect. 2.6.6 for details.

Another option to get benchmark data is to create synthetic or artificial data. We make a distinction between the two. Synthetic data refers to data generated by realistic simulators of real systems. For example, a simulator of a biological process (e.g. a gene network or an artificial neural network), a chemical process, or a physical process. See Sect. 2.6.2. In contrast, artificial data refers to data generated by a structural equation model (a.k.a. functional causal model). No knowledge of biology, physics, or chemistry is needed, this is a purely mathematical abstraction. All is needed is to "noise" distributions and functional mechanisms. See Sect. 2.6.3. Still, there are important design issues concerning: how to balance data to include a diversity of types of variables (continuous, binary, categorial), types of distributions, types of functional mechanisms, and signal to noise ratios. Finally, artificial datasets are not except of the risk of introducing biases. All of these issues are discussed in Sect. 2.6.3.

In the best of all worlds, synthetic or artificial data should be indistinguishable from real data, and could serve to augment datasets of real data, since real data are scarce. A central problem is therefore whether it is possible to "adjust" the distributions of artificial data to that of real data, to create large homogeneous datasets. We explain in Sect. 2.6.5 our attempts to make the distributions of real and artificial data similar.

2.6.2 Realistic Synthetic Data

Most authors use structural equations models to generate artificial data. It is questionable whether such data are realistic. It is necessary to put more effort in this direction to obtain large quantities of realistic data, which can serve to train causation coefficients, calibrate them, or conduct statistical test.

Another approach to obtain realistic data is to use **physical models**. One of the earliest causal benchmark studies using simulators was obtained for genomics data simulators. DREAM challenges http://dreamchallenges.org/ have made use of such data over the years. For example, cause-effect pairs {transcription factor, activated gene} have been used in [59, 60] and were part of the dataset of the cause-effect pair challenge [29, 30]. It has been made available as part of the Causality Workbench repository.[17] Another example is the neural connectomics dataset, which was use in the ChaLearn connectomics challenge.[18] A relatively realistic simulator of neural activity was use to generate spike trains. A physical model of fluorescence imaging was then used to generate simulated data of observed neural activities in neural cultures, imitating real experimental data. The goal was to unravel neuron interconnections from the sole information of their activity [2, 27]. Some authors created ad-hoc simulators using differential equations describing their system, e.g. [37]. Other valuable resources of biological models that could be used for causal studies include the bio-model database.[19] Of course, simulators of real systems are not limited to biology. There are many simulators in physics, chemistry, and engineering, e.g. chemical plants.[20]

---

[17]Causality Workbench repo: http://www.causality.inf.ethz.ch/repository.php.

[18]Connectomics challenge: http://connectomics.chalearn.org/.

[19]Bio-model database: http://www.ebi.ac.uk/biomodels-main/.

[20]Chemical plant simulator: http://depts.washington.edu/control/LARRY/TE/download.html.

Recently many bridges have been made between causal studies and reinforcement learning (RL). This is quite natural since the goal of RL is to create agents learning to act in given environments by developing appropriate policies (i.e. mappings of state to action) to attain particular goals or accrue rewards. This is equivalent to unravel cause-effect relationships $cause = action \rightarrow effect = reward$. In this context, simulators developed for RL are resources for causal discovery benchmarks, although it is some work to create causal discovery tasks from RL simulators. Examples of RL simulators include:

- GYM: https://gym.openai.com/envs/
- RLlab: https://rllab.readthedocs.io/en/latest/#
- Pypownet: https://github.com/MarvinLer/pypownet
- EPIMOD: http://idmod.org/software

The Carnegie Mellon school of causal studies, who contributed over the years several members of the Causality Workbench, has continued to be very active to gather case studies of interest, including via the workshop organized by Richard Scheines.[21] Contributors to the workshop presented econometrics, brain imaging, and climate simulators.

Unfortunately, harnessing simulators and creating cause-effect pair data from them is a huge endeavor. Except for the genomics transcriptome data, cause-effect pairs from realistic simulators have not been incorporated yet in benchmark data. However, this may happen soon in the context of the "Cause me" project.[22]

2.6.3 Artificial Data

In this section, we now turn to purely artificial data generators found in the literature, including those of Table 2.7, then describe in more details the dataset of the cause-effect pair challenge that we are most familiar with, and whose description was not published yet elsewhere.

2.6.3.1 General Setting

To make notations less heavy, we do not always fully specify the double random process. It will be assumed implicitly that, for each data generative model:

1. We draw a data generative process $\mathcal{P}_{\Pi=\pi}(X, Y)$ from a mother distribution $\mathcal{P}_{\mathcal{M}}$.
2. We draw n samples $S_{\Pi=\pi}(X, Y) = \{(x_1, y_1), (x_2, y_2), \cdots, (x_n, y_n)\}$ (a *scatter plot*) from $\mathcal{P}_{\Pi=\pi}(X, Y)$.

---

[21]CMU case studies: https://www.cmu.edu/dietrich/philosophy/events/workshops-conferences/causal-discovery/index.html.

[22]http://causeme.uv.es/index.html.

Table 2.7 Cause-effect pair datasets

Origin	Type	Causal relation	Data	Date	Ref.
Tuebingen dataset CE-Tueb	Real	$X \to Y$ $X \leftarrow Y$	108 pairs	2013–15	[46]
Janzing et al.	Artificial	$X \to Y$ $X \leftarrow Y$	CODE	2012	[36]
CE pair challenge CE-Cha	Real & artificial	$X \to Y$ $X \leftarrow Y$ $X \leftrightarrow Y$ $X \perp Y$	24299 pairs & CODE	2013–14	This chapter
Mooij et al. CE-Gauss	Artificial	$X \to Y$ $X \leftarrow Y$	400 pairs & CODE	2016	[46]
Chalupka et al.	Artificial	$X \to Y$ $X \leftarrow Y$ $X \leftrightarrow Y$ $X \perp Y$	CODE	2016	[8]
Goudet et al. CE-Multi	Artificial	$X \to Y$ $X \leftarrow Y$ $X \leftrightarrow Y$ $X \perp Y$	CODE	2017	[22]
Lopez Paz et al. CE-Net CE-Multi	Artificial	$X \to Y$ $X \leftarrow Y$	600 pairs & CODE	2017	[44] [21]
Ttagasovska et al.	Artificial	$X \to Y$ $X \leftarrow Y$	CODE	2018	[61]

The nicknames CE-Cha, CE-Tueb, CE-Net, CE-Gauss, CE-Multi are used in Chap. 3

$\mathcal{P}_\Pi(X, Y)$ is parameterized by Π, which includes the choice of ground truth (causal graph) $g \in \mathcal{G} \subset \{X \to Y, X \leftarrow Y, X \leftrightarrow Y, X \perp Y\}$, input distribution $P(X) \in \mathcal{X}$ or $P(Y) \in \mathcal{Y}$, noise or hidden variable distribution(s) $P(N_x) \in \mathcal{N}_x$, $P(N_y) \in \mathcal{N}_y$, $P(N_z) \in \mathcal{N}_z$, and function(s) $f \in \mathcal{F}$, and $h \in \mathcal{H}$. When not specified, all noise variables are independent of one another and the input is independent of the noise variable(s).

Most authors generate data using structural equation models (functional causal models) of the type:

$$
\mathcal{P}_{\Pi=\pi}(X, Y) \begin{cases} g = [X \to Y]: x \sim P(X), n_y \sim P(N_y) \;\; y := f(x, n_y) \\ g = [X \leftarrow Y]: y \sim P(Y), n_x \sim P(N_x) \;\; x := f(y, n_x) \\ \qquad\qquad\quad\; n_x \sim P(N_x), \\ g = [X \leftrightarrow Y]: \quad n_y \sim P(N_y), \qquad x := f(n_x, n_z), \; y := h(n_y, n_z) \\ \qquad\qquad\quad\; n_z \sim P(N_z), \\ g = [X \perp Y]: \;\; x \sim P(X), y \sim P(Y) \end{cases}
$$

(2.15)

This paradigm corresponds to lumping the effect of all latent variables in the "noise" variables N_x and N_y (see e.g. [50]). In [36], the authors take another angle:

they generate data from a multivariate graphical model, then isolate cause-effect pairs. We focus here on the first paradigm consisting in generating pairs in isolation.

2.6.4 Cause Effect Pairs: $\mathcal{G} = \{X \to Y, X \leftarrow Y\}$

Initial work on (non-linear) additive noise models (Eq. (2.16))) [33, 49] was limited to $\mathcal{G} = \{X \to Y, X \leftarrow Y\}$:

$$\begin{cases} g = [X \to Y] : x \sim P(X), n_y \sim P(N_y), X \perp N_y, \quad y := f(x) + n_y \\ g = [X \leftarrow Y] : y \sim P(Y), n_x \sim P(N_x), Y \perp N_x, \quad x := f(y) + n_x. \end{cases} \quad (2.16)$$

In [42], to make data more realistic, the author fit the parameters of their models to obtain more realistic scatter plots. The use (unlabeled) real data scatter plots and minimize a distance between embeddings of synthetic scatter plots and real scatter plots (drawn from the Tuebingen dataset).

The independence assumption $X \perp N_y$ and $Y \perp N_x$ may be lifted to account for partial confounding. For instance, for the $X \to Y$ case, this could be represented by:

$$g = [X \to Y] : x \sim P(X|N_y), n_y \sim P(N_y), \quad y := f(x) + n_y, \quad (2.17)$$

where x could be simply generated with $x := h(n_y) + n_x, n_x \sim P(N_x)$.

Another popular model for generating pairs is the post-non-linear (PNL) model [66]:

$$g = [X \to Y] : x \sim P(X), n_y \sim P(N_y), X \perp N_y, \quad y := f(h(x)+n_y). \quad (2.18)$$

In [46] (CE-Gauss), the authors remove the additive noise restriction:

$$g = [X \to Y] : n_x \sim P(N_x), n_y \sim P(N_y), N_x \perp N_y, \quad x := h(n_x), y := f(x, n_y), \quad (2.19)$$

In that paper, random functions are sampled from a Gaussian process. Independent noise distributions are obtained by mapping a standard-normal distribution through a random function sampled from a Gaussian Process. Finally, Gaussian measurement noise is added to both X and Y. The authors of [46] also consider a partial confounding case:

$$g = [X \to Y] : n_x \sim P(N_x), n_y \sim P(N_y), n_z \sim P(N_z),$$
$$x := h(n_x, n_z), y := f(x, n_y, n_z). \quad (2.20)$$

with all noise variables drawn from independent variables: $N_x \perp N_y, N_x \perp N_z$, $N_y \perp N_z$. This generalizes Eq. (2.17). The authors consider several scenarios:

SIM, SIM-c, SIM-ln, and SIM-G SIM is the default scenario without confounders. SIM-c includes a one-dimensional confounder, whose influences on X and Y are typically equally strong as the influence of X on Y. The setting SIM-ln has low noise levels, and one can expect IGCI to work well in this scenario. Finally, SIM-G has approximate Gaussian distributions for the cause X and approximately additive Gaussian noise (on top of a nonlinear relationship between cause and effect); it is expected that methods which make these Gaussianity assumptions will work well in this scenario. Figure 2.8 shows examples of this dataset. The authors provide data and code, see Table 2.7, which is very valuable for further research.

Other authors have provided data for the cases $X \rightarrow Y$ abd $X \leftarrow Y$ with or without partial confounding. In [61], the authors consider three types of models, with additive or multiplicative noise:

$$g = [X \rightarrow Y] : x \sim P(X), n_y \sim P(N_y), X \perp N_y, \begin{cases} (1) y := f(x) + n_y \\ (2) y := f(x) + h(x) . n_y \\ (3) y := f(x) . n_y \end{cases}$$
(2.21)

Similarly, in [21, 22], the authors of the CE-Multi dataset generated 300 artificial pairs using pre- or post- additive or multiplicative noise (two of these cases correspond to the Additive Noise Model (ANM) and the Post Non-Linear

Fig. 2.8 SIM datasets. We show a few examples of scatter plots from [46]. From left to right and top to bottom, SIM, SIM-c, SIM-G, and SIM-ln (see text)

model (PNL)); the mechanism f is linear or polynomial of degree 2 with random coefficients:

$$g = [X \to Y] : x \sim P(X), n_y \sim P(N_y), X \perp N_y, \begin{cases} (1)y := f(x) + n_y \ (ANM) \\ (2)y := f(x) . n_y \\ (3)y := f(x + n_y) \ (PNL) \\ (4)y := f(x . n_y) \end{cases}$$

$$(2.22)$$

In [44], the authors generalize this type of data generative process to image data.

Other authors have generated pairs using a neural network, following the generic structural equation model:

$$g = [X \to Y] : x \sim P(X), n_y \sim P(N_y) \quad y := f(x, n_y) \qquad (2.23)$$

For instance, in [21] the authors of the CE-Net dataset generated 300 artificial pairs with a neural network initialized with random weights and used for $P(X)$ distributions drawn randomly from the set {*exponential*, *gamma*, *lognormal*, *laplace*}.

2.6.5 All Pairs: $\mathcal{G} = \{X \to Y, X \leftarrow Y, X \leftrightarrow Y, X \perp Y\}$

In contrast with other authors, [8] consider the full set $\mathcal{G} = \{X \to Y, X \leftarrow Y, X \leftrightarrow Y, X \perp Y\}$. They consider only categorical variables (multinomial distributions). Their data generative processes are of the type:

$$\begin{cases} g = [X \to Y] : x \sim P(X), \forall x, y \sim P(Y|X = x) \\ g = [X \leftarrow Y] : y \sim P(Y), \forall y, x \sim P(X|Y = y) \\ g = [X \leftrightarrow Y] : h \sim P(H), \forall h, x \sim P(X|H = h), y \sim P(Y|H = h) \\ g = [X \perp Y] : \ x \sim P(X), y \sim P(Y), \end{cases}$$

$$(2.24)$$

where all distributions $P(X)$, $P(Y)$, $P(H)$, $P(Y|X = x)$, $P(X|Y = y)$, $P(X|H = h)$, and $P(Y|H = h)$ are all drawn from Dirichlet priors.

The scripts of [22] provide an option to build confounding pairs or independent pairs (although this is not used in the paper):

$$\begin{cases} g=[X \leftrightarrow Y] : \ n_x \sim P(N_x), n_y \sim P(N_y), h \sim P(H), y := f(h, n_x), y := f(h, n_y) \\ g = [X \perp Y] : n_x \sim P(N_x), n_y \sim P(N_y), x := f(n_x), y := f(n_y). \end{cases}$$

$$(2.25)$$

The most comprehensive dataset for all pairs is the cause-effect-pair challenge dataset [29, 30]. It is the only dataset we know of, which considers the full set $\mathcal{G} = \{X \to Y, X \leftarrow Y, X \leftrightarrow Y, X \perp Y\}$ that mixes continuous and categorical variables. In that respect it is significantly more difficult than other datasets. The dataset released for the challenge included 80% artificial data and 20% real data. We describe here the artificial data. The real data is described in Sect. 2.6.6.

Real Exogenous Variables The first step in the dataset construction was to collect a large pool of 15,552 real variables from multiple datasets of machine learning and data mining, to obtain a rich collection of distributions of real variables, each having 10,000 samples (**pool$_1$**). Another pool of 15,552 variables was created from the original variables using randomly drawn functions from the library to get 15,552 smooth continuous variables (**pool$_2$**). Those were used to draw data for exogenous (noise) variables $P(N_x)$, $P(N_y)$, $P(N_z)$, instead of using synthetic data. Thus all input and noise distributions of continuous variables are **real**.

To get ordinal (discrete numerical), categorical, and binary variables from continuous variables **x**, a discretization algorithm Δ was implemented:

$$\Delta(\mathbf{x}; t, r) = \begin{cases} \text{round}(r.(\mathbf{x} - \bar{\mathbf{x}})/\sigma_x) & \text{if } t = Numerical \\ \text{reassign}(\text{round}(r.(\mathbf{x} - \bar{\mathbf{x}})/\sigma_x)) & \text{if } t = Categorical \end{cases} \tag{2.26}$$

where t is the desired variable type $t \in \{Numerical, Categorical\}$, r is a discretization parameter, and the *reassign* function randomly reassigns each (discrete) value to an arbitrary categorical label.

Structural Equation Model The second step was to implement a library of diverse functions of two variables $y = f(x_1, x_2)$ producing continuous values y, $f \in \{$ line, parabola, cubic, sqrt, sine, hyperbola, log, exp, tanh, atanh, rbf $\}$.

Noise was mixed in one of four ways:

$$\begin{cases} (1) f(x, n_y) = f(\alpha.x + \beta.n_y) & \text{``preadd'' (PNL model)} \\ (2) f(x, n_y) = f(x^\alpha . n_y^\beta) & \text{``premult''} \\ (3) f(x, n_y) = \alpha.f(x) + \beta.n_y & \text{``postadd'' (ANM model)} \\ (4) f(x, n_y) = f(x)^\alpha . n_y^\beta & \text{``postmult''} \end{cases} \tag{2.27}$$

where parameter α and β control the signal to noise ratio. The noise level s2n was varied in the range $\{0.25, 0.5, 1, 2\}$ and the parameters calculated as $\beta = 1/(1+s2n)$ and $\alpha = 1 - \beta$.

The ground truth g was drawn uniformly in the set $\mathcal{G} = \{X \to Y, X \leftarrow Y, X \leftrightarrow Y, X \perp Y\}$ and pairs were generated as follows:

Postprocessing The pairs of variables prepared as indicated before, undergo the following postprocessing steps:

- The number of points in each scatter plot is reduced to n, $500 \le n \le 8000$ by drawing a subset of points without replacement. The value of n is drawn uniformly on a log2 scale in the interval chosen.
- Pairs having at least one variable with only 1 value are eliminated.
- Variables with 2 values are considered binary and mapped to 0/1.

G	Generative model	
$X \to Y$	$n_x \sim U(\textbf{pool}_2), n_y \sim U(\textbf{pool}_1),$ $r, r' \sim P(R), t, t' \sim P(T)$	$x := \Delta(n_x, r, t), y := \Delta(f(x, n_y), r', t')$
$X \leftarrow Y$	Same as $[X \to Y]$, swapping the roles of x and y	
$X \leftrightarrow Y$	$n_x \sim U(\textbf{pool}_1), n_y \sim U(\textbf{pool}_1),$ $n_z \sim U(\textbf{pool}_1),$ $r, r' \sim P(R), t, t' \sim P(T)$	$x := \Delta(f(n_x, n_z), r, t), y := \Delta(h(n_y, n_z), r', t')$
$X \perp Y$	Use $[X \to Y]$ or $[X \leftarrow Y]$ pairs and permute values independently	

Table 2.8 Cause-effect pair challenge data statistics

Dataset	All pairs	$X \to Y$	$X \leftarrow Y$	$X \leftrightarrow Y$	$X \perp Y$	Real CE
Training	4050	965	1033	1010	1042	354
Validation	4050	986	1034	1014	1016	332
Test	4050	1041	1025	1007	977	364
Sup1 (artif, numeric)	5998	1514	1485	1500	1499	0
Sup2 (artif, mixed)	5989	1529	1466	1497	1497	0
Sup3 (real)	162	42	39	41	40	81
Total	24, 299	6077	6082	6069	6071	1131

- Categorical variables with C values are assigned randomly class numbers between 1 and C.
- Numerical variables (discrete or continuous) are **standardized** (the mean is subtracted and then the result is divided by the standard deviation) and then **quantized** by multiplying the result by 10,000 and rounding to the nearest integer.

Examples of pairs from this dataset are shown in Fig. 2.1. For the challenges, several data sets were released, including two datasets containing only artificial data SUP1 and SUP2 (Table 2.8). SUP1data: contains only continuous variables (CE-Cha used in Chap. 4 is a subset of those pairs). SUP2 data contains mixed binary, categorical, and continuous variables. For illustrative purposes, we show all the statistics of the SUP2 data in Table 2.9.

A trained human eye gets about 0.7 AUC score on SUP1data (a sample of which is shown in Fig. 2.9 under the name CE-Cha). SUP2 data are much more difficult for the human eye (see Fig. 2.1).

Quality Control One danger when generating artificial data is to introduce artifacts that can easily be picked up by a learning machine, making the problem of separating the classes of artificial pairs trivial, but delivering useless causation coefficients. In particular, the marginal distributions of the variables X and Y should not betray the causal direction. The most obvious thing to do is to standardize variables to avoid at least biases in the mean or standard deviation (this is done as post-processing and does not alter the causal relationships.)

Table 2.9 Statistics on the SUP2 data [29]

G	Num. pairs	Pearson corr.
All pairs	5989	0.23
$X \rightarrow Y$	1529	0.36
$X \leftarrow Y$	1466	0.38
$X \leftrightarrow Y$	1497	0.17
$X \perp Y$	1497	0.02

Num. pairs	Binary	Categorical	Discrete	Numerical
Binary	102	83	117	433
Categorical	93	92	95	463
Discrete	124	93	128	461
Numerical	465	457	453	2330

Sample size	500–1000	1000–2000	2000–4000	4000–8000
Num. pairs	1486	1563	1508	1432

S2N	0.25	0.50	1.00	2.00
% pairs	23	27	25	25

These are artificial pairs, distributed similarly to those of the cause-effect pair challenge

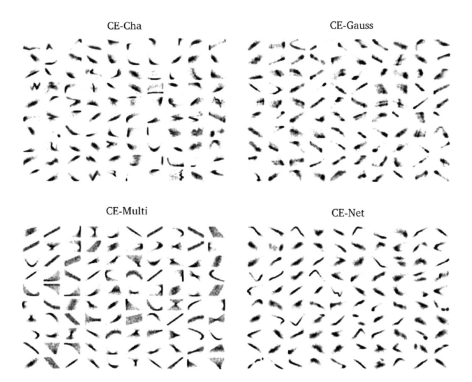

Fig. 2.9 CHA datasets. We show a few examples of scatter plots from [21]

During the first challenge [29], participants identified one such flaw: the number of unique values of X was smaller that of Y, on average, for pairs $X \rightarrow Y$. This was a consequence from using "real" variables for X (some of which were quantized) and passing them through functions returning continuous values. Interestingly, this problem is also found in real data, see Sect. 2.6.6. This motivated the new implementation of discretization and quantization described in the previous section.

The discretization parameters were drawn from the same distribution for all $g \in \{X \rightarrow Y, X \leftarrow Y, X \leftrightarrow Y, X \perp Y\}$. In this way, the distribution of unique values of variables is the same in all causal categories, as verified by QQplots (Fig. 2.10).

A new version of the dataset was released to the 313 challenge participants and scrutinized for further problems of "data leakage" (trivial features revealing the causal categories). Nothing new was found, so this gives confidence that this dataset is free of trivial biases. This does not mean of course that the pairs are realistic and resemble real data.

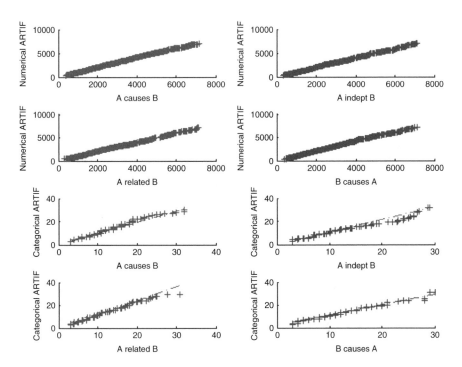

Fig. 2.10 SUP2 dataset QQ plots. These plots were made as a sanity check for the cause-effect pair challenge data in [29]. They show that in all quantiles, the distribution of unique values of X and Y is similar, for all types of causal categories. Each cross represents thresholds u_x and u_y on the number of unique values U_x and U_y of random variables X and Y for a given value of k such that $Pr[U_x < u_x] \leq k/q$ and $Pr[U_y < u_y] \leq k/q$, given q quantiles. If the distributions of unique values of X and Y are identical, the points should be on the diagonal (red dashed lines)

We know of one attempt to make data more realistic by adjusting hyper-parameters of the data generative model to minimize the distance between the distribution of real data and of artificially generated data [42]. More effort must be put in this direction.

2.6.6   Real Data

The first sizeable dataset of real cause-effect pairs has been the Tuebingen dataset [46]. It has been carefully manually curated and is used as a benchmark in many publications. However, because of its small size ($\simeq$ 100 $pairs$), there is a high risk of overfitting if training is used or of multiple testing if many methods are compared. In this dataset, the pairs are not independent. This is compensated for by giving weights to each pair. A small fraction of the pairs include multivariate data for X and Y.

A larger dataset of real pairs was prepared for the cause-effect pair challenges [29, 30]. Real data came from miscellaneous sources: including the UCI repository, past challenges (KDD cup, ChaLearn, Kaggle, DREAM, etc.), R datasets, and NYU transcriptome data [59, 60]. The pairs were drawn from a wide variety of domains of application. Examples include:

Demographics

Sex → Height
Age → Wages
Native country → Education
Latitude → Infant mortality

Ecology

City elevation → Temperature
Water level → Algal frequency
Elevation → Vegetation type
Distance to hydrology → Fire

Econometrics

Mileage → Car resell price
Number of rooms → House price
Trade price last day → Trade price

Medicine

Cancer volume → Recurrence
Metastasis → Prognosis
Age → Blood pressure
Genomics (mRNA level): transcription factor → protein induced

Engineering

Car model year $\rightarrow$ Horsepower
Number of cylinders $\rightarrow$ MPG
Cache memory $\nrightarrow$ Compute power
Roof area $\nrightarrow$ Heating load
Cement used $\rightarrow$ Compressive strength

However, the data are not well balanced with respect to application domains (see Table 2.10). In particular, a very large number of pairs are drawn from the NYU transcriptome dataset [59, 60], which provided an abundant source of pairs of "transcription factor $\rightarrow$ protein induced". All other pairs were manually curated (Fig. 2.11).

There is no guarantee that cause-effect pairs thus collected from real data are not partially confounded by hidden variables. However, the are considered $X \rightarrow Y$ and $X \leftarrow Y$ pairs for the purpose of the dataset construction. As described in Fig. 2.12, the dataset was augmented with semi-artificial $X \perp Y$ and $X \leftrightarrow Y$ pairs, in the following way: A random subset of half of the original pairs was selected to create $X \perp Y$ pairs by randomly permuting independently the values of X and Y. The $X \leftrightarrow Y$ pairs were obtained from a random selection of half of the original pairs to which an algorithm that preserves the marginal distributions while destroying the causal relationships was applied:

- Generate an artificial $X \leftrightarrow Y$ pair according the method described in Sect. 2.6.5, with n samples.
- Randomly select two real variables X_r and Y_r from real data and resample the data to obtained n samples.

Table 2.10 Number of pairs variables coming from the various data sources, in the cause-effect-pair challenge dataset

ADA	42	FIRE	4	PROCA	23
AIDS	6	GAGURINE	1	QUINE	4
BLOOD	3	GLASS	9	RADIA	36
BOND	10	IMPORTS1	9	SITKA	3
CAR	36	IMPORTS2	37	SURVEY	5
CLAIM	29	IMPORTS3	4	SYLVA	48
COIL	71	LEMON	21	TITANIC	27
CONCRETE	8	MISC	1	VETERAN	11
CPU	14	MPI0001 - DWD	81	VIT2005	12
CREDIT	15	NLSCHOOLS	5	YEAST	2779
ECOLI	1713	PIMA	12		
ENERGY	13	PROCA2	6		
TOTAL	5098	TOTAL NYU	4492	TOTAL other	606

A very large fraction of pairs is coming from the transcriptome data of NYU (YEAST and ECOLI) [59, 60]

Fig. 2.11 Tuebingen dataset. We show a few examples of the Tuebingen dataset, called CAUSEEFFECTPAIRS benchmark data in [46]

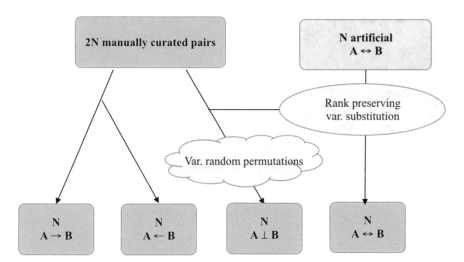

Fig. 2.12 Process for generating semi-artificial real data in the cause-effect pair challenge [29, 30]. The $X \rightarrow Y$ and $X \leftarrow Y$ pairs are real (though post-process). Other pairs are semi-artificial. $X \perp Y$ pairs are obtained by random shuffling or real variables. $X \leftrightarrow Y$ pairs are obtained from artificial $X \leftrightarrow Y$ pairs but their marginal distributions are back-fitted to marginal distributions of real variables

- Replace the values of the samples of X by the values of samples of X_r, respecting the rank ordering of values (i.e. smallest X replaced by smallest X_r values, second smallest X replaced by second smallest X_r values, etc.), and likewise for Y and Y_r.

It is worth mentioning that even real data can be biased. As mentioned in Sect. 2.6.5 the cause-effect pair challenge participants discovered bias in the first dataset that was released: the number of unique values of X was smaller that that of Y, on average, for pairs $X \rightarrow Y$. This was true both for artificial data and for real data. To compensate for this bias, we applied to real data pairs the same discretization and quantization technique described in Sect. 2.6.5. We verified that the distribution of unique values was reasonably well balanced using QQ plots. We show an example of such plots for the SUP3 dataset, which was provided to the participant as additional training data. It includes that pairs of the Tuebingen dataset, postprocessed to even out the number of unique values of X and Y and augmented with semi-artificial $X \rightarrow Y$ and $X \leftarrow Y$ pairs (Fig. 2.13).

Overall the artificial pairs remain significantly easier than the real pairs, as can be seen from the performance of the top ranking participants (Table 2.11). The score used in this table were calculated as follows: we call C the causation coefficient provided by the participants and T the target values ($-1, 0, 1; -1$ for $X \leftarrow Y, +1$ for $X \rightarrow Y$ and 0 otherwise) (Fig. 2.14).

- **(challenge) Score:** The score of the challenge, that is the average of two AUCs for the separation of $X \rightarrow Y$ vs. everything else and $X \leftarrow Y$ vs. everything else.

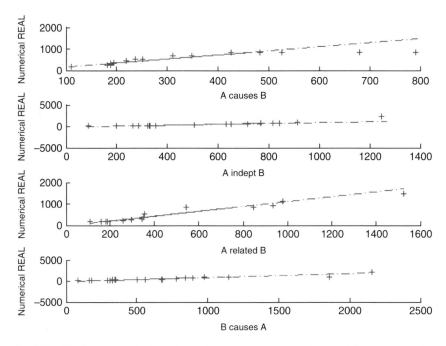

Fig. 2.13 SUP3 dataset QQ plots. These plots were made as a sanity check for the cause-effect pair challenge data in [29]. The dataset is constructed from real pairs of the Tuebingen dataset. The plots show that in all quantiles, the distribution of unique values of X and Y is similar, for all types of causal categories

Table 2.11 Results of the top ranking teams on real and artificial data (round 1 on Kaggle)

Rank	Team	Dependency	Confounding	Causality	Score
Real data					
1	ProtoML	0.88057	0.65432	0.75756	0.70420
2	Jarfo	0.95721	0.70386	0.73312	0.68642
3	HiDloN	0.91476	0.69209	0.74774	0.69669
4	FirfiD	0.92352	0.69547	0.73960	0.68274
5	Mouse	0.87689	0.64211	0.75008	0.69259
6	Domcasto & Sayani	0.85339	0.65786	0.78075	0.71355
Artificial data					
1	ProtoML	0.95372	0.76944	0.90946	0.84206
2	Jarfo	0.98063	0.83663	0.89425	0.83499
3	HiDloN	0.94416	0.76777	0.89466	0.82883
4	FirfiD	0.97644	0.80086	0.88644	0.82249
5	Mouse	0.94966	0.75831	0.86722	0.80620
6	Domcasto & Sayani	0.91789	0.72655	0.86299	0.79507

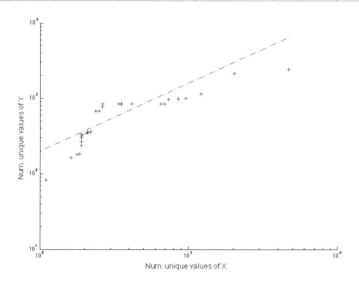

Fig. 2.14 Tuebingen dataset QQ plot. By comparison with Fig. 2.13 the QQ plots show that the distribution of unique values of X and Y differ in the original data

- **Causality (score):** Similar to the score of the challenge, but limited to the pairs $X \rightarrow Y$ and $X \leftarrow Y$. To compute this score, the $X \rightarrow Y$ and $X \leftarrow Y$ pairs are removed.
- **Confounding (score):** AUC for the separation of $X \leftrightarrow Y$ vs. $(X \rightarrow Y$ or $X \leftarrow Y)$ using abs(C). To compute this score, the $X \perp Y$ pairs are removed.

- **Dependency (score):** AUC for the separation of $X \perp Y$ *vs.* $(X \rightarrow Y$ or $X \leftarrow Y)$ using abs(C). To compute this score, the $X \leftrightarrow Y$ pairs are removed.

Notice that we do not have a score that could measures how well $X \leftrightarrow Y$ and $X \perp Y$ are separated since these two classes were lumped together with the same target 0.

For the cause-effect pair challenges, the artificial data were mixed with real data in the proportion 20% of real data and 80% of artificial data. Samples were evenly split in three sets of equal sizes called training (provided with labels), validation (for the public leaderboard), and test set (for the private leaderboard), each including 4050 pairs. We computed the average absolute value of the Pearson correlation coefficient for the pairs of continuous variables, in the various causal categories. For pairs of independent variable we found 0.02. For $X \rightarrow Y$ and $X \leftarrow Y$, we obtained 0.35. For non causally related dependent variables $X \leftrightarrow Y$ we found 0.16. The last category can therefore be separated from $X \rightarrow Y$ and $X \leftarrow Y$ on the basis of correlation alone. However, this is not an easy separation, as the performance results of Table 2.11 indicate.

2.7   Conclusion

In this chapter, we have introduced methods for evaluating causal discovery algorithms, which uncover causal relationships from observed samples of only two variables. Starting from a "mechanistic" definition of causal discovery cast in the framework of structural equation models (a.k.a. functional causal models), we have brought the problem of cause-effect pairs to a pattern recognition problem, in which samples of (X, Y) pairs of variables (scatter plots) are patterns in a supervised learning problem with ground truth G being the causal graphs in $\{X \rightarrow Y, X \leftarrow Y, X \leftrightarrow Y, X \perp Y\}$. Pairs of patterns and labels are drawn i.i.d. from the joint distribution of (X, Y) and G, called mother distribution. Given the symmetry of the problem, one can bring it back to a binary classification problem $X \rightarrow Y$ *vs.* other cases and define discriminant functions, called "causation coefficients" having large positive values if $X \rightarrow Y$, small negative values if $X \leftarrow Y$ and values near zero otherwise. We introduce the notion of Bayes-optimal coefficients from which we derive a notion of identifiability of causal relationships related to the Bayes optimal classification accuracy. In this sense, identifiability is a property of the mother distribution and causal discovery algorithms seek to approximate as well as possible optimal Bayesian causation coefficients. These notions can help characterize new algorithms and compare them, given data generated artificially or semi-artificially and/or from real data. We give many pointers to such benchmark data. Practitioners interested in testing the validity of causal assumptions made on *particulars pairs* can also use empirical mother distributions to derive *ad hoc* statistical tests.

Our framework rests upon the existence of mother distributions. Does it push the problem further without solving it? In many application areas of pattern recognition it seems natural to have a training set and a test set drawn from the same (but unknown) probability distribution. What is different for causal discovery? One important difference is that, in applications, we generally have no or very few labeled examples of our "mother distribution". hence we must resort to "few short learning" or "zero short learning" or learning from simulated data resembling data drawn from out mother distribution, and hope that we operate quality "transfer learning". Thus, causation coefficients should "generalize" well not only for data drawn from the same mother distribution, but also for data generated from other mother distributions. This pushes the problem even further, in the direction of defining a "grand-mother distribution" of mother distributions...

Another limitation of this framework is that it addresses only pairs of variables. However, it can be generalized and one can consider the orientation of pairs of variables within a graph in a similar way. In that case though, it becomes even more important to test algorithms on pairs not drawn from the same mother distribution, i.e. drawn from other systems of variables related via different causal graphs in training and in test data.

Acknowledgements The authors would like to thank Dominik Janzing and Berna Batu for their careful review of this chapter.

Appendix 1: Derivation of Bayes Optimal Causation Coefficients

We derive the Bayes optimal causation coefficients introduced in Sect. 2.3.2.

The Bayes optimal decision rule prescribes the following:

Classify pair (X_π, Y_π) as $[X \rightarrow Y]$ iff

$$P_\mathcal{M}\left(G = [X \rightarrow Y] \mid (X_\pi, Y_\pi)\right) > \quad P_\mathcal{M}\left(G \neq [X \rightarrow Y] \mid (X_\pi, Y_\pi)\right).$$

(2.28)

Given a classification problem of patterns z (in our case $z = (X_\pi, Y_\pi)$ pairs), with ground truth g_1 and g_0 (in our case $g_1 = [X \rightarrow Y]$ and $g_0 = \neg[X \rightarrow Y]$), we define a "discriminant function" as a function $g(z)$ taking values in $\mathbb{R}$ such that we predict class g_1 if $g(z) > \theta$ and class g_0 otherwise. Important: with our definition, θ is a real number not necessarily equal to 0 (as is commonly used). In this context,

$$P_\mathcal{M}\left(G = [X \rightarrow Y] \mid (X_\pi, Y_\pi)\right) - P_\mathcal{M}\left(G \neq [X \rightarrow Y] \mid (X_\pi, Y_\pi)\right)$$

is a Bayes optimal discriminant function and because:

$$P_\mathcal{M}\left(G = [X \rightarrow Y] \mid (X_\pi, Y_\pi)\right) = 1 - P_\mathcal{M}\left(G \neq [X \rightarrow Y] \mid (X_\pi, Y_\pi)\right),$$

the following is also a Bayes optimal discriminant function:

$$2 \, P_{\mathcal{M}}\Big(G = [X \to Y] \mid (X_\pi, Y_\pi)\Big) - 1$$

and therefore, so is:

$$P_{\mathcal{M}}\Big(G = [X \to Y] \mid (X_\pi, Y_\pi)\Big).$$

Also note that we could have considered the symmetric problem of classifying $Y \to X$ *vs.* all other cases. If we assume that the mother distribution is perfectly symmetrical, i.e. that for each pair (X, Y) labeled $X \to Y$ we have the symmetric pair (Y, X) labeled $Y \to X$ and for all pairs (X, Y) labeled $X \leftrightarrow Y$, we have the same pair labeled $Y \leftrightarrow X$ and for all pairs (X, Y) labeled $X \perp Y$, we have the same pair labeled $Y \perp X$, then, the ranking of all pairs (X_π, Y_π) by sorting according to $P_{\mathcal{M}}\Big(G = [X \to Y] \mid (X_\pi, Y_\pi)\Big)$ should be in reverse order as the ranking with $P_{\mathcal{M}}\Big(G = [X \leftarrow Y] \mid (X_\pi, Y_\pi)\Big)$. Consequently we obtain the same ranking with:

$$\boxed{C_{\mathcal{B}1}(X_\pi, Y_\pi) = \Phi\Big(P_{\mathcal{M}}\Big(G = [X \to Y]|(X_\pi, Y_\pi)\Big)\Big) - \Phi\Big(P_{\mathcal{M}}\Big(G = [X \leftarrow Y]|(X_\pi, Y_\pi)\Big)\Big)}$$

$$(2.29)$$

where $\Phi(.)$ is any strictly monotonically increasing function.

It is important to note that, because we consider four possible truth values for G, $G \in \{X \to Y, X \leftarrow Y, X \leftrightarrow Y, X \perp Y\}$, $P_{\mathcal{M}}\Big(G = [X \to Y] \mid (X_\pi, Y_\pi)\Big)$ is NOT equal to $(1 - P_{\mathcal{M}}\Big(G = [X \leftarrow Y] \mid (X_\pi, Y_\pi)\Big)$.

It may also be convenient to define an Bayes optimal causation coefficient in terms of data generative model. To that end, notice that if $a - b$ is a discriminant function, so is $a/b - 1$. Therefore,

$$P_{\mathcal{M}}\Big(G = [X \to Y] \mid (X_\pi, Y_\pi)\Big) \Big/ P_{\mathcal{M}}\Big(G = [X \leftarrow Y] \mid (X_\pi, Y_\pi)\Big) - 1$$

is also a Bayes optimal discriminant function. Using Bayes' rule again,

$$P_{\mathcal{M}}\Big(G = [X \to Y] \mid (X_\pi, Y_\pi)\Big) =$$
$$P_{\mathcal{M}}\Big((X_\pi, Y_\pi) \mid G = [X \to Y]\Big) P_{\mathcal{M}}\Big(G = [X \to Y]\Big) \Big/ P_{\mathcal{M}}\Big((X_\pi, Y_\pi)\Big)$$

and further assuming that the mother distribution is not biased towards a particular causal direction:

$$P_{\mathcal{M}}\Big(G = [X \to Y]\Big) = P_{\mathcal{M}}\Big(G = [Y \to X]\Big)$$

the following is also a Bayes optimal discriminant function:

$$P_{\mathcal{M}}\Big((X_\pi, Y_\pi) \mid G = [X \to Y]\Big)/P_{\mathcal{M}}\Big((X_\pi, Y_\pi) \mid G = [Y \to X]\Big) - 1$$

and so is, for any strictly monotonically increasing function $\Phi(.)$:

$$C_{\mathcal{B}2}(X_\pi, Y_\pi) = \Phi\Big(P_{\mathcal{M}}\big((X_\pi, Y_\pi) | G = [X \to Y]\big)\Big) - \Phi\Big(P_{\mathcal{M}}\big((X_\pi, Y_\pi) | G = [Y \to X]\big)\Big)$$

(2.30)

Appendix 2: Proof of Theorem 2.1: $\mathcal{B}$-Identifiability Implies (α, β)-Identifiability

Given the hypotheses of the theorem (symmetrical mother distribution), we can choose $C_{\mathcal{B}2}$ as causation coefficient (Eq. (2.8)) and apply it to $\mathcal{B}_\Pi(X, Y)$:

$$C_{\mathcal{B}2}(X_\pi, Y_\pi) = P_{\mathcal{M}}\Big(\mathcal{B}_\Pi(X, Y) \mid G = [X \to Y]\Big)$$
$$- P_{\mathcal{M}}\Big(\mathcal{B}_\Pi(X, Y) \mid G = [Y \to X]\Big).$$

Imposing $\alpha = \beta = \theta = 0$, as per the definition of (α, β)-identifiability, the causal direction is (α, β)-identifiable for $P_{\mathcal{M}}\Big(\mathcal{B}_\Pi(X, Y), G\Big)$ iff:

$$Pr(C_{\mathcal{B}2}(X_\pi, Y_\pi) > 0 \mid G = [X \leftarrow Y]) = 0. \quad \text{(Type I errors)}$$
$$Pr(C_{\mathcal{B}2}(X_\pi, Y_\pi) < 0 \mid G = [X \to Y]) = 0. \quad \text{(Type II errors)}$$

In other words, (α, β)-identifiability with $\alpha = \beta = \theta = 0$ for $\mathcal{B}_\Pi(X, Y)$ is equivalent to:

$$G = [X \to Y]$$
$$\Rightarrow P_{\mathcal{M}}\Big(\mathcal{B}_\Pi(X, Y) \mid G = [X \to Y]\Big) > P_{\mathcal{M}}\Big(\mathcal{B}_\Pi(X, Y) \mid G = [Y \to X]\Big).$$

(2.31)

and vice versa if we invert the roles of X and Y. If $\mathcal{B}$-identifiability holds, then:

$$G = [X \to Y] \Rightarrow \begin{cases} \exists\, (f \in \mathcal{F} \land P(N) \in \mathbb{N}) \text{ s.t. } Y := f(X, N) \\ \nexists\, (f \in \mathcal{F} \land P(N) \in \mathbb{N}) \text{ s.t. } X := f(Y, N). \end{cases}$$

(2.32)

which can be equivalently re-written, for the given pair (X_π, Y_π), as:

$$G = [X \to Y] \Rightarrow \begin{cases} P_{\mathcal{M}}\Big(\mathcal{B}_\Pi(X, Y) \mid G = [X \to Y]\Big) > 0 \\ P_{\mathcal{M}}\Big(\mathcal{B}_\Pi(X, Y) \mid G = [Y \to X]\Big) = 0. \end{cases}$$

(2.33)

It can easily be seen that if Eq. (2.33) is satisfied then Eq. (2.31) holds. Thus we have proved that $\mathcal{B}$-identifiability implies (α, β)-identifiability with $\alpha = \beta = \theta = 0$ for $\mathcal{B}_\Pi(X, Y)$. Let us prove now the reciprocal statement.

Starting from Eq. (2.31), if we swap the role of X and Y, we obtain: $G = [Y \to X] \Rightarrow P_{\mathcal{M}}\Big(\mathcal{B}_\Pi(X, Y) \mid G = [Y \to X]\Big) > P_{\mathcal{M}}\Big(\mathcal{B}_\Pi(X, Y) \mid G = [X \to Y]\Big)$; and if we contrapose Eq. (2.31) we obtain: $P_{\mathcal{M}}\Big(\mathcal{B}_\Pi(X, Y) \mid G = [Y \to X]\Big) > P_{\mathcal{M}}\Big(\mathcal{B}_\Pi(X, Y) \mid G = [X \to Y]\Big) \Rightarrow G = [Y \to X]$, since when data are generated with a binary process $\neg(G = [X \to Y])$ is equivalent to $G = [Y \to X]$.

Thus we have an equivalence, both for the previous formula and for Eq. (2.31):

$$G = [X \to Y] \Leftrightarrow P_{\mathcal{M}}\Big(\mathcal{B}_\Pi(X, Y) \mid G = [X \to Y]\Big)$$
$$> P_{\mathcal{M}}\Big(\mathcal{B}_\Pi(X, Y) \mid G = [Y \to X]\Big) \geq 0.$$

(2.34)

In this last formula, if $P_{\mathcal{M}}\Big(\mathcal{B}_\Pi(X, Y) \mid G = [Y \to X]\Big) \neq 0$, then $\exists (X, Y)$ s.t. $G = [Y \to X]$. This would contradicts that $G = [X \to Y]$. Hence we must have $P_{\mathcal{M}}\Big(\mathcal{B}_\Pi(X, Y) \mid G = [Y \to X]\Big) = 0$. Therefore, if Eq. (2.34) holds, then Eq. (2.33) holds too, or equivalently Eq. (2.32). Thus, we have proved that (α, β)-identifiability with $\alpha = \beta = \theta = 0$ implies $\mathcal{B}$-identifiability. $\square$

Appendix 3: Examples of Cause-Effect Pairs

In this section, we should graphically how the some of the causation coefficient filters are computed. The examples are drawn from Tables 2.1 and 2.2. It can be observed that, depending on the type of data generative model, one or the other assumption is violated. Hence the causation coefficient filters generally disagree on the causal direction. Even though the small decision tree of Fig. 7.7 performs relatively well on the challenge data, it is very easy to construct pairs to make it fail. In the following chapters, we will see more advanced method (Figs. 2.15, 2.16, 2.17, 2.18, 2.19, 2.20, 2.21, 2.22, 2.23, 2.24, 2.25 and 2.26).

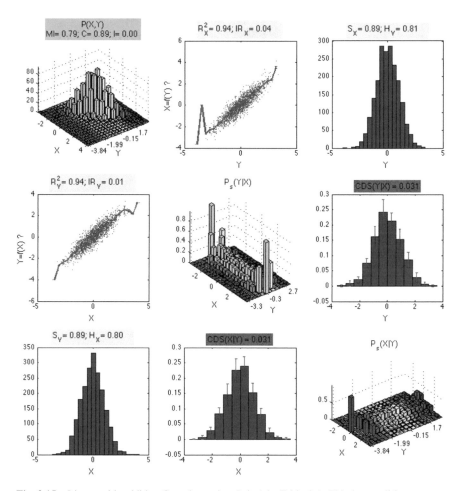

Fig. 2.15 Linear with additive Gaussian noise. Pair 1 in Table 2.1. This is a well-known non identifiable pair. However, due to the finite sample size, wrong decisions might be made

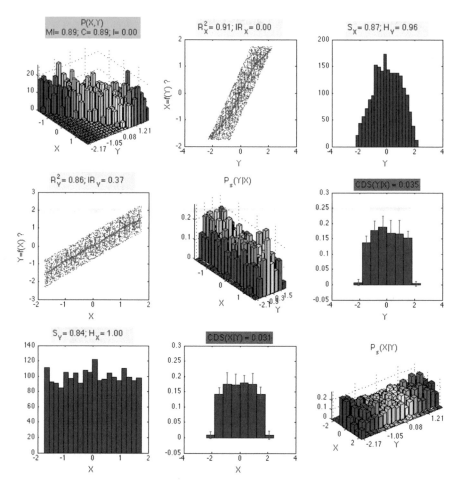

Fig. 2.16 Linear with additive uniform noise. Pair 2 in Table 2.1. Unlike the previous pair, this one is identifiable with the Additive Noise Model (ANM): $IR_Y > IR_X$, there is a better independence between the input and the residual in the correct direction. However the R^2 is better in the wrong direction!

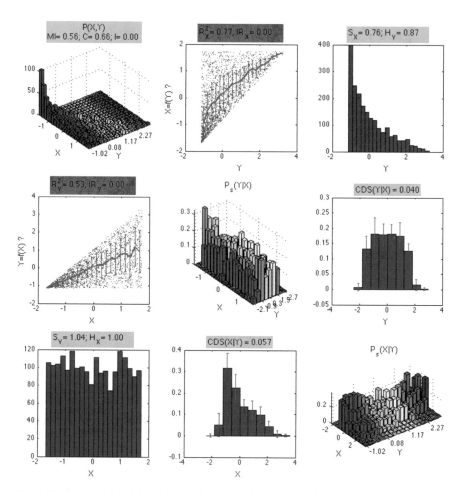

Fig. 2.17 Linear with multiplicative uniform noise. Pair 3 in Table 2.1. The ANM has difficulties, but the CDA works

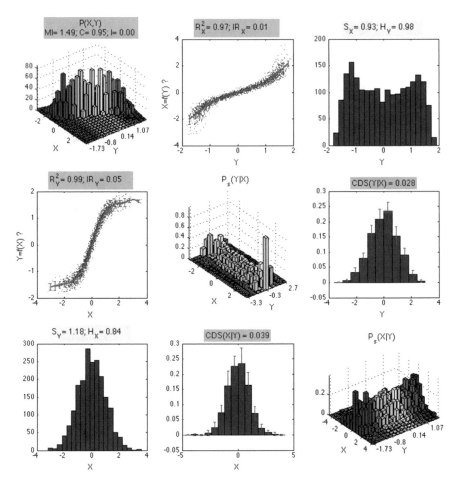

Fig. 2.18 S-shaped function with Gaussian input violating the independence of input density and function. Pair 4 in Table 2.1. The IGCI entropy criterion fails, but the IGCI slope criterion works

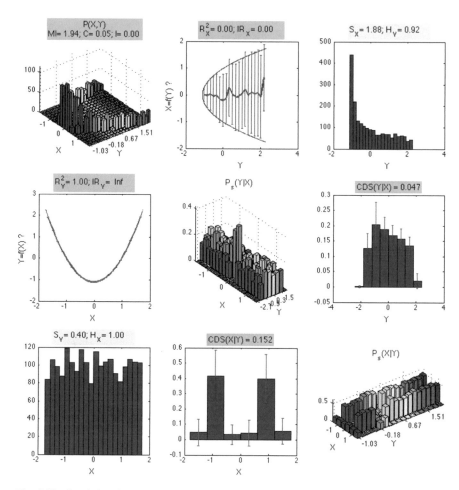

Fig. 2.19   Parabola with very small noise. Pair 5 in Table 2.1. The IGCI slope criterion fails, because the function is ntn invertible

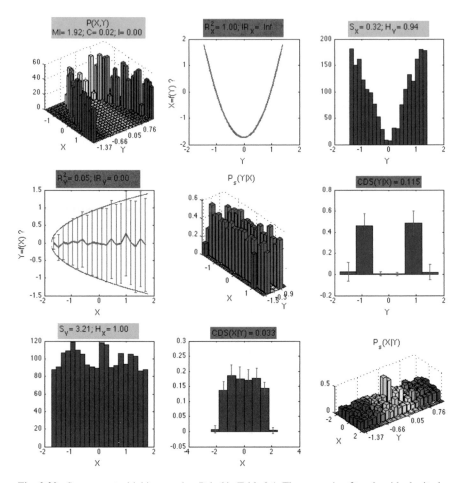

Fig. 2.20 Square root with binary noise. Pair 6 in Table 2.1. The regression fit and residual criteria fail as well as the CDS. But the IGCI criteria work

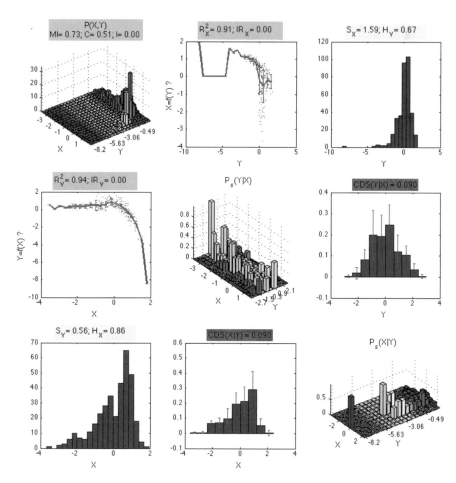

Fig. 2.21 Altitude *vs.* temperature of German cities. Pair 1 in Table 2.2. The IGCI slope criterion fails, because the function is not invertible. More surprisingly, CDS fails too, probably because of outliers

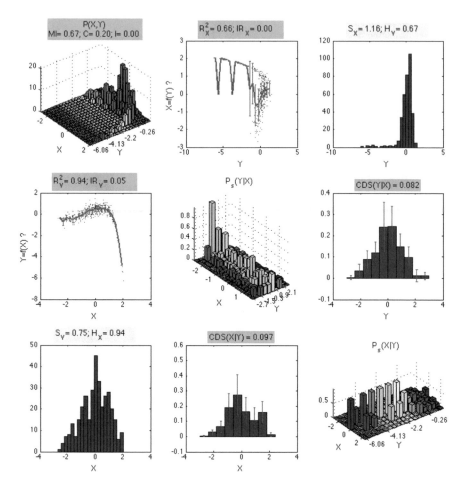

Fig. 2.22 Simulated altitude *vs.* temperature. Pair 2 in Table 2.2. Only the IGCI slope criterion fails, because the function is not invertible

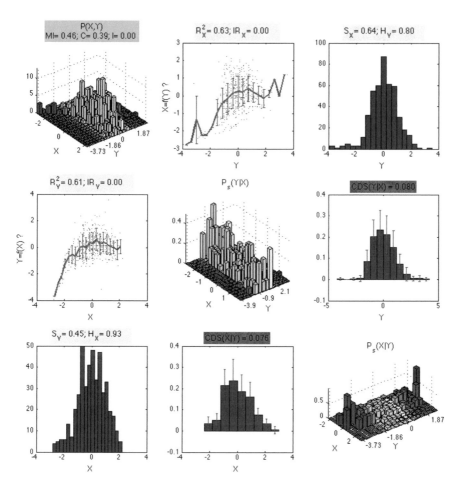

Fig. 2.23 Real weight *vs.* age pair. Pair 3 in Table 2.2. Only *H* really works on that pair (*IR* is neutral)

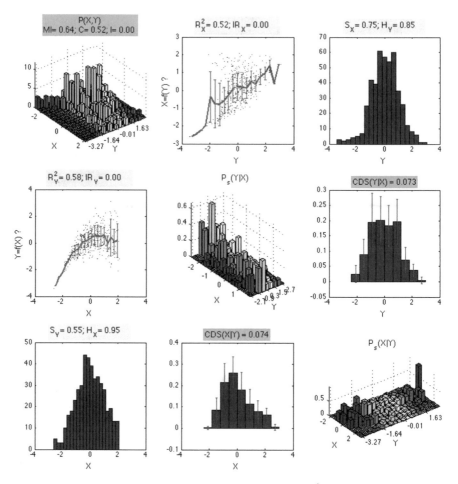

Fig. 2.24 Simulated weight *vs.* age pair. Pair 4 in Table 2.2. Only R^2 and H work on that pair

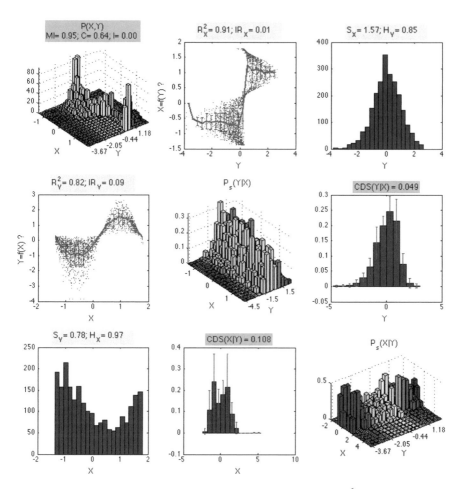

Fig. 2.25 Real pair "hill shade at 3 pm" *vs.* aspect. Pair 5 in Table 2.2. R^2 fails because of the multiplicative noise and S fails because the function is not invertible

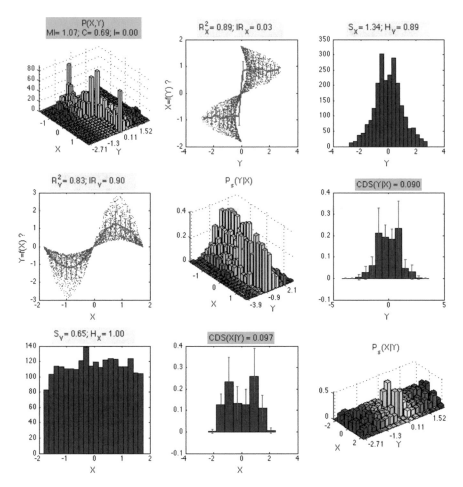

Fig. 2.26 Simulated pair "hill shade at 3 pm" *vs.* aspect. Pair 6 in Table 2.2. The only pair in which all diagnoses agree between real and synthetic data

References

1. Constantin F. Aliferis, Ioannis Tsamardinos, Alexander R. Statnikov, and Laura E. Brown. Causal explorer: A causal probabilistic network learning toolkit for biomedical discovery. In *Proceedings of the International Conference on Mathematics and Engineering Techniques in Medicine and Biological Sciences, METMBS '03, June 23 - 26, 2003, Las Vegas, Nevada, USA*, pages 371–376, 2003.
2. Demian Battaglia, Isabelle Guyon, Vincent Lemaire, Javier Orlandi, Bisakha Ray, and Jordi Soriano. *Neural Connectomics Challenge*. Springer Publishing Company, Incorporated, 1st edition, 2017. ISBN 3319530690, 9783319530697.
3. J A Blackard and D J Dean. Comparative accuracies of artificial neural networks and discriminant analysis in predicting forest cover types from cartographic variables. *Computers and Electronics in Agriculture*, vol.24:131–151, 1999.

4. Patrick Bloebaum, Dominik Janzing, Takashi Washio, Shohei Shimizu, and Bernhard Schoelkopf. Cause-effect inference by comparing regression errors. In *International Conference on Artificial Intelligence and Statistics*, pages 900–909, 2018.
5. C Bonferroni. Teoria statistica delle classi e calcolo delle probabilita. *Pubblicazioni del R Istituto Superiore di Scienze Economiche e Commericiali di Firenze*, 8:3–62, 1936.
6. Gianluca Bontempi. From dependency to causality: a machine learning approach. In *Proc. NIPS 2013 workshop on causality*, http://clopinet.com/isabelle/Projects/NIPS2013/, December 2013.
7. P. B. Burns, R. J. Rohrich, and K. C. Chung. The levels of evidence and their role in evidence-based medicine. *Plastic and reconstructive surgery*, 128(1):305–310, 2011.
8. Krzysztof Chalupka, Frederick Eberhardt, and Pietro Perona. Estimating causal direction and confounding of two discrete variables. *arXiv preprint arXiv:1611.01504*, 2016.
9. Povilas Daniusis, Dominik Janzing, Joris Mooij, Jakob Zscheischler, Bastian Steudel, Kun Zhang, and Bernhard Schölkopf. Inferring deterministic causal relations. *arXiv preprint arXiv:1203.3475*, 2012.
10. Diogo Moitinho de Almeida. Automated feature engineering applied to causality. In *Proc. NIPS 2013 workshop on causality*, http://clopinet.com/isabelle/Projects/NIPS2013/, December 2013.
11. Suzana de Siqueira Santos, Daniel Yasumasa Takahashi, Asuka Nakata, and André Fujita. A comparative study of statistical methods used to identify dependencies between gene expression signals. *Briefings in Bioinformatics*, 15(6):906–918, 2014. doi: 10.1093/bib/bbt051. URL http://dx.doi.org/10.1093/bib/bbt051.
12. R. O. Duda, P. E. Hart, and D. G. Stork. *Pattern Classification*. John Wiley & Sons, USA, 2nd edition, 2001.
13. B. Efron. Estimating the error rate of a prediction rule: Improvement on cross-validation. *Journal of the American Statistical Association*, 78:316–331, 1983.
14. Bradley Efron and Robert J Tibshirani. *An introduction to the bootstrap*. CRC press, 1994.
15. Guy Fagherazzi, Alice Vilier, Daniela Saes Sartorelli, Martin Lajous, Beverley Balkau, and Françoise Clavel-Chapelon. Consumption of artificially and sugar-sweetened beverages and incident type 2 diabetes in the etude epidémiologique auprès des femmes de la mutuelle générale de l'education nationale–european prospective investigation into cancer and nutrition cohort. *The American Journal of Clinical Nutrition*, 97(3):517–523, March 2013.
16. Ronald A. Fisher. *The Design of Experiments*. 1935.
17. José A. R. Fonollosa. Conditional distribution variability measure for causality detection. In *Proc. NIPS 2013 workshop on causality*, http://clopinet.com/isabelle/Projects/NIPS2013/, December 2013.
18. José AR Fonollosa. Conditional distribution variability measures for causality detection. *arXiv preprint arXiv:1601.06680*, 2016.
19. U.S. Preventive Services Task Force. Guide to clinical preventive services: report of the u.s. preventive services task force. 1989.
20. Stuart Geman, Elie Bienenstock, and René Doursat. Neural networks and the bias/variance dilemma. *Neural Comput.*, 4(1):1–58, 1992. ISSN 0899-7667. doi: https://doi.org/10.1162/neco.1992.4.1.1.
21. Olivier Goudet. Causality pairwise inference datasets. replication data for: "learning functional causal models with generative neural networks", 2017. URL http://dx.doi.org/10.7910/DVN/3757KX.
22. Olivier Goudet, Diviyan Kalainathan, Philippe Caillou, Isabelle Guyon, David Lopez-Paz, and Michèle Sebag. Causal generative neural networks. *arXiv preprint arXiv:1711.08936*, 2017.
23. Clive WJ Granger. Investigating causal relations by econometric models and cross-spectral methods. *Econometrica: Journal of the Econometric Society*, pages 424–438, 1969.
24. A. Gretton, K. Fukumizu, CH. Teo, L. Song, B. Schölkopf, and AJ. Smola. A kernel statistical test of independence. In *Advances in neural information processing systems 20*, pages 585–592, Red Hook, NY, USA, September 2008. Max-Planck-Gesellschaft, Curran.

25. Arthur Gretton, Ralf Herbrich, Alexander Smola, Olivier Bousquet, and Bernhard Schölkopf. Kernel methods for measuring independence. *Journal of Machine Learning Research*, 6(Dec):2075–2129, 2005.
26. I. Guyon, C. Aliferis, G. Cooper, A. Elisseeff, J.-P. Pellet, P. Spirtes, and A. Statnikov. Design and analysis of the causality pot-luck challenge. In *JMLR W&CP*, volume 5: NIPS 2008 causality workshop, Whistler, Canada, December 12 2008.
27. I. Guyon, D. Battaglia, A. Guyon, V. Lemaire, J. G. Orlandi, B. Ray, M. Saeed, J. Soriano, A. Statnikov, and O. Stetter. Design of the first neuronal connectomics challenge: From imaging to connectivity. In *2014 International Joint Conference on Neural Networks (IJCNN)*, pages 2600–2607, July 2014. https://doi.org/10.1109/IJCNN.2014.6889913.
28. Isabelle Guyon. A practical guide to model selection, 2010.
29. Isabelle Guyon. Chalearn cause effect pairs challenge, 2013. URL http://www.causality.inf.ethz.ch/cause-effect.php.
30. Isabelle Guyon. Chalearn fast causation coefficient challenge. 2014.
31. Isabelle Guyon and et al. Results and analysis of the 2013 chalearn cause-effect pair challenge. In *Proc. NIPS 2013 workshop on causality*, Workshop URL: http://clopinet.com/isabelle/Projects/NIPS2013/; Challenge URL: http://www.causality.inf.ethz.ch/cause-effect.php, December 2013.
32. Isabelle Guyon, Steve Gunn, Masoud Nikravesh, and Lotfi A. Zadeh. *Feature Extraction: Foundations and Applications (Studies in Fuzziness and Soft Computing)*. Springer-Verlag, Berlin, Heidelberg, 2006. ISBN 3540354875.
33. Patrik O Hoyer, Dominik Janzing, Joris M Mooij, Jonas Peters, and Bernhard Schölkopf. Nonlinear causal discovery with additive noise models. In *Neural Information Processing Systems (NIPS)*, pages 689–696, 2009.
34. P. Illari, F. Russo, and J. Williamson. *Causality in the Sciences*. Oxford University Press, 2011.
35. Dominik Janzing and Bernhard Scholkopf. Causal inference using the algorithmic markov condition. *IEEE Transactions on Information Theory*, 56(10):5168–5194, 2010.
36. Dominik Janzing, Joris Mooij, Kun Zhang, Jan Lemeire, Jakob Zscheischler, Povilas Daniušis, Bastian Steudel, and Bernhard Schölkopf. Information-geometric approach to inferring causal directions. *Artif. Intell.*, 182-183:1–31, May 2012. ISSN 0004-3702. doi: 10.1016/j.artint.2012.01.002. URL http://dx.doi.org/10.1016/j.artint.2012.01.002.
37. Mingyu Chung Gabriela K. Fragiadakis Jonathan Fitzgerald Birgit Schoeberl Garry P. Nolan Claire Tomlin Karen Sachs, Solomon Itani. Experiment design in static models of dynamic biological systems. In *NIPS2013 workshop on causality*, 2013.
38. Shachar Kaufman, Saharon Rosset, Claudia Perlich, and Ori Stitelman. Leakage in data mining: Formulation, detection, and avoidance. *ACM Transactions on Knowledge Discovery from Data (TKDD)*, 6(4):15, 2012.
39. Ron Kohavi. Scaling up the accuracy of naive-bayes classifiers: a decision-tree hybrid. In *PROCEEDINGS OF THE SECOND INTERNATIONAL CONFERENCE ON KNOWLEDGE DISCOVERY AND DATA MINING*, pages 202–207. AAAI Press, 1996.
40. S. Kpotufe, E. Sgouritsa, D. Janzing, and B. Schölkopf. Consistency of causal inference under the additive noise model. In *Proceedings of the 31st International Conference on Machine Learning, W&CP 32 (1)*, pages 478–495. JMLR, 2014.
41. John Langford. Tutorial on practical prediction theory for classification. *J. Mach. Learn. Res.*, 6:273–306, December 2005. ISSN 1532-4435. URL http://dl.acm.org/citation.cfm?id=1046920.1058111.
42. David Lopez-Paz, Krikamol Muandet, and Benjamin Recht. The randomized causation coefficient. *J. Mach. Learn. Res.*, 16(1):2901–2907, January 2015a. ISSN 1532-4435. URL http://dl.acm.org/citation.cfm?id=2789272.2912092.
43. David Lopez-Paz, Krikamol Muandet, Bernhard Schölkopf, and Ilya O Tolstikhin. Towards a learning theory of cause-effect inference. In *ICML*, pages 1452–1461, 2015b.
44. David Lopez-Paz, Robert Nishihara, Soumith Chintala, Bernhard Schölkopf, and Léon Bottou. Discovering causal signals in images. *arXiv preprint arXiv:1605.08179;*, 2016.

45. Bram Minnaert. Feature importance in causal inference for numerical and categorical variables. In *Proc. NIPS 2013 workshop on causality*, http://clopinet.com/isabelle/Projects/NIPS2013/, December 2013.

46. Joris M Mooij, Jonas Peters, Dominik Janzing, Jakob Zscheischler, and Bernhard Schölkopf. Distinguishing cause from effect using observational data: methods and benchmarks. *Journal of Machine Learning Research*, 17(32):1–102, 2016.

47. J. Pearl. *Causality: Models, Reasoning, and Inference*. Cambridge University Press, 2000.

48. J. Peters, D. Janzing, and B. Schölkopf. *Elements of Causal Inference: Foundations and Learning Algorithms*. MIT Press, Cambridge, MA, USA, 2017a.

49. Jonas Peters, Dominik Janzing, and Bernhard Scholkopf. Causal inference on discrete data using additive noise models. *IEEE Transactions on Pattern Analysis and Machine Intelligence*, 33(12):2436–2450, 2011.

50. Jonas Peters, Dominik Janzing, and Bernhard Schölkopf. *Elements of causal inference: foundations and learning algorithms*. MIT press, 2017b.

51. Karl Popper. *Conjectures and refutations: The growth of scientific knowledge*. routledge, 2014.

52. Hans Reichenbach. *The direction of time*. Dover Publications, 1956.

53. Paul R. Rosenbaum and Donald B. Rubin. The central role of the propensity score in observational studies for causal effects. *Biometrika*, 70(1):41–55, 1983.

54. Donald Rubin. Estimating causal effects of treatments in randomized and nonrandomized studies. *Journal of Educational Psychology*, 66(5):688–701, 1974.

55. Spyridon Samothrakis, Diego Perez, and Simon Lucas. Training gradient boosting machines using curve fitting and information-theoretic features for causal direction detection. In *Proc. NIPS 2013 workshop on causality*, http://clopinet.com/isabelle/Projects/NIPS2013/, December 2013.

56. K. F. Schulz, D. G. Altman, D. Moher, and for the CONSORT Group. Consort 2010 statement: updated guidelines for reporting parallel group randomised trials. *Ann. Int. Med.*, 2010.

57. P. Spirtes, C. Glymour, and R. Scheines. *Causation, Prediction, and Search*. The MIT Press, Cambridge, Massachusetts, London, England, 2000.

58. Alexander Statnikov, Mikael Henaff, Nikita I Lytkin, and Constantin F Aliferis. New methods for separating causes from effects in genomics data. *BMC Genomics*, 13, 2012a.

59. Alexander Statnikov, Mikael Henaff, Nikita I Lytkin, and Constantin F Aliferis. New methods for separating causes from effects in genomics data. *BMC genomics*, 13(8):S22, 2012b.

60. Alexander Statnikov, Sisi Ma, Mikael Henaff, Nikita Lytkin, Efstratios Efstathiadis, Eric R. Peskin, and Constantin F. Aliferis. Ultra-scalable and efficient methods for hybrid observational and experimental local causal pathway discovery. *J. Mach. Learn. Res.*, 16(1):3219–3267, January 2015. ISSN 1532-4435. URL http://dl.acm.org/citation.cfm?id=2789272.2912102.

61. Natasa Tagasovska, Thibault Vatter, and Valérie Chavez-Demoulin. Nonparametric quantile-based causal discovery. *arXiv preprint arXiv:1801.10579*, 2018.

62. https://en.wikipedia.org/wiki/Evidence-based_medicine. Evidence-based medicine.

63. Yi Wang, Yi Li andHongbao Cao, Momiao Xiong, Yin Yao Shugart, and Li Jin. Efficient test for nonlinear dependence of two continuous variables. *BMC Bioinformatics*, 16(260), 2015.

64. K. Zhang, B. Schölkopf, K. Muandet, and Z. Wang. Domain adaptation under target and conditional shift. In *Proceedings of the 30th International Conference on Machine Learning, W&CP 28 (3)*, page 819–827. JMLR, 2013.

65. Kun Zhang. Causal learning and machine learning. In Antti Hyttinen, Joe Suzuki, and Brandon Malone, editors, *Proceedings of The 3rd International Workshop on Advanced Methodologies for Bayesian Networks*, volume 73 of *Proceedings of Machine Learning Research*, pages 4–4. PMLR, 20–22 Sep 2017. URL http://proceedings.mlr.press/v73/zhang17a.html.

66. Kun Zhang and Aapo Hyvärinen. On the identifiability of the post-nonlinear causal model. In *Proceedings of the twenty-fifth conference on uncertainty in artificial intelligence*, pages 647–655. AUAI Press, 2009.

67. Kun Zhang, Zhikun Wang, Jiji Zhang, and Bernhard Schölkopf. On estimation of functional causal models: general results and application to the post-nonlinear causal model. *ACM Transactions on Intelligent Systems and Technology (TIST)*, 7(2):13, 2016.

Chapter 3
Learning Bivariate Functional Causal Models

Olivier Goudet, Diviyan Kalainathan, Michèle Sebag, and Isabelle Guyon

3.1 Introduction

A natural approach to address the cause-effect pair problem is from a reverse engineering perspective: given the available measurements $\{(x_i, y_i)\}_{i=1}^{n}$ of the two variables X and Y, the task is to discover the underlying causal process that led the variables to take the values they have. To find this model, one needs implicitly to answer two questions:

1. First, is there a causal relationship between X and Y and what is the *causal direction*? Was X generated first and then Y generated from X, or the opposite?
2. Second, what is the *causal mechanism* that can explain the behavior of the system? *How* was Y generated from X or X generated from Y?

Therefore this approach for causal discovery goes beyond finding the causal structure, as it requires also to define a generative model of the data, which do not seem mandatory at first sight if one is only interested in finding if $X \rightarrow Y$ or $Y \rightarrow X$.

This type of generative model has notably been formalized with the framework of Functional Causal Models (FCMs) [21], also known as Structural Equation Models (SEMs), that can well represent the underlying data-generating process, supports interventions and allows counterfactual reasoning.

O. Goudet (✉) · D. Kalainathan · M. Sebag
Team TAU - CNRS, INRIA, Université Paris Sud, Université Paris Saclay, Orsay, France
e-mail: Diviyan.kalainathan@lri.fr; sebag@lri.fr

I. Guyon
Team TAU - CNRS, INRIA, Université Paris Sud, Université Paris Saclay, Orsay France

ChaLearn, Berkeley, CA, USA
e-mail: guyon@chalearn.org

© Springer Nature Switzerland AG 2019   101
I. Guyon et al. (eds.), *Cause Effect Pairs in Machine Learning*,
The Springer Series on Challenges in Machine Learning,
https://doi.org/10.1007/978-3-030-21810-2_3

3.1.1   Toy Example: Recovering the Underlying Generative Process

Let us first introduce a simple cause-effect example depicted on Fig. 3.1. This bivariate example was generated using an artificial causal mechanism from one variable to another.[1] Interestingly enough, the correlation coefficient between X and Y is zero, but one can immediately see what could be the causal direction.

Indeed it seems very intuitive to prefer the causal direction $X \rightarrow Y$. And this is true in this case as the data were generated from X to Y according the following stochastic process with quadratic deterministic mechanism:

$$X \sim \mathscr{U}(-1, 1) \tag{3.1}$$

$$N_Y \sim \mathscr{U}(-1, 1)/3 \tag{3.2}$$

$$Y := 4 \times (X^2 - 0.5)^2 + N_Y, \tag{3.3}$$

where $\mathscr{U}(-1, 1)$ denotes uniform distribution between -1 and 1. Here we use the symbol ":=" when writing the model to signify that it has to be seen as an assignment from cause to effect.

The correlation coefficient is equal to zero, but there is a nonlinear dependency between X and Y. Moreover, if one assumes that this dependency is due to the influence of one of the variable on the other and not due to a third variable

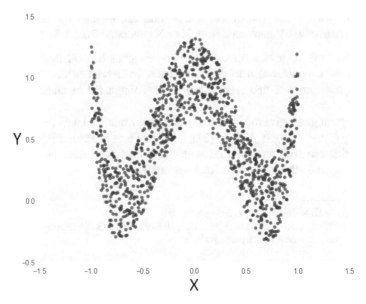

Fig. 3.1 Data generated with the quadratic model of Eq. (3.3)

---

[1]Example coming from https://en.wikipedia.org/wiki/Correlation_and_dependence.

influencing both, one of the two following causal hypotheses holds as stated in Chap. 1 of this book:

- $Y := f_Y(X, N_Y)$ with $N_Y \perp\!\!\!\perp X$ (hypothesis 1, $X \rightarrow Y$),
- $X := f_X(Y, N_X)$ with $N_X \perp\!\!\!\perp Y$ (hypothesis 2, $Y \rightarrow X$),

where the noise variable N_Y (respectively N_X) summarizes *all the other unobserved influences* on X (respectively on Y).

In order to recover the causal mechanism, one can propose to search in the class of polynomial functions of degree 4 by fitting regression models $y = \hat{f}_Y(x)$ and $x = \hat{f}_X(y)$ on the data with mean squared error loss (Fig. 3.2).

The expected mean squared error is lower for the model $\hat{f}_Y$ from X to Y than for the other model $\hat{f}_X$ from Y to X. The residuals of each polynomial regression are displayed on Fig. 3.3.

To some extent, as the residual $Y - \hat{f}_Y(X)$ is independent of X, one can build an explanatory model of the data as : $Y := \hat{f}_Y(X) + N_Y$, with $\hat{f}_Y$ quadratic and with almost $N_Y \perp\!\!\!\perp X$ and $N_Y \sim \mathscr{U}(-1, 1)/3$. In this case the underlying data generative process of the data corresponding to the *true* model (see Eq. (3.3)) is recovered. The causal direction $X \rightarrow Y$ is identified and one has also built a simulator close to the *true* mechanism (up to small parameter adjustments) that can be used to simulate the effect of interventions on the system. Indeed with this functional model, one can now compute $Y^{do(X=x)} = \hat{f}_Y(x) + N_Y$, with $N_Y \sim \mathscr{U}(-1, 1)/3$. It should give results on average similar to the *true* model of Eq. (3.3).

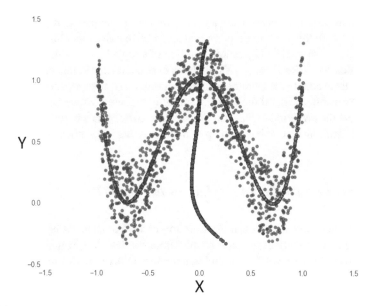

Fig. 3.2 Data generated with the *true* quadratic model (blue points). Polynomial fit of degree 4 of Y on X is depicted as green curve. Polynomial fit of degree 4 of X on Y is depicted as red curve. The *best* fit appears with the green curve. Better seen in color

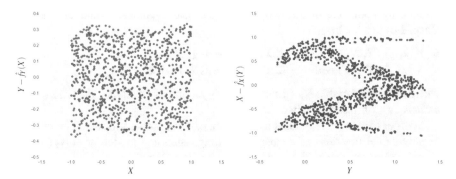

Fig. 3.3 Left: error $Y - \hat{f}_Y(X)$ is almost independent of X. Right: error $X - \hat{f}_X(Y)$ is not independent of Y. Better seen in color

In the opposite direction, as the residual is not independent of Y, one cannot build any model such as $X := \hat{f}_X(Y) + N_X$ with $N_X \perp\!\!\!\perp Y$. However we will see later in this chapter that it is possible to prove that a model $X := \hat{f}_X(Y, N_X)$ with $N_X \perp\!\!\!\perp Y$ exists in this case, but its expression may be more complex as the noise term is not additive and the mechanism $\hat{f}_X$ is not continuous on its definition domain. Therefore, from an explanatory perspective, the additive noise model $Y := \hat{f}_Y(X) + N_Y$ (hypothesis 1) offers a simpler explanation of the phenomenon than the other explanation $X := \hat{f}_X(Y, N_X)$ (hypothesis 2) with a non additive noise. For this reason, it seems intuitive to "prefer" hypothesis 1 to hypothesis 2. It is not a formal proof of causality, as it comes from an "Occam razor principle" that favors a simple explanation with the prior assumption that an additive noise model is simpler than a non additive noise model [12]. Another notion of simplicity could be preferred such as multiplicative noise $Y := f_Y(X) \times N_Y$ as explained later in this chapter.

Given the available measurements, the goal is to recover an *explanatory model* of the data by using statistical tools to test causal hypotheses. However, even if in this toy example the preferred explanatory model also corresponds to the model with the best predictive power, one has to keep in mind that this is not always the case.

3.1.2   Real Example: To Explain or to Predict?

Let us introduce now a real example well known in "the cause-effect pair community": the first cause-effect real pair of the Tübingen database.[2] Figure 3.4 displays collected data on altitude (X-axis) and temperature (Y-axis) in the atmosphere from 349 meteorological stations in Germany over the years 1961–1990.

---

[2]This database is composed of more than one hundred real cause-effect pairs with known ground truth and is available online at https://webdav.tuebingen.mpg.de/cause-effect/.

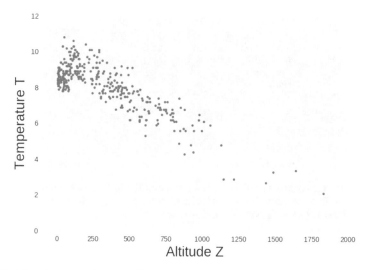

Fig. 3.4 349 real couples of points (altitude, temperature) collected from meteorological stations in Germany over the years 1961–1990

T is the temperature and Z the corresponding altitude. We assume for this simple example that the observed dependency between T and Z is only due to a direct causal relation from one of the two variables to the other. We will see later in this chapter that it is not actually obvious and the model may be actually more complex, as at least one hidden variable latitude may also have an impact on both variables.

In order to test causal hypotheses, the data are re-scaled with zero mean and unit variance, the dataset are split a large number of times between train (80%) and test sets (20%) and two alternative nonlinear Gaussian process regression models are learned on the train set.[3] When regressing the temperature on altitude one obtains the model $t = \hat{f}_t(z)$ (Fig. 3.5-left) and when regressing the altitude on the temperature one obtains the model $z = \hat{f}_z(t)$ (Fig. 3.6-left).

Interestingly enough, the expected mean squared error on the train and test sets averaged over 100 runs are lower for the *false* causal orientation $T \rightarrow Z$ than for the *true* causal orientation $Z \rightarrow T$. Therefore the overall predictive accuracy measured in term of mean squared error is better, even if the model $z = \hat{f}_z(t)$ does not seem to accurately reproduce the data generative process notably in the non-reversible part of the relation (circled area on Fig. 3.6-left).

The best predictive model does not necessarily corresponds to the true causal orientation [29]. It comes from the fact that minimizing a predictive score such as an expected mean squared error does not give necessarily an explanation of the data

---

[3] *GaussianProcessRegressor* algorithm with default parameters from python library scikit-learn 0.19.1 [23] are used.

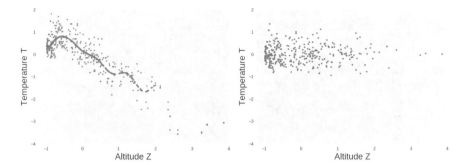

Fig. 3.5 Left: real couples of points (altitude, temperature) in blue and regression model $t = \hat{f}_t(z)$ in green. To some extent this residual is independent of the altitude Z. Therefore, the causal hypothesis $T := \hat{f}_T(Z) + N_T$ with $N_T \perp\!\!\!\perp T$ may hold

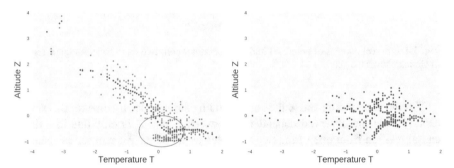

Fig. 3.6 Left: real couples of points (altitude, temperature) in blue and regression model $z = \hat{f}_z(t)$ in red. Right: residual of the non-linear regression of the altitude on temperature (red). The circled area corresponds to the non-reversible part of the relation (Z,T). To some extent this residual is not independent of the temperature T. Therefore, the causal hypothesis $Z := \hat{f}_Z(T) + N_Z$ with $N_Z \perp\!\!\!\perp T$ does not hold

generative process and then may lead to misunderstandings when it comes to causal interpretation.[4]

If one uses the same nonlinear regression model, but rather than looking at the mean squared error on the test set, one looks at the residuals on the test set defined respectively as $n_t(z) = t(z) - \hat{f}_t(z)$ and $n_z(t) = z(t) - \hat{f}_z(t)$, one can see that a causal footprint may be detected. Indeed, the residual N_Z is almost independent of Z (Fig. 3.5-right), while the residual N_T is not independent of T (Fig. 3.6-right).

---

[4]Let us note however that a recent work of [2] shows that comparing mean square error after fitting regression models in both direction can achieve overall good results when specific assumptions are satisfied such as the function ϕ that represents the causal mechanism is monotonically increasing (or decreasing) and a specific independence postulate between the variance of the noise and the derivative ϕ' is satisfied (see Sect. 3.5.3.4 for a description of this method). A wide comparative evaluation of all the methods, including this method RECI, will also be proposed in Sect. 3.6.

It confirms, to some extent, that the causal hypothesis $T := \hat{f}_T(Z) + N_T$ with $N_T \perp\!\!\!\perp Z$ holds, while the causal hypothesis $Z := \hat{f}_z(T) + N_Z$ with $N_Z \perp\!\!\!\perp T$ does not hold. Therefore, from an explanatory perspective, using the same conclusion as in the previous example, the additive noise model $T := \hat{f}_T(Z) + N_T$ (model 1) is preferred to the other explanation $Z := \hat{f}_Z(T, N_Z)$ (model 2) with non additive noise.

From a probabilistic point of view, the model $T := \hat{f}_T(Z) + N_T$ corresponds to the stochastic model $P_{T|Z}$ that accounts for uncertainty about the mechanism involved. Indeed for a given altitude there are several values of temperature possible, because the temperature may depend on other unobserved factors such as the latitude, the type of vegetation, the type of soil, the degree of humidity in the air, etc. In order to characterize a full *generative model*, one may consider that the altitude depends from other unknown variables such as the variations in terrain elevation: $Z := \hat{f}_Z(N_Z)$, where N_Z models latent source causes. It gives a distribution of P_Z, which when combined with $P_{T|Z}$ gives a full generative model $P_Z P_{T|Z} = P_{Z,T}$, that can be used as a simulator to draw samples (z, t) in the region.

This explanatory model may recover a causal interpretation, formally defined with the *do-notation* [22]. The temperature T is said to be a cause of Z if:

$$P_T^{\text{do}(Z=z)} \neq P_T^{\text{do}(Z=z')}, \tag{3.4}$$

for some z, z' [20]. An intervention, denoted as do$(Z = z)$, forces the variable altitude Z to take the value z, while the rest of the system remains unchanged. Concretely this mathematical formulation can be translated into: "*all other things being equal*", when modifying the altitude (climbing a mountain), it has an impact on the temperature (it decreases)". However $P_Z^{\text{do}(T=t)} = P_Z$ as modifying the temperature (heating the air) does not increase the altitude. Nevertheless this causal implication would not be true for hot air balloons! Indeed in causality "random variables" cannot be isolated from their context, because they are intimately related to an underlying specific system.

Moreover this functional causal model could also be used to derive counterfactual statements [22]. Indeed, for any specific meteorological station with a couple of datapoints altitude and temperature, (z_i, t_i), if one knows f_T, one can calculate the value n_T^i such that $t_i = f_T(z_i) + n_T^i$, and therefore for any specific station, one can answer the question "what would have been the temperature t_i' in this meteorological station if the altitude had changed from z_i to z_i'?" by using the mathematical expression $t_i' = f_T(z_i') + n_T^i$. This counterfactual reasoning on specific individuals would not be possible when having only a model $P_{T|Z}$ at the population level and not the underlying functional causal model including both causal orientation $(Z \rightarrow T)$ and mechanism f_T.

3.1.3 Comparing Alternative Data Generating Models

As shown with this real introductory example, finding the causal direction, when assuming that there are no confounding effects, consists in comparing two alternative data generating models and deciding whether the causal process $Z \rightarrow T$ is more natural or simpler than the backward process $T \rightarrow Z$. Intuitively, we can think of it as a rudimentary physical model that generates the temperature (effect) from the altitude (cause), which provides a better explanation in some way (more natural or simpler) than generating the altitude from the temperature.

In order to compare these alternatives models, an *Occam's razor principle* is always invoked in one way or another in the literature. Generally speaking, an *Occam's razor principle* can be seen as a general heuristic used in science to guide the modeler to find the *simplest explanation* when *testing different causal hypotheses on the data*. In order to apply this principle, two things must be defined : what do we mean by *simplest explanation*, which refers to the notion of the **complexity of a model**? And what do we mean by *testing a causal hypothesis on the data*, which refers to the notion of the **fit of a model**? These two notions of complexity and model fit have been formalized in different ways in the literature. We will detail them in this chapter.

Furthermore, one has always to keep in mind however that this heuristic choice is not an irrefutable principle. It is impossible in the cause-effect pair problem from purely observational data to formally prove that an explainable causal model is true. It is easy to find examples where *Occam's razor principle* favors the wrong theory given available data. Indeed in the introductory example with altitude and temperature, the *true causal mechanism* could have been $Z := f_Z(T, N_Z)$ (as shown later on in this chapter one can always exhibit such mechanism f_Z and variable N_Z with $N_Z \perp\!\!\!\perp T$) and a conclusion based on the idea that $T := f_T(Z) + N_T$ is simpler would have led to a false conclusion.

However this Occam razor principle has been implemented in the literature with good empirical success on artificial and real data [20]. By looking at the overall picture, we can distinguish three types of methods implementing this principle in different ways. The first class of methods uses fixed complexity of models and chooses the causal direction corresponding to the model that best fits the data. A second type of methods evaluates a weighted aggregation between two criteria: complexity and fit of the model. The last approaches exhibit two candidate models that are assumed to perfectly correspond to the data generative process and compare their complexities.

In Sect. 3.2, we introduce the bivariate problem setting with the usual assumptions invoked. In Sect. 3.3 we discuss the specific problem of identifiability that appears in this problem. The following Sect. 3.4 is devoted to the general method developed in the literature to tackle this identifiability issue. It will allow us to define a typology of the cause-effect inference methods that we will present more in detail in Sect. 3.5 with their practical implementations. In Sect. 3.6 we propose a benchmark of various methods presented in this chapter on artificial and real data.

The next Sect. 3.7 is a discussion on open problems and extensions for the cause-effect pair setting. The last Sect. 3.8 concludes.

3.2   Problem Setting

In this section, we present the cause-effect pair problem from the generative approach perspective. We first introduce the notations used in the chapter as well as the main assumptions usually involved. Then we present the general bivariate structural model.

3.2.1   Notations and Assumptions

X and Y are two one-dimensional random variables in $\mathbb{R}$ with joint distribution $P_{X,Y}$.

3.2.1.1   Identically and Distributed Samples

The given observations $\mathscr{D} = \{(x_i, y_i)\}_{i=1}^{n}$ of the random variables X and Y are independent and identically distributed drawn from $P_{X,Y}$.

3.2.1.2   Time

The time for which the observed data have been collected is not available. It is then impossible to exploit Granger causality tests for time series relying on the principle that if $X \rightarrow Y$, then the predictions of the value of Y based on its own past values and on the past values of X are better than predictions of Y based only on its own past values [8]. In the approaches presented in this chapter, time is not explicitly modeled, even though it is assumed that causes precede their effects.

3.2.1.3   Faithfulness Assumption

This is the classical faithfulness assumption used in graphical causal inference, transposed for two variables: "if there is a causal relation between X and Y, the two variables are not independent".

Pathological cases could arise for example as depicted on Fig. 3.7. The altitude has negative effect on temperature, but the altitude could have also negative impact on the degree of humidity in the air, which could have a negative effect on the temperature (as strange as it may seem, but this is an illustrative case). In this

Fig. 3.7 Example of
unfaithful case

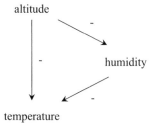

scenario the altitude would directly inhibit the temperature and indirectly improve
it, which would result in a statistical independence between altitude and temperature
by coincidence even if it is well known that altitude causes temperature.

In this chapter we will consider only pair effect problems where the two variables
X and Y are statistically dependent. When detecting a dependency between X and
Y five main cases may arise:

1. X causes Y
2. Y causes X
3. Selection bias: there is a unobserved common effect W of both X and Y on which
   X and Y were conditioned during the data acquisition. This selection bias creates
   a spurious dependency between X and Y.
4. Confounder: X and Y are both common consequences of a same third variable
   $X \leftarrow Z \rightarrow Y$
5. Feedback loop: X is a cause of Y and Y is a cause of X.
6. Constraint relation: X and Y are linked together, but there is no causal relationship between them.

Let us note that multiple combinations such as case 1 and 4 may arise at the same
time, X causes Y *and* both variables are also caused by an unobserved variable Z.

3.2.1.4 Selection Bias

A selection bias corresponds to an unobserved variable on which the two variables
X and Y were implicitly conditioned: graph $X \rightarrow W \leftarrow Y$ (Fig. 3.8-(3)). In our
introductory example, we may imagine for example that the variable temperature is
in fact independent of the variable altitude. However the temperature has an impact
on the number of dwarf mountain pines present in the region because this type
of trees grows only in cold region. The altitude has also an impact of this type
of vegetation as this type of trees grows only in mountains. Then if the weather
stations were only constructed in area with this type of vegetation (as strange as it
may seem), when collecting the data, an artificial dependency link would be created
between altitude and temperature (Fig. 3.9).

Throughout this chapter, it is assumed that the sample $\{(x_i, y_i)\}_{i=1}^{n}$, corresponding to the variables X and Y, was collected without selection bias.

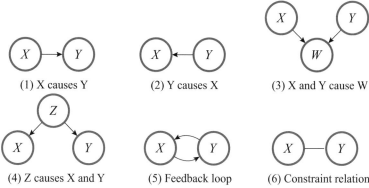

Fig. 3.8 Five main cases when detecting a dependency between X and Y

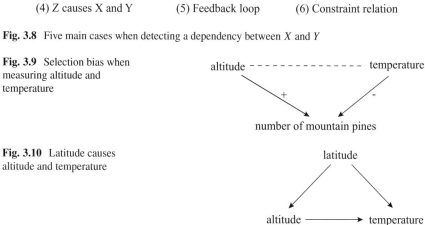

Fig. 3.9 Selection bias when measuring altitude and temperature

Fig. 3.10 Latitude causes altitude and temperature

3.2.1.5 Causal Sufficiency Assumption

Under this assumption it is assumed that X and Y are not common consequences of the same hidden variables (case corresponding to $X \leftarrow Z \rightarrow Y$ (Fig. 3.8-(4)) excluded).

   This causal sufficiency assumption is made by many methods of the cause-effect pair literature that we will review in this chapter as it allows to considerably simplify the cause-effect pair problem. However there are many realistic cases where there are potential confounding effects that can affect both variables (the most typical examples of confounding factors are the age or the gender in epidemiological studies). In this regard, if we come back to our introductory example, a confounding effect may be present as illustrated on Fig. 3.10. Indeed, the hidden variable latitude is known to be a cause of the temperature, but it is also a cause of the altitude, because in Germany all the mountains are situated in the south of the country. Therefore the link between altitude and temperature could be completely spurious and disappears when conditioned on the latitude variable. However it is not the case with this example as we still have a well known causal effect from altitude to temperature, but it highlights the fact that for the cause-effect pair analysis, one should always study the relationship between X and Y after conditioning on the potential observed confounding variables. In Sect. 3.7, we will provide a discussion on the confounding case, which is a great challenge and the problem is far from being solved for the cause-effect pair setting. To keep the problem simple in the first instance and clearly explain the cause-effect pair problem where only $X \rightarrow Y$ or $Y \rightarrow X$ are considered, we will first assume in this chapter that the confounding case is excluded.

3.2.1.6 Feedback Loops

A feedback loop appears when both X causes Y and Y cause X: graph $X \rightleftharpoons Y$ (Fig. 3.8-(5)). Even if the notion of time is not present, this case may happen for example in cross-sectional studies where data are collected over a certain period of time. Mooij et al. [20] give an example where the two variables are the temperature and the amount of sea ice: "an increase of the global temperature causes sea ice to melt, which causes the temperature to rise further (because ice reflects more sun light)".

We will assume in this chapter that this case is excluded. Therefore the causal graph between X and Y refers to the literature on Directed Acyclic Graph (DAG) (with only two variables).

3.2.1.7 Constraint Relation

This case of dependency with a relation $X - Y$ (Fig. 3.8-(4)) may arise for example if the two variables are linked by a logical or mathematical formula, and not related by a causal relation. As an example, if we write that the productivity P in a firm is equal to the total added value VA of the firm divided by the total number of employees N, the two variables P and VA are linked by a mathematical expression: $P = \frac{VA}{N}$. By observing VA and knowing N we can immediately deduce P, but the opposite is also true as knowing P and N gives VA, with equivalent mathematical relation, without any notion of an underlying system that could have generated one of the variable from the other. We do not consider this case in this chapter.

3.2.1.8 Measurement Noise

In general in the literature, it is assumed that there are no measurement noise. Such measurement noise may happen if for example the altitude is not measured precisely, but its noisy version noted $\tilde{Z}$. However the variable temperature T is still a function of the original variable Z that is not corrupted by measurement noise. This problem is related to a cause-effect pair problem between T and $\tilde{Z}$ in presence of a latent hidden variable which is the original Z. We refer the reader to [20] who propose a benchmark that verify the robustness of various cause-effect algorithms in presence of small perturbations of the data.

3.2.1.9   Variables Units

The orders of magnitude of the variable as well as their physical units are not considered in the problem. In most methods, the variables X and Y are re-scaled with zero mean and unit variance.

3.2.2   *Bivariate Functional Causal Models*

In the literature on causality, if $\mathcal{G}$ denotes an acyclic causal graph (DAG) obtained by drawing arrows from causes $X_{\mathrm{Pa}(i;\mathcal{G})}$ towards their effects X_i, it is often assumed that the effects are expressed as a linear function of their cause and an additive Gaussian noise. These models are linear structural equation models, where each variable is continuous and modeled as:

$$X_i := \sum_{j \in \mathrm{Pa}(i;\mathcal{G})} \alpha_j X_j + N_i, \ \text{for } i = 1, \ldots, d, \tag{3.5}$$

with $\mathrm{Pa}(i;\mathcal{G})$ the subset of index of the parents of each variable X_i in graph $\mathcal{G}$ and N_i a random noise variable, meant to account for all unobserved variables. The parameters α_j are real values. Each equation characterizes the direct causal relation explaining variable X_i from the set of its causes $X_{\mathrm{Pa}(i;\mathcal{G})}$, based on some linear *causal mechanisms*. These models are used a lot in social science fields such as econometric and sociology. Although this simplified model with linear mechanisms and additive Gaussian noise appears to be very convenient from a theoretical point of view, it is not often realistic as the interactions between cause and noise may be more complex in reality. Therefore a more general framework has been proposed by Pearl [21] with potential nonlinear interactions between cause and effect:

$$X_i := f_i(X_{\mathrm{Pa}(i;\mathcal{G})}, N_i), \ \text{for } i = 1, \ldots, d. \tag{3.6}$$

When the DAG $\mathcal{G}$ is reduced to $X \to Y$, this system of equation refers to a bivariate structural model.

Definition 3.1   A bivariate structural model noted $\mathcal{B}_{\mathcal{G}, f, P_N}$ is a triplet $(\mathcal{G}, f, P_N)$, where $\mathcal{G}$ is the causal graph $X \to Y$ or $Y \to X$, $f = (f_X, f_Y)$ is a couple of possibly nonlinear functions and (N_X, N_Y) are two independent random variables drawn according to continuous distribution $P_N = (P_{N_X}, P_{N_Y})$, such that:

- $X := f_X(N_X)$ and $Y := f_Y(X, N_Y)$ if $X \to Y$
- $Y := f_Y(N_Y)$ and $X := f_X(Y, N_X)$ if $Y \to X$

One can notice that this definition holds for any type of continuous distribution of the noise P_N. For example P_{N_Y} can be set to the uniform distribution on $[0, 1]$ and this is not a general restriction, since one can always write $N_Y = g_Y(\tilde{N}_Y)$, for some function g_Y, with $\tilde{N}_Y \sim \mathcal{U}[0, 1]$ and $\tilde{f}_Y = f_Y(\cdot, g_Y(\cdot))$ [31].

Without loss of generality, we could also write $X := N_X$, with $P_{N_X} = P_X$, but in the following we prefer to keep the formulation with two functions (f_X, f_Y) in order to stay consistent with the general formulation of FCM given by Eq. (3.6).

According to [20], the assumption that N_X and N_Y are independent, is justified by the assumptions that there is no confounding effect, no selection bias, and no feedback between X and Y (see Sect. 3.2.1).

3.3   The Problem of Identifiability with Two Variables

Given the formulation of the processes described in Sect. 3.2.2, the task is to identify the causal structure $X \rightarrow Y$ or $Y \rightarrow X$ that could have generated the observed data. By *identifying* we mean proving that f and P_N exist so that the hypothesis $\mathscr{B}_{\mathscr{G}, f, P_N}$ holds in the causal direction $\mathscr{G}$ with respect to the observed data while there do not exist any f' and P'_N so that $\mathscr{B}_{\mathscr{G}', f', P'_N}$ holds in the opposite causal direction $\mathscr{G}'$.

This problem faces two difficulties. The first is a classical empirical problem because in general one has access to a finite sample size $\mathscr{D} = \{(x_j, y_j)\}_{j=1}^n$ making impossible to evaluate perfectly $P_{X,Y}$. This is why the evaluation will rely on the definition of a model $Q_{X,Y}$ of the data distribution, which we will discuss later on. The second difficulty is more profound as it is related to the inference of a DAG when only two variables are observed. In this case, it is impossible to identify the causal direction by using classical conditional independence tests (e.g. as in the PC algorithm of [30]), because the two graphs $X \rightarrow Y$ and $Y \rightarrow X$ are Markov equivalent.

3.3.1   The Particular Linear Gaussian Case

A first well known identifiability issue arises in the linear Gaussian case because it induces a perfectly symmetric distribution after rescaling (Fig. 3.11).

A linear Gaussian generative bivariate FCM is defined by the system of equations:

$$\begin{cases} X := \alpha_X N_X \text{ with } N_X \sim \mathcal{N}(\mu_X, \sigma_X) \\ Y := \beta_Y X + \alpha_Y N_Y, \text{ with } N_Y \sim \mathcal{N}(\mu_Y, \sigma_Y), \end{cases} \tag{3.7}$$

with $\alpha_X, \alpha_Y, \beta_Y \in \mathscr{R}^3$. As shown by Mooij et al. [20], it is always possible in this case to find parameters $\alpha'_X, \alpha'_Y, \beta'_X, \mu'_X, \mu'_Y, \sigma'_X, \sigma'_Y$ such that:

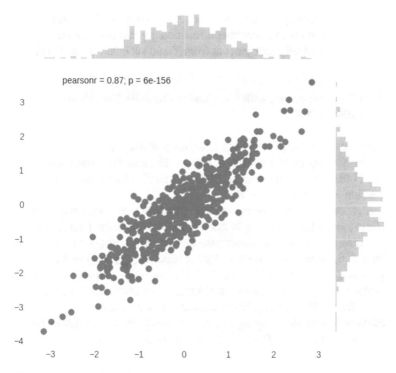

Fig. 3.11 Pairwise linear Gaussian case

$$\begin{cases} Y := \alpha'_Y N_Y \text{ with } N_Y \sim \mathcal{N}(\mu'_Y, \sigma'_Y) \\ X := \beta'_X Y + \alpha'_X N_X, \text{ with } N_X \sim \mathcal{N}(\mu'_X, \sigma'_X). \end{cases} \tag{3.8}$$

Therefore, for this pair a perfect symmetric generative model exists in both directions (that can only be dissociated by the values of its parameters) and it is impossible to determine the causal direction from these observational data.

3.3.2 General Case

Given any two random variables X and Y with continuous support, [36] shows that if $F_{Y|X}$ is the conditional cumulative distribution function of Y given X and q an arbitrary continuous and strictly monotonic function with a non-zero derivative, then the quantity $\tilde{N} = q \circ F_{Y|X}$, where $\circ$ denotes function composition is independent from X. Furthermore, the transformation from (X, Y) to $(X, \tilde{N})$ is always invertible, in the sense that Y can be uniquely reconstructed from $(X, \tilde{N})$.

Stated in another way, given any two random variables X and Y with continuous support, one can always construct a function f_Y and another variable, denoted by

N_Y, which is statistically independent from X and such that $Y := f_Y(X, N_Y)$. And equivalently, on can always construct a function f_X and another variable, denoted by N_X, which is statically independent from Y and such that $X := f_X(Y, N_X)$.

3.3.2.1 Characterization with Continuous Quantile Functions and Uniform Noise

More specifically if the joint density function h of $P_{X,Y}$ is continuous and strictly positive on a compact and convex subset of $\mathbb{R}^2$, and zero elsewhere, the model $\mathcal{B}_{\mathcal{G},f,P_N}$ holds with a couple of continuous quantile functions $f = (f_X, f_Y)$ in any direction $X \to Y$ and $Y \to X$.

Indeed, if one considers the cumulative distribution F_X defined over the domain of X ($F_X(x) = Pr(X < x)$). F_X is strictly monotonous as the joint density function is strictly positive therefore its inverse, the quantile function $Q_X : [0, 1] \mapsto dom(X)$ is defined. If n_X is drawn in $\mathcal{U}[0, 1]$, by construction, $Q_X(n_X) = F_X^{-1}(n_X)$ and by setting $f_X = Q_X$, we obtain $X = f_X(N_X)$. For any noise value n_X let x be the value of X defined from n_X. The conditional cumulative distribution $F_Y(y|X = x) = Pr(Y < y|X = x)$ is strictly continuous and monotonous with respect to y, and can be inverted using the same argument as above. Then we can define $f_Y(x, n_y) = F_Y^{-1}(x, n_y)$ and we obtain $Y := f_Y(X, N_Y)$. In an equivalent manner, we can show that there exists a set $f = (f_X, f_Y)$ such that $Y := f_Y(N_Y)$ and $X := f_X(Y, N_X)$.

Furthermore, it has been shown by Goudet et al. [7] that under the same assumptions on $P_{X,Y}$ for both candidate generative bivariate FCM $X \to Y$ and $Y \to X$, the functions f_X and f_Y defined above are continuous on their definition domain.

An example of a continuous joint density function $P_{X,Y}$, strictly positive on a compact and convex subset of $\mathbb{R}^2$ and zero elsewhere is depicted on Fig. 3.12. On

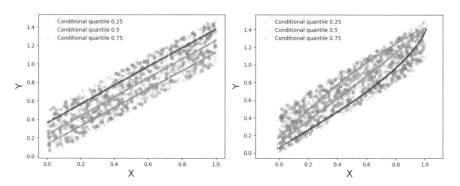

Fig. 3.12 Cause-effect pair with quantile regressions 0.25 (orange), 0.5 (green) and 0.75 (red) in both directions $X \to Y$ (left) and $Y \to X$ (right). Better seen in color

the left part of the Figure is shown a quantile regression of the variable Y on X with fraction 0.25 (orange curve), 0.5 (green curve) and 0.75 (red curve). It corresponds to the estimation of the FCM $y := f_Y(x, n_y)$ with uniform noise and where n_y is respectively set to the values 0.25, 0.5 and 0.75. On the right part of this Figure is shown the quantile regression of X on Y, corresponding to the estimation of the FCM $x := f_X(y, n_x)$, with n_x set to the values 0.25 (orange curve), 0.5 (green curve) and 0.75 (red curve). It highlights the fact that continuous FCM may be recovered in both directions in this case. However for the causal orientation $X \to Y$, the FCM is linear for any fixed noise value n_y, while for the causal orientation $Y \to X$, the FCM is more complicated as it seems to be only linear for $n_x = 0.5$ (green curve).

3.3.2.2 How to Overcome This Identifiability Problem?

This identifiability problem is a negative result for the cause-effect pair problem, because without any additional assumptions the problem is unsolvable.

However, even if both $\mathcal{B}_{X \to Y, f, P_N}$ and $\mathcal{B}_{Y \to X, f', P'_N}$ hold, there is almost always an asymmetry in the data generative process $X \to Y$ and $Y \to X$, because in general the mechanisms f and f' do not belong to the same class of functions (except in the linear Gaussian case mentioned before).

If we go back to the introductory example with altitude and temperature, there exist two plausible causal models:

$$\begin{cases} Z := f_Z(N_Z) \\ T := f_T(Z, N_T), \ with \ N_T \perp\!\!\!\perp Z \end{cases} \tag{3.9}$$

$$\begin{cases} T := f_T(N_T) \\ Z := f_Z(T, N_Z), \ with \ N_Z \perp\!\!\!\perp T \end{cases} \tag{3.10}$$

However, the first model of Eq. (3.9) can be rewritten *to some extent* with an additive mechanism:

$$\begin{cases} Z := f_Z(N_Z) \\ T := f_T(Z) + N_T, \ with \ N_T \perp\!\!\!\perp Z, \end{cases} \tag{3.11}$$

while the alternative causal model with causal orientation $T \to Z$ cannot be expressed using the same type of expression with additive noise. If one accepts the fact that an additive mechanism is a "simpler" form of conditional, we may prefer the causal orientation $Z \to T$ according to Occam's Razor principle.

In general, one can see that the factorization of the joint density function $P_{X,Y}$ into $P_X P_{Y|X}$ or $P_Y P_{X|Y}$ may lead to models with different complexities, with respect to some appropriate notion of complexity to be defined.

3.4 Computing a Trade-Off Fit/Complexity

The determination of the best explainable model is then based in the literature on these main lines:

- Different candidate bivariate models (hypotheses) are evaluated in both directions.
- For each candidate model one evaluates a score monitoring the trade-off between the fit of the model (meaning its adequacy to the observational data) and the complexity of the mechanisms involved.
- The model with the best score is returned, with its corresponding causal arrow $X \to Y$ or $Y \to X$.

3.4.1 Defining Candidate Bivariate Models and Sampling Data

In order to model such continuous underlying bivariate generative process $\mathcal{B}_{\mathcal{G}, f, P_N}$ which is assumed to have generated the data, we introduce the notion of candidate model $\mathcal{B}_{\widehat{\mathcal{G}}, \hat{f}, Q_N}$ described by:

- a structure defined by a causal orientation $X \to Y$ or $Y \to X$
- its estimated mechanisms modeled by $\hat{f}$
- an estimated distribution of noise Q_N

3.4.1.1 Structure of a Candidate Model

We note θ_X and θ_X the vectors of parameters of the estimated mechanisms $\hat{f}_X$ and $\hat{f}_Y$. And we note respectively θ_{N_X} and θ_{N_Y} the vectors of parameters of the distribution of the modeled noise variables Q_{N_X} and Q_{N_Y}. The noise variables are independent. The global vector of parameters of the model is noted $\theta = (\theta_X, \theta_Y, \theta_{N_X}, \theta_{N_Y})$.

When $\mathcal{G} = X \to Y$, this candidate generative model depicted on Fig. 3.13 generates a distribution $Q_{X,Y}(\theta) = Q_X(\theta_X, \theta_{N_X}) Q_{Y|X}(\theta_Y, \theta_{N_Y})$. When $\mathcal{G} = Y \to X$, this candidate model generates a distribution $Q_{X,Y}(\theta) = Q_Y(\theta_Y, \theta_{N_Y}) Q_{X|Y}(\theta_X, \theta_{N_X})$.

In some approaches proposed in the literature, the cause variable is not modelled but taken as the observed variable. In this case, $Q_X = P_X$. We refer the reader to Chap. 1 of this book explaining why it could be a problem for cause-effect inference.

Fig. 3.13 Candidate
generative model with causal
orientation $X \to Y$

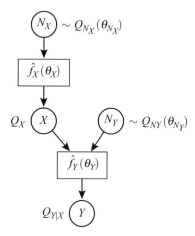

3.4.1.2 Mechanisms

After having defined the overall structure, one needs to model the mechanisms:

- A first characterization that needs to be specified is related to the type of interaction between the noise variable and the cause. Indeed in the literature, we distinguish mainly *additive noise interaction* of the form $Y := \hat{f}_Y(X) + N_Y$ or *complex noise interaction* of the form $Y := \hat{f}_Y(X, N_Y)$, where the cause variable and the noise are mixed with a non-linear mechanism.
- The second characterization concerns the class of functions used to define $\hat{f}$. It may range from linear mechanisms as in LiNGAM algorithm [28] to complex non-linear mechanisms modeled with Gaussian processes [31] or neural networks [16]. In general, the more complex the mechanisms are, the more the candidate model can fit the data and the more the model is general (meaning that it can be applied to a wide variety of cases). However, it may result in more difficulty to assess the causal orientation because the candidate model has more chances to fit equally well the data in both directions. A method for controlling the complexity of the mechanisms involved will be discussed later on in Sect. 3.4.3.

3.4.1.3 Sampling Data Points with a Candidate Model

Now we have all the ingredients required to sample data points of the estimated distribution $Q_{X,Y}$ with the **generative model** depicted in Fig. 3.13 by proceeding as follow:

1. Draw $\{(n_{X,j}, n_{Y,j})\}_{j=1}^n$, n samples independent and identically distributed from the joint distribution $Q_{N_X}(\theta_{N_X}) \times Q_{N_Y}(\theta_{N_Y})$ of independent noise variables (N_X, N_Y).

2. Generate n samples $\widehat{\mathscr{D}} = \{(\hat{x}_j, \hat{y}_j)\}_{j=1}^n$, where each estimated sample $\hat{x}_j$ of variable X is computed from $\hat{f}_X(\theta_X)$ with the j-th estimated samples $n_{X,j}$; then each estimated sample $\hat{y}_j$ of variable Y is computed from $\hat{f}_Y(\theta_Y)$ with the j-th estimated samples $n_{Y,j}$ and $\hat{x}_j$.

Generative candidate models support interventions, that is, freezing the variable X to some constant v_i. The resulting joint distribution noted $Q_Y^{\text{do}(X=v_i)}$, called *interventional distribution* [22], can be computed from this model by clamping the value of X to the value v_i. However when freezing the value of Y to some constant w_i, it has no impact on X: $Q_X^{\text{do}(Y=w_i)} = Q_X$. Generative candidate models support also counterfactual reasoning [22] as explained with the introductory example.

3.4.2 Model Fitness Score

In order to evaluate the quality of a candidate generative model, we introduce a fit score $S_{\widehat{\mathscr{B}}}(\theta)$ of a candidate model $\widehat{\mathscr{B}}_{\widehat{\mathscr{G}}, \hat{f}, Q_N}(\theta)$. This score has been implemented in different ways in the literature. It has always the property to be minimal when $P = Q$ (perfect fit in the large sample limit).

3.4.2.1 Log-Likelihood Parametric Scores

An example of score used in [31, 32] is the negative log-likelihood score defined for a candidate generative model with causal orientation $X \to Y$ by:

$$
\begin{aligned}
S_{\widehat{\mathscr{B}}}(\theta) &= -\log \hat{f}(\mathscr{D}|\theta) \\
&= -\sum_{i=1}^n \left[\log Q_{X=x^i}(\theta_X, \theta_{N_X}) + \log Q_{Y=y^i|X=x^i}(\theta_Y, \theta_{N_Y}) \right].
\end{aligned}
\tag{3.12}
$$

This likelihood score is often computed in a parametric context with special constraints imposed on the class of densities for the distribution of the cause Q_X and the distribution of the conditional $Q_{Y|X}$. For example in [31], a Gaussian mixture model is used as a prior distribution of the cause and a Gaussian process with a zero mean function and a squared-exponential covariance function is chosen as prior of the conditional.

3.4.2.2   Implicit Fit Score Computed as an Independence Score Between Cause and Noise Variable

If one considers a model with causal orientation $X \rightarrow Y$, [36] shows that computing this maximum likelihood score of the model with respect to the observational data is equivalent to minimizing a mutual information term $I(X, \hat{N}_Y; \theta)$ between the estimated noise $\hat{N}_Y$ and the cause X. We re-transcribed here the theoretical justification given by Zhang et al. [36] with our notations.

We consider a candidate model $\widehat{\mathscr{B}}_{\widehat{\mathcal{G}}, \hat{f}, Q_N}(\theta)$ with causal orientation $X \rightarrow Y$ and where the distribution of the source cause is not modelled and taken as P_X.

One can write $Q_{X, N_Y} = P_X Q_{N_Y}$ as in this model X and N_Y are assumed to be independent. Therefore, the Jacobian matrix of the transformation from (X, N_Y) to (X, Y) is:

$$\mathbf{J}_{X \rightarrow Y} = \begin{pmatrix} \frac{\delta X}{\delta X} & \frac{\delta X}{\delta N_Y} \\ \frac{\delta Y}{\delta X} & \frac{\delta Y}{\delta N_Y} \end{pmatrix} = \begin{pmatrix} 1 & 0 \\ \frac{\delta f_Y}{\delta X} & \frac{\delta f_Y}{\delta N_Y} \end{pmatrix}. \tag{3.13}$$

The absolute value of its determinant is $|\mathbf{J}_{X \rightarrow Y}| = |\frac{\delta f_Y}{\delta N_Y}|$. Then,

$$Q_{X,Y} = Q_{X, N_Y} / |\mathbf{J}_{X \rightarrow Y}| = P_X Q_{N_Y} |\frac{\delta f_Y}{\delta N_Y}|^{-1}, \tag{3.14}$$

which implies

$$Q_{Y|X} = Q_{N_Y} |\frac{\delta f_Y}{\delta N_Y}|^{-1}. \tag{3.15}$$

As the transformation from (X, N_Y) to (X, Y) is invertible, given any parameter set θ_Y involved in the function f_Y, the noise N_Y can be recovered, and the authors denote by $\hat{N}_Y$ the estimated noise variable. For any parameter set $\theta = (\theta_Y, \theta_{N_Y})$, using Eq. (3.15) the negative log-likelihood score attained by the model is:

$$
\begin{aligned}
S_{\widehat{\mathscr{B}}}(\theta) &= -\log \hat{f}(\mathscr{D}|\theta) \\
&= -\sum_{i=1}^{n} \left[\log P_{X=x^i} + \log Q_{Y=y^i|X=x^i}(\theta_Y, \theta_{N_Y})\right] \\
&= -\sum_{i=1}^{n} \log P_{X=x^i} - \sum_{i=1}^{n} \log Q_{N_Y=\hat{n}_Y^i}(\theta_{N_Y}) \\
&\quad + \sum_{i=1}^{n} \log |\frac{\delta f_Y}{\delta N_Y}_{X=x^i, N_Y=\hat{n}_Y^i}(\theta_Y)|.
\end{aligned} \tag{3.16}
$$

Now the fit of the model can be seen differently. Instead of fitting the model (Sect. 3.2.2) by modeling the noise N_Y which is independent of X and then modeling the conditional $Q_{Y|X}$, one can start from the true distribution $P_{X,Y}$ and look for such an estimate $\hat{N}_Y$ that $\hat{N}_Y$ and X are independent. In this approach, (X, Y) is recovered from $(X, \hat{N}_Y)$ as:

$$P_{X,Y} = Q_{X,\hat{N}_Y} | \frac{\delta f}{\delta N_Y} |^{-1}. \tag{3.17}$$

In order to make $\hat{N}_Y$ and X independent, one can compute the mutual information between X and $\hat{N}_Y$ that depends of the parameters θ of the model:

$$\begin{aligned} I(X, \hat{N}_Y; \theta) &= \mathbb{E}_{x \sim P_X, \hat{n}_Y \sim Q_{\hat{N}_Y}} \left[\log \frac{Q_{X=x, \hat{N}_Y=\hat{n}_Y}}{P_{X=x} Q_{\hat{N}_Y=\hat{n}_Y}} \right] \\ &= -\mathbb{E}_{x \sim P_X} \log P_{X=x} - \mathbb{E}_{\hat{n}_Y \sim Q_{\hat{N}_Y}} \log Q_{\hat{N}_Y=\hat{n}_Y} \\ &\quad + \mathbb{E}_{x \sim P_X, \hat{n}_Y \sim Q_{\hat{N}_Y}} \log Q_{X=x, \hat{N}_Y=\hat{n}_Y}. \end{aligned} \tag{3.18}$$

By using the sample version of this quantity and Eq. (3.17) the authors obtain:

$$\begin{aligned} \hat{I}(X, \hat{N}_Y; \theta) &= -\frac{1}{n} \sum_{i=1}^{n} \log P_{X=x^i} - \frac{1}{n} \sum_{i=1}^{n} \log Q_{\hat{N}_Y=\hat{n}_Y^i}(\theta_{N_Y}) \\ &\quad + \frac{1}{n} \sum_{i=1}^{n} \log | \frac{\delta f_Y}{\delta N_Y}_{X=x^i, N_Y=\hat{n}_Y^i} (\theta_Y) | + \frac{1}{n} \sum_{i=1}^{n} \log P(X=x^i, Y=y^i). \end{aligned} \tag{3.19}$$

Thus,

$$S_{\widehat{\mathscr{B}}}(\theta) = n \hat{I}(X, \hat{N}_Y; \theta) - \sum_{i=1}^{n} \log P(X=x^i, Y=y^i). \tag{3.20}$$

As the term $\sum_{i=1}^{n} \log P(X=x^i, Y=y^i)$ does not depend on the parameters θ of the model, minimizing the likelihood score $S_{\widehat{\mathscr{B}}}(\theta)$ amounts to minimizing the mutual information between the cause X and the estimated noise $\hat{N}_Y$.

This kind of evaluation score with an independence test is used to fit the model ANM [12] and PNL [35] presented in Sect. 3.5.1.

3.4.2.3 Non-parametric Scores

Other methods such as [7, 16] use a non-parametric approach. In these methods the authors do not specify any type of distribution for the model of the data $Q_{X,Y}$, but instead compare directly with a two sample test the observed data sample $\mathscr{D}$ with the generated data sample $\widehat{\mathscr{D}}$ coming from any candidate model.

In [16], the score of the model is non-parametric and computed with Conditional Generative Adversarial Networks, or CGANs [18] (see Sect. 3.5.2.2). It has been shown by Goodfellow et al. [6] that in the large sample limit, the Generative Adversarial Networks allows to approximate the Jensen-Shannon divergence between the true distribution P and the generated distribution Q:

$$S_{\widehat{\mathscr{B}}}(\theta) \simeq JSD(P, Q). \tag{3.21}$$

The Jensen–Shannon divergence is an information theory method of measuring the similarity between two probability distributions. This metric is always positive and equal to zero when $P = Q$.

Goudet et al. [7] used the empirical Maximum Mean Discrepancy (MMD) [10], a kernel based metric between distribution, as a two sample test to compare $\mathscr{D}$ and $\widehat{\mathscr{D}}$ (see Sect. 3.5.2.3).

3.4.3 Complexity of the Model

Now we introduce a term of complexity of a candidate bivariate model $\widehat{\mathscr{B}}_{\widehat{\mathscr{G}}, \hat{f}, Q_N}(\theta)$ that we note $C_{\widehat{\mathscr{B}}}(\theta)$. This complexity notion refers to a simplicity prior on the underlying data generative process. It has been handled in different ways in the literature from fix a class of admissible mechanisms to more flexible criteria.

3.4.3.1 Explicit Class of Admissible Mechanisms

A first type of methods in the literature defines a rudimentary notion of complexity: all mechanisms $\hat{f}$ belonging to a particular class $\mathscr{F}$ of bivariate FCM are assumed to be simple, while the others are assumed to be complex. In [12], for a causal model with orientation $X \to Y$, a mechanism is assumed to be simple if it can be written under the form $Y := \hat{f}_Y(X) + N_Y$ with $X \perp\!\!\!\perp N_Y$ (additive noise model). A more general class of mechanism is defined by the Post-Nonlinear model (PNL) [35], involving an additional nonlinear function on the top of an additive noise: $Y := \hat{g}_Y(\hat{f}_Y(X) + N_Y)$, with $\hat{g}_Y$ an invertible function and $X \perp\!\!\!\perp N_Y$. For these methods, we write $C_{\widehat{\mathscr{B}}}(\theta) = 0$ if $\hat{f} \in \mathscr{F}$ and $C_{\widehat{\mathscr{B}}}(\theta) = 1$ otherwise.

In [7] (CGNN), the class of functional causal model is defined as $Y := \hat{f}_Y(X, N_Y)$ where $\hat{f}_Y$ is a one hidden unit neural network with RelU activation functions and $N_Y \sim \mathscr{N}(0, 1)$ with $X \perp\!\!\!\perp N_Y$. The class of admissible mechanisms is variable as it is measured as a number of hidden units n_h in this one hidden layer neural network. In this framework, the complexity term can be expressed as $C_{\widehat{\mathscr{B}}}(\theta) = n_h$.

3.4.3.2 Kolmogorov Complexity

In the previous section, the complexity term was defined in term of an explicit class of functionals, but another approach coming from the information theory has been developed in the literature.

In this information theory framework, the basic postulate that "the factorization of the joint density function $P_{\text{cause,effect}}$ into $P_{\text{cause}} P_{\text{effect}|\text{cause}}$ should lead to a simpler model than $P_{\text{effect}} P_{\text{cause}|\text{effect}}$", can be expressed with the Kolmogorov complexity framework as shown by [14]:

$$K(P_{\text{cause}}) + K(P_{\text{effect}|\text{cause}}) \overset{+}{\leq} K(P_{\text{effect}}) + K(P_{\text{cause}|\text{effect}}). \qquad (3.22)$$

This inequality comes from the postulate of algorithmic independence between the distribution of the cause P_{cause} and the distribution of the causal mechanism $P_{\text{effect}|\text{cause}}$ stated by Janzing and Schölkopf [14] as:

$$I(P_{\text{cause}} : P_{\text{effect}|\text{cause}}) \overset{+}{=} 0. \qquad (3.23)$$

where $I(P_{\text{cause}} : P_{\text{effect}|\text{cause}})$ denotes algorithmic mutual information.

Kolmogorov complexity and algorithmic mutual information are not computable in practice but they have led to two different practical implementations in the literature.

Model Selection with Minimum Message Length Principle (MML)

A first practical implementation of the postulate defined in Eq. (3.22) is the Minimum Message Length principle (MML), which can be seen as an information theory restatement of Occam's Razor principle.

For a candidate bivariate generative model $\mathcal{B}_{\widehat{\mathcal{G}}, \hat{f}, Q_N}$, we have defined a family of functions $\hat{f}$ (i.e. linear mechanisms, neural networks, Gaussian processes) and a family of noise distributions Q_N. The overall model (mechanisms and noise distributions) is parametrized by the vector of parameter $\theta \in \Theta$. Furthermore one can also define a prior probability distribution π of θ over Θ, that can be seen as a simplicity prior over the parameter space. Now according to the MML principle, the modeling problem of transmitting the observed data $\mathcal{D} = \{(x^i, y^i)\}_{i=1}^n$ to a receiver can be decomposed into two parts:

1. First, the model $\mathcal{B}_{\widehat{\mathcal{G}}, \hat{f}, Q_N}$ with parameter θ from the parameter space Θ is send by the transmitter to the receiver (assertion). According to [33] the complexity of this model seen in term of total code length can be approximated as:

$$C_{\widehat{\mathcal{B}}}(\theta) \approx -\log\pi(\theta) + \frac{1}{2}\log|\mathbf{J}_\theta| - \frac{k}{2}\log(2\pi) + \frac{1}{2}\log(k\pi), \qquad (3.24)$$

where $|\mathbf{J}_\theta|$ is the determinant of the Fisher information matrix defined as the matrix of expected second derivatives of the negative log-likelihood function with respect to all continuous parameters of the model, with entry (i, j) given by:

$$I(\theta)_{i,j} = -\int_{(x,y)\in\mathbb{R}^2} \hat{f}((x, y)|\theta)\frac{\delta^2}{\delta\theta_{i,j}}\log\hat{f}((x, y)|\theta)dxdy. \qquad (3.25)$$

2. Second, the data $\mathscr{D}$ are transmitted to the receiver using this model. The length of the detail, which encodes the data using the model defined by the set of parameter θ, corresponds to the negative log-likelihood of the data according to the model defined previously in Eq. (3.12) as $S_{\widehat{\mathscr{B}}}(\theta) = -\log\hat{f}(\mathscr{D}|\theta)$.

This MML principle is used for example by Stegle et al. [31] to select the model associated to $X \rightarrow Y$ or $Y \rightarrow X$ with the lower total code length $\mathscr{A}_{\widehat{\mathscr{B}}}(\theta) = C_{\widehat{\mathscr{B}}}(\theta) - \log\hat{f}(\mathscr{D}|\theta)$ (see Sect. 3.5.2).

Independence Between Cause and Mechanism

Another characterization of complexity comes from the algorithmic independence principle of Eq. (3.23) to derive the idea that if $X \rightarrow Y$, the marginal probability distribution of the causal mechanism $P_{Y|X}$ should be independent of the cause P_X, hence estimating a model $Q_{Y|X}$ from P_X should hardly be possible, while estimating a model $Q_{Y|X}$ based on P_X may be possible.

This complexity measure has been evaluated directly as a covariance estimation between $Q_{Y|X}$ and P_X in [4] or by a characterization of the variance of the kernel embedding of $Q_{Y|X}$ when X varies according in its definition domain [19] (see Sect. 3.5.3).

One can see that there is a direct connection between "the postulate of independence between the cause and the mechanism" and the complexity of the mechanism, as when $P_{Y|X}$ is independent on P_X, the function $\hat{f}_Y$ required to model $Q_{Y|X}$ takes in general a simpler form than the function $\hat{f}_X$ required to model $Q_{X|Y}$.

3.4.4 Bi-objective Trade-Off for Cause-Effect Inference

In the previous section, we have defined the complexity $C_{\widehat{\mathscr{B}}}(\theta)$ and the fit $S_{\widehat{\mathscr{B}}}(\theta)$ of a candidate bivariate model parameterized by the vector of parameters θ. From a general point of view, we can now frame the model selection as a bi-objective trade-off with a Pareto front of optimal models (cf. Fig. 3.14).

This general bi-objective trade-off between fit and complexity is very general in science. It has been seen from two different angles. Some of the modeling approaches favor models of lower complexity, while others favor models with better explanatory power (Fig. 3.14):

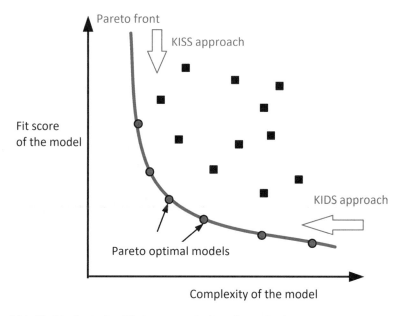

Fig. 3.14 Bi-objective trade-off between complexity and reproduction

- The first is the KISS approach (*Keep It Simple, Stupid*) proposed by Axelrod and Hamilton [1] and stating that the models should include the minimal number of parameters and mechanisms and only add new ones only if required.
- On the other hand, the KIDS principle (*Keep It Descriptive, Stupid*) is an anti-simplistic approach that favors the accuracy of the model and states that all parameters and mechanisms that appear relevant should be included, but parameters that do not add quality of the model should be removed [5].

When transposing these modeling approaches to the cause-effect problem, we can see that some methods favor models with low complexity and low explanatory power such as linear Gaussian models while others have a better explanatory power as they can model complex interactions between noise and causes (for example when using generative neural networks as in [16]), but at the cost of more complex mechanisms.

In the cause-effect pair literature, we can distinguish three different approaches used to deal with this complexity/fit trade-off:

- Methods such as those by [7, 12, 16, 35] that reason at fixed complexity $C_{\widehat{\mathscr{B}}}(\theta)$ and choose the causal direction according to the best fit. For any candidate model $\mathscr{B}_{\widehat{\mathscr{G}},\hat{f},\varrho_N}$, we note $\hat{\theta}$ the set of parameters that minimizes the score $S_{\widehat{\mathscr{B}}}(\theta)$ and for the purposes of simplified notations, we note $S_{X \to Y}(\hat{\theta})$ the best fit score corresponding to the model $\mathscr{B}_{\widehat{\mathscr{G}},\hat{f},\varrho_N}$ with $\widehat{\mathscr{G}} = X \to Y$.

If $S_{X \to Y}(\hat{\theta}) < S_{Y \to X}(\hat{\theta})$, it is decided that $X \to Y$, otherwise it is decided that $Y \to X$.

- Methods such as those by [4, 27] that assume a comparative fit $P = Q$ in both directions and choose the causal direction by comparing the complexity terms. In this case, for any candidate model $\mathscr{B}_{\hat{\mathscr{G}}, \hat{f}, Q_N}$, we note $\hat{\theta}$ the set of parameters that minimizes the score $C_{\hat{\mathscr{B}}}(\theta)$ and $C_{X \to Y}(\hat{\theta})$ the lowest complexity score corresponding to the model $\mathscr{B}_{\hat{\mathscr{G}}, \hat{f}, Q_N}$ with $\hat{\mathscr{G}} = X \to Y$.

If $C_{X \to Y}(\hat{\theta}) < C_{Y \to X}(\hat{\theta})$, it is decided that $X \to Y$, otherwise it is decided that $Y \to X$.

- Methods such as those by Stegle et al. [31] that compute a weighted bi-criteria aggregation between fit and complexity $\mathscr{A}_{\hat{\mathscr{B}}}(\theta) = S_{\hat{\mathscr{B}}}(\theta) + \lambda C_{\hat{\mathscr{B}}}(\theta)$. We use the same notation $\hat{\theta}$ for the set of parameters that minimizes the score $\mathscr{A}_{\hat{\mathscr{B}}}(\theta)$. If $\mathscr{A}_{X \to Y}(\hat{\theta}) < \mathscr{A}_{Y \to X}(\hat{\theta})$, it is decided that $X \to Y$, otherwise it is decided that $Y \to X$.

This bi-objective aggregation corresponds for example to cause-effect inference based on the MML principle. In this case, the total score is directly $S_{\hat{\mathscr{B}}}(\theta) + C_{\hat{\mathscr{B}}}(\theta)$, without any aggregation parameter λ. However this aggregation parameter is "implicitly" set in the chosen prior $\pi(\theta)$.

With all these different approaches, a *causal score* that measures the confidence of the approach in the causal orientation can be defined as the difference between the two scores evaluated in each direction. For example for the methods that reason at fixed complexity and compare the fit scores if $S_{X \to Y}(\hat{\theta}) < S_{Y \to X}(\hat{\theta})$, $X \to Y$ is preferred with causal score $\Delta_{X \to Y} = S_{Y \to X}(\hat{\theta}) - S_{X \to Y}(\hat{\theta}) > 0$.

3.5 Review of the Main Pairwise Methods

According to the complexity/fit trade-off framework defined in the previous section we can propose a reading grid for the main algorithms developed in the literature (Table 3.1).

We introduce a taxonomy of methods according to the type of functional involved, their fit scores, their complexity scores and their way to deal with the trade-off fit/complexity.

Three main families of methods emerge:

1. Methods with a restricted class of mechanisms.
2. Non-parametric methods.
3. Methods exploiting the independence between cause and mechanism.

We present with more details these families in the next Sects. 3.5.1–3.5.3.

Table 3.1 Classification of the main algorithms for cause-effect inference proposed in the literature

Method	Reference	Interaction noise/cause	Mechanism	Fit score	Complexity score	Trade-off F/C
1) Restricted class						
Lingam	[28]	Additive noise	Linear regression	Log-likelihood	Restricted class	Compare fit scores
ANM-HSIC	[12]	Additive noise	Gaussian process	Indep. noise/cause	Restricted class	Compare fit scores
PNL	[34]	Post additive noise	Neural network	Indep. noise/cause	Restricted class	Compare fit scores
Markov kernel	[32]	Mixed noise	Markov kernel	Log-likelihood	Restricted class	Compare fit scores
II) Non-parametric						
GPI-MML	[31]	Mixed noise	Gaussian process	Log-likelihood	MML	Aggregation
CGAN-C2ST	[16]	Mixed noise	Neural networks	GAN	Flexible class	Compare fit scores
CGNN	[7]	Mixed noise	Neural networks	MMD	Flexible class	Compare fit scores
III) Indep. cause/mech						
IGCI	[4]	Deterministic function	Invertible function	–	Indep. cause/mech.	Compare complexities
CURE	[27]	Mixed noise	Gaussian process	Log-likelihood	Indep. cause/mech.	Compare complexities
CRACK	[17]	Mixed noise	–	MDL	Indep. cause/mech.	Aggregation
KCDC	[19]	Mixed noise	Kernel embedding	–	Indep. cause/mech.	Compare complexities
RECI	[2]	Mixed noise	Conditional expectation	–	Indep. cause/mech.	Compare complexities

3.5.1   Methods with a Restricted Class of Mechanisms

This first class of methods developed from 2006 to 2010 rely on restrictive class of admissible mechanisms $\mathcal{F}$ and focus on identifiability results. The main idea is to show that in some cases there exist $f \in \mathcal{F}$ and Q_N such that the hypothesis $\mathcal{B}_{\mathcal{G}, f, Q_N}$ holds in the causal direction $\mathcal{G}$ with respect to the observed data while there do not exist any $f' \in \mathcal{F}$ nor Q'_N such that $\mathcal{B}_{\mathcal{G}', f', Q'_N}$ holds in the opposite causal direction $\mathcal{G}'$.

These methods range from very simple class of functions with LINGAM [28] to more complex class of functions such as PNL [34], with each time a trade-off between the identifiability and the generality of the proposed approach as depicted on Fig. 3.15.

Indeed, when the class of function is very restricted, there are fewer non identifiable cases, but the model can only successfully be used when encountering very specific observed data (such as data generated by linear mechanisms). When the class of functions becomes larger, the model becomes more general and can be used for more types of distribution, but at the cost of more non identifiable cases. In the extreme case of a completely general model without restriction on the class of mechanisms, all pairs become non identifiable as shown in Sect. 3.3.

3.5.1.1   Pairwise LiNGAM Inference

The LiNGAM [28] method was first developed for directed acyclic graph orientation for more than two variables. LiNGAM handles linear structural equation models, where each variable is continuous and modeled as:

$$X_i := \sum_k \alpha_k P_a^k(X_i) + E_i, i \in [\![1, n]\!], \tag{3.26}$$

with $P_a^k(X_i)$ the k-th parent of X_i and α_k a real value. Assuming further that all probability distributions of source nodes in the causal graph are non-Gaussian, [28] show that the causal structure is fully identifiable (all edges can be oriented).

Fig. 3.15 Diagram on the identifiability/generality trade-off

Model

In the bivariate case, the authors assume that the variables X and Y are non Gaussian, as well as standardized to zero mean and unit variance. The goal is to distinguish between candidate linear causal models.

The first is denoted by $X \rightarrow Y$ and defined as:

$$Y := \rho X + N_Y \text{ with } X \perp\!\!\!\perp N_Y. \tag{3.27}$$

The second model with orientation $Y \rightarrow X$ is defined as:

$$X := \rho Y + N_X \text{ with } Y \perp\!\!\!\perp N_X. \tag{3.28}$$

The parameter ρ is the same in the two models because it is equal to the correlation coefficient between X and Y.

Identifiability Result

A theoretical identifiability has been derived by Shimizu et al. [28] who prove that if $P_{X,Y}$ admits the linear model $Y := aX + N_Y$ with $X \perp\!\!\!\perp N_Y$ (model 1), then there exist $b \in \mathbb{R}$ and a random variable N_X such that $X := bY + N_X$ with $Y \perp\!\!\!\perp N_X$ (model 2) if and only if X and N_Y are Gaussian.

In different words there is only one non-identifiable case corresponding to the linear Gaussian case presented in Sect. 3.3.1. Moreover if X or N_Y is non-Gaussian, when the candidate linear model with orientation $X \rightarrow Y$ holds, the candidate linear model with orientation $Y \rightarrow X$ does not hold.[5]

Practical Evaluation

The candidate models correspond to a restrictive class of mechanism and the comparison of the candidate models is based on comparison of fit scores at fixed complexity. The fit score used for comparison is the likelihood score as defined in Sect. 3.4.2.1 and derived by Hyvärinen and Smith [13] in this case as:

$$S_{X \rightarrow Y} = - \left[\sum_{i=1}^{n} G_X(x^i) + G_{N_Y}\left(\frac{y^i - \rho x^i}{\sqrt{1 - \rho^2}}\right) \right] + n\log(1 - \rho^2), \tag{3.29}$$

---

[5]However as discuss in Sect. 3.3.2 there always exists a potential nonlinear model $Y \rightarrow X$ that holds ($X := f_Y(Y, N_X)$) but this model is assumed to be more complex and is rejected due to the prior assumption that linear mechanisms are simpler.

where $G_X(u) = \log P_X(u)$ and G_{N_Y} is the standardized log probability distribution function of the residual when regressing Y on X. $S_{Y \to X}$ is computed similarly and the causal direction is decided by comparing $S_{X \to Y}$ with $S_{Y \to X}$.

3.5.1.2 Additive Noise Model

An extension of the previous model to deal with nonlinear mechanism has been derived by Hoyer et al. [12].

Model

A bivariate additive noise model (ANM) $X \to Y$ is defined as:

$$Y := f_Y(X) + N_Y \text{ with } X \perp\!\!\!\perp N_Y. \tag{3.30}$$

$f_Y : \mathbb{R} \to \mathbb{R}$ is a Borel measurable function.

Identifiability Result

Hoyer et al. [12] proved that the ANM model is generally identifiable, saying that if $P_{X,Y}$ satisfies an additive noise model with orientation $X \to Y$, $P_{X,Y}$ cannot satisfy an additive model with orientation $Y \to X$.

However, specific cases have been identified where ANM is non-identifiable (see [35]). In particular the linear Gaussian case presented in Sect. 3.3.1 is non identifiable.

Practical Evaluation Based on Independence Score (ANM-HSIC)

In the original paper of [12] the ANM is seen as a discriminative model and the fit score is based on an independence test between noise and cause (Sect. 3.4.2.2). More precisely for the two alternatives $X \to Y$ and $Y \to X$, the estimated mechanisms $\hat{f}_Y$ and $\hat{f}_X$ are obtained via Gaussian process regressions. These estimated regression functions are used to estimate the residuals $\hat{n}_Y = y - \hat{f}_Y(x)$ and $\hat{n}_X = x - \hat{f}_X(y)$. The scores $S_{X \to Y}$ and $S_{Y \to X}$ correspond respectively to kernel HSIC independence test [9] between $\hat{n}_Y$ and x (for $X \to Y$) and between $\hat{n}_X$ and y (for $Y \to X$).

If $S_{X \to Y} < S_{Y \to X}$ it is decided that $X \to Y$. If $S_{X \to Y} > S_{Y \to X}$ it is decided that $Y \to X$.

3.5.1.3 Post Nonlinear Model

The ANM may fail to recover the causal direction when the noise is not additive. Therefore a generalization of ANM called Post-NonLinear model (PNL) that takes into account nonlinear interactions between the cause and the noise has been proposed by Zhang and Hyvärinen [34].

Model

A bivariate Post-NonLinear Model (PNL) $X \to Y$ is defined as:

$$Y := \hat{g}_Y(\hat{f}_Y(X) + N_Y) \text{ with } X \perp\!\!\!\perp N_Y. \tag{3.31}$$

$\hat{f}_Y : \mathbb{R} \to \mathbb{R}$ and $\hat{g}_Y : \mathbb{R} \to \mathbb{R}$ are two Borel measurable functions. $\hat{g}_Y$ is assumed to be invertible.

One can notice that LiNGAM and ANM are special cases of PNL. Indeed by setting $\hat{g}_Y$ to the identity function we recover the ANM. By choosing also $\hat{f}_Y$ to be linear and one of X or N_Y to be non Gaussian we recover the LiNGAM model.

Identifiability Result

Zhang and Hyvärinen [35] proved that the PNL model is generally identifiable, saying that if $P_{X,Y}$ satisfies a PNL model $X \to Y$, $P_{X,Y}$ cannot satisfy a PNL $Y \to X$, except when specific conditions are encountered. The set of non-identifiable distribution $P_{X,Y}$ is larger than for ANM. However PNL is more general and can handle more types of observed distribution.

Practical Evaluation

The model has been evaluated in [34] using an independence score between cause and noise (cf. Sect. 3.4.2.2).

As $\hat{g}_Y$ is assumed to be invertible, the idea is that the noise variable in Eq. (3.31) can be recovered from $P_{X,Y}$ as:

$$\hat{N}_Y = g_Y^{-1}(Y) - f_Y(X). \tag{3.32}$$

The noise variable is then estimated by functions l_1 and l_2 such as $\hat{N}_Y = l_1(Y) - l_2(X)$ with $\hat{N}_Y$ independent of X. It comes back to solve a constrained nonlinear ICA problem, that can be achieved by minimizing $I(X, \hat{N}_Y; \theta)$, the mutual information between X and $\hat{N}_Y$ [34] with respect to the parameter of the model θ. Symmetrically, an optimization of $I(Y, \hat{N}_X; \theta)$ is performed.

The causal direction $X \to Y$ is preferred if $I(X, \hat{N}_Y; \hat{\theta}) < I(Y, \hat{N}_X; \hat{\theta})$, $Y \to X$ otherwise.

3.5.1.4 Causal Inference by Choosing Graphs with Most Plausible Markov Kernel

In [32], the generative candidates model are derived from plausible Markov kernels and evaluated with log-likelihood scores.

Model

For a generative bivariate model $X \to Y$, the evaluation of cause and mechanism are the following:

- the distribution of the modeled cause Q_X is recovered by maximizing the entropy $H(Q_X)$ under constraints on the first and second moments of Q_X to make them correspond to those of the observed data P_X.
- following the same idea the distribution of the mechanism $Q_{Y|X}$ is modeled by maximizing the entropy $H(Q_{Y|X})$ under constraints on the first and second moments.

Evaluation

Once the model is recovered, log-likelihood scores of the model $Q_X Q_{Y|X}$ and $Q_Y Q_{X|Y}$ are computed as explained in Sect. 3.4.2.1 and the causal direction is determined by comparing the two scores.

3.5.2 Non-parametric Methods

The methods presented in the last section always assumed that the causal mechanisms belong to a restricted class of functions $\mathscr{F}$. However, this a priori restriction poses serious practical limitations when the task is to infer the causal direction on real data. Indeed in reality the mechanisms are often far from linearity and the interaction between noise and cause may be more complex than additive or even post-nonlinear noise. This is why more general methods have been proposed following pioneer works by Stegle et al. [31]. These methods in general offer better overall results on real data as they are more flexible, but they come with a loss of theoretical identifiability results, as no explicit restriction on the class of function is imposed (Sect. 3.3). The causal direction is often recovered by setting a smooth prior on the complexity of the mechanisms.

3.5.2.1 Probabilistic Latent Variable Models

A fully non-parametric Bayesian approach was proposed by Stegle et al. [31]. The name of the algorithm is GPI for Gaussian Process Inference.

Model

The approach aims to address the most general formulation of generative bivariate model with orientation $X \to Y$ with complex interaction between cause and noise: $Y := f_Y(X, N_Y)$.

The distribution of cause in GPI if modeled with a Gaussian mixture model with k modes:

$$Q(x^i|\theta_X) = \sum_{j=1}^{k} \alpha_j \mathcal{N}(x^i|\mu_j, \sigma_j^2),$$ (3.33)

with parameters $\theta_X = \{(\alpha_j, \mu_j, \sigma_j)\}_{j=1}^{k}$.

The mechanism of GPI is a Gaussian process with zero mean and square exponential covariance function $\mathbf{K}_{\theta_Y}$ whose entry (i, j) is:

$$k_{\theta_Y}((x^i, n_Y^i), (x^j, n_Y^j)) = \lambda_Y^2 \exp\left(-\frac{(x^j - x^i)^2}{2\lambda_X^2}\right) \exp\left(-\frac{(n_Y^j - n_Y^i)^2}{2\lambda_N^2}\right),$$ (3.34)

where $\theta_Y = (\lambda_X, \lambda_Y, \lambda_N)$ are hyper parameters. Gamma priors are set on all these lambda parameters.

Practical Evaluation

The model is then evaluated using the MML framework exposed in Sect. 3.4.3.2. According to [31], for a GPI model in the direction $X \to Y$, the global aggregated MML score between fit and complexity can be expressed as:

$$\mathscr{A}_{X \to Y} = \mathscr{A}_X + \mathscr{A}_{Y|X},$$ (3.35)

where the MML score for the cause is:

$$\mathscr{A}_X = \min_{\theta_X} \left(\sum_{j=1}^{k} \log(\frac{n\alpha_j}{12}) + \frac{k}{2}\log\frac{N}{12} + \frac{3k}{2} - \log Q(x|\theta_X) \right).$$ (3.36)

The MML score for the mechanism is:

$$\mathscr{A}_{Y|X} = \min_{\theta_Y, n_Y} \left(-\log \pi(\theta_Y) - \log \mathscr{N}(n_Y|0, \mathbf{I}) \right.$$

$$\left. -\log \mathscr{N}(y|0, \mathbf{K}_{\theta_Y}) + \sum_{i=1}^{n} \log|M_i \mathbf{K}_{\theta_Y}^{-1} y| \right), \tag{3.37}$$

where the matrix M is defined for index (i, j) as $M_{i,j} = \frac{\delta k_{\theta_Y}}{\delta n_Y}((x^i, n_Y^i), (x^j, n_Y^j))$.
If $\mathscr{A}_{X \to Y} < \mathscr{A}_{Y \to X}$, it is decided that $X \to Y$, $Y \to X$ otherwise.

3.5.2.2 Conditional GAN for Causal Discovery

Lopez-Paz and Oquab [16] propose to use Conditional Generative Adversarial Networks, or CGANs [18] in order to model realistic causal mechanisms.

Model

The model with direction $X \to Y$ takes the form of a discriminative model, where the causal mechanism is defined by a one hidden unit neural network $\hat{f}_Y$ with parameter θ_Y. The variable Y is generated as:

$$Y := \hat{f}_Y(X, N_Y). \tag{3.38}$$

N_Y is independent from X and drawn according to standard normal distribution $\mathscr{N}(0, 1)$. X is the conditioning variable input to the generator and follow the observed distribution P_X.

Evaluation

In order to train this conditional GAN, a discriminative neural network d with parameter ω is used and the problem amounts to solve this min max optimization problem:

$$S_{X \to Y}(\hat{\theta}) = \min_{\theta} \max_{\omega} \left(\mathbb{E}_{x,y}[\log d_\omega(x, y)] + \mathbb{E}_{x,n_Y}[\log(1 - d_\omega(x, \hat{f}_Y(x, n_Y; \theta)))] \right). \tag{3.39}$$

Then the principle used for causal discovery is to learn two CGANs: one with a generator $\hat{f}_Y$ from X to Y to synthesize the dataset $\widehat{\mathscr{D}}_{X \to Y} = \{(x^i, \hat{y}^i)\}_{i=1}^n$, and the other with a generator $\hat{f}_X$ from Y to X to synthesize the dataset $\widehat{\mathscr{D}}_{Y \to X} = \{(\hat{x}^i, y^i)\}_{i=1}^n$. Then, the causal direction is decided to be $X \to Y$ if the two-sample test statistic between the real sample $\mathscr{D} = \{(x^i, y^i)\}_{i=1}^n$ and $\widehat{\mathscr{D}}_{X \to Y}$ is smaller than the one between $\mathscr{D}$ and $\widehat{\mathscr{D}}_{Y \to X}$.

3.5.2.3 Causal Generative Neural Network

Goudet et al. [7] proposed and extension of [16] for multivariate causal discovery called CGNN for Causal Generative Neural Network. As in [16] the mechanisms are modelled with generative neural networks.

If the joint density function h of $P_{X,Y}$ is continuous and strictly positive on a compact and convex subset of $\mathbb{R}^2$, and zero elsewhere, it has been shown that there exist two CGNNs $X \rightarrow Y$ and $Y \rightarrow X$, that approximates $P_{X,Y}$ with arbitrary accuracy. This result highlights the generality of the approach. However it raises also the issue that the CGNN can reproduce equally well the observational distribution in both directions. This non-identifiability issue is empirically mitigated by restricting the class of CGNNs considered, and specifically limiting the number n_h of hidden neurons in each causal mechanism. This parameter n_h can be seen as a complexity parameter that governs the CGNN ability to model the causal mechanisms: too small n_h, and data patterns may be missed; too large n_h, and overly complicated causal mechanisms may be retained.

Practical Evaluation

For practical use in the cause-effect pair setting n_h is empirically set to 30 hidden units in [7]. The fit score of the model is evaluated with a kernel two sample test between the sample $\mathscr{D}$ coming from observed distribution $P_{X,Y}$ and the sample $\widehat{\mathscr{D}}$ coming from the generated distribution $Q_{X,Y}$:

$$S_{X \rightarrow Y}(\theta) = \widehat{\text{MMD}}_k(\mathscr{D}, \widehat{\mathscr{D}}), \tag{3.40}$$

where $\widehat{\text{MMD}}_k(\mathscr{D}, \widehat{\mathscr{D}})$ is the empirical Maximum Mean Discrepancy (MMD) [10] defined as:

$$\widehat{\text{MMD}}_k(\mathscr{D}, \widehat{\mathscr{D}}) = \frac{1}{n^2} \sum_{i,j=1}^{n} k(\mathbf{z}_i, \mathbf{z}_j) + \frac{1}{n^2} \sum_{i,j=1}^{n} k(\hat{\mathbf{z}}_i, \hat{\mathbf{z}}_j) - \frac{2}{n^2} \sum_{i,j=1}^{n} k(\mathbf{z}_i, \hat{\mathbf{z}}_j),$$
$$\tag{3.41}$$

where $\mathbf{z} = [x, y]$ is the two dimensional vector composed of x and y. The kernel k is usually taken as the Gaussian kernel ($k(\mathbf{z}, \mathbf{z}') = \exp(-\gamma \|\mathbf{z} - \mathbf{z}'\|_2^2)$).

For a fix number of hidden units n_h in each mechanism $\hat{f}_X$ and $\hat{f}_Y$, the causal direction is then based on the comparison of these best fit scores $S_{X \rightarrow Y}(\hat{\theta})$ and $S_{Y \rightarrow X}(\hat{\theta})$ in both directions.

3.5.3 Methods That Exploit Independence Between Cause and Mechanism

This class of methods exploits the notion of complexity of the causal mechanisms from a different perspective. They are based on the principle stated in Sect. 3.4.3.2 saying that when $X \rightarrow Y$ the distribution of the cause P_X should not contain information that can be useful to derive the conditional model $Q_{Y|X}$ on the data.

3.5.3.1 NonLinear Deterministic Mechanism

One of the first method that exploits the postulate of independence between cause and mechanism is the Information Geometric Causal Inference algorithm (IGCI) [4].

Model

When $X \rightarrow Y$, the authors assume that Y was generated from X by a nonlinear deterministic and invertible function:

$$Y := h(X). \tag{3.42}$$

Then the authors exploit a certain type of independence between P_X and the estimate of the function h. In particular, they interpret $x \rightarrow P_X(x)$ and $x \rightarrow \log h'(x)$ as random variables on the probability space $[0, 1]$. Then they compute the covariance of these two random variables with respect to the uniform distribution on $[0, 1]$:

$$\mathrm{Cov}(\log h', P_X) = \mathbb{E}(\log h' \dot{P}_X) - \mathbb{E}(\log h')\mathbb{E}(P_X)$$

$$= \int_0^1 \log h'(x) \dot{P}_X(x)dx - \int_0^1 \log h'(x)dx \int_0^1 P_X(x)dx. \tag{3.43}$$

The authors show that if $\mathrm{Cov}(\log h', P_X)$ is close to zero, meaning that P_X does not contain information about $Q_{Y|X}$. Moreover it implies that for the reverse direction P_Y and $\log h'^{-1}$ are positively correlated. Therefore P_Y contains information about $Q_{X|Y}$, which implies an asymmetry between X and Y.

Practical Evaluation

To evaluate this model, the authors compute:

$$C_{X \to Y} = \int_0^1 \log h'(x) P_X(x) dx. \tag{3.44}$$

$$C_{Y \to X} = \int_0^1 \log h'^{-1}(y) P_Y(y) dy = -S_{X \to Y}. \tag{3.45}$$

The algorithm IGCI infers $X \to Y$ whenever $C_{X \to Y}$ is negative. The authors also show that the evaluation can be simplified into:

$$C_{X \to Y} = H(Y) - H(X). \tag{3.46}$$

Then it is decided that $X \to Y$ if $H(X) > H(Y)$ and $Y \to X$ otherwise.

3.5.3.2 Unsupervised Inverse Regression

Sgouritsa et al. [27] propose a method based on the idea that if $X \to Y$, P_X should not contain information about $P_{Y|X}$, while P_Y may contain information about $P_{X|Y}$. Therefore the estimation of $Q_{Y|X}$ based on P_X should be less accurate than the estimation of $Q_{X|Y}$ based on P_Y.

Model

The causal mechanism $Q_{Y|X}$ is modeled with a Gaussian process latent variable model whose likelihood function with respect to the data is given by:

$$Q(y|x, \theta_Y) = \mathcal{N}(y|0, \mathbf{K}(x) + \sigma_n^2 \mathbf{I})). \tag{3.47}$$

The entry (i, j) of $\mathbf{K}$ is:

$$k((x^i), (x^j)) = \sigma_f^2 \exp\left(-\frac{(x^j - x^i)^2}{\ell^2}\right), \tag{3.48}$$

with the set of parameters $\theta_Y = (\ell, \sigma_f, \sigma_n)$.

The idea is then to estimate $Q_{X|Y}^{unsup}$ based only on the sample $\mathbf{y}* = \{y^i\}_{i=1}^n$ of P_Y with unsupervised Gaussian process regression and to compare it with the estimate $Q_{X|Y}^{sup}$ based on the sample $\mathscr{D} = \{(x^i, y^i)\}_{i=1}^n$ of $P_{X,Y}$. Negative log-likelihoods scores of both models are then computed as $C_{X|Y}^{unsup} = -\frac{1}{n}\sum_{i=1}^n \log Q_{X|Y}^{unsup}(x^i|y^i)$ and $C_{X|Y}^{sup} = -\frac{1}{n}\sum_{i=1}^n \log Q_{X|Y}^{sup}(x^i|y^i)$. The accuracy of the estimation of $Q_{X|Y}$ based only on P_Y is then accessed by computing $C_{X|Y} = C_{X|Y}^{unsup} - C_{X|Y}^{sup}$. A symmetric evaluation is done for $C_{Y|X}$. The causal direction $X \to Y$ is then preferred to $Y \to X$ if $C_{X|Y} < C_{Y|X}$.

3.5.3.3 Causal Inference via Kernel Deviance Measures

Mitrovic et al. [19] exploit the same postulate that $Q_{Y|X}$ should be independent of P_X whenever $X \to Y$. The idea is that the estimate of the conditional distribution $\{Q_{Y|X=x^i}\}_{i=1}^n$ should be less sensitive to the different values x^i taken by the variable X than the conditional $\{Q_{X|Y=y^i}\}_{i=1}^n$ is sensitive to the different values of $Y = y^i$.

Model

For $i = 1..n$, $\{Q_{Y|X=x^i}\}_{i=1}^n$ is evaluated with a conditional RBF kernel embedding into the Hilbert space of infinitely differentiable functions.

Evaluation

A score for the causal direction $X \to Y$ is evaluated as the deviance of this set of conditional embeddings with respect to the Reproducing Kernel Hilbert Space (RKHS) norm as:

$$C_{X \to Y} = \frac{1}{n} \sum_{i=1}^n \left(\| \mu_{Y|X=x^i} \|_{\mathcal{H}_{\mathcal{Y}}} - \frac{1}{n} \sum_{j=1}^n \| \mu_{Y|X=x^j} \|_{\mathcal{H}_{\mathcal{Y}}} \right)^2. \qquad (3.49)$$

$C_{Y \to X}$ is computed analogously and the causal direction $X \to Y$ is preferred if $C_{X \to Y} < C_{Y \to X}$.

3.5.3.4 Cause-Effect Inference by Comparing Regression Errors

A new method proposed by Bloebaum et al. [2] called RECI is based on a slightly different idea than the assumption of independence between cause and mechanism. The authors assume that the causal mechanism represents *a law of nature* that persists when the distribution of the cause and the distribution of the noise "change due to changing background conditions".

Model

They denote by ϕ the function that minimizes the expected least-squares error when predicting Y from X, $\phi(x) = \mathbb{E}[Y|X=x]$, and ψ the minimizer of the least-squares error for predicting X from Y, $\phi(y) = \mathbb{E}[X|Y=y]$.
For a model with the causal orientation $X \to Y$, the authors rewrite the bivariate functional causal model of Definition 3.1 under the following new form:

$$Y_\alpha := \phi(X) + \alpha N, \tag{3.50}$$

where $\alpha \in \mathbb{R}^+$ and N is a noise variable not necessarily independent of X.

They show under the regime of almost deterministic relations (when $\alpha \to 0$) that it implies:

$$\mathbb{E}\left[(Y - \phi(X))^2\right] \leq \mathbb{E}\left[(X - \psi(Y))^2\right], \tag{3.51}$$

which can be translated into "the MSE of regressing Y on X is lower that the MSE of regressing X on Y".

To obtain this result, the authors make the main following assumptions that we briefly summarize here:

- **Invertible function**: ϕ is a strictly monotonically increasing (or decreasing) twice differentiable function.
- **Compact supports**: the distribution of X has compact support.
- **Independence postulate**: the functions $x \mapsto \phi'(x)$ and $x \mapsto \text{Var}[N|X = x]$ $p_X(x)$ that define random variables are assumed to be uncorrelated, which is formally stated after re-scaling of the variables between 0 and 1 as:

$$\int_0^1 \phi'(x)\text{Var}[N|X{=}x]\,p_X(x)dx - \int_0^1 \phi'(x)dx \int_0^1 \text{Var}[N|X{=}x]\,p_X(x)dx{=}0. \tag{3.52}$$

Practical Evaluation

The method RECI consists in fitting a non-linear regression model on both directions after re-scaling between 0 and 1 both variables and comparing the mean squared error losses. The regression models used by the authors may be logistic functions, polynomial functions or neural networks. In practice the authors report better empirical results with simple polynomial regression models such as the shifted monomial functions $ax^3 + c$.

3.6 Experimental Comparison of Cause-Effect Inference Algorithms

In the last section we have presented an overview of the main methods proposed for the cause-effect pair problem. Now we propose to evaluate the different algorithms whose code are available online on several cause-effect pair datasets.

3.6.1 Datasets

Five datasets with continuous variables are considered [6]:

- *CE-Cha*: 300 continuous variable pairs from the cause-effect pair challenge [11] that will be presented with more details in the next chapter. Here we only consider pairs with label $+1$ ($X \rightarrow Y$) and -1 ($Y \rightarrow X$) (notably the confounding case is excluded).
- *CE-Net*: 300 artificial pairs generated with a neural network initialized with random weights and random distribution for the cause (exponential, gamma, lognormal, laplace...).
- *CE-Gauss*: 300 artificial pairs without confounder sampled with the generator of [20]: $Y := f_Y(X, N_Y)$ and $X := f_X(N_X)$ with $N_X \sim P_{N_X}$ and $N_Y \sim P_{N_Y}$. P_{N_X} and P_{N_Y} are randomly generated Gaussian mixture distributions. Causal mechanisms f_X and f_Y are randomly generated Gaussian processes.
- *CE-Multi*: 300 artificial pairs generated with linear and polynomial mechanisms. The effect variables are built with post additive noise setting ($Y := f_Y(X) + N_Y$), post multiplicative noise ($Y := f_Y(X) \times N_Y$), pre-additive noise ($Y := f_Y(X + N_Y)$) or pre-multiplicative noise ($Y := f_Y(X \times N_Y)$).
- *CE-Tueb*: 99 real-world cause-effect pairs from the *Tuebingen cause-effect pairs* dataset, version August 2016 [20]. This version of this dataset is taken from various domains: climate, census, medicine data.

For all variable pairs, the size n of the data sample is set with a maximum of 1500 for the sake of an acceptable overall computational load. To provide an overview of the type of pairs encountered in each dataset, one hundred pairs of each of them are displayed in Fig. 3.16 (the real pair with altitude and temperature given as introductory example corresponds to the first pair in the top left corner of *CE-Tueb*).

3.6.2 Algorithms

We compare the performance of the following algorithms presented in this chapter:

- **Best mse**: the method presented in the introduction that consists in fitting a non-linear Gaussian process regression model on both directions after re-scaling with zero mean and unit variance and comparing the mean squared error loss (mse). The direction corresponding to the fit with the lowest mse is preferred.

---

[6]The first four datasets are available at http://dx.doi.org/10.7910/DVN/3757KX. The *Tuebingen cause-effect pairs* dataset with real pairs is available at https://webdav.tuebingen.mpg.de/cause-effect/.

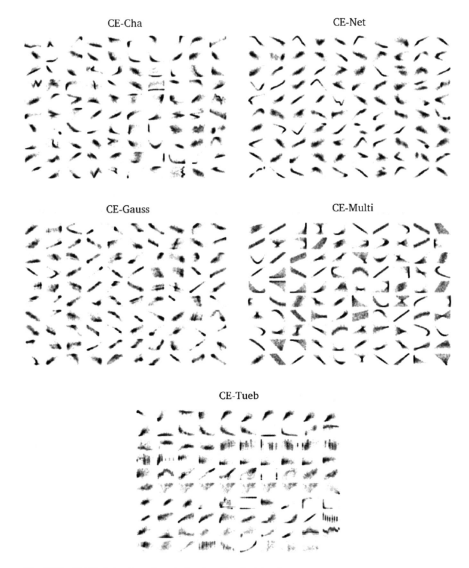

Fig. 3.16 (X,Y) plots of one hundred pairs of each dataset

- **RECI**: the practical implementation of this method is equivalent to the **Best mse** method except that the re-scaling is made between 0 and 1 and Gaussian process regression is replaced by polynomial regression with monomial function $ax^3 + c$ [2] (see Sect. 3.5.3.4).
- **LiNGAM**: a pairwise version of the method developed by Shimizu et al. [28] relying on Independent Component Analysis to identify the linear relations between variables (see Sect. 3.5.1.1).

- **ANM**: the Additive Noise Model [20] with Gaussian process regression and HSIC independence test of the residual (see Sect. 3.5.1.2).
- **IGCI**: the Information Geometric Causal Inference algorithm [4] with entropy estimator and Gaussian reference measure (see Sect. 3.5.3.1).
- **PNL**: the Post-NonLinear model with HSIC independence test [35] (see Sect. 3.5.1.3).
- **GPI**: the Gaussian Process Inference algorithm [31] based on the Minimum message length principle (see Sect. 3.5.2.1).
- **CGNN**: the Causal Generative Neural method [7] using neural networks to model causal mechanisms and Maximum Mean Discrepancy as fit score (see Sect. 3.5.2.3).

For the methods **Best mse** and **RECI** we use the implementation provided in the CausalDiscoveryToolbox.[7] For the implementation of the algorithms **ANM**, **IGCI**, **PNL**, **GPI** and **LiNGAM** we use the R program available at https://github.com/ssamot/causality. For **CGNN** we use the code available on github at https://github.com/GoudetOlivier/CGNN. We use default authors parameters for each algorithm implementation.

3.6.3 Performance Metric

The task of orienting each pair observed pair as $X \rightarrow Y$ or $Y \rightarrow X$ is a binary classification problem. We propose to use two scores to evaluate the performance of the algorithms:

- The **accuracy score** computed as the ratio of well oriented edges over the total number of edges for the datasets *CE-Cha*, *CE-Net*, *CE-Gauss* and *CE-Multi*. For the *CE-Tueb* dataset, a weighted accuracy is computed as in [20] in order to take into account dependent pairs from the same domain.
- The **area under the ROC curve** computed using the causal score given by each model that measures the confidence of the approach in the causal orientation for each pair. This score is defined as the difference between the two scores of each candidate model evaluated in both directions (cf. Sect. 3.4).

---

[7] Available online at https://github.com/Diviyan-Kalainathan/CausalDiscoveryToolbox.

3.6.4 Results

Table 3.2 reports the area under the roc curve (AUROC) and the accuracy (in parenthesis) for each benchmark and each algorithm. The corresponding ROC curves are displayed in Fig. 3.17.

The method **LiNGAM** is outperformed as it uses linear mechanisms to model the data generative process which is in many cases unrealistic. **IGCI** does not seem to be very robust: it takes advantage of some specific features of the dataset, (e.g. the cause entropy being lower than the effect entropy in *CE-Multi*), but remains near chance level otherwise. The method **ANM** yields good results when the additive assumption holds (e.g. on *CE-Gauss*), but fails otherwise. **PNL**, less restrictive than **ANM**, yields overall good results compared to the former methods. The method **RECI** based on comparison of mean square error scores after proper re-scaling provides overall good results too. However it fails for more complex pairs due to restrictive assumptions on the causal mechanisms involved. Lastly, methods like **GPI** and **CGNN** that admit the most flexible class of causal mechanisms and non-parametric metrics to match the distributions perform well on most datasets, including the real-world cause-effect pairs *CE-Tueb*, in counterpart for a higher computational cost (resp. 32 min on CPU for GPI and 24 min on GPU for CGNN).[8]

Let us note that better scores for the dataset Tübingen (*CE-Tueb*) are reported in recent papers such as [16] (accuracy of 82.0%) and [19] (accuracy of 78.7%) using ensemble methods with the algorithms presented in Sects. 3.5.2.2 and 3.5.3.3.

Table 3.2 Area under the Precision Recall curve and accuracy in parenthesis on the five datasets and for all the algorithms

Methods	CE-Cha	CE-Net	CE-Gauss	CE-Multi	CE-Tueb	All
Best mse	50.0 (46.7)	86.4 (76.7)	18.7 (23.7)	46.9 (36.3)	61.3 (61.7)	61.3 (61.7)
RECI	59.0 (56.0)	66.0 (60.3)	71.0 (64.3)	94.7 (85.3)	70.5 (70.8)	73.8 (66.7)
LiNGAM	57.8 (55.7)	3.3 (36.7)	72.2 (77.3)	62.3 (63.3)	31.1 (44.3)	54.8 (57.8)
IGCI	55.6 (55.0)	57.4 (57.0)	16.0 (21.3)	77.8 (68.0)	63.1 (62.6)	52.8 (50.7)
ANM	43.7 (46.0)	87.8 (78.0)	90.7 (83.3)	25.5 (38.0)	63.9 (62.7)	60.7 (61.4)
PNL	78.6 (76.0)	75.6 (65.3)	84.7 (78.3)	51.7 (56.3)	73.8 (66.2)	71.9 (68.9)
GPI	71.5 (67.0)	88.1 (79.0)	90.2 (82.0)	73.8 (77.7)	70.6 (62.5)	79.9 (76.0)
CGNN	76.2 (71.6)	86.3 (75.3)	89.3 (81.0)	94.7 (87.3)	76.6 (75.9)	**86.5 (78.8)**

Underline values corresponds to best score for each dataset. *Bold* value corresponds to best overall score on all dataset.

---

[8]Computational times are measured on Intel Xeon 2.7Ghz (CPU) or on Nvidia GTX 1080Ti graphics card (GPU).

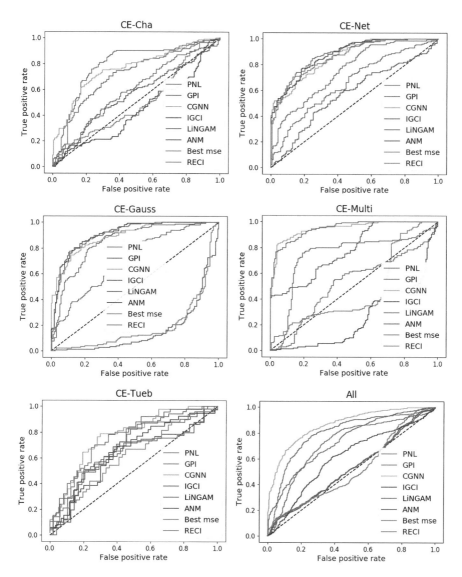

Fig. 3.17 ROC curves for the algorithms PNL, GPI, CGNN, IGCI, LiNGAM, ANM and Best mse on the different datasets. The last plot corresponds to the overall score on the five datasets

3.7 Discussion and Open Problems

The cause-effect inference problem is relatively new in the Machine Learning literature and there are still a lot of open problems to be addressed in order to build a robust tool that can be used by the practitioner to confirm for example if a given treatment has an impact or not on a given disease or to discover if a gene has a regulatory power on an other one.

3.7.1 Relax the Causal Sufficiency Assumption

To build such useful tools for practitioners, one of the first assumption that needs to be relaxed is the causal sufficiency assumption as in a lot of real problems it is very rare to find a cause-effect problem that is not affected by hidden common confounder that can affect both variables such as age or gender.

One idea proposed in the literature is to model confounders by introducing correlation between the noise variables N_X and N_Y that affect X and Y as in [26] or by modelling all the unobserved confounding effects by a new noise variable N_{XY} entering in the generation process of X and Y [7, 15].

If we reformulate the generative bivariate framework of Sect. 3.4.1.1 in presence of confounders three alternative candidate models must be considered:

1. If $\mathcal{G} = X \to Y$:

   - $X := \hat{f}_X(N_X, N_{XY})$ with $N_X \sim Q_{N_X}$, $N_{XY} \sim Q_{N_{XY}}$ and $N_X \perp\!\!\!\perp N_{XY}$
   - then $Y := \hat{f}_Y(X, N_Y, N_{XY})$ with $N_Y \sim Q_{N_Y}$ and $N_Y \perp\!\!\!\perp N_{XY}$

2. If $\mathcal{G} = Y \to X$:

   - $Y := \hat{f}_Y(N_Y, N_{XY})$ with $N_Y \sim Q_{N_Y}$, $N_{XY} \sim Q_{N_{XY}}$ and $N_Y \perp\!\!\!\perp N_{XY}$
   - then $X := \hat{f}_X(Y, N_X, N_{XY})$ with $N_X \sim Q_{N_X}$ and $N_X \perp\!\!\!\perp N_{XY}$

3. If $\mathcal{G} = Y \leftrightarrow X$,

   - $X := \hat{f}_X(N_X, N_{XY})$ with $N_X \sim Q_{N_X}$, $N_{XY} \sim Q_{N_{XY}}$ and $N_X \perp\!\!\!\perp N_{XY}$
   - $Y := \hat{f}_Y(N_Y, N_{XY})$ with $N_Y \sim Q_{N_Y}$ and $N_Y \perp\!\!\!\perp N_{XY}$

A diagram of the model is presented in Fig. 3.18. We use the same notation for the vector of parameters as in Sect. 3.4.1.1 but with a new set of parameters $\theta_{N_{XY}}$ for the distribution of the common noise variable N_{XY}.

The same approach with a trade-off between fit and complexity could be used to compare these three alternative models in presence of potential confounders. An additional penalty term depending on the total number of edges $|\widehat{G}|$ in the model could be introduced like in score based methods for multivariate inference [3], in order to remove the eventual spurious link due to the confounding effect between X and Y. We have indeed $|\widehat{G}| = 1$ for the models with structures $X \to Y$ or $Y \to X$, and $|\widehat{G}| = 0$ for the models with structure $Y \leftrightarrow X$.

This framework could also take into account known variables as confounders. In this case the variable N_{XY} would be replaced by a set of observed variables (e.g. the latitude in the introductory example of this chapter with altitude and temperature).

Furthermore one can notice that this extension of the generative approach in presence of the confounding effect would not be possible for discriminative

Fig. 3.18 Candidate generative models $X \rightarrow Y$ with a potential confounding effect modelled with the noise variable N_{XY}

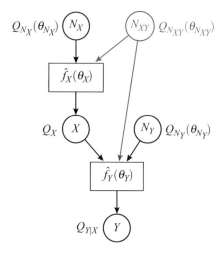

approaches where the source cause is not modelled (when only comparing $P_{Y|X}$ with $P_{X|Y}$).

3.7.2 Need for Real Datasets of a Big Size

Another important problem that is often overlooked in the "cause-effect pair community" concerns benchmarking. As of the writing of this chapter, the main real data benchmark used to compare the different methods by the community is the Tübingen Dataset,[9] composed of only 100 hundred pairs which are often very similar. It is indeed very difficult to collect cause-effect pairs with enough data points from the real world with an authenticated known ground truth. But one must to keep in mind that it is very easy for most of the methods presented in this chapter to tune their hyper parameters (even unintentionally) in order to obtain the best results. This overfitting problem is often compounded by the fact that this dataset is, most of the time, not separated into train/validation/test sets. To overcome this problem a Cause-effect Pair Challenge has been proposed by Guyon [11] with real and artificial data generated with various mechanisms. It will be discussed in the next chapter.

---

[9]https://webdav.tuebingen.mpg.de/cause-effect/.

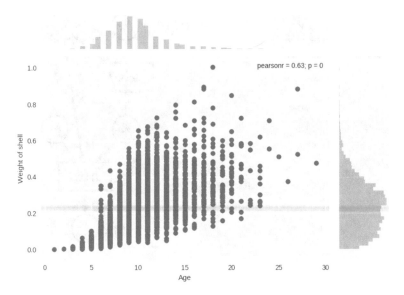

Fig. 3.19 Age of a snail (X-axis) and corresponding weight of its shell (Y-axis)

3.7.3 Biased Assessment Due to Artifacts in Data

It is often observed that the cause variable is discrete ordinal while the other is continuous. This induces an artificial asymmetry between cause and effect which could lead to biased assessments.

Let us consider for example real abalone data[10] representing the age of snails (X-axis) and the corresponding weight of its shell (Y-axis) as depicted in Fig. 3.19. The ground truth is *age* causes *weight of the shell*.

We see that due to the experimental conditions when collecting the data, the variable age is discrete (categorical ordered variable or ordinal variable) and not continuous. Because of this artifact on the age variable, the conditional $P_{\text{weight}|\text{age}}$ has really more chance to be simpler than $P_{\text{age}|\text{weight}}$. Therefore it favors approaches that compare only $P_{Y|X}$ with $P_{X|Y}$ and it may lead to inconsistent methods for the cause-effect pair problem as stated in Chap. 1 of this book.

An open problem could be to find a way to correct this bias when one encounters this type of data. This was done in the design of the dataset of the Cause-effect Pair Challenge.

---

[10]https://archive.ics.uci.edu/ml/datasets/Abalone.

3.7.4 Extension of the Generative Approach for Categorical Variables

In this chapter we have discussed the cause-effect pair problem for continuous variables, but the same idea could be used for categorical variables or mixed variables. To the best of our knowledge, only few attempts have been made to solve the cause-effect pair problem with categorical data [17, 24].

It may be explained by the fact that the cause-effect problem for categorical data may be really harder than for continuous data, because there is in general less information to exploit in the distribution of the noise and in the asymmetry of the causal mechanisms.

If one considers for example the extreme case of two binary variables, what kind of causal information can be really exploited from a matrix of size (2,2) that represents the repartition of the data points into the 4 different cases (1,0), (0,1), (1,1) and (0,0) ?

3.7.5 Extension of the Pairwise Setting for Complete Graph Inference

There is a need for methods that can really cross the bridge between the cause-effect pair problem and the complete problem of causal discovery with more than two variables. A way of research could be to propose an efficient approach for the general multivariate case that can potentially exploit all the information available, including the asymmetry between cause and effect and the conditional independence relations.

In this direction, an extension of the bivariate Post-NonLinear model (PNL) has been proposed [35], where an FCM is trained for any plausible causal structure, and each model is tested a posteriori for the required independence between errors and causes, but the main limitation is its super-exponential cost with the number of variables [35]. Another hybrid approach uses a constraint based algorithm to identify a Markov equivalence class, and thereafter uses bivariate modeling to orient the remaining edges [35]. For example, the constraint-based PC algorithm [30] can identify the v-structure, enabling the bivariate PNL method to further infer the remaining arrows that are not identifiable with conditional independence tests. However an effective combination of constraint-based and bivariate approaches requires a final verification phase to test the consistency between the v-structures and the edge orientations based on asymmetry.

An extension of the ANM model (Sect. 3.5.1.2) called CAM [25] proposed a consistent framework that can exploit the interaction and the asymmetry of the cause and effect, but the approach is restricted to the assumption of causal additive noise. The CGNN algorithm presented in Sect. 3.5.2.3 can be extended in the multivariate case [7]. It is more general than the CAM algorithm, but needs to start from a supposed known skeleton of the causal graph and employ simple exploratory heuristic to explore the space of DAG due to computational reasons.

3.7.6 Computational Complexity Limitations

Some methods suffer from computational complexity limitations. In the bivariate case, there are only two alternative DAGs to compare, but for the multivariate case with more than 1000 variables, the number of different DAGs to consider grows exponentially. Therefore it is a real challenge to make the successful methods of the cause-effect problem scale for big data problem. In particular the methods that can model complex interactions between cause and noise, such as those using Gaussian process regressions or neural networks are often really slow to compute and do not scale well in term of number of variables and number of data points.

3.7.7 Relax Restrictive Assumptions on Causal Mechanisms

Another open problem concerns the fact that all these methods rely on specific assumptions on the underlying data generative process. All of them can work well when these specific assumptions are encountered in the observed data. This is why a new Machine Learning approach, presented in the next chapter, has appeared in recent years. It is based on the idea to combine all the successful algorithms presented in this chapter into a single meta algorithm that could benefit from the advantages of each of them.

3.8 Conclusion

We have briefly explained the difference between explanatory models and predictive models and seen that causal discovery consists in finding the best explanatory model of the data. We have then defined the problem of cause-effect inference in the bivariate setting and the main assumptions usually involved in the literature. Under these assumptions we have formalized the notion of bivariate structural equation model. We have then seen that the task of recovering the good causal direction from $X \rightarrow Y$ or $Y \rightarrow X$ consists in comparing alternative candidate models estimated from data. This comparison is always based in one way or another on a complexity/fit trade-off. We have reviewed how the complexity and the fit terms are usually evaluated in order to compute a causal score in both directions. It has led us to propose a reading grid of the main methods proposed in the literature.

   Three main families have emerged: (1) methods that restrict the class of admissible causal mechanisms and focus on identifiability results; (2) methods that do not explicitly restrict the class of admissible mechanisms and focus on the generality of the approach at the expense of theoretical identifiability guaranties; and (3) lastly methods that exploit the postulate that the cause should be independent of the causal mechanism.

We have then compared the main methods of the literature whose code is available online. It appears that methods that allow for flexible causal mechanism and complex realistic interactions can obtain consistent scores on a wide range of cause-effect problems (artificial and real data). These results need however to be confirmed on real datasets of bigger size with known ground truth.

One fruitful way of research could be to extend the best generative approach for causal discovery presented in this chapter to deal with potential confounding effects. Another interesting way of research could be to provide a theoretical framework that can unify the cause-effect pair methods presented in this chapter with the multivariate methods for causal discovery using conditional independence tests.

Software Packages

- R package including ANM, IGCI, PNL, GPI and LiNGAM algorithms available at the URL:

  https://github.com/ssamot/causality.

- Python package including Best mse, RECI, CGNN, ANM, IGCI and LiNGAM algorithms available at the URL:

  https://github.com/Diviyan-Kalainathan/CausalDiscoveryToolbox.

Acknowledgements The authors would like to thank Daniel Rolland for proofreading this document, as well as the reviewers for their constructive feedback.

References

1. Robert Axelrod and William Donald Hamilton. The evolution of cooperation. *science*, 211(4489):1390–1396, 1981.
2. Patrick Bloebaum, Dominik Janzing, Takashi Washio, Shohei Shimizu, and Bernhard Schölkopf. Cause-effect inference by comparing regression errors. In *International Conference on Artificial Intelligence and Statistics*, pages 900–909, 2018.
3. David Maxwell Chickering. Optimal structure identification with greedy search. *Journal of machine learning research*, 3(Nov):507–554, 2002.
4. Povilas Daniušis, Dominik Janzing, Joris Mooij, Jakob Zscheischler, Bastian Steudel, Kun Zhang, and Bernhard Schölkopf. Inferring deterministic causal relations. In *Proceedings of the Twenty-Sixth Conference on Uncertainty in Artificial Intelligence*, UAI'10, pages 143–150, Arlington, Virginia, United States, 2010. AUAI Press. ISBN 978-0-9749039-6-5. http://dl.acm.org/citation.cfm?id=3023549.3023566.
5. Bruce Edmonds and Scott Moss. From kiss to kids–an 'anti-simplistic' modelling approach. In *International workshop on multi-agent systems and agent-based simulation*, pages 130–144. Springer, 2004.
6. Ian Goodfellow, Jean Pouget-Abadie, Mehdi Mirza, Bing Xu, David Warde-Farley, Sherjil Ozair, Aaron Courville, and Yoshua Bengio. Generative adversarial nets. In *Neural Information Processing Systems (NIPS)*, pages 2672–2680, 2014.

7. Olivier Goudet, Diviyan Kalainathan, Philippe Caillou, Isabelle Guyon, David Lopez-Paz, and Michèle Sebag. Causal generative neural networks. *arXiv preprint arXiv:1711.08936*, 2017.
8. Clive WJ Granger. Investigating causal relations by econometric models and cross-spectral methods. *Econometrica: Journal of the Econometric Society*, pages 424–438, 1969.
9. Arthur Gretton, Olivier Bousquet, Alex Smola, and Bernhard Schölkopf. Measuring statistical dependence with Hilbert-Schmidt norms. In *International conference on algorithmic learning theory*, pages 63–77. Springer, 2005.
10. Arthur Gretton, Karsten M Borgwardt, Malte Rasch, Bernhard Schölkopf, Alexander J Smola, et al. A kernel method for the two-sample-problem. 19:513, 2007.
11. Isabelle Guyon. Chalearn cause effect pairs challenge, 2013. http://www.causality.inf.ethz.ch/cause-effect.php.
12. Patrik O Hoyer, Dominik Janzing, Joris M Mooij, Jonas Peters, and Bernhard Schölkopf. Nonlinear causal discovery with additive noise models. In *Neural Information Processing Systems (NIPS)*, pages 689–696, 2009.
13. Aapo Hyvärinen and Stephen M Smith. Pairwise likelihood ratios for estimation of non-gaussian structural equation models. *Journal of Machine Learning Research*, 14(Jan):111–152, 2013.
14. Dominik Janzing and Bernhard Schölkopf. Causal inference using the algorithmic Markov condition. *IEEE Transactions on Information Theory*, 56(10):5168–5194, 2010.
15. Dominik Janzing and Bernhard Schölkopf. Detecting confounding in multivariate linear models via spectral analysis. *Journal of Causal Inference*, 6(1), 2018.
16. David Lopez-Paz and Maxime Oquab. Revisiting classifier two-sample tests. *arXiv preprint arXiv:1610.06545*, 2016.
17. Alexander Marx and Jilles Vreeken. Causal inference on multivariate and mixed-type data. *arXiv preprint arXiv:1702.06385*, 2017.
18. Mehdi Mirza and Simon Osindero. Conditional generative adversarial nets. *arXiv preprint arXiv:1411.1784*, 2014.
19. Jovana Mitrovic, Dino Sejdinovic, and Yee Whye Teh. Causal inference via kernel deviance measures. *arXiv preprint arXiv:1804.04622*, 2018.
20. Joris M Mooij, Jonas Peters, Dominik Janzing, Jakob Zscheischler, and Bernhard Schölkopf. Distinguishing cause from effect using observational data: methods and benchmarks. *Journal of Machine Learning Research*, 17(32):1–102, 2016.
21. Judea Pearl. Causality: models, reasoning and inference. *Econometric Theory*, 19(675–685):46, 2003.
22. Judea Pearl. *Causality*. Cambridge university press, 2009.
23. F. Pedregosa, G. Varoquaux, A. Gramfort, V. Michel, B. Thirion, O. Grisel, M. Blondel, P. Prettenhofer, R. Weiss, V. Dubourg, J. Vanderplas, A. Passos, D. Cournapeau, M. Brucher, M. Perrot, and E. Duchesnay. Scikit-learn: Machine learning in Python. *Journal of Machine Learning Research*, 12:2825–2830, 2011.
24. Jonas Peters, Dominik Janzing, and Bernhard Schölkopf. Causal inference on discrete data using additive noise models. *IEEE Transactions on Pattern Analysis and Machine Intelligence*, 33(12):2436–2450, 2011.
25. Jonas Peters, Joris M Mooij, Dominik Janzing, and Bernhard Schölkopf. Causal discovery with continuous additive noise models. *The Journal of Machine Learning Research*, 15(1):2009–2053, 2014.
26. Dominik Rothenhäusler, Christina Heinze, Jonas Peters, and Nicolai Meinshausen. Backshift: Learning causal cyclic graphs from unknown shift interventions. In *Advances in Neural Information Processing Systems*, pages 1513–1521, 2015.
27. Eleni Sgouritsa, Dominik Janzing, Philipp Hennig, and Bernhard Schölkopf. Inference of cause and effect with unsupervised inverse regression. In *Artificial Intelligence and Statistics*, pages 847–855, 2015.
28. Shohei Shimizu, Patrik O Hoyer, Aapo Hyvärinen, and Antti Kerminen. A linear non-gaussian acyclic model for causal discovery. *Journal of Machine Learning Research*, 7(Oct):2003–2030, 2006.

29. Galit Shmueli et al. To explain or to predict? *Statistical science*, 25(3):289–310, 2010.
30. Peter Spirtes, Clark N Glymour, and Richard Scheines. *Causation, prediction, and search.* MIT press, 2000.
31. Oliver Stegle, Dominik Janzing, Kun Zhang, Joris M Mooij, and Bernhard Schölkopf. Probabilistic latent variable models for distinguishing between cause and effect. In *Neural Information Processing Systems (NIPS)*, pages 1687–1695, 2010.
32. Xiaohai Sun, Dominik Janzing, and Bernhard Schölkopf. Causal inference by choosing graphs with most plausible Markov kernels. In *ISAIM*, 2006.
33. Chris S Wallace and Peter R Freeman. Estimation and inference by compact coding. *Journal of the Royal Statistical Society. Series B (Methodological)*, pages 240–265, 1987.
34. Kun Zhang and Aapo Hyvärinen. Distinguishing causes from effects using nonlinear acyclic causal models. In *Proceedings of the 2008th International Conference on Causality: Objectives and Assessment-Volume 6*, pages 157–164. JMLR. org, 2008.
35. Kun Zhang and Aapo Hyvärinen. On the identifiability of the post-nonlinear causal model. In *Proceedings of the twenty-fifth conference on uncertainty in artificial intelligence*, pages 647–655. AUAI Press, 2009.
36. Kun Zhang, Zhikun Wang, Jiji Zhang, and Bernhard Schölkopf. On estimation of functional causal models: general results and application to the post-nonlinear causal model. *ACM Transactions on Intelligent Systems and Technology (TIST)*, 7(2):13, 2016.

Chapter 4
Discriminant Learning Machines

Diviyan Kalainathan, Olivier Goudet, Michèle Sebag, and Isabelle Guyon

4.1 Introduction

Distinguish causes from effects is of utmost importance in order to understand mechanisms and provide unbiased predictions, or to be able to make recommendations. In order to ascertain causal relationships, randomized controlled experiments represent the gold standard. However those experiments are often costly, unethical, or even unfeasible, leaving only available observational data. Causal discovery out of observational data has been thoroughly studied in the graph setting[1] [11, 35, 47], but we will focus in this chapter on the particular case where we have only access to two variables without time information to determine their causal relationship. This setting is relevant when only two variables are available, or when only two variables are of interest and are already conditioned on the covariates.

To tackle this problem, the literature proposed generative models for causal discovery which aim to find models matching the empirical distribution of the data (c.f. Chapter III). These models are sought in a model class, that needs to be restrictive after [53]: actually, too general a class might allow to learn an accurate

---

[1]Where more than two variables are available and conditional independencies can be exploited to recover the causal structure of the graph.

D. Kalainathan · O. Goudet (✉) · M. Sebag
Team TAU - CNRS, INRIA, Université Paris Sud, Université Paris Saclay, Orsay, France
e-mail: Diviyan.kalainathan@lri.fr; olivier.goudet@inria.fr; sebag@lri.fr

I. Guyon
Team TAU - CNRS, INRIA, Université Paris Sud, Université Paris Saclay, Orsay France

ChaLearn, Berkeley, CA, USA
e-mail: guyon@chalearn.org

© Springer Nature Switzerland AG 2019
I. Guyon et al. (eds.), *Cause Effect Pairs in Machine Learning*,
The Springer Series on Challenges in Machine Learning,
https://doi.org/10.1007/978-3-030-21810-2_4

generative model whatever the hypothesized causal dependencies, hindering the identification of the true causal mechanisms. Therefore, generative models explicitly assume the simplicity of the sought causal mechanism. For instance, the Additive Noise Model (ANM) [21] identifies causal relationships when the total of external contributions influence linearly the mechanism:

$$Y = f(X) + E \tag{4.1}$$

where Y represents the effect, X the cause and E a random noise variable accounting for the unobserved variables. The ANM explicitly models the direct effect between the variables through the possibly non-linear causal mechanism f.

Another issue related to simple model classes is the testability of the underlying assumptions[2] which proved itself to be difficult, even though pioneering has been done by Scheines [43], Zhang and Spirtes [52], and Uhler et al. [49].

As said, generative models strongly rely on the simplicity assumption, stating that the causal mechanism is the simplest model that generates one variable from the other(s). Here "simplicity" could be formalized in terms of Kolmogorov Complexity (K), stating that the causal direction is the direction holds the lowest K. For instance, Janzing and Schölkopf [22][3] states that:

$$K(P_{\text{cause}}) + K(P_{\text{effect|cause}}) \leq K(P_{\text{effect}}) + K(P_{\text{cause|effect}}) \tag{4.2}$$

This strong assumption does not always hold true in real-world settings, due to e.g. missing intermediate variables or complex causal mechanisms.

These limitations have been addressed through a new learning approach to pairwise causal discovery, formalized through the Cause Effect Pairs (CEP) Challenge [19, 20] (c.f. Appendix 1). Considering two variables X and Y and (a sample of) their joint distribution, the CEP goal is to determine the category of their causal relationship (whether X causes Y, or Y causes X, or neither causes the other one). Thereby the causal discovery problem is shifted from modeling the causal mechanism relating given variables, to a classification problem where any joint distribution is associated a causal class. Accordingly, by leveraging Machine Learning algorithms, a classifier is trained to leverage causally relevant features from joint distributions of pairs of variables sampled from a Mother Distribution (Sect. 4.2.5) for classification. Such classification approaches come in two modes: (1) ensemble learning methods build upon statistical features and pre-existing generative models; (2) discriminant learning methods build on top of representation learning and distribution embeddings.

This chapter first formalizes the pairwise cause-effect inference problem as a classification task (Sect. 4.2), and thoroughly presents the various approaches for feature construction in Sect. 4.3. The different approaches and algorithms developed

---

[2]C.f. Sect. 4.2.2.
[3]Refer to Chapter III for details.

to address these challenges are presented in Sect. 4.4. The limitations of these approaches are discussed and some perspectives for further research are presented in Sect. 4.5.

The appendices consist in: Appendix 1 describes the Cause Effect Pairs Challenges organized by Guyon [19, 20], Appendix 2 refers to the traditional learning bounds [50] and Appendix 3 extends these bounds for our problem of learning out of distributions, with a kernel based feature construction step (Sect. 4.4.2).

4.2 Problem Setting

This section formalizes pairwise causal discovery as a learning task. You are given a dataset $((d_1, g_1), (d_2, g_2), \ldots, (d_n, g_n))$; each d_j is itself a dataset of pairs $(x_{1j}, y_{1j}), \ldots, (x_{pj}, y_{pj})$ and the label g_i represents the causal mechanism at play in the dataset d_i, defined after Reichenbach's Principle of Common Cause [2]: (i) causal class $(X \rightarrow Y)$; (ii) anti-causal class $(X \leftarrow Y)$; (iii) there exists a confounding variable Z such that $X \leftarrow Z \rightarrow Y$; (iv) X and Y are independent $(X \perp\!\!\!\perp Y)$. Classes (iii) and (iv) are merged in the following; we shall return to this point in Sect. 4.5.

The examples are exploited using mainstream classification algorithms; eventually the trained classifier is used to predict the causal class associated with a new joint distribution $P_{X', Y'}$.

4.2.1 Notations

We will briefly introduce the various notations that we will use throughout this chapter.

- X and Y denote random variables with values in $\mathbb{R}$. Unless specified otherwise, X is considered as the cause and Y as the effect of X.
- P_X represents the probability distribution of X.
- $S_j = \{x_{ij}, y_{ij}\}_{i=1}^{n_j}$ depicts a empirical distribution, based on which the algorithms infer the causal direction of the pair.
- (S_j, g_j) depicts a empirical distribution along with its label g_j, based on which the algorithms learn the causal direction of the pair. g_j represents the ground truth of the causal relation between the two variables (encoded as described in Sect. 4.2.3). This set of data points and label is also called **causal pair**.
- $S = \{S_j, g_j\}_{j=1}^{n}$ denotes the dataset of causal pairs.
- $\mu(P_{S_j})$ represents a single vector of features (of potentially infinite dimension) encoding the embedding of the empirical distribution $\{x_{ij}, y_{ij}\}_{i=1}^{n_j}$.
- $C(X, Y)$ represents the causal coefficient (c.f. Sect. 4.2.4) for the (X, Y) pair of variables.

4.2.2 Causal Assumptions

We will define here the various assumptions made in this chapter, some of which traditionally made are not explicitly made by the presented framework. However, some of the assumptions are made by the presented algorithms in Sect. 4.4.

Reichenbach's Principle
Reichenbach's principle states that if two variables X and Y are dependent, then either: (i) $X \to Y$, (ii) $Y \to X$, (iii) $\exists Z, X \leftarrow Z \to Y$, Z being a confounding variable. The presented framework does not make this assumption,[4] therefore including the case in which there can be dependency without any causal relationship, e.g. constraint or equilibrium (c.f. Chap. 7).

Causal Sufficiency
Causal sufficiency assumes that the direct dependency between two variables is the result of a direct causal influence between the two variables, and not the result of a confounding effect from a hidden variable (case (iii)) in Reichenbach's principle). We will not make this assumption in this chapter, as we will consider this case during classification.

Causal Faithfulness
Causal faithfulness states that if two variables X, Y are causally related, then they are dependent. A typical case where this hypothesis does not hold true is if X influences both Y and an auxiliary variable Z, and Z influences Y in such a way that the direct effect of X is counteracted by the influence of Z.

Causal Markov
Causal Markov assumes that if two variables X and Y are dependent, then they are d-connected. Under the abovementioned additional assumptions, it comes down to four cases:

1. $X \to Y$
2. $Y \to X$
3. $\exists Z, X \leftarrow Z \to Y$, Z being a confounding variable
4. $X \leftrightarrow Y$, denoting a feedback loop or a 2-cycle.

In this study, we will exclude the case of cycles between the variables of interest; i.e. there exists no paths between X and Y such as $X \to \ldots \to Y$ and $Y \to \ldots \to X$, therefore excluding the fourth case.

---

[4]Even though many algorithms make this assumption.

4.2.3 Causal Discovery as a Classification Task

Let $\mathscr{S}$ denote an example associated with a pair of variables X, Y. Its description $\left(\{(x_i, y_i)_{i=1}^m\}, g_i \right)$ is an iid sample drawn after joint distribution $P_{X,Y}$ along with its associated label g_i. g_i is 1 i.f.f. X causes Y ($X \to Y$), -1 if Y causes X ($X \leftarrow Y$) and 0 otherwise (if X and Y are independent, $X \perp\!\!\!\perp Y$; or there exists a third variable Z causing both X and Y, $X \leftarrow Z \to Y$) (Fig. 4.1).

Note that the label g_i primarily depends on the relationship between both variables X and Y: if $X \to Y$ and there exists a third variable Z such that $X \leftarrow Z \to Y$ (Fig. 4.1(5) and (6)), distribution $P_{X,Y}$ is labelled as 1 (c.f. Chap. 1).

From a training set made of examples $\mathscr{S}_1, \ldots, \mathscr{S}_n$, mainstream classification algorithms are leveraged to train a classifier, used to associate a causal scenario with any sample coming from a new joint distribution $P_{X',Y'}$.

This problem setting casts causal discovery as a regular supervised learning task. After the usual methodology, the **training set** is used to train a classifier with given hyper-parameters; a **validation set** is used to optimize the hyper-parameters of the learning algorithm; and the performance of the trained classifier is assessed using a **test set**. Notably, this setting accommodates heterogeneous causal discovery problems: examples can involve distribution samples of different sizes, associated with continuous, categorical, ordinal or binary variables.

In order to compensate for this heterogeneity, some pre-processing step (feature construction) can be applied in order to map any joint distribution sample onto a k-dimensional real-valued vector. Appendix 2 highlights the bounds obtained for a learning problem, for an optimal feature construction step out of distributions.

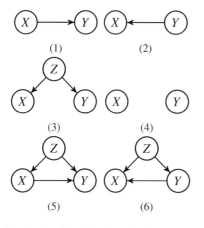

(7) Table of correspondence between causal scenarios and classes

Configuration	Class
(a)	1
(b)	−1
(c)	0
(d)	0
(e)	1
(f)	−1

Fig. 4.1 A pair of variable X and Y is associated with one out of six causal scenarios, falling in three classes

4.2.4 Causation Coefficient

While each example falls into one out of three causal classes (Fig. 4.1), for convenience one most often associates to each variable pair X, Y a continuous *causation coefficient* $C(X, Y) \in \mathbb{R}$, such that:

- $C(X, Y) > 0$ corresponds to $X \rightarrow Y$
- $C(X, Y) < 0$ corresponds to $X \leftarrow Y$
- $C(X, Y) \approx 0$ corresponds to $X \perp\!\!\!\perp Y$ or $\exists Z, X \leftarrow Z \rightarrow Y$

The advantage of using a continuous causation coefficient is twofold. On one hand, the absolute value $|C(X, Y)|$ is interpreted as the confidence of the prediction. When $|C(X, Y)|$ goes to 0, the causal direction is unclear; variables could be considered as either independent, or dependent because of a confounding effect; we shall return to this in Sect. 4.5.

On the other hand, $C(X, Y)$ is used to rank pairs of variables, supporting the definition of confidence based scores such as the precision-recall score or the area under the ROC curve score. From a practitioner's viewpoint, $C(X, Y)$ can be used to prioritize experiments in order to assess causal predictions. Additionally, $C(X, Y)$ allows practitioners to orient edges in partially oriented causal graphs.

4.2.5 Mother Distributions

After [29], the proposed causal discovery setting is amenable to a theoretical analysis rooted in statistical learning theory and risk minimization [50]. The analysis relies on the notion of Mother Distribution. Let $\mathcal{M}$ be a distribution defined on $\mathcal{P} \times \mathcal{G}$, where $\mathcal{P}$ depicts the set of joint distributions of causally related pairs of variables, and $\mathcal{G}$ denotes the set of causal labels (Fig. 4.1). For simplicity, only the case $\mathcal{G} = \{1, -1\}$ is considered in the following; the extension to multi-classes follows from [29]. All n examples $\{(\mathcal{S}_1, g_1), \ldots (\mathcal{S}_n, g_n)\}$ are independently sampled from $\mathcal{M}$, called the **Mother distribution** of the causal discovery problem.

As said, feature construction[5] is commonly used to map each $\mathcal{S}_j$ onto a k-dimensional real-valued vector in $\mathbb{R}^k$. The problem of learning from empirical joint distributions is thus shifted to a standard supervised learning problem of classification $\mathbb{R}^k \mapsto \mathcal{G}$.

---

[5]Representation learning, mapping each distribution sample onto a latent space, will be also considered in Sect. 4.4.2.

Fig. 4.2 General structure of discriminant learning algorithms for pairwise causal discovery

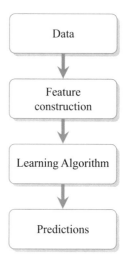

4.2.6 Learning Algorithms for This Classification Problem

A distinctive characteristic of the causal pairwise classification problem compared to the traditional classification problem is the nature of the samples points. In a regular classification problem a sample is a vector representing the position of the example in the feature space $\mathbb{R}^d$, where d represents the number of features. In our pairwise classification problem, a sample is an empirical distribution, a set of points $\{x_i, y_i\}_{i=1}^{n_j}$.

Therefore, a feature construction step is added between the data and the learning algorithm, making the structure of algorithms as shown in Fig. 4.2.

4.3 Feature Construction out of Distributions for Pairwise Classification

In order to apply regular learning tools for classification, features have to be extracted out of the data distribution samples. This step is a feature construction step, and the literature has taken three different approaches to extract such features: firstly, the manual construction of causally relevant features to classify the pairs. Secondly, the embedding of the sample distributions into a fixed size feature vector: the resulting manifold will be mapped to the target classes using the training set, allowing to classify unseen examples using the same embedding. Finally, the third approach is to not only use embeddings of distributions, but to also automatically learn and identify classification patterns using the training set.

Sine-Based Pairwise Example Dataset In this section, we will illustrate the inner workings of the various features using a simple dataset, as all the mechanisms

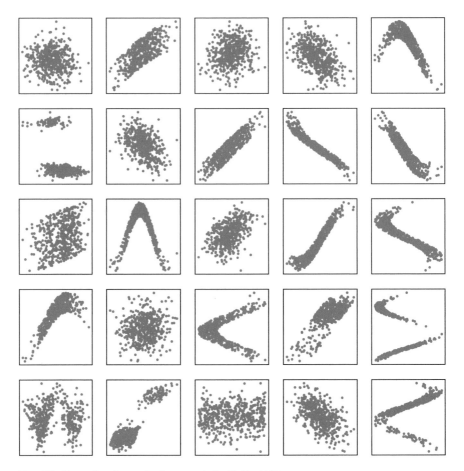

Fig. 4.3 Examples of causal pairs generated with Eq. (4.3)

are sine functions. The causes follow either a Gaussian distribution or a Gaussian mixture distribution; and the noise is additive and is sampled from a Gaussian or a uniform distribution. The causal mechanisms sums up to:

$$Y = \sin(\omega X + \varphi) + E \tag{4.3}$$

with E the noise variable, ω and φ the frequency and phase parameters of the sine function, sampled in $\mathcal{N}_{0,1} \times \mathcal{U}[-\pi, \pi]$. Examples of generated pairs is given in Fig. 4.3. One of the perks of this dataset is the varying complexity of the generated pairs: as ω tends to 0, some of the generated pairs tend to the unidentifiable case of Gaussian input, Gaussian noise and linear mechanism. On the opposite end, when ω takes high values the pairs come down to high frequency sinuses, in which the noise might confuse the pair.

All code of experiments performed in this section is available at: https://github.com/Diviyan-Kalainathan/ChapterV-Causal-Pairs-Book.

4.3.1 Handcrafted Causal Features

An intuitive way to obtain features out of empirical distributions for this new learning problem is to use the output of preexisting causal discovery algorithms, but also feature characterizing the joint and marginal distributions of the samples. In this section we will discuss the different types of features that can be employed as features for the classifier, while giving some examples of those features.

4.3.1.1 Statistical Features of the Distributions

In the Cause-Effect pair challenge (Appendix 1), all participants included independence tests in their algorithms: either to avoid testing for causal relationships if the variables are independent,[6] or to maximize the accuracy of the predictions as a class in the challenge was dedicated to independent pairs.

The independence test statistics used consist in mainly two types: the correlation-based and the kernel-based tests. Firstly, the correlation-based tests consist in the well-known statistic tests such as the Pearson's correlation and the Spearman's correlation, but also tests based on mutual information. The challenges contained all types of data, including continuous data. In order to compute mutual information out of the empirical distributions, algorithms binned their continuous variables prior to computing mutual information based features. In this section we will consider U, V, obtained by binning X and Y. Examples of these features are mutual information, normalized mutual information [27] and adjusted mutual information [51].

Mutual Information Mutual information is a quantity measuring dependence in information theory, basing itself on how the knowledge of one variable reduces the uncertainty on the other variable. In our case, this quantity can be expressed as:

$$I(U, V) = \sum_{i=1}^{|U|} \sum_{j=1}^{|V|} \frac{|U_i \cap V_j|}{N} \log \frac{N|U_i \cap V_j|}{|U_i||V_j|} \tag{4.4}$$

where U, V represent the input variables and U_i, V_j represent the categories of the variables.

---

[6]Therefore assuming Causal Markov.

Normalized Mutual Information Normalized mutual information [27] is a variation of the mutual information score, normalized to range from 0, representing no mutual information, to 1, representing perfect correlation.

$$NMI(U, V) = \frac{2I(U, V)}{H(U) + H(V)} \tag{4.5}$$

where H represents the entropy. However, this score does not account for chance.

Adjusted Mutual Information Adjusted mutual information has been proposed by Vinh et al. [51] to solve this issue, that takes into account the number of samples in each category:

$$AMI(U, V) = \frac{I(U, V) - E(I(U, V))}{\frac{1}{2}(H(U) + H(V)) - E(I(U, V))} \tag{4.6}$$

4.3.1.2 Statistical Asymmetries in the Distribution

In the cause effect pairs challenge, many statistical quantities have been used to highlight patterns and asymmetries that might provide hints of the causal direction. These features come in different natures: information theory, regression based or statistical properties. The latter denotes features such as moments of the empirical distributions, and moments of regression residuals. These quantities are computed for the learning machine following in the pipeline (Fig. 4.2) to lever these features in order to detect causal patterns in the distributions.

Regression Based Features Regression based features represent the majority of features in algorithms using predefined features. They come in various forms, such as the errors of polynomial regressions of various degrees, independence of the residuals with the cause of the polynomial regression. Features of conditional distribution variability have been introduced by Fonollosa [13]. One of those, called **standard deviation of the conditional distributions** (CDS) manages to achieve good performance even when used alone. The CDS score measures the spread of the conditional distributions after normalization of the bins:

$$CDS(X, Y) = \sqrt{\frac{1}{M} \sum_{y=0}^{M-1} var_x(p_n(Y = y | X = x))} \tag{4.7}$$

where $p_n(Y = y | X = x)$ represents the normalized conditional probability and var_x the sample variance over x. This feature proved itself very useful for causality detection, as it captures the distribution asymmetry; typically, it standalone yields a score of 0.69 on the Tübingen dataset [33].

4.3.1.3   Preexisting Pairwise Causal Discovery Algorithms

Many approaches basing their inference on predefined features [13, 40] use as input of the classifier already known models for pairwise causal discovery in a stacked classifier fashion. Examples of used algorithms are the Additive Noise Model (ANM) model [21] or the Information Geometric Causal Inference (IGCI) model [12]. These two models are the most employed, as they represent a decent tradeoff between performance and computational cost.

   We will briefly present these two algorithms, as a more detailed description is made in Chapter III.

Additive Noise Model Additive noise model [21] is one of most popular approaches for pairwise causal discovery. As said, it bases itself of the hypothesis that the causal mechanism is a structural equation model based on a additive noise:

$$Y = f(X) + E \qquad (4.8)$$

where f is a (possibly non-linear) function and E is a noise variable independent from the cause X. If the ANM fits in one direction and not in the other, the causal direction is identifiable.

Information Geometric Causal Inference Information geometric causal inference [12] takes on another approach to infer the causal direction in the pairwise setting. It bases itself on the independence between the cause and the causal mechanism: under the strong assumption that X and Y are related by a bijective relation,[7] the cause P_X is independent from the mechanism $P_{Y|X}$ and not in the opposite direction. This approach can also be related to a complexity approach on the mechanisms [33].

4.3.1.4   Applying Transformations to Variables

Beyond computing all the above-mentioned features on the empirical distributions given as input, Almeida [1] and Fonollosa [13] also compute additional sets of the same features, but by changing the input variables by applying transformations. These transformations come in various forms, such as conversions from one type of variable to another, aggregating the distributions, or computing regressions and using the residuals as the new variables.

   This kind of transformations allow for computing higher order statistics and to grow the number of features considerably, as such transformations can be stacked multiple times before computing the various features.

---

[7]Therefore assuming minimal noise.

4.3.2 Building Distribution Embeddings

Another approach to feature construction for pairwise causal discovery is to use distribution embeddings to represent the distribution samples in a latent space as a vector with a fixed number of features. Unlike computing a custom set of variables (Sect. 4.3.1), this approach represents each distribution in a latent space and the learning algorithm learns to split this latent space into the different classes. Inference of unseen pairs consist in applying the embedding to the distribution and reporting the label assigned to the region in the latent space corresponding to the image of the sample. One could see this operation as to look for the closest distribution in the training set to the sample and assign its label. Appendix 3 develops the bounds given in Appendix 2 for a kernel-based preprocessing instead of assuming the optimality of the feature construction.

In this section, we will focus on two types of embeddings: kernel-based embeddings of the joint distribution (Sect. 4.3.2.1) and embeddings of the conditional distributions (Sect. 4.3.2.2).

4.3.2.1   Kernel Based Embeddings

Kernel embeddings for learning machines have proven themselves to achieve great performance through strong representational power [6, 44]. To leverage this performance, Lopez-Paz et al. [29] introduced kernel-based embedding for feature construction in pairwise causal discovery. Starting from the dataset of empirical distributions $S = \{(x_{ij}, y_{ij})_{j=1}^{n_i}\}_{i=1}^{n}$, a kernel mean embedding allows to project all those empirical distributions into the same Reproducing Kernel Hilbert Space (RKHS) $\mathcal{H}_k$. To obtain a homogeneous and low dimension embedding, Lopez-Paz et al. [29] uses random cosine based embeddings that approximate empirical kernel mean embeddings in low dimension:

$$\mu_{k,m}(P_{S_j}) = \frac{2C_k}{|S|} \sum_{x_{ij}, y_{ij} \in S_j} (\cos(w_j^x * x_{ij} + w_j^y * y_{ij} + b_j))_{j=1}^{m} \in \mathbb{R}^m \qquad (4.9)$$

where $\{w_j, b_j\}_{j=1}^{m}$ are the kernel parameters sampled i.i.d. in $\mathbb{N}_{0,2} \times [0, 2\pi]$, as well as their number m defining the number of dimensions of the output space, P_S is the empirical distribution, and $C_k = \int_{\mathcal{X}} p_k(w)dw$, with $p_k : \mathbb{R}^d \mapsto \mathbb{R}$ the positive and integrable Fourier transform of the chosen kernel k, equal to 1 in this case.

Illustration Using the Sine Dataset (Sect. 4.3)   We will now highlight the performance of the kernel mean embeddings using the dataset introduced at the beginning of this section. By applying the embedding and by reducing the dimension of the output feature space using T-SNE [31], we obtain Fig. 4.4. T-SNE is a projection technique that allows for visualization of high dimension spaces, compressing information into local information: close points in the original space are close in

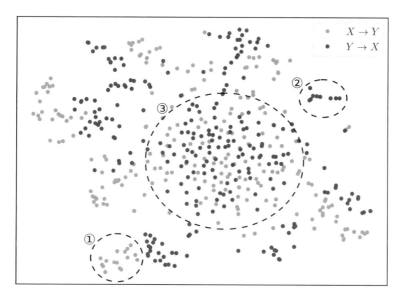

Fig. 4.4 T-SNE of the sine dataset with random mean kernel embeddings. Each point represents a causal pair $\{x_i, y_i\}_{i=1}^{n_j}$ sampled following Eq. (4.3) and a unique set of parameters ω and ϕ. The label of the respective pair is represented by its color

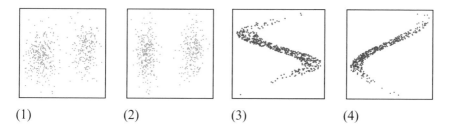

Fig. 4.5 Scatter plots of causal pairs in distinct clusters, their number refer to those in Fig. 4.4. (1) $X \rightarrow Y$ pair in ①. (2) $X \rightarrow Y$ pair in ①. (3) $Y \rightarrow X$ pair in ②. (4) $Y \rightarrow X$ pair in ②

the projected space. One can notice on Fig. 4.4 that multiple small homogeneous clusters (from the same class) emerge (such as ① and ②), along with a large central heterogeneous cluster (③). The small clusters highlight the efficiency of the embedding approach to distinguish classes: Fig. 4.5 shows examples of pairs from these distinct clusters, which causal direction is easily identifiable. The pairs composing the same cluster present also the same characteristics of distributions. However, the embedding shows the large cluster ③ is composed by samples from both classes, making these hard to distinguish. Indeed, as shown by scatter plots of some of those pairs in Fig. 4.6, those pairs are hardly identifiable, even though they were labelled and generated by Eq. (4.3). These pairs represent distributions sampled from Eq. (4.3), using a small value of ω and a small signal/noise ratio.

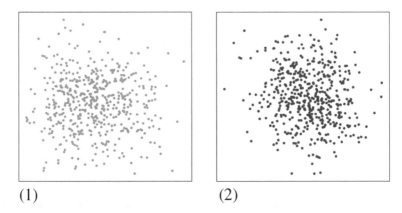

(1)   (2)

Fig. 4.6 Scatter plots of causal pairs in the middle cluster in Fig. 4.4. The causal direction is unclear as seen on the scatter plots. (1) $X \to Y$ pair in ③. (2) $Y \to X$ pair in ③

4.3.2.2 Embeddings of the Conditional Distributions

In order to highlight the asymmetries in the distributions, Mitrovic et al. [32] has introduced embeddings on the conditional distributions $P_{Y|X}$ and $P_{X|Y}$ instead of the joint distribution. This allows for distinguishing asymmetries along with building an embedding of the distribution. In [32], the proposed conditional embedding is based on the Gaussian kernel along with an α quantity that performs as conditioning:

$$\mu_{k,M}(P_{S_j}) = \left\{ \sum_{j=1}^{n_i} \alpha_j(y) k_m(\cdot, x_j), \sum_{j=1}^{n_i} \alpha_j(x) k_m(\cdot, y_j) \right\}_{m \in M} \tag{4.10}$$

with $\alpha(y) = (\mathbf{L} + n\lambda\mathbf{I})^{-1}\mathbf{l}_y$, $\mathbf{L} = [l(y_i, y_j)]_{i,j=1}^n$, $\mathbf{l}_y = [l(y_1, y), \ldots, l(y_n, y)]^T$, $\alpha(\cdot) = [\alpha_1(\cdot), \ldots, \alpha_n(\cdot)]^T$, regularization parameter λ, identity matrix $\mathbf{I}$, and M the set of parameters for the kernel k.

4.3.3 Automatic Feature Construction out of Distributions

Kernel embeddings allow for a general and strong representation of the distributions. However, these representation are not specific to the problem of pairwise causal discovery and therefore some patterns might be missed by those. Therefore, adapting the embeddings to the given distributions and to the task through learning allow the algorithms to automatically distinguish relevant patterns in the distributions, thus merging the last two steps of the four-step procedure described in Fig. 4.2.

This paradigm fits with "Deep Learning" or more generally into the "Automatic Machine Learning" concept in which only the data has to be fed to the algorithm with no further domain specific knowledge. This merges representation learning and supervised learning: the algorithms learn their own features based on the given data and task.

4.3.3.1   Learning an Custom Embedding from the Samples

Going from empirical distributions to a fixed-size vector representing the learnt relevant features implies a dimension reduction operation. Lopez-Paz et al. [30] leverages mean embeddings to perform this operation: after applying a transformation to each point in the sample, all outputs are averaged to produce the feature vector representing the sample. This process can be summed up by the following equation:

$$\mu(P_{S_j}) = \frac{1}{n_j} \sum_{i=1}^{n_j} f(x_i, y_j) \tag{4.11}$$

where f is a function with learnable parameters, n_j is the number of points in the sample $S_j = \{x_i, y_i\}_{i=1}^{n_j}$. In [30], the f function is represented by a neural network learnt by backpropagation.

Application on the Sine Dataset   By applying the same methodology as in Sect. 4.4.2, we train neural network-based mean embeddings using NCC (c.f. Sect. 4.4.3.1) [30], and then we plot the embeddings (in 20 dimensions) of the pairs using T-SNE [31]. The results shown in Fig. 4.7, denotes a much clearer separation between the two classes than in Fig. 4.4, therefore highlighting the effectiveness of such automatic feature construction.

4.3.3.2   Visual Patterns on the Joint Distribution

Another idea to represent the empirical distribution into a fixed-size two dimensional object would be to represent the pair given as input as a scatter plot; the algorithms would then try to visually identify causal patterns in the drawn scatter plot. This approach, exploited by Singh et al. [46] through a deep convolutional neural network, aligns itself with the examples and the idea that non-invertible causal mechanisms (a visually noticeable feature) give away the causal direction.

Many different visual representations of the distributions are available to the practitioners, and little is known on their influence. We will focus on two of them: the "raw" scatter plot of the data, where a pixel is either 1 or 0 depending on whether a data point is present in the region represented by the pixel. The second is obtained by considering a Gaussian distribution centered on each point, with a relatively low

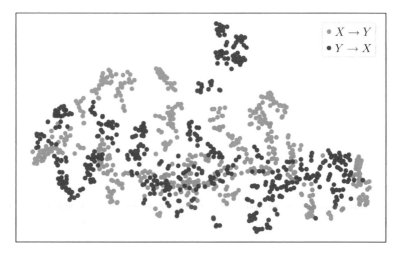

Fig. 4.7 T-SNE of the sine dataset with trained kernel embeddings after 2000 epochs. Each point represents a causal pair $\{x_i, y_i\}_{i=1}^{n_j}$ and the label of the respective pair is represented by its color

variance. The following equations sum up these two approaches:

$$\mu_{\text{raw}}[i, j] = \begin{cases} 1 \text{ if } \exists (x, y) \in S, (x * r, y * r) \in [i, i + 1] \times [j, j + 1] \\ 0 \text{ otherwise} \end{cases} \quad (4.12)$$

where r represents the chosen resolution of the image.

$$\mu_{\text{gaussian}}[i, j] = A \sum_{x, y \in S} e^{-\left(\frac{(x-i)^2}{2\sigma_1^2} + \frac{(y-j)^2}{2\sigma_2^2}\right)} \quad (4.13)$$

where A and $\sigma_1, sigma_2$ represent respectively the amplitude and the standard deviation of the Gaussian distributions.

The outputs given by those two approaches is illustrated in Fig. 4.8. Singh et al. [46] highlighted the influence of some preprocessing methods; they claim that "raw" scatter plot are better for numerical variables as it allows for detection of subtle causal patterns (Fig. 4.8(1), (2)), whereas density based scatter plots are more suited to categorical variables, as "raw" scatter plot can sum up to grid-like images (Fig. 4.8(3), (4)).

Experiment Using Gradient Visualization We will now perform an experiment consisting in training a convolutional neural network on the above-mentioned sine dataset, and in a second step visualize which pattern triggers the prediction of a causal direction by using Grad-CAM [45], a recent visualization technique. The convolutional neural network consists in three convolutional layers, taking as input 64×64 pixels images and producing 4096 features fed into three layers of dense

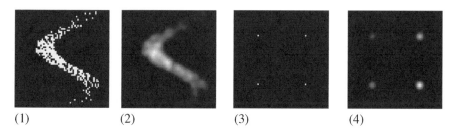

(1)   (2)   (3)   (4)

Fig. 4.8 Scatter plots using either Eq. (4.12) for (1, 3) and Eq. (4.13) for (2, 4). (1) Raw scatter plot. (2) Density based plot. (3) Raw scatter plot of a binary pair. (4) Density based plot of a binary pair

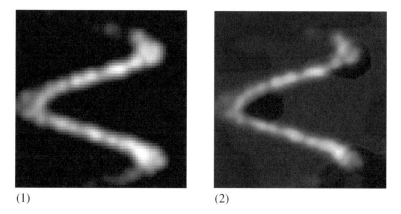

(1)   (2)

Fig. 4.9 Gradient sensitivity analysis of a $Y \rightarrow X$ causal pair using Grad-CAM [45], X being on the X-axis and Y on the Y-axis. (1) Original scatter plot of a $Y \rightarrow X$ pair given as input. (2) Heatmap of the gradient for the $Y \rightarrow X$ class

layers. The network is trained using Adam [26], and converges rather quickly using minibatches of 32 images. After applying Grad-CAM, we obtain Fig. 4.9(2), which highlights that the network uses the non-invertible characteristic of the given causal pair as it looks vertically for the point where a value of X has multiple images in Y, therefore highlighting the non-injectivity of the mechanism function in the $Y = F(X, E)$ hypothesis.

4.4 Overview of Algorithms Using the Mother Distribution Framework

This section reviews the main pairwise causal discovery algorithms participating in the Challenges (Appendix 1), distinguishing three categories of pre-processing methodologies: (1) manually defined features describing the empirical distributions

(Sect. 4.3.1); (2) features based on the kernelization of the empirical distributions (Sect. 4.4.2); and (3) latent features based on neural net-based change of representations (Sect. 4.4.3). As said, standard learning algorithms are used on the top of the pre-processing phase (Sect. 4.4.1) to learn classifiers and predict the causal label associated with an empirical joint distribution. To avoid redundancy with the previous section, the feature construction step of algorithms will be briefly presented.

4.4.1 Learning Algorithms

For the sake of self-containedness, this section briefly presents the long known supervised learning algorithms used in causal discovery algorithms, referring the reader to [5] for a more comprehensive introduction. Throughout this section, we will refer to the original software provided by the authors, but many of them are available at https://github.com/Diviyan-Kalainathan/CausalDiscoveryToolbox.

4.4.1.1 Decision Trees

A decision tree is a tree-like graph model, hierarchically testing conditions on the data features until arriving in a tree leaf, here associated with a causal class (Fig. 4.10). Decision tree learning [8] iteratively proceeds by determining the most informative feature depending on the current training set. In a classification context, one selects the feature maximizing an information score (e.g. information gain or Gini score; $f^* = \arg\min \sum_v p(f(x) = v) \sum_c p(y = c|f(x) = v)log(p(y = c|f(x) = v))$ and the training data is split according to the value of the selected feature; in a regression context, one selects the feature maximizing the variance of the label conditionally to the feature value ($f^* = \arg\min \sum_v Var(y|f(x) = v)$).

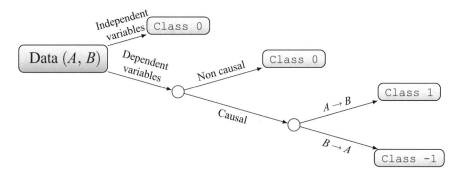

Fig. 4.10 Example of decision tree based on two features: an independence test and a confounder test; the class is the causal label

4.4.1.2 Random Forests

Random forests [9] address the main limitation of decision trees, namely their potential to overfit small- or medium-sized data through hyper-parameter setting. Given d features, random forests build a large number of decision trees, independently learned using a fraction of the available features (classically, $\sqrt{d}$) and a random subset of the training samples; these trees are aggregated using a vote procedure (bagging). Random forests are celebrated for their excellent empirical performance and computational efficiency. An extension of random forests, ExtraTrees [17] proceed by selecting the splitting condition uniformly (uniformly selecting the feature and the splitting condition in the feature range).

4.4.1.3 Neural Networks

Like decision trees, neural nets (NNs) have extensively been used since the 1980s for their computational efficiency, versatility and performance. A neural net is a set of interconnected computational units called neurons, delivering an output computed in a non-linear way from its weighted input. NN learning consists of adjusting the weights in order to optimize the learning criterion (e.g. cross-entropy in the classification context; mean-square error in the regression context). In the standard case of feedforward NN (acyclic computational graph), the weights are optimized using stochastic gradient descent as long as all terms involved in the learning criterion are differentiable. The computational efficiency of large neural net learning is related to the use of highly parallel computational architectures such as Graphical Processing Units (GPUs) [38]. The stacking of many neuronal layers, yielding deep NNs, supports the building of increasingly abstract features and delivers applicative breakthroughs (see [18] for an overview).

4.4.1.4 Boosting Methods

Boosting [42] is a term to qualify meta-algorithms that base themselves on many small algorithms, added sequentially as an ensemble method. To each classifier a weight is assigned to measure its relevance for the current classification task. The misclassified training examples are weighted so the following classifiers added to the ensemble improve the performance of the ensemble by focusing on those examples. Well known examples of boosting methods are Adaboost [14] and Xgboost [10].

Two methods, using decision trees on the top of manually defined features, with good performance in the Cause-Effect pairs challenges, are **ProtoML** (Sect. 4.4.1.5) and **Jarfo** (Sect. 4.4.1.6).

4.4.1.5 ProtoML

Description ProtoML [1] won the 2013 Cause-Effect pairs challenge on Kaggle. It is based on a pipeline, generating and selecting and generating very many features (up to 20,000+), and achieving supervised learning on the top of the selected features; overall, it aims at minimal human intervention.

Feature Construction Feature construction is based on multiple feature patterns, a feature pattern being a valid set of conversion functions followed by an aggregation function if the feature function outputs a multi-dimensional value. All possible feature patterns are applied to the data.

Learning Algorithm Learning algorithm is a gradient boosted decision tree ensemble [15] is learned on the top of the extensive set of features thus created, and the learned classifier predicts the causal direction associated with an empirical distribution.

Computational Cost Computational cost is the main limitation of the approach is its learning and prediction computational times (as all features involved in the learned classifier have to be computed for each sample). After the competition, another algorithm named **autocause** based on ProtoML was proposed by the same author, using much fewer features with a huge computational gain at the expense of a slight performance loss.

4.4.1.6 Jarfo

Description Jarfo [13], one of the best performing algorithms over both challenges, operates as follows: (1) a type-dependent preprocessing of the input variables is applied; (2) information theoretic measures and other causally relevant features are computed; (3) a gradient boosting classifier. It is rather popular due to the robust performance/computational cost ratio that it offers.

Feature Construction The preprocessing of the initial variables goes as follows. Numerical variables are normalized and binned along 19 intervals to compute features such as discrete mutual information or discrete entropy. Categorical variables are relabelled with sorted probabilities to obtain numerical variables. Information-theoretic measures include discrete entropy, mutual information, divergence, and standard deviation on conditional distributions (CDS). Extra features, commonly used in conditional discovery, are computed: Hilbert Schmit Independence Criterion (HSIC), moments, the IGCI score [23] for causal discovery, a Pearson correlation and a polynomial fit on the variables, and the obtained residual of the fit.

Learning Algorithm Learning algorithm is a gradient boosting classifier based on the previous features is trained using a tenfold cross-validation.

Computational Cost Computational cost is average, and is dependent on the number of computed features.

4.4.2   Learning over Distribution Embeddings

The second category of pre-processing uses kernel-based representations of distributions. This randomized functional representation of distributions, exploited using random forest learning, yields the Random Causation Coefficient (RCC) [29] with good accuracy and computational efficiency. This idea was extended by Mitrovic et al. [32] for embeddings of conditional distributions.

4.4.2.1   Randomized Causation Coefficient

Description   RCC [29] introduces kernel embeddings of distributions to pairwise causal discovery, while producing robust performance: standalone precision score above 0.80 on the Tüebingen dataset, and third place on the fast causation challenge [20].

Feature Construction   Feature construction is based on projecting empirical distributions into a RKHS using random mean kernel embeddings, the causal pairs being classified in this new space (c.f. Sect. 4.4.2).

Learning Algorithm   Learning algorithm is a decision tree learning directly over the kernel space.

Computational Cost   Computational cost for this approach is very attractive as the feature construction step is summed up as a projection into a latent space using a random feature matrix.

4.4.2.2   Kernel Conditional Deviance for Causal Inference

Description   Kernel Conditional Deviance for Causal Inference (KCDC) [32] is an algorithm that extends the approach of [29] regarding embeddings of distributions, by applying it to conditional distributions instead of the joint distributions. It achieves an accuracy score of 78.7% the Tüebingen dataset.

Feature Construction   As explained more throughoutly in Sect. 4.3.2.2, the embedding is built using the Gaussian kernel along with a conditioning quantity α.

Learning Algorithm   Learning algorithm ranges from a difference between scores of different parameter sets to a random forest algorithms depending on the version of the algorithm used. Another well performing algorithm is a majority vote between the outputs of the scores.

Computational Cost   Computational cost is rather low as the algorithm has a simple decision algorithm and the feature construction step is straightforward.

4.4.3 Mapping Distributions onto Latent Spaces

A general trend in Machine Learning, best exemplified by Deep Learning [18], aims to seamlessly and autonomously integrate representation learning and supervised learning. This subsection presents two algorithms mapping the empirical joint distributions onto a latent space.

4.4.3.1 Neural Causal Coefficient

Description As said (Eq. (4.21)), the random causation coefficient approach proposed by Lopez-Paz et al. [29] is based on a predefined kernel matrix capturing the distribution sample. In a further work, Lopez-Paz et al. [30] learn this feature matrix using a multilayer perceptron. The data sample is sequentially supplied to the NN, and the corresponding outputs are averaged to define a single point, submitted to the classifier NCC:

$$\text{NCC}(\{(x_i, y_i)\}_{i=1}^m) = \psi \left(\frac{1}{m} \sum_{i=1}^m \phi(x_i, y_i) \right), \tag{4.14}$$

where both classifier ψ and representation ϕ are simultaneously trained as neural networks from the sample data.

Feature Construction Feature construction is a neural network, processing each data point before computing the average of all points of a distribution sample (c.f. Sect. 4.3.3.1).

Learning Algorithm Learning algorithm is also a neural network, taking as input the mean embedding of the pairs.

Computational Cost On the one hand, the NCC approach linearly scales with the size of the training set, using stochastic gradient descent to train both classifier ψ and representation ϕ. On the other hand, neural training is known to require large sized datasets. Empirically, NCC standalone achieves a score of 0.79 precision on the Tüebingen dataset [33], matching the score of RCC at a fraction of its cost.

4.4.3.2 Convolutional Neural Networks

Description Finally, another possibility is to view the empirical distribution as an image, and to exploit convolutional neural architectures extensively used in computer vision to learn from such images. Singh et al. [46] exploits scatter plots built from the empirical distributions and uses these to train a convolutional neural network architecture (CNN).

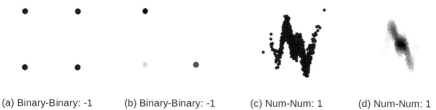

(a) Binary-Binary: -1   (b) Binary-Binary: -1   (c) Num-Num: 1   (d) Num-Num: 1

Fig. 4.11 Scatter plots of binary-binary (**a**, **b**) and numerical-numerical (**c**, **d**) empirical distributions. Raw scatter plots (i.e. data points) are represented in (**a**) and (**c**); colored scatter plots in (**b**) and (**d**) associate to each point its frequency [46]

Feature Construction For numerical variables, the scatter plot is used after a standard normalization. For categorical or binary variables, scatter plots usually are uninformative (Fig. 4.11), and this issue is addressed by coloring the points with the normalized frequency of the observations.

Learning Algorithm The CNN is used together with a gradient boosted classifier inspired from **Jarfo** [13], delivering a score of 0.825 on the Cause-effect pairs challenge. This score, obtained after the end of the challenge, outperforms that of the challenge winner **ProtoML** [1].

Computational Cost The computational cost is rather low as it leverages the computational efficiency of convolutional neural networks. However the proposed solution as a ensemble method with Jarfo (Sect. 4.4.1.6) makes it quite computationally heavy.

4.5 Discussion

Within the Mother Distribution framework (Sect. 4.2), the pairwise causal discovery problem is cast as a supervised learning problem. The advances made along this formalization, leveraging machine learning algorithms and due to the efforts of all participants to both causality challenges, are impressive (Table 4.1). This section analyses their current limitations and discusses some research perspectives to address them.

4.5.1 Sensitivity to Mother Distributions and Generalization

A primary limitation is due to the examples used to train the classifiers. As widely known, the accuracy of trained classifiers depends on the quality of the training examples. In quite a few causal examples however, the joint distributions present

Table 4.1 The two causality challenges: winning algorithms

(a) Top algorithms of the Cause-Effect Pairs challenge, ProtoML manages to top the leaderboard, having however a significant computational cost

Algorithm	Author	Ladder score
ProtoML[a]	Diogo Moitinho de Almeida	0.820
Jarfo[b]	José A.R. Fonollosa	0.811
FirfID[c]	Spyridon Samothrakis, et al.	0.800

(b) Top algorithms of the Fast Causation Coefficient challenge. RCC manages to obtain a good score while being almost six times faster than Jarfo

Algorithm	Author	Ladder score	Execution time
Jarfo[b]	José A.R. Fonollosa	0.826	1891 s
FastCausation[d]	Wei Zhang	0.818	1057 s
RCC[e]	David Lopez-Paz	0.719	316 s

typical features giving away the causality label, a phenomenon referred to as *data leakage*. Another issue would be the presence of biases in the training set of the classifiers. For example, if the causal pairs with one categorical variable and one numerical variable are always labelled such as categorical $\rightarrow$ numerical, the learning algorithms might learn biased features on distributions due to the training set.

For instance, if we take an example with two numerical quantities but one is sampled regularly; e.g. a physical experiment evaluating the influence of voltage on the perceived luminance of a light bulb typically proceeds by setting the voltage value using a regular grid. The acquisition process thus introduces a substantial bias in the data through the marginal distribution of the cause (Fig. 4.12), with a number of unique values much lower for the cause than for the effect variable.

Such biases hinder the generality of the causality classifiers, as they might be exploited by learning algorithms and induce biased hypotheses.

A second limitation related with the data is their insufficient amount. As far as neural nets and deep learning are involved in the learning process, the quantity of examples also becomes essential. Given the comparatively few variable pairs for which the causality label is known from prior knowledge, many authors thus rely on data augmentation, generating new artificial examples from scratch or by perturbing the available examples [29].

However, theoretical results require that causal classifiers be trained and evaluated on examples following the same Mother Distribution. The empirical results (Table 4.2) also confirm that the classifier accuracy is much better when applied on data following the same Mother Distribution as the training examples. As in all machine learning problem, the simplest setting is the i.i.d. setting in which training and test data are drawn from the same distribution. The same applies to the cause-effect pair problem: higher performance is attained when the pairs are drawn from the same mother distribution. Unfortunately, in many real world applications, one does not know from which "mother distribution" a new incoming pair to be

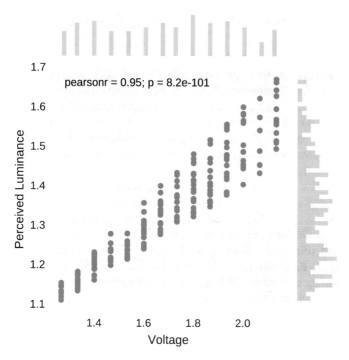

Fig. 4.12   Joint and marginal plots of the voltage/luminance of the light bulb example

Table 4.2 Post-challenge (cause-effect pairs) experiment based on a new 3648 pairs dataset generated with GeneNetWeaver [41]

	Algorithm	Experiment 1	Experiment 2
AUC	Jarfo	**0.873**	**0.997**
	FirfiD	0.596	0.984
	ProtoML	0.8085	0.991
Time	Jarfo	**5 h**	**5 h**
	FirfiD	7 h	8 h
	ProtoML	10 h	12 h

Bold denotes best performance

classified is drawn and one does not have labeled examples of cause-effect pairs from the "mother distribution" of interest.

Both limitations, regarding the quality and the quantity of the training data, can be addressed using Domain Adaptation and Transfer Learning principles [4, 16], adapting classifiers trained from abundant artificial and diversified Mother Distributions to focused application domains.

4.5.2 Refining the Supervised Learning Problem

Variable pairs (X, Y) actually fall in one out of four cases: the causal case $X \to Y$, the anti-causal case $X \leftarrow Y$, the independent case $X \perp\!\!\!\perp Y$, and the confounder case $X \leftarrow Z \to Y$. For convenience, the four cases are handled using a single continuous causation coefficient $L(X, Y)$, positive in the causal case and negative in the anti-causal case, and both the independence and the confounder case are associated with a low absolute value of $L(X, Y)$. In all generality however, a low value of $L(X, Y)$ might reflect either the independence of both variables, or the uncertainty regarding the causal direction.

A perspective for further research thus consists in extending the proposed framework, and associate with each variable pair (X, Y) two continuous scores, noted $(\lambda_{X,Y}, \lambda_{Y,X}) \in \mathbb{R}_+^2$, respectively characterizing the causal and anti-causal strength of the link between both variables. This pair of scores lends itself to a clear interpretation (Fig. 4.13), enabling to distinguish the independence region where both scores are low, from the region of 2-cycles where both scores are high, from the confounding case where both scores are neither low nor high but similar, from the causal and anti-causal region.

4.5.3 Explaining the Causal Mechanism

Another perspective for further research concerns the explanation of the causal mechanism. Quite a few causal algorithms proceed by identifying the potential

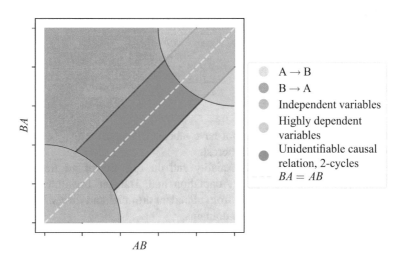

Fig. 4.13 Representation of a two dimension causal coefficient $(\lambda_{AB}, \lambda_{BA})$ and the associated causal interpretations depending on the values of each dimension. Taken from [24]

causal mechanism leading from X to Y and vice-versa, and selecting the causal label depending on the causal mechanism best fitting the data (subject to some limitations on its complexity, as noted in the introduction). It is of utmost interest to the practitioner to "open the black-box" and understand the nature of the underlying causal mechanism, typically distinguishing four cases depending on the influence of the noise variable E:

- $Y = f(X) + E$ (Post-additive)
- $Y = f(X) \times E$ (Post-multiplicative)
- $Y = f(X + E)$ (Pre-additive)
- $Y = f(X \times E)$ (Pre-multiplicative)

A potential approach would be to extend and apply the Automated Statistician [25, 28] to uncover the nature of the causal mechanism, making a leap towards explainable causal learning.

4.6 Conclusion

Pairwise causal discovery has shown itself as a slightly particular machine learning problem: in fact, the samples are not represented by single vectors of features, but by empirical distributions which number of samples is not fixed. However, literature has quickly adapted itself through the cause-effect pair challenges [19, 20] by adding a feature construction step before its traditional learning algorithm. Algorithms have taken different paths to build their features: off the shelf features of distributions, embeddings of distributions, or even learning those embeddings. Finally, discriminative learning machines have proven themselves to be quite useful for pairwise causal discovery as their accuracy exceeded 80%.

Acknowledgements The authors want to thank David Lopez-Paz for many discussions and insights, and Corentin Tallec for his insightful feedback. The second author was funded on a grant from *La Fabrique de l'Industrie*.

Appendix 1: The Cause-Effect Pair Challenges

Two challenges pioneering the above causal setting were organized by ChaLearn [19, 20]. This section reports on the data and the experimental setting of both challenges, together with their results.

Kaggle Cause-Effect Pair Challenge

The Cause-Effect Pair Challenge organized in 2013 on the Kaggle platform by Guyon [19] is the first competition focusing on pairwise causal discovery, pioneering the supervised learning setting presented in Sect. 4.2. The training data involves 12,081 pairs of variables; the test data involves 4050 other pairs of variables. Each pair of variables is associated its ground truth causal label, ranging in four classes respectively corresponding to $X \rightarrow Y$, $X \leftarrow Y$, $X \perp\!\!\!\perp Y$ and $\exists Z, X \leftarrow Z \rightarrow Y$.

The training and test pairs of variables included circa 18% real pairs and 82% artificial pairs with continuous, categorical and binary variables.

Real Data Real data originate from multiple domains: demographics, medicine, ecology, genetics, economics and engineering. The causal labels are determined by considering exogenous variables as causes or independent variables, and using prior knowledge to assess the plausibility of the causal relationship. For example, the causal label of pair $(Age, Wage)$ is $Age \rightarrow Wage$ as (1) interventions on the $Wage$ variable do not affect the Age variable; (2) Age increase does increase the $Wage$ due to the seniority bonus. The circa 4000 real pairs included in the challenge are equidistributed among the three causal relationship classes. Independent pairs are built by randomly shuffling one of the variables, thus breaking the causal relationship. The generation of pairs falling in class 4 (involving a confounding variable) proceeds by (1) considering a real pair X, Y; (2) generating three artificial variables $Z, \tilde{X}, \tilde{Y}$ such that $\tilde{X} \leftarrow Z \rightarrow \tilde{Y}$; (3) replacing $\tilde{X}$ values by X values using a monotonous transformation, and likewise replacing $\tilde{Y}$ values by Y values. Care was taken to make sure that the causal relationship between X and Y could not be determined solely on the basis of simple statistics of the marginal distributions of X and Y: all variables were standardized and quantized on a number of levels distributed similarly for X and Y in all four causal relationship classes.

Artificial Data Artificial data are generated by perturbing real-world data as follows. The cause variable X is selected among the real variables, and the effect variable Y is generated using four causal equations involving a fixed causal mechanism f and an additive or multiplicative noise E:

1. $Y = f(X) + E$
2. $Y = f(X) \times E$
3. $Y = f(X + E)$
4. $Y = f(X \times E)$

Performance Metric The hypothesis learned by either a classification or a regression algorithm associates with each variable pair X, Y an estimated causation coefficient $\widehat{C(X, Y)}$ in $\mathbb{R}$; a positive $\widehat{C(X, Y)}$ is interpreted as X causing Y while a negative $\widehat{C(X, Y)}$ is interpreted as Y causing X. Two criteria are considered: L_1 denotes the Area Under the ROC Curve (AUC) associated with the prediction of $X \rightarrow Y$ against the other three classes, and L_2 denotes the AUC associated with the prediction of $X \leftarrow Y$ against the other three classes. The score of the algorithm is the half sum of both AUCs. While this score does not directly account for class 0 (independent variables or dependent variables due to a confounding variable), this class is implicitly taken into account through the pair ordering based on $\widehat{C(X, Y)}$, as wrongly classified independent pairs penalize one of the AUC scores.

Codalab Fast Causation Coefficient Challenge

Most approaches submitted to the Cause-Effect Pair Challenge involve a heavy feature construction process, associating to each sample of any joint distribution $P(X, Y)$ a real-valued vector of feature values (up to 20,000 features), on the top of which a standard learning algorithm is used. Due to the high computational effort required to achieve this statistical feature construction, a follow-up 2-month challenge, the Fast Causation Coefficient challenge has been proposed by Guyon [20], aimed at algorithms achieving a reasonable trade-off between predictive causal accuracy and computational efficiency. The assessment of algorithms was made possible as the Fast Causation Coefficient challenge (with same setting as the previous challenge) was hosted on the Codalab challenge platform. This Codalab platform allows participants to submit an executable code, that can therefore be assessed in a fair and reproducible way.

Results of the Challenges

The Cause-Effect Pair Challenge spanned over 5 months in 2013. Two hundred and sixty-six teams participated to the competition and submitted over 4578 entries. As said, most submissions relied on a two step procedure: (1) data pre-processing and computation of predefined statistical features describing the empirical distributions; (2) learning of a classifier on top of these features. The pre-processing and the feature extraction were diversified, ranging from normalization, binning numerical variables and grouping categorical variables, to independence tests, entropy measures, and computing fit residuals. On the contrary, the classifiers used were mainly based on decision trees or random forests (85%).

The results obtained[8] were quite promising (Table 4.1) with a final score of 0.82 on the test set (where the score is the half sum of the AUCs associated with the $X \to Y$ and the $X \leftarrow Y$ classes).

The best performing algorithms were further tested using an additional 3648 new cause-effect pair benchmark generated by the organizers using the GeneNetWeaver 3.0 software [41] based on the E. Coli transcriptional regulatory network. Two

---

[8]The monetary rewards ranged from 1500 USD (with 1000 USD for travel expenses) to 500 USD for the best performing teams that made their software publicly available.

experiments were performed: the first one was to apply the given algorithms with no training on the new dataset and the second experiment was to train the algorithms on one half of the dataset and to test on the other half. The experiments were conclusive (Table 4.2): the AUC score for the first experiment was of 0.80 for ProtoML and of 0.87 for Jarfo, and over 0.99 for both algorithms on the second experiment. These experiments empirically establish the merit of the winning algorithms.

The goal of the follow-up Fast Causation Coefficient challenge is to reduce the computational cost of causal discovery with no performance loss compared to the first challenge. This challenge attracted seven participants, who were given a light version of the **Jarfo** algorithm,[9] achieving the best performance *vs* computational cost tradeoff on the first challenge. As shown in Table 4.1b, the original version of **Jarfo** by Fonollosa [13] came on top of the ranking. The second algorithm, **FastCausation**, managed to almost preserve **Jarfo** predictive accuracy while reducing the computational cost by 44%. The third **RCC** algorithm used a distribution embedding instead of manual feature extraction, and achieved a score of 0.72 for 17% of the computational cost of **Jarfo**. This follow-up challenge thus deliver practical algorithms, with decent predictive accuracy at an affordable computational cost.

Appendix 2: Error Bounds for a Classical Classification Problem

In this section, we will remind the error bounds for a traditional learning problem, where the goal is to classify samples $\{x_i\}_{i=1}^n$ in the label space $\mathcal{G}$, where x_i is a k-dimensional feature vector. Given a loss function $\mathcal{L}$, the learning goal thus is to find a classifier $h : \mathbb{R}^k \to \mathcal{G}$ with minimal expected risk $R(h)$ [50]:

$$R(h) = \mathbb{E}_{x,g \sim \mathbb{R}^k \times L}[\mathcal{L}(h(x), g)] \tag{4.15}$$

with $g \in \mathcal{G}$ The expected risk is classically related to the empirical risk $\hat{R}(h)$ measured on the available training set:

$$\hat{R}(h) = \frac{1}{n} \sum_{i=1}^{n} \mathcal{L}(h(x_i), g_i) \tag{4.16}$$

The standard loss function is the 0–1 loss $\mathcal{L}_{01}(\hat{g}, g) = |\hat{g} - g|$, for which $R(h)$ comes down to the probability of misclassification. While the consistency of the 0–1 loss is established [7], it defines a non-convex optimization problem. For tractability, real-valued classifiers $f : \mathbb{R}^k \mapsto \mathbb{R}$ are considered [48], and margin-based loss

---

[9]Version that does not include some of the most computationally expensive features.

functions $varphi : \mathbb{R} \rightarrow \mathbb{R}_+$, with $\varphi(f(x), g) = [m - f(x)g]_+$ (where $[A]_+ = max(A, 0)$) are used [3], inducing a smooth optimization problem. The associated expected and empirical risks respectively read:

$$R_\varphi(f) = \mathbb{E}_{x, g \sim \mathbb{R}^k \times \mathscr{L}}[\varphi(f(x), g)] \tag{4.17}$$

$$\hat{R}_\varphi(f) = \frac{1}{n} \sum_{i=1}^{n} \varphi(f(x_i), g_i) \tag{4.18}$$

Letting f^* (respectively $\hat{f}_n$) denote the hypothesis minimizing the expected risk, Eq. (4.17) (resp. the empirical risk, Eq. (4.18)), the excess risk $\mathscr{E}_{\mathscr{F}}(\hat{f}_n)$ is bounded after [7]:

Theorem 4.1 *Let $\mathscr{F}$ be a class of functions mapping $\mathbb{R}^k$ onto $\mathbb{R}$. Let $\varphi : \mathbb{R} \rightarrow \mathbb{R}^+$ be a κ-Lipschitz function such that $\varphi(\epsilon) \geq \mathbb{1}_{\epsilon > 0}$. Let B be a uniform upper bound on $\varphi(-f(\epsilon)\ell)$. Let $\{(x_i, \ell_i)\}_{i=1}^{n} \sim \mathbb{R}^k \times L$ and $\{\sigma_i\}_{i=1}^{n}$ be i.i.d. in $\{1, -1\}$ (Rademacher random signs). Then, with probability at least $1 - \delta$,*

$$\mathscr{E}_{\mathscr{F}}(\hat{f}_n) = R_\varphi(\hat{f}_n) - R_\varphi(f^*) \leq 4\kappa e \left[\sup_{f \in \mathscr{F}} \frac{1}{n} \left| \sum_{i=1}^{n} \sigma_i f(x_i) \right| \right] + B \sqrt{\frac{\log(1/\delta)}{2n}},$$

where the expectation is taken w.r.t. $\{\sigma_i, x_i\}_{i=1}^{n}$.

Naturally, in our case of learning through empirical distributions, the expected risk (and thus the performance of $\hat{f}_n$) crucially depends on the feature construction step mapping each data distribution sample $\mathscr{S}_j$ onto a k-dimensional real-valued vector.

Appendix 3: Error Bounds in the Cause-Effect Pairs Setting for Kernel-Based Embeddings

Lopez-Paz et al. [29] exploits functional representations of empirical distributions based on Reproducing Kernel Hilbert Spaces (RKHS). Letting k denote a kernel on the sample space, given an n-sample $x_1 \ldots x_n$ drawn iid from distribution P, a functional representation of these samples is given as:

$$\mu_k(P) = \frac{1}{n} \sum_{i=1}^{n} k(x_i, \cdot) \tag{4.19}$$

with $\mu_k(P)$ being a function in the RKHS $\mathscr{H}_k$ associated with kernel k. This representation enables to refine Theorem 4.1 as follows:

Theorem 4.2 ([29]) *With same notations as in Theorem 4.1, let $\mathcal{H}_k$ denote the RKHS associated with some bounded, continuous kernel function k, such that $\sup_z k(z,z) \leq 1$. Let $\mathcal{F}_k$ be a class of functions mapping $\mathcal{H}_k$ to $\mathbb{R}$ with Lipschitz constant uniformly bounded by $\kappa_{\mathcal{F}}$. Let $\varphi\colon \mathbb{R} \to \mathbb{R}^+$ be a κ-Lipschitz function such that $\phi(\epsilon) \geq \mathbb{1}_{\epsilon>0}$. Let $\varphi\big(-f(\epsilon)\ell\big) \leq B$ for every $f \in \mathcal{F}_k$, $\epsilon \in \mathcal{H}_k$, and $\ell \in L$. Then, with probability greater than $1 - \delta$ (over all sources of randomness)*

$$\mathcal{E}_{\mathcal{F}}(\hat{f}_n) = R_\varphi(\hat{f}_n) - R_\varphi(f^*) \leq 4\kappa\, R_n(\mathcal{F}_k) + 2B\sqrt{\frac{\log(2/\delta)}{2n}}$$

$$+ \frac{4\kappa\kappa_{\mathcal{F}}}{n} \sum_{i=1}^n \left(\sqrt{\frac{\mathrm{e}_{z\sim P_{S_j}}[k(z,z)]}{n_i}} + \sqrt{\frac{\log(2n/\delta)}{2n_i}} \right),$$

with $R_n(\mathcal{F}_k) = \mathrm{e}\left[\sup_{f\in\mathcal{F}_k} \frac{1}{n} \left| \sum_{i=1}^n \sigma_i f(x_i) \right| \right]$ the Rademacher complexity of $\mathcal{F}_k$.

Theorem 4.2 represents the bound for our causal pairs learning problem with kernel embeddings as features. Compared to Theorem 4.1, an additional term is added to cope with the feature construction step: if the kernel embedding manages to capture all information out of the distributions useful for the classification of the causal pairs, then we obtain the bound given by Theorem 4.1.

Lopez-Paz et al. [29] goes towards a more scalable approach for kernel computation relying on Fourier-based approximations of real-valued and shift invariant kernels [39], defined as:

$$\forall x, x' \in \mathbb{R}^d, k(x, x') = 2C_k\, \mathrm{e}_{w,b}\big[\cos(\langle w, x\rangle + b)\cos(\langle w, x'\rangle + b)\big] \qquad (4.20)$$

where $w \sim \frac{1}{C_k} p_k$, $b \sim \mathcal{U}[0, 2\pi]$, $p_k\colon \mathbb{R}^d \to \mathbb{R}$ is the positive and integrable Fourier transform of k, and $C_k = \int_{\mathbb{Z}} p_k(w)dw$.

For example, the shift-invariant Gaussian kernel with kernel width γ can be approximated using Eq. (4.20) with $p_k(w) = Pr(w|\mathcal{N}(0, 2\gamma I))$, and $C_k = 1$ [29, 36, 37], with linear complexity, as:

$$\hat{v}_m^x(\cdot) = \frac{1}{m} \sum_{i=1}^m 2C_k \cos(\langle w, x\rangle + b)\cos(\langle w, \cdot\rangle + b) \qquad (4.21)$$

with (w_j, b_j) iid sampled in $\mathbb{N}_{0,2} \times [0, 2\pi]$. After [29], this approximation enables to refine Theorem 4.1:

Lemma 4.1 ([29]) *Let $\mathbb{Z} = \mathbb{R}^d$. For any shift-invariant kernel k s.t. $\sup_{z\in\mathbb{Z}} k(z,z) \leq 1$, any fixed $S = \{z_i\}_{i=1}^n \subset \mathbb{Z}$, any probability distribution Q on $\mathbb{Z}$, and any $\delta > 0$, it comes:*

$$\left\| \mu_k(P_S) - \frac{1}{n} \sum_{i=1}^{n} \hat{g}_m^{z_i}(\cdot) \right\|_{L_2(Q)} \leq \frac{2C_k}{\sqrt{m}} \left(1 + \sqrt{2 \log(n/\delta)} \right)$$

with probability greater than $1 - \delta$ over $\{(w_i, b_i)\}_{i=1}^{m}$.

References

1. Diogo Montinho Almeida. Pattern-based causal feature extraction. *Cause-effect Pairs*, (Chapter 10), 2018.
2. Frank Arntzenius. Reichenbach's common cause principle. In Edward N. Zalta, editor, *The Stanford Encyclopedia of Philosophy*. Metaphysics Research Lab, Stanford University, fall 2010 edition, 2010.
3. Peter L Bartlett, Michael I Jordan, and Jon D McAuliffe. Convexity, classification, and risk bounds. *Journal of the American Statistical Association*, 101(473):138–156, 2006.
4. Shai Ben-David, John Blitzer, Koby Crammer, Alex Kulesza, Fernando Pereira, and Jennifer Wortman Vaughan. A theory of learning from different domains. *Machine Learning*, 79(1):151–175, 2010.
5. Chris Bishop. *Pattern Recognition and Machine Learning*. Springer-Verlag New York, 2006.
6. Bernard Boser, Isabelle Guyon, and Vladimir Vapnik. Pattern recognition system using support vectors, July 15 1997. US Patent 5,649,068.
7. Stéphane Boucheron, Olivier Bousquet, and Gábor Lugosi. Theory of classification: A survey of some recent advances. *ESAIM: probability and statistics*, 9:323–375, 2005.
8. Leo Breiman. Classification and regression trees. 1984.
9. Leo Breiman. Random forests. *Machine learning*, 45(1):5–32, 2001.
10. Tianqi Chen and Carlos Guestrin. Xgboost: A scalable tree boosting system. In *Proceedings of the 22nd ACM SIGKDD international conference on knowledge discovery and data mining*, pages 785–794. ACM, 2016.
11. David Maxwell Chickering. Optimal structure identification with greedy search. *JMLR*, 2002.
12. Povilas Daniusis, Dominik Janzing, Joris Mooij, Jakob Zscheischler, Bastian Steudel, Kun Zhang, and Bernhard Schölkopf. Inferring deterministic causal relations. *arXiv*, 2012.
13. José Fonollosa. Conditional distribution variability measures for causality detection. *arXiv*, 2016.
14. Yoav Freund and Robert E Schapire. A decision-theoretic generalization of on-line learning and an application to boosting. *Journal of computer and system sciences*, 55(1):119–139, 1997.
15. Jerome H Friedman. Greedy function approximation: a gradient boosting machine. *Annals of statistics*, pages 1189–1232, 2001.
16. Yaroslav Ganin, Evgeniya Ustinova, Hana Ajakan, Pascal Germain, Hugo Larochelle, François Laviolette, Mario Marchand, and Victor Lempitsky. Domain-adversarial training of neural networks. *Journal of Machine Learning Research*, 17(59):1–35, 2016.
17. Pierre Geurts, Damien Ernst, and Louis Wehenkel. Extremely randomized trees. *Machine learning*, 63(1):3–42, 2006.
18. Ian Goodfellow, Yoshua Bengio, and Aaron Courville. *Deep Learning*. MIT Press, 2016. http://www.deeplearningbook.org.
19. Isabelle Guyon. Chalearn cause effect pairs challenge, 2013. URL http://www.causality.inf.ethz.ch/cause-effect.php.
20. Isabelle Guyon. Chalearn fast causation coefficient challenge. *Codalab platform, ChaLearn*, 2014.
21. Patrik O Hoyer, Dominik Janzing, Joris M Mooij, Jonas Peters, and Bernhard Schölkopf. Nonlinear causal discovery with additive noise models. *NIPS*, 2009.

22. Dominik Janzing and Bernhard Schölkopf. Causal inference using the algorithmic markov condition. *IEEE Transactions on Information Theory*, 56(10):5168–5194, 2010.
23. Dominik Janzing, Joris Mooij, Kun Zhang, Jan Lemeire, Jakob Zscheischler, Povilas Daniušis, Bastian Steudel, and Bernhard Schölkopf. Information-geometric approach to inferring causal directions. *Artificial Intelligence*, 182:1–31, 2012.
24. D. Kalainathan, O. Goudet, I. Guyon, D. Lopez-Paz, and M. Sebag. SAM: Structural Agnostic Model, Causal Discovery and Penalized Adversarial Learning. *ArXiv e-prints*, March 2018.
25. Hyunjik Kim and Yee Whye Teh. Scaling up the Automatic Statistician: Scalable structure discovery using Gaussian processes. In *AISTATS*, volume 84 of *Proceedings of Machine Learning Research*, pages 575–584, 2018.
26. Diederik P Kingma and Jimmy Ba. Adam: A method for stochastic optimization. *arXiv preprint arXiv:1412.6980*, 2014.
27. Tarald O Kvalseth. Entropy and correlation: Some comments. *IEEE Transactions on Systems, Man, and Cybernetics*, 17(3):517–519, 1987.
28. James Robert Lloyd, David Duvenaud, Roger Grosse, Joshua B. Tenenbaum, and Zoubin Ghahramani. Automatic construction and natural-language description of nonparametric regression models. In *AAAI*, 2014.
29. David Lopez-Paz, Krikamol Muandet, Bernhard Schölkopf, and Ilya O Tolstikhin. Towards a learning theory of cause-effect inference. *ICML*, 2015.
30. David Lopez-Paz, Robert Nishihara, Soumith Chintala, Bernhard Schölkopf, and Léon Bottou. Discovering causal signals in images. *CVPR*, 2017.
31. Laurens van der Maaten and Geoffrey Hinton. Visualizing data using t-SNE. *Journal of machine learning research*, 9(Nov):2579–2605, 2008.
32. Jovana Mitrovic, Dino Sejdinovic, and Yee Whye Teh. Causal inference via kernel deviance measures. *arXiv preprint arXiv:1804.04622*, 2018.
33. Joris M Mooij, Jonas Peters, Dominik Janzing, Jakob Zscheischler, and Bernhard Schölkopf. Distinguishing cause from effect using observational data: methods and benchmarks. *JMLR*, 2016.
34. Krikamol Muandet, Kenji Fukumizu, Bharath Sriperumbudur, Bernhard Schölkopf, et al. Kernel mean embedding of distributions: A review and beyond. *Foundations and Trends® in Machine Learning*, 10(1–2):1–141, 2017.
35. Judea Pearl. *Causality*. 2009.
36. Ali Rahimi and Benjamin Recht. Random features for large-scale kernel machines. In *Advances in neural information processing systems*, pages 1177–1184, 2008.
37. Ali Rahimi and Benjamin Recht. Weighted sums of random kitchen sinks: Replacing minimization with randomization in learning. In *Advances in neural information processing systems*, pages 1313–1320, 2009.
38. Rajat Raina, Anand Madhavan, and Andrew Y Ng. Large-scale deep unsupervised learning using graphics processors. In *Proceedings of the 26th annual international conference on machine learning*, pages 873–880. ACM, 2009.
39. Walter Rudin. *Fourier Analysis on Groups*. Wiley, 1962.
40. Spyridon Samothrakis, Diego Perez, and Simon Lucas. Training gradient boosting machines using curve-fitting and information-theoretic features for causal direction detection. 2013.
41. Thomas Schaffter, Daniel Marbach, and Dario Floreano. Genenetweaver: In silico benchmark generation and performance profiling of network inference methods. *Bioinformatics*, 27(16):2263–2270, 2011. wingx.
42. Robert E Schapire. A brief introduction to boosting. 1999.
43. Richard Scheines. An introduction to causal inference. 1997.
44. Bernhard Schölkopf, Alexander Smola, and Klaus-Robert Müller. Kernel principal component analysis. In *International Conference on Artificial Neural Networks*, pages 583–588. Springer, 1997.
45. Ramprasaath R Selvaraju, Michael Cogswell, Abhishek Das, Ramakrishna Vedantam, Devi Parikh, Dhruv Batra, et al. Grad-cam: Visual explanations from deep networks via gradient-based localization. 2017.

46. Karamjit Singh, Garima Gupta, Lovekesh Vig, Gautam Shroff, and Puneet Agarwal. Deep convolutional neural networks for pairwise causality. *arXiv preprint arXiv:1701.00597*, 2017.
47. Peter Spirtes, Clark N Glymour, Richard Scheines, David Heckerman, Christopher Meek, Gregory Cooper, and Thomas Richardson. *Causation, prediction, and search*. MIT Press, 2000.
48. Ingo Steinwart and Andreas Christmann. Support vector machines. *Information Science and Statistics*, 1, 2008.
49. Caroline Uhler, Garvesh Raskutti, Peter Bühlmann, and Bin Yu. Geometry of the faithfulness assumption in causal inference. *The Annals of Statistics*, pages 436–463, 2013.
50. Vladimir N Vapnik. *Statistical learning theory*. Adaptive and learning systems for signal processing, communications and control series. John Wiley & Sons, New York. A Wiley-Interscience Publication, 1998.
51. Nguyen Xuan Vinh, Julien Epps, and James Bailey. Information theoretic measures for clusterings comparison: Variants, properties, normalization and correction for chance. *Journal of Machine Learning Research*, 11(Oct):2837–2854, 2010.
52. Jiji Zhang and Peter Spirtes. Strong faithfulness and uniform consistency in causal inference. In *Proceedings of the Nineteenth conference on Uncertainty in Artificial Intelligence*, pages 632–639. Morgan Kaufmann Publishers Inc., 2002.
53. Kun Zhang and Aapo Hyvärinen. On the identifiability of the post-nonlinear causal model. *UAI*, 2009.

Chapter 5
Cause-Effect Pairs in Time Series with a Focus on Econometrics

Nicolas Doremus, Alessio Moneta, and Sebastiano Cattaruzzo

5.1 Introduction

Let us consider two scalar stochastic processes x_t and y_t, $t \in \mathbb{Z}$, each observed for T realizations. We assume that x_t and y_t are covariance stationary or that Δx_t and Δy_t are covariance stationary. Most time series observed in macroeconomics, for example, belong to this class of processes (see e.g. [29]). If we exclude the possibility that the future can cause the past, but we allow contemporaneous feedback loops due for example to temporal aggregation, there are several possibilities as regards the causal structure between x_t and y_t, which we list here below. We denote causal relationships[1] with directed edges ($\rightarrow$), following the graphical causal models terminology [64].

---

[1]When referring to "causal relationships", we endorse here, in the spirit of Hoover [32], Pearl [55], a structural account of causality: causal relationships are the fundamental, but usually latent, building blocks of the mechanism that has generate the observed data, which we aim at representing through a structural (or causal) model. While a structural model entails probabilistic relations, it contains more information than a statistical model, because it allows us to analyze the effect of interventions (cf. [58]).

N. Doremus (✉)
IUSS Pavia, Pavia, Italy
e-mail: nicolas.doremus@iusspavia.it

A. Moneta
Sant'Anna School of Advanced Studies, Pisa, Italy
e-mail: a.moneta@santannapisa.it

S. Cattaruzzo
Rovira i Virgili University, Tarragona, Spain
e-mail: sebastiano.cattaruzzo@urv.cat

© Springer Nature Switzerland AG 2019
I. Guyon et al. (eds.), *Cause Effect Pairs in Machine Learning*,
The Springer Series on Challenges in Machine Learning,
https://doi.org/10.1007/978-3-030-21810-2_5

(i) The series x_t has a contemporaneous or lagged causal effect on y_t, i.e. $x_i \rightarrow y_{i+s}$ for some i, s such that $i \geq 0, s \geq 0$.

(ii) The series y_t has a contemporaneous or lagged causal effect on x_t, i.e. $y_i \rightarrow x_{i+s}$ for some i, s such that $i \geq 0, s \geq 0$.

(iii) A not-measured series z_t has a contemporaneous or lagged causal effect on both x_t and y_t.

(iv) The causal structure between x_t and y_t can be described by any combination of (i)–(iii).

(v) There is no causal link or path (of any type) linking x_t and y_{t+s}, for any $s \in \mathbb{N}$.

In principle, other, more involute, causal structures are possible between x_t and y_t. For example, the data generating process may have a frequency that is different from the frequency of data collection, so that there are hidden causal structures between the observed variables. This class of structures has been considered in the literature on temporal aggregation in econometrics (see e.g. [17, 18, 50]) and in the literature on subsampling in machine learning (see [10, 36]), but will not be further discussed in this paper. We will also limit our discussion on structures in which variables are well-defined (i.e. they are not aggregate of variables with diverse causal roles) and the causal structures are *time invariant*: i.e. if $x_i \rightarrow w_{i+s}$ given any $s \in \mathbb{Z}$, then this true for all $i \in \mathbb{Z}$, where w can be any variable (included x itself). We will also typically assume that each observed series w_t will be directly causally influenced by its own past, until a certain lag and that each variable at each time unit will be affected, in an additive manner, by one or more independent shock. In other words, we focus on *additive noise models*.

The causal structure between two time series can be represented by a causal graph consisting of nodes for $x_t, \ldots, x_{t-p}, y_t, \ldots, y_{t-p}$, where p is the largest lag by which x_t or y_t can be directly causally influenced. Using the terminology proposed by Chu and Glymour [7], this graph is called a *unit causal graph*. Examples for unit causal graphs are shown in Figs. 5.1 and 5.2, for $p = 2$. Figure 5.1 represents the case in which (i) is true, while Fig. 5.2 represents the case in which (iii) is true. Chu and Glymour [7] notice that a unit causal graph can be extended to *repetitive causal graph* (not shown), including the variables x_t and y_t at a potentially infinite time units. The repetitive causal graph corresponding to the unit causal graph of Fig. 5.1, for example, would include nodes for $x_{t-3}, x_{t-4}, \ldots$, for $y_{t-3}, y_{t-4}, \ldots$ and direct edges from x_{t-s} to y_{t-s}, as well as $x_{t-s-2} \rightarrow y_{t-s}$ and $x_{t-s-1} \rightarrow y_{t-s}$, for any $s \in \mathbb{Z}$.

Fig. 5.1 Unit causal graph for bi-variate time series with both lagged and contemporaneous effects

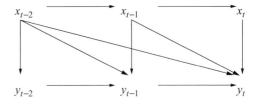

Fig. 5.2 Unit causal graph
for bi-variate time series with
a latent series z_t

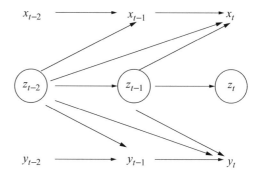

How do we detect which of the five cases listed above (i)–(v) is true? How do we learn which causal graph better represents the data generating process? How do we learn to what extent an intervention on one variable at time t propagates on all the variables at time $t + h$ for any value of $h > 0$? These are the typical questions that concern, for example, the applied macro-econometrician. In this paper we discuss possible manners to address these questions. We review methods that are able to disentangle among different causal structures, under different assumptions.

Some causal discovery methods developed for i.i.d. data cannot be applied, without further modification, to the time series setting, due to the fact that, even in a simple setting of causal pairs, there is the possibility of causal relationships with different effects at different lags. Furthermore, the autocorrelation (or self-dependence) structure underlying the data introduces some complications in standard statistical inference that reduce the efficiency of simple regression estimation or conditional independence testing [26]. Nevertheless, the time series setting is not necessarily a curse, and is actually a blessing in specific contexts of causal inference. Indeed, if one accepts the assumption that the future cannot cause the past (whose acceptance in economics involves a careful taking into account of expectational variables, see [33]), exploiting the arrow of time allows one to solve many *orientation* problems, i.e. problems where it is known that there is a causal dependence between two variables, but not the direction. Moreover, in the case of causal pairs, the possibility of observing past values of the variables allows us to condition on more than two variables, which is not possible in the context of i.i.d. causal pairs.

We shall also notice that if the framework is the one of a causal time-series pair in which only one direction of causal influence is admitted: either $x_t \rightarrow y_s$ (for one or more values of s such that $s \geq t$) or $y_t \rightarrow x_s$ ($s \geq t$) and one is only interested in the "summary graph" [58], i.e. in ascertaining whether x causes y or y causes x at any time unit, then the problem can be solved in a relatively easy fashion in many settings. Using a simple regression analysis, it will be sufficient to regress x_t on lagged values of itself and of the other variable, as well as to regress y_t on lagged values of itself and of the other variable. Since all the covariates in the two regressions are pre-determined there are no endogeneity problems here and the error terms will be independent of the regressors. Therefore, by simple testing the hypothesis of non-zero statistical influence of one lagged variable (e.g. x_{t-1}) on another (e.g. y_t) and the hypothesis of a zero statistical influence on the symmetric regression (e.g. of y_{t-1} on x_t), we will be able to detect a genuine causal influence (at some unknown time unit) from one variable to another (e.g. from x to y). This framework is identical to the vector autoregressive framework that we will discuss below and also related to an interpretation of Granger non-causality test that we will also discuss below. Notice, however, than in many fields like economics the assumption of causality running in only one direction between time series, without the possibility of a feedback at a different time unit, is a toy example, with very poor empirical applicability. This is why our discussion framework will be larger, including the possibility of structures like $y_{t-1} \to x_t \to y_t$.

In reviewing different methods we distinguish between methods that filter the series through a vector autoregressive model (Sect. 5.2.1) and methods that apply causal search directly to time series data (Sect. 5.3).

5.2 Vector-Autoregressive Framework

5.2.1 The VAR Model

One of the most popular approaches to identify dynamic causal effects in time series econometrics is structural vector autoregressive (VAR) analysis. Structural VAR analysis is based on the assumption that the statistical properties of a data generating process can be well approximated by a reduced-form VAR model.

Let us consider a vector Y_t of k time series variables. For example, $Y_t = (x_t, y_t)'$, in which case $k = 2$. We assume that Y_t follows a stochastic process that can be well approximated by a linear VAR process of the form

$$Y_t = \mu + A_1 Y_{t-1} + \cdots + A_p Y_{t-p} + u_t, \tag{5.1}$$

where μ is a $k \times 1$ vector of constants, A_i $(i = 1, \ldots, p)$ is a $k \times k$ matrix and u_t is a $k \times 1$ vector of white noise, whose elements are referred to as *reduced-form residuals*. Each element of u_t is in turn assumed to be a linear combination of latent structural shocks, $\epsilon_{1t}, \epsilon_{2t}, \ldots$, which are the sources of variation of the system. In macroeconomics these shocks have special meaning such as, for example, the productivity shock, the monetary policy shock, the fiscal policy shock, etc. It is standard in the VAR literature to assume that the number of shocks is equal to the number of measured variables. Another usual assumptions is that $\epsilon_{1t}, \ldots, \epsilon_{kt}$ are mutually independent, although orthogonality is sufficient in many applications. Thus we have:

$$u_t = B\varepsilon_t, \tag{5.2}$$

where B is a $k \times k$ invertible matrix (the *impact* or *mixing* matrix) and $\varepsilon_t = (\epsilon_{1t}, \ldots, \epsilon_{kt})'$ is a vector of independent shocks. Let W be B^{-1}. By pre-multiplying Eq. (5.1) by W we get the structural VAR form:

$$WY_t = \mu' + \Gamma_1 Y_{t-1} + \cdots + \Gamma_p Y_{t-p} + \varepsilon_t, \tag{5.3}$$

where $\mu' = W\mu$ and $\Gamma_i = WA_i$ for $i = 1, \ldots, p$. From Eq. (5.1) it is evident that the matrix W incorporates information about the contemporaneous causal structure, while the matrices Γ_i's incorporate information about the lagged causal structure. Since Sims [62], econometricians have focused their attention on the identification of the effect of ε_t on Y_t over time. These are called *impulse response functions*, and we will be discussed in a subsequent Sect. 5.2.4.

Since Eq. (5.3) cannot be directly estimated because of endogeneity problem, the idea of VAR analysis is to follow a two-step procedure: first Eq. (5.1) is estimated through standard regression methods. From this stage one obtains an estimate of the reduced-form residuals u_t. Second, the parameters of Eq. (5.3) (in particular the coefficients entering in W and Γ_i) can be recovered by analyzing the relationships among the elements of u_t, which, under some conditions, may allow identifying the matrix B entering in Eq. (5.2). Notice that, having estimated (5.1), knowing B is sufficient for identifying (5.3).

For example, Swanson and Granger [68], Bessler and Lee [3], Demiralp and Hoover [11], Moneta [52] propose a two-step identification method, consisting in first estimating the reduced-form VAR residuals, and then applying to the estimated u_t (which should share characteristics of i.i.d. data) conditional independence tests, in the spirit of a causal search based on graphical causal models [64]. This allows them to find out which entries of B are zero.

For $k = 2$, as is the case of causal pairs, independence tests between u_{1t} and u_{2t} can only discriminate between the presence and the absence of a causal link between the contemporaneous variables, but are not of any help in finding causal directions. In other words, they find zero entries in B only in the case when u_{1t} and u_{2t} are mutually independent (corresponding to the absence of contemporaneous causal relations).

5.2.2 ICA-Based Identification

An alternative method to identify B in the same two-step framework is to apply Independent Component Analysis (ICA) to the estimated reduced-form residuals u_t. Since, as shown in (5.2), $u_t = B\varepsilon_t$, it is possible to apply ICA to recover the coefficients that linearly mix the elements of ε_t to produce u_t [9, 37, 39]. ICA has been applied to a VAR setting by Hyvärinen et al. [40], Moneta et al. [53], Gouriéroux et al. [22], among others.

ICA is based on a theorem, see [9, Th. 11], [15, Th. 3], [22, p.112], according to which if B is invertible, and if the components of ε_t ($\epsilon_{1t}, \ldots, \epsilon_{kt}$) are independent, with at most one Gaussian distribution, then the matrix B is identifiable up to a post multiplication by DP, where P is a permutation matrix and D a diagonal matrix with non zero diagonal elements.

There are many ICA approaches to estimate the mixing matrix B (cfr. [39] for an overview), most popular of which are the fastICA algorithm [38], which is based on minimization of mutual information and maximization of negentropy, the JADE algorithm [5], which maximizes a measure of non-Gaussianity based on the fourth moments, and the product density ICA algorithm [28], which is based on maximum likelihood principle. Alternative approaches have been also recently proposed in econometrics, e.g. the distance covariance approach by Matteson and Tsay [51], the Cramer-von-Mises distance approach by Herwartz [30], the maximum likelihood approach by Lanne et al. [48], and the pseudo ML approach by Gouriéroux et al. [22].

Assuming that B is invertible implies that each observed variable u_{it} is affected by at least one shock ϵ_{it} and that each ϵ_{it} influences at least one variable. In other words, there is always a column-permutation of the mixing matrix $\tilde{B}$ output of ICA such that all the elements in the main diagonal are significantly different from zero. This assumption is in tune with the standard VAR framework.

In the case of causal pairs ($k = 2$), with matrix B of dimension 2×2, it is therefore very useful to test which entries in B are significantly close to zero and check their row position. The significance test can be done with a bootstrap procedure, by performing a nonparametric quantile test in order to decide whether 0 is an outlier, as proposed by Lacerda et al. [47]. Alternatively, one can test a zero restriction in B by exploiting the asymptotic distribution of the pseudo ML estimator of B, as proposed by Gouriéroux et al. [22].

Let us continue to assume that $Y_t = (x_t, y_t)'$. On the basis of tests on zero restrictions in B, one can distinguish among four different cases: (1) If there is only one zero entry in B and this lies in the first row, this means that the first element of u_t, which we call u_{xt}, is affected only by one shock, while the second element of u_t, which we call u_{yt}, is affected by both shocks. This means that x_t causes y_t. (2) Symmetrically, if the only zero entry of B lies in the second row, y_t causes x_t. (3) If there are two zero entries in B, which, by construction, must lie either in its main or anti-diagonal, then x_t and y_t are not (contemporaneously) causally related. (4) If there are no zero entries in B, some other structures are possibilities: there could be a feedback loop between x_t and y_t, or a latent variable z_t affecting both x_t and y_t, possibly also including causal relationships between x_t and y_t.

If there is a latent variable z_t, this means that the shocks affecting the system are potentially three, while the observed variables are still two. Attempting to identify the structural model would bring us outside the VAR framework. It is worth noting, however, that the ICA framework has been extended to the cases where the number of sources is greater than the number of mixtures (*overcomplete ICA*) (see [39, ch.16]). The identification of the rectangular mixing matrix potentially allows distinguishing between the case of feedback loop between x_t and y_t (two shocks affecting the system) and the case of a latent variable (three shocks affecting the system with at least one idiosyncratic shock).

If it is known that, underlying the structural model, there is a recursive contemporaneous structure, that is either x_t causes y_t or y_t causes x_t (equivalently, there is a permutation of the matrices B and W that make them lower triangular), then, a valid and efficient alternative to the test of zero-coefficient suggested above, is performing a LiNGAM (short for Linear Non-Gaussian Acyclic Model) analysis, as proposed by Shimizu et al. [61]. LiNGAM is an algorithm that incorporates ICA in the first step, and then search for the right row-permutation of the unmixing matrix W that yields a lower triangular matrix. Lacerda et al. [47] propose an extension of this algorithm to the cyclic case (in which feedback loops are allowed), called LiNG. Hoyer et al. [34] propose an extension of basic LiNGAM to the case in which latent common cause are allowed, called LvLiNGAM.

5.2.3 Nonlinear Framework

The standard VAR framework, as proposed in the econometric literature, is a linear model. In economics and in many other fields, however, there is no compelling substantive reason why a variable should depend *only linearly* on current values of other variables, on past values of itself and of other variables. Thus, a class of nonlinear structural VAR models has been proposed (see [44, ch. 18]) that allows nonlinear dependence among measured time-series but with an additive white noise error terms. In this case, we can apply a two-step identification procedure similar to linear case: in a first step one estimates a reduced-form nonlinear VAR model, and in a second step one extracts from the estimated additive errors information in order to recover the structural VAR model. A general nonlinear VAR model with additive errors can be written as:

$$Y_t = F_t(Y_{t-1}, \ldots, Y_{t-p}) + u_t, \qquad (5.4)$$

where the nonlinear function $F_t(\cdot)$ may depend on t. Most nonlinear VAR models considered in the econometric literature deal with time-varying coefficients (see e.g. [59]) which are able to capture very general nonlinear dynamics, while keeping linear the mixing structure between reduced-form and structural residuals.

We do not review here this literature (see [27, 43], and references therein). Rather, we point out a method to identify the contemporaneous causal direction that exploits the nonlinear dependence among the variables and is based on two assumptions: (i) there is a contemporaneous, nonlinear causal relationship between x_t and y_t in only one direction (either $x_t \longrightarrow y_t$ or $y_t \longrightarrow x_t$), (ii) the structural form model can be written as $Y_t = F(Y_{t-1}, \ldots, Y_{t-p}) + G(Y_t) + \varepsilon_t$, where $F(\cdot)$ and $G(\cdot)$ are two linear functions with $\epsilon_{1t} \perp\!\!\!\perp \epsilon_{2t}$.

The method follows a two-step procedure, as is typical of a VAR-based approach. In the first step the lagged effects are filtered out through nonlinear or nonparametric estimates of the regressions $x_t = f_1(x_{t-1}, \ldots, x_{t-p}, y_{t-1}, \ldots, y_{t-p}) + u_{1t}$ and $y_t = f_2(x_{t-1}, \ldots, x_{t-p}, y_{t-1}, \ldots, y_{t-p}) + u_{2t}$, in order to obtain estimates of u_{1t}

and u_{2t}. In the second step one the contemporaneous causal direction is detected through a nonlinear additive noise model (see [35, 58]). Indeed we will have that if the contemporaneous causal relation is $x_t \to y_t$

$$u_{2t} = f_y(u_{1t}) + N_y \tag{5.5}$$

where N_y is an unobserved noise term and $N_t^y \perp\!\!\!\perp u_{1t}$. Likewise, if the contemporaneous causal relation is $y_t \to x_t$

$$u_{1t} = f_x(u_{2t}) + N_x, \tag{5.6}$$

where N_x is an unobserved noise term and $N_x \perp\!\!\!\perp u_{2t}$.

Thus, once u_{1t} and u_{2t} are estimated through a nonlinear or nonparametric VAR model, one regress them on each other, using a nonparametric estimator, and obtains estimated of N_x and N_y. If, on the basis of a nonparametric independence test (see e.g. [25]), the independence between N_y and u_{1t} is not rejected, while the independence between N_x and u_{2t} is rejected, one infer $x_t \to y_t$. If, the independence between N_x and u_{2t} is not rejected, while the independence between N_y and u_{1t} is rejected, one infer $y_t \to x_t$.

5.2.4 Impulse Response Functions

Having identified the mixing matrix B and the structural shocks ε_t, econometricians are mostly interested in the responses over time of each element of $Y_t = (x_t, y_t)'$ to a one-time impulse in each element of $\varepsilon_t = (\epsilon_{1t}, \epsilon_{2t})'$. These impulse response functions are defined [44, p. 110] as:

$$\frac{\partial Y_{t+i}}{\partial \varepsilon_t'} = \Theta_i \quad i = 0, 1, 2, \ldots, H, \tag{5.7}$$

where, in the case of two variables, Θ_i is a 2×2 matrix, whose four elements are: $\frac{\partial x_{t+i}}{\partial \epsilon_{1t}}, \frac{\partial y_{t+i}}{\partial \epsilon_{1t}}$ (first column), $\frac{\partial x_{t+i}}{\partial \epsilon_{2t}}, \frac{\partial y_{t+i}}{\partial \epsilon_{2t}}$ (second column).

Consider, for simplicity, a linear VAR model with one lag (p=1) and no intercept:

$$Y_t = A_1 Y_{t-1} + u_t. \tag{5.8}$$

By recursive substitution it can be written:

$$Y_{t+i} = A_1^{i+1} Y_{t-1} + \sum_{j=0}^{i} A_1^j u_{t+i-j}. \tag{5.9}$$

The responses of Y_t to reduced-form errors (also referred to as forecast errors) i periods ago[2] are then captured by the matrix $\Phi_i = A_1^i$. If Y_t is a stable process (all eigenvalues of A have modulus less than 1), i.e. each element of Y_t is covariance stationary, Eq. (5.8) can be equivalently expressed according to the moving average (MA) representation (Wold decomposition):

$$Y_t = \sum_{i=0}^{\infty} \Phi_i u_{t-i}, \tag{5.10}$$

where Φ_i is calculated as above (for the one-lag case), with $\Phi_0 = I$. From Eqs. (5.10), (5.2) and (5.7) it follows

$$Y_t = \sum_{i=0}^{\infty} \Phi_i B B^{-1} u_{t-i} = \sum_{i=0}^{\infty} \Phi_i B \varepsilon_{t-i} = \sum_{i=0}^{\infty} \Theta_i \varepsilon_{t-i}. \tag{5.11}$$

If the VAR is not stable, the infinite Wold representation is not allowed, but the same approach to calculate Φ_i and Θ_i will work, because Eq. (5.9) does not depend on stationarity. In case of unstable process, the impulse response functions will not be tied to the MA representation and will not converge to zero for $i \to \infty$. In particular if Δx_t is stationary the impulse response function to Δx_t will converge to a finite number.

This framework to calculate impulse response functions can be easily extended to the case of more lags using a "companion matrix" representation (see [44, p. 25]) and is not substantively affected by the presence of a constant in (5.8). However, it cannot be applied to nonlinear VAR models, due to its reliance on Eq. (5.9).

Thus structural impulse responses in a nonlinear setting are defined in an alternative manner, using the concept of conditional expectation [44, 45, p. 615]. Denoting by Ω_{t-1} the information set available at date $t-1$ and by δ the magnitude of the impulse of which one wants to study the response (e.g. $\delta =$ standard deviation (ϵ_{1t})), the structural response of x_{t+i} to the structural shock ϵ_{1t} is defined as

$$I_x(i, \delta, \Omega_{t-1}) = \mathbb{E}(x_{t+i}|\epsilon_{1t} = \delta, \Omega_{t-1}) - \mathbb{E}(x_{t+i}|\Omega_{t-1}) \quad i = 0, \dots, H. \tag{5.12}$$

Having estimated a nonlinear reduced form VAR model (5.4) and having recovered the structural shocks (for example on the basis of additive noise model framework, see end of Sect. 5.2.3), one can evaluate (5.12) using a Monte Carlo procedure [44, pp. 615–616]. In this procedure, one simulates two time paths: in a first path the shock of interest is set at time 0 to a particular value δ and the subsequent realizations of the variables of interest are estimated; in a second time path the value of the shock of interest is drawn from an empirically estimated marginal distribution.

---

[2]Or, equivalently, the responses of Y_{t+i} to forecast errors at time t.

Thus, Eq. (5.12) is estimated by subtracting the average outcome of the second path from the first.

5.2.5 Granger Causality in a VAR Framework

VAR models have also been used for a type of causal analysis that does not involve the identification of a structural model like Eq. (5.3). This approach is based on a notion of causal relationship proposed by Granger [23, 24], which is referred to as *Granger causality*. Granger's general definition of causality relies on two general principles: (i) the effect does not precede its cause in time; (ii) the causal time series contains unique information about the series being caused that is not available otherwise (see [13]). A corollary of these principles is that x_t Granger causes y_t if x_t is helpful for predicting future values of y_t. Incidentally, these tenets share profound similarities with probabilistic theories of causality proposed in the philosophy of science literature [20, 21, 67] (see also [65]).

Although the definition of Granger causality is more general (see Sect. 5.3.1 below), several empirical studies and statistical software make it operational in a linear VAR framework. Consider a bivariate VAR with p lags:

$$\begin{pmatrix} x_t \\ y_t \end{pmatrix} = \sum_{i=1}^{p} \begin{bmatrix} a_{11,i} & a_{12,i} \\ a_{21,i} & a_{22,i} \end{bmatrix} \begin{pmatrix} x_{t-i} \\ y_{t-i} \end{pmatrix} + u_t. \tag{5.13}$$

In this framework x_t is said to be non-Granger-causal for y_t if and only if $a_{21,i} = 0$ for $i = 1, \ldots, p$ [49, p. 154]. This amounts to say that the information set available until time $t-1$ to forecast y_t comprises only x_{t-1} (with more lagged terms) and y_{t-1} (with more lagged terms), and one wants to check whether excluding or not lagged x_t from the information set makes a difference in predicting y_t. The zero restrictions can be tested with standard Wald χ^2- or F-tests, which have standard asymptotic properties if the series are stationary [49, p. 154].

A main limitation of this framework is that lagged x_t may make a difference in forecasting y_t (so that to infer that x_t Granger-causes y_t) because it contains information that is not contained in the information set comprising lagged y_t and lagged x_t, but it is always possible that if one considered a larger set of information, for example one containing lagged values of a series z_t, x_t would not bring a further contribution for the prediction of y_t. If z_t is a common cause of both x_t and y_t one would have wrongly inferred that x_t causes y_t. Thus, although scholars have worked in this direction, introducing concepts such as conditional independencies and higher-order interactions, causal sufficiency is still a fundamental tenet of this approach; this is particularly true, if the focus on causality goes beyond what sometimes is referred to as "predictive causality."

Granger-causality in causal pairs is a very powerful method in a setting in which, as mentioned in the introduction, the presence of a causal relationship between the two variables, until some lag $p \geq 0$, is known, but is unknown whether it is x_{t-p} that causes y_t or it is y_{t-p} that causes x_t.

Suppose, for example, that is known that x_{t-p} causes y_t with $p = 0$ or 1 and there are no causal relationships from y_t to x_t at any lag. Then in all the 3 admitted cases in which x_t can cause y_t ((i) $x_{t-1} \rightarrow y_t$; (ii) $x_t \rightarrow y_t$; (iii) i $\cup$ ii), the coefficient $a_{12,1}$, estimated by regressing equation (5.13), is expected to be not significantly different from zero, while the other coefficients of the same matrix will be non-zero. Symmetrically, if y_{t-p} causes x_t with $p = 0, 1$ (and no feedback from x_t to y_t at any lag), then the only coefficient of the same matrix, obtained by regressing the same equation, which is expected to be zero is $a_{21,1}$.

Standard Granger-causality in a VAR framework neglects, by choice, the contemporaneous causal link, which is considered by the structural VAR approach. Geweke [19], however, proposes an extension of the Granger-causality concept to detect linear contemporaneous feedback between two time-series, x_t and y_t.

Jacobs et al. [41] and Hoover [32, pp. 151–152] present examples of bivariate, one-lag structural VAR models in which $x_{t-1} \rightarrow y_t$; $y_{t-1} \rightarrow x_t$; $x_t \rightarrow y_t$, but, for particular configurations of the parameters, in the reduced form VAR the coefficient corresponding to the influence of y_{t-1} on x_t ($a_{11,1}$ in Eq. (5.13)) is zero. One could exclude these types of parameters configuration as "measure-zero." This assumption would be similar to the faithfulness assumption in the graphical causal model literature [64], where configurations of parameters that yield statistical independence actually corresponding to causal dependence are ruled out. Hoover [32] argues further that specific configurations of parameters for which Granger non-causality does not match structural non-causality may correspond to theoretical economic models and thus cannot be easily dismissed.

5.3 Direct Causal Search

In this section we discuss methods for causal pairs search that are applied directly to time series data, without filtering them through a vector autoregressive model. Skipping VAR estimation has the clear advantage of not being tied to the imposition of a functional form (e.g. linear VAR), when estimating the relationship between current and lagged values of the variables of interest. On the other hand, direct causal search deals directly with autocorrelated data.

5.3.1 Granger Causality

As mentioned above (Sect. 5.2.5), the central notion in Granger causality is "incremental predictability" [32, p.150]: if a time series y_{t+1} is better predicted by the set of all information available up to time t than by the same information set less the series x_t, then x_t *Granger-causes* y_{t+1}. The general definition given by Granger [24, p. 49] is that x_t is said to cause y_{t+1} if

$$P(y_{t+1} \in A|\Omega_t) \neq P(y_{t+1} \in A|\Omega_t - x_t), \qquad (5.14)$$

where Ω_t is all the knowledge in the universe available at time t, $\Omega_t - x_t$ is the same information set except the values taken by a x_t up to time t, where $x_t \in \Omega_t$, and A is any set of values that y_{t+1} can take. We can also write that x_t does *not* Granger-causes y_{t+1} if [13]

$$y_{t+1} \perp\!\!\!\perp \Omega_t | \Omega_t - x_t, \qquad (5.15)$$

otherwise x_t is said to Granger-cause y_{t+1}. As Granger [24] admits, this general definition of causality is not operational, i.e. it cannot be implemented with actual data. A practical solution is to consider Ω_t as incorporating only current and past values (until certain lags) of x_t, y_t and of a set of observed variables Z_t. Thus we have that x_t is Granger-noncausal for y_{t+1} if [16, 66]

$$y_{t+1} \perp\!\!\!\perp \{x_t, \ldots, x_{t-q}\} | \{y_t, \ldots, y_{t-p}, Z_t, \ldots, Z_{t-r}\}, \qquad (5.16)$$

given lags p, q, r, where by $\{x_t, \ldots, x_{t-q}\}$ we denote the σ-field generated by the vector of random variables $(x_t, \ldots, x_{t-q})$, and similarly for $\{y_t, \ldots\}$. The σ-field generated by a random variable is the set of events that may be described in terms of that random variable [16, p. 588]. Let us suppose that the background knowledge available at time t comprises only two time series: x_t and y_t. Then, given lags p and q, x_{t-1} does not Granger causes y_t if

$$y_t \perp\!\!\!\perp \{x_{t-1}, \ldots, x_{t-q}\} | \{y_{t-1}, \ldots, y_{t-p}\}. \qquad (5.17)$$

Assuming that x_t and y_t are stationary and ergodic, many studies have proposed nonparametric tests of (5.17), without assuming a linear structure (which could be treated in a linear VAR framework) (see [1, 2, 4, 12, 31, 66, 70]). In case of $p, q = 1$ the proposed tests have high performance, which tends to decline for high p and q for data with limited sample size [6]. The assumption of Ω_t as comprising only two time series is, of course, a strong assumption in empirical contexts where causal sufficiency may fail.

5.3.2 Graphical Models for Time Series

Since Granger-causality faces fundamental hurdles in case of unmeasured causal variables, one possible solution is to rely on causal inference procedures that are designed to perform well in presence of latent variables. One algorithm that is asymptotically correct in the presence of latent variables is the Fast Causal Inference

(FCI) algorithm proposed by Spirtes et al. [64]. This method belongs to the more general approach of graphical causal models based on conditional independence tests, also known as "constraint-based causal search" (see [63]). We have mentioned this approach in Sect. 5.2.1, noticing that it was of little use when applied to pairs of estimated VAR reduced-form residuals. This approach, however, has larger applicability when applied directly to pairs of time series data (not filtered by a VAR model), because it can exploit the possibility of conditioning both on lagged and contemporaneous variables. An interesting method, in this setting, is the adaptation of the FCI algorithm that Entner and Hoyer [14] propose for time series.

In case of causal sufficiency (and no feedback loops), constraint-based causal search moves from the assumption that the data generating process can be described by a directed acyclic graph (DAG) and a joint distribution $P(\mathbf{X})$, where $\mathbf{X} = (X_1, \ldots, X_n)$ is the set of observable variables represented by the set V of n vertices of the DAG. Causal inference is based on two assumptions: *Markov* and *faithfulness* condition. Markov condition states that if vertices i and j of a DAG $\mathscr{G}$ given some subset $W \subseteq V \backslash \{i, j\}$ are *d-separated* (a graphical criterion defined by Pearl [54]), then we have $X_i \perp\!\!\!\perp X_j | \{X_w : w \in W\}$. Faithfulness condition states that all (conditional and unconditional) independence relations in $P(\mathbf{X})$ are entailed by the Markov condition. In this setting, the PC algorithm [64], on the base of these assumptions, starts from a complete graph (all vertices connected by undirected edges) over all variables, and performs a series of independence tests that allows the removal of edges between pairs of variables that are independent conditionally on any set of variables (included the empty set). Then it makes use of some rules which allow us to orient edges among triple of vertices, and in particular to distinguish between collider ($\cdot \rightarrow \cdot \leftarrow \cdot$) structure and fork/chain structures ($\cdot \leftarrow \cdot \rightarrow \cdot$, or $\cdot \leftarrow \cdot \leftarrow \cdot$, or $\cdot \rightarrow \cdot \rightarrow \cdot$). This is also done on the basis of conditional independence tests and the two conditions above. The outcome of the algorithm is a set of DAGs that share the same (conditional) independence relations, i.e. a class of *Markov equivalent* DAGs.

Relaxing the assumption of causal sufficiency, the FCI algorithm [64] moves also from the assumption that the process underlying the data can be described by a DAG, but this DAG may contain vertices that correspond to latent variables. Richardson and Spirtes [60] (see also [8]) introduced a new class of graphs whose vertices are observed variables, but in which the causal relationships may involve latent variables. These graphs, in which a latent cause Z affecting the observed variables X and Y is represented by $X \leftrightarrow Y$, are called *maximal ancestral graphs* (MAGs). The idea is that any DAG whose vertices include latent variables can be transformed in a unique MAG whose vertices comprise only observed variables. Moreover, MAGs encode conditional independence relations among the observed variables through m-separation, a generalization of d-separation [8, 60]. A MAG is a graph $\mathscr{M}$ with the following properties: (i) $\mathscr{M}$ is a *mixed* graph (it contains not only directed ($\rightarrow$), but also undirected ($-$) and bi-directed ($\leftrightarrow$) edges); (ii) $\mathscr{M}$ is an *ancestral* graph (there is no vertex i which is a ancestor of any of its parents nor any of its spouse[3]); (iii) for every pair of variables $\langle X_i, X_j \rangle$ there is an edge between i and j in $\mathcal{M}$ if and only if there does not exist a set of vertices $W \subseteq V \backslash \{i, j\}$ in $\mathcal{M}$ such that $X_i \perp\!\!\!\perp X_j | \{X_w : w \in W\}$ [14, 60].

Similarly to PC algorithm, the output of the FCI algorithm is a class of MAGs that entail the same set of conditional independence relationships. This class of MAGs is represented by a *partial ancestral graph* (PAG), which is a graph which have a third edge mark, besides arrowtail ($-$) and arrowhead ($>$), namely a circle ($\circ$). Excluding feedback loops or selection bias (hence undirected edges), a PAG can only incorporate these types of edges: $\rightarrow$, $\leftrightarrow$, $\circ\!\rightarrow$, and $\circ\!-\!\circ$. If $X_i \leftrightarrow X_j$ then neither variable is ancestor of the other and there is a latent variable between X_i and X_j. The circle ($\circ$) denotes the case where it is undecided whether in the underlying data generating process there is an arrowtail or an arrowhead next to the vertex where the circle appear. This means that the PAG contains a MAG with ($-$) and a MAG with ($>$) at that location. Like the PC algorithm, the FCI in a first step removes edges from a complete graph on the base of conditional independence tests, and in a second step it orients edges so that the inferred causal structures are in tune with the Markov and faithfulness assumptions (all the conditional independence relations must be derived from m-separation).

Entner and Hoyer [14] adapt the FCI in a time series framework, which they call tsFCI. Suppose the observed time series variables are $\{x_t\} = x_1, \ldots, x_T$ and $\{y_t\} = y_1, \ldots, y_T$. The algorithm starts from a complete graph on a time window of the time series, i.e. the set of vertices are $x_t, x_{t-1}, \ldots, x_{t-p}, y_t, y_{t-1}, \ldots y_{t-p}$. It then remove edges from this complete graph, as in a standard FCI algorithm, on the basis of conditional independence test, but with the addition that if the contemporaneous edge is eliminated, this will be eliminated at all time units $(t, t-1, \ldots, t-p)$. If a lagged edge with lag l is eliminated (for example from x_{t-l} to y_t), this is eliminated at all time units (for example from x_{t-l-1} to y_{t-1}). Orientation makes use not only of the orientation rules of the standard FCI algorithm, but also makes use of the "arrow of time": if there is an undirected edge between two lagged variable, it will be put an arrowtail at the variable coming before and an arrowhead at the variable coming after. Moreover, if an edge is oriented contemporaneously at time t, this will be oriented in the same manner for all time units $(t, t-1, \ldots)$. If a lagged edge with lag l is oriented (for example $x_{t-l} \rightarrow y_t$), this is oriented in the same manner for all time units (for example $x_{t-l-1} \rightarrow y_{t-1}$).

Thus, exploiting the assumption that an effect cannot precede a cause and the assumption of repetition of causal structures over time (time invariance), one can reach a more detailed description of the data generating process than the one that would be provided by a standard application of constraint based algorithm. However, since these methods ultimately rely on conditional independence tests

---

[3]A vertex i is an ancestor of j if there is a sequence of directed edges ($\rightarrow$) between i and j. A vertex i is a parent of j if $i \rightarrow j$. A vertex i is a spouse of j (and j a spouse of i) if there is a bi-directed edge between i and j.

is crucial that they are designed taking into account the specificity of testing self-dependence in a time series context (see [46]).

5.3.3 Additive Noise Models

We consider in this subsection the problem of distinguishing among different causal structures over the time-series pair $\{x_t, y_t\}$, using a specific class of structural equation models. We assume that: (i) there are no latent common causes between x_t and y_t (at any lag); (ii) no contemporaneous causal feedback loops (i.e. either $x_t \rightarrow y_t$ or $x_t \leftarrow y_t$, but it is possible that $x_{t-s} \rightarrow y_t \rightarrow x_{t+h}$, for $s \geq 0, h \geq 1$); (iii) each variable x_t and y_t causally depends on its own past (respectively $x_{t-1}, \dots$ and $y_{t-1}, \dots$) until a lag p; (iv) both contemporaneous and lagged causal structures recur over time: if $x_{t-i} \rightarrow y_t$ then $x_{t-i-s} \rightarrow y_{t-s}$, for $i \geq 0, s \geq 1$. To simplify the illustration, we also assume here that (v) p = 1. In Fig. 5.3 we show the 12 directed acyclic graphs (DAGs) corresponding to all the possible causal structures related to the data generating process (represented as unit graphs) under these assumptions. We also assume that (vi) x_t and y_t are stationary and ergodic processes. We also assume that the data generating process can be formalized as a specific type of structural equation model (or *functional equation model*, see [55]), namely as an *additive noise model* [35, 56, 57], where

$$x_t = f_x(\mathbf{PA}^x) + N_t^x \tag{5.18}$$

and

$$y_t = f_y(\mathbf{PA}^y) + N_t^y, \tag{5.19}$$

where $\mathbf{PA}^x$ are the graphical parents of x_t (and $\mathbf{PA}^y$ of y_t) in the DAG representing the data generating process, and N_t^x and N_t^y are independent white noise processes. We assume (vii) $N_t^x \perp\!\!\!\perp \mathbf{PA}^x$, $N_t^y \perp\!\!\!\perp \mathbf{PA}^y$, and $N_t^x \perp\!\!\!\perp N_t^y$; (viii) $f_x(\cdot)$ and $f_y(\cdot)$ are either nonlinear functions or linear but with the additional assumption that N_t^x and N_t^y have non-Gaussian distribution.[4]

   In Fig. 5.3, below each DAG it is shown the set of corresponding structural equations and the set of implied (conditional or unconditional) independence relationships. Hoyer et al. [35] (see also Sect. 5.2.3) proposes a procedure to check if a DAG corresponding to a nonlinear additive noise model is consistent with the data: first one constructs a nonlinear regression of each variable on its parents, then one tests whether the estimated residuals are independent of the covariates and among

---

[4]Specific nonlinear functions $f_x(\cdot)$ and distributions of the noise terms have also to be excluded. A precise specification can be found in Peters et al. [57, Proposition 23] and Zhang and Hyvärinen [69].

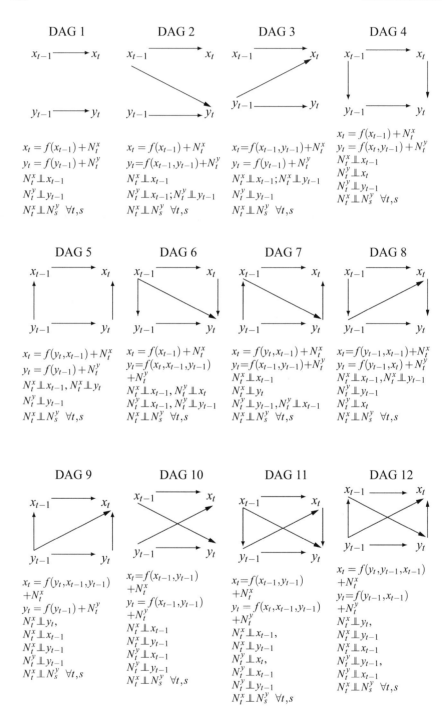

Fig. 5.3 Unit graphs of all the possible structural equations models under assumption (i)–(viii)

each other. If any independence test is rejected the DAG is rejected, if none of the independence tests are rejected, the DAG is consistent with the data.

Thus, in principle, one could run the regressions corresponding to the equations indicated below each DAG in Fig. 5.3 to check whether a specific DAG is consistent with the data. Let us analyze some specific cases.

If the data are generated by DAG 1 (see Fig. 5.3), and the data generating process were not known to the observer, by constructing the nonparametric regressions[5]:

$$x_t = f_1(x_{t-1}) + N_t^{x,1} \tag{5.20}$$

$$y_t = f_1(y_{t-1}) + N_t^{y,1} \tag{5.21}$$

and by not rejecting the independence relations:

$$\widehat{N_t^{x,1}} \perp\!\!\!\perp x_{t-1}, \tag{5.22}$$

$$\widehat{N_t^{y,1}} \perp\!\!\!\perp y_{t-1}, \tag{5.23}$$

$$\widehat{N_{t-i}^{x,1}} \perp\!\!\!\perp \widehat{N_{t-j}^{y,1}} \quad \text{for} \langle i, j \rangle = \langle 0, 0 \rangle, \langle 1, 0 \rangle, \langle 0, 1 \rangle, \tag{5.24}$$

one would conclude the DAG 1 is consistent with the data. Are other DAGs consistent with these findings? If we run the same regressions but using data generated by DAG 2, we will not necessarily reject: $\widehat{N_t^{x,1}} \perp\!\!\!\perp x_{t-1}$, $\widehat{N_t^{y,1}} \perp\!\!\!\perp y_{t-1}$. Indeed these regressions may suffer of omitted variable bias, but not of reverse causality. However, we will have that $\widehat{N_{t-1}^{x,1}} \not\perp\!\!\!\perp \widehat{N_t^{y,1}}$. Indeed $\widehat{N_t^{y,1}}$ results from a regression in which it is omitted x_{t-1}. Hence $N_t^{y,1}$ is dependent on x_{t-1}, and since x_{t-1} is in turn dependent on $\widehat{N_{t-1}^{x,1}}$, then $\widehat{N_{t-1}^{x,1}} \not\perp\!\!\!\perp \widehat{N_t^{y,1}}$. If we run the same regressions (Eqs. (5.20), (5.21)) using data generated by any other DAG (from DAG 3 to DAG 12), for analogous lines of reasoning we would reach the same conclusion: $\widehat{N_{t-i}^{x,1}} \not\perp\!\!\!\perp \widehat{N_{t-j}^{y,1}}$ for some $\langle i, j \rangle = \langle 0, 0 \rangle, \langle 1, 0 \rangle, \langle 0, 1 \rangle$.

Let us now suppose that DAG 1 has been found not consistent with the data and one runs the nonparametric regressions (also indicated below DAG 2 in Fig. 5.3):

$$x_t = f_2(x_{t-1}) + N_t^{x,2}, \tag{5.25}$$

$$y_t = f_2(x_{t-1}, y_{t-1}) + N_t^{y,2}. \tag{5.26}$$

By not rejecting:

---

[5]Here and below the subscript i in the function $f_i(\cdot)$, as well as the superscript i in the noise term $N_t^{\cdot,i}$, indicate that these functions and noise terms enter in the additive noise model associated to DAG i (see Fig. 5.3).

$$\widehat{N_t^{x,2}} \perp\!\!\!\perp x_{t-1}, \tag{5.27}$$

$$\widehat{N_t^{y,2}} \perp\!\!\!\perp x_{t-1}, \tag{5.28}$$

$$\widehat{N_t^{y,2}} \perp\!\!\!\perp y_{t-1}, \tag{5.29}$$

$$\widehat{N_{t-i}^{x,2}} \perp\!\!\!\perp \widehat{N_{t-j}^{y,2}} \quad \text{for} \langle i, j \rangle = \langle 0, 0 \rangle, \langle 1, 0 \rangle, \langle 0, 1 \rangle, \tag{5.30}$$

one would conclude the DAG 2 is consistent with the data. If the data were generated by DAG 3, we would have that $\widehat{N_t^{x,2}} \not\perp\!\!\!\perp \widehat{N_{t-1}^{y,2}}$, because in regressing x_t on x_{t-1} we are omitting y_{t-1}, which is a graphical parent of x_t in DAG 3. If the data were generated by any DAG containing the contemporaneous causal link (DAG 4–DAG 12, except DAG 10), we would have that $\widehat{N_t^{x,2}} \not\perp\!\!\!\perp \widehat{N_t^{y,2}}$. If DAG 10 were generating the data, we would have that $\widehat{N_t^{x,2}} \not\perp\!\!\!\perp \widehat{N_{t-1}^{y,2}}$, because, again, we would omit y_{t-1} in the regression of x_t on x_{t-1}.

Let us suppose now that DAG 4 is the data generating process. By running the nonparametric regressions,

$$x_t = f_4(x_{t-1}) + N_t^{x,4} \tag{5.31}$$

$$y_t = f_4(x_t, y_{t-1}) + N_t^{y,4} \tag{5.32}$$

and not rejecting

$$\widehat{N_t^{x,4}} \perp\!\!\!\perp x_{t-1} \tag{5.33}$$

$$\widehat{N_t^{y,4}} \perp\!\!\!\perp x_t \tag{5.34}$$

$$\widehat{N_t^{y,4}} \perp\!\!\!\perp y_{t-1} \tag{5.35}$$

$$\widehat{N_{t-i}^{x,4}} \perp\!\!\!\perp \widehat{N_{t-j}^{y,4}} \quad \text{for} \langle i, j \rangle = \langle 0, 0 \rangle, \langle 1, 0 \rangle, \langle 0, 1 \rangle, \tag{5.36}$$

we would conclude that DAG 4 is consistent with the data. If the data generating process were any DAG with opposite contemporaneous causal link (DAG 5, 7, 9, 12), running the same regressions ((5.31), (5.32)) and tests ((5.33)–(5.36)), we would get $\widehat{N_t^{y,4}} \not\perp\!\!\!\perp x_t$. If the data generating process were any DAG among DAG 2, 3, 6, 8, 10, 11, there would be no reverse contemporaneous causal link, but an omitted lagged variables in one (or both) of the two regressions. This would imply that $\widehat{N_{t-i}^{x,4}} \not\perp\!\!\!\perp \widehat{N_{t-j}^{y,4}}$ for some $\langle i, j \rangle = \langle 1, 0 \rangle, \langle 0, 1 \rangle$.

These examples should already suggest that, under the framework of the 12 possible DAGs of Fig. 5.3, under the assumptions listed above, with an exhaustive search of independence relationships derived by the possible DAGs, one is able to uniquely identify the model that has generated the data. Based on these considerations, we propose a search procedure formalized in the algorithm described in the Table here below. The algorithm avoids an exhaustive causal search, but at the same time is able to uniquely identify, among the 12 DAGs represented in Fig. 5.3, the one that has generated the data.

The search algorithm is able to efficiently infer one of the 12 DAGs on the base of a limited number of nonparametric regressions and tests of unconditional independence. Once the algorithms outputs DAG number i, however, we suggest to check its consistency with the data through the nonparametric regressions and (conditional and unconditional) independence tests indicated in Fig. 5.3 under the inferred DAG number.

For a more general framework in which there are k possible time series and p lags of causal influence, Peters et al. [56] propose a search procedure based on additive noise models called TiMINO, i.e. time series models with independent noise. The

---

Search Algorithm

1. **Input**: Samples from a 2-dimensional time series of length T, maximal order $p = 1$.
2. Run nonpar. regressions: $x_t = f_1(x_{t-1}) + N_t^{x,1}$; $y_t = f_1(y_{t-1}) + N_t^{y,1}$, get $\widehat{N_t^{x,1}}$, $\widehat{N_t^{y,1}}$
3. Test: $\widehat{N_t^{x,1}} \perp\!\!\!\perp \widehat{N_t^{y,1}}$
4. If $\widehat{N_t^{x,1}} \perp\!\!\!\perp \widehat{N_t^{y,1}}$
5.   Test: $\widehat{N_{t-i}^{x,1}} \perp\!\!\!\perp \widehat{N_{t-j}^{y,1}}$ for $\langle i, j \rangle = \langle 1, 0 \rangle, \langle 0, 1 \rangle$
6.   If $\widehat{N_{t-i}^{x,1}} \perp\!\!\!\perp \widehat{N_{t-j}^{y,1}}$ for $\langle i, j \rangle = \langle 1, 0 \rangle, \langle 0, 1 \rangle$, break, output DAG 1
7.   If $\widehat{N_t^{x,1}} \perp\!\!\!\perp \widehat{N_{t-1}^{y,1}}$ and $\widehat{N_{t-1}^{x,1}} \not\!\perp\!\!\!\perp \widehat{N_t^{y,1}}$, then break, output DAG 2
8.   If $\widehat{N_{t-1}^{x,1}} \perp\!\!\!\perp \widehat{N_t^{y,1}}$ and $\widehat{N_t^{x,1}} \not\!\perp\!\!\!\perp \widehat{N_{t-1}^{y,1}}$, then break, output DAG 3
9.   Else break, output DAG 10
10. If $\widehat{N_t^{x,1}} \not\!\perp\!\!\!\perp \widehat{N_t^{y,1}}$
11.   Run nonp. reg.: $x_t = f_4(x_{t-1}) + N_t^{x,4}$; $y_t = f_4(x_t, y_{t-1}) + N_t^{y,4}$, get $\widehat{N_t^{x,4}}$, $\widehat{N_t^{y,4}}$
12.   Test: $\widehat{N_t^{y,4}} \perp\!\!\!\perp x_t$
13.   If $\widehat{N_t^{y,4}} \perp\!\!\!\perp x_t$
14.   Test: $\widehat{N_{t-i}^{x,4}} \perp\!\!\!\perp \widehat{N_{t-j}^{y,4}}$ for $\langle i, j \rangle = \langle 0, 0 \rangle, \langle 1, 0 \rangle, \langle 0, 1 \rangle$
15.   If $\widehat{N_{t-i}^{x,4}} \perp\!\!\!\perp \widehat{N_{t-j}^{y,4}}$ for $\langle i, j \rangle = \langle 0, 0 \rangle, \langle 1, 0 \rangle, \langle 0, 1 \rangle$, break, output DAG 4
16.   If $\widehat{N_{t-i}^{x,4}} \perp\!\!\!\perp \widehat{N_{t-j}^{y,4}}$ only for $\langle i, j \rangle = \langle 0, 0 \rangle, \langle 0, 1 \rangle$, break, output DAG 6
17.   If $\widehat{N_{t-i}^{x,4}} \perp\!\!\!\perp \widehat{N_{t-j}^{y,4}}$ only for $\langle i, j \rangle = \langle 0, 0 \rangle, \langle 1, 0 \rangle$, break, output DAG 8
18.   Else break, output DAG 11
19.   If $\widehat{N_t^{y,4}} \not\!\perp\!\!\!\perp x_t$
20.   Run $x_t = f_5(x_{t-1}, y_t) + N_t^{x,5}$; $y_t = f_5(y_{t-1}) + N_t^{y,5}$, get $\widehat{N_t^{x,5}}$, $\widehat{N_t^{y,5}}$
21.   Test: $\widehat{N_{t-i}^{x,5}} \perp\!\!\!\perp \widehat{N_{t-j}^{y,5}}$ for $\langle i, j \rangle = \langle 0, 0 \rangle, \langle 1, 0 \rangle, \langle 0, 1 \rangle$
22.   If $\widehat{N_{t-i}^{x,5}} \perp\!\!\!\perp \widehat{N_{t-j}^{y,5}}$ for $\langle i, j \rangle = \langle 0, 0 \rangle, \langle 1, 0 \rangle, \langle 0, 1 \rangle$, break, output DAG 5
23.   If $\widehat{N_{t-i}^{x,5}} \perp\!\!\!\perp \widehat{N_{t-j}^{y,5}}$ only for $\langle i, j \rangle = \langle 0, 0 \rangle, \langle 0, 1 \rangle$, break, output DAG 7
24.   If $\widehat{N_{t-i}^{x,5}} \perp\!\!\!\perp \widehat{N_{t-j}^{y,5}}$ only for $\langle i, j \rangle = \langle 0, 0 \rangle, \langle 1, 0 \rangle$, break, output DAG 9
25.   Else break, output DAG 12
26. **Output**: One DAG among DAG 1 - DAG 12.

output of TiMINO is however, a *summary* graph. This means that it is not possible to disentangle between contemporaneous and lagged causal effects. The advantage of our search algorithm is that it is possible to distinguish between these two types of effects, but only under the specific framework of time series pairs.

5.3.4 Local Projections

Local projections were introduced by Jorda [42] to compute impulse responses (see Sect. 5.2.4) without specifying and estimating a VAR model. Furthermore, any attempt of representing the data generating process through a multivariate time series structural system is eschewed in local projections. The idea here is to focus on the estimation of impulse responses through regression methods that are applied at each period of interest, without hinging on a pre-specified or pre-estimated time series model.

Let be $Y_t = (x_t, y_t)'$, as in Sect. 5.2.1. Jorda [42] considered projecting Y_{t+s} onto the linear space generated by $(Y_{t-1}, \ldots, Y_{t-p})'$ for a certain choice of lag p, namely

$$Y_{t+s} = \alpha^s + P_1^{s+1} Y_{t-1} + P_2^{s+1} Y_{t-2} + \ldots + P_p^{s+1} Y_{t-p} + u_{t+s}^s, \tag{5.37}$$

where α^s is a (2×1) vector of constant, P_i^{s+1} are (2×2) matrices of coefficients, and u_{t+s}^s is a (2×1) vector of errors by construction uncorrelated with the regressors. Superscripts here are meant to denote the time window where the regression is performed.

Impulse response functions are defined as the difference between two forecasts, which is an idea consistent with Eq. (5.12). More specifically, we have that the impulse response of x_{t+s} to a shock at time t, $s \in Z$ is

$$IR(t, s, \delta) = E(x_{t+s}|v_{1t} = \delta, Y_t) - E(x_{t+s}|v_{1t} = 0, Y_t) \quad i = 0, \ldots, H. \tag{5.38}$$

where $E(\cdot|\cdot)$ denotes the best, mean squared predictor, v_{1t} is a disturbance shock, and d is the magnitude of the shock the impact of which one wants to measure.

The impulse responses estimated from (5.37) are

$$IR(t, s, \delta) = \hat{P}_1^s \delta. \tag{5.39}$$

As noted by Kilian and Lütkepohl [44, chapter 12], these impulse responses will be relative to a reduced-form error ($v_{it} = u_{it}$) and not to the true shock affecting the system, if they are estimated directly through a least square regression of Eq. (5.38). Thus, it is fundamental in this context to transform the reduced-form residuals in a mixture of structural shocks. But here the problem is analogous to the problem of identification of the structural VAR model and the literature on local projections seems not to have found a method yet that bypasses this step.

5.4   Conclusions

In this paper we have addressed the problem of causal inference from data that are realizations of bivariate time series processes. We have focused on the setting typically encountered in econometrics, namely stationary or difference-stationary autoregressive processes with additive noises. The standard approach in econometrics to address this problem is structural vector autoregressive analysis. This allows the researcher to filter the time-series data, in order to apply causal search algorithms to the i.i.d. filtered data. Since the time structure is filtered out, the output of this causal search is a contemporaneous causal structure, which, in a second step, gives the possibility of recovering the entire structural autoregressive model. In a causal pair setting, however, causal search in this framework is limited. For example, in the case of Gaussian data, the linear causal structure between the two filtered time series is not identifiable. We have shown that identification is possible under non-Gaussianity (exploiting independent component analysis) or under non-linearity (exploiting non-linear additive noise model). But we have also shown that in a setting of bivariate time series, an alternative valid approach is to address the problem of causal inference by avoiding the vector autoregressive framework. This is possible by applying graphical models algorithms (like FCI) or nonlinear additive noise models algorithms (like the one presented in this paper) directly to the data, without filtering them. We have also shown the possibility of applications of Granger non-causality testing and local projections in a framework in which VAR models are not necessarily estimated. The latter two techniques, however, deviate for many aspects, from a structural interpretation of causality (see footnote 1), i.e. from a framework which allows intervention, while they are closer to a notion of predictability. A study of the relative merits of the different methods presented above with empirical and simulated data is left to future research.

Acknowledgements   The authors want to thank Isabelle Guyon, Alexander Statnikov, and Daniele Marinazzo for very valuable comments on a first draft.

References

1. Ehung Baek and William Brock.   A general test for nonlinear Granger causality: Bivariate model. *Iowa State University and University of Wisconsin at Madison Working Paper*, 1992.
2. David Bell, Jim Kay, and Jim Malley.   A non-parametric approach to non-linear causality testing. *Economics Letters*, 51(1):7–18, 1996.
3. David A Bessler and Seongpyo Lee.   Money and prices: US data 1869–1914 (a study with directed graphs). *Empirical Economics*, 27(3):427–446, 2002.
4. Taoufik Bouezmarni, Jeroen VK Rombouts, and Abderrahim Taamouti. Nonparametric copula-based test for conditional independence with applications to Granger causality. *Journal of Business & Economic Statistics*, 30(2):275–287, 2012.
5. Jean-François Cardoso and Antoine Souloumiac.   Blind beamforming for non-Gaussian signals.   In *IEE proceedings F (radar and signal processing)*, volume 140, pages 362–370. IET, 1993.

6. Nadine Chlaß and Alessio Moneta. Can graphical causal inference be extended to nonlinear settings? In *EPSA Epistemology and Methodology of Science*, pages 63–72. Springer, 2009.
7. Tianjiao Chu and Clark Glymour. Search for additive nonlinear time series causal models. *Journal of Machine Learning Research*, 9(May):967–991, 2008.
8. Diego Colombo, Marloes H Maathuis, Markus Kalisch, and Thomas S Richardson. Learning high-dimensional directed acyclic graphs with latent and selection variables. *The Annals of Statistics*, pages 294–321, 2012.
9. Pierre Comon. Independent component analysis, a new concept? *Signal processing*, 36(3):287–314, 1994.
10. David Danks and Sergey Plis. Learning causal structure from undersampled time series. *JMLR: Workshop and Conference Proceedings (NIPS Workshop on Causality)*, 2013.
11. Selva Demiralp and Kevin D Hoover. Searching for the causal structure of a vector autoregression. *Oxford Bulletin of Economics and statistics*, 65(s1):745–767, 2003.
12. Cees Diks and Valentyn Panchenko. A new statistic and practical guidelines for nonparametric Granger causality testing. *Journal of Economic Dynamics & Control*, 30:1647–1669, 2006.
13. Michael Eichler. Causal inference in time series analysis. *Causality: Statistical Perspectives and Applications*, pages 327–354, 2012.
14. Doris Entner and Patrik O Hoyer. On causal discovery from time series data using FCI. *Probabilistic graphical models*, pages 121–128, 2010.
15. Jan Eriksson and Visa Koivunen. Identifiability, separability, and uniqueness of linear ICA models. *IEEE signal processing letters*, 11(7):601–604, 2004.
16. Jean-Pierre Florens and Michel Mouchart. A note on noncausality. *Econometrica*, pages 583–591, 1982.
17. Claudia Foroni, Eric Ghysels, and Massimiliano Marcellino. Mixed-frequency vector autoregressive models. In *VAR Models in Macroeconomics–New Developments and Applications: Essays in Honor of Christopher A. Sims*, pages 247–272. Emerald Group Publishing Limited, 2013.
18. Andrea Gazzani and Alejandro Vicondoa. Proxy-svar as a bridge between mixed frequencies. *Unpublished Manuscript*, 2016.
19. John Geweke. Measurement of linear dependence and feedback between multiple time series. *Journal of the American Statistical Association*, 77(378):304–313, 1982.
20. Irving John Good. A causal calculus (i). *The British Journal for the Philosophy of Science*, 11(44):305–318, 1961a.
21. Irving John Good. A causal calculus (ii). *The British Journal for the Philosophy of Science*, 12(45):43–51, 1961b.
22. Christian Gouriéroux, Alain Monfort, and Jean-Paul Renne. Statistical inference for independent component analysis: Application to structural VAR models. *Journal of Econometrics*, 196(1):111–126, 2017.
23. Clive WJ Granger. Investigating causal relations by econometric models and cross-spectral methods. *Econometrica*, pages 424–438, 1969.
24. Clive WJ Granger. Testing for causality: a personal viewpoint. *Journal of Economic Dynamics and control*, 2:329–352, 1980.
25. Arthur Gretton, Kenji Fukumizu, Choon H Teo, Le Song, Bernhard Schölkopf, and Alex J Smola. A kernel statistical test of independence. In *Advances in neural information processing systems*, pages 585–592, 2008.
26. James Douglas Hamilton. *Time Series Analysis*, volume 2. Princeton university press Princeton, NJ, 1994.
27. Wolfgang Härdle, Helmut Lütkepohl, and Rong Chen. A review of nonparametric time series analysis. *International Statistical Review*, 65(1):49–72, 1997.
28. Trevor Hastie and Rob Tibshirani. Independent components analysis through product density estimation. In *Advances in neural information processing systems*, pages 665–672, 2003.
29. David F Hendry. *Dynamic Econometrics*. Oxford University Press on Demand, 1995.
30. Helmut Herwartz. Hodges–Lehmann detection of structural shocks–an analysis of macroeconomic dynamics in the Euro area. *Oxford Bulletin of Economics and Statistics*, 2018.

31. Craig Hiemstra and Jonathan D Jones. Testing for linear and nonlinear Granger causality in the stock price-volume relation. *The Journal of Finance*, 49(5):1639–1664, 1994.
32. Kevin D Hoover. *Causality in Macroeconomics*. Cambridge University Press, 2001.
33. Kevin D Hoover. Economic theory and causal inference. In Uskali Mäki, editor, *Philosophy of Economics*. North Holland, 2012.
34. Patrik O Hoyer, Shohei Shimizu, Antti J Kerminen, and Markus Palviainen. Estimation of causal effects using linear non-gaussian causal models with hidden variables. *International Journal of Approximate Reasoning*, 49(2):362–378, 2008.
35. Patrik O Hoyer, Dominik Janzing, Joris M Mooij, Jonas Peters, and Bernhard Schölkopf. Nonlinear causal discovery with additive noise models. In *Advances in neural information processing systems*, pages 689–696, 2009.
36. Antti Hyttinen, Sergey Plis, Matti Järvisalo, Frederick Eberhardt, and David Danks. Causal discovery from subsampled time series data by constraint optimization. *JMLR: Workshop and Conference Proceedings (PGM)*, 2016.
37. Aapo Hyvärinen. Independent component analysis: recent advances. *Phil. Trans. R. Soc. A*, 371(1984):20110534, 2013.
38. Aapo Hyvärinen and Erkki Oja. A fast fixed-point algorithm for independent component analysis. *Neural computation*, 9(7):1483–1492, 1997.
39. Aapo Hyvärinen, Juha Karhunen, and Erkki Oja. *Independent Component Analysis. Series on Adaptive and Learning Systems for Signal Processing, Communications, and Control*. Wiley, 2001.
40. Aapo Hyvärinen, Kun Zhang, Shohei Shimizu, and Patrik O Hoyer. Estimation of a structural vector autoregression model using non-gaussianity. *Journal of Machine Learning Research*, 11(May):1709–1731, 2010.
41. Rodney L Jacobs, Edward E Leamer, and Michael P Ward. Difficulties with testing for causation. *Economic Inquiry*, 17(3):401–413, 1979.
42. Oscar Jorda. Estimation and inference of impulse responses by local projections. *American Economic Review*, 95(1):161–182, 2005.
43. Maria Kalli and Jim E Griffin. Bayesian nonparametric vector autoregressive models. *Journal of Econometrics*, 203(2):267–282, 2018.
44. Lutz Kilian and Helmut Lütkepohl. *Structural Vector Autoregressive Analysis*. Cambridge University Press, 2017.
45. Gary Koop, M Hashem Pesaran, and Simon M Potter. Impulse response analysis in nonlinear multivariate models. *Journal of Econometrics*, 74(1):119–147, 1996.
46. RJ Kulperger and RA Lockhart. Tests of independence in time series. *Journal of Time Series Analysis*, 19(2):165–185, 1998.
47. Gustavo Lacerda, Peter L Spirtes, Joseph Ramsey, and Patrik O Hoyer. Discovering cyclic causal models by independent components analysis. In *Proc. Conf. on Uncertainty in Artificial Intelligence (UAI-08)*, pages 366–374, 2008.
48. Markku Lanne, Mika Meitz, and Pentti Saikkonen. Identification and estimation of non-gaussian structural vector autoregressions. *Journal of Econometrics*, 196(2):288–304, 2017.
49. Helmut Lütkepohl. Vector autoregressive models. In Nigar Hashimzade and Michael A. Thornton, editors, *Handbook of Research Methods and Applications in Empirical Macroeconomics*, pages 139–164. Edward Elgar, 2013.
50. Massimiliano Marcellino. Some consequences of temporal aggregation in empirical analysis. *Journal of Business & Economic Statistics*, 17(1):129–136, 1999.
51. David S Matteson and Ruey S Tsay. Independent component analysis via distance covariance. *Journal of the American Statistical Association*, 112(518):623–637, 2017.
52. Alessio Moneta. Graphical causal models and vars: an empirical assessment of the real business cycles hypothesis. *Empirical Economics*, 35(2):275–300, 2008.
53. Alessio Moneta, Doris Entner, Patrik O Hoyer, and Alex Coad. Causal inference by independent component analysis: Theory and applications. *Oxford Bulletin of Economics and Statistics*, 75(5):705–730, 2013.

54. Judea Pearl. *Probabilistic reasoning in intelligent systems: Networks of plausible reasoning.* Morgan Kaufmann Publishers, Los Altos, 1988.
55. Judea Pearl. *Causality: Models, Reasoning, and Inference.* Cambridge University Press, 2009.
56. Jonas Peters, Dominik Janzing, and Bernhard Schölkopf. Causal inference on time series using restricted structural equation models. In *Advances in Neural Information Processing Systems,* pages 154–162, 2013.
57. Jonas Peters, Joris M Mooij, Dominik Janzing, and Bernhard Schölkopf. Causal discovery with continuous additive noise models. *The Journal of Machine Learning Research,* 15(1):2009–2053, 2014.
58. Jonas Peters, Dominik Janzing, and Bernhard Schölkopf. *Elements of Causal Inference: Foundations and Learning Algorithms.* MIT press, 2017.
59. Giorgio E Primiceri. Time varying structural vector autoregressions and monetary policy. *The Review of Economic Studies,* 72(3):821–852, 2005.
60. Thomas Richardson and Peter Spirtes. Ancestral graph markov models. *The Annals of Statistics,* 30(4):962–1030, 2002.
61. Shohei Shimizu, Patrik O. Hoyer, Aapo Hyvärinen, and Antti Kerminen. A linear non-Gaussian acyclic model for causal discovery. *Journal of Machine Learning Research,* 7:2003–2030, 2006.
62. Christopher A Sims. Macroeconomics and reality. *Econometrica,* pages 1–48, 1980.
63. Peter Spirtes and Kun Zhang. Causal discovery and inference: concepts and recent methodological advances. In *Applied informatics,* volume 3, page 3. SpringerOpen, 2016.
64. Peter Spirtes, Clark N Glymour, and Richard Scheines. *Causation, Prediction, and Search.* MIT press, 2000.
65. Wolfgang Spohn. Probabilistic causality: From Hume via Suppes to Granger. In M. Galvotti and G. Gambetta, editors, *Causalità e modelli probabilistici,* pages 69–87. Clueb, 1983.
66. Liangjun Su and Halbert White. A nonparametric Hellinger metric test for conditional independence. *Econometric Theory,* 24(4):829–864, 2008.
67. Patrick Suppes. *A probabilistic theory of causality.* North-Holland, Amsterdam, 1970.
68. Norman R Swanson and Clive WJ Granger. Impulse response functions based on a causal approach to residual orthogonalization in vector autoregressions. *Journal of the American Statistical Association,* 92(437):357–367, 1997.
69. Kun Zhang and Aapo Hyvärinen. On the identifiability of the post-nonlinear causal model. In *Proceedings of the twenty-fifth conference on uncertainty in artificial intelligence,* pages 647–655. AUAI Press, 2009.
70. Kun Zhang, Jonas Peters, Dominik Janzing, and Bernhard Schölkopf. Kernel-based conditional independence test and application in causal discovery. In *Proceedings of the Twenty-Seventh Conference on Uncertainty in Artificial Intelligence,* pages 804–813. AUAI Press, 2011.

Chapter 6
Beyond Cause-Effect Pairs

Frederick Eberhardt

6.1   Introduction

This volume has focused on the identification of cause-effect pairs. The original cause-effect pair challenge at the NIPS 2008 Causality workshop considered the specific case of determining the edge orientation between two causal variables: $X \to Y$ vs. $X \leftarrow Y$ (that is, the blue partition in Fig. 6.1). The unconnected case $X \quad Y$ (case (c)) can be easily excluded with a suitable independence test. The NIPS 2013 challenge extended this setting to three classes, $X \to Y$, $X \leftarrow Y$ or the null class, which, for the purposes of that challenge, consisted of the unconnected case $X \quad Y$ or the case of pure confounding $X \leftrightarrow Y$ (this notation is used as shorthand for $X \leftarrow H \to Y$, where H is unobserved, but where neither X or Y cause each other). That is, it combined cases (c) and (d) in Fig. 6.1 into one class, which had to be distinguished from (a) and (c), resulting in the red partition.

As Dominik Janzing already noted in Chap. 1, the identification of the causal relation between two variables can, of course, be more complex than just determining whether one causes the other. The variables that cause each other may in addition be confounded (cases (e) and (f)), they might stand in a feedback relation, where each causes the other ($X \leftrightarrows Y$), or a combination of feedback and confounding. Moreover, dependencies between the two variables may arise for other reasons, such as sample selection bias, ill-defined variables or other non-causal relations, such as e.g. logical relations.

This chapter reverses the specific focus on determining the cause among a pair of variables by connecting the ideas that have come out of the NIPS 2013 challenge to the broader question of how to learn causal graph structures over multiple variables,

F. Eberhardt (✉)
Caltech, Pasadena, CA, USA
e-mail: fde@caltech.edu

© Springer Nature Switzerland AG 2019   215
I. Guyon et al. (eds.), *Cause Effect Pairs in Machine Learning*,
The Springer Series on Challenges in Machine Learning,
https://doi.org/10.1007/978-3-030-21810-2_6

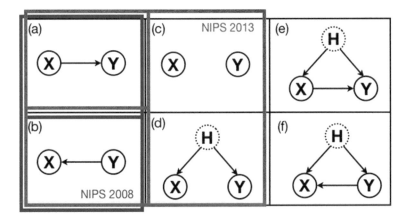

Fig. 6.1 The Cause-Effect Pair challenge and its extensions. The original 2008 proposal focused on the distinction between X causing Y and Y causing X, cases (**a**) and (**b**), the blue partition. The NIPS 2013 challenge had three output classes, (**a**) vs. (**b**) vs. {(**c**), (**d**)}, i.e. the red partition, H is assumed to be unobserved. The six depicted causal structures linking X and Y were distinguished by the classification method developed in Chalupka et al. [5], but they assumed that X, Y and H are all discrete. Of course, there are other possible causal structures among the two variables, such as a feedback loop (alone or in combination with unobserved confounding), and observed dependencies between two variables may have other non-causal sources, such as sample selection bias or ill-defined variables

and by placing the cause-effect pair challenge in the context of a variety of other causal discovery challenges.

In many ways, the generalization to learning the causal structure over a set of variables is anachronistic, as the development of methods for learning causal *graphs* from observational data preceded most of the methods for causal *pairs* discussed in this volume. Prior to the focus on causal pairs, causal discovery algorithms primarily used the independence structure over a set of variables to infer something about the underlying causal structure (see, e.g. the discovery algorithms discussed in Spirtes et al. [33]). The independence structure often (though not always!) underdetermines the orientations of edges and consequently two or more different causal structures cannot be distinguished. These are then said to be Markov equivalent, as are, in particular, $X \to Y$ and $X \leftarrow Y$. Consequently, a significant motivation for studying causal pairs came from a desire to improve the number of edges that could be oriented for a discovery algorithm that outputs equivalence classes of causal graphs. This challenge then resulted in several methods to solve the Cause-Effect-Pair problem, distinguishing whether $X \to Y$, $X \leftarrow Y$ or neither. However, as is evident from the possible output classes of the NIPS 2013 challenge, the solution proposals were developed under the explicit assumption that confounding does not co-occur with a direct causal relation between the variables: Either one of the variables causes the other, or (exclusive or!) there is confounding or (inclusive or!) independence. There was no need to be sensitive to the distinction between cases (a) and (e) or (b) and (f) in Fig. 6.1. My understanding is that training data was only generated from these three classes. Consequently, it is by no means obvious that methods that are successful at solving the cause-effect pair challenge would similarly work as a post-processing step to orient causal edges in a structure learning graph that returns unoriented edges that may, in addition, be confounded.

This chapter then aims to achieve the following: In Sect. 6.2 we explore whether and how the winning methods from the NIPS 2013 cause-effect pair challenge could be generalized to consider more classes. Section 6.3 briefly discusses the existing approaches (and their challenges) that apply to the cause-effect pair challenge, but have in fact been generalized to graph learning methods. Section 6.4 considers the generalization of the Cause-Effect Pair challenge in a different direction—not as an expansion to more variables, but posing it as a challenge in new types of discovery scenarios over a pair of variables. And finally, Sect. 6.5 considers an inverted version of the cause-effect pair challenge: how can one construct a cause-effect pair if in fact one has a large number of individual variables that one would like to aggregate into a pair of cause and effect variables?

6.2 How to Extend the Winning Methods Beyond the Cause-Effect Pair Case?

Figure 6.1 illustrates in red the partition of the output that was considered in the NIPS 2013 challenge. A natural initial extension is to ask whether there are straightforward adaptations of the methods that succeeded at that challenge to address, for example, the distinction among all six possible causal structures. That is, in particular, are these methods extendable to distinguish cases that have unobserved confounding in combination with a causal relation? I omit the case involving feedback here primarily because the presence of feedback raises separate questions about how exactly the data was sampled (e.g. as a time series or in equilibrium?) and what exactly the feedback graph means. Chapter 5 considers these issues in more detail.

6.2.1 Classification-Based Causal Discovery

Remarkably, all the winning or highly ranked methods of the actual competition discussed in this volume treated the challenge as a pure classification task [7, 22, 23, 29]. In part, as Janzing describes in Chap. 1, converting the causal discovery problem to a classification task was a deliberate aim of the challenge, since it vastly simplified the comparative evaluation between methods.

The highly ranked approaches applied relatively standard machine learning methods of the time to generate and select between 20 and 20,000 features using the training data, which were then in turn applied to classifying the test data.

The winning method [23] deliberately did not select features associated with well-understood justifications for their relevance to causal inference, but instead used feature patterns, which generated features from a set of simple measures of the data (that is, features were generated from e.g. means, correlations, various loss functions etc.). In contrast, the second placed method [7] at least used some features that were based on the assumption that when in fact $X \rightarrow Y$, then the conditional distribution $P(Y|X)$ is simpler than the conditional distribution $P(X|Y)$. Such an assumption derives from the "independent mechanisms" assumption discussed in Chap. 1. This approach is echoed, though with different features, in a subsequent paper [11].

The extension of these pure classification-based approaches to the problem when the pair of causal variables may (also) be confounded is conceptually trivial. It merely extends the classification problem from two (or three) classes (the blue or red partition in Fig. 6.1) to however many more constellations of two variables one intends to distinguish. One would expect that with more classes, more features might have to be generated, but to the extent that there is any marker in the data that provides a basis for distinctions between the underlying causal structures, there will be suitable classifiers (if not the present ones) that distinguish the classes.

This, however, is the crux of this approach: We know from basic results about the identifiability of causal models that for linear Gaussian and multinomial parameterizations, the underlying causal structure remains underdetermined by the Markov equivalence class, i.e. by the set of causal models that share the same independence structure. Under the assumption that the causal model is acyclic and that there are no unmeasured common causes, Geiger and Pearl [8] and Meek [21] proved the completeness of independence based methods for continuous and discrete causal models, respectively:

Theorem 6.1 (Markov Completeness) *For linear Gaussian and multinomial causal relations, an algorithm that identifies the set of causal graphs with the same independence structure is complete.*

That is, if the value of each variable in the causal graph is determined by a linear function of its parents in the graph plus a Gaussian error term, or if the model is multinomial, then the independence structure contains all the information about the causal structure that there is. So, in particular, for these parameterizations, $X \rightarrow Y$ and $X \leftarrow Y$ cannot be distinguished in principle. In fact, this underdetermination is worsened if there can be unmeasured common causes. So for a causal pair, no matter whether in fact there is an edge one way or the other, or confounding, within the class of linear Gaussian or multinomial models, any of those structures can be fit to the data. As we will see in Sect. 6.3 this is not true for other specific model classes (such as e.g. for additive noise models). For those model classes, the underlying causal model can be uniquely (or close to uniquely) identified. For many other classes of models the identifiability is simply unknown.

What do these types of identifiability results imply for classification based causal discovery methods?—Most obviously, unless some additional assumption about, for example, the parameterization of the causal relations is made, such classifiers will exhibit an irreducible baseline error, a misclassification error that cannot be avoided.

In the strict sense of the statistical term then, these methods cannot be consistent, since the models are not uniquely identifiable.

In classification tasks in machine learning, such a baseline error is standard and widely accepted as an unavoidable difficulty of the problem to be solved—after all, not all images of dogs can be distinguished from all images of cats. But for causal discovery, the challenge for any extension along these lines is that if there is no theoretical justification for the features being used, it remains unclear what the magnitude of the irreducible error of the method is. The estimation of such an error hinges on the appropriateness of the assumption that the training and test data accurately represent the manifold of causal models that the algorithm is subsequently applied to. Of course, the appropriateness of the training and test data is an issue every classification algorithm faces for any domain (e.g. are 20% of the images I will have to classify really going to be dogs, as my training/test datasets suggest?). But in the causal case this problem is exacerbated due to the dearth of real data for which the true causal model is known. For dogs and cats we have a sense of the manifold that any image of them will lie on. The manifold of causal models we encounter in our data is much more elusive, not least because for many datasets we have no idea what the ground truth is. Unlike for images of cats and dogs where a simple inspection of the image can generally determine the label, the true causal structure is not written into the data in any obvious way. This is why the Tübingen causal pairs data set [24] proves so useful—it starts to address the question of what real data looks like in cases where we know (or have good reason to think we know) the causal ground truth.

Thus, while traditional causal discovery methods use background assumptions about the underlying causal model (say, linearity, Gaussianity etc.) as basis for the identifiability results, classification-based approaches to causal discovery have to replace these with an assumption that the training/test data is appropriate for the actual application of the algorithm and have to hope that the classes (the different underlying causal models) can indeed be distinguished (with a low misclassification error).

The assumption of independent mechanisms (discussed in Chap. 1) provides a basis for this latter hope, as it offers a reason to expect detectable features in the data that indicate what the underlying causal model is. These features might track the complexities of the conditional distributions or identify particular independencies between residuals in the data. Nevertheless, even under this assumption it remains quite unclear how to obtain well-justified estimates of the inevitable misclassification error, since the notion of independence in the assumption of independent mechanisms, or the notion of complexity for the conditionals, is only understood either in very abstract form (in terms of Kolmogorov complexity) or for very restricted settings (with a specific computable measure). Chapter 1 discusses some of these issues and provides useful references.

6.2.2 Extensions

In light of the previous considerations, what can we say about the extension
of classification based causal discovery algorithms beyond the cause-effect pair
challenge?

Obviously, one can build a classifier with more classes and generate training
and test data for which one knows that the classes are identifiable, thereby
guaranteeing in principle a zero misclassification error. Alternatively, one could
train a classification algorithm on a dataset with more varied ground truth causal
structures and hope for the best that (1) they are distinguishable, and (2) that the
examples are representative of the domain of application. This latter approach is
essentially the route Lopez-Paz et al. [18] took when they trained a neural net on
the features of a kernel mean embedding of the distribution of a pair of variables
to address the causal pair task. They suggest that their approach can be extended to
the more general case of also distinguishing confounding by simply adding more
classes, but they do not actually show any results for the confounded case.

In Chalupka et al. [5] we took a somewhat different approach in trying to
classifying the six cases shown in Fig. 6.1, for discrete data. Obviously, for general
multinomial distributions, these models are not identifiable (except for case (c)).
Motivated by the assumption of "independent mechanisms", we made the following
assumptions:

1. $P(\text{effect} \mid \text{cause}) \perp\!\!\!\perp P(\text{cause})$
2. $P(\text{effect} \mid \text{cause} = c)$ is sampled from an uninformative hyperprior for each c.
3. $P(\text{cause})$ is sampled from an uninformative hyperprior

In fact, (2) is often not taken to be part of the independent mechanisms assumption, instead allowing for additional structure within the generating conditional
distribution. In the case of finite discrete variables, the uninformative hyperprior is
given by the Dirichlet distribution with all parameters set to 1. Under these generating assumptions the causal models (a) vs. (b) in Fig. 6.1 are not strictly identifiable,
but we were able to derive an analytic classification boundary with a well-defined
irreducible misclassification error. Without putting significant restrictions on the
nature of the confounder, we could not derive analytical classification boundaries
for all six cases in Fig. 6.1, but instead used a neural net trained on distributions
generated under the assumptions given above.

The approach we took is intermediate between the case of making sufficient
background assumptions that guarantee full identifiability, and one where the
irreducible misclassification error is completely unknown. We leveraged the fact that
the training and test data is known to contain features that distinguish the classes,
even if a baseline error remains. As can be seen in Fig. 6.2, the biggest "confusion"
for the classifier arises, unsurprisingly, in distinguishing the orientation. But as noted
above, while we can estimate the inevitable misclassification error in this way for
the general problem of classifying the six causal structures in Fig. 6.1, it remains

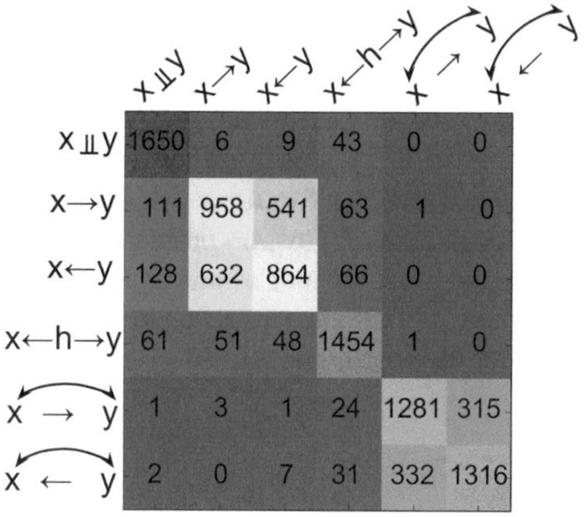

Fig. 6.2 Confusion matrix for the classification method developed in Chalupka et al. [5] (their figure) to address the causal discovery task of distinguishing the six causal structures in Fig. 6.1. The test set contained 10,000 distributions, with all the classes sampled with equal probability. For the confusion matrix presented here X and Y are binary discrete variables. There is significantly less confusion when the cardinality of the variables is increased. When each variable has more than 10 states, there is hardly any misclassification error—see the reference for details

unclear how reasonable these data generating assumptions are for any domain of application.

The only other approach that I am aware of (thanks to an anonymous reviewer) that attempts to tackle the full set of structures shown in Fig. 6.1 is in Janzing and Schoelkopf [15]. Here the authors take X, Y and H to be high-dimensional continuous variables, and apply spectral analysis. But rather than a lack of effort, I suspect that the dearth of attempts to extend the classification-based approach likely indicates the following realization: While these classification approaches are straightforwardly generalizable to include more possibilities of the causal relation between two variables (confounding, feedback, selection bias etc.), we generally have little insight about the manifold that causal structures in any domain may be described by. Consequently, our training data for these causal classification algorithms is a somewhat arbitrary guess about the distribution of causal models we expect to encounter. In contrast, in the case of the standard domains of application of classification algorithms, such as image or text classification, we have a relatively good understanding of the manifold that our samples come from, and we can more easily explore the classification boundaries actively.

On the other hand, if there is a justification for the features that the classification is based on—generally these are motivated by some version of the independent mechanisms assumption—then for simple cases the irreducible misclassification error can be quantified (such as in Hernandez-Lobato et al. [11] and Chalupka et al. [5]), but these analytic results are often not easily generalized beyond the very simple cases.

6.3   Established Extensions to Graph Search

The previous section considered the generalization of the cause-effect pair challenge to more than just the two possible relationships between two variables $X \to Y$ and $X \leftarrow Y$. One may think that the search for causal graphs, i.e. a structure over a set of variables, is then just a repeated classification problem of the relationship between any two variables in the graph. I am not aware of any such approach using the types of feature-based classification algorithms suggested by the winning methods of the NIPS challenge, but the recent publication of Goudet et al. [10] goes in this direction.

6.3.1   Additive Noise Models

There are a variety of methods based on the Additive Noise Model (see Peters et al. [26] for an overview of ANMs) that both apply to the cause-effect pair challenge *and* have been extended to the general graph search. In fact, in the case of the "LiNGAM" discovery method for Linear non-Gaussian Models (a subclass of the additive noise models), the method was developed for graph search from the outset [32].

One way of looking at the ANM-based methods is to return to Geiger & Pearl's limiting result (Theorem 6.1 above) that indicates that for *linear Gaussian* models the Markov equivalence class of the true model is the best one can hope for from a causal discovery algorithm. This limiting result says nothing about the case when the causal relations are *non*-linear or *non*-Gaussian.

Shimizu et al. [32] considered precisely one of these cases and showed that if the functional relation still remains linear, but the error terms are anything but Gaussian (LiNGAM), then the causal graph is uniquely identifiable. That is, the causal graph is identifiable if for each variable $y \in \mathbf{V}$, y is given by

$$y = \sum_{x_i \in pa(y)} a_i x_i + \epsilon_y \quad \text{with} \quad \epsilon_y \sim NonGauss(\theta),$$

where $pa(y)$ are the parents of y in the graph and $NonGauss(\theta)$ is some non-degenerate distribution that is not Gaussian. So, in particular, $X \to Y$ and $X \leftarrow Y$ can be distinguished in this model class.

With slightly weaker identifiability results, LiNGAM has been extended to acyclic causal structures with latent variables [13] and to causal structures with cycles (but without latent confounding) [17]. So in many ways the LiNGAM method is precisely what one would have hoped to discover in the cause-effect pair challenge, since it addresses that particular challenge, but could also be extended usefully to more general scenarios. But it preceded the challenge.

The identifiability results for the non-linear ANMs take the other alternative of avoiding Theorem 6.1 by exploring the role of the function. They assume that for each variable $y \in \mathbf{V}$, y is given by

$$y = f_y(pa(y)) + \epsilon_y$$

where $f_y(.)$ is a continuous function and ϵ_y is an additive error term with some positive distribution. Hoyer et al. [12] then show that in general (i.e. except for very special cases, that include the linear Gaussian case) $X \rightarrow Y$ can be distinguished from $X \leftarrow Y$. Peters et al. [25] extended the identifiability result to graph structures.

It is worth noting an important aspect to the non-linear ANMs that is rarely discussed in any detail: Unlike the LiNGAM model or traditional linear Gaussian or multinomial causal models, non-linear ANMs are not (in general) closed under marginalization. This effectively makes them inapplicable to scenarios with unmeasured confounding, or, for that matter, any unobserved variable. If the true model is a non-linear ANM, the marginalized observable model is, in general, not. This feature then places a strong demand on having exactly the right set of variables: if the world is indeed well-described by non-linear ANMs, then there is exactly one level of correct causal description. Note, for example that the approach to confounder detection considered by Janzing et al. [16] only considers non-linear ANMs where there is no causal connection between the observed variables, and therefore the marginalization problem does not arise. Of course, one might take the unique level of causal description implied by non-linear ANMs as a virtue, useful to detect truly direct causal relations, rather than as problem of this model class. In that case, it would be of interest to develop an argument why we should expect the world to be structured in this way.

While the LiNGAM methods in their original incarnation identified the graph directly on the basis of matrix operations on the data, the extensions of non-linear ANMs to identifying the graph are really just an iterative procedure of applying the pairwise result, taking into account that any edge might now also be subject to confounding from a variable higher up in the graph structure. In the Causal Additive Model (CAM) approach of Bühlmann et al. [2], which considers non-linear ANMs with Gaussian errors, the search method first determines the (partial) order of the variables in the causal graph using maximum likelihood estimation, and then subsequently the specific parents of each variable are determined using sparse regression.

Other approaches based on the LiNGAM model echo this division of labor and also outsource the search for graph structure to methods that use the independence structure (such as the PC algorithm) and then only attempt to resolve the orientations. For example, Zhang and Chan [35] and Zhang and Hyvärinen [34] consider the case where the data is generated by a linear non-Gaussian model and then subject to a non-linear invertible transformation. This post-nonlinear model is in general identifiable. The generalization from the pairwise case to a graph is simply done by using another method like the PC-algorithm to search for the adjacency structure among the variables and then applying the post-non-linear test to each undirected edge. A similar approach is taken by various other methods implemented in the Tetrad code package [1].

While these identifiability results are remarkable and constitute significant theoretical advances, the success of these methods at orienting edges in practice remains unclear. Perhaps the most thorough empirical investigation of the Additive Noise Methods was done in Mooij et al. [24] with a specific focus on the cause-effect pair challenge. The results were mixed, with the method described in Hoyer et al. [12] obtaining the best results. I am not aware of investigations that systematically considered graph search.

The LiNGAM methods and variations of them have been applied in a variety of real-world settings or realistic simulations and the authors report results on edge orientations that are consistent with background knowledge (see e.g. Shimizu and Bollen [31] and Ramsey et al. [27]). However, I am not aware of any application of these methods where an edge orientation that was not determinable from the independence structure, was subsequently confirmed, e.g. by experimentation. It remains an open question just how good these orientation methods are in practice.

6.4 More Causal Challenges for Pairs of Variables

Section 6.2 discussed the possibility of extending the methods developed for the cause-effect pair challenge to other causal scenarios among pairs of variables. Although we did not discuss cases of selection bias or feedback cycles in any detail, these are all cases that can be well described within the framework of causal graphical models. This section considers two cases of the search for cause-effect pairs that do not neatly fit this framework, but are still of significant interest to causal discovery.

6.4.1 Discovery of Dynamical Causal Relations

Chapter 5 already discussed causal discovery in time series data. Time series data has the advantage of providing a time order over the samples and therefore somewhat restricts the possible causal influences among variables. But this time order usually comes in fixed discrete intervals and in general there is no reason to think that the measurement interval has anything to do with the speed of the causal process. As a result, even if the causal inference algorithm works well, the discovered causal effects should be thought of as causal effects relative to the particular sampling rate. Various attempts have then been made to determine what the actual causal process looks like if the time series subsamples the causal process, i.e. when the causal effects occur faster than the sampling rate [9, 14].

In the extreme of infinitesimal time delay between cause and effect, the system can be described as a dynamical causal process. Time is continuous, and—at least in principle—one could obtain measurements at any time granularity. However, the data is not independent and identically distributed (i.i.d.), there is no stationary distribution or any of the other niceties that come with (or are generally assumed for) standard causal (even time series) data sets. Nevertheless, the cause-effect pair challenge still remains: How can we learn the causal relation between X and Y (if any) when they both have continuous-in-time trajectories?

As with the standard cause-effect pair challenge, one might define the ground truth in terms of the results of interventions: X is a cause of Y if an intervention that sets X to a particular value results in a change in Y. But can such a causal relation be learned from just observing a suitably long trajectory? If so, how?

Despite the fact that dynamical models are ubiquitous in the natural sciences, there are only very few approaches to causal discovery in dynamical systems. Roy and Jantzen [28] provide an explicitly causal treatment of the problem for the case of first order differential equation models. The challenge they pose can be easily stated: Suppose one has measurements in (continuous) time of two variables x and y, that may be unidirectionally coupled by a first order autonomous system, such as:

$$\dot{x} = \alpha(x, \dot{y}, y)$$
$$\dot{y} = \beta(y)$$

Clearly, y has an influence on x but not vice-versa (hence, unidirectional coupling). Given measurements of x and y in continuous time, and the assumption that we are only considering first order autonomous systems (i.e. no unmeasured variables), how can one determine that $y \rightarrow x$ and not vice versa? The authors propose a method based on symmetry transformations and compare their approach to methods based on Transfer Entropy and the Convergent Cross Map. This opens the door to address much more general questions of causal discovery in dynamical systems.

6.4.2 Discovery of Relational Causes

The second setting also concerns a non-i.i.d. scenario for the data collection, but the issue is rather different from the case of dynamical systems. Consider a relational database that contains individuals that have properties, e.g. whether they smoke or not, and relations, e.g. which other individuals they are friends with. A causal question about an individual I that one may hope to address with such a database is: Is it the friends that I has that cause I to smoke, or does I's smoking cause I's friends to smoke, or is there a common cause of I's own and I's friends' smoking, for example, the friendship relation itself? There may of course be other, even causal, explanations, but we can start with these.

The challenge in addressing these types of relational causal discovery questions arises from the fact that in addition to the causal relations, there are logical relations between the individuals, in this case the friendship relation, that need to be taken into account. These logical relations can introduce dependencies in the data that are not in fact causal. Similar such constraints may arise from boundary conditions or conservation laws, such as that the total energy in a physical system is constant or that there are resource constraints in economic models.

With a few very notable exceptions [19, 30], this task of relational causal learning has been completely neglected, even though it might be one of the most important causal questions when it comes to social science and social network data. The most thorough investigation in this direction has been done in a variety of publications Maier, Marazopolou and Jensen (see e.g. Maier et al. [20]. They have extended the PC algorithm to relational causal models. To my knowledge there has been no attempt to consider any of the insights from the cause-effect pair approaches in the relational setting.

6.5 Construction of Cause Effect Pairs

Finally, I will invert the cause-effect pair challenge to ask how we obtain our cause and effect pair variables in the first place. This question is motivated by a concern that I think has been neglected in the discussion of causal models:

What makes a random variable causal?

The previous section already suggested that there can be logical relations among variables in addition to causal ones. It follows from the definition of a random variable that every function of a random variable is a random variable. But the same is not true in the same way for causal variables: We do not consider X and the variable Y that is *defined* as $Y = 2X$ as two distinct causal variables. We might consider them to be two descriptions of the same variable, or a translation of one another, but we do not have two separate causal variables. In addition to the features of ordinary random variables, causal variables play a role in supporting interventions and counterfactuals. One cannot intervene on X without intervening on Y (as defined above), nor are the counterfactuals between definitionally related variables analogous to the counterfactuals between causally related variables. These points are generally emphasized when structural equations are introduced to describe causal relations: The authors generally point out that these equations should be understood as *assignments*, often marked by the symbol ":=", rather than as mathematical equations where quantities can be exchanged between sides of the equal sign. The reason, though not always explicitly stated, is that the causal relations permit interventions and counterfactual statements that are, in general, not symmetric.

Obviously, any dependence between X and Y (as $2X$) should be attributed to their mathematical relation, and not to any causal connection. But this realization leads us to a concern for causal discovery: Before applying any causal discovery methods to a dataset, we need to ensure that the variables are indeed all distinct and appropriate causal variables to be combined in a model, they should not be definitionally related. The approaches to relational causal learning in the previous section provide one avenue to address this challenge. I will here consider a different approach motivated not by relational databases, but by the challenge of constructing causal variables.

Consider the following example: There have been several studies exploring which features of a face lead to judging that face to be attractive. Subjects are shown a variety of portraits and asked to rate them on a scale of how attractive they consider the faces to be. What is the (visual) cause of such an attractiveness judgment? In this case we have an effect variable (the judgment), but it is unclear what the cause is. Is each pixel of the image a cause? Is the presence of a smile in the picture the cause? Is there a correct level of description at which to identify the cause?—Commonly, the symmetry of facial features is cited as a candidate cause of attractiveness judgments. (See e.g. the overview here: https://en.wikipedia.org/wiki/Facial_symmetry. The proposal is supported by evidence that changes in the symmetry of the depicted faces lead to changes in the attractiveness judgment.

One may well wonder whether symmetry tells the whole story. There is evidence that perfect symmetry appears uncanny and that slight asymmetries in the face score higher on attractiveness. For our purposes here, the key question is about how this search for causes should be approached in the first place. If we just consider candidate causal hypotheses that are easily described in a few words, then even if we find that they have some effect on the attractiveness judgment, they might only describe *aspects* or *indicators* of the full (visual) cause of the attractiveness judgment.

In current machine learning circles this concern would be approached using a deep neural net to identify possibly very complex features in the portrait images that do strongly predict the attractiveness judgment, even if the features themselves do not lend themselves to a simple description in natural language. Since the studies use an experimental set-up in which the evaluating subjects were shown portrait images in a lab setting that minimizes any confounding, the predictive features such a deep neural net detects can be considered to be causes of the attractiveness judgments, not merely predictive features. The appropriate description of the cause of the attractiveness judgment is not at the level of the pixels of the image, but at the level of the features of the image. The pixels *constitute* the features in the images, but the individual pixels are not causes of the attractiveness judgment. Manipulating an individual pixel will not change the attractiveness judgment (unless it is a very coarse image).

Here then is an attempt to give a coherent causal account of how we might identify and construct the cause of the attractiveness judgment from a low level pixel space: The pixels of the image containing the face describe a high dimensional state space $\mathscr{I}$. An image of a face specifies a state $I = i$ in the pixel state space $\mathscr{I}$, where I is the variable ranging over the state space. We can use a neural net to identify the features in pixel space that predict the attractiveness judgment E. The features identified by the neural net then provide a partition Π of the state space of the pixels $\mathscr{I}$. The cause C of the attractiveness judgment E is then a variable, whose state-space stands in a bijection to the labels of the cells of the partition Π identified by the neural net. So the cause C of the attractiveness judgment E *supervenes* on the pixel state space $\mathscr{I}$, in the sense that any change in the cause C necessitates a change of at least one pixel, but there may be changes of the pixels that do not affect the cause of the attractiveness judgment E. Importantly, the relationship between the pixels and the cause of the attractiveness judgment is a mathematical one, not a causal one. That is, the variable I ranging over the pixel state space $\mathscr{I}$ is related to C, the cause of the attractiveness judgment, by a mathematical (definitional) relation, not a causal one: $C = f(I)$. Figure 6.3 illustrates the relations, including the possibility the effect may also supervene on a much higher dimensional space $\mathscr{J}$. For example, the (mental) attractiveness judgment is presumably defined in terms of the underlying neural activity. In general, there may also be unobserved confounding between C and E, which complicates the inference from I to C, since some features of I now may be merely predictive of E, but no longer causes of E.

In the scenario of judging the attractiveness of images of faces shown in a lab setting, the features that a neural net identifies are obviously causal because the set-up is experimental: the pictures of faces are shown to the judge in experimental conditions. There is no confounding between content in the picture and the

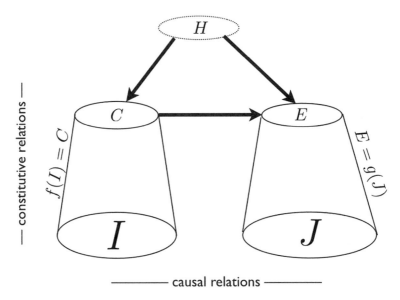

Fig. 6.3 Construction of cause effect pairs: Consider I and J to be very high-dimensional measurement variables, such as, for example images, or temperature maps, or neural recordings. In many cases only coarser descriptions of the underlying system are relevant to the causal questions we are interested in. For example, for the causal question "What makes a face look attractive?" we are not interested in the pixel values of the image depicting the face, but in candidate higher level features. Similarly, on the effect side, we are interested in the attractiveness judgment, not necessarily in the neural details that implement the attractiveness judgment. So we have a cause C of an effect E (which may in principle also be confounded by an unobserved H), but C and E supervene on the low level measurement spaces I and J, respectively. While the relations among C and E (and H) are causal, the relation between I and C is not causal, but constitutive (similarly, for J and E). Any intervention on C necessarily is an intervention on I. Given I and J, can we nevertheless construct a causal pair C and E?

attractiveness judgment. In these conditions, a simple application of a neural net an appropriate way to identify causal relations, since the predictive features correspond to the causal ones. But what if the data were non-experimental? For example, suppose we have a temperature map and a wind map over a specific geographical region that specify the temperature/windspeed for each location in the region. We obtained this data by observation, not experimentation, and for all we know, the two maps may be heavily confounded by the location of the sun or other geological activity. Can we still analyze the causal effect of the wind on the temperature?

One approach would be to consider the causal relations at the "pixel" level. Each individual "pixel" of the wind map would be a candidate cause for any of the "pixels" of the temperature map. If we allow for feedback, then the reverse relations would also have to be considered, and there could be confounding. But even leaving feedback relations and confounding aside, this approach would be equivalent to claiming in our earlier example of attractiveness judgments that each pixel of the image of the face individually may be a cause of the attractiveness judgment. While it is possible that our judgments of attractiveness are that sensitive, it seems implausible. The cause of the attractiveness judgment is a feature that *supervenes* on the pixels, it is a function of the pixels, the pixels themselves are not the relevant causal variables. Analogously then, a causal analysis of the relationship between wind and temperature over a geographical area may well exist at a coarser level of description than the "pixel level" of measurement. How then can we construct a cause-effect pair from two high-dimensional spaces of observational low level measurement variables?

In Chalupka et al. [3] we addressed this problem in the following way: Given high-dimensional measurement variables I and J, we wanted to find a method that could determine whether there are coarser variables C and E such that C is a cause of E, i.e. $C \rightarrow E$, and $C = f(I)$ and $E = g(J)$ for some surjective functions f and g. One of the criteria of identifying such a macro-level cause C of E is that we have to be able to define intervention distributions $P(E|do(C))$. That is, in order to define C, we have to be able to make sense of what it means to intervene on C and specify a well-defined effect for such an intervention.

We started with an approach similar to the one proposed above for the case of attractiveness judgments: Given the observational conditional probability distribution $P(J|I)$, we clustered states of I and J according to the following two equivalences:

$$i_1 \sim i_2 \iff \forall j \in J, \quad P(j|i_1) = P(j|i_2)$$
$$j_1 \sim j_2 \iff \forall i \in I, \quad P(j_1|i) = P(j_2|i)$$

That is, we clustered states of I if they implied the same conditional probability distribution for J, and we clustered states of J if for any i they had the same conditional probability distribution. This clustering can be performed by a neural net, and results in a partition $\Pi_o(I)$ of the state space of I and a partition $\Pi_o(J)$ of the state space of J. If the probabilities in the above equivalences had been interventional probabilities, i.e. $P(J|do(I))$, then the discovered partitions would already describe the states of C and E, respectively. But so far, the partitions only describe the dependencies between I and J in a maximally succinct form. These dependencies could still be entirely due to confounding between I and J.

So the questions is, how do the observational partitions Π_o defined by the equivalences above, differ from the causal partitions Π_c of the state spaces of I and J defined by:

$$i_1 \sim i_2 \Longleftrightarrow \forall j \in J, \quad P(j|do(i_1)) = P(j|do(i_2))$$

$$j_1 \sim j_2 \Longleftrightarrow \forall i \in I, \quad P(j_1|do(i)) = P(j_2|do(i))$$

The state space of C is defined as a bijection to the labels of the cells of the partition $\Pi_c(I)$ implied by the first equivalence: While there may be several different states of I that map to the same state of C, those differences are causally irrelevant to E.

We showed in the Causal Coarsening Theorem (see proof in Chalupka et al. [6]) that under relatively weak assumptions, if indeed there are descriptions of the causal system at a coarser level, then the causal partitions Π_c are a *coarsening* of the observational partitions Π_o. That is, the distinctions in the state space of I that are found by clustering on the basis of $P(J|I)$ are a superset of the distinctions in the state space of I that have a causal influence on J.

This should not come as a surprise: all dependencies between two variables, whether due to a causal relation or confounding, can be useful for predicting one variable from another. This is the reason why we use a barometer to predict the weather tomorrow: The distinctions it makes (in tracking pressure) are useful for prediction. But we do not think that the barometer reading is a cause of the weather tomorrow. The observational partition of the readings of the barometer needle are very fine, but the causal partition of the barometer readings is maximally coarse, since every reading has the same causal effect on the weather tomorrow, namely none.

The Causal Coarsening Theorem provides the basis for an efficient experimental method to check which distinctions in the observational partition are actually causally relevant. One does not have to check every possible state of I, but only the different distinctions of the observational partition. In cases where one cannot intervene, the methods developed as a result of the cause-effect pair challenge provide a natural basis to start detecting which features are causal and which are due to confounding.

The approach provides an account of how to construct causal variables with well-defined intervention distributions from low level measurement data. In Chalupka et al. [4] we extend this approach to consider cases where there might be multiple levels of causal description at various levels of analysis. But these results by no means provide a full-fledged account of how to identify causal variables. As they stand, they are restricted to discrete variables without feedback.

6.6 Final Remarks

My view is that the cause-effect pair challenge at the NIPS 2013 workshop failed in an interesting way: It did not produce winning methods with interesting generalizable insights for the field of causal discovery. However, this failure highlighted an important point about the limits of existing causal discovery methods: that for specific settings with well-established training and test data, brute force black box machine learning methods will outperform causal discovery algorithms. What is one to make of that?—Unlike the case of image or text classification, we rarely have a good understanding of what the ground truth causal relations look like. So the success of black box machine learning methods on these sorts of challenges provides very limited assurance of their success in general. This raises the question of how to structure causal discovery challenges in future? The Tübingen test data set seems like a step in the right direction. But we now need to go from the "causal MNIST" dataset to the "causal ImageNet". So which domains could provide large and varied datasets with known causal ground truth?

With regard to the general question of where we stand with regard to handling causal structures that are observationally Markov equivalent, I think the field has made enormous steps forward, largely driven by the careful analysis of the Additive Noise Model framework (which I frame broadly to include the LiNGAM methods). But on that front, the advance on the theoretical side has not yet been matched by broad successes in application.

References

1. Tetrad code package. URL http://www.phil.cmu.edu/tetrad/about.html.
2. Peter Bühlmann, Jonas Peters, Jan Ernest, et al. Cam: Causal additive models, high-dimensional order search and penalized regression. *The Annals of Statistics*, 42(6):2526–2556, 2014.
3. K. Chalupka, P. Perona, and F. Eberhardt. Visual causal feature learning. In *Proceedings of UAI*, 2015.
4. K. Chalupka, P. Perona, and F. Eberhardt. Multi-level cause-effect systems. In *Proceedings of AISTATS*, 2016a.
5. Krzysztof Chalupka, Frederick Eberhardt, and Pietro Perona. Estimating causal direction and confounding of two discrete variables. *arXiv preprint arXiv:1611.01504*, 2016b.
6. Krzysztof Chalupka, Frederick Eberhardt, and Pietro Perona. Causal feature learning: an overview. *Behaviormetrika*, 44(1):137–164, 2017.
7. José AR Fonollosa. Conditional distribution variability measures for causality detection. *arXiv preprint arXiv:1601.06680*, 2016.
8. D. Geiger and J. Pearl. On the logic of causal models. In *Proceedings of UAI*, 1988.
9. Mingming Gong, Kun Zhang, Bernhard Schoelkopf, Dacheng Tao, and Philipp Geiger. Discovering temporal causal relations from subsampled data. In *International Conference on Machine Learning*, pages 1898–1906, 2015.

10. Olivier Goudet, Diviyan Kalainathan, Philippe Caillou, Isabelle Guyon, David Lopez-Paz, and Michele Sebag. Learning functional causal models with generative neural networks. In *Explainable and Interpretable Models in Computer Vision and Machine Learning*, pages 39–80. Springer, 2018.
11. Daniel Hernandez-Lobato, Pablo Morales Mombiela, David Lopez-Paz, and Alberto Suarez. Non-linear causal inference using gaussianity measures. *Journal of Machine Learning Research*, 2016.
12. P.O. Hoyer, D. Janzing, J.M. Mooij, J.R. Peters, and B. Schölkopf. Nonlinear causal discovery with additive noise models. In D. Koller, D. Schuurmans, Y. Bengio, and L. Bottou, editors, *Advances in Neural Information Processing Systems 21*, pages 689–696. 2008a.
13. P.O. Hoyer, S. Shimizu, A.J. Kerminen, and M. Palviainen. Estimation of causal effects using linear non-Gaussian causal models with hidden variables. *International Journal of Approximate Reasoning*, 49:362–378, 2008b.
14. Antti Hyttinen, Sergey Plis, Matti Järvisalo, Frederick Eberhardt, and David Danks. A constraint optimization approach to causal discovery from subsampled time series data. *International Journal of Approximate Reasoning*, 90:208–225, 2017.
15. Dominik Janzing and Bernhard Schoelkopf. Detecting confounding in multivariate linear models via spectral analysis. *arXiv preprint arXiv:1704.01430*, 2017.
16. Dominik Janzing, Jonas Peters, Joris Mooij, and Bernhard Schölkopf. Identifying confounders using additive noise models. In *Proceedings of the Twenty-Fifth Conference on Uncertainty in Artificial Intelligence*, pages 249–257. AUAI Press, 2009.
17. G Lacerda, P Spirtes, J Ramsey, and P. O. Hoyer. Discovering cyclic causal models by independent components analysis. In *Proceedings of UAI*, pages 366–374, 2008.
18. David Lopez-Paz, Krikamol Muandet, Bernhard Schölkopf, and Ilya O. Tolstikhin. Towards a learning theory of cause-effect inference. In *ICML*, pages 1452–1461, 2015.
19. Marc Maier. *Causal Discovery for Relational Domains: Representation, Reasoning, and Learning*. PhD thesis, 2014.
20. Marc Maier, Katerina Marazopoulou, David Arbour, and David Jensen. A sound and complete algorithm for learning causal models from relational data. *arXiv preprint arXiv:1309.6843*, 2013.
21. C. Meek. Strong completeness and faithfulness in bayesian networks. In *Proceedings of UAI*, pages 411–418. Morgan Kaufmann Publishers Inc., 1995.
22. Bram Minnaert. Feature importance in causal inference for numerical and categorical variables.
23. Diogo Moitinho de Almeida. Pattern-based causal feature extraction.
24. Joris M Mooij, Jonas Peters, Dominik Janzing, Jakob Zscheischler, and Bernhard Schölkopf. Distinguishing cause from effect using observational data: methods and benchmarks. *The Journal of Machine Learning Research*, 17(1):1103–1204, 2016.
25. Jonas Peters, Joris M Mooij, Dominik Janzing, and Bernhard Schölkopf. Causal discovery with continuous additive noise models. *The Journal of Machine Learning Research*, 15(1):2009–2053, 2014.
26. Jonas Peters, Dominik Janzing, and Bernhard Schölkopf. *Elements of causal inference: foundations and learning algorithms*. MIT press, 2017.
27. Joseph D Ramsey, Stephen José Hanson, and Clark Glymour. Multi-subject search correctly identifies causal connections and most causal directions in the dcm models of the smith et al. simulation study. *NeuroImage*, 58(3):838–848, 2011.
28. Subhradeep Roy and Benjamin Jantzen. Detecting causality using symmetry transformations. *Chaos: An Interdisciplinary Journal of Nonlinear Science*, 28(7):075305, 2018.
29. Spyridon Samothrakis, Diego Perez, and Simon Lucas. Training gradient boosting machines using curve-fitting and information-theoretic features for causal direction detection.
30. Oliver Schulte and Hassan Khosravi. Learning graphical models for relational data via lattice search. *Machine Learning*, 88(3):331–368, 2012.
31. Shohei Shimizu and Kenneth Bollen. Bayesian estimation of causal direction in acyclic structural equation models with individual-specific confounder variables and non-gaussian distributions. *The Journal of Machine Learning Research*, 15(1):2629–2652, 2014.

32. Shohei Shimizu, Patrik O Hoyer, Aapo Hyvärinen, and Antti Kerminen. A linear non-gaussian acyclic model for causal discovery. *Journal of Machine Learning Research*, 7(Oct):2003–2030, 2006.
33. P. Spirtes, C. Glymour, and R. Scheines. *Causation, Prediction and Search*. MIT Press, 2 edition, 2000.
34. K. Zhang and A. Hyvärinen. On the identifiability of the post-nonlinear causal model. In *Proceedings of UAI*, pages 647–655. AUAI Press, 2009.
35. Kun Zhang and Lai-Wan Chan. Extensions of ICA for causality discovery in the Hong Kong stock market. In *International Conference on Neural Information Processing*, pages 400–409. Springer, 2006.

Chapter 7
Results of the Cause-Effect Pair Challenge

Isabelle Guyon and Alexander Statnikov

7.1 Introduction

The problem of attributing causes to effects is pervasive in science, medicine, economy and almost every aspects of our everyday life involving human reasoning and decision making. What affects your health? the economy? climate changes? The gold standard to establish causal relationships is to perform randomized controlled experiments. However, experiments are costly while non-experimental "observational" data collected routinely around the world are readily available. Unraveling potential cause-effect relationships from such observational data could save a lot of time and effort.

Consider for instance a target variable Y, like occurrence of "lung cancer" in patients. The goal would be to find whether a factor X, like "smoking", might cause Y. The objective of the challenge we organized on "cause-effect pairs" is to rank pairs of variables $\{X, Y\}$ to prioritize experimental verification of the conjecture that X causes Y. As is known, "correlation does not mean causation". More generally, observing a statistical dependency between X and Y does not imply that X causes Y or that Y causes X; X and Y could be consequences of a common cause. But, is it possible to determine from the joint observation of samples of two variables X and Y that X should be a cause of Y?

I. Guyon
Team TAU - CNRS, INRIA, Université Paris Sud, Université Paris Saclay, Orsay France

ChaLearn, Berkeley, CA, USA
e-mail: guyon@chalearn.org

A. Statnikov (✉)
SoFi, San Francisco, CA, USA

© Springer Nature Switzerland AG 2019
I. Guyon et al. (eds.), *Cause Effect Pairs in Machine Learning*,
The Springer Series on Challenges in Machine Learning,
https://doi.org/10.1007/978-3-030-21810-2_7

There are new algorithms that have appeared in the literature in the past few years that tackle this problem. This challenge has been an opportunity to the public to evaluate them and propose new techniques to improve on them. We provided hundreds of pairs of real variables with known causal relationships from domains as diverse as chemistry, climatology, ecology, economy, engineering, epidemiology, genomics, medicine, physics, and sociology. Those were intermixed with controls (pairs of independent variables and pairs of variables that are dependent but not causally related) and semi-artificial cause-effect pairs (real variables mixed in various ways to produce a given outcome).

This challenge was limited to pairs of variables **deprived of their context**. Thus constraint-based methods relying on conditional independence tests and/or graphical models were not applicable. The goal was to push the state-of-the art in complementary methods, which can eventually disambiguate Markov equivalence classes. The idea was to create a "causation coefficient", analogous to a correlation coefficient, but indicative not only of statistical dependency, but also of causal orientation. The cause-effect pair challenges [8, 9] attracted a large number of participants in the first round on Kaggle[1] focusing on accuracy (over 300) and only a few participants in the second round with code submission organized on Codalab,[2] with emphasis on code efficiency. The participants adopted a machine learning approach, which contrasted, at the time, with previously published model-based methods. They extracted numerous features of the joint empirical distribution of X and Y and built a classifier to separate pairs belonging to the class $X \rightarrow Y$ from other cases ($X \leftarrow Y$, $X \leftrightarrow Y$, and $X \perp Y$). The classifier was trained from examples provided by the organizers and tested on independent test data for which the truth values of causal relationships was known only to the organizers. The participants achieved an Area under the ROC Curve (AUC) over 0.8 in the first phase deployed on the Kaggle platform, which ran from March through September 2013, significantly outperforming baseline methods that reach an AUC around 0.6. The participants were then invited to improve upon the code efficiency by submitting fast causation coefficients on the Codalab platform (April through June 2014). The causation coefficients developed by the winners have been made available under open source licenses and the methods were presented at a NIPS workshop.[3] The challenge resources including data, code submitted by participants, and challenge platform remain available for students and researchers at http://www.causality.inf.ethz.ch/cause-effect.php.

7.1.1 Dataset

The design of the challenge dataset for round 1 (Table 7.1) is described in details in Chap. 2. The dataset, which is freely available for download,[4] can be very useful to

---

[1]https://www.kaggle.com/c/cause-effect-pairs.

[2]https://competitions.codalab.org/competitions/1381.

[3]http://clopinet.com/isabelle/Projects/NIPS2013/.

[4]Download the data http://www.causality.inf.ethz.ch/CEdata/AllDataCode/.

Table 7.1 Cause-effect pair challenge data statistics (round 1)

Dataset	All pairs	$X \to Y$	$X \leftarrow Y$	$X \leftrightarrow Y$	$X \perp Y$	real CE
Training	4050	965	1033	1010	1042	354
Validation	4050	986	1034	1014	1016	332
Test	4050	1041	1025	1007	977	364
Sup1 (artif, numeric)	5998	1514	1485	1500	1499	0
Sup2 (artif, mixed)	5989	1529	1466	1497	1497	0
Sup3 (real)	162	42	39	41	40	81
Total	24, 299	6077	6082	6069	6071	1131

continue evaluating methods and serve as a "mother distribution" for confirmatory analysis.

Briefly, we provided hundreds of pairs of real variables with known causal relationships, including real and semi-artificial pairs (80% semi-artificial data and 20% real data). Real data came from miscellaneous sources: including the UCI repository, past challenges (KDD cup, ChaLearn, Kaggle, DREAM, etc.), R datasets, and NYU transcriptome data [21, 22]. The pairs were drawn from a wide variety of domains of application (chemistry, climatology, ecology, economy, engineering, epidemiology, genomics, medicine, physics, and sociology). Semi-artificial data complemented the real data. They were obtained from real exogenous variables from machine learning and data mining datasets, which were passed through a wide variety of functions (line, parabola, cubic, sqrt, sine, hyperbola, log, exp, tanh, atanh, rbf) and noise mechanisms (pre- or post-multiplication with real exogenous variables). Both for real and artificial data, care was taken to disguise the marginal distributions so it would be impossible from such information alone to guess the causal direction. In particular, variables were standardized and the distribution of number of unique values was approximately balanced across causal classes. Specifically, all variables were post-processed in the same way:

- A random sub-sample of the *num_val* values original values was drawn without replacement uniformly on a log2 scale between *min_size* and *max_size*, where *min_size*=500 and *max_size*=8000. Pairs with less than 500 examples were not sub-sampled.
- Pairs having at least one variable with only one value were eliminated.
- Variables with two values were considered binary and mapped to 0/1.
- Categorical variables with C values were assigned randomly class numbers between 1 and C.
- Numerical variables (discrete or continuous) were standardized (the mean is subtracted and then the result is divided by the standard deviation) and then quantized by multiplying the result by 10,000 and rounding to the nearest integer.

The data were evenly split in three sets of equal sizes called training, validation, and test set, each including 4050 pairs. We computed the average absolute value of the Pearson correlation coefficient for the pairs of continuous variables, in the various causal categories. For pairs of independent variable we found 0.02. For $X \rightarrow Y$ and $X \leftarrow Y$, we obtained 0.35. For non causally related dependent variables $X \leftrightarrow Y$ we found 0.16. The last category can therefore be separated from $X \rightarrow Y$ and $X \leftarrow Y$ on the basis of correlation alone. However, this is not an easy separation, as the performance results indicate.

We provided two additional training datasets artificially generated. Those training datasets have balanced number of unique values across all classes. SUP1data includes ~6000 pairs of numerical variables. SUP2data includes ~6000 pairs of mixed variables (numerical, categorical, binary). We provided one additional training datasets generated from real data (SUP3data), except for the $X \leftrightarrow Y$ pairs that are semi-artificial.

The SUP3 data was analogous to other "real data" provided in the training, validation, and test sets. They were created from the Tuebingen dataset [15], publicly available at the time of the challenge. The role of X and Y was reversed in half of them to create both $X \rightarrow Y$ and $X \leftarrow Y$ pairs. A random subset of half of the original pairs was selected to create $X \perp Y$ pairs by randomly permuting independently the values of X and Y. The $X \leftrightarrow Y$ pairs were obtained from a random selection of half of the original pairs to which an algorithm that preserves the marginal distributions while destroying the causal relationships was applied. Pairs of artificially generated dependent variables that are not in a causal relationship were used. Their values were replaced by the values of the real variables in a way that preserves the rank ordering of the values (i.e. the smallest value in the artificial variable is the smallest in the real variable, the second smallest artificial value is the second smallest real value, etc.).

In round 2 (with code submission) fresh data were generated in a similar way for training, validation, and test, and in the same amount (4050/4150/4150).

7.1.2 Challenge Protocol

We briefly outline the challenge protocols. More details can be found on the websites of the challenge: http://www.causality.inf.ethz.ch/cause-effect.php.

1. **Kaggle version (first round)**: The first event that lasted 5 months (end of March to end of August 2013) was a "classical" data science challenge in which the problem was to submit predictions to a classification problem. During the development phase, the participants submitted results on the "validation set". The results were scored automatically on the platform and the corresponding scores were shown on the "public leaderboard". During the final phase, the participants had to submit executable code capable of reproducing their results BEFORE the organizers revealed the decryption key of the test data, then they submitted the predictions on test data. The official final ranking was obtained using test set scores kept on a "private leaderboard" visible to the organizers only, which was revealed after the challenge ended once the results were validated. To validate

the results, the organizers ran the code provided by the participants for the top 10 participants.

2. **Codalab version (second round)**: The second event lasted 2 months (mid April to mid June 2013). It made use of the capability of the Codalab platform to submit code (rather than just predictions). The participants had to submit either Python code or Windows compiled executables, which computed a "causation coefficient". Training was performed off-line by the participants (using training data supplied by the organizers). The code was tested on the platform using a new edition of the validation and test data, not supplied to the participants. The results on validation data and the execution time were provided as soon as the execution completed. The results on final test data were not revealed until the completion of the final phase.

The organizers encouraged the dissemination of results in several ways, by inviting the participants:

- to fill out "fact sheets" (a brief survey on methods used in the challenge) to which 27 participants responded;
- to submit contributions to one of two workshops (IJCNN 2013, August 4–9, 2013, and/or NIPS 2013, December 9, 2013).
- to submit short proceedings papers or full length papers to a special topic of the Journal of Machine Learning Research (JMLR).

We also proposed a data donation track. However, it was canceled because of insufficient participation.

7.1.3   Scoring Metrics

For the purpose of the challenge, variables X and Y are considered causally related if:

$$Y = f(Y, \text{noise}) \text{ or } X = f(Y, \text{noise}) .$$

If the former case, X is a cause of Y, and in the latter case Y is a cause of X. All other factors are lumped into the "noise" variable. Samples of joint observations of X and Y were provided, not organized in a time series. Feed-back loops were excluded and only four types of causal relationships considered: $\mathcal{G} = \{X \rightarrow Y , X \leftarrow Y , X \leftrightarrow Y , X \perp Y \}$, as previously defined. The problem was brought back to a 2-class classification problem: for each pair of variable (X, Y), determine whether $X \rightarrow Y$ or not.

The participants were expected to produce a score between $-$ inf and $+$ inf, large positive values indicating $X \rightarrow Y$ with certainty, large negative values indicating that $X \leftarrow Y$ with certainty, middle range scores (near zero) indicating $X \leftrightarrow Y$ or $X \perp Y$.

For each pair of variables, there is a ternary truth value indicating whether $X \rightarrow Y$ $(+1)$, $X \leftarrow Y$ (-1), or neither (0). The scores provided by the participants was used as ranking criterion. Their entries were evaluated with two Area Under the ROC curve (AUC) scores: Let $\hat{Y}$ be the predicted score $\hat{Y} \in [-\inf, +\inf]$ and Y the target values $Y \in \{-1, 01\}$. We define $Y_1 = Y$; $Y_1(Y == 0) = -1$; and $Y_2 = Y$; $Y_2(Y == 0) = +1$;. Then, the score of the challenge is defined as:

$$\text{Score} = \text{Bidirectional AUC} = 0.5 \left(AUC(\hat{Y}, Y_1) + AUC(\hat{Y}, Y_2) \right) \quad (7.1)$$

The Forward AUC $AUC(\hat{Y}, Y_1)$ measures the success at correctly detecting that $X \rightarrow Y$ rather than $\{X \leftarrow Y, X \leftrightarrow Y, X \perp Y\}$. The Backward AUC $AUC(\hat{Y}, Y_2)$ measures the success at correctly detecting that $X \leftarrow Y$ rather than $\{X \rightarrow Y, X \leftrightarrow Y, X \perp Y\}$. Since the problem is symmetric, we average both Forward and Backward AUC.

The organizers also computed various other score for analysis purpose, but they were not used to rank the participants. These other scores assessed the capability of the methods to identify not only the causal direction, but to detect independence and confounding. Let is call C the causation coefficient provided by the participants and T the target values $\{-1, 0, 1\}$ (-1 for $X \leftarrow Y$, $+1$ for $X \rightarrow Y$ and 0 otherwise).

- **(challenge) Score:** The score of the challenge, that is the average of two AUCs for the separation of $X \rightarrow Y$ vs. everything else and $X \leftarrow Y$ vs. everything else.
- **Causality (score):** Similar to the score of the challenge, but limited to the pairs $X \rightarrow Y$ and $X \leftarrow Y$. To compute this score, the $X \rightarrow Y$ and $X \leftarrow Y$ pairs are removed.
- **Confounding (score):** AUC for the separation of $X \leftrightarrow Y$ vs. ($X \rightarrow Y$ or $X \leftarrow Y$) using abs(C). To compute this score, the $X \perp Y$ pairs are removed.
- **Dependency (score):** AUC for the separation of $X \perp Y$ vs. ($X \rightarrow Y$ or $X \leftarrow Y$) using abs(C). To compute this score, the $X \leftrightarrow Y$ pairs are removed.

Notice that there is no score measuring how well $X \leftrightarrow Y$ and $X \perp Y$ are separated since these two classes were lumped together with the same target 0.

The teams HiDloN and Bruce Cragin returned a causation coefficient not centered on zero (a mere ranking of the pairs, smallest rank corresponding to most likely $X \leftarrow Y$ cases and highest rank to most likely $X \rightarrow Y$ cases. This did not affect the calculation of the score of the challenge. However, this prevented us to compute the dependency and confounding score. To allows us to do that, we just centered their prediction coefficient by subtracting its mean over all pairs.

7.1.4   Top Performing Causation Coefficients

The results of both challenge rounds are shown in Tables 7.3 and 7.5.

Round 1: Cause-effect Pair Challenge (on Kaggle)

In Fig. 7.1, we plotted the ROC curves for Round 1. They all present a strange inflexion point that is uncommon and attributable to the non-homogeneity of the data distribution, including four sub-classes $\mathcal{G} = \{X \rightarrow Y , X \leftarrow Y , X \leftrightarrow Y , X \perp Y \}$. The multi-modal nature of the distribution is also visible in Fig. 2.4.

The three winners of Round 1 are:

1. **Team ProtoML-score = 0.8196**, which ranked first (Diogo Moitinho de Almeida) [2], with a method using nearly 20,000 features created automatically based on curve fitting residuals using various models, then processed by a Gradient Boosting Machine (GBM) [1, 5, 6].
2. **Team Jarfo-score = 0.8105**, which ranked second (José Adrián Rodríguez Fonollosa) [3, 4], with a method largely based on information theoretic features and statistics of the conditional distribution, also followed by a GBM classifier.

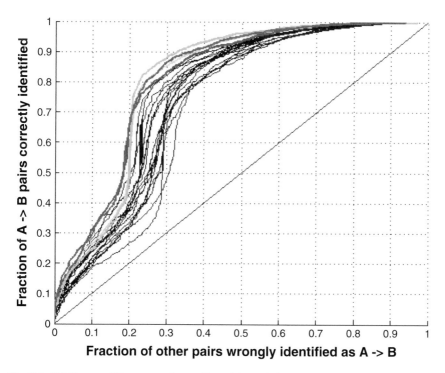

Fig. 7.1 ROC curves. We compare the top 20 participants ROC curves for the separation $X \rightarrow Y$ vs. other cases. The four best curves are color-coded: Red = ProtoML, Green = Jarfo, Blue = HiDloN, Cyan = FirfiD

3. **Team FirfID-score = 0.7996**, which ranked fourth (Spyridon Samothrakis, Diego Perez, and Simon Lucas) [18] also used a method based on curve fitting and information theoretic features, followed by a GBM.

In Round 1, 44 participants out of 267 submitted code for verification, including all top 10 ranking participants. For the most part, the code was written in Python, but we also received R and Matlab code. The organizers could reproduce the results of all top 10 ranking teams, except for those of the HiDLoN team, which they could not get to work. Because of lack of time to debug the problem, the HiDLoN team decided to drop out. The prizes went to the teams ProtoML, Jarfo and FirfID, who made their code publicly available under an open source license.

All three winning methods are remarkably similar. It may be more than a coincidence that all three used GBM as a classifier, a method based on ensembles of decision trees. An overwhelming majority of participants used ensembles of decision trees (85%). This may have been biased by the Python sample code that provided an example using Random Forests [11]. However, the top ranking participants report better performances using GBM.

One may wonder if additional performance increase could still be gained. To partially answer this question, we averaged the predictions of the top ranking participants. Specifically, we first replaced the predicted values by their rank, as a mean of normalizing them. We then averaged the ranks, using the validation set accuracy to weigh their importance. The maximum score obtained is **0.8452**, a notable improvement over the final test score of the winner 0.8196, and the next value to beat!

In post-challenge experiments, Alexander Statnikov and Sisi Ma of NYU performed tests on fresh data, not used in the challenge (Table 7.2). The datasets used in these experiments have been released on the Causality Workbench repository (ECOLI and YEAST). Two experiments were conducted on the three winning algorithms. Both experiments utilize a dataset (GNW_E.Coli dataset) with 3648 cause effect pairs (with 3616 number of one-sided edges and 32 double-sided edges) where each pair has 1565 samples. This dataset was generated with GeneNetWeaver

Table 7.2 Post-challenge (Cause-Effect Pairs) experiments: results on a new 3648 pairs dataset generated with GeneNetWeaver [19]

	Algorithm	Experiment 1 NO retraining	Experiment 2 Retraining
AUC	Jarfo	0.8730	0.9972
	FirfiD	0.5963	0.9845
	ProtoML	0.8085	0.9908
Time	Jarfo	~5 h	~5 h
	FirfiD	~7 h	~8 h
	ProtoML	~10 h	~12 h

3.0 [19], based on the E.coli transcriptional regulatory network. This dataset were not available to participants at the time of the competition. For **Experiment 1**, models were trained with a training set of 4050 cause effect pairs, provided by the cause effect challenge (which contains pairs of REAL data of Yeast and E.coli transcriptional data) and were tested on the whole GNW_E.Coli dataset (3648 cause effect pairs). For **Experiment 2**, the GNW_E.Coli dataset was split into a training set of 1824 cause effect pairs and a test set of 1824 cause effect pairs, respectively. AUCs were computed on the predictions of test sets as a performance metric for individual algorithms. Double sided edges were excluded when computing the AUC. These experiments show that the Jarfo coefficient is robust to changes in data distribution. All algorithms do well when retraining, but they are less capable of generalizing across datasets than the Jarfo coefficient.

Round 2: Fast Causation Coefficient Challenge (on Codalab)
The code of Jarfo, which was the most computationally efficient and robust to changes in data distribution among the top ranking methods of Round 1, was chosen to become the baseline to beat in Round 2 (Fast causation coefficient challenge), whose objective was to obtain a practical method running in reasonable time.

The three winners of Round 2 are:

1. **Team Jarfo-score = 0.8264 (1891 s)** of Jossé Adrián Rodríguez Fonollosa, which was the baseline to beat [3, 4] and ranked first by score but was the slowest method.
2. **Team wzhang009-score = 0.8178 (1057 s)**, of Wei Zhang, which managed to do almost as well as Jarfo with a similar method, while reducing the computational time by 44%. This was achieved by making feature extraction more computationally efficient: (1) a lot of features were computed from a common transformation of the data including normalization, discretization, etc., (2) anti-symmetric features (contributing to characterize $X \leftarrow Y$ when there is one already characterizing $X \rightarrow Y$) were removed, (3)the code for some features, e.g. HSICwas re-written.
3. **Team david.lopez.paz-score = 0.7193 (316 s)**, of David Lopez Paz, which reduced the computational time by a factor of five, using a method called Randomized Causation Coefficient (RCC) [14] based on a randomized approximation [17] of the empirical kernel mean embedding of probability distributions [20] to summarise each given dataset into a k-dimensional real feature vector. These feature vectors are then passed by to a general Gradient Boosting Classifier.

In summary, the cause-effect pair challenges yielded better performing causation coefficients: the Jarfo coefficient, whose robustness was tested in post-challenge experiments and the fast causation coefficient RCC.

7.1.5 Analyses

We visualized the results in various ways to understand the results better. These analyses are based on the results of Round 1 for which we have more data.

Overfitting Because the participants practice for a long time using as feed-back the performances on the "public leaderboard", there is always some chance that they would overfit the validation set. We remind the reader that, in both rounds, there were 4050 example in both the validation set and the test set. However, as illustrated in Fig. 7.2a showing a scatter plot of round 1 results, there is no noticeable overfitting. The correlation between results on validation and test data is very high: 0.97 (p value 3×10^{-29}) (Tables 7.3, 7.4, 7.5).

Real vs. Artificial Pairs Table 7.4 shows a comparison of the results on real and artificial data (for round 1). For all three scores (Dependency, Causality, and Confounding), the results on artificial data are better than on real data. However, even on real data, they are significantly better than chance for the best entrants. To evaluate this, we performed a permutation test. We re-computed the scores 500 hundred times for each of the top 20 participants after randomly permuting the order of the truth values of the causal relationships. This generated 10,000 points for each score. In Fig. 7.2b we show the Dependency, Causality, and Confounding for the 20

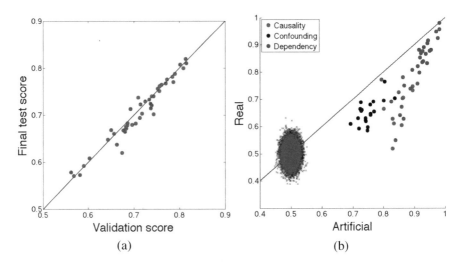

(a)   (b)

Fig. 7.2 Score comparisons (Round 1). Each point represents a participant. (**a**) Correlation between validation and final test results. (**b**) Comparison of final test results on real and artificial data (top 20 participants only). We also show the results of permutation tests (crosses): All participants performed significantly better than chance

Table 7.3   Final evaluation scores (round 1 on Kaggle)

Rank	Team name	Validation	Final test	Entries
1	ProtoML +	0.81367	0.8196	25
2	Jarfo +	0.81464	0.81052	123
3	HiDLoN +	0.80191	0.8072	59
4	FirfiD +	0.80867	0.79957	221
5	Mouse +	0.79026	0.78782	30
6	Domcastro & Sayani +	0.78467	0.78133	324
7	nor +	0.77297	0.77595	20
8	LucaToni +	0.78671	0.77081	126
9	Rangel Dokov +	0.76993	0.7678	32
10	Liubenyuan & Abhishek +	0.76108	0.76502	70
11	Saeh & Xing +	0.7571	0.76181	33
12	Rahan +	0.75295	0.75666	48
13	Bruce Cragin +	0.75639	0.75194	60
14	E-L +	0.7438	0.74047	63
15	Dirk Gently +	0.73976	0.74035	53
16	Mr. Wolf +	0.7096	0.73741	53
17	furiouseskimo +	0.73386	0.73373	11
18	borg	0.72463	0.72943	8
19	RamSud +	0.73689	0.7244	81
20	Issam Laradji	0.71449	0.72271	13
21	kinnskogr + john backus mayes +	0.73939	0.72124	43
22	Vik Paruchuri +	0.73736	0.71499	2
23	n_m	0.69233	0.71339	4
24	Delta	0.71759	0.70316	99
25	Gurupad Hegde	0.74388	0.70233	7
26	sbachish +	0.71325	0.69436	76
27	DieselBoy	0.68673	0.68336	90
28	Attila Balogh +	0.70397	0.68262	46
29	David Low	0.69602	0.67981	14
30	kosklain	0.68552	0.67844	26
31	jajo	0.68274	0.67581	13
32	AndreyICT +	0.68361	0.67239	19
33	Ali Hassane	0.68077	0.66944	27
34	LM +	0.65093	0.66825	18
35	cmna +	0.67731	0.66778	52
36	zzol +	0.68063	0.66486	5
37	ikretus +	0.65725	0.66106	26
38	YCSU	0.64352	0.64844	34

(continued)

Table 7.3 (continued)

Rank	Team name	Validation	Final test	Entries
39	Sexteentons +	0.6632	0.6379	27
40	Anatoliy	0.67483	0.62032	46
41	Jeong-Yoon & Damian +	0.60236	0.60823	75
42	Tony Liu	0.58991	0.59242	8
43	Christopher Nowzohour +	0.56205	0.57848	3
44	Jason Sumpter	0.58151	0.57312	59
	Basic Python Benchmark	0.56809	0.57099	

Results of the teams who beat the "basic Python benchmark". Teams marked with + uploaded their code

top ranking participants and the results of the permutation test as crosses. It can be seen that for artificial data, even the worst participant's scores outperform all results of the permutation test. Considering that there are N = 44 entrants in the final phase, even after Bonferroni correction, the hypothesis that the results of any of the top 20 participants was obtained by chance can be rejected in artificial data for all scores with high confidence (p value 44×10^{-4}). In real data, this is also the case for the Dependency score for all top 20 ranking participants, for the Causality score in all top 14 participants, and for the Confounding score in all 17 top ranking participants.

It is worth noticing that all the participants did not perform as well with respect to all the scores in artificial and real data. Notably, Domcastro & Sayani obtained the best results on real data and achived the smallest difference between real and artificial data in the top ranking participants. Jarfo (overall ranked second) has a particularly high Dependency score (0.96 on rel data and 0.98 on artificial data).

Factor Sensitivity Analysis By design the cause-effect pair challenge dataset spanned a variety of difficulties. In particular, variable type, sample size, and signal to noise ratio were drawn randomly and independently, in an approximate factorial design (Table 2.9). In Fig. 7.3, we show the influence of these various factors on the performance of the top ranking participants:

- **Type of variables:** It is very important to us to notice that the performances on pairs of categorical or binary variables are better than chance. Some participants do well on those pairs, almost as well as they do as on continuous variables. The top ranking participants are not the best on those pairs.The pairs (categorical, categorical) are the hardest, but there is a confounding factor: there were more numerical variables that binary or categorical, so there was less training data for those pairs.

Table 7.4 Results of the top ranking teams, split between real and artificial data (Round 1 on Kaggle)

Rank	Team	Dependency	Confounding	Causality	Score
Real data					
1	ProtoML	0.88057	0.65432	0.75756	0.70420
2	Jarfo	0.95721	0.70386	0.73312	0.68642
3	HiDloN	0.91476	0.69209	0.74774	0.69669
4	FirfiD	0.92352	0.69547	0.73960	0.68274
5	Mouse	0.87689	0.64211	0.75008	0.69259
6	Domcasto & Sayani	0.85339	0.65786	0.78075	0.71355
7	nor	0.94847	0.68080	0.70586	0.67200
8	LucaToni	0.83910	0.63084	0.70434	0.65773
9	Rangel Dokov	0.86599	0.61937	0.67195	0.63402
10	Liubenyuan & Abhishek	0.87618	0.64650	0.62838	0.60271
11	Saeh & Xing	0.82162	0.62352	0.72561	0.66813
12	Rahan	0.86864	0.68940	0.60430	0.58837
13	Bruce Cragin	0.79769	0.59270	0.64157	0.60025
14	E-L	0.90563	0.66048	0.61041	0.59288
15	Dirk Gently	0.80719	0.60958	0.69212	0.64297
16	Mr. Wolf	0.89109	0.63047	0.62772	0.60258
17	Furioso	0.83247	0.59798	0.54983	0.53855
18	borg	0.88118	0.66425	0.77271	0.70920
19	RamSud	0.98007	0.76478	0.66464	0.63072
20	Issam Laradji	0.83585	0.58518	0.51904	0.50935
Artificial data					
1	ProtoML	0.95372	0.76944	0.90946	0.84206
2	Jarfo	0.98063	0.83663	0.89425	0.83499
3	HiDloN	0.94416	0.76777	0.89466	0.82883
4	FirfiD	0.97644	0.80086	0.88644	0.82249
5	Mouse	0.94966	0.75831	0.86722	0.80620
6	Domcasto & Sayani	0.91789	0.72655	0.86299	0.79507
7	nor	0.97087	0.75676	0.86348	0.79669
8	LucaToni	0.92839	0.74099	0.86214	0.79270
9	Rangel Dokov	0.93696	0.74265	0.85856	0.79289
10	Liubenyuan & Abhishek	0.92646	0.75771	0.86497	0.79620
11	Saeh & Xing	0.91056	0.74140	0.84961	0.78034
12	Rahan	0.92175	0.72586	0.85874	0.78958
13	Bruce Cragin	0.91653	0.71915	0.85376	0.78059
14	E-L	0.94194	0.72921	0.83312	0.76984
15	Dirk Gently	0.89369	0.69167	0.82472	0.75937
16	Mr. Wolf	0.93073	0.71590	0.82960	0.76326
17	Furioso	0.94129	0.74834	0.83904	0.76958
18	borg	0.91559	0.72371	0.79323	0.73381
19	RamSud	0.98097	0.80423	0.80100	0.74399
20	Issam Laradji	0.92615	0.74768	0.82929	0.76495

Table 7.5 Results of the top ranking teams above baseline (Round 2 on Codalab)

Rank	Team	Execution time	Forward AUC	Reverse AUC	Bidirectional AUC
Validation set					
1	jose.fonollosa	1942.34	0.820183	0.84349	0.831836
2	wzhang009	1069.58	0.823987	0.836836	0.830412
3	irjudson	3868.45	0.818943	0.83457	0.826756
	reference	295.43	0.550647	0.565181	0.557914
Final test set					
1	jose.fonollosa	1890.75	0.831516	0.82131	0.826413
2	wzhang009	1057.17	0.821189	0.814409	0.817799
3	**david.lopez.paz**	**316.24**	0.718142	0.720575	0.719359
4	aiolli	3343.26	0.679862	0.667509	0.673685
	reference	289.64	0.57412	0.584624	0.579372

We outline in bold the winner of the fastest causaltion coefficient contest

- **Sample size:** Above $\simeq 1000$ samples, performances are largely independent of sample size. Then they start breaking down. The top ranking participants have more robust methods: their performances degrade less for small sample sizes.
- **Signal to noise ratio:** In the range of signal to noise ratio (S2N) investigated, performances do not degrade drammatically as a function of S2N. Although some methods are less robust to bas S2N than others, all the top ranking participants do really well, down to S2N = 0.25.

Fact Sheets We analyzed the information provided by the participants in the fact sheets of Round 1. The bulk of the effort in this challenge has gone into feature engineering. Most submissions followed the same workflow: (1) data pre-processing and feature extraction; (2) training a classifier. The pre-processing and the feature extraction were very diverse (Fig. 7.4). In contrast, the classifiers used were mainly based on ensembles of decision trees (85%).

Explainability and Interpretability Because the models of the top ranking participants are based of a large number of features and ensembles of decision trees, the models are difficult to interpret and the decisions they make hard to explain. We attempted to perform an analysis of the Jarfo coefficient [3, 4], the strongest method according to the results of both rounds (Fig. 7.5).

The heterogeneity of the data makes it difficult to come up with simple rules. To simplify the problem, we focused on a subset of the dataset (Fig. 7.6) and used it to train a Jarfo coefficient. Then we performed a feature selection. The most compact

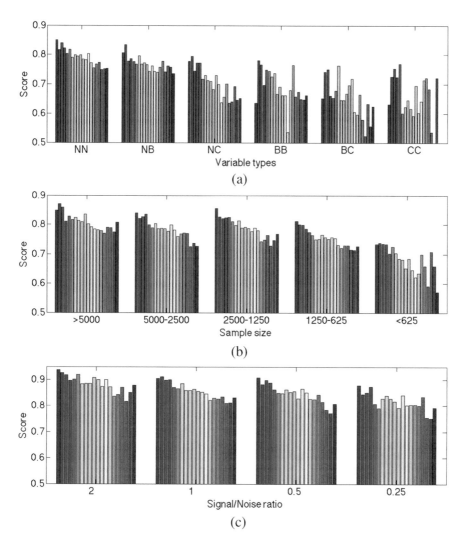

Fig. 7.3 Histogram of performances of the top 20 participants in Round 1 as a function of number of (**a**) Variable types. (**b**) Sample size. (**c**) Signal to noise ratio. The score is the Bi-directional AUC

set of features we could obtain without sacrificing performance too much was a set of three features, selected with a combination of a univariate filter (S2N, with a threshold on signal to noise ratio of 2 [7]) and a forward selection method (Gram-

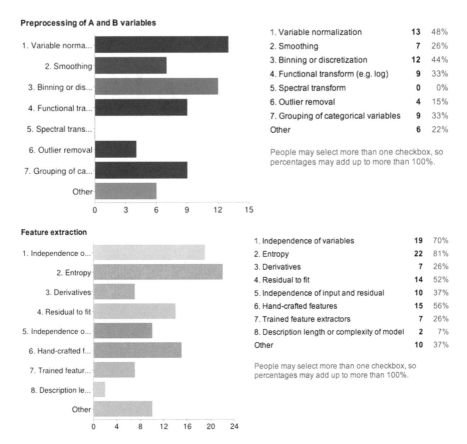

Fig. 7.4 Preprocessing and feature extraction. These results were extracted from the fact sheets of Round 1

Schmidt Relief [10]). We then trained a decision tree using the selected features and a symmetrized dataset (Fig. 7.7). The root of the tree is thus the most imformative feature: the Conditional Distribution Similarity (CDS) [4]. It is complemented by the difference and the max of the marginal entropy.

This result is consistent with findings of other authors: Marginal entropy is the basis of one of the IGCI criteria [13]. CDS can be considered a generalization of the ANM criterion [12, 16], testing independence of the input and the noise (called IR in this chapter). ANM has been found superior to IGCI in other benchmarks [15]. CDS works also, to some extent, for non additive noise.

A->B or B->A

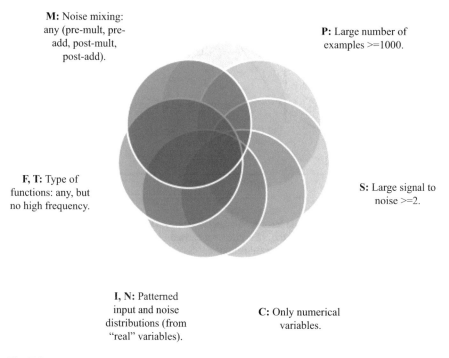

M: Noise mixing: any (pre-mult, pre-add, post-mult, post-add).

P: Large number of examples >=1000.

F, T: Type of functions: any, but no high frequency.

S: Large signal to noise >=2.

I, N: Patterned input and noise distributions (from "real" variables).

C: Only numerical variables.

Fig. 7.5 Subset of the data. We reduced the dataset to conduct and explainability and interpretability study

Given the design of the cuase-effect pair challenge, the $X \rightarrow Y$ and $X \leftarrow Y$ pairs are not partially confounded in artificial data, so testing the independence of the input and the noise should be a good method. Since we have both cases of mutliplicative and additive noise in the dataset, it is natural that CDS does better than IR. We think that entropy works well because of the choice of functions that generated the artificial data. Most are invertible.

7.2 Conclusion

The cause-effect pair challenge attained its goal to devise "causation coefficients". Its novel protocol casting the cause-effect pair problem as a pattern recognition problem and providing training and test data changed completely the angle that

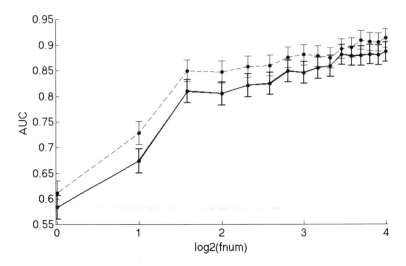

Fig. 7.6 Feature selection on the Jarfo coefficient. We reduced the number of predictive features. After pre-selecting features with the S2N filter, we carried out a forward selection with Gram-Schmidt Relief. We show AUC on the validation set (dashed) and test set (solid). Given the error bars, not much performance is gained with more than three features

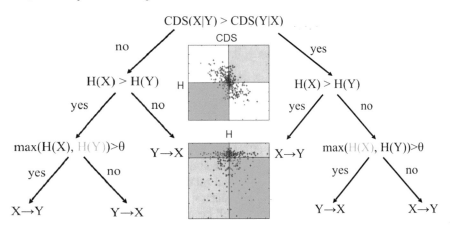

Fig. 7.7 Simplified decision tree extracted from the Jarfo coefficient. The decisions are based on the CDS and the marginal entropy (one implementation of the IGCI principle). The first split is using CDS, the most informative feature and the second one entropy. If the two criteria disagree, the opinion of CDS prevails, unless the entropy is very large

researchers took to solve the problem. Rather than using model-based methods, they learned the causation coefficients from examples of cause-effect pairs (scatter plots), thought of as patterns. All winning methods in the first round were remarkably similar. It may be more than a coincidence that all three used GBM as a classifier, a method based on ensembles of decision trees. An overwhelming majority of participants used ensembles of decision trees (85%). This may have been biased by the Python sample code that provided an example using Random Forests. However, the top ranking participants reported better performance using GBM. In the second round a more original method emerged with the Randomized Causation Coefficient (RCC) [14], which opened a new direction of research. Results indicated that causation coefficients trained on real data do not necessarily generalize well on artificial data and vice versa, but post-challenge analyses on new data gave promising results. Further benchmark efforts should focus on drifts in the mother distribution and transfer learning. Other directions to be pursued are the organization of a time series challenge and a series of challenge on experimental design in which the participants can conduct virtual experiments on artificial systems.

Acknowledgements We are very grateful to all those who contributed time to make this challenge happen. The initial impulse for this challenge was given by Joris Mooij, Dominik Janzing, and Bernhard Schoelkopf, from the Max Planck Institute who devised a cause-effect pair task, which was part of the NIPS 2008 Pot-Luck challenge http://www.causality.inf.ethz.ch/pot-luck. php. Examples of algorithms and data were supplied by Povilas Daniusis, Arthur Gretton, Patrik O. Hoyer, Dominik Janzing, Antti Kerminen, Joris Mooij, Jonas Peters, Bernhard Schoekopf, Shohei Shimizu, Oliver Stegle, and Kun Zhang, and Jakob Zscheischler. The datasets were prepared by Isabelle Guyon, Mehreen Saeed, Mikael Henaff, Sisi Ma, and Alexander Statnikov. The website and the sample code were prepared by Isabelle Guyon and Ben Hamner. The challenge protocol and implementation was tested and/or reviewed by Marc Boullé, Léon Bottou, Hugo Jair Escalante, Frederick Eberhardt, Seth Flaxman, Patrik Hoyer, Dominik Janzing, Richard Kennaway, Vincent Lemaire, Joris Mooij, Jonas Peters, Florin, Peter Spirtes, Ioannis Tsamardinos, Jianxin Yin,and Kun Zhang. The second round was supported by Microsoft Research. We are very grateful to Evelyne Viegas for her help and advice.

References

1. Leo Breiman. Arcing the edge. Technical report, Technical Report 486, Statistics Department, University of California at Berkeley, 1997.
2. Diogo Moitinho de Almeida. Automated feature engineering applied to causality. In *Proc. NIPS 2013 workshop on causality*, http://clopinet.com/isabelle/Projects/NIPS2013/, December 2013.
3. José A. R. Fonollosa. Conditional distribution variability measure for causality detection. In *Proc. NIPS 2013 workshop on causality*, http://clopinet.com/isabelle/Projects/NIPS2013/, December 2013.
4. José AR Fonollosa. Conditional distribution variability measures for causality detection. *arXiv preprint arXiv:1601.06680*, 2016.
5. Jerome H Friedman. Greedy function approximation: a gradient boosting machine. *Annals of statistics*, pages 1189–1232, 2001.
6. Jerome H Friedman. Stochastic gradient boosting. *Computational Statistics & Data Analysis*, 38(4):367–378, 2002.
7. Todd R Golub, Donna K Slonim, Pablo Tamayo, Christine Huard, Michelle Gaasenbeek, Jill P Mesirov, Hilary Coller, Mignon L Loh, James R Downing, Mark A Caligiuri, et al. Molecular classification of cancer: class discovery and class prediction by gene expression monitoring. *science*, 286(5439):531–537, 1999.
8. Isabelle Guyon. Chalearn cause effect pairs challenge, 2013. URL http://www.causality.inf. ethz.ch/cause-effect.php.

9. Isabelle Guyon. Chalearn fast causation coefficient challenge. 2014.
10. Isabelle Guyon, Hans-Marcus Bitter, Zulfikar Ahmed, Michael Brown, and Jonathan Heller. Multivariate non-linear feature selection with kernel multiplicative updates and gram-schmidt relief. In *BISC Flint-CIBI 2003 Workshop*. *Berkeley*, pages 1–11, 2003.
11. Tin Kam Ho. Random decision forests. In *Proceedings of the Third International Conference on Document Analysis and Recognition (Volume 1) - Volume 1*, ICDAR '95, pages 278–, Washington, DC, USA, 1995. IEEE Computer Society. ISBN 0-8186-7128-9. URL http://dl.acm.org/citation.cfm?id=844379.844681.
12. Patrik O Hoyer, Dominik Janzing, Joris M Mooij, Jonas Peters, and Bernhard Schölkopf. Nonlinear causal discovery with additive noise models. In *Neural Information Processing Systems (NIPS)*, pages 689–696, 2009.
13. Dominik Janzing, Joris Mooij, Kun Zhang, Jan Lemeire, Jakob Zscheischler, Povilas Daniušis, Bastian Steudel, and Bernhard Schölkopf. Information-geometric approach to inferring causal directions. *Artif. Intell.*, 182–183:1–31, May 2012. ISSN 0004-3702. https://doi.org/10.1016/j.artint.2012.01.002. URL http://dx.doi.org/10.1016/j.artint.2012.01.002.
14. David Lopez-Paz, Krikamol Muandet, and Benjamin Recht. The randomized causation coefficient. *J. Mach. Learn. Res.*, 16(1):2901–2907, January 2015. ISSN 1532-4435. URL http://dl.acm.org/citation.cfm?id=2789272.2912092.
15. Joris M Mooij, Jonas Peters, Dominik Janzing, Jakob Zscheischler, and Bernhard Schölkopf. Distinguishing cause from effect using observational data: methods and benchmarks. *Journal of Machine Learning Research*, 17(32):1–102, 2016.
16. Jonas Peters, Dominik Janzing, and Bernhard Scholkopf. Causal inference on discrete data using additive noise models. *IEEE Transactions on Pattern Analysis and Machine Intelligence*, 33(12):2436–2450, 2011.
17. Ali Rahimi and Benjamin Recht. Random features for large-scale kernel machines. In *Advances in neural information processing systems*, pages 1177–1184, 2008.
18. Spyridon Samothrakis, Diego Perez, and Simon Lucas. Training gradient boosting machines using curve fitting and information-theoretic features for causal direction detection. In *Proc. NIPS 2013 workshop on causality*, http://clopinet.com/isabelle/Projects/NIPS2013/, December 2013.
19. Thomas Schaffter, Daniel Marbach, and Dario Floreano. Genenetweaver: In silico benchmark generation and performance profiling of network inference methods. *Bioinformatics*, 27(16): 2263–2270, 2011. wingx.
20. Alex Smola, Arthur Gretton, Le Song, and Bernhard Schölkopf. A hilbert space embedding for distributions. In *International Conference on Algorithmic Learning Theory*, pages 13–31. Springer, 2007.
21. Alexander Statnikov, Mikael Henaff, Nikita I Lytkin, and Constantin F Aliferis. New methods for separating causes from effects in genomics data. *BMC genomics*, 13(8):S22, 2012.
22. Alexander Statnikov, Sisi Ma, Mikael Henaff, Nikita Lytkin, Efstratios Efstathiadis, Eric R. Peskin, and Constantin F. Aliferis. Ultra-scalable and efficient methods for hybrid obser-vational and experimental local causal pathway discovery. *J. Mach. Learn. Res.*, 16(1): 3219–3267, January 2015. ISSN 1532-4435. URL http://dl.acm.org/citation.cfm?id=2789272.2912102.

Chapter 8
Non-linear Causal Inference Using Gaussianity Measures

Daniel Hernández-Lobato, Pablo Morales-Mombiela, David Lopez-Paz, and Alberto Suárez

8.1 Introduction

The inference of causal relationships from data is one of the current areas of interest in the artificial intelligence community, e.g. [3, 15, 22]. The reason for this surge of interest is that discovering the causal structure of a complex system provides an explicit description of the mechanisms that generate the data, and allows us to understand the consequences of interventions in the system [25]. More precisely, automatic causal inference can be used to determine how modifications of the value of certain relevant variables (the causes) influence the values of other related variables (the effects). Therefore, understanding cause-effect relations is of paramount importance to control the behavior of complex systems and has applications in industrial processes, medicine, genetics, economics, social sciences or meteorology.

The vast majority of the work was done while being at the Max Planck Institute for Intelligent Systems and at Cambridge University

D. Hernández-Lobato (✉) · A. Suárez
Universidad Autónoma de Madrid, Madrid, Spain
e-mail: daniel.hernandez@uam.es; alberto.suarez@uam.es

P. Morales-Mombiela
Quantitative Risk Research, Madrid, Spain
e-mail: pablo.morales@estudiante.uam.es

D. Lopez-Paz
Facebook AI Research, Paris, France
e-mail: dlp@fb.com

© Springer Nature Switzerland AG 2019
I. Guyon et al. (eds.), *Cause Effect Pairs in Machine Learning*,
The Springer Series on Challenges in Machine Learning,
https://doi.org/10.1007/978-3-030-21810-2_8

257

Causal relations can be determined in complex systems in three different ways. First, they can be inferred from domain knowledge provided by an expert, and incorporated in an ad-hoc manner in the description of the system. Second, they can be discovered by performing interventions in the system. These are controlled experiments in which one or several variables of the system are forced to take particular values. Interventions constitute a primary tool for identifying causal relationships. However, in many situations they are unethical, expensive, or technically infeasible. Third, they can be estimated using causal discovery algorithms that use as input purely uncontrolled and static data.

This last approach for causal discovery has recently received much attention from the machine learning community [10, 28, 33]. These methods assume a particular model for the *mapping mechanisms* that link causes to effects. By specifying particular conditions on the mapping mechanism and the distributions of the cause and noise variables, the causal direction becomes identifiable Chen et al. [3]. For instance, Hoyer et al. [10] assume that the effect is a non-linear transformation of the cause plus some independent additive noise. A potential drawback of these methods is that the assumptions made by the particular model considered could be unrealistic for the data under study.

In this paper we propose a general method for causal inference that belongs to the third of the categories described above. Specifically, we assume that the cause and the effect variables have the same distribution and are linked by a linear relationship contaminated with non-Gaussian noise. For the univariate case we prove that, under these assumptions, the magnitude of the cumulants of the residuals of order higher than two is smaller for the linear fit in the anti-causal direction than in the causal one. Since the Gaussian is the only distribution whose cumulants of order higher than two are zero, statistical tests based on measures of Gaussianity can be used for causal inference. An antecedent of this result is the observation that, when cause and effect have the same distribution, the residuals of a fit in the anti-causal direction have higher entropy than in the causal direction [12, 17]. Since the residuals of the causal and anti-causal linear models have the same variance and the Gaussian is the distribution that maximizes the entropy for a fixed variance, this means that the distribution of the latter is more Gaussian than the former.

For multivariate cause-effect pairs that have the same distribution and are related by a linear model with additive non-Gaussian noise the proof given by Hyvärinen and Smith [12] and Kpotufe et al. [17] can be extended to show that the entropy of the vector of residuals of a linear fit in the anti-causal direction is larger than the corresponding residuals of a linear fit in the causal direction. We conjecture that also in this case there is a reduction of the magnitude of the tensor cumulants of the anti-causal multivariate residuals and provide some numerical evidence of this effect in two dimensions.

The problem of non-linear causal inference is addressed by embedding the original problem in an expanded feature space. We then make the assumption that the non-linear relation between causes and effects in the original space is linear in the expanded feature space. The computations required to make inference on the causal direction based on this embedding can be readily carried out using kernel methods.

In summary, the proposed method for causal inference proceeds by first making a transformation of the original variables so that causes and effects have the same distribution. Then we perform kernel ridge regression in both the causal and the anti-causal directions. The dependence between causes and effects, which is non-linear in the original space, is assumed to be linear in the kernel-induced feature space. A statistical test is then used to quantify the degree of similarity between the distributions of these residuals and a Gaussian distribution with the same variance. Finally, the direction in which the residuals are less Gaussian is identified as the causal one.

The performance of this method is evaluated in both synthetic and real-world cause-effect pairs. From the results obtained it is apparent that the anti-causal residuals of a linear fit in the expanded feature space are more Gaussian than the causal residuals. In general, it is difficult to estimate the entropy from a finite sample [1]. Empirical estimators of high order cumulants involve high order moments, which means they often have large variance. As an alternative, we propose to use statistical tests based on the *energy distance* to characterize the Gaussianization effect for the residuals of linear fits in the causal and anti-causal directions. Tests based on the energy distance were analyzed in depth by Székely and Rizzo [31]. They have been shown to be related to homogeneity tests based on embeddings in a Reproducing Kernel Hilbert Space [8]. An advantage of energy distance-based statistics is that they can be readily estimated from a sample by computing expectations of pairwise Euclidean distances. The energy distance generally provides better results than the entropy or cumulant-based Gaussianity measures. In the problems investigated, the accuracy of the proposed method, using the energy distance to the Gaussian, is comparable to other state-of-the-art techniques for causal discovery.

The rest of the paper is organized as follows: Sect. 8.2 illustrates that, under certain conditions, the residuals of a linear regression fit are closer to a Gaussian in the anti-causal direction than in the causal one, based on a reduction of the high-order cumulants and on an increment of the entropy. This section considers both the univariate and multivariate cases. Section 8.3 adopts a kernel approach to carry out a feature expansion that can be used to detect non-linear causal relationships. We also show here how to compute the residuals in the expanded feature space, and how to choose the different hyper-parameters of the proposed method. Section 8.4 contains a detailed description of the implementation. In Sect. 8.6 we present the results of an empirical assessment of the proposed method in both synthetic and real-world cause-effect data pairs. Finally, Sect. 8.7 summarizes the conclusions and puts forth some ideas for future research.

8.2 Asymmetry Based on the Non-Gaussianity of the Residuals of Linear Models

Let $\mathscr{X}$ and $\mathscr{Y}$ be two random variables that are causally related. The direction of the causal relation is not known. Our goal is to determine whether $\mathscr{X}$ causes $\mathscr{Y}$, i.e., $\mathscr{X} \to \mathscr{Y}$ or, alternatively $\mathscr{Y}$ causes $\mathscr{X}$, i.e., $\mathscr{Y} \to \mathscr{X}$. For this purpose, we exploit an asymmetry between causes an effects. This type of asymmetry can be uncovered using statistical tests that measure the non-Gaussianity of the residuals of linear regression models obtained from fits in the causal and in the anti-causal direction.

To motivate the methodology that we have developed, we will proceed in stepwise manner. First we analyze a special case in one dimension: We assume that $\mathscr{X}$ and $\mathscr{Y}$ have the same distribution and are related via a linear model contaminated with additive i.i.d. non-Gaussian noise. The noise is independent of the cause. Under these assumptions we show that the distribution of the residuals of a linear fit in the incorrect (anti-causal) direction is closer to a Gaussian distribution than the distribution of the residuals in the correct (causal) direction. For this, we use an argument based on the reduction of the magnitude of the cumulants of order higher than 2. The cumulants are defined as the derivatives of the logarithm of the moment-generating function evaluated at zero [4, 20].

The Gaussianization effect can be characterized also in terms of an increase of the entropy. The proof is based on the results of [12], which are extended in this paper to the multivariate case. In particular, we show that the entropy of the residuals of a linear fit in the anti-causal direction is larger or equal than the entropy of the residuals of a linear fit in the causal direction. Since the Gaussian it the distribution that has maximum entropy, given a particular covariance matrix, an increase of the entropy of the residuals means that their distribution becomes closer to the Gaussian.

Finally, we note that it is easy to guarantee that $\mathscr{X}$ and $\mathscr{Y}$ have the same distribution in the case that these variables are unidimensional and continuous. To this end we only have to transform one of the variables (typically the cause random variable) using the probability integral transform, as described in Sect. 8.4. However, after the data have been transformed, the relation between the variables will no longer be linear in general. Thus, to address non-linear cause-effect problems involving univariate random variables the linear model is formulated in an expanded feature space, where the multivariate analysis of the Gaussianization effect is also applicable. In this feature space all the computations required for causal inference can be formulated in terms of kernels. This can be used to detect non-linear causal relations in the original input space and allows for an efficient implementation of the method. The only assumption is that the non-linear relation in the original input space is linear in the expanded feature space induced by the selected kernel.

8.2.1   Analysis of the Univariate Case Based on Cumulants

Let $\mathscr{X}$ and $\mathscr{Y}$ be one-dimensional random variables that have the same distribution. Without further loss of generality, we will assume that they have zero mean and unit variance. Let $\mathbf{x} = (x_1, \ldots, x_N)^{\mathrm{T}}$ and $\mathbf{y} = (y_1, \ldots, y_N)^{\mathrm{T}}$ be N paired samples drawn i.i.d. from $P(\mathscr{X}, \mathscr{Y})$. Assume that the causal direction is $\mathscr{X} \to \mathscr{Y}$ and that the measurements are related by a linear model

$$y_i = wx_i + \epsilon_i, \qquad \epsilon_i \perp x_i, \quad \forall i, \tag{8.1}$$

where $w = \mathrm{corr}(\mathscr{X}, \mathscr{Y}) \in [-1, 1]$ and ϵ_i is independent i.d. non-Gaussian additive noise.

A linear model in the opposite direction, i.e., $\mathscr{Y} \to \mathscr{X}$, can be built using least squares

$$x_i = wy_i + \tilde{\epsilon}_i, \tag{8.2}$$

where $w = \mathrm{corr}(\mathscr{Y}, \mathscr{X})$ is the same coefficient as in the previous model. The residuals of this reversed linear model are defined as $\tilde{\epsilon}_i = x_i - wy_i$.

Following an argument similar to that of [9] we show that the residuals $\{\tilde{\epsilon}_i\}_{i=1}^{N}$ in the anti-causal direction are more Gaussian than the residuals $\{\epsilon_i\}_{i=1}^{N}$ in the actual causal direction $\mathscr{X} \to \mathscr{Y}$ based on a reduction of the magnitude of the cumulants. The proof is based on establishing a relation between the cumulants of the distribution of the residuals in both the causal and the anti-causal direction. First, we show that $\kappa_n(y_i)$, the n-th order cumulant of $\mathscr{Y}$, can be expressed in terms of $\kappa_n(\epsilon_i)$, the n-th order cumulant of the residuals:

$$\kappa_n(y_i) = w^n \kappa_n(x_i) + \kappa_n(\epsilon_i) = w^n \kappa_n(y_i) + \kappa_n(\epsilon_i) = \frac{1}{1 - w^n} \kappa_n(\epsilon_i). \tag{8.3}$$

To derive this relation we have used (8.1), that x_i and y_i have the same distribution (and hence have the same cumulants), and standard properties of cumulants [4, 20]. Furthermore,

$$\kappa_n(\tilde{\epsilon}_i) = \kappa_n(x_i - wy_i) = \kappa_n(x_i - w^2 x_i - w\epsilon_i) = (1 - w^2)^n \kappa_n(x_i) + (-w)^n \kappa_n(\epsilon_i) \tag{8.4}$$

$$= (1 - w^2)^n \kappa_n(y_i) + (-w)^n \kappa_n(\epsilon_i) = \frac{(1 - w^2)^n}{1 - w^n} \kappa_n(\epsilon_i) + (-w)^n \kappa_n(\epsilon_i) \tag{8.5}$$

$$= c_n(w) \kappa_n(\epsilon_i), \tag{8.6}$$

where we have used the definition of $\tilde{\epsilon}_i$ and (8.3) In Fig. 8.1 the value of

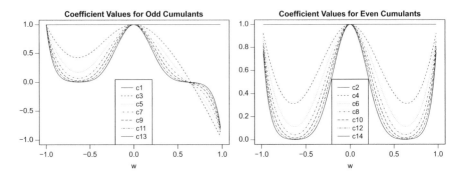

Fig. 8.1 Values of the function $c_n(\cdot)$ as a function of w for each cumulant number n (odd in the left plot, even in the right plot). All values for $c_n(\cdot)$ lie in the interval $[-1, 1]$

$$c_n(w) = \frac{(1 - w^2)^n}{1 - w^n} + (-w)^n. \tag{8.7}$$

is displayed as a function of $w \in [-1, 1]$. Note that $c_1(w) = c_2(w) = 1$ independently of the value of w. This means that the mean and the variance of the residuals are the same in both the causal and anti-causal directions. For $n > 2$, $|c_n(w)| \leq 1$ with equality only for $w = 0$ and $w = \pm 1$. The result is that the high-order cumulants of the residuals in the anti-causal direction are smaller in magnitude that the corresponding cumulants in the causal direction. Using the observation that all the cumulants of the Gaussian distribution of order higher than two are zero [19], we conclude that the distribution of the residuals in the anti-causal direction is closer to the Gaussian distribution than in the causal direction.

In summary, we can infer the causal direction by (1) fitting a linear model in each possible direction, i.e., $\mathscr{X} \rightarrow \mathscr{Y}$ and $\mathscr{Y} \rightarrow \mathscr{X}$, and (2) carrying out statistical tests to detect the level of Gaussianity of the two corresponding residuals. The direction in which the residuals are less Gaussian is expected to be the correct one.

8.2.2 Analysis of the Multivariate Case Based on Cumulants

In this section we argue that the Gaussianization effect of the residuals in the anti-causal direction also takes place when the two random variables $\mathscr{X}$ and $\mathscr{Y}$ are multidimensional. We will assume that these variables follow the same distribution and, without further loss of generality, that they have been whitened (i.e., they have a zero mean vector and the identity matrix as the covariance matrix). Let $\mathbf{X} = (\mathbf{x}_1, \ldots, \mathbf{x}_N)^T$ and $\mathbf{Y} = (\mathbf{y}_1, \ldots, \mathbf{y}_N)^T$ be N paired samples drawn i.i.d. from $P(\mathscr{X}, \mathscr{Y})$. In this case, the model assumed for the actual causal relation is

$$\mathbf{y}_i = \mathbf{A}\mathbf{x}_i + \boldsymbol{\epsilon}_i, \quad \boldsymbol{\epsilon}_i \perp \mathbf{x}_i, \quad \forall i, \tag{8.8}$$

where $\mathbf{A} = \text{corr}(\mathscr{Y}, \mathscr{X})$ is a $d \times d$ matrix of model coefficients and ϵ_i is i.i.d. non-Gaussian additive noise. The model in the anti-causal direction is the one that results from the least squares fit:

$$\mathbf{x}_i = \tilde{\mathbf{A}}\mathbf{y}_i + \tilde{\epsilon}_i \,, \tag{8.9}$$

where we have defined $\tilde{\epsilon}_i = \mathbf{x}_i - \tilde{\mathbf{A}}\mathbf{y}_i$ and $\tilde{\mathbf{A}} = \text{corr}(\mathscr{X}, \mathscr{Y}) = \mathbf{A}^\mathrm{T}$.

As in the univariate case, we start by expressing the cumulants of $\mathscr{Y}$ in terms of the cumulants of the residuals. However, the cumulants are now tensors [20]:

$$\kappa_n(\mathbf{y}_i) = \kappa_n(\mathbf{A}\mathbf{x}_i) + \kappa_n(\epsilon_i) \,. \tag{8.10}$$

In what follows, the notation $\text{vect}(\cdot)$ stands for the vectorization of a tensor. For example, in the case of a tensor $\mathbf{T}$ with dimensions $d \times d \times d$

$$\text{vect}(\mathbf{T}) = (T_{1,1,1}, T_{2,1,1}, \cdots, T_{d,1,1}, T_{1,2,1}, \cdots, T_{d,d,d})^\mathrm{T}.$$

Using this notation we obtain

$$\text{vect}(\kappa_n(\mathbf{y}_i)) = \mathbf{A}^n \text{vect}(\kappa_n(\mathbf{x}_i)) + \text{vect}(\kappa_n(\epsilon)) = (\mathbf{I} - \mathbf{A}^n)^{-1} \text{vect}(\kappa_n(\epsilon)) \,, \tag{8.11}$$

where $\mathbf{A}^n = \mathbf{A} \otimes \mathbf{A} \otimes \mathbf{A} \cdots \otimes \mathbf{A}$, n times, is computed using the Kronecker matrix product. To derive this expression we have used (8.8), the fact that $\mathscr{Y}$ and $\mathscr{X}$ are equally distributed and hence have the same cumulants. We also have used the properties of the tensor cumulants $\text{vect}(\kappa_n(\mathbf{A}\mathbf{x}_i)) = \mathbf{A}^n \text{vect}(\kappa_n(\mathbf{x}_i))$, where the powers of the matrix $\mathbf{A}$ are computed using the Kronecker product [20].

Similarly, for the reversed linear model

$$\kappa_n(\tilde{\epsilon}_i) = \kappa_n(\mathbf{x}_i - \mathbf{A}^\mathrm{T}\mathbf{y}_i) = \kappa_n(\mathbf{x}_i - \mathbf{A}^\mathrm{T}\mathbf{A}\mathbf{x}_i - \mathbf{A}^\mathrm{T}\epsilon_i) = \kappa_n((\mathbf{I} - \mathbf{A}^\mathrm{T}\mathbf{A})\mathbf{x}_i - \mathbf{A}^\mathrm{T}\epsilon_i) \tag{8.12}$$

$$= \kappa_n((\mathbf{I} - \mathbf{A}^\mathrm{T}\mathbf{A})\mathbf{x}_i) + \kappa_n(-\mathbf{A}^\mathrm{T}\epsilon_i) \,. \tag{8.13}$$

Using again the notation for the vectorized tensor cumulants

$$\text{vect}(\kappa_n(\tilde{\epsilon}_i)) = (\mathbf{I} - \mathbf{A}^\mathrm{T}\mathbf{A})^n \text{vect}(\kappa_n(\mathbf{x}_i)) + (-1)^n (\mathbf{A}^\mathrm{T})^n \text{vect}(\kappa_n(\epsilon_i)) \tag{8.14}$$

$$= (\mathbf{I} - \mathbf{A}^\mathrm{T}\mathbf{A})^n (\mathbf{I} - \mathbf{A}^n)^{-1} \text{vect}(\kappa_n(\epsilon_i)) + (-1)^n (\mathbf{A}^\mathrm{T})^n \text{vect}(\kappa_n(\epsilon_i)) \tag{8.15}$$

$$= \left((\mathbf{I} - \mathbf{A}^\mathrm{T}\mathbf{A})^n (\mathbf{I} - \mathbf{A}^n)^{-1} + (-1)^n (\mathbf{A}^\mathrm{T})^n \right) \text{vect}(\kappa_n(\epsilon_i)) \,, \tag{8.16}$$

where the powers of matrices are computed using the Kronecker product as well, and where we have used (8.11) and that $\mathscr{Y}$ and $\mathscr{X}$ are equally distributed and have the same cumulants.

We now give some evidence to support that the magnitude of $\text{vect}(\kappa_n(\tilde{\boldsymbol{\epsilon}}_i))$ is smaller than the magnitude of $\text{vect}(\kappa_n(\boldsymbol{\epsilon}_i))$ in terms of the ℓ_2-norm, for cumulants of order higher than 2. That is, the tensors corresponding to high-order cumulants become closer to a tensor with all its components equal to zero. For this, we introduce the following definition:

Definition 8.1 The operator norm of a matrix $\mathbf{M}$ induced by the ℓ_p vector norm is $||\mathbf{M}||_{\text{op}} = \min\{c \geq 0 : ||\mathbf{M}\mathbf{v}||_p \leq c||\mathbf{v}||_p, \forall \mathbf{v}\}$, where $||\cdot||_p$ denotes the ℓ_p-norm for vectors.

The consequence is that $||\mathbf{M}||_{\text{op}} \geq ||\mathbf{M}\mathbf{v}||_p/||\mathbf{v}||_p, \forall \mathbf{v}$. This means that $||\mathbf{M}||_p$ can be understood as a measure of the size of the matrix $\mathbf{M}$. In the case of the ℓ_2-norm, the operator norm of a matrix $\mathbf{M}$ is equal to its largest singular value or, equivalently, to the square root of the largest eigenvalue of $\mathbf{M}^{\mathsf{T}}\mathbf{M}$. Let $\mathbf{M}_n = (\mathbf{I} - \mathbf{A}^{\mathsf{T}}\mathbf{A})^n (\mathbf{I} - \mathbf{A}^n)^{-1} + (-1)^n (\mathbf{A}^{\mathsf{T}})^n$. That is, $\mathbf{M}_n$ is the matrix that relates the cumulants of order n of the residuals in the causal and anti-causal directions in (8.16). We now evaluate $||\mathbf{M}_n||_{\text{op}}$, and show that in most cases its value is smaller than one for high-order cumulants $\kappa_n(\cdot)$, leading to a Gaussianization of the residuals in the anti-causal direction. From (8.16) and the definition given above, we know that $||\mathbf{M}_n||_{\text{op}} \geq ||\text{vect}(\kappa_n(\tilde{\boldsymbol{\epsilon}}_i))||_2/||\text{vect}(\kappa_n(\boldsymbol{\epsilon}_i))||_2$. This means that if $||\mathbf{M}_n||_{\text{op}} < 1$ the cumulants of the residuals in the incorrect causal direction are shrunk to the origin. Because the multivariate Gaussian distribution has all cumulants of order higher than two equal to zero [20], this translates into a distribution for the residuals in the anti-causal direction that is closer to the Gaussian distribution.

In the causal direction, we have that $\mathbb{E}[\mathbf{y}\mathbf{y}^T] = \mathbb{E}[(\mathbf{A}\mathbf{x}_i + \boldsymbol{\epsilon}_i)(\mathbf{A}\mathbf{x}_i + \boldsymbol{\epsilon}_i)^{\mathsf{T}}] = \mathbf{A}\mathbf{A}^T + \mathbf{C} = \mathbf{I}$, where $\mathbf{C}$ is the positive definite covariance matrix of the actual residuals.[1] Thus, $\mathbf{A}\mathbf{A}^T = \mathbf{I} - \mathbf{C}$ and hence the singular values of $\mathbf{A}$, denoted $\sigma_1, \dots, \sigma_d$, satisfy $0 \leq \sigma_i = \sqrt{1 - \alpha_i} \leq 1$, where α_i is the corresponding positive eigenvalue of $\mathbf{C}$. Assume that $\mathbf{A}$ is symmetric (this also means that $\mathbf{M}_n$ is symmetric). Denote by $\lambda_1, \dots, \lambda_d$ to the eigenvalues of $\mathbf{A}$. That is, $\sigma_i = \sqrt{\lambda_i^2}$ and $0 \leq \lambda_i^2 \leq 1, i = 1, \dots, d$. For a fixed cumulant of order n we have that

$$||\mathbf{M}_n||_{\text{op}} = \max_{\mathbf{v} \in \mathscr{S}} \left| \prod_{j=1}^{n} \frac{\left[1 - \lambda_{v_j}^2\right]}{1 - \prod_{i=1}^{n} \lambda_{v_i}} + (-1)^n \prod_{j=1}^{n} \lambda_{v_j} \right|, \tag{8.17}$$

where $\mathscr{S} = \{1, \dots, d\}^n$, $|\cdot|$ denotes absolute value, and we have employed standard properties of the Kronecker product about eigenvalues and eigenvectors [18]. Note that this expression does not depend on the eigenvectors of $\mathbf{A}$, but only on its eigenvalues.

Figure 8.2 shows, for symmetric $\mathbf{A}$, the value of $||\mathbf{M}_n||_{\text{op}}$ for $n = 3, \dots, 8$, and $d = 2$ when the two eigenvalues of $\mathbf{A}$ range in the interval $(-1, 1)$. We observe that $||\mathbf{M}_n||_{\text{op}}$ is always smaller than one. As described before, this will lead to a

---

[1]We assume such matrix exists and that it is positive definite.

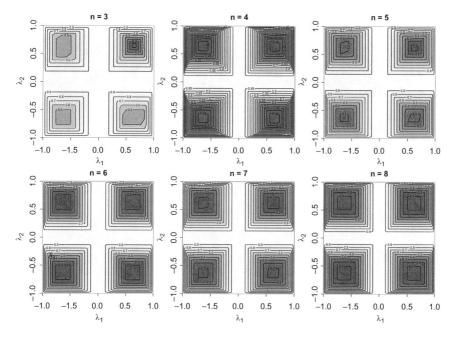

Fig. 8.2 Contour curves of the values of $||\mathbf{M}_n||_{op}$ for $d = 2$ and for $n > 2$ as a function of λ_1 and λ_2, i.e., the two eigenvalues of $\mathbf{A}$. $\mathbf{A}$ is assumed to be symmetric. Similar results are obtained for higher-order cumulants

reduction in the ℓ_2-norm of the cumulants in the anti-causal direction due to (8.16), and will in consequence produce a Gaussianization effect on the distribution of the residuals. For $n \leq 2$ it can be readily shown that $||\mathbf{M}_1||_{op} = ||\mathbf{M}_2||_{op} = 1$.

In general, the matrix $\mathbf{A}$ need not be symmetric. In this case, $||\mathbf{M}_1||_{op} = ||\mathbf{M}_2||_{op} = 1$ as well. However, the evaluation of $||\mathbf{M}_n||_{op}$ for $n > 2$ is more difficult, but feasible for small n. Figure 8.3 displays the values of $||\mathbf{M}_n||_{op}$, for $d = 2$, as the two singular values of $\mathbf{A}$, σ_1 and σ_2, vary in the interval $(0, 1)$. The left singular vectors and the right singular vectors of $\mathbf{A}$ are chosen at random. In this figure a dashed blue line highlights the boundary of the region where $||\mathbf{M}_n||_{op}$ is strictly smaller than one. We observe that for most values of σ_1 and σ_2, $||\mathbf{M}_n||_{op}$ is smaller than one, leading to a Gaussianization effect in the distribution of the residuals in the anti-causal direction. However, for some singular values, $||\mathbf{M}_n||_{op}$ is strictly larger than one. Of course, this does not mean that there is not such a Gaussianization effect also in those cases. The definition given for $||\mathbf{M}_n||_{op}$ assumes that all potential vectors $\mathbf{v}$ represent valid cumulants of a probability distribution, which need not be the case in practice. For example, it is well known that cumulants exhibit some form of symmetry [20]. This can be seen in the second order cumulant, which is a covariance matrix. The consequence is that $||\mathbf{M}_n||_{op}$ is simply an upper bound on the reduction of the ℓ_2-norm of the cumulants in the anti-causal model. Thus,

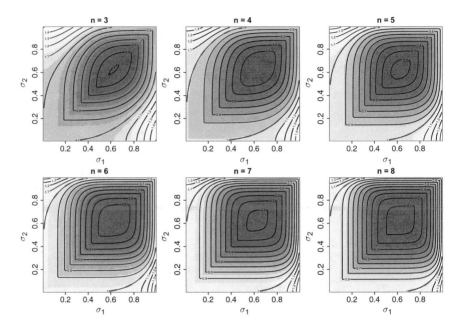

Fig. 8.3 Contour curves of the values of $||\mathbf{M}_n||_{\mathrm{op}}$ for $d=2$ and for $n>2$ as a function of σ_1 and σ_2, i.e., the two singular values of $\mathbf{A}$. $\mathbf{A}$ is not assumed to be symmetric. The singular vectors of $\mathbf{A}$ are chosen at random. A dashed blue line highlights the boundary of the region where $||\mathbf{M}_n||_{\mathrm{op}}$ is strictly smaller than one

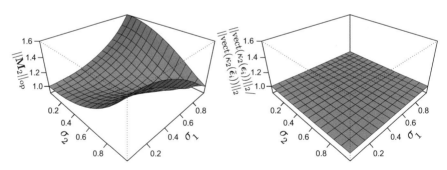

Fig. 8.4 (**left**) Value of $||\mathbf{M}_2||_{\mathrm{op}}$, for $d=2$, as a function of σ_1 and σ_2, i.e., the two singular values of $\mathbf{A}$. (**right**) Actual ratio between $||\mathrm{vect}(\kappa_2(\boldsymbol{\epsilon}_i))||_2$ and $||\mathrm{vect}(\kappa_2(\tilde{\boldsymbol{\epsilon}}_i))||_2$, for $d=2$, as a function of σ_1 and σ_2. $\mathbf{A}$ is not assumed to be symmetric. The singular vectors of $\mathbf{A}$ are chosen at random

we also expect a Gaussianization effect to occur also for these cases. Furthermore, the numerical simulations presented in Sect. 8.6 provide evidence of this effect for asymmetric $\mathbf{A}$.

The fact that $||\mathbf{M}_n||_{\mathrm{op}}$ is only an upper bound is illustrated in Fig. 8.4. This figure considers the particular case of the second cumulant $\kappa_2(\cdot)$, which can be analyzed in detail. On the left plot the value of $||\mathbf{M}_2||_{\mathrm{op}}$ is displayed as a function of σ_1 and σ_2, the two singular values of $\mathbf{A}$. We observe that $||\mathbf{M}_2||_{\mathrm{op}}$ takes values that are larger than one. In this case it is possible to evaluate in closed form the ℓ_2-norm of $\text{vect}(\kappa_2(\epsilon_i))$ and $\text{vect}(\kappa_2(\tilde{\epsilon}_i))$, i.e., the vectors that contain the second order cumulant of the residuals in each direction. In particular, it is well known that the second order cumulant is equal to the covariance matrix [20]. In the causal direction, the covariance matrix of the residuals is $\mathbf{C} = \mathbf{I} - \mathbf{AA}^T$, as shown in the previous paragraphs. The covariance matrix of the residuals in the anti-causal direction, denoted by $\tilde{\mathbf{C}}$, can be computed similarly. Namely, $\tilde{\mathbf{C}} = \mathbf{I} - \mathbf{A}^T\mathbf{A}$. These two matrices, i.e., $\mathbf{C}$ and $\tilde{\mathbf{C}}$, respectively give $k_2(\epsilon_i)$ and $k_2(\tilde{\epsilon}_i)$. Furthermore, they have the same singular values. This means that $||\text{vect}(k_2(\epsilon_i))||_2/||\text{vect}(k_2(\tilde{\epsilon}_i))||_2 = 1$, as illustrated by the right plot in Fig. 8.4. Thus, $||\mathbf{M}_2||_{\text{op}}$ is simply an upper bound on the actual reduction of the ℓ_2-norm of the second order cumulant of the residuals in the anti-causal direction. The same behavior is expected for $||\mathbf{M}_n||_{\text{op}}$, with $n > 2$. In consequence, one should expect that the cumulants of the distribution of the residuals of a model fitted in the anti-causal direction are smaller in magnitude. This will lead to an increased level of Gaussianity measured in terms of a reduction of the magnitude of the high-order cumulants.

8.2.3 Analysis of the Multivariate Case Based on Information Theory

The analysis of the multivariate case carried out in the previous section is illustrative. Nevertheless, it does not prove that the distribution of the residuals in the anti-casual direction is more Gaussian based on a reduction of the magnitude of the cumulants. Further evidence of this increased level of Gaussianity can be obtained based on an increase of the entropy obtained by using information theory. In this case we also assume that the multi-dimensional variables $\mathscr{X}$ and $\mathscr{Y}$ follow the same distribution, but unlike in the previous section, they need not be whitened, only centered. Here we closely follow Sect. 2.4 of the work by Hyvärinen and Smith [12] and extend their results to the multivariate case.

Under the assumptions specified earlier, the model in the causal direction is $\mathbf{y}_i = \mathbf{A}\mathbf{x}_i + \epsilon_i$, with $\mathbf{x}_i \perp \epsilon_i$ and $\mathbf{A} = \text{Cov}(\mathscr{Y}, \mathscr{X})\text{Cov}(\mathscr{X}, \mathscr{X})^{-1}$. Similarly, the model in the anti-causal direction is $\mathbf{x}_i = \tilde{\mathbf{A}}\mathbf{y}_i + \tilde{\epsilon}_i$ with $\tilde{\mathbf{A}} = \text{Cov}(\mathscr{X}, \mathscr{Y})\text{Cov}(\mathscr{Y}, \mathscr{Y})^{-1}$. By making use of the causal model it is possible to show that $\tilde{\epsilon}_i = (\mathbf{I} - \tilde{\mathbf{A}}\mathbf{A})\mathbf{x}_i - \tilde{\mathbf{A}}\epsilon_i$, where $\mathbf{I}$ is the identity matrix. Thus, the following equations are satisfied:

$$\begin{pmatrix} \mathbf{x}_i \\ \mathbf{y}_i \end{pmatrix} = \mathbf{P} \begin{pmatrix} \mathbf{x}_i \\ \epsilon_i \end{pmatrix} = \begin{pmatrix} \mathbf{I} & \mathbf{0} \\ \mathbf{A} & \mathbf{I} \end{pmatrix} \begin{pmatrix} \mathbf{x}_i \\ \epsilon_i \end{pmatrix}, \tag{8.18}$$

and

$$\begin{pmatrix} \mathbf{y}_i \\ \tilde{\epsilon}_i \end{pmatrix} = \tilde{\mathbf{P}} \begin{pmatrix} \mathbf{x}_i \\ \epsilon_i \end{pmatrix} = \begin{pmatrix} \mathbf{A} & \mathbf{I} \\ \mathbf{I} - \tilde{\mathbf{A}}\mathbf{A} & -\tilde{\mathbf{A}} \end{pmatrix} \begin{pmatrix} \mathbf{x}_i \\ \epsilon_i \end{pmatrix}. \tag{8.19}$$

Let $H(\mathbf{x}_i, \mathbf{y}_i)$ be the entropy of the joint distribution of the two random variables associated with samples $\mathbf{x}_i$ and $\mathbf{y}_i$. Because (8.18) is a linear transformation, we can use the entropy transformation formula [12] to get that $H(\mathbf{x}_i, \mathbf{y}_i) = H(\mathbf{x}_i, \epsilon_i) + \log|\det\mathbf{P}|$, where $\det\mathbf{P} = \det\mathbf{I} = 1$. Thus, we have that $H(\mathbf{x}_i, \mathbf{y}_i) = H(\mathbf{x}_i, \epsilon_i)$. Conversely, if we use (8.19) we have $H(\mathbf{y}_i, \epsilon_i) = H(\mathbf{x}_i, \epsilon_i) + \log|\det\tilde{\mathbf{P}}|$, where $\det\tilde{\mathbf{P}} = \det\mathbf{A} \cdot \det(-\tilde{\mathbf{A}} - (\mathbf{I} - \tilde{\mathbf{A}}\mathbf{A})\mathbf{A}^{-1}\mathbf{I}) = -\det\mathbf{I} = -1$, under the assumption that $\mathbf{A}$ is invertible. The result is that $H(\mathbf{x}_i, \mathbf{y}_i) = H(\mathbf{y}_i, \epsilon_i) = H(\mathbf{x}_i, \epsilon_i)$.

Denote the mutual information between the cause and the noise with $I(\mathbf{x}_i, \epsilon_i)$. Similarly, let $I(\mathbf{y}_i, \tilde{\epsilon}_i)$ be the mutual information between the random variables corresponding to the observations $\mathbf{y}_i$ and $\tilde{\epsilon}_i$. Then,

$$I(\mathbf{x}_i, \epsilon_i) - I(\mathbf{y}_i, \tilde{\epsilon}_i) = H(\mathbf{x}_i) + H(\epsilon_i) - H(\mathbf{x}_i, \epsilon_i) - H(\mathbf{y}_i) - H(\tilde{\epsilon}_i) + H(\mathbf{y}_i, \tilde{\epsilon}_i)$$
(8.20)

$$= H(\mathbf{x}_i) + H(\epsilon_i) - H(\mathbf{y}_i) - H(\tilde{\epsilon}_i). \tag{8.21}$$

Furthermore, from the actual causal model assumed we know that $I(\mathbf{x}_i, \epsilon_i) = 0$. By contrast, we have that $I(\mathbf{y}_i, \tilde{\epsilon}_i) \geq 0$, since both $\mathbf{y}_i$ and $\tilde{\epsilon}_i$ depend on $\mathbf{x}_i$ and ϵ_i. We also know that $H(\mathbf{x}_i) = H(\mathbf{y}_i)$ because we have made the hypothesis that both $\mathscr{X}$ and $\mathscr{Y}$ follow the same distribution. The result is that:

$$H(\epsilon_i) \leq H(\tilde{\epsilon}_i), \tag{8.22}$$

with equality iff the residuals are Gaussian. We note that an alternative but equivalent way to obtain this last result is to consider a multivariate version of Lemma 1 by Kpotufe et al. [17], under the assumption of the same distribution for the cause and the effect. In particular, even though [17] assume univariate random variables, their work can be easily generalized to multiple variables.

Although the random variables corresponding to ϵ_i and $\tilde{\epsilon}_i$ have both zero mean, they need not have the same covariance matrix. Denote with $\text{Cov}(\epsilon_i)$ and $\text{Cov}(\tilde{\epsilon}_i)$ to these matrices and let $\hat{\epsilon}_i$ and $\hat{\tilde{\epsilon}}_i$ be the whitened residuals (i.e., the residuals multiplied by the Cholesky factor of the inverse of the corresponding covariance matrix). Then,

$$H(\hat{\epsilon}_i) \leq H(\hat{\tilde{\epsilon}}_i) - \frac{1}{2}\log|\det\text{Cov}(\tilde{\epsilon}_i)| + \frac{1}{2}\log|\det\text{Cov}(\epsilon_i)|. \tag{8.23}$$

As shown in Appendix 1, although not equal, the matrices $\text{Cov}(\epsilon_i)$ and $\text{Cov}(\tilde{\epsilon}_i)$ have the same determinant. Thus, the two determinants cancel in the equation above. This gives,

$$H(\hat{\epsilon}_i) \leq H(\hat{\tilde{\epsilon}}_i). \tag{8.24}$$

The consequence is that the entropy of the whitened residuals in the anti-causal direction is expected to be higher or equal than the entropy of the whitened residuals in the causal direction. Because the Gaussian distribution is the continuous distribution with the highest entropy for a fixed covariance matrix, we conclude that the level of Gaussianity of the residuals in the anti-causal direction, measured in terms of differential entropy, has to be larger or equal to the level of Gaussianity of the residuals in the causal direction.

In summary, if the causal relation between the two identically distributed random variables $\mathscr{X}$ and $\mathscr{Y}$ is linear the residuals of a least squares fit in the anti-causal direction are more Gaussian than those of a linear fit in the causal direction. This Gaussianization can be characterized by a reduction of the magnitude of the corresponding high-order cumulants (although we have not formally proved this, we have provided some evidence that this is the case) and by an increase of the entropy (we have proved this in this section). A causal inference method can take advantage of this asymmetry to determine the causal direction. In particular, statistical tests based on measures of Gaussianity can be used for this purpose. However and importantly, these measures of Gaussianity need not be estimates of the differential entropy or the high-order cumulants. In particular, the entropy is a quantity that is particularly difficult to estimate in practice [1]. The same occurs with the high-order cumulants. Their estimators involve high-order moments, and hence suffer from high variance.

When the distribution of the residuals in (8.8) is Gaussian, the causal direction cannot be identified. In this case, it is possible to show that the distribution of the reversed residuals $\tilde{\epsilon}_i$, the cause $\mathbf{x}_i$, and the effect $\mathbf{y}_i$, is Gaussian as a consequence of (8.11) and (8.16). This non-identifiability agrees with the general result of [28], which indicates that non-Gaussian distributions are strictly required in the disturbance variables to carry out causal inference in linear models with additive independent noise.

Finally, the fact that the Gaussianization effect is also expected in the multivariate case suggests a method to address causal inference problems in which the relationship between cause and effect is non-linear: It consists in mapping each observation x_i and y_i to a vector in an expanded feature space. One can them assume that the non-linear relation in the original input space is linear in the expanded feature space and compute the residuals of kernel ridge regressions in both directions. The direction in which the residuals are less Gaussian is identified as the causal one.

8.3 A Feature Expansion to Address Non-linear Causal Inference Problems

We now proceed to relax the assumption that the causal relationship between the unidimensional random variables $\mathscr{X}$ and $\mathscr{Y}$ is linear. For this purpose, instead of working in the original space in which the samples $\{(x_i, y_i)\}_{i=1}^{N}$ are observed, we will assume that the model is linear in some expanded feature space $\{(\phi(x_i), \phi(y_i))\}_{i=1}^{N}$ for some mapping function $\phi(\cdot) : \mathbb{R} \rightarrow \mathbb{R}^d$. Importantly, this map preserves the property that if x_i and y_i are equally distributed, so will be $\phi(x_i)$ and $\phi(y_i)$. According to the analysis presented in the previous section, the residuals of a linear model in the expanded space should be more Gaussian in the anti-causal direction than the residuals of a linear model in the causal direction, based on an increment of the differential entropy and on a reduction of the magnitude of the cumulants. The assumption we make is that the non-linear relation between $\mathscr{X}$ and $\mathscr{Y}$ in the original input space is linear in the expanded feature space.

In this section we focus on obtaining the normalized residuals of linear models formulated in the expanded feature space. For this purpose, we assume that a kernel function $k(\cdot, \cdot)$ can be used to evaluate dot products in the expanded feature space. In particular, $k(x_i, x_j) = \phi(x_i)^\mathsf{T}\phi(x_j)$ and $k(y_i, y_j) = \phi(y_i)^\mathsf{T}\phi(y_j)$ for arbitrary x_i and x_j and y_i and y_j. Furthermore, we will not assume in general that $\phi(x_i)$ and $\phi(y_i)$ have been whitened, only centered. Whitening is a linear transformation which is not expected to affect to the level of Gaussianity of the residuals. However, once these residuals have been obtained they will be whitened in the expanded feature space. Later on we describe how to center the data in the expanded feature space. For now on, we will assume this step has already been done.

8.3.1 Non-linear Model Description and Fitting Process

Assume that the relation between $\mathscr{X}$ and $\mathscr{Y}$ is linear in an expanded feature space

$$\phi(y_i) = \mathbf{A}\phi(x_i) + \boldsymbol{\epsilon}_i, \quad \boldsymbol{\epsilon}_i \perp x_i, \tag{8.25}$$

where $\boldsymbol{\epsilon}_i$ is i.i.d. non-Gaussian additive noise.

Given N paired observations $\{(x_i, y_i)\}_{i=1}^{N}$ drawn i.i.d. from $P(\mathscr{X}, \mathscr{Y})$, define the matrices $\boldsymbol{\Phi}_x = (\phi(x_1), \ldots, \phi(x_N))$ and $\boldsymbol{\Phi}_y = (\phi(y_1), \ldots, \phi(y_N))$ of size $d \times N$. The estimate of $\mathbf{A}$ that minimizes the sum of squared errors is $\hat{\mathbf{A}} = \boldsymbol{\Gamma}\boldsymbol{\Sigma}^{-1}$, where $\boldsymbol{\Gamma} = \boldsymbol{\Phi}_y\boldsymbol{\Phi}_x^\mathsf{T}$ and $\boldsymbol{\Sigma} = \boldsymbol{\Phi}_x\boldsymbol{\Phi}_x^\mathsf{T}$. Unfortunately, when $d > N$, where d is the number of variables in the feature expansion, the matrix $\boldsymbol{\Sigma}^{-1}$ does not exist and $\hat{\mathbf{A}}$ is not unique. This means that there is an infinite number of solutions for $\hat{\mathbf{A}}$ with zero squared error.

To avoid the indetermination described above and also to alleviate over-fitting, we propose a regularized estimator. Namely,

$$\mathscr{L}(\mathbf{A}) = \sum_{i=1}^{N} \frac{1}{2}||\phi(y_i) - \mathbf{A}\phi(x_i)||_2^2 + \tau\frac{1}{2}||\mathbf{A}||_{\mathscr{F}}^2, \tag{8.26}$$

where $||\cdot||_2$ denotes the ℓ_2-norm and $||\cdot||_{\mathscr{F}}$ denotes the Frobenius norm. In this last expression $\tau > 0$ is a parameter that controls the amount of regularization. The minimizer of (8.26) is $\hat{\mathbf{A}} = \boldsymbol{\Gamma}\boldsymbol{\Sigma}^{-1}$, where $\boldsymbol{\Gamma} = \boldsymbol{\Phi}_y\boldsymbol{\Phi}_x^\mathsf{T}$ and $\boldsymbol{\Sigma} = \tau\mathbf{I} + \boldsymbol{\Phi}_x\boldsymbol{\Phi}_x^\mathsf{T}$. The larger the value of τ, the closer the entries of $\hat{\mathbf{A}}$ are to zero. Furthermore, using the matrix inversion lemma we have that $\boldsymbol{\Sigma}^{-1} = \tau^{-1}\mathbf{I} - \tau^{-1}\boldsymbol{\Phi}_x\mathbf{V}^{-1}\boldsymbol{\Phi}_x^{\mathrm{T}}$, where $\mathbf{V} = (\tau\mathbf{I} + \mathbf{K}_{x,x})^{-1}$ and $\mathbf{K}_{x,x} = \boldsymbol{\Phi}_x^{\mathrm{T}}\boldsymbol{\Phi}_x$ is a kernel matrix whose entries are given by $k(x_i, x_j)$. After some algebra it is possible to show that

$$\hat{\mathbf{A}} = \boldsymbol{\Gamma}\boldsymbol{\Sigma}^{-1} = \boldsymbol{\Phi}_y\mathbf{V}\boldsymbol{\Phi}_x^{\mathrm{T}}, \tag{8.27}$$

which depends only on the matrix $\mathbf{V}$. This matrix be computed with cost $\mathcal{O}(N^3)$. We note that the estimate obtained in (8.27) coincides with the kernel conditional embedding operator described by Song et al. [30] for mapping conditional distributions into infinite dimensional feature spaces using kernels.

8.3.2 Obtaining the Matrix of Inner Products of the Residuals

A first step towards obtaining the whitened residuals in feature space (which will be required for the estimation of their level of Gaussianity) is to compute the matrix of inner products of these residuals (kernel matrix). For this, we define $\epsilon_i = \phi(y_i) - \hat{\mathbf{A}}\phi(x_i)$. Thus,

$$\epsilon_i^{\mathrm{T}}\epsilon_j = \left[\phi(y_i) - \hat{\mathbf{A}}\phi(x_i)\right]^{\mathrm{T}}\left[\phi(y_j) - \hat{\mathbf{A}}\phi(x_j)\right] \tag{8.28}$$

$$= \phi(y_i)^{\mathrm{T}}\phi(y_j) - \phi(y_i)^{\mathrm{T}}\hat{\mathbf{A}}\phi(x_j) - \phi(x_i)^{\mathrm{T}}\hat{\mathbf{A}}\phi(y_j) + \phi(x_i)^{\mathrm{T}}\hat{\mathbf{A}}\hat{\mathbf{A}}\phi(x_j), \tag{8.29}$$

for two arbitrary residuals ϵ_i and ϵ_j in feature space. In general, if we denote with $\mathbf{K}_\epsilon$ to the matrix whose entries are given by $\epsilon_i^{\mathrm{T}}\epsilon_j$ and define $\mathbf{K}_{y,y} = \boldsymbol{\Phi}_y^{\mathrm{T}}\boldsymbol{\Phi}_y$, we have that

$$\mathbf{K}_\epsilon = \mathbf{K}_{y,y} - \mathbf{K}_{y,y}\mathbf{V}\mathbf{K}_{x,x} - \mathbf{K}_{x,x}\mathbf{V}\mathbf{K}_{y,y} + \mathbf{K}_{x,x}\mathbf{V}\mathbf{K}_{y,y}\mathbf{V}\mathbf{K}_{x,x}, \tag{8.30}$$

where we have used the definition of $\hat{\mathbf{A}}$ in (8.27). This expression only depends on the kernel matrices $\mathbf{K}_{x,x}$ and $\mathbf{K}_{y,y}$ and the matrix $\mathbf{V}$, and can be computed with cost $\mathcal{O}(N^3)$.

8.3.3 Centering the Input Data and Centering and Whitening the Residuals

An assumption made in Sect. 8.2 was that the samples of the random variables $\mathscr{X}$ and $\mathscr{Y}$ are centered, i.e., they have zero mean. In this section we show how to carry out this centering process in feature space. Furthermore, we also show how to center the residuals of the fitting process, which are also whitened. Whitening is a standard procedure in which the data are transformed to have the identity matrix as the covariance matrix. It also corresponds to projecting the data onto all the principal components, and scaling them to have unit standard deviation.

We show how to center the data in feature space. For this, we follow Schölkopf et al. [27] and work with:

$$\tilde{\phi}(x_i) = \phi(x_i) - \frac{1}{N} \sum_{j=1}^{N} \phi(x_j), \quad \tilde{\phi}(y_i) = \phi(y_i) - \frac{1}{N} \sum_{j=1}^{N} \phi(y_j). \quad (8.31)$$

The consequence is that now the kernel matrices $\mathbf{K}_{x,x}$ and $\mathbf{K}_{y,y}$ are replaced by

$$\tilde{\mathbf{K}}_{x,x} = \mathbf{K}_{x,x} - \mathbf{1}_N \mathbf{K}_{x,x} - \mathbf{K}_{x,x} \mathbf{1}_N + \mathbf{1}_N \mathbf{K}_{x,x} \mathbf{1}_N, \quad (8.32)$$

$$\tilde{\mathbf{K}}_{y,y} = \mathbf{K}_{y,y} - \mathbf{1}_N \mathbf{K}_{y,y} - \mathbf{K}_{y,y} \mathbf{1}_N + \mathbf{1}_N \mathbf{K}_{y,y} \mathbf{1}_N, \quad (8.33)$$

where $\mathbf{1}_N$ is a $N \times N$ matrix with all entries equal to $1/N$. The residuals can be centered also in a similar way. Namely, $\tilde{\mathbf{K}}_\epsilon = \mathbf{K}_\epsilon - \mathbf{1}_N \mathbf{K}_\epsilon - \mathbf{K}_\epsilon \mathbf{1}_N + \mathbf{1}_N \mathbf{K}_\epsilon \mathbf{1}_N$.

We now explain the whitening of the residuals, which are now assumed to be centered. This process involves the computation of the eigenvalues and eigenvectors of the $d \times d$ covariance matrix $\mathbf{C}$ of the residuals. This is done as in kernel PCA [27]. Denote by $\tilde{\boldsymbol{\epsilon}}_i$ to the centered residuals. The covariance matrix is $\mathbf{C} = N^{-1} \sum_{i=1}^{N} \tilde{\boldsymbol{\epsilon}}_i \tilde{\boldsymbol{\epsilon}}_i^T$. The eigenvector expansion implies that $\mathbf{C} \mathbf{v}_i = \lambda_i \mathbf{v}_i$, where $\mathbf{v}_i$ denotes the i-th eigenvector and λ_i the i-th eigenvalue. The consequence is that $N^{-1} \sum_{k=1}^{N} \tilde{\boldsymbol{\epsilon}}_k \tilde{\boldsymbol{\epsilon}}_k^T \mathbf{v}_i = \lambda_i \mathbf{v}_i$. Thus, the eigenvectors can be expressed as a combination of the residuals. Namely, $\mathbf{v}_i = \sum_{j=1}^{N} b_{i,j} \tilde{\boldsymbol{\epsilon}}_j$, where $b_{i,j} = N^{-1} \tilde{\boldsymbol{\epsilon}}_j^T \mathbf{v}_i$. Substituting this result in the previous equation we have that $N^{-1} \sum_{k=1}^{N} \tilde{\boldsymbol{\epsilon}}_k \tilde{\boldsymbol{\epsilon}}_k^T \sum_{j=1}^{N} b_{i,j} \tilde{\boldsymbol{\epsilon}}_j = \lambda_i \sum_{j=1}^{N} b_{i,j} \tilde{\boldsymbol{\epsilon}}_j$. When we multiply both sides by $\tilde{\boldsymbol{\epsilon}}_l^T$ we obtain $N^{-1} \sum_{k=1}^{N} \tilde{\boldsymbol{\epsilon}}_l^T \tilde{\boldsymbol{\epsilon}}_k \tilde{\boldsymbol{\epsilon}}_k^T \sum_{j=1}^{N} b_{i,j} \tilde{\boldsymbol{\epsilon}}_j = \lambda_i \sum_{j=1}^{N} b_{i,j} \tilde{\boldsymbol{\epsilon}}_l^T \tilde{\boldsymbol{\epsilon}}_j$, for $l = 1, \ldots d$, which is written in terms of kernels as $\tilde{\mathbf{K}}_\epsilon \tilde{\mathbf{K}}_\epsilon \mathbf{b}_i = \lambda_i N \tilde{\mathbf{K}}_\epsilon \mathbf{b}_i$, where $\mathbf{b}_i = (b_{i,1}, \ldots, b_{i,N})^T$. A solution to this problem is found by solving the eigenvalue problem $\tilde{\mathbf{K}}_\epsilon \mathbf{b}_i = \lambda_i N \mathbf{b}_i$. We also require that the eigenvectors have unit norm. Thus, $1 = \mathbf{v}_i^T \mathbf{v}_i = \sum_{j=1}^{N} \sum_{k=1}^{N} b_{i,j} b_{i,k} \tilde{\boldsymbol{\epsilon}}_j^T \tilde{\boldsymbol{\epsilon}}_k = \mathbf{b}_i^T \tilde{\mathbf{K}}_\epsilon \mathbf{b}_i = \lambda_i N \mathbf{b}_i^T \mathbf{b}_i$, which means that $\mathbf{b}_i$ has norm $1/\sqrt{\lambda_i N}$. Consider now that $\tilde{\mathbf{b}}_i$ is one eigenvector of $\tilde{\mathbf{K}}_\epsilon$. Then, $\mathbf{b}_i = 1/\sqrt{\lambda_i N} \tilde{\mathbf{b}}_i$. Similarly, let $\tilde{\lambda}_i$ be an eigenvalue of $\tilde{\mathbf{K}}_\epsilon$. Then $\lambda_i = \tilde{\lambda}_i/N$. In summary, λ_i and $b_{i,j}$, with $i = 1, \ldots, N$ and $j = 1, \ldots, N$ can be found with cost $\mathcal{O}(N^3)$ by finding the eigendecomposition of $\tilde{\mathbf{K}}_\epsilon$.

The whitening process is carried out by projecting each residual $\tilde{\boldsymbol{\epsilon}}_k$ onto each eigenvector $\mathbf{v}_i$ and then multiplying by $1/\sqrt{\lambda_i}$. The corresponding i-th component for the k-th residual, denoted by $Z_{k,i}$, is $Z_{k,i} = 1/\sqrt{\lambda_i} \mathbf{v}_i^T \tilde{\boldsymbol{\epsilon}}_k = 1/\sqrt{\lambda_i} \sum_{j=1}^{N} b_{i,j} \tilde{\boldsymbol{\epsilon}}_j^T \tilde{\boldsymbol{\epsilon}}_k$, and in consequence, the whitened residuals are $\mathbf{Z} = \tilde{\mathbf{K}}_\epsilon \mathbf{BD} = N \mathbf{BD}^{-1} = \sqrt{N} \tilde{\mathbf{B}}$, where $\mathbf{B}$ is a matrix whose columns contain each

$\mathbf{b}_i$, $\tilde{\mathbf{B}}$ is a matrix whose columns contain each $\tilde{b}_i$ and $\mathbf{D}$ is a diagonal matrix whose entries are equal to $1/\sqrt{\lambda_i}$. Each row of $\mathbf{Z}$ now contains the whitened residuals.

8.3.4 Inferring the Most Likely Causal Direction

After having trained the model and obtained the matrix of whitened residuals $\mathbf{Z}$ in each direction, a suitable Gaussianity test can be used to determine the correct causal relation between the variables $\mathscr{X}$ and $\mathscr{Y}$. Given the theoretical results of Sect. 8.2 one may be tempted to use tests based on entropy or cumulants estimation. Such tests may perform poorly in practice due to the difficulty of estimating high-order cumulants or differential entropy. In particular, the estimators of the cumulants involve high-order moments and hence, suffer from high variance. As a consequence, in our experiments we use a statistical test for Gaussianity based on the *energy distance* [31], which has good power, is robust to noise, and does not have any adjustable hyper-parameters. Furthermore, in Appendix 2 we motivate that in the anti-causal direction one should also expect a smaller energy distance to the Gaussian distribution.

Assume $\mathscr{X}$ and $\mathscr{Y}$ are two independent random variables whose probability distribution functions are $F(\cdot)$ and $G(\cdot)$. The energy distance between these distributions is defined as

$$D^2(F, G) = 2\mathbb{E}[||\mathscr{X} - \mathscr{Y}||] - \mathbb{E}[||\mathscr{X} - \mathscr{X}'||] - \mathbb{E}[||\mathscr{Y} - \mathscr{Y}'||], \tag{8.34}$$

where $|| \cdot ||$ denotes some norm, typically the ℓ_2-norm; $\mathscr{X}$ and $\mathscr{X}'$ are independent and identically distributed (i.i.d.); $\mathscr{Y}$ and $\mathscr{Y}'$ are i.i.d; and $\mathbb{E}$ denotes expected value. The energy distance satisfies all axioms of a metric and hence characterizes the equality of distributions. Namely, $D^2(F, G) = 0$ if and only if $F = G$. Furthermore, in the case of univariate random variables the energy distance is twice the Cramér-von Mises distance given by $\int (F(x) - G(x))^2 \, dx$.

Assume $\mathbf{X} = (\mathbf{x}_1, \ldots, \mathbf{x}_N)^{\mathrm{T}}$ is a matrix that contains N random samples (one per each row of the matrix) from a d dimensional random variable with probability density f. The statistic described for testing for Gaussianity, i.e., $H_0 : f = \mathscr{N}(\cdot|\mathbf{0}, \mathbf{I})$ vs $H_1 : f \neq \mathscr{N}(\cdot|\mathbf{0}, \mathbf{I})$, that is described by Székely and Rizzo [31] is:

$$\text{Energy}(\mathbf{X}) = N \left(\frac{2}{N} \sum_{j=1}^{N} \mathbb{E}[||\mathbf{x}_j - \mathscr{Y}||] - \mathbb{E}[||\mathscr{Y} - \mathscr{Y}'||] - \frac{1}{N^2} \sum_{j,k=1}^{N} ||\mathbf{x}_j - \mathbf{x}_k|| \right), \tag{8.35}$$

where $\mathscr{Y}$ and $\mathscr{Y}'$ are independent random variables distributed as $\mathscr{N}(\cdot|\mathbf{0}, \mathbf{I})$ and $\mathbb{E}$ denotes expected value. Furthermore, the required expectations with respect to the Gaussian random variables $\mathscr{Y}$ and $\mathscr{Y}'$ can be efficiently computed as described by Székely and Rizzo [31]. The idea is that if f is similar to a Gaussian density $\mathcal{N}(\cdot|0, \mathbf{I})$, then Energy$(\mathbf{X})$ is close to zero. Conversely, the null hypothesis H_0 is rejected for large values of Energy$(\mathbf{X})$.

The data to test for Gaussianity is in our case $\mathbf{Z}$, i.e., the matrix of whitened residuals, which has size $N \times N$. Thus, the whitened residuals have N dimensions. The direct introduction of these residuals into a statistical test for Gaussianity is not expected to provide meaningful results, as a consequence of the high dimensionality. Furthermore, in our experiments we have observed that it is often the case that a large part of the total variance is explained by the first principal component (see the supplementary material for evidence supporting this). That is, λ_i, i.e., the eigenvalue associated to the i-th principal component, is almost negligible for $i \geq 2$. Additionally, we motivate in Appendix 3 that one should also obtain more Gaussian residuals, after projecting the data onto the first principal component, in terms of a reduction of the magnitude of the high-order cumulants. Thus, in practice, we consider only the first principal component of the estimated residuals in feature space. This is the component i with the largest associated eigenvalue λ_i. We denote such N-dimensional vector by $\mathbf{z}$.

Let $\mathbf{z}_{x \to y}$ be the vector of coefficients of the first principal component of the residuals in feature space when the linear fit is performed in the direction $\mathcal{X} \to \mathcal{Y}$. Let $\mathbf{z}_{y \to x}$ be the vector of coefficients of the first principal component of the residuals in feature space when the linear fit is carried out in the direction $\mathcal{Y} \to \mathcal{X}$. We define the measure of Gaussianization of the residuals as $\mathcal{G} =$ Energy$(\mathbf{z}_{x \to y})/N -$ Energy$(\mathbf{z}_{y \to x})/N$, where Energy$(\cdot)$ computes the statistic of the energy distance test for Gaussianity described above. Note that we divide each statistic by N to cancel the corresponding factor that is considered in (8.35). Since in this test larger values for the statistic corresponds to larger deviations from Gaussianity, if $\mathcal{G} > 0$ the direction $\mathcal{X} \to \mathcal{Y}$ is expected to be more likely the causal direction. Otherwise, the direction $\mathcal{Y} \to \mathcal{X}$ is preferred.

The variance of $\mathcal{G}$ will depend on the sample size N. Thus, ideally one should use the difference between the p-values associated to each statistic as the confidence in the decision taken. Unfortunately, computing these p-values is expensive since the distribution of the statistic under the null hypothesis must be approximated via random sampling. In our experiments we measure the confidence of the decision in terms of the absolute value of $\mathcal{G}$, which is faster to obtain and we have found to perform well in practice.

8.3.5 Parameter Tuning and Error Evaluation

Assume that a squared exponential kernel is employed in the method described above. This means that $k(x_i, x_j) = \exp\left(-\gamma(x_i - x_j)^2\right)$, where $\gamma > 0$ is the bandwidth of the kernel. The same is assumed for $k(y_i, y_j)$. Therefore, two hyper-parameters require adjustment in the method described. These are the ridge regression regularization parameter τ and the kernel bandwidth γ. They must be tuned in some way to produce the best possible fit in each direction. The method chosen to guarantee this is a grid search guided by a 10-fold cross-validation procedure, which requires computing the squared prediction error over unseen data. In this section we detail how to evaluate these errors.

Assume that M new paired data instances are available for validation. Let the two matrices $\boldsymbol{\Phi}_{y^{\text{new}}} = (\phi(y_1^{\text{new}}), \ldots, \phi(y_M^{\text{new}}))$ and $\boldsymbol{\Phi}_{x^{\text{new}}} = (\phi(x_1^{\text{new}}), \ldots, \phi(x_M^{\text{new}}))$ summarize these data. Define $\boldsymbol{\epsilon}_i^{\text{new}} = \phi(y_i^{\text{new}}) - \hat{\mathbf{A}}\phi(x_i^{\text{new}})$. After some algebra, it is possible to show that the sum of squared errors for the new instances is:

$$E = \sum_{i=1}^{M} (\boldsymbol{\epsilon}_i^{\text{new}})^{\text{T}} \boldsymbol{\epsilon}_i^{\text{new}} = \text{trace}\bigg(\mathbf{K}_{y^{\text{new}}, y^{\text{new}}} - \mathbf{K}_{y^{\text{new}}, y} \mathbf{V} \mathbf{K}_{x^{\text{new}}, x}^{\text{T}} - \tag{8.36}$$

$$\mathbf{K}_{x^{\text{new}}, x} \mathbf{V} \mathbf{K}_{y^{\text{new}}, y}^{\text{T}} + \mathbf{K}_{x^{\text{new}}, x} \mathbf{V} \mathbf{K}_{y, y} \mathbf{V} \mathbf{K}_{x^{\text{new}}, x}^{\text{T}} \bigg). \tag{8.37}$$

where $\mathbf{K}_{y^{\text{new}}, y^{\text{new}}} = \boldsymbol{\Phi}_{y^{\text{new}}}^{\text{T}} \boldsymbol{\Phi}_{y^{\text{new}}}$, $\mathbf{K}_{y^{\text{new}}, y} = \boldsymbol{\Phi}_{y^{\text{new}}}^{\text{T}} \boldsymbol{\Phi}_{y}$ and $\mathbf{K}_{x, x^{\text{new}}} = \boldsymbol{\Phi}_x^{\text{T}} \boldsymbol{\Phi}_{x^{\text{new}}}$.

Of course, the new data must be centered before computing the error estimate. This process is similar to the one described in the previous section. In particular, centering can be simply carried out by working with the modified kernel matrices:

$$\tilde{\mathbf{K}}_{x^{\text{new}}, x} = \mathbf{K}_{x^{\text{new}}, x} - \mathbf{M}_N \mathbf{K}_{x, x} - \mathbf{K}_{x^{\text{new}}, x} \mathbf{1}_N + \mathbf{M}_N \mathbf{K}_{x, x} \mathbf{1}_N , \tag{8.38}$$

$$\tilde{\mathbf{K}}_{y^{\text{new}}, y} = \mathbf{K}_{y^{\text{new}}, y} - \mathbf{M}_N \mathbf{K}_{y, y} - \mathbf{K}_{y^{\text{new}}, y} \mathbf{1}_N + \mathbf{M}_N \mathbf{K}_{y, y} \mathbf{1}_N , \tag{8.39}$$

$$\tilde{\mathbf{K}}_{y^{\text{new}}, y^{\text{new}}} = \mathbf{K}_{y^{\text{new}}, y^{\text{new}}} - \mathbf{M}_N \mathbf{K}_{y, y^{\text{new}}} - \mathbf{K}_{y^{\text{new}}, y} \mathbf{M}_N^{\text{T}} + \mathbf{M}_N \mathbf{K}_{y, y} \mathbf{M}_N^{\text{T}} , \tag{8.40}$$

where $\mathbf{M}_N$ is a matrix of size $M \times N$ with all components equal to $1/N$. In this process, the averages employed for the centering step are computed using only the observed data.

A disadvantage of the squared error is that it strongly depends on the kernel bandwidth parameter γ. This makes it difficult to choose this hyper-parameter in terms of such a performance measure. A better approach is to choose both γ and τ in terms of the explained variance by the model. This is obtained as follows: Explained-Variance $= 1 - E/M \text{Var}_{y\text{new}}$, where E denotes the squared prediction error and $\text{Var}_{y\text{new}}$ the variance of the targets. The computation of the error E is done as described previously and $\text{Var}_{y\text{new}}$ is simply the average of the diagonal entries in $\tilde{\mathbf{K}}_{y^{\text{new}}, y^{\text{new}}}$.

8.3.6 Finding Pre-images for Illustrative Purposes

The kernel method described above expresses its solution as feature maps of the original data points. Since the feature map $\phi(\cdot)$ is usually non-linear, we cannot guarantee the existence of a pre-image under $\phi(\cdot)$. That is, a point y such that

$\phi(y) = \hat{\mathbf{A}}\phi(x)$, for some input point x. An alternative to amend this issue is to find approximate pre-images, which can be useful to make predictions or plotting results [26]. In this section we describe how to find this approximate pre-images.

Assume that we have a new data instance x_{new} for which we would like to know the associated target value y_{new}, after our kernel model has been fitted. The predicted value in feature space is:

$$\phi(y_{\text{new}}) = \boldsymbol{\Phi}_y \mathbf{V} \boldsymbol{\Phi}_x^{\mathsf{T}} \phi(x_{\text{new}}) = \boldsymbol{\Phi}_y \mathbf{V} \mathbf{k}_{x,x_{\text{new}}} = \sum_{i=1}^{n} \alpha_i \phi(y_i), \qquad (8.41)$$

where $\mathbf{k}_{x,x_{\text{new}}}$ contains the kernel evaluations between each entry in $\mathbf{x}$ (i.e., the observed samples of the random variable $\mathscr{X}$) and the new instance. Finally, each α_i is given by a component of the vector $\mathbf{V}\mathbf{k}_{x,x_{\text{new}}}$. The approximate pre-image of $\phi(y_{\text{new}})$, y_{new}, is found by solving the following optimization problem:

$$y_{\text{new}} = \arg\min_{u} \; \|\phi(y_{\text{new}}) - \phi(u)\|_2^2 = \arg\min_{u} \; -2\boldsymbol{\alpha}^{\mathsf{T}}\mathbf{k}_{y,u} + k(u,u),$$
$$(8.42)$$

where $\mathbf{k}_{y,u}$ is a vector with the kernel values between each y_i and u, and $k(u,u) = \phi(u)^{\mathsf{T}}\phi(u)$. This is a non-linear optimization problem than can be solved approximately using standard techniques such as gradient descent. In particular, the computation of the gradient of $\mathbf{k}_{y,u}$ with respect to u is very simple in the case of the squared exponential kernel.

8.4 Data Transformation and Detailed Causal Inference Algorithm

The method for causal inference described in the previous section relies on the fact that both random variables $\mathscr{X}$ and $\mathscr{Y}$ are equally distributed. In particular, if this is the case, $\phi(x_i)$ and $\phi(y_i)$, i.e., the maps of x_i and y_i in the expanded feature space, will also be equally distributed. This means that under such circumstances one should expect residuals that are more Gaussian in the anti-causal direction due to a reduction of the magnitude of the high order cumulants and an increment of the differential entropy. The requirement that $\mathscr{X}$ and $\mathscr{Y}$ are equally distributed can be easily fulfilled in the case of continuous univariate data by transforming $\mathbf{x}$, the samples of $\mathscr{X}$, to have the same empirical distribution as $\mathbf{y}$, the samples of $\mathscr{Y}$.

Consider $\mathbf{x} = (x_1, \ldots, x_N)^{\mathsf{T}}$ and $\mathbf{y} = (y_1, \ldots, y_N)^{\mathsf{T}}$ to be N paired samples of $\mathscr{X}$ and $\mathscr{Y}$, respectively. To guarantee the same distribution for these samples we only have to replace $\mathbf{x}$ by $\tilde{\mathbf{x}}$, where each component of $\tilde{\mathbf{x}}$, $\tilde{x}_i$, is given by $\tilde{x}_i = \hat{F}_y^{-1}(\hat{F}_x(x_i))$, with $\hat{F}_y^{-1}(\cdot)$ the empirical quantile distribution function of the random variable $\mathscr{Y}$, estimated using $\mathbf{y}$. Similarly, $\hat{F}_x(\cdot)$ is the empirical cumulative distribution function of $\mathscr{X}$, estimated using $\mathbf{x}$. This operation is known as the probability integral transform.

One may wonder why should $\mathbf{x}$ be transformed instead of $\mathbf{y}$. The reason is that by transforming $\mathbf{x}$ the additive noise hypothesis made in (8.1) and (8.8) is preserved. In particular, we have that $y_i = f(\hat{F}_x^{-1}(\hat{F}_y(\tilde{x}_i))) + \epsilon_i$. On the other hand, if $\mathbf{y}$ is transformed instead, the additive noise model will generally not be valid anymore. More precisely, the transformation that computes $\tilde{y}$ in such a way that it is distributed as $\mathbf{x}$ is $\tilde{y}_i = \hat{F}_x^{-1}(\hat{F}_y(y_i))$, $\forall i$. Thus, under this transformation we have that $\tilde{y}_i = \hat{F}_x^{-1}(\hat{F}_y(f(x_i) + \epsilon_i))$, which will lead to the violation of the additive noise model.

Of course, transforming $\mathbf{x}$ requires the knowledge of the causal direction. In practice, we will transform both $\mathbf{x}$ and $\mathbf{y}$ and consider that the correct transformation is the one that leads to the highest level of Gaussianization of the residuals in the feature space, after fitting the model in each direction. That is, the transformation that leads to the highest value of $\mathscr{G}$ is expected to be the correct one. We expect that when $\mathbf{y}$ is transformed instead of $\mathbf{x}$, the Gaussianization effect of the residuals is not as high as when $\mathbf{x}$ is transformed, as a consequence of the violation of the additive noise model. This will allow to determine the causal direction. We do not have a theoretical result confirming this statement, but the good results obtained in Sect. 8.6.1 indicate that this is the case.

The details of the complete causal inference algorithm proposed are given in Algorithm 1. Besides a causal direction, e.g., $\mathscr{X} \rightarrow \mathscr{Y}$ or $\mathscr{Y} \rightarrow \mathscr{X}$, this algorithm also outputs a confidence level in the decision made which is defined as $\max(|\mathscr{G}_{\tilde{x}}|, |\mathscr{G}_{\tilde{y}}|)$, where $\mathscr{G}_{\tilde{x}} = \mathrm{Energy}(\mathbf{z}_{\tilde{x} \rightarrow y})/N - \mathrm{Energy}(\mathbf{z}_{y \rightarrow \tilde{x}})/N$ denotes the estimated level of Gaussianization of the residuals when $\mathbf{x}$ is transformed to have the same distribution as $\mathbf{y}$. Similarly, $\mathscr{G}_{\tilde{y}} = \mathrm{Energy}(\mathbf{z}_{\tilde{y} \rightarrow x})/N - \mathrm{Energy}(\mathbf{z}_{\tilde{y} \rightarrow x})/N$ denotes the estimated level of Gaussianization of the residuals when $\mathbf{x}$ and $\mathbf{y}$ are swapped and $\mathbf{y}$ is transformed to have the same distribution as $\mathbf{x}$. Here $\mathbf{z}_{\tilde{x} \rightarrow y}$ contains the first principal component of the residuals in the expanded feature space when trying to predict $\mathbf{y}$ using $\tilde{\mathbf{x}}$. The same applies for $\mathbf{z}_{y \rightarrow \tilde{x}}$, $\mathbf{z}_{\tilde{y} \rightarrow x}$ and $\mathbf{z}_{x \rightarrow \tilde{y}}$. However, the residuals are obtained this time when trying to predict $\tilde{\mathbf{x}}$ using $\mathbf{y}$, when trying to predict $\mathbf{x}$ using $\tilde{\mathbf{y}}$ and when trying to predict $\tilde{\mathbf{y}}$ using $\mathbf{x}$, respectively. Recall that the reason for keeping only the first principal component of the residuals is described in Sect. 8.3.4.

Assume $|\mathscr{G}_{\tilde{x}}| > |\mathscr{G}_{\tilde{y}}|$. In this case we prefer the transformation of $\mathbf{x}$ to guarantee that the cause and the effect have the same distribution. The reason is that it leads to a higher level of Gaussianization of the residuals, as estimated by the energy statistical test. Now consider that $\mathscr{G}_{\tilde{x}} > 0$. We prefer the direction $\mathscr{X} \rightarrow \mathscr{Y}$ because the residuals of a fit in that direction are less Gaussian and hence have a higher value of the statistic of the energy test. By contrast, if $\mathscr{G}_{\tilde{x}} < 0$ we prefer the direction $\mathscr{Y} \rightarrow \mathscr{X}$ for the same reason. In the case that $|\mathscr{G}_{\tilde{x}}| < |\mathscr{G}_{\tilde{y}}|$ the reasoning is the same and we prefer the transformation of $\mathbf{y}$. However, because we have swapped $\mathbf{x}$ and $\mathbf{y}$ for

---

Algorithm 1: Causal inference based on the Gaussianity of the residuals (GR-AN)

Data: Paired samples $\mathbf{x}$ and $\mathbf{y}$ from the random variables $\mathscr{X}$ and $\mathscr{Y}$.
Result: An estimated causal direction alongside with a confidence level.

1 Standardize $\mathbf{x}$ and $\mathbf{y}$ to have zero mean and unit variance;

2 Transform $\mathbf{x}$ to compute $\tilde{\mathbf{x}}$;   `// This guarantees that x̃ is`
`distributed as y.`

3 $\hat{\mathbf{A}}_{\tilde{x}\to y} \leftarrow$ FitModel($\tilde{\mathbf{x}}, \mathbf{y}$); `// This also finds the hyper-parameters`
τ and γ.

4 $\mathbf{z}_{\tilde{x}\to y} \leftarrow$ ObtainResiduals($\tilde{\mathbf{x}}, \mathbf{y}, \hat{\mathbf{A}}_{\tilde{x}\to y}$);   `// First PCA component in`
`feature space.`

5 $\hat{\mathbf{A}}_{y\to\tilde{x}} \leftarrow$ FitModel($\mathbf{y}, \tilde{\mathbf{x}}$); `// Fit the model in the other direction`

6 $\mathbf{z}_{y\to\tilde{x}} \leftarrow$ ObtainResiduals($\mathbf{y}, \tilde{\mathbf{x}}, \hat{\mathbf{A}}_{y\to\tilde{x}}$);   `// First PCA component in`
`feature space.`

7 $\mathscr{G}_{\tilde{x}} \leftarrow$ Energy($\mathbf{z}_{\tilde{x}\to y}$)$/N -$ Energy($\mathbf{z}_{y\to\tilde{x}}$)$/N$; `// Get the Gaussianization`
`level.`

8 Swap $\mathbf{x}$ and $\mathbf{y}$ and repeat lines 2–7 of the algorithm to compute $\mathscr{G}_{\tilde{y}}$.

9 **if** $|\mathscr{G}_{\tilde{x}}| > |\mathscr{G}_{\tilde{y}}|$ **then**
10   **if** $\mathscr{G}_{\tilde{x}} > 0$ **then**
11 | **Output**: $\mathscr{X} \to \mathscr{Y}$ with confidence $|\mathscr{G}_{\tilde{x}}|$
12   **else**
13 | **Output**: $\mathscr{Y} \to \mathscr{X}$ with confidence $|\mathscr{G}_{\tilde{x}}|$
14   **end**
15 **else**
16   **if** $\mathscr{G}_{\tilde{y}} > 0$ **then**
17 | **Output**: $\mathscr{Y} \to \mathscr{X}$ with confidence $|\mathscr{G}_{\tilde{y}}|$
18   **else**
19 | **Output**: $\mathscr{X} \to \mathscr{Y}$ with confidence $|\mathscr{G}_{\tilde{y}}|$
20   **end**
21 **end**

---

computing $\mathscr{G}_{\tilde{y}}$, the decision is the opposite as the previous one. Namely, if $\mathscr{G}_{\tilde{y}} > 0$ we prefer the direction $\mathscr{Y} \to \mathscr{X}$ and otherwise we prefer the direction $\mathscr{X} \to \mathscr{Y}$. The confidence in the decision (i.e., the estimated level of Gaussianization) is always measured by $\max(|\mathscr{G}_{\tilde{x}}|, |\mathscr{G}_{\tilde{y}}|)$.

The algorithm uses a squared exponential kernel with bandwidth parameter γ and the actual matrices $\hat{\mathbf{A}}_{\tilde{x}\to y}$ and $\hat{\mathbf{A}}_{y\to\tilde{x}}$, of potentially infinite dimensions, need not be evaluated in closed form in practice. As indicated in Sect. 8.3, all computations are carried out efficiently with cost $\mathscr{O}(N^3)$ using inner products, which are evaluated in terms of the corresponding kernel function. All hyper-parameters, i.e., τ and γ, are chosen using a grid search method guided by a 10-fold cross-validation process. This search maximizes the explained variance of the left-out data and 10 potential values are considered for both τ and γ.

8.5 Related Work

The Gaussianity of residuals was first employed for causal inference by Hernández-Lobato et al. [9]. These authors analyze auto-regressive (AR) processes and show that a similar asymmetry as the one described in this paper can be used to determine the temporal direction of a time series in the presence of non-Gaussian noise. Namely, when fitting an AR process to a reversed time series, the residuals obtained follow a distribution that is closer to a Gaussian distribution. Nevertheless, unlike the work described here, the method proposed by Hernández-Lobato et al. [9] cannot be used to tackle multidimensional or non-linear causal inference problems. In their work, Hernández-Lobato et al. [9] show some advantages of using statistical tests based on measures of Gaussianity to determine the temporal direction of a time series, as a practical alternative to statistical tests based on the independence of the cause and the residual. The motivation for these advantages is that the former tests are one-sample tests while the later ones are two-sample tests.

The previous paper is extended by Morales-Mombiela et al. [22] to consider multidimensional AR processes. However, this work lacks a theoretical result that guarantees that the residuals obtained when fitting a vectorial AR process in the reversed (anti-chronological) direction will follow a distribution closer to a Gaussian distribution. In spite of this issue, extensive experiments with simulated data suggest the validity of such conjecture. Furthermore, a series of experiments show the superior results of the proposed rule to determine the direction of time, which is based on measures of Gaussianity, and compared with other state-of-the-art methods based on tests of independence.

The problem of causal inference under continuous-valued data has also been analyzed by Shimizu et al. [28]. The authors propose a method called LINGAM that can identify the causal order of several variables when assuming that (a) the data generating process is linear, (b) there are no unobserved co-founders, and (c) the disturbance variables have non-Gaussian distributions with non-zero variances. These assumptions are required because LINGAM relies on the use of Independent Component Analysis (ICA). More specifically, let $\mathbf{x}$ denote a vector that contains the variables we would like to determine the causal order of. LINGAM assumes that $\mathbf{x} = \mathbf{B}\mathbf{x} + \mathbf{e}$, where $\mathbf{B}$ is a matrix that can be permuted to strict lower triangularity if one knows the actual causal ordering in $\mathbf{x}$, and $\mathbf{e}$ is a vector of non-Gaussian independent disturbance variables. Solving for $\mathbf{x}$, one gets $\mathbf{x} = \mathbf{A}\mathbf{e}$, where $\mathbf{A} = (\mathbf{I} - \mathbf{B})^{-1}$. The $\mathbf{A}$ matrix can be inferred using ICA. Furthermore, given an estimate of $\mathbf{A}$, $\mathbf{B}$ can be obtained to find the corresponding connection strengths among the observed variables, which can then be used to determine the true causal ordering. LINGAM has been extended to consider linear relations among groups of variables [6, 16].

In real-world data, causal relationships tend to be non-linear, a fact that questions the usefulness of linear methods. Hoyer et al. [10] show that a basic linear framework for causal inference can be generalized to non-linear models. For non-linear models with additive noise, almost any non-linearities (invertible or not) will typically yield identifiable models. In particular, Hoyer et al. [10] assume that $y_i = f(x_i) + \epsilon_i$, where $f(\cdot)$ is a possibly non-linear function, x_i is the cause variable, and ϵ_i is some independent and random noise. The proposed causal inference mechanism consists in performing a non-linear regression on the data to get an estimate of $f(\cdot)$, $\hat{f}(\cdot)$, and then calculate the corresponding residuals $\hat{\epsilon}_i = y_i - \hat{f}(x_i)$. Then, one may test whether $\hat{\epsilon}_i$ is independent of x_i or not. The same process is repeated in the other direction. The direction with the highest level of independence is chosen as the causal one. In practice, the estimate $\hat{f}(\cdot)$ is obtained using Gaussian processes for regression, and the HSIC test [7] is used as the independence criterion. This method has obtained good performance results [15] and it has been extended to address problems where the model is $y_i = h(f(x_i)+\epsilon_i)$, for some invertible function $h(\cdot)$ [33]. A practical difficulty is however that such a model is significantly harder to fit to the data.

In the work by Mooij et al. [21], a method for causal inference is proposed based on a latent variable model, used to incorporate the effects of un-observed noise. In this context, it is considered that the effect variable is a function of the cause variable and an independent noise term, not necessarily additive, that is, $y_i = f(x_i, \epsilon_i)$, where x_i is the cause variable and ϵ_i is some independent and random noise. The causal direction is then inferred using standard Bayesian model selection. In particular, the preferred direction is the one under which the corresponding model has the largest marginal likelihood, where the marginal likelihood is understood as a proxy for the Kolmogorov complexity. This method suffers from several implementation difficulties, including the intractability of the marginal likelihood computation. However, it has shown encouraging results on synthetic and real-world data.

Janzing et al. [14] consider the problem of inferring linear causal relations among multi-dimensional variables. The key point here is to use an asymmetry between the distributions of the cause and the effect that occurs if the covariance matrix of the cause and the matrix mapping the cause to the effect are independently chosen. This method exhibits the nice property that applies to both deterministic and stochastic causal relations, provided that the dimensionality of the involved random variables is sufficiently high. The method assumes that $\mathbf{y}_i = \mathbf{A}\mathbf{x}_i + \boldsymbol{\epsilon}_i$, where $\mathbf{x}_i$ is the cause and $\boldsymbol{\epsilon}_i$ is additive noise. Namely, denote with $\hat{\boldsymbol{\Sigma}}$ to the empirical covariance matrix of the variables in each $\mathbf{x}_i$. Given an estimate of $\mathbf{A}$, $\hat{\mathbf{A}}$, the method computes $\boldsymbol{\Delta}_{\mathbf{x}\to\mathbf{y}} = \log \operatorname{trace}(\hat{\mathbf{A}}\,\hat{\boldsymbol{\Sigma}}\,\hat{\mathbf{A}}^{\mathrm{T}}) - \log \operatorname{trace}(\hat{\boldsymbol{\Sigma}}) + \log \operatorname{trace}(\hat{\mathbf{A}}\hat{\mathbf{A}}^{\mathrm{T}}) + d$, where d is the dimension of $\mathbf{x}_i$. This process is repeated to compute $\boldsymbol{\Delta}_{\mathbf{y}\to\mathbf{x}}$ where $\mathbf{x}_i$ and $\mathbf{y}_i$ are swapped. The asymmetry described states that $\boldsymbol{\Delta}_{\mathbf{x}\to\mathbf{y}}$ should be close to zero while $\boldsymbol{\Delta}_{\mathbf{y}\to\mathbf{x}}$ should not. Thus, if $|\boldsymbol{\Delta}_{\mathbf{x}\to\mathbf{y}}| > |\boldsymbol{\Delta}_{\mathbf{y}\to\mathbf{x}}|$, $\mathbf{x}_i$ is expected to be the cause. Otherwise, the variables in $\mathbf{y}_i$ are predicted to be cause instead. Finally, a kernelized version of this method is also described by Chen et al. [2].

Most of the methods introduced in this section assume some form of noise in the generative process of the effect. Thus, their use is not justified in the case of noiseless data. Janzing et al. [15] describe a method to deal with these situations. In particular, the method makes use of information geometry to identify an asymmetry that can be used for causal inference. The asymmetry relies on the idea that the marginal distribution of the cause variable, denoted by $p(x)$, is expected to be chosen independently from the mapping mechanism producing the effect variable, denoted by the conditional distribution $p(y|x)$. Independence is defined here as orthogonality in the information space, which allows to describe a dependence that occurs between $p(y)$ and $p(x|y)$ in the anti-causal direction. This dependence can be then used to determine the causal order. A nice property of this method is that this asymmetry between the cause and the effect becomes very simple if both random variables are deterministically related. Remarkably, the method also performs very well in noisy scenarios, although no theoretical guarantees are provided in this case.

A similar method for causal inference to the last one is described by Chen et al. [3]. These authors also consider that $p(x)$ and $p(y|x)$ fulfill some sort of independence condition, and that this independence condition does not hold for the anti-causal direction. Based on this, they define an uncorrelatedness criterion between $p(x)$ and $p(y|x)$, and show an asymmetry between the cause and the effect in terms of a certain complexity metric on $p(x)$ and $p(y|x)$, which is less than the same complexity metric on $p(y)$ and $p(x|y)$. The complexity metric is calculated in terms of a reproducing kernel Hilbert space embedding (EMD) of probability distributions. Based on the complexity metric, the authors propose an efficient kernel-based algorithm for causal discovery.

In Sect. 8.2.3 we have shown that in the multivariate case one should expect higher entropies in the anti-causal direction. Similar results have been obtained in the case of non-linear relations and the univariate data case [12, 17]. Assume $x, y \in \mathbb{R}$ and the actual causal model to be $y = f(x) + d$, with $x \perp d$ and $f(\cdot)$ an arbitrary function. Let e be the residual of a fit performed in the anti-causal direction. Section 5.2 of the work by Hyvärinen and Smith [12] shows that the likelihood ratio R of each model (i.e., the model fitted in the causal direction and the model fitted in the anti-causal direction) converges in the presence of infinite data to the difference between the sum of the entropies of the independent variable and the residual in each direction. Namely, $R \to -H(x) - H(d/\sigma_d) + H(y) + H(e/\sigma_e) + \log \sigma_d - \log \sigma_e$, where σ_d and σ_e denote the standard deviation of the errors in each direction. If $R > 0$, the causal direction is chosen. By contrast, if $R < 0$ the anti-causal direction is preferred. The process of evaluating R involves the estimation of the entropies of four univariate random variables, i.e., x, d, y and e and the standard deviation of the errors d and e, which need not be equal. The non-linear functions are estimated as in the work by Hoyer et al. [10] using a Gaussian process. The entropies are obtained using a maximum entropy approximation under the hypothesis that the distributions of these variables are not far from Gaussian [11]. The resulting method is called non-linear maximum entropy (NLME). A practical difficulty is however that the estimation of the entropy is a very difficult task, even in one dimension [1]. Thus, the NLME method is adapted in an *ad-hoc* manner with the aim of obtaining better results in certain difficult situations with sparse residuals. More precisely, if $H(x)$ and $H(y)$ are ignored and Laplacian residuals are assumed $R \to \log \sigma_e - \log \sigma_d$. That is, the model with the minimum error is preferred. The errors are estimated however in terms of the absolute deviations (because of the Laplacian assumption).

This method is called mean absolute deviation (MAD). Finally, [17] show the consistency of the noise additive model, give a formal proof for $R \geq 0$ (see Lemma 1), and propose to estimate $H(x)$, $H(y)$, $H(d)$ and $H(e)$ using kernel density estimators. Note that if x and y are equally distributed, $H(x) = H(y)$ and the condition $R \geq 0$ implies $H(e) \geq H(d)$. Nevertheless, σ_d and σ_e are in general different (see the supplementary material for an illustrative example). This means that in the approach of [12] and [17] it is not possible to make a decision directly on the basis of a Gaussianization effect on the residuals.

The proposed method GR-AN, introduced in Sect. 8.4, differs from the approaches described in the previous paragraph in that it does not have to deal with the estimation of four univariate entropies, which can be a particularly difficult task. By contrast, it relies on statistical tests of deviation from Gaussianity to infer the causal direction. Furthermore, the tests employed in our method need not be directly related to entropy estimation. This is particularly the case of the energy test suggested in Sect. 8.3.4. Not having to estimate differential entropies is an advantage of our method confirmed by the results that are obtained in the experiments section. In particular, we have empirically observed that GR-AN performs better than the two methods for causal inference NLME and MAD that have been described in the previous paragraph. GR-AN also performs better than GR-ENT, a method that uses, instead of statistical tests of Gaussianity, a non-parametric estimator of the entropy [29].

8.6 Experiments

We carry out experiments to validate the method proposed in this paper, and empirically verify that the model residuals in the anti-causal direction are more Gaussian that the model residuals in the causal direction due to a reduction of the high-order cumulants and an increment of the differential entropy. From now on, we refer to our method as GR-AN (Gaussianity of the Residuals under Additive Noise). Furthermore, we compare the performance of GR-AN with four other approaches from the literature on causal inference, reviewed in Sect. 8.5. First, LINGAM [28], a method which assumes an additive noise model, but looks for independence between the cause and the residuals. Second, IR-AN (Independence of the Residuals under Additive Noise), by Hoyer et al. [10]. Third, a method based on information geometry, IGCI [15]. Fourth, a method based on Reproducing Kernel Hilbert Space Embeddings (EMD) of probability distributions [3]. Fifth, the two methods for non-linear causal inference based on entropy estimation described by Hyvärinen and Smith [12], NLME and MAD. Sixth, the same GR-AN method, but where we omit the transformation to guarantee that the random variables $\mathscr{X}$ and $\mathscr{Y}$ are equally distributed. This method is called GR-AN*. Last, we also compare results with two variants of GR-AN that are not based on the energy distance to measure the level of Gaussianity of the residuals. These are GR-K4, which uses the empirical estimate of the fourth cumulant (kurtosis) to determine the causal direction (it chooses the direction with the largest estimated fourth cumulant); and GR-ENT, which uses a non-parametric estimator of the entropy [29] to determine the causal direction (the direction with the smallest entropy is preferred).

The hyper-parameters of the different methods are set as follows. In LINGAM, we use the parameters recommended by the implementation provided by the authors. In IR-AN, NLME and MAD we employ a Gaussian process whose hyper-parameters are found by type-II maximum likelihood. Furthermore, in IR-AN the HSIC test is used to assess independence between the causes and the residuals. In NLME the entropy estimator is the one described by Hyvärinen [11]. In IGCI, we test different normalizations (uniform and Gaussian) and different criteria (entropy or integral) and report the best observed result. In EMD and synthetic data, we follow Chen et al. [3] to select the hyper-parameters. In EMD and real-world data, we evaluate different hyper-parameters and report the results for the best combination found. In GR-AN, GR-K4 and GR-ENT the hyper-parameters are found via cross-validation, as described in Sect. 8.4. The number of neighbors in the entropy estimator of GR-ENT is set to 10, a value that we have observed to give a good trade-off between bias and variance. Finally, in GR-AN, GR-K4, and GR-ENT we transform the data so that both variables are equally distributed, as indicated in Sect. 8.4.

The confidence in the decision is computed as indicated by Janzing et al. [15]. More precisely, in LINGAM the confidence is given by the maximum absolute value of the entries in the connection strength matrix **B**. In IGCI we employ the absolute value of the difference between the corresponding estimates (entropy or integral) in each direction. In IR-AN the confidence level is obtained as the maximum of the two p-values of the HSIC test. In EMD we use the absolute value of the difference between the estimates of the corresponding complexity metric in each direction, as described in [3]. In NLME and MAD the confidence level is given by the absolute value of the difference between the outputs of the entropy estimators in each direction [12]. In GR-K4 we use the absolute difference between the estimated fourth cumulants. In GR-ENT we use the absolute difference between the estimates of the entropy. Finally, in GR-AN we follow the details given in Sect. 8.4 to estimate the confidence in the decision.

To guarantee the exact reproducibility of the different experiments described in this paper, the source-code for all methods and data sets is available in the public repository https://bitbucket.org/dhernand/gr_causal_inference.

8.6.1 Experiments with Synthetic Data

We carry out a first batch of experiments on synthetic data. In these experiments, we employ the four causal mechanisms that map $\mathscr{X}$ to $\mathscr{Y}$ described by Chen et al. [3]. They involve linear and non-linear functions, and additive and multiplicative noise effects:

- M_1: $y_i = 0.8x_i + \epsilon_i$.
- M_2: $y_i = x_i\epsilon_i$.
- M_3: $y_i = 0.3x_i^3 + \epsilon_i$.
- M_4: $y_i = \text{atan}(x_i)^3 + \epsilon_i$.

The noise ϵ_i can follow four different types of distributions: (1) A generalized Gaussian distribution with shape parameter equal to 10 (an example of a sub-Gaussian distribution); (2) a Laplace distribution (an example of a super-Gaussian distribution); (3) a Gaussian distribution; and (4) a bimodal distribution with density $p(\epsilon_i) = 0.5\mathcal{N}(\epsilon_i|m, s) + 0.5\mathcal{N}(\epsilon_i| - m, s)$, where $m = 0.63$ and $s = 0.1$. The Laplace distribution and the Gaussian distribution are adjusted to have the same variance as the generalized Gaussian distribution. The bimodal distribution already has the same variance as the generalized Gaussian distribution.

As indicated by Chen et al. [3], in these experiments, the samples from the cause variable $\mathcal{X}$ are generated from three potential distributions:

- $p_1(x) = \frac{1}{\sqrt{2\pi}}\exp\{-x^2/2\}$.
- $p_2(x) = \frac{1}{2\sqrt{0.5\pi}}\exp\{-(x + 1)^2/0.5\} + \frac{1}{2\sqrt{0.5\pi}}\exp\{-(x - 1)^2/0.5\}$.
- $p_3(x) = \frac{1}{4\sqrt{0.5\pi}}\exp\{-(x + 1.5)^2/0.5\} + \frac{1}{2\sqrt{0.5\pi}}\exp\{-x^2/0.5\}$
  $+ \frac{1}{4\sqrt{0.5\pi}}\exp\{-(x - 1.5)^2/0.5\}$.

These are unimodal, bimodal, and trimodal distributions, respectively.

Figure 8.5 displays a representative example of the plots of different combinations of distributions and mapping mechanisms when the noise follows a generalized Gaussian distribution with shape parameter equal to 10. The plots for Laplace, Gaussian or bimodal distributed noise look similar to these ones. The assumptions made by proposed method, i.e., GR-AN, are valid in the case of all the causal mechanisms, except for M2, which considers multiplicative noise, and in the case of all cause distributions, p_1, p_2 and p_3. The only type of noise that violates the assumptions made by GR-AN is the case of Gaussian noise. In particular, under Gaussian noise GR-AN cannot infer the causal direction using Gaussianity measures because the actual residuals are already Gaussian.

The average results of each method on 100 repetitions of each potential causal mechanism, distribution for the effect, and noise distribution are displayed in Table 8.1. The size of each paired samples of $\mathcal{X}$ and $\mathcal{Y}$ is set to 500 in these experiments. We observe that when the assumptions made by the proposed method, GR-AN, are satisfied, it identifies the causal direction on a very high fraction of the 100 repetitions considered. However, when these assumptions are not valid, e.g., in the case of the M2 causal mechanism, which has multiplicative noise, the performance worsens. The same happens when the distribution of the residuals is Gaussian. In these experiments, LINGAM tends to fail when the causal relation is strongly non-linear. This is the case of the causal mechanism M3. LINGAM also has problems when all the independent variables are Gaussian. Furthermore, all methods generally fail in the case of independent Gaussian variables that are linearly related. This corresponds to the causal mechanism M1, the distribution $p_1(x)$ for

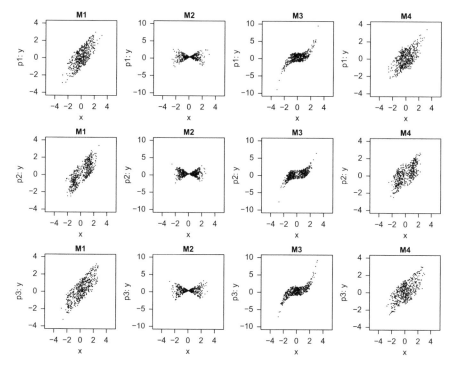

Fig. 8.5 Plots of different distributions and mechanisms when the noise follows a generalized Gaussian distribution with shape parameter equal to 10

the cause, and the Gaussian distribution for the noise. The reason for this is that in this particular scenario the causal direction is not identifiable [28]. IGCI and EMD sometimes fail in the case of the causal mechanism M1 and M4. However, they typically correctly identify the causal direction in the case of the mechanism M2, which has non-additive noise, and where the other methods tend to fail. Finally, IR-AN performs slightly better than GR-AN, especially in the case of additive Gaussian noise, where GR-AN is unable to identify the causal direction. MAD provides very bad results for some of the mechanism considered, i.e., M1 and M4. Surprisingly this is the case even for Laplacian additive noise, which is the hypothesis made by MAD. This bad behavior is probably a consequence of ignoring the entropies of $\mathscr{X}$ and $\mathscr{Y}$ in this method. NLME and GR-ENT give worse results than GR-AN in some particular cases, e.g., $p1$ and the causal mechanism M3. We believe this is related to the difficulty of estimating differential entropies in practice. GR-AN* performs very similar to GR-AN. This indicates that in practice one may ignore the transformation that guarantees that $\mathscr{X}$ and $\mathscr{Y}$ are equally distributed. GR-K4 also gives similar results to GR-AN, probably because in these experiments the tails of the residuals are not very heavy.

Table 8.1 Accuracy on the synthetic data for each method, causal mechanisms and type of noise

Noise Algorithm	Generalized Gaussian mechanism				Laplacian mechanism				Gaussian mechanism				Bimodal mechanism			
	M1	M2	M3	M4	M1	M2	M3	M4	M1	M2	M3	M4	M1	M2	M3	M4
$p_1(x)$																
LINGAM	100%	1%	7%	93%	100%	0%	26%	89%	58%	0%	11%	12%	100%	0%	3%	100%
IGCI	28%	100%	100%	34%	73%	100%	100%	96%	49%	100%	100%	63%	29%	98%	100%	44%
EMD	34%	96%	100%	43%	70%	100%	100%	77%	48%	100%	100%	50%	50%	99%	100%	55%
IR-AN	100%	31%	100%	99%	99%	26%	100%	97%	45%	34%	100%	75%	100%	46%	100%	100%
NLME	100%	31%	22%	100%	100%	20%	15%	100%	45%	22%	8%	96%	100%	42%	17%	100%
MAD	0%	94%	100%	0%	100%	99%	100%	100%	50%	99%	100%	97%	0%	92%	97%	0%
GR-AN	100%	46%	95%	100%	100%	44%	80%	100%	48%	47%	6%	20%	100%	51%	100%	100%
GR-AN*	100%	0%	94%	100%	100%	0%	94%	100%	45%	0%	1%	17%	100%	0%	100%	100%
GR-K4	100%	70%	94%	100%	99%	51%	96%	100%	52%	56%	2%	19%	100%	53%	100%	100%
GR-ENT	100%	71%	76%	97%	93%	52%	51%	93%	41%	58%	26%	29%	100%	50%	84%	99%
$p_2(x)$																
LINGAM	100%	32%	68%	100%	100%	30%	99%	100%	100%	13%	91%	100%	100%	53%	91%	100%
IGCI	40%	97%	100%	71%	98%	100%	100%	99%	72%	100%	100%	97%	39%	99%	100%	54%
EMD	96%	99%	100%	98%	96%	100%	100%	98%	94%	100%	100%	90%	92%	95%	100%	95%
IR-AN	100%	55%	100%	100%	100%	42%	100%	100%	100%	44%	100%	100%	100%	43%	100%	100%
NLME	100%	47%	100%	100%	95%	36%	100%	100%	99%	36%	100%	100%	100%	38%	100%	100%
MAD	0%	100%	100%	13%	5%	100%	100%	100%	2%	100%	100%	95%	0%	100%	85%	0%
GR-AN	100%	46%	100%	100%	98%	32%	96%	100%	29%	40%	16%	54%	100%	32%	100%	100%
GR-AN*	100%	0%	94%	100%	100%	0%	65%	100%	39%	0%	0%	6%	100%	0%	100%	100%
GR-K4	100%	50%	100%	100%	87%	44%	100%	98%	26%	51%	23%	47%	100%	30%	100%	100%
GR-ENT	96%	56%	90%	98%	78%	40%	73%	92%	46%	45%	42%	48%	100%	36%	97%	100%

$p_3(x)$																
LINGAM	100%	0%	19%	100%	100%	0%	98%	100%	92%	0%	56%	67%	100%	8%	7%	100%
IGCI	76%	100%	100%	83%	100%	100%	100%	100%	92%	100%	100%	97%	67%	100%	100%	87%
EMD	90%	100%	100%	94%	98%	100%	100%	100%	92%	100%	100%	97%	96%	100%	100%	94%
IR-AN	100%	40%	100%	100%	100%	26%	100%	100%	96%	35%	100%	100%	100%	45%	100%	100%
NLME	100%	44%	100%	100%	100%	26%	100%	100%	74%	34%	98%	100%	100%	43%	99%	100%
MAD	0%	97%	100%	1%	100%	100%	100%	100%	38%	98%	100%	98%	0%	95%	99%	0%
GR-AN	100%	52%	90%	100%	100%	58%	100%	100%	46%	53%	36%	45%	100%	54%	98%	100%
GR-AN*	100%	0%	100%	100%	100%	0%	100%	100%	51%	0%	12%	26%	100%	0%	100%	100%
GR-K4	100%	64%	94%	100%	99%	47%	100%	97%	43%	54%	15%	24%	100%	57%	100%	100%
GR-ENT	100%	60%	42%	95%	94%	54%	86%	91%	47%	48%	48%	32%	100%	47%	43%	99%

An overall comparison of the different methods evaluated is shown in Fig. 8.6. This figure displays several radar charts that indicate the average accuracy of each method for the different types of noise considered and for each mechanism M1, M2, M3 and M4. In particular, for a given method and a given type of noise, the radius of each portion of the pie is proportional to the corresponding average accuracy of the method across the distributions p_1, p_2 and p_3 for the cause. The pie at the bottom corresponds to 100% accuracy for each causal mechanism. The conclusions derived from this figure are similar to the ones obtained from Table 8.1. In particular, IR-AN performs very well, except for multiplicative noise (M3), closely followed by GR-AN, GR-AN*, and GR-K4, which give similar results. The methods perform very poorly in the case of additive Gaussian noise, since they cannot infer the actual causal direction in that situation. NLME and GR-ENT have problems in the case of the causal mechanism M3 and MAD in the case of the mechanisms M1 and M4. LINGAM also performs bad in the case of M3 and IGCI and EMD have problems in the case of the mechanisms M1 and M4. IGCI, EMD and MAD are the only methods performing well in the case of M2, the mechanism with non-additive noise.

We have repeated these experiments for other samples sizes, e.g., 100, 200 300 and 1000. The results obtained are very similar to the ones reported here, except when the number of samples is small and equal to 100. In that case NLME performs slightly better than the proposed approach GR-AN, probably because with 100 samples it is very difficult to accurately estimate the non-linear transformation that is required to guarantee that $\mathcal{X}$ and $\mathcal{Y}$ are equally distributed. These results of these additional experiments are found in the supplementary material.

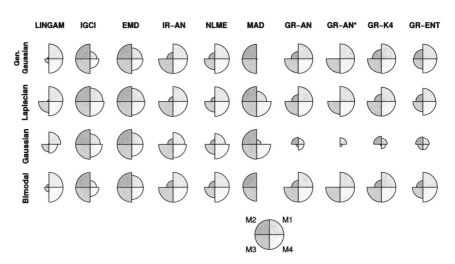

Fig. 8.6 Radar charts showing the average accuracy of each method for the different types of noise considered and for each mechanism M1, M2, M3 and M4. For a particular method and type of noise, the radius of each portion of the pie is proportional to the corresponding average accuracy of the method across the distributions p_1, p_2 and p_3 for the cause. The pie at the bottom corresponds to 100% accuracy for each mechanism

In summary, the good results provided by GR-AN and its variants in the experiments described indicate that (1) when the assumptions made by GR-AN are valid, the method has a good performance and (2) there is indeed a Gaussianization effect in the residuals when the model is fitted under the anti-causal direction. Because GR-AN* also performs well in these experiments, this indicates that a Gaussianization of the residuals may happen even when $\mathcal{X}$ and $\mathcal{Y}$ do not follow the same distribution.

We give further evidence of the Gaussianization of the distribution of the residuals obtained when fitting the model under the anti-causal direction. For this, we analyze in detail three particular cases of GR-AN corresponding to the causal mechanism M3, the distribution $p_2(x)$ for the cause and each of the three types of additive noise considered. Namely, generalized Gaussian noise, Laplacian noise and bimodal noise. Figure 8.7 shows the predicted pre-images for new data instances when the model has been fitted in the causal ($\tilde{\mathcal{X}} \rightarrow \mathcal{Y}$) and the anti-causal ($\mathcal{Y} \rightarrow \tilde{\mathcal{X}}$) direction alongside with a histogram of the first principal component of the residuals in feature space. A Gaussian approximation is also displayed as a solid

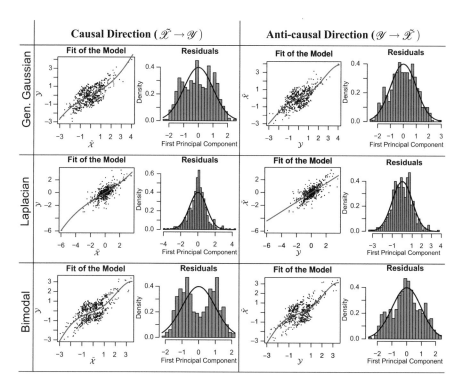

Fig. 8.7 (left column) Predicted pre-images obtained in the casual direction $\tilde{\mathcal{X}} \rightarrow \mathcal{Y}$ alongside with a histogram of the first principal component of the residuals in feature space. A Gaussian fit is displayed as a solid black line. Results are shown for each type of additive noise considered. (right column) Same plots for the anti-causal direction $\mathcal{Y} \rightarrow \tilde{\mathcal{X}}$

black line on top of the histogram. In this case **x**, i.e., the samples of $\mathscr{X}$, have been transformed to be equally distributed to **y**, i.e., the samples from $\mathscr{Y}$. We observe that the distribution of the residuals in the anti-causal direction ($\mathscr{Y} \to \tilde{\mathscr{X}}$) is more similar to a Gaussian distribution. Furthermore, for the direction $\tilde{\mathscr{X}} \to \mathscr{Y}$ the statistic of the energy based Gaussianity test for the first principal component of the residuals is respectively 4.02, 4.64 and 11.46, for generalized Gaussian, Laplacian and bimodal noise. Recall that the larger the value the larger the deviation from Gaussianity. In the case of the direction $\mathscr{Y} \to \tilde{\mathscr{X}}$, the energy statistic associated to the residuals is 0.97, 0.68 and 1.31, respectively. When **y** is transformed to have the same distribution as **x** similar results are observed (results not shown). However, the Gaussianization effect is not as strong as in this case, probably because it leads to the violation of the additive noise assumption. In summary, the figure displayed illustrates in detail the Gaussianization effect of the residuals when fitting the model in the anti-causal direction.

8.6.2   Experiments with Real Cause-Effect Pairs

A second batch of experiments is performed on the cause-effect pairs from the ChaLearn challenge.[2] This challenge contains 8073 cause-effect data pairs with a labeled causal direction. From these pairs, we consider a subset for our experiments. In particular, we select the 184 pairs that have (1) at least 500 samples, and (2) a fraction of repeated instances for each random variable of at most 1%. The first criterion guarantees that there is enough data to make a decision with high confidence. The second criterion removes the pairs with discrete random variables, motivated by the transformation required by the GR-AN method to guarantee the equal distribution of $\mathscr{X}$ and $\mathscr{Y}$. In particular, this transformation cannot be carried out on discrete data. Another advantage is that this filtering process of the data facilitates the experiments since several of the methods considered in the comparison (i.e., GR-AN, GR-ENT, GR-K4, IR-AN, NLME, MAD and EMD) are computationally very expensive. More precisely, they have a cubic cost with respect to the number of samples and they require tuning several hyper-parameters. The consequence is that evaluating these methods on the 8073 pairs available is therefore not feasible.

Using these 184 pairs we evaluate each of the methods considered in the previous section and report the corresponding accuracy as a function of the decisions made. In these experiments we sample at random 500 instances from each cause-effect pair. This is a standard number of samples that has been previously employed by other authors in their experiments with cause-effect pairs [15]. Furthermore, a threshold value is fixed and the obtained confidence in the decision by each method is compared to such threshold. Only if the confidence is above the threshold value, the

---

[2]See https://www.codalab.org/competitions/1381 for more information.

cause-effect pair is considered in the evaluation of the accuracy of the corresponding method. A summary of the results is displayed in Fig. 8.8. This figure shows for each method, as a fraction of the decisions made, the accuracy on the filtered data sets on which the confidence on the decision is above the threshold value. A gray area has been drawn to indicate accuracy values that are not statistically different from random guessing (accuracy equal to 50%) using a binomial test (p-value above 5%). We observe that IR-AN obtains the best results, followed by GR-AN, GR-AN*, GR-K4, GR-ENT, IGCI, NLME and EMD. NLME, IGCI and EMD perform worse than GR-AN and GR-AN* when a high number of decisions are made. The differences in performance between IR-AN and GR-AN, when 100% of the decisions are made, are not statistically significant (a paired t-test returns a p-value equal to 25%). The fact that the performance of GR-AN* is similar to the performance of GR-AN also indicates that there is some Gaussianization of the residuals even though the two random variables $\mathscr{X}$ and $\mathscr{Y}$ are not equally distributed. We observe that the results of LINGAM and MAD are not statistically different from random guessing. This remarks the importance of non-linear models and questions the practical utility of the MAD method. In these experiments, GR-ENT and GR-K4 perform worse than GR-AN, which remarks the benefits of using the energy distance to estimate the deviation from the Gaussian distribution, as a practical alternative to entropy or cumulant based measures.

In summary, the results displayed in Fig. 8.8 confirm that the level of Gaussianity of the residuals, estimated using statistical tests, is a useful metric that can be used to identify the causal order of two random variables. Furthermore, this figure also validates the theoretical results obtained in Sect. 8.2 which state that one should

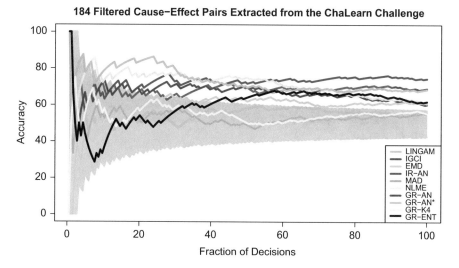

Fig. 8.8 Accuracy of each method, as a fraction of the decisions made, on the 184 filtered cause-effect pairs extracted from the ChaLearn challenge. The number of samples of each pair is equal to 500. Best seen in color

expect residuals whose distribution is closer to the Gaussian distribution when performing a fit in the anti-causal direction.

In the supplementary material we include additional results for other sample sizes. Namely, 100, 200 and 300 samples. The results obtained are similar to the ones reported in Fig. 8.8. However, the differences between GR-ENT, NLME, GR-AN and GR-AN* are smaller. Furthermore, when the number of samples is small (i.e., equal to 100) GR-AN performs worse than NLME, probably because with such a small number of samples it is difficult to estimate the non-linear transformation that guarantees that $\mathscr{X}$ and $\mathscr{Y}$ are equality distributed.

In this section we have also evaluated the different methods compared in the previous experiments on a random subset of 184 cause-effect pairs chosen across the 8073 pairs of the ChaLearn challenge (results not shown). In this case, the ranking of the curves obtained looks similar to the ranking displayed in Fig. 8.8, i.e., IR-AN performs best followed by GR-AN, GR-AN*, NLME and EMD. However, all methods obtain worse results in general and none of them, except IR-AN, perform significantly different from random guessing.

Finally, we also have evaluated the different methods in a subset of 82 cause-effect pairs extracted from the Tübingen cause-effect pairs.[3] We only considered those pairs with scalar cause and effect. The results obtained are displayed in Fig. 8.9. In this case, the performance of the different methods is worse than the one displayed in Fig. 8.8. Only IR-AN, IGCI and MAD perform significantly better

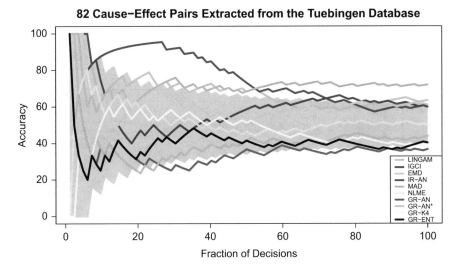

Fig. 8.9 Accuracy of each method, as a fraction of the decisions made, on the 82 cause-effect pairs extracted from the Tuebingen database. Best seen in color

---

[3] See http://webdav.tuebingen.mpg.de/cause-effect/ for more details.

than random guessing. Furthermore, GR-AN and GR-AN* do not perform well in this set of cause-effect pairs. This is also the case of NLME. We believe that the reason for this bad performance is that in most of these pairs some of the variables take discrete or repeated values. In the case of GR-AN this makes infeasible to transform the two random variables, $\mathscr{X}$ and $\mathscr{Y}$, so that they are equally distributed. Furthermore, the discrete random variables may have a strong impact in the tests for Gaussianity and in the estimation of the differential entropy. This could explain the bad performance of GR-AN*, NLME and GR-ENT.

In summary, the results reported in this section have shown that in some cause-effect pairs, when the assumptions made by the proposed method are satisfied, there is indeed a Gaussianization effect in the residuals obtained when fitting the model in the anti-causal direction, and this asymmetry is useful to carry out causal inference on both synthetic and real inference problems. Our experiments also show that the transformation employed to guarantee that $\mathscr{X}$ and $\mathscr{Y}$ are equally distributed can be ignored in some cases without decreasing the performance. This indicates that our statement about the increased level of Gaussianity of the residuals, in terms of the increase of the entropy and the reduction of the high-order cumulants, may be true under more general assumptions.

8.7 Conclusions

In this paper we have shown that in the case of cause-effect pairs with additive non-Gaussian noise there is an asymmetry that can be used for causal inference. In particular, assuming that the cause and the effect are equally distributed random variables, that are linearly related, the residuals of a least squares fit in the anti-causal direction are more Gaussian than the residuals of a linear fit in the causal direction due a reduction of the magnitude of the high-order cumulants. Furthermore, by extending the results of [12] based on information theory, we have shown that this Gaussianization effect is also present when the two random variables are multivariate due to an increment of the differential entropy. This motivates the use of kernel methods to work in an expanded feature space. This enables addressing non-linear cause-effect inference problems using simple techniques. Specifically, kernel methods allow to fit a linear model in an expanded feature space which will be non-linear in the original input space.

Taking advantage of the asymmetry described, we have designed a method for non-linear causal inference, GR-AN (Gaussianity of the Residuals under Additive Noise). The method consists in computing the residuals of a linear model in an expanded feature space in both directions, i.e., $\mathscr{X} \rightarrow \mathscr{Y}$ and $\mathscr{Y} \rightarrow \mathscr{X}$. The expected causal direction is the one in which the residuals appear to be more Gaussian (i.e., the magnitude of the high-order cumulants is reduced and the entropy is increased). Thus, a suitable statistical test that measures the level of non-Gaussianity of the residuals can be used to determine the causal direction. In principle, one may be tempted to use statistical tests based on entropy or cumulant estimation. However, our experiments show that one can obtain better results by using a test based on an *energy distance* to quantify the Gaussianity of the residuals. In particular, entropy estimation is an arguably difficult task and the estimators of the cumulants involve high-order moments which can lead to high variance.

The effectiveness of the proposed method GR-AN has been illustrated in both synthetic and real-world causal inference problems. We have shown that in certain problems GR-AN is competitive with state-of-the-art methods and that it performs better than related methods based on entropy estimation [12]. The entropy can be understood as a measure of non-Gaussianity. Nevertheless, it is very difficult to estimate in practice. By contrast, the statistical test employed by GR-AR is not directly related to entropy estimation. This may explain the improvements observed. A limitation of the current formulation of GR-AN is that the distributions of the cause and the effect have to be equal. In the case of continuous univariate variables finding a transformation to make this possible is straightforward. Additionally, our experiments show that such a transformation can be side-stepped in some cases without a deterioration in performance. In any case, further research is needed to extend this analysis to remove this restriction.

Finally, the performance of GR-AN on cause-effect pairs with discretized values is rather poor. We believe this is due to the fact that in this case, finding a transformation so that the cause and the effect are equally distributed is infeasible. Furthermore, the discretization process probably has a strong impact on the Gaussianity tests. Further evidence that make these observations more plausible is the fact that discretization has also a strong negative impact in the performance of the methods based on entropy estimation.

Acknowledgements Daniel Hernández-Lobato and Alberto Suárez gratefully acknowledge the use of the facilities of Centro de Computación Científica (CCC) at Universidad Autónoma de Madrid. These authors also acknowledge financial support from the Spanish Plan Nacional I+D+i, Grants TIN2013-42351-P and TIN2015-70308-REDT, and from Comunidad de Madrid, Grant S2013/ICE-2845 CASI-CAM-CM. David Lopez-Paz acknowledges support from *Fundación la Caixa*.

Appendix 1

In this appendix we show that if $\mathcal{X}$ and $\mathcal{Y}$ follow the same distribution and they have been centered, then the determinant of the covariance matrix of the random variable corresponding to ϵ_i, denoted with $\mathrm{Cov}(\epsilon_i)$, coincides with the determinant of the covariance matrix corresponding to the random variable $\tilde{\epsilon}_i$, denoted with $\mathrm{Cov}(\tilde{\epsilon}_i)$.

From the causal model, i.e., $\mathbf{y}_i = \mathbf{A}\mathbf{x}_i + \epsilon_i$, we have that:

$$\mathrm{Cov}(\mathcal{Y}) = \mathbf{A}\mathrm{Cov}(\mathcal{X})\mathbf{A}^{\mathrm{T}} + \mathrm{Cov}(\epsilon_i)\,. \tag{8.43}$$

Since $\mathscr{X}$ and $\mathscr{Y}$ follow the same distribution we have that $\mathrm{Cov}(\mathscr{Y}) = \mathrm{Cov}(\mathscr{X})$. Furthermore, we know from the causal model that $\mathbf{A} = \mathrm{Cov}(\mathscr{Y}, \mathscr{X})\mathrm{Cov}(\mathscr{X})^{-1}$. Then,

$$\mathrm{Cov}(\boldsymbol{\epsilon}_i) = \mathrm{Cov}(\mathscr{X}) - \mathrm{Cov}(\mathscr{Y}, \mathscr{X})\mathrm{Cov}(\mathscr{X})^{-1}\mathrm{Cov}(\mathscr{X}, \mathscr{Y}) . \tag{8.44}$$

In the case of $\tilde{\boldsymbol{\epsilon}}_i$ we know that the relation $\tilde{\boldsymbol{\epsilon}}_i = (\mathbf{I} - \tilde{\mathbf{A}}\mathbf{A})\mathbf{x}_i - \tilde{\mathbf{A}}\boldsymbol{\epsilon}_i$ must be satisfied, where $\tilde{\mathbf{A}} = \mathrm{Cov}(\mathscr{X}, \mathscr{Y})\mathrm{Cov}(\mathscr{Y})^{-1} = \mathrm{Cov}(\mathscr{X}, \mathscr{Y})\mathrm{Cov}(\mathscr{X})^{-1}$. Thus, we have that:

$$\mathrm{Cov}(\tilde{\boldsymbol{\epsilon}}_i) = (\mathbf{I} - \tilde{\mathbf{A}}\mathbf{A})\mathrm{Cov}(\mathscr{X})(\mathbf{I} - \mathbf{A}^{\mathrm{T}}\tilde{\mathbf{A}}^{\mathrm{T}}) + \tilde{\mathbf{A}}\mathrm{Cov}(\boldsymbol{\epsilon}_i)\tilde{\mathbf{A}}^{\mathrm{T}} \tag{8.45}$$

$$= \mathrm{Cov}(\mathscr{X}) - \mathrm{Cov}(\mathscr{X})\mathbf{A}^{\mathrm{T}}\tilde{\mathbf{A}}^{\mathrm{T}} - \tilde{\mathbf{A}}\mathbf{A}\mathrm{Cov}(\mathscr{X}) + \tilde{\mathbf{A}}\mathbf{A}\mathrm{Cov}(\mathscr{X})\mathbf{A}^{\mathrm{T}}\tilde{\mathbf{A}}^{\mathrm{T}} \tag{8.46}$$

$$+ \tilde{\mathbf{A}}\mathrm{Cov}(\mathscr{X})\tilde{\mathbf{A}}^{\mathrm{T}} - \tilde{\mathbf{A}}\mathrm{Cov}(\mathscr{Y}, \mathscr{X})\mathrm{Cov}(\mathscr{X})^{-1}\mathrm{Cov}(\mathscr{X}, \mathscr{Y})\tilde{\mathbf{A}}^{\mathrm{T}} \tag{8.47}$$

$$= \mathrm{Cov}(\mathscr{X}) - \mathrm{Cov}(\mathscr{X})\mathbf{A}^{\mathrm{T}}\tilde{\mathbf{A}}^{\mathrm{T}} - \tilde{\mathbf{A}}\mathbf{A}\mathrm{Cov}(\mathscr{X}) + \tilde{\mathbf{A}}\mathrm{Cov}(\mathscr{X})\tilde{\mathbf{A}}^{\mathrm{T}} \tag{8.48}$$

$$= \mathrm{Cov}(\mathscr{X}) - \mathrm{Cov}(\mathscr{X}, \mathscr{Y})\mathrm{Cov}\mathscr{X}^{-1}\mathrm{Cov}(\mathscr{Y}, \mathscr{X}) \tag{8.49}$$

$$- \mathrm{Cov}(\mathscr{X}, \mathscr{Y})\mathrm{Cov}\mathscr{X}^{-1}\mathrm{Cov}(\mathscr{Y}, \mathscr{X}) \tag{8.50}$$

$$+ \mathrm{Cov}(\mathscr{X}, \mathscr{Y})\mathrm{Cov}\mathscr{X}^{-1}\mathrm{Cov}(\mathscr{Y}, \mathscr{X}) \tag{8.51}$$

$$= \mathrm{Cov}(\mathscr{X}) - \mathrm{Cov}(\mathscr{X}, \mathscr{Y})\mathrm{Cov}(\mathscr{X})^{-1}\mathrm{Cov}(\mathscr{Y}, \mathscr{X}) . \tag{8.52}$$

By the matrix determinant theorem we have that $\mathrm{detCov}(\tilde{\boldsymbol{\epsilon}}_i) = \mathrm{detCov}(\boldsymbol{\epsilon}_i)$. See [23, p. 117] for further details.

Appendix 2

In this Appendix we motivate that, if the distribution of the residuals is not Gaussian, but is close to Gaussian, one should also expected more Gaussian residuals in the anti-causal direction in terms of the energy distance described in Sect. 8.3.4. For simplicity we will consider the univariate case. We use the fact that the energy distance in the one-dimensional case is the squared distance between the cumulative distribution functions of the residuals and a Gaussian distribution [32]. Thus,

$$\tilde{D}^2 = \int_{-\infty}^{\infty} \left[\tilde{F}(x) - \Phi(x) \right]^2 dx , \quad D^2 = \int_{-\infty}^{\infty} [F(x) - \Phi(x)]^2 dx , \tag{8.53}$$

where $\tilde{D}^2$ and D^2 are the energy distances to the Gaussian distribution in the anti-causal and the causal direction respectively; $\tilde{F}(x)$ and $F(x)$ are the c.d.f. of the residuals in the anti-causal and the causal direction, respectively; and finally, $\Phi(x)$ is the c.d.f. of a standard Gaussian.

One should expect that $\tilde{D}^2 \leq D^2$. To motivate this, we use the Gram-Charlier series and compute an expansion of $\tilde{F}(x)$ and $F(x)$ around the standard Gaussian distribution [24]. Such an expansion only converges in the case of distributions that are close to be Gaussian (see Sect. 17.6.6a of [5] for further details). Namely,

$$\tilde{F}(x) = \Phi(x) - \phi(x) \left(\frac{\tilde{a}_3}{3!} H_2(x) + \frac{\tilde{a}_4}{4!} H_3(x) + \cdots \right), \tag{8.54}$$

$$F(x) = \Phi(x) - \phi(x) \left(\frac{a_3}{3!} H_2(x) + \frac{a_4}{4!} H_3(x) + \cdots \right), \tag{8.55}$$

where $\phi(x)$ is the p.d.f. of a standard Gaussian, $H_n(x)$ are Hermite polynomials and $\tilde{a}_n$ and a_n are coefficients that depend on the cumulants, e.g., $a_3 = \kappa_3$, $a_4 = \kappa_4$, $\tilde{a}_3 = \tilde{\kappa}_3$, $\tilde{a}_4 = \tilde{\kappa}_4$. Note, however, that coefficients a_n and $\tilde{a}_n$ for $n > 5$ depend on combinations of the cumulants. Using such an expansion we find:

$$\tilde{D}^2 = \int_{-\infty}^{\infty} \phi(x)^2 \left[-\sum_{n=3}^{\infty} \frac{\tilde{a}_n}{n!} H_{n-1}(x) \right]^2 dx \approx \int_{-\infty}^{\infty} \phi(x)^2 \left[-\sum_{n=3}^{4} \frac{\tilde{\kappa}_n}{n!} H_{n-1}(x) \right]^2 dx \tag{8.56}$$

$$\approx \frac{\tilde{\kappa}_3^2}{36} \mathbb{E}[H_2(x)^2 \phi(x)] + \frac{\tilde{\kappa}_4^2}{576} \mathbb{E}[H_3(x)^2 \phi(x)], \tag{8.57}$$

where $\mathbb{E}[\cdot]$ denotes expectation with respect to a standard Gaussian and we have truncated the Gram-Charlier expansion after $n = 4$. Truncation of the Gram-Charlier expansion after $n = 4$ is a standard procedure that is often done in the ICA literature for entropy approximation. See for example Sect. 5.5.1 of [13]. We have also used the fact that $\mathbb{E}[H_3(x) H_2(x) \phi(x)] = 0$. The same approach can be followed in the case of D^2, the energy distance in the causal direction. The consequence is that $D^2 \approx \kappa_3^2/36 \cdot \mathbb{E}[H_2(x)^2 \phi(x)] + \kappa_4^2/576 \cdot \mathbb{E}[H_3(x)^2 \phi(x)]$. Finally, the fact that one should expect $\tilde{D}^2 \leq D^2$ is obtained by noting that $\tilde{\kappa}_n = c_n \kappa_n$, where c_n is some constant that lies in the interval $(-1, 1)$, as indicated in Sect. 8.2.1. We expect that this result extends to the multivariate case.

Appendix 3

In this Appendix we motivate that one should expect also more Gaussian residuals in the anti-causal direction, based on a reduction of the cumulants, when the residuals in feature space are projected onto the first principal component. That is, when they are multiplied by the first eigenvector of the covariance matrix of the residuals, and scaled by the corresponding eigenvalue. Recall from Sect. 8.2.2 that these covariance matrices are $\mathbf{C} = \mathbf{I} - \mathbf{A}\mathbf{A}^{\mathrm{T}}$ and $\tilde{\mathbf{C}} = \mathbf{I} - \mathbf{A}^{\mathrm{T}}\mathbf{A}$, in the causal and anti-causal direction respectively. Note that both matrices have the same eigenvalues.

If $\mathbf{A}$ is symmetric we have that both $\mathbf{C}$ and $\tilde{\mathbf{C}}$ have the same matrix of eigenvectors $\mathbf{P}$. Let $\mathbf{p}_1^n$ be the first eigenvector multiplied n times using the Kronecker product. The cumulants in the anti-causal and the causal direction, after projecting the data onto the first eigenvector are $\tilde{\kappa}_n^{\mathrm{proj}} = (\mathbf{p}_1^n)^{\mathrm{T}}\mathbf{M}_n \mathrm{vect}(\tilde{\kappa}_n) = c(\mathbf{p}_1^n)^{\mathrm{T}}\mathrm{vect}(\tilde{\kappa}_n)$ and $\kappa_n^{\mathrm{proj}} = (\mathbf{p}_1^n)^{\mathrm{T}}\mathrm{vect}(\kappa_n)$, respectively, where $\mathbf{M}_n$ is the matrix that relates the cumulants in the causal and the anti-causal direction (see Sect. 8.2.2) and c is one of the eigenvalues of $\mathbf{M}_n$. In particular, if $\mathbf{A}$ is symmetric, it is not difficult to show that $\mathbf{p}_1^n$ is one of the eigenvectors of $\mathbf{M}_n$. Furthermore, we also showed in that case that $||\mathbf{M}_n||_{\mathrm{op}} < 1$ for $n \geq 3$ (see Sect. 8.2.2). The consequence is that $c \in (-1, 1)$, which combined with the fact that $||\mathbf{p}_1^n|| = 1$ leads to smaller cumulants in magnitude in the case of the projected residuals in the anti-causal direction.

If $\mathbf{A}$ is not symmetric we motivate that one should also expect more Gaussian residuals in the anti-causal direction due to a reduction in the magnitude of the cumulants. For this, we derive a smaller upper bound on their magnitude. This smaller upper bound is based on an argument that uses the operator norm of vectors.

Definition 8.2 The operator norm of a vector $\mathbf{w}$ induced by the ℓ_p norm is $||\mathbf{w}||_{\mathrm{op}} = \min\{c \geq 0 : ||\mathbf{w}^{\mathrm{T}}\mathbf{v}||_p \leq c||\mathbf{v}||_p, \forall\mathbf{v}\}$.

The consequence is that $||\mathbf{w}||_{\mathrm{op}} \geq ||\mathbf{w}^{\mathrm{T}}\mathbf{v}||_p/||\mathbf{v}||_p, \forall\mathbf{v}$. Thus, the smallest the operator norm of $\mathbf{w}$, the smallest the expected value obtained when multiplying any vector by the vector $\mathbf{w}$. Furthermore, it is clear that $||\mathbf{w}||_{\mathrm{op}} = ||\mathbf{w}||_2$, in the case of the ℓ_2-norm. From the previous paragraph, in the anti-causal direction we have $||\tilde{\kappa}_n^{\mathrm{proj}}||_2 = ||(\tilde{\mathbf{p}}_1^n)^{\mathrm{T}}\mathbf{M}_n\mathrm{vect}(\kappa_n)||_2$, where $\tilde{\mathbf{p}}_1$ is the first eigenvector of $\tilde{\mathbf{C}}$, while in the causal direction we have $||\kappa_n^{\mathrm{proj}}||_2 = ||(\mathbf{p}_1^n)^{\mathrm{T}}\mathrm{vect}(\kappa_n)||_2$, where $\mathbf{p}_1$ is the first eigenvector of $\mathbf{C}$. Thus, because the norm of each vector $\tilde{\mathbf{p}}_1^n$ and $\mathbf{p}_1^n$ is one, we have that $||\mathbf{p}_1^n||_{\mathrm{op}} = 1$. However, because we expect $\mathbf{M}_n$, to reduce the norm of $(\tilde{\mathbf{p}}_1^n)^{\mathrm{T}}$, as motivated in Sect. 8.2.2, $||(\tilde{\mathbf{p}}_1^n)^{\mathrm{T}}\mathbf{M}_n||_{\mathrm{op}} < 1$ should follow. This is expected to lead to smaller cumulants in magnitude in the anti-causal direction.

References

1. J. Beirlant, E. J. Dudewicz, L. Györfi, and E. C. Van Der Meulen. Nonparametric entropy estimation: An overview. *International Journal of Mathematical and Statistical Sciences*, 6 (1):17–39, 1997.
2. Z. Chen, K. Zhang, and L. Chan. Nonlinear causal discovery for high dimensional data: A kernelized trace method. In *IEEE 13th International Conference on Data Mining*, pages 1003–1008, 2013.
3. Z. Chen, K. Zhang, L. Chan, and B. Schölkopf. Causal discovery via reproducing kernel Hilbert space embeddings. *Neural Computation*, 26(7):1484–1517, 2014.
4. E. A. Cornish and R. A. Fisher. Moments and cumulants in the specification of distributions. *Revue de l'Institut International de Statistique / Review of the International Statistical Institute*, 5(4):307–320, 1938.

5. H. Cramér. *Mathematical methods of statistics*. PhD thesis, 1946.
6. D. Entner and P. O. Hoyer. Estimating a causal order among groups of variables in linear models. In *Internatinal Conference on Artificial Neural Networks*, pages 84–91. 2012.
7. A. Gretton, K. Fukumizu, C. H. Teo, L. Song, B. Schölkopf, and A. J. Smola. A kernel statistical test of independence. In *Advances in Neural Information Processing Systems 20*, pages 585–592. 2008.
8. A. Gretton, K. M. Borgwardt, M. J. Rasch, B. Schölkopf, and A. Smola. A kernel two-sample test. *Journal of Machine Learning Research*, 13:723–773, 2012.
9. J. M. Hernández-Lobato, P. Morales-Mombiela, and A. Suárez. Gaussianity measures for detecting the direction of causal time series. In *International Joint Conference on Artificial Intelligence*, pages 1318–1323, 2011.
10. P. O. Hoyer, D. Janzing, J. M. Mooij, J. Peters, and B. Schölkopf. Nonlinear causal discovery with additive noise models. In *Advances in Neural Information Processing Systems 21*, pages 689–696, 2009.
11. A. Hyvärinen. New approximations of differential entropy for independent component analysis and projection pursuit. In *Advances in Neural Information Processing Systems 10*, pages 273–279. MIT Press, 1998.
12. A. Hyvärinen and S. M. Smith. Pairwise likelihood ratios for estimation of non-Gaussian structural equation models. *Journal of Machine Learning Research*, 14(1):111–152, 2013.
13. A. Hyvärinen, J. Karhunen, and E. Oja. *Independent Component Analysis*. John Wiley & Sons, 2004.
14. D. Janzing, P. O. Hoyer, and B. Schölkopf. Telling cause from effect based on high-dimensional observations. In *International Conference on Machine Learning*, pages 479–486, 2010.
15. D. Janzing, J. M. Mooij, K. Zhang, J. Lemeire, J. Zscheischler, P. Daniušis, B. Steudel, and B. Schölkopf. Information-geometric approach to inferring causal directions. *Artificial Intelligence*, 182–183:1–31, 2012.
16. Y. Kawahara, K. Bollen, S. Shimizu, and T. Washio. GroupLiNGAM: Linear non-Gaussian acyclic models for sets of variables. 2012. arXiv:1006.5041.
17. S. Kpotufe, E. Sgouritsa, D. Janzing, and B. Schölkopf. Consistency of causal inference under the additive noise model. In *International Conference on Machine Learning*, pages 478–486, 2014.
18. A. J. Laub. *Matrix Analysis For Scientists And Engineers*. Society for Industrial and Applied Mathematics, Philadelphia, PA, USA, 2004. ISBN 0898715768.
19. J. T. Marcinkiewicz. Sur une propriété de la loi de gauss. *Mathematische Zeitschrift*, 44:612–618, 1938.
20. P. McCullagh. *Tensor methods in statistics*. Chapman and Hall, 1987.
21. J. M. Mooij, O. Stegle, D. Janzing, K. Zhang, and B. Schölkopf. Probabilistic latent variable models for distinguishing between cause and effect. In *Advances in Neural Information Processing Systems 23*, pages 1687–1695. 2010.
22. P. Morales-Mombiela, D. Hernández-Lobato, and A. Suárez. Statistical tests for the detection of the arrow of time in vector autoregressive models. In *International Joint Conference on Artificial Intelligence*, 2013.
23. K. Murphy. *Machine Learning: a Probabilistic Perspective*. The MIT Press, 2012.
24. J. K. Patel and C. B. Read. *Handbook of the normal distribution*, volume 150. CRC Press, 1996.
25. J. Pearl. *Causality: Models, Reasoning, and Inference*. Cambridge University Press, New York, NY, USA, 2000. ISBN 0-521-77362-8.
26. B. Schölkopf and A. J. Smola. *Learning with Kernels: Support Vector Machines, Regularization, Optimization, and Beyond*. MIT Press, Cambridge, MA, USA, 2002. ISBN 0262194759.
27. B. Schölkopf, A. Smola, and K.-R. Müller. Kernel principal component analysis. In *International Conference on Artificial Neural Networks*, pages 583–588. Springer, 1997.
28. S. Shimizu, P. O. Hoyer, A. Hyvärinen, and A. Kerminen. A linear non-Gaussian acyclic model for causal discovery. *Journal of Machine Learning Research*, 7:2003–2030, 2006.

29. H. Singh, N. Misra, V. Hnizdo, A. Fedorowicz, and E. Demchuk. Nearest neighbor estimates of entropy. *American journal of mathematical and management sciences*, 23(3–4):301–321, 2003.
30. L. Song, K. Fukumizu, and A. Gretton. Kernel embeddings of conditional distributions: A unified kernel framework for nonparametric inference in graphical models. *Signal Processing Magazine, IEEE*, 30:98–111, 2013.
31. G. J. Székely and M. L. Rizzo. A new test for multivariate normality. *Journal of Multivariate Analysis*, 93(1):58–80, 2005.
32. G. J. Székely and M. L. Rizzo. Energy statistics: A class of statistics based on distances. *Journal of Statistical Planning and Inference*, 143(8):1249–1272, 2013.
33. K. Zhang and A. Hyvärinen. On the identifiability of the post-nonlinear causal model. In *International Conference on Uncertainty in Artificial Intelligence*, pages 647–655, 2009.

Chapter 9
From Dependency to Causality: A Machine Learning Approach

Gianluca Bontempi and Maxime Flauder

9.1 Introduction

The relationship between statistical dependency and causality lies at the heart of all statistical approaches to causal inference and can be summarized by two famous statements: *correlation (or more generally statistical association) does not imply causation* and *causation induces a statistical dependency between causes and effects (or more generally descendants)* [31]. In other terms it is well known that statistical dependency is a necessary yet not sufficient condition for causality. The unidirectional link between these two notions has been used by many formal approaches to causality to justify the adoption of statistical methods for detecting or inferring causal links from observational data. The most influential one is the Causal Bayesian Network approach, detailed in [20] which relies on notions of independence and conditional independence to detect causal patterns in the data. Well known examples of related inference algorithms are the constraint-based methods like the PC algorithms [35] and IC [27]. These approaches are founded on probability theory and have been shown to be accurate in reconstructing causal patterns in many applications [30], notably in bioinformatics [12]. At the same time they restrict the set of configurations which causal inference is applicable to. Such boundary is essentially determined by the notion of *distinguishability* which defines the set of Markov equivalent configurations on the basis of conditional independence tests. Typical examples of indistinguishability are the two-variable setting and the

G. Bontempi (✉) · M. Flauder
Machine Learning Group, Computer Science Department, ULB, Université Libre de Bruxelles, Brussels, Belgium
e-mail: gbonte@ulb.ac.be

© Springer Nature Switzerland AG 2019
I. Guyon et al. (eds.), *Cause Effect Pairs in Machine Learning*,
The Springer Series on Challenges in Machine Learning,
https://doi.org/10.1007/978-3-030-21810-2_9

completely connected triplet configuration [16] where it is impossible to distinguish between cause and effects by means of conditional or unconditional independence tests.

If on one hand the notion of indistinguishability is probabilistically sound, on the other hand it should not prevent us from addressing interesting yet indistinguishable causal patterns. In fact, indistinguishability results rely on two main aspects: (1) they refer only to specific features of dependency (notably conditional or unconditional independence) and (2) they state the conditions (e.g. faithfulness) under which it is possible to distinguish (or not) *with certainty* between configurations. Accordingly, indistinguishability results do not prevent the existence of statistical algorithms able to *reduce the uncertainty about the causal pattern* even in indistinguishable configurations. This has been made evident by the appearance in recent years of a series of approaches which tackle the cause-effect pair inference, like ANM (Additive Noise Model) [17], IGCI (Information Geometry Causality Inference) [10, 18], LiNGAM (Linear Non Gaussian Acyclic Model) [34] and the algorithms described in [25] and [36].[1] What is common to these approaches is that they use alternative statistical features of the data to detect causal patterns and reduce the uncertainty about their directionality. A further important step in this direction has been represented by the recent organization of the ChaLearn cause-effect pair challenge [14]. The good (and significantly better than random) accuracy obtained on the basis of observations of pairs of causally related (or unrelated) variables supports the idea that alternative strategies can be designed to infer with success (or at least significantly better than random) indistinguishable configurations.

It is worthy to remark that the best ranked approaches[2] in the ChaLearn competition share a common aspect: they infer from statistical features of the bivariate distribution the probability of the existence and then of the directionality of the causal link between two variables. The success of these approaches shows that the problem of causal inference can be successfully addressed as a supervised machine learning approach where the inputs are features describing the probabilistic dependency and the output is a class denoting the existence (or not) of a directed causal link. Once sufficient training data are made available, conventional feature selection algorithms [15] and classifiers can be used to return a prediction better than random.

The effectiveness of machine learning strategies in the case of pairs of variables encourages the extension of the strategy to configurations with a larger number of variables. In this paper we propose an original approach to learn from multivariate observations the probability that a variable is a direct cause of another. This task is undeniably more difficult because

- the number of parameters needed to describe a multivariate distribution increases rapidly (e.g. quadratically in the Gaussian case),

---

[1] A more extended list of recent algorithms is available in http://www.causality.inf.ethz.ch/cause-effect.php?page=help.

[2] We took part in the ChaLearn challenge and we ranked eighth in the final leader board.

- information about the existence of a causal link between two variables is returned also by the nature of the dependencies existing between the two variables and the remaining ones.

The second consideration is evident in the case of a collider configuration $z_1 \rightarrow z_2 \leftarrow z_3$: in this case the dependency (or independency) between z_1 and z_3 tells us more about the link $z_1 \rightarrow z_2$ than the dependency between z_1 and z_2. This led us to develop a machine learning strategy (described in Sect. 9.2) where descriptors of the relation existing between members of the Markov blankets of two variables are used to learn the probability (i.e. a score) that a causal link exists between two variables. The approach relies on the asymmetry of some conditional (in)dependence relations between the members of the Markov blankets of two variables causally connected. The resulting algorithm (called D2C and described in Sect. 9.3) predicts the existence of a direct causal link between two variables in a multivariate setting by (1) creating a set of of features of the relationship based on asymmetric descriptors of the multivariate dependency and (2) using a classifier to learn a mapping between the features and the presence of a causal link.

In Sect. 9.4 we report the results of a set of experiments assessing the accuracy of the D2C algorithm. Experimental results based on synthetic and published data show that the D2C approach is competitive and often outperforms state-of-the-art methods.

9.2 Learning the Relation Between Dependency and Causality in a Configuration with $n > 2$ Variables

This section presents an approach to learn, from a number of observations, the relationships existing between the n variate distribution of $\mathbf{Z} = [z_1, \ldots, z_n]$ and the existence of a directed causal link between two variables z_i and z_j, $1 \leq i \neq j \leq n$, in the case of no confounding, no selection bias and no feedback configurations. Several parameters may be estimated from data in order to represent the multivariate distribution of $\mathbf{Z}$, like the correlation or the partial correlation matrix. Some problems however arise in this case like: (1) these parameters are informative in case of Gaussian distributions only, (2) identical (or close) causal configurations could be associated to very different parametric values, thus making difficult the learning of the mapping and (3) different causal configurations may lead to identical (or close) parametric values.

In other terms it is more relevant to describe the distribution in structural terms (e.g. with notions of conditional dependence/independence) rather than in parametric terms. Two more aspects have to be taken into consideration. First since we want to use a learning approach to identify cause-effect relationships we need some quantitative features to describe the structure of the multivariate distribution. Second, since asymmetry is a distinguishing characteristic of a causal relationship, we expect that effective features should share the same asymmetric properties.

In this paper we will use information theory to represent and quantify the notions of (conditional) dependence and independence between variables and to derive a set of asymmetric features to reconstruct causality from dependency.

9.2.1 Notions of Information Theory

Let us consider three continuous random variables z_1, z_2 and z_3 having a joint Lebesgue density.[3] Let us start by considering the relation between z_1 and z_2. The mutual information [8] between z_1 and z_2 is defined in terms of their probabilistic density functions $p(z_1)$, $p(z_2)$ and $p(z_1, z_2)$ as

$$I(z_1; z_2) = \int \int \log \frac{p(z_1, z_2)}{p(z_1)p(z_2)} p(z_1, z_2) dz_1 dz_2 = H(z_1) - H(z_1|z_2) \quad (9.1)$$

where H is the *entropy* and the convention $0\log\frac{0}{0} = 0$ is adopted. This quantity measures the amount of stochastic dependence between z_1 and z_2 [8]. Note that, if z_1 and z_2 are Gaussian distributed the following relation holds

$$I(z_1; z_2) = -\frac{1}{2}\log(1 - \rho^2) \quad (9.2)$$

where ρ is the Pearson correlation coefficient between z_1 and z_2.

Let us now consider a third variable z_3. The *conditional mutual information* [8] between z_1 and z_2 once z_3 is given is defined by

$$I(z_1; z_2|z_3) = \int \int \int \log \frac{p(z_1, z_2|z_3)}{p(z_1|z_3)p(z_2|z_3)} p(z_1, z_2, z_3) dz_1 dz_2 dz_3 =$$
$$= H(z_1|z_3) - H(z_1|z_2, z_3) \quad (9.3)$$

The conditional mutual information is null if and only if z_1 and z_2 are conditionally independent given z_3.

A structural notion which can be described in terms of conditional mutual information is the notion of Markov Blanket (MB). The Markov Blanket of variable z_i in an n dimensional distribution is the smallest subset of variables belonging to $Z \setminus z_i$ (where $\setminus$ denotes the set difference operator) which makes z_i conditionally independent of all the remaining ones. In information theoretic terms let us consider a set Z of n random variables, a variable z_i and a subset $M_i \subset Z \setminus z_i$. The subset M_i is said to be a *Markov blanket* of z_i if it is the minimal subset satisfying

---

[3] Boldface denotes random variables.

$$I(\mathbf{z}_i; (\mathbf{Z} \setminus (\mathbf{M}_i \cup \mathbf{z}_i)) | \mathbf{M}_i) = 0$$

Effective algorithms have been proposed in literature to infer a Markov Blanket from observed data [38]. Feature selection algorithms are also useful to construct a Markov blanket of a given target variable once they rely on notions of conditional independence to select relevant variables [24].

9.2.2 Causality and Asymmetric Dependency Relationships

The notion of causality is central in science and also an intuitive notion of everyday life. The remarkable property of causality which distinguishes it from dependency is asymmetry.

In probabilistic terms a variable $\mathbf{z}_i$ is dependent on a variable $\mathbf{z}_j$ if the density of $\mathbf{z}_i$, conditional on the observation $\mathbf{z}_j = z_j$, is different from the marginal one

$$p(z_i | \mathbf{z}_j = z_j) \neq p(z_i)$$

In information theoretic terms the two variables are dependent if $I(\mathbf{z}_i; \mathbf{z}_j) = I(\mathbf{z}_j; \mathbf{z}_i) > 0$. This implies that dependency is *symmetric*. If $\mathbf{z}_i$ is dependent on $\mathbf{z}_j$, then $\mathbf{z}_j$ is dependent on $\mathbf{z}_i$ too as shown by

$$p(z_j | \mathbf{z}_i = z_i) \neq p(z_j)$$

The formal representation of the notion of causality demands an extension of the syntax of the probability calculus as done by [26] with the introduction of the operator do which allows to distinguish the observation of a value of $\mathbf{z}_j$ (denoted by $\mathbf{z}_j = z_j$) from the manipulation of the variable $\mathbf{z}_j$ (denoted by $\mathrm{do}(\mathbf{z}_j = z_j)$). Once this extension is accepted we say that a variable $\mathbf{z}_j$ is a cause of a variable $\mathbf{z}_i$ (e.g. "diseases cause symptoms") if the distribution of $\mathbf{z}_i$ is different from the marginal one when we set the value $\mathbf{z}_j = z_j$

$$p(z_i | \mathrm{do}(\mathbf{z}_j = z_j)) \neq p(z_i)$$

but not vice versa (e.g. "symptoms do not cause disease")

$$p(z_j | \mathrm{do}(\mathbf{z}_i = z_i)) = p(z_j)$$

The extension of the probability notation made by Pearl allows to formalize the intuition that causality is *asymmetric*. Another notation which allows to represent causal expression is provided by graphical models or more specifically by Directed Acyclic Graphs (DAG) [20]. In this paper we will limit to consider causal relationships modeled by DAG, which proved to be convenient tools to understand and use the notion of causality. Furthermore we will make the assumption that the set of causal relationships existing between the variables of interest can be described by a Markov and faithful DAG [27]. This means that the DAG is an accurate map of dependencies and independencies of the represented distribution and that using the notion of *d-separation* it is possible to read from the graph if two sets of nodes are (in)dependent conditioned on a third.

The asymmetric nature of causality suggests that if we want to infer causal links from dependency we need to find some features (or descriptors) which describe the dependency and share with causality the property of asymmetry. Let us suppose that we are interested in predicting the existence of a directed causal link $\mathbf{z}_i \to \mathbf{z}_j$ where $\mathbf{z}_i$ and $\mathbf{z}_j$ are components of an observed n-dimensional vector $\mathbf{Z} = [\mathbf{z}_1, \ldots, \mathbf{z}_n]$.

We define as *dependency descriptor* of the ordered pair $\langle i, j \rangle$ a function $d(i, j)$ of the distribution of $\mathbf{Z}$ which depends on i and j. Example of dependency descriptors are the correlation $\rho(i, j)$ between $\mathbf{z}_i$ and $\mathbf{z}_j$, the mutual information $I(\mathbf{z}_i; \mathbf{z}_j)$ or the partial correlation between $\mathbf{z}_i$ and $\mathbf{z}_j$ given another variable $\mathbf{z}_k$, $i \neq j$, $j \neq k$, $i \neq k$.

We call a dependency descriptor *symmetric* if $d(i, j) = d(j, i)$ otherwise we call it *asymmetric*. Correlation and mutual information are symmetric descriptors since

$$d(i, j) = I(\mathbf{z}_i; \mathbf{z}_j) = I(\mathbf{z}_j; \mathbf{z}_i) = d(j, i)$$

Because of the asymmetric property of causality, if we want to maximize our chances to reconstruct causality from dependency we need to identify relevant asymmetric descriptors. In order to define useful asymmetric descriptors we have recourse to the Markov Blankets of the two variables $\mathbf{z}_i$ and $\mathbf{z}_j$.

Let us consider for instance the portion of a DAG represented in Fig. 9.1 where the variable $\mathbf{z}_i$ is a direct cause of $\mathbf{z}_j$. The figure shows also the Markov Blankets of the two variables (denoted M_i and M_j respectively) and their components, i.e. the direct causes (denoted by $\mathbf{c}$), the direct effects ($\mathbf{e}$) and the spouses ($\mathbf{s}$) [28].

In what follows we will make two assumptions: (1) the only path between the sets $\mathbf{z}_i \cup M_i$ and $\mathbf{z}_j \cup M_j$ is the edge $\mathbf{z}_i \to \mathbf{z}_j$ and (2) there is no common ancestor of $\mathbf{z}_i$ ($\mathbf{z}_j$) and its spouses $\mathbf{s}_i$ ($\mathbf{s}_j$). We will discuss these assumptions at the end of the section. Given these assumptions and because of d-separation [13], a number of asymmetric conditional (in)dependence relations holds between the members of M_i and M_j (Table 9.1). For instance (first line of Table 9.1), by conditioning on the effect $\mathbf{z}_j$ we create a dependence between $\mathbf{z}_i$ and the direct causes of $\mathbf{z}_j$ while by conditioning on the $\mathbf{z}_i$ we d-separate $\mathbf{z}_j$ and the direct causes of $\mathbf{z}_i$.

The relations in Table 9.1 can be used to define the following set of asymmetric descriptors,

$$d_1^{(k)}(i, j) = I(\mathbf{z}_i; \mathbf{c}_j^{(k)} | \mathbf{z}_j), \tag{9.4}$$

$$d_2^{(k)}(i, j) = I(\mathbf{e}_i^{(k)}; \mathbf{c}_j^{(k)} | \mathbf{z}_j), \tag{9.5}$$

$$d_3^{(k)}(i, j) = I(\mathbf{c}_i^{(k)}; \mathbf{c}_j^{(k)} | \mathbf{z}_j), \tag{9.6}$$

$$d_4^{(k)}(i, j) = I(\mathbf{z}_i; \mathbf{c}_j^{(k)}), \tag{9.7}$$

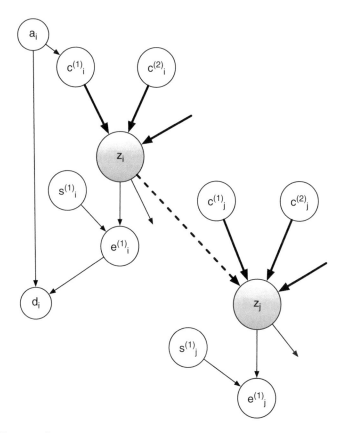

Fig. 9.1 Two causally connected variables and their Markov blankets

whose asymmetry is given by

$$d_1^{(k)}(i, j) = I(\mathbf{z}_i; \mathbf{c}_j^{(k)}|\mathbf{z}_j) > 0, \quad d_1^{(k)}(j, i) = I(\mathbf{z}_j; \mathbf{c}_i^{(k)}|\mathbf{z}_i) = 0, \qquad (9.8)$$

$$d_2^{(k)}(i, j) = I(\mathbf{e}_i^{(k)}; \mathbf{c}_j^{(k)}|\mathbf{z}_j) > 0, \quad d_2^{(k)}(j, i) = I(\mathbf{e}_i^{(k)}; \mathbf{c}_i^{(k)}|\mathbf{z}_i) = 0, \qquad (9.9)$$

$$d_3^{(k)}(i, j) = I(\mathbf{c}_i^{(k)}; \mathbf{c}_j^{(k)}|\mathbf{z}_j) > 0, \quad d_3^{(k)}(j, i) = I(\mathbf{c}_j^{(k)}; \mathbf{c}_i^{(k)}|\mathbf{z}_i) = 0, \qquad (9.10)$$

$$d_4^{(k)}(i, j) = I(\mathbf{z}_i; \mathbf{c}_j^{(k)}) = 0, \quad d_4^{(k)}(j, i) = I(\mathbf{z}_j; \mathbf{c}_i^{(k)}) > 0. \qquad (9.11)$$

At the same time we can write a set of symmetric conditional (in)dependence relations (Table 9.2) and the equivalent formulations in terms of mutual information terms:

$$I(\mathbf{z}_j; \mathbf{e}_i^{(k)}) > 0, \qquad (9.12)$$

$$I(\mathbf{z}_i; \mathbf{e}_j^{(k)}) > 0, \qquad (9.13)$$

Table 9.1 Asymmetric (un)conditional (in)dependance relationships between members of the Markov Blankets of $\mathbf{z}_i$ and $\mathbf{z}_j$ in Fig. 9.1

Relation i, j	Relation j, i
$\forall k \quad \mathbf{z}_i \not\perp\!\!\!\perp \mathbf{c}_j^{(k)}\vert \mathbf{z}_j$	$\forall k \quad \mathbf{z}_j \perp\!\!\!\perp \mathbf{c}_i^{(k)}\vert \mathbf{z}_i$
$\forall k \quad \mathbf{e}_i^{(k)} \not\perp\!\!\!\perp \mathbf{c}_j^{(k)}\vert \mathbf{z}_j$	$\forall k \quad \mathbf{e}_j^{(k)} \perp\!\!\!\perp \mathbf{c}_i^{(k)}\vert \mathbf{z}_i$
$\forall k \quad \mathbf{c}_i^{(k)} \not\perp\!\!\!\perp \mathbf{c}_j^{(k)}\vert \mathbf{z}_j$	$\forall k \quad \mathbf{c}_j^{(k)} \perp\!\!\!\perp \mathbf{c}_i^{(k)}\vert \mathbf{z}_i$
$\forall k \quad \mathbf{z}_i \perp\!\!\!\perp \mathbf{c}_j^{(k)}$	$\forall k \quad \mathbf{z}_j \not\perp\!\!\!\perp \mathbf{c}_i^{(k)}$

Table 9.2 Symmetric (un)conditional (in)dependance relationships between members of the Markov Blankets of $\mathbf{z}_i$ and $\mathbf{z}_j$ in Fig. 9.1

Relation i, j	Relation j, i
$\forall k \quad \mathbf{z}_i \not\perp\!\!\!\perp \mathbf{e}_j^{(k)}$	$\forall k \quad \mathbf{z}_j \not\perp\!\!\!\perp \mathbf{e}_i^{(k)}$
$\forall k \quad \mathbf{z}_i \perp\!\!\!\perp \mathbf{s}_j^{(k)}$	$\forall k \quad \mathbf{z}_j \perp\!\!\!\perp \mathbf{s}_i^{(k)}$
$\forall k \quad \mathbf{z}_i \perp\!\!\!\perp \mathbf{e}_j^{(k)}\vert \mathbf{z}_j$	$\forall k \quad \mathbf{z}_j \perp\!\!\!\perp \mathbf{e}_i^{(k)}\vert \mathbf{z}_i$
$\forall k \quad \mathbf{z}_i \perp\!\!\!\perp \mathbf{s}_j^{(k)}\vert \mathbf{z}_j$	$\forall k \quad \mathbf{z}_j \perp\!\!\!\perp \mathbf{s}_i^{(k)}\vert \mathbf{z}_i$
$\forall k \quad \mathbf{e}_i^{(k)} \perp\!\!\!\perp \mathbf{e}_j^{(k)}\vert \mathbf{z}_i$	$\forall k \quad \mathbf{e}_j^{(k)} \perp\!\!\!\perp \mathbf{e}_i^{(k)}\vert \mathbf{z}_j$
$\forall k \quad \mathbf{e}_i^{(k)} \perp\!\!\!\perp \mathbf{s}_j^{(k)}\vert \mathbf{z}_j$	$\forall k \quad \mathbf{e}_j^{(k)} \perp\!\!\!\perp \mathbf{s}_i^{(k)}\vert \mathbf{z}_i$

$$I(\mathbf{z}_j; \mathbf{s}_i^{(k)}) = I(\mathbf{z}_i; \mathbf{s}_j^{(k)}) = 0, \tag{9.14}$$

$$I(\mathbf{z}_i; \mathbf{e}_j^{(k)}\vert \mathbf{z}_j) = I(\mathbf{z}_j; \mathbf{e}_i^{(k)}\vert \mathbf{z}_i) = I(\mathbf{z}_i; \mathbf{s}_j^{(k)}\vert \mathbf{z}_j) = I(\mathbf{z}_j; \mathbf{s}_i^{(k)}\vert \mathbf{z}_i) = 0, \tag{9.15}$$

$$I(\mathbf{e}_j^{(k)}; \mathbf{e}_i^{(k)}\vert \mathbf{z}_i) = I(\mathbf{e}_i^{(k)}; \mathbf{e}_j^{(k)}\vert \mathbf{z}_j) = I(\mathbf{e}_i^{(k)}; \mathbf{s}_j^{(k)}\vert \mathbf{z}_j) = I(\mathbf{e}_j^{(k)}; \mathbf{s}_i^{(k)}\vert \mathbf{z}_i) = 0. \tag{9.16}$$

9.2.3 From Asymmetric Relationships to Distinct Distributions

The asymmetric properties of the four descriptors (9.4)–(9.7) is encouraging if we want to exploit dependency related features to infer causal properties from data. However, this optimism is undermined by the fact that all the descriptors require already the capability of distinguishing between the causes (i.e. the terms $\mathbf{c}$) and the effects (i.e. the terms $\mathbf{e}$) of the Markov Blanket of a given variable. Unfortunately this discriminating capability is what we are looking for!

In order to escape this circularity problem we consider two solutions. The first is to have recourse to a preliminary phase that prioritizes the components of the Markov Blanket and then use this result as starting point to detect asymmetries and then improve the classification of causal links. This is for instance feasible by using a filter selection algorithm, like mIMR [3, 5], which aims to prioritize the direct causes in the Markov Blanket by searching for pairs of variables with high relevance and low interaction.

The second solution is related to the fact that the asymmetry of the four descriptors induces a difference in the distributions of some information theoretic terms which do not require the distinction between causes and effects within the Markov Blanket. The consequence is that we can replace the descriptors (9.4)–(9.7) with other descriptors (denoted with the letter D) that can be actually estimated from data.

Let $\mathbf{m}^{(k)}$ denote a generic component of the Markov Blanket with no distinction between cause, effect or spouse. It follows that a population made of terms depending on $\mathbf{m}^{(k)}$ is a mixture of three subpopulations, the first made of causes, the second made of effects and the third of spouses, respectively. It follows that the distribution of the population is a *finite mixture* [23] of three distributions, the first related to the causes, the second to the effects and the third to the spouses. Since the moments of the finite mixture are functions of the moments of each component, we can derive some properties of the resulting mixture from the properties of each component. For instance if we can show that all the subpopulations but one are identical (e.g. all the elements of the third subpopulation in the first mixture are larger than the elements of the analogous subpopulation in the second mixture), we can derive that the two mixture distributions are different.

Consider for instance the quantity $I(\mathbf{z}_i; \mathbf{m}_j^{(k_j)}|\mathbf{z}_j)$ where $\mathbf{m}_j^{(k_j)}$, $k_j = 1, \ldots, K_j$ is a member of the set $M_j \setminus \mathbf{z}_i$. From (9.8) and (9.15) it follows that the mixture distribution associated to the populations $D_1(i, j) = \{I(\mathbf{z}_i; \mathbf{m}_j^{(k_j)}|\mathbf{z}_j), k_j = 1, \ldots, K_j\}$ and $D_1(j, i) = \{I(\mathbf{z}_j; \mathbf{m}_i^{(k_i)}|\mathbf{z}_i), k_i = 1, \ldots, K_i\}$ are different since

$$
\begin{cases}
I(\mathbf{z}_i; \mathbf{m}_j^{(k_j)}|\mathbf{z}_j) > I(\mathbf{z}_j; \mathbf{m}_i^{(k_i)}|\mathbf{z}_i), & \text{if } \mathbf{m}_j^{(k_j)} = \mathbf{c}_j^{(k_j)} \wedge \mathbf{m}_i^{(k_i)} = \mathbf{c}_i^{(k_i)} \\
I(\mathbf{z}_i; \mathbf{m}_j^{(k_j)}|\mathbf{z}_j) = I(\mathbf{z}_j; \mathbf{m}_i^{(k_i)}|\mathbf{z}_i), & \text{else}
\end{cases}
$$

$$(9.17)$$

It follows that even if we are not able to distinguish between a cause $\mathbf{c}_j \in M_j$ and an effect $\mathbf{e}_j \in M_j$, we know that the distribution of the population $D_1(i, j)$ differs from the distribution of the population $D_1(j, i)$. We can therefore use the population $D_1(i, j)$ (or some of its moments) as descriptor of the causal dependency.

Similarly we can replace the descriptors (9.5), (9.6) with the distributions of the population $D_2(i, j) = \{I(\mathbf{m}_i^{(k_i)}; \mathbf{m}_j^{(k_j)}|\mathbf{z}_j), k_j = 1, \ldots, K_j, k_i = 1, \ldots, K_i\}$. From (9.9), (9.10) and (9.16) we obtain that the distributions of the populations $D_2(i, j)$ and $D_2(j, i)$ are different.

If we make the additional assumption that $I(\mathbf{z}_j; \mathbf{e}_i^{(k)}) = I(\mathbf{z}_i; \mathbf{e}_j^{(k)}) > 0$ from (9.11) we obtain also that the distribution of the population $D_3(i, j) = \{I(\mathbf{z}_i; \mathbf{m}_j^{(k_j)}), k_j = 1, \ldots, K_j\}$ is different from the one of $D_3(j, i) = \{I(\mathbf{z}_j; \mathbf{m}_i^{(k_i)}), k_i = 1, \ldots, K_i\}$.

The previous results are encouraging and show that though we are not able to distinguish between the different components of a Markov Blanket, we can notwithstanding compute some quantities (in this case distributions of populations) whose asymmetry is informative about the causal relationships $z_i \rightarrow z_j$.

As a consequence by measuring from observed data some statistics (e.g. quantiles) related to the distribution of these asymmetric descriptors, we may obtain some insight about the causal relationship between two variables. This idea is made explicit in the algorithm described in the following section.

Though these results rely on the two assumptions made before (i.e. single path and no common ancestors), two considerations are worthy to be made. First, the main goal of the approach is to shed light on the existence of dependency asymmetries also in multivariate contributions. Secondly we expect that the second layer (based on supervised learning) will eventually compensate for configurations not compliant with the assumptions and take advantage of complementarity or synergy of the descriptors in discriminating between causal configurations.

9.3 The D2C Algorithm

The rationale of the D2C algorithm is to predict the existence of a causal link between two variables in a multivariate setting by (1) creating a set of features of the relationship between the members of the Markov Blankets of the two variables and (2) using a classifier (e.g. a Random Forest as in our experiments) to learn a mapping between the features and the presence of a causal link.

We use two sets of features to summarize the relation between the two Markov blankets: the first one accounts for the presence (or the position if the MB is obtained by ranking) of the terms of M_j in M_i and vice versa. For instance it is evident that if z_i is a cause of z_j we expect to find z_i highly ranked between the causal terms of M_j but z_j absent (or ranked low) among the causes of M_i. The second set of features is based on the results of the previous section and is obtained by summarizing the distributions of the asymmetric descriptors with a set of quantiles.

We propose then an algorithm (D2C) which for each pair of measured variables z_i and z_j:

1. infers from data the two Markov Blankets (e.g. by using state-of-the-art approaches) M_i and M_j and the subsets $M_i \setminus z_j = \{\mathbf{m}^{(k_i)}, k_i = 1, \ldots, K_i\}$ and $M_j \setminus z_i = \{\mathbf{m}^{(k_j)}, k_j = 1, \ldots, K_j\}$. Most of the existing algorithms associate to the Markov Blanket a ranking such that the most strongly relevant variables are ranked before.
2. computes a set of (conditional) mutual information terms describing the dependency between z_i and z_j

$$I = [I(z_i; z_j), I(z_i; z_j | M_j \setminus z_i), I(z_i; z_j | M_i \setminus z_j)] \tag{9.18}$$

3. computes the positions $P_i^{(k_i)}$ of the members $\mathbf{m}^{(k_i)}$ of $M_i \setminus \mathbf{z}_j$ in the ranking associated to $M_j \setminus \mathbf{z}_i$ and the positions $P_j^{(k_j)}$ of the terms $\mathbf{m}^{(k_j)}$ in the ranking associated to $M_i \setminus \mathbf{z}_j$. Note that in case of the absence of a term of M_i in M_j, the position is set to $K_j + 1$ (respectively $K_i + 1$).

4. computes the populations based on the asymmetric descriptors introduced in Sect. 9.2.3:

   (a) $D_1(i, j) = \{I(\mathbf{z}_i; \mathbf{m}_j^{(k_j)} | \mathbf{z}_j), k_j = 1, \dots, K_j\}$

   (b) $D_1(j, i) = \{I(\mathbf{z}_j; \mathbf{m}_i^{(k_i)} | \mathbf{z}_i), k_i = 1, \dots, K_i\}$

   (c) $D_2(i, j) = \{I(\mathbf{m}_i^{(k_i)}; \mathbf{m}_j^{(k_j)} | \mathbf{z}_j), k_i = 1, \dots, K_i, k_j = 1, \dots, K_j\}$ and

   (d) $D_2(j, i) = \{I(\mathbf{m}_j^{(k_j)}; \mathbf{m}_i^{(k_i)} | \mathbf{z}_i), k_i = 1, \dots, K_i, k_j = 1, \dots, K_j\}$

   (e) $D_3(i, j) = \{I(\mathbf{z}_i; \mathbf{m}_j^{(k_j)}), k_j = 1, \dots, K_j\}$,

   (f) $D_3(j, i) = \{I(\mathbf{z}_j, \mathbf{m}_i^{(k_i)}), k_i = 1, \dots, K_i\}$

5. creates a vector of descriptors

$$x = [I, \mathcal{Q}(\hat{P}_i), \mathcal{Q}(\hat{P}_j), \mathcal{Q}(\hat{D}_1(i, j)), \mathcal{Q}(\hat{D}_1(j, i)),$$

$$\mathcal{Q}(\hat{D}_2(i, j)), \mathcal{Q}(\hat{D}_2(j, i)), \mathcal{Q}(\hat{D}_3(i, j)), \mathcal{Q}(\hat{D}_3(j, i))] \qquad (9.19)$$

where $\hat{P}_i$ and $\hat{P}_j$ are the empirical distributions of the populations $\{P_i^{(k_i)}\}$ and $\{P_j^{(k_j)}\}$, $\hat{D}_h(i, j)$ denotes the empirical distribution of the corresponding population $D_h(i, j)$ and $\mathcal{Q}$ returns a set of sample quantiles of a distribution (in the experiments we set the quantiles to 0.1, 0.25, 0.5, 0.75, 0.9).

The vector x can be then derived from observational data and used to create a vector of descriptors to be used as inputs in a supervised learning paradigm.

The rationale of the algorithm is that the asymmetries between M_i and M_j (e.g. Table 9.1) induce an asymmetry on the distributions $\hat{P}$ and $\hat{D}$ and that the quantiles of those distributions provide information about the directionality of causal link ($\mathbf{z}_i \rightarrow \mathbf{z}_j$ or $\mathbf{z}_j \rightarrow \mathbf{z}_i$). In other terms we expect that the distribution of these variables should return useful information about which is the cause and the effect. Note that these distributions would be more informative if we were able to rank the terms of the Markov Blankets by prioritizing the direct causes (i.e. the terms $\mathbf{c}_i$ and $\mathbf{c}_j$) since these terms play a major role in the asymmetries of Table 9.1. The D2C algorithm can then be improved by choosing an appropriate Markov Blanket selector algorithms, like the mIMR filter.

In the experiments (Sect. 9.4) we derive the information terms as difference between (conditional) entropy terms (see Eqs. 9.1 and 9.3) which are themselves estimated by a Lazy Learning regression algorithm [4] by making an assumption of Gaussian noise. Lazy Learning returns a leave-one-out estimation of conditional variance which can be easily transformed in entropy under the normal assumption [8]. The (conditional) mutual information terms are then obtained by using the relations (9.1) and (9.3).

9.3.1 Complexity Analysis

In this subsection we make a complexity analysis of the approach: first it is important to remark that since the D2C approach relies on a classifier, its learning phase can be time-consuming and dependent on the number of samples and dimension. However, this step is supposed to be performed only once and from the user perspective it is more relevant to consider the cost in the testing phase. Given two nodes for which a test of the existence of a causal link is required, three steps have to be performed:

1. computation of the Markov blankets of the two nodes. The information filters we used have a complexity $O(Cn^2)$ where C is the cost of the computation of mutual information [24]. In case of very large n this complexity may be bounded by having the filter preceded by a ranking algorithm with complexity $O(Cn)$. Such ranking may limit the number of features taken into consideration by the filters to $n' < n$ reducing then considerably the cost.
2. once a number K_i (K_j) of members of MB_i (MB_j) have been chosen, the rest of the procedure has a complexity related to the estimation of a number $O(K_i K_j)$ of descriptors. In this paper we used a local learning regression algorithm to estimate the conditional entropies terms. Given that each regression involves at most three terms, the complexity is essentially related linearly to the number N of samples
3. the last step consists in the computation of the Random Forest predictions on the test set. Since the RF has been already trained, the complexity of this step depends only on the number of trees and not on the dimensionality or number of samples.

For each test, the resulting complexity has then a cost of the order $O(Cn + Cn'^2 + K_i K_j N)$. It is important to remark that an advantage of D2C is that, if we are interested in predicting the causal relation between two variables only, we are not forced to infer the entire adjacency matrix (as typically the case in constraint-based methods). This mean also that the computation of the entire matrix can be easily made parallel.

9.4 Experimental Validation

In this section the D2C (Sect. 9.3) algorithm is assessed in a set of synthetic experiments and published data sets.

9.4.1 Synthetic Data

This experimental session addresses the problem of inferring causal links from synthetic data generated for linear and non-linear DAG configurations of different sizes. All the variables are continuous, and the dependency between children and parents is modelled by the additive relationship

$$x_i = \sum_{j \in par(i)} f_{i,j}(x_j) + \epsilon_i, \qquad i = 1, \ldots, n \qquad (9.20)$$

where the noise $\epsilon_i \sim N(0, \sigma_i)$ is Normal, $f_{i,j}(x) \in L(x)$ and three sets of continuous functions are considered:

- linear: $L(x) = \{f \mid f(x) = a_0 + a_1 x\}$
- quadratic: $L(x) = \{f \mid f(x) = a_0 + a_1 x + a_2 x^2\}$
- sigmoid: $L(x) = \{f \mid f(x) = \frac{1}{1+exp(a_0+a_1 x)}\}$

In order to assess the accuracy with respect to dimensionality, we considered three network sizes:

- small: number of nodes n is uniformly sampled in the interval $[20, 30]$,
- medium: number of nodes n is uniformly sampled in the interval $[100, 200]$,
- large: number of nodes n is uniformly sampled in the interval $[500, 1000]$,

The assessment procedure relies on the generation of a number of DAG structures[4] and the simulation, for each of them, of N (uniformly random in $[100, 500]$) node observations according to the dependency (9.20). In each data set we removed the observations of 5% of the variables in order to introduce unobserved variables.

For each DAG, on the basis of its structure and the data set of observations, we collect a number of pairs $\langle x_d, y_d \rangle$, where x_d is the descriptor vector returned by (9.19) and y_d is the class denoting the existence (or not) of the causal link in the DAG topology.

Several sizes of training set are considered. The largest D2C training set is made of $D = 60,000$ pairs $\langle x_d, y_d \rangle$ and is obtained by generating DAGs and storing for each of them the descriptors associated to at most four positives examples (i.e. a pair where the node z_i is a direct cause of z_j) and at most six negatives examples (i.e. a pair where the node z_i is not a direct cause of z_j). A Random Forest classifier is trained on the balanced data set: we use the implementation from the R package randomForest [21] with default setting.

The test set is obtained by considering a number of independently simulated DAGs. We consider 190 DAGs for the small and medium configurations and 90 for the large configuration. For each testing DAG we select four positives examples (i.e. a pair where the node z_i is a direct cause of z_j) and six negatives examples (i.e. a pair where the node z_i is not a direct cause of z_j). The predictive accuracy of the trained Random Forest classifier is then assessed on the test set.

---

[4]We used the function random_dag from the R package gRbase [11].

The D2C approach is compared in terms of classification accuracy (Balanced Error Rate (BER)) to several state-of-the-art approaches:

- ANM: Additive Noise Model [17] using a Gaussian process with RBF kernel and the Hilbert-Schmidt Independence Criterion (p value = 0.02)[5]
- DAGL1: DAG-Search score-based algorithm with potential parents selected with a L1 penalization [32].[6]
- DAGSearch: unrestricted DAG-Search score-based algorithm (multiple restart greedy hill-climbing, using edge additions, deletions, and reversals) [32] (see footnote 6),
- DAGSearchSparse: DAG-Search score-based algorithm with potential parents restricted to the ten most correlated features [32] (see footnote 6),
- gs: Grow-Shrink constraint-based structure learning algorithm [22],[7]
- hc: hill-climbing score-based structure learning algorithm [9] (see footnote 7),
- iamb: incremental association MB constraint-based structure learning algorithm [38] (see footnote 7),
- mmhc: max-min hill climbing hybrid structure learning algorithms [39] (see footnote 7),
- PC: Estimate the equivalence class of a DAG using the PC algorithm[8] (this method was used only for the small size configuration (Fig. 9.2) for computational time reasons)
- si.hiton.pc: Semi-Interleaved HITON-PC local discovery structure learning algorithms [37] (see footnote 7),
- tabu: tabu search score-based structure learning algorithm (see footnote 7).

The BER of six versions of the D2C method are compared to the BER of state-of-the-art methods in Figs. 9.2 (small), 9.3 (medium), and 9.4 (large). The six versions of D2C are obtained by considering two types of training data (i.e. one based on linear dependency and one based on the same dependency used for testing) and three training set sizes (equal to 400, 3000 and 60,000 respectively) Each subfigure corresponds to the three types of stochastic dependency (top: linear, middle: quadratic, bottom: sigmoid).

A series of considerations can be made on the basis of the experimental results:

- the n-variate approach D2C obtains competitive results with respect to several state-of-the-art techniques in the linear case,
- the improvement of D2C wrt state-of-the-art techniques (often based on linear assumptions) tends to increase when we move to more nonlinear configurations, In particular the accuracy of the D2C algorithm is able to generalize to DAG with

---

[5]The code is available in https://staff.fnwi.uva.nl/j.m.mooij/code/additive-noise.tar.gz.

[6]The code is available in http://www.cs.ubc.ca/~murphyk/Software/DAGlearn/.

[7]The code is available in the R package bnlearn [33].

[8]The code is available in the R package pcalg [19].

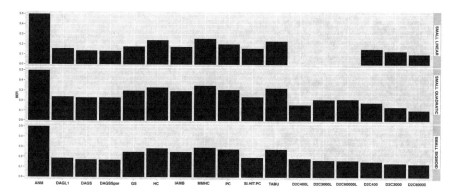

Fig. 9.2 Balanced Error Rate of the different methods for small size DAGs and three types of dependency (top: linear, middle: quadratic, bottom: sigmoid). The notation D2Cx stands for D2C with a training set of size x and where training and test sets are based on DAGs with the same type of dependency. The notation D2Cx_lin stands for D2C with a training set of size x based on DAGs with linear dependency only

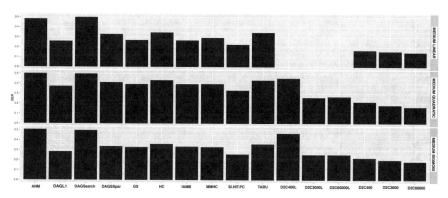

Fig. 9.3 Balanced Error Rate of the different methods for medium size DAGs and three types of dependency (top: linear, middle: quadratic, bottom: sigmoid). The notation D2Cx stands for D2C with a training set of size x and where training and test sets are based on DAGs with the same type of dependency. The notation D2Cx_lin stands for D2C with a training set of size x based on DAGs with linear dependency only

different number of nodes and different distributions also when trained only on data observed for linear DAGs (see accuracy of D2Cx$_{lin}$ in the second and third row of Figs. 9.2, 9.3, and 9.4)

- the accuracy of the D2C approach improves by increasing the number of training examples,
- with a small number of examples (i.e. $N = 400$) it is already possible to learn a classifier D2C whose accuracy is competitive with state-of-the-art methods,
- the ANM approach is not able to return accurate information about causal dependency by taking into consideration only bivariate information,

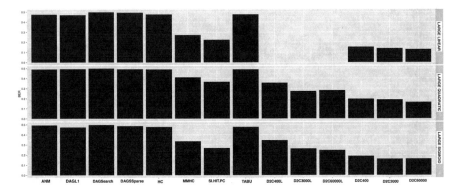

Fig. 9.4 Balanced Error Rate of the different methods for large size DAGs and three types of dependency (top: linear, middle: quadratic, bottom: sigmoid). The notation D2Cx stands for D2C with a training set of size x and where training and test sets are based on DAGs with the same type of dependency. The notation D2Cx_lin stands for D2C with a training set of size x based on DAGs with linear dependency only

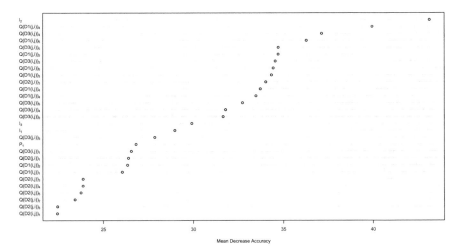

Fig. 9.5 Importance of D2C features returned by the Random Forest mean decrease accuracy. I_i denotes the ith component of the descriptor vector (9.18) while $Q(Dx(i, j))_k$ denotes the kth quantile of the population of descriptor $Dx(i, j)$

- the analysis of the importance of the D2C descriptors (based on the Mean Decrease Accuracy of the Random Forest in Fig. 9.5) shows that the most relevant variables in the vector (9.19) are the terms in I, D_1 and D_3.

The D2C code is available in the CRAN R package D2C [6].

9.4.2 Published Data

The second part of the assessment relies on the simulated and resimulated data sets proposed in Table 11 of [1]. These 103 data sets were obtained by simulating data from known Bayesian networks and also by resimulation, where real data is used to elicit a causal network and then data is simulated from the obtained network. We split the 103 data sets in two portions: a training portion (made of 52 sets) and a second portion (made of 51 sets) for testing. This was done in order to assess the accuracy of two versions of the D2C algorithm: the first uses as training set only 40,000 synthetic samples generated as in the previous section, the second includes in the training set also the 52 data sets of the training portion. The goal is to assess the generalization accuracy of the D2C algorithm with respect to DAG distributions never encountered before and not included in the training set. In this section we compare D2C to a set of algorithms implemented by the *Causal Explorer* software [2][9]:

- GS: Grow/Shrink algorithm
- IAMB: Incremental Association-Based Markov Blanket
- IAMBnPC: IAMB with PC algorithm in the pruning phase
- interIAMBnPC: IAMB with PC algorithm in the interleaved pruning phase

and two filters based on information theory, mRMR [29] and mIMR [3]. The comparison is done as follows: for each data set and for each node (having at least a parent) the causal inference techniques return the ranking of the inferred parents. The ranking is assessed in terms of the average of Area Under the Precision Recall Curve (AUPRC) and a t-test is used to assess if the set of AUPRC values is significantly different between two methods. Note that the higher the AUPRC the more accurate is the inference method.

The summary of the paired comparisons is reported in Table 9.3 for the D2C algorithm trained on the synthetic data only and in Table 9.4 for the D2C algorithm trained on both synthetic data and the 52 training data sets.

It is worthy to remark that

- the D2C algorithm is extremely competitive and outperforms the other techniques taken into consideration,

Table 9.3 D2C trained on synthetic data only: number of data sets for which D2C has an AUPRC (significantly (p-val < 0.05)) higher/lower than the method in the column

	GS	IAMB	IAMBnPC	interIAMBnPC	mRMR	mIMR
W-L	48-3 (32-0)	43-8 (21-0)	46-5 (26-0)	46-5 (25-0)	42-9 (17-0)	34-17 (12-0)

W-L stands for Wins-Losses

---

[9]Note that we use *Causal Explorer* here because, unlike bnlearn which estimates the entire adjacency matrix, it returns a ranking of the inferred causes for a given node.

Table 9.4 D2C trained on synthetic data and 52 training data sets: number of data sets for which the D2C has an AUPRC (significantly (p-val < 0.05)) higher/lower than the method in the column

	GS	IAMB	IAMBnPC	interIAMBnPC	mRMR	mIMR
W-L	49-2 (36-0)	49-2 (27-0)	49-2 (32-0)	49-2 (32-0)	42-9 (17-0)	46-5 (19-1)

W-L stands for Wins-Losses

- the D2C algorithm is able to generalize to DAG with different number of nodes and different distributions also when trained only on synthetic data simulated on linear DAGs,
- the D2C algorithm takes advantage from the availability of more training data and in particular of training data related to the causal inference task of interest, as shown by the improvement of the accuracy from Table 9.3 to Table 9.4,
- the two filters (mRMR and mIMR) algorithm appears to be the least inaccurate among the state-of-the-art algorithms,
- though the D2C is initialized with the results returned by the mIMR algorithm, it is able to improve its output and to significantly outperform it.

9.5 Conclusion

Two attitudes are common with respect to causal inference for observational data. The first is pessimistic and motivated by the consideration that *correlation (or dependency) does not imply causation*. The second is optimistic and driven by the fact that *causation implies correlation (or dependency)*. This paper belongs evidently to the second school of thought and relies on the confidence that causality leaves footprints in the form of stochastic dependency and that these footprints can be detected to retrieve causality from observational data. The results of the ChaLearn challenge and the preliminary results of this paper confirm the potential of machine learning approaches in predicting the existence of causality links on the basis of statistical descriptors of the dependency. We are convinced that this will open a new research direction where learning techniques may be used to reduce the degree of uncertainty about the existence of a causal relationships also in indistinguishable configurations which are typically not addressed by conditional independence approaches.

Further work will focus on (1) discovering additional features of multivariate distributions to improve the accuracy (2) addressing and assessing other related classification problems (e.g. predicting if a variable is an ancestor or descendant of a given one) (3) extending the work to partial ancestral graphs [40] (e.g. exploiting the logical relations presented in [7]) extending the validation to real data sets and configurations with a still larger number of variables (e.g. network inference in bioinformatics).

Acknowledgements This work was supported by the ARC project "Discovery of the molecular pathways regulating pancreatic beta cell dysfunction and apoptosis in diabetes using functional genomics and bioinformatics" funded by the Communauté Française de Belgique and the BridgeIRIS project funded by INNOVIRIS, Brussels Region. The authors wishes to thank the editor and the anonymous reviewers for their insightful comments and remarks.

References

1. C. F. Aliferis, A. Statnikov, I. Tsamardinos, S. Mani, and X. D. Koutsoukos. Local causal and markov blanket induction for causal discovery and feature selection for classification. *Journal of Machine Learning Research*, 11:171–234, 2010.
2. C.F. Aliferis, I. Tsamardinos, and A. Statnikov. Causal explorer: A probabilistic network learning toolkit for biomedical discovery. In *Proceedings of METMBS*, 2003.
3. G. Bontempi and P.E. Meyer. Causal filter selection in microarray data. In *Proceedings of ICML*, 2010.
4. G. Bontempi, M. Birattari, and H. Bersini. Lazy learning for modeling and control design. *International Journal of Control*, 72(7/8):643–658, 1999.
5. G. Bontempi, B. Haibe-Kains, C. Desmedt, C. Sotiriou, and J. Quackenbush. Multiple-input multiple-output causal strategies for gene selection. *BMC Bioinformatics*, 12(1):458, 2011.
6. G. Bontempi, C. Olsen, and M. Flauder. *D2C: Predicting Causal Direction from Dependency Features*, 2014. URL http://CRAN.R-project.org/package=D2C. R package version 1.1.
7. T. Claassen and T. Heskes. A logical characterization of constraint-based causal discovery. In *Proceedings of UAI*, 2011.
8. T. M. Cover and J. A. Thomas. *Elements of Information Theory*. John Wiley, New York, 1990.
9. R. Daly and Q. Shen. Methods to accelerate the learning of bayesian network structures. In *Proceedings of the UK Workshop on Computational Intelligence*, 2007.
10. P. Daniusis, D. Janzing, J. Mooij, J. Zscheischler, B. Steudel, K. Zhang, and B. Scholkopf. Inferring deterministic causal relations. In *Proceedings of UAI*, pages 143–150, 2010.
11. C. Dethlefsen and S. Højsgaard. A common platform for graphical models in R: The gRbase package. *Journal of Statistical Software*, 14(17):1–12, 2005. URL http://www.jstatsoft.org/v14/i17/.
12. N. Friedman, M. Linial, I. Nachman, and Dana Pe'er. Using bayesian networks to analyze expression data. *Journal of Computational Biology*, 7, 2000.
13. D. Geiger, T. Verma, and J. Pearl. Identifying independence in bayesian networks. *Networks*, 20, 1990.
14. I. Guyon. Results and analysis of the 2013 ChaLearn cause-effect pair challenge. In *Proceedings of NIPS 2013 Workshop on Causality: Large-scale Experiment Design and Inference of Causal Mechanisms*, 2014.
15. I. Guyon and A. Elisseeff. An introduction to variable and feature selection. *Journal of Machine Learning Research*, 3:1157–1182, 2003.
16. I. Guyon, C. Aliferis, and A. Elisseeff. *Computational Methods of Feature Selection*, chapter Causal Feature Selection, pages 63–86. Chapman and Hall, 2007.
17. PO Hoyer, D. Janzing, J. Mooij, J. Peters, and B. Scholkopf. Nonlinear causal discovery with additive noise models. In *Advances in Neural Information Processing Systems*, pages 689–696, 2009.
18. D. Janzing, J. Mooij, K. Zhang, J. Lemeire, J. Zscheischler, P. Daniusis, B. Steudel, and B. Scholkopf. Information-geometric approach to inferring causal directions. *Artificial Intelligence*, 2012.
19. M. Kalisch, M. Mächler, D. Colombo, M. H. Maathuis, and P. Bühlmann. Causal inference using graphical models with the R package pcalg. *Journal of Statistical Software*, 47(11):1–26, 2012. URL http://www.jstatsoft.org/v47/i11/.

20. D. Koller and N. Friedman. *Probabilistic Graphical Models*. The MIT Press, 2009.
21. A. Liaw and M. Wiener. Classification and regression by randomforest. *R News*, 2(3):18–22, 2002. URL http://CRAN.R-project.org/doc/Rnews/.
22. D. Margaritis. *Learning Bayesian Network Model Structure from Data*. PhD thesis, School of Computer Science, Carnegie-Mellon University, Pittsburgh, PA, 2003.
23. G.J. McLaughlan. *Finite Mixture Models*. Wiley, 2000.
24. P.E. Meyer and G. Bontempi. *Biological Knowledge Discovery Handbook*, chapter Information-theoretic gene selection in expression data. IEEE Computer Society, 2014.
25. JM Mooij, O. Stegle, D. Janzing, K. Zhang, and B. Scholkopf. Probabilistic latent variable models for distinguishing between cause and effect. In *Advances in Neural Information Processing Systems*, 2010.
26. J. Pearl. Causal diagrams for empirical research. *Biometrika*, 82:669–710, 1995.
27. J. Pearl. *Causality: Models, Reasoning, and Inference*. Cambridge University Press, 2000.
28. J.P. Pellet and A. Elisseeff. Using markov blankets for causal structure learning. *Journal of Machine Learning Research*, 9:1295–1342, 2008.
29. H. Peng, F. Long, and C. Ding. Feature selection based on mutual information: Criteria of max-dependency,max-relevance, and min-redundancy. *IEEE Transactions on Pattern Analysis and Machine Intelligence*, 27(8):1226–1238, 2005.
30. O. Pourret, P. Nam, and B. Marcot. *Bayesian Networks: A Practical Guide to Applications*. Wiley, 2008.
31. H. Reichenbach. *The Direction of Time*. University of California Press, Berkeley, 1956.
32. M. Schmidt, A. Niculescu-Mizil, and K. Murphy. Learning graphical model structure using l1-regularization paths. In *Proceedings of AAAI*, 2007.
33. Marco Scutari. Learning bayesian networks with the bnlearn R package. *Journal of Statistical Software*, 35(3):1–22, 2010. URL http://www.jstatsoft.org/v35/i03/.
34. S. Shimizu, P.O. Hoyer, A. Hyvrinen, and A.J. Kerminen. A linear, non-gaussian acyclic model for causal discovery. *Journal of Machine Learning Research*, 7:2003–2030, 2006.
35. P. Spirtes, C. Glymour, and R. Scheines. *Causation, Prediction and Search*. Springer Verlag, Berlin, 2000.
36. A. Statnikov, M. Henaff, N.I. Lytkin, and C. F. Aliferis. New methods for separating causes from effects in genomics data. *BMC Genomics*, 13(S22), 2012.
37. I. Tsamardinos, CF Aliferis, and A Statnikov. Time and sample efficient discovery of markov blankets and direct causal relations. In *Proceedings of KDD*, pages 673–678, 2003.
38. I. Tsamardinos, C.F. Aliferis, and A. Statnikov. Algorithms for large scale markov blanket discovery. In *Proceedings of FLAIRS*, 2003.
39. I. Tsamardinos, LE Brown, and CF Aliferis. The max-min hill-climbing bayesian network structure learning algorithm. *Machine Learning*, 65(1):31–78, 2010.
40. J. Zhang. Causal reasoning with ancestral graphs. *Journal of Machine Learning Research*, 9:1437–1474, 2008.

Chapter 10
Pattern-Based Causal Feature Extraction

Diogo Moitinho de Almeida

10.1 Introduction

From the competition homepage [2]: The problem of attributing causes to effects is pervasive in science, medicine, economy and almost every aspects of our everyday life involving human reasoning and decision making…However, experiments are costly while non-experimental "observational" data collected routinely around the world are readily available. Unraveling potential cause-effect relationships from such observational data could save a lot of time and effort…The objective of the challenge is to rank pairs of variables A, B to prioritize experimental verification of the conjecture that A causes B. Contestants were given over 20,000 training pairs of variables deprived of their context of both real variables with known causal relationships from diverse domains and artificially generated variables and their respective causal relationships. Contestants were to use this data in order to calculate a ranking of each pairs of variables were the highest ranked pairs had the first variable, A, cause the second variable, B, and the lowest ranked pairs have B cause A. The rankings that we provided were judged by the average of the AUC's of predicting whether or not A causes B and B causes A. The competition has both a public and private leaderboard, each of which coming with 4050 pairs of variables which contestants were not able to see the labels of. The public leaderboard was available for the duration of the competition, where contestants could submit rankings twice a day in order to see how well their algorithms perform on that dataset. Because competitors could potentially overfit on that dataset, the

D. M. de Almeida (✉)
Google, Menlo Park, CA, USA

© Springer Nature Switzerland AG 2019
I. Guyon et al. (eds.), *Cause Effect Pairs in Machine Learning*,
The Springer Series on Challenges in Machine Learning,
https://doi.org/10.1007/978-3-030-21810-2_10

final winner was determined by only one submission on the private leaderboard, whose data was only made available after competitors submitted their algorithms to be tested.

10.2 Method

Our method was able to attain the second highest score in the public leaderboard and the highest score in the private leaderboard. Our final solution involved not only the feature extraction process outlined in this paper, but also a process for the elimination of features, which turned out to be unnecessary, and scikit-learn's [4] gradient boosted decision tree ensemble [3] classifier with hyper-parameters tuned by Spearmint [5] for the final rankings (Table 10.1).

The focus of this paper will solely be on the feature extraction methodology, because the feature extraction process contains all of our novel contributions for and we feel that the rest of our pipeline was fairly standard for a kaggle competition.

10.2.1 Algorithm

Our process revolves around general algorithm templates that one would use to generate causal features, which we call Feature Patterns. These Feature Patterns take in algorithms/functions as parameters and create new algorithms that can then generate features. By simply creating the architecture for a few patterns and changing the parameterization of each pattern, many unique features could be generated with this approach.

In addition to the architecture sharing that occurs within a Feature Pattern, the commonalities between Feature Patterns allow even greater code reuse and more importantly for the creation of more complex work flows than we could generate from scratch. Take for example our simplest Feature Pattern: a unary function that takes in a numerical variable. This pattern would require the unary function, functions to convert categorical, binary, and numerical variables to numerical, and an aggregation function for the case when the return value of one the transforms is

Table 10.1 Leaderboard scores of top submissions

Submission	Public	Private
Our submission (1st place): w/ feature selection +	0.81367	0.8196
Our 2nd best submission: w/o feature selection +	0.81279	0.81743
Our 3rd best submission: w/ feature selection +	0.81238	0.81681
Team jarfo (2nd place): Top submissions +	0.81464	0.81052
Team HiDLoN (3rd place): Top submissions +	0.80191	0.80720

multidimensional (for example, if the transform from categorical to numerical is a one-encoding), in which case we would apply the unary transform to each column of the resulting matrix, and apply the aggregation function to combine the results. Afterwards, we would do the same function with the variables reversed, and then passing the two resulting values to a relative feature function (for example, taking the difference between the two variables, or only returning second of the two). Since all Feature Patterns would have to handle the conversion between numerical, categorical, and binary, as well as handle the relative features and aggregation, if any, afterwards, relatively little effort is needed to create more complex features (Table 10.2).

In addition to sharing architecture, the same benefit can also be attained through the unification of the possible values for similar/equivalent parameters. By doing so, the number of features would grow at a rate greater than linearly for each possible value of a shared parameters and thus, it would require less parameters to get an equivalent number of unique features (Table 10.3).

The feature extraction process is then completed by simply iterating over each Feature Pattern and parameter combination to generate valid features for each observation.

Table 10.2 Feature patterns

Feature pattern	Example parameters
N unary function	N unary function, N/B/C-to-N transforms, aggregator
NN binary function	NN binary function, N/B/C-to-N transforms, 2 aggregators
CN binary function	CN binary function, N/B/C-to-N/C transforms, 2 aggregators
Regression metric	Regression predictor, Metric, N/B/C-to-N transform, aggregator
Classification metric	Classifier, metric, N/B/C-to-N/C transform, 2 aggregators

N, B, and C are used for numerical, binary, and categorical

Table 10.3 Examples of pattern parameters used

Parameter type	Examples
Aggregation functions	Mean, max, min, median, sum
Regression predictors	Ridge regression, random forest, k-NN
Classification predictors	Logistic regression, random forest, naive Bayes
Classification metrics	Accuracy, AUC, hinge loss
Regression metrics	Mean squared error, mean absolute error
Clustering metrics	Mutual information score, homogeneity score
Statistical tests	Pearson's R, χ^2 test, ANOVA
Distance metrics	Euclidean distance, cosine distance
Unary functions	Normalized entropy, skew, kurtosis

10.2.2 Justification

The assumed definition of causality for this section is that which was provided in the competition site [2]: if $B = f(A, noise)$, then A is the $cause$ of B, and vice-versa. While each feature extraction algorithm created from each Feature Pattern would have its own justification, we believe a specific set of patterns, namely "Regression Metric" and "Classification Metric", deserve special attention. This is because these patterns have the most parameters, and thus contributed the largest amount of features to the final feature sets, and as shown in the experimental results, these features seemed to be the most important for performance. The gist of these patterns is that a model is trained to predict one variable from the other variable, that model is used to generate predictions for that variable, and a function (generally a goodness-of-fit measure) is applied to those predictions (Fig. 10.1).

Our motivation behind this class of goodness-of-fit features are the assumptions that the features would be especially good at detecting how likely it is that a function from one variable to the other (namely f in the assumed definition of causality) can exist and that the likelihood that that function exists is a good feature for causal discovery. The first assumption makes sense because the existing machine learning algorithms which are used to provide the fit generally perform quite well at estimating hypothesis functions on real-world data. The second assumption similarly makes sense because B = f(A, noise) or A = f(B, noise) being true relies on the such an f existing.

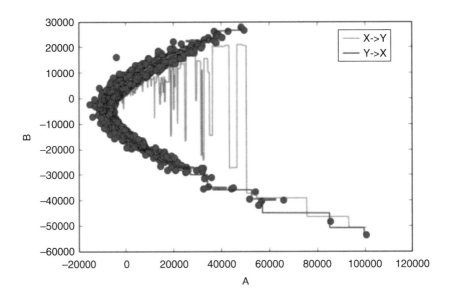

Fig. 10.1 Difference between goodness of fit of invertible and non-invertible functions

10.2.3   Considerations

Due to the time constraints of the competition and the limitations of the effort
that we could afford to spend, the motivation for creating our process was
to easily, quickly, and reproducibly go from insight to features with minimal
human intervention. As such, we made the decision to trade off computational
time in order minimize human time. The result is our algorithm can be quite
inefficient since features generated from similar parameters in general would be
quite similar/redundant, though the exact computational cost would depend on the
Feature Patterns and parameters used. Another downside of our approach is that
bookkeeping on individual features quickly loses human interpretability, since it is
so far removed from the original data.

10.2.4   autocause

Because the competition code was mostly hacked together and did not take full
advantage of sharing both architecture and parameters, we refactored the codebase
of the feature extraction process into its own package: autocause.[1] This allowed us to
declaratively iterate different settings and publish the settings in a human-readable,
unix-diff-able format as well for further analysis.[2]

10.3   Experiments

Because of the aforementioned difficulty of interpreting the individual features,
we chose to perform analyses on classes of features that might provide insight
into the most effective parts of our feature extraction process and the underlying
mechanisms of causal discovery. These analyses were performed by varying the
available parameters to Feature Patterns in order to either find which of a set
of parameters are most important, or by removing an entire set of parameters,
eliminating all Feature Patterns that depend on those parameters. Each set of features
was scored by being trained by both a linear model and gradient boosted decision
tree ensemble with both models optimized for speed on 80% of the final training
data of the competition, and having their predictions score on the final 20% of the
data using the same metric as in the competition (Table 10.4).

---

[1] Available at https://github.com/diogo149/autocause.
[2] See the configs subdirectory of https://github.com/diogo149/CauseEffectPairsPaper.

Table 10.4 Experimental results

Description	#Feat	GBM score	Linear score
Competition features	8686	0.692483139268	0.663782901707
autocause default	21,207	0.696014248897	0.694080271398
Efficient parameters	324	0.682581676518	0.687203189251
Effective parameters	14,442	0.676321066209	0.681059838814

Table 10.5 Results of experiment on fit features

Description	#Feat	GBM score	Linear score
Both together	21,186	0.713640109365	0.700135374168
Only fit default	18,612	0.693269150278	0.680996251976
No fit	2574	0.687915176559	0.611305285221

As shown in the experimental results table, after refactoring the code, a lot more features were able to be generated with the same number of parameters. This is good to confirm that the features generated by autocause are comparable to that of the software used during the competition. The results for a set of parameters that were chosen by combining insights from several dozen experiments (see the Appendix) for a mix of relatively low dimensionality for the final feature set and good accuracy are also included in the table. This parameter set allows us to get over 98% of the accuracy of the default model using only 1.5% of the number of features. Using the same methodology as in the last paragraph, we tried to construct a parameter set to only maximize accuracy by only keeping the changes that improved accuracy by a noticeable amount. This unfortunately led to features that performed significantly worse than the default settings. This indicates that the methodology of picking and choosing parameters by looking at each individually and combining them after the fact is flawed, and that better means of creating parameter sets should be used (Table 10.5).

One notable set of results from experiments is that of the results between features that rely on only classification/regression predictors and those that don't at all, because the experiments show the performance of different Feature Patterns. The "No Fit" features contain all the unary/binary function patterns, while the "Only Fit" features contain "Regression Metric" and "Classification Metric" Feature Patterns. The scores of each show the "Only Fit" features to perform significantly better, indicating that its Feature Pattern likely contributed more to the accuracy of our winning submission than the others.

10.4   Conclusion

From the approach of feature extraction for accuracy, there are still more Feature Patterns that could be added to our approach, such as those underlying the previous state of the art features [1], and Feature Patterns such as those described in this paper may just be the tip of the iceberg, both in terms of quality and quantity. During the competition, we were certainly biased towards the "Regression Metric" and "Classification Metric" Feature Patterns. Despite them performing the best in our limited experimental results, it may be the case that we haven't appropriately represented other Feature Patterns. There seems to be even more work remaining from the perspective of understanding why our process works as well as it does. We were able to get comparable performance to our 20k-dimensional features with only 324 features, but that still is too many for us to dive deep and find the truly important ones, and even if we did do so, the features generated may be too far removed from the original data to retain any human interpretable meaning.

Acknowledgment Special thanks to the organizers of the ChaLearn Cause-Effect Pair Challenge hosted by Kaggle.

Appendix

Results

See Tables 10.6, 10.7, 10.8, 10.9, 10.10, 10.11, 10.12, and 10.13.

Table 10.6 Results of experiment on meta-features

Description	#Feat	GBM score	Linear score
autocause default	21,207	0.696014248897	0.694080271398
No metafeatures	21,186	0.713640109365	0.700135374168
Only metafeatures	21	0.513249437852	0.514610878117

Table 10.7 Results of experiment on relative features

Description	#Feat	GBM score	Linear score
No metafeatures	21,186	0.713640109365	0.700135374168
Only difference features	7062	0.699178700923	0.707910542983
Only A to B	7062	0.646039719086	0.619346087547
Only B to A	7062	0.675171907802	0.633300654009

Table 10.8 Results of experiment on aggregation features

Description	#Feat	GBM score	Linear score
Only mean	4743	0.703366341099	0.66190548093
Only mode	4743	0.702727813568	0.664183581517
Only median	4743	0.691697784105	0.670042628328
Only min	4743	0.700988250898	0.660565019326
Only sum	4743	0.701434552265	0.673035609828
Only max	4743	0.691870225179	0.651876362553
All of the above	25,773	0.709451429787	0.695304807716
No aggregation features	1077	0.676581730474	0.623828720773

Table 10.9 Results of experiment on numerical vs categorical features

Description	#Feat	GBM score	Linear score
autocause default	21,207	0.696014248897	0.694080271398
Numerical only	6321	0.656714283634	0.611395370877
Categorical only	5451	0.579135168216	0.607908620448

Table 10.10 Results of experiment on numerical to categorical transformation

Description	#Feat	GBM score	Linear score
Discretization into 10 (default)	5451	0.579135168216	0.607908620448
KMeans into 10	5451	0.632243266485	0.622365613862
KMeans into 3	5451	0.614931332437	0.587218538488
KMeans with gap statistic	5451	0.583693386727	0.582386249005

Table 10.11 Results of experiment on categorical to numerical transformation

Description	#Feat	GBM score	Linear score
One-hot encoding (default)	6321	0.656714283634	0.611395370877
Identity	921	0.671054122146	0.592442871034
PCA to 1 dimension	921	0.66682459185	0.606938680493
Reshuffling	921	0.651080073736	0.599028952216

Table 10.12 Results of experiment on classifiers

Description	#Feat	GBM score	Linear score
Only naive Bayes	996	0.578082139243	0.59122957333
Only GBM	996	0.633170335784	0.607150621346
Only RandomForest	996	0.646001448959	0.607517231438
Only k-NN	996	0.607753059361	0.572566617101
Only logistic regression	996	0.620826820564	0.600463299695
Only decision tree	996	0.637150678151	0.61158719868
All of the above	5451	0.632243266485	0.622365613862
No classifier features	105	0.581141154559	0.572462173005

Table 10.13 Results of experiment on regression predictors

Description	#Feat	GBM score	Linear score
Only RandomForest	261	0.643682857561	0.568762197986
Only GBM	261	0.657848458945	0.596995045661
Only DecisionTree	261	0.618929711403	0.550528710645
Only k-NN	261	0.638331347172	0.577983408646
Only ridge	261	0.62702149139	0.578773516607
Only linear regression	261	0.624841890148	0.577198194394
All of the above	921	0.66682459185	0.606938680493
No regression predictor features	129	0.619709098921	0.540686641005

References

1. Causality Workbench causality challenge #3: Cause-effect pairs - help. http://www.causality.inf.ethz.ch/cause-effect.php?page=help. Accessed: 2013.
2. Cause-Effect Pairs, howpublished = http://www.kaggle.com/c/cause-effect-pairs, note = Accessed: 2013.
3. Jerome H Friedman. Greedy function approximation: a gradient boosting machine. *Annals of statistics*, pages 1189–1232, 2001.
4. Fabian Pedregosa, Gaël Varoquaux, Alexandre Gramfort, Vincent Michel, Bertrand Thirion, Olivier Grisel, Mathieu Blondel, Peter Prettenhofer, Ron Weiss, Vincent Dubourg, et al. Scikit-learn: Machine learning in python. *Journal of machine learning research*, 12(Oct):2825–2830, 2011.
5. Jasper Snoek, Hugo Larochelle, and Ryan P Adams. Practical Bayesian optimization of machine learning algorithms. In *Advances in neural information processing systems*, pages 2951–2959, 2012.

Chapter 11
Training Gradient Boosting Machines Using Curve-Fitting and Information-Theoretic Features for Causal Direction Detection

Spyridon Samothrakis, Diego Perez, and Simon Lucas

11.1   Introduction

Humanity's effort to understand causality and its relationship to knowledge can be observed in almost every academic field, including philosophy (e.g. [2]:"we think we have knowledge of a thing only when we have grasped its cause" quoting Aristotle) or Anthropology (e.g. see the ability for associative thinking in [3]). One can formulate the problem of attributing causality between events in the spirit of [7] as a Markov Decision Process (MDP). A (finite) Markov Decision Process is a tuple $< S, C, T, R >$, where $c \in C$ is the set of actions an agent can perform, $s \in S$ a set of states and $R(s'|s)$ is the reward at each state/action pair. $T(s'|s, c)$ is a transition function that denotes the probability of an agent moving from state s to another state s' given an action c. To apply MDPs to the problem of causality we make the following instantiation: All actions come from two sets $C_1 = A, C_2 = B$ and states $S_1 = A, S_2 = B$. Thus, there is a transition function that has the form $T(b|s, a)$ and $T(a|s, b)$. The MDP runs for one step, with both agents being at dummy state s initially. The agent takes an action that either leads it to one group of states A or B, followed by a second action that takes it to either B or A, respectively. Let's assume we are trying to learn a generative model of the transition function, in order to use it later in some policy scheme. If $T(A|s, B) = T(A)$, we claim A does **not** cause B.

S. Samothrakis (✉)
University of Essex, Wivenhoe Park, Colchester, Essex, UK
e-mail: ssamot@essex.ac.uk

D. Perez · S. Lucas
University of Essex, Wivenhoe Park, Colchester, Essex, UK

School of Electronic Engineering and Computer Science, Queen Mary University of London, London, UK
e-mail: diego.perez@qmul.ac.uk; simon.lucas@qmul.ac.uk

© Springer Nature Switzerland AG 2019   331
I. Guyon et al. (eds.), *Cause Effect Pairs in Machine Learning*,
The Springer Series on Challenges in Machine Learning,
https://doi.org/10.1007/978-3-030-21810-2_11

Otherwise, if the actions taken from set B impact T, i.e. the previous equation does not hold, we claim that A causes B. In other words if an agent is able to effectively control a process given the possibility of doing so, we can claim that the agent's actions are causal to the states of the process.

It is not always easy to perform the controlled process mentioned above, but it might be the case that we have a number of observations of actions each agent took, following uniform random policy (i.e. nature is the agent). This in effect turns our problem into one of prediction. Does the knowledge of action A help me predict action B and/or the reverse? Obviously, assuming the transition function is stochastic, there can be no proof of this. We could possibly try to infer the causal direction if we assume some sensible set of priors over the transition function, mostly taking a view reminiscent of the work of Kolmogorov, i.e. assuming nature prefers simple mechanisms. In this paper we try to infer causal structure using a machine learning approach on features extracted from the random variables provided.

The rest of the paper is organised as follows: In Sect. 11.2 we present the method we used for inferring causal direction. In Sect. 11.3 we present some experimental results and analyse the resulting classifiers. We conclude with a short discussion in Sect. 11.4.

11.2 Methodology

There are some core concepts behind the methodology followed. Firstly, we are trying to find whether the mapping $F : A \rightarrow B$ is more probable than $F : B \rightarrow A$. This can be captured by trying to fit different classifiers at each direction of the data. This implicitly assumes that machine learning classifiers tend to prefer simpler models. The second concept is that information theoretic features about the data should be able to capture some of the characteristics of the underlying distributions, thus helping our overall classification task.

11.2.1 Data and Data Pre-processing

Our data source was the union of all samples provided by the "Kaggle Causality Challenge" and can be found here: http://www.kaggle.com/c/cause-effect-pairs/ data. The amount of data provided is doubled by reversing all the examples provided. The total number of labelled data is 32,399 samples. Each labelled sample belongs to either class 1 (A causes B), class -1 (B causes A) or class 0 (where respectively the events are independent; are influenced by a third cause or we cannot tell). The type of variable in each data sample is also known (i.e. categorical, binary or continuous).

11.2.2   *Feature Extraction*

What follows is a brief exposition of the features used:

1. *Spearman ρ*: The correlation coefficient ρ.
2. *Number of Unique Samples A*: Number of unique samples of variable A.
3. *Number of Unique Samples B*: Number of unique samples of variable B.
4. *Noise Independence A $\rightarrow$ B (trees)*: The mutual information of an additive noise model [5]. Uses k-means++([1]) to discretise noise. Modelling is performed using Regression or Decision Trees.
5. *Noise Independence B $\rightarrow$ A (trees)*: As in feature 4, but trying to predict A using B.
6. *Noise Independence A $\rightarrow$ B (SVM)*: As in feature 4, with a support vector classifier or regressor as the modelling function.
7. *Noise Independence B $\rightarrow$ A (SVM)*: As in feature 5, but trying to predict A using B.
8. *Noise Independence A $\rightarrow$ B (trees)—spearman*: As in feature 4 but, instead of mutual information, using spearman ρ as an independence test.
9. *Noise Independence B $\rightarrow$ A (trees)—spearman*: As in feature 5, but trying to predict A using B.
10. *Entropy A*: Entropy of Variable A. If the variable is continuous, k-means is performed and distance is measured from closest centre as a method for discretisation.
11. *Entropy B*: Entropy of Variable B. Same discretisation method as with feature 10.
12. *Uncertainty Coefficient A*: Uncertainty Coefficient of Variable A. In case of continuous variable, the k-means trick from feature 10 is used.
13. *Uncertainty Coefficient B*: Uncertainty Coefficient of Variable B. In case of continuous variable, the k-means trick from feature 10 is used.
14. *Predicts A $\rightarrow$ B (trees)*: Fraction of correctly classified examples or R^2, depending on whether B is categorical or continuous. In all tree examples a decision tree regressor or a decision tree classifier is used.
15. *Predicts B $\rightarrow$ A (trees)*: As in feature 14, but trying to predict A using B.
16. *Predicts U $\rightarrow$ B (trees)*: Predict B using just random variables that come from a distribution as close to A as possible.
17. *Predicts U $\rightarrow$ A (trees)*: As above but with reversed direction.
18. *Predicts A $\rightarrow$ B (SVM)*: Exactly as in the case of labelit:pred, but this time with support vector machines.
19. *Predicts B $\rightarrow$ A (SVM)*: See above.
20. *Predicts U $\rightarrow$ B (SVM)*: See above.
21. *Predicts U $\rightarrow$ A (SVM)*: See above.
22. *Uniform Symmetrised Divergence A*: Symmetrised KL Divergence between A and the Uniform distribution. As usual, discretisation is performed using k-means.

23. *Uniform Symmetrised Divergence B*: Symmetrised KL Divergence between B and the Uniform distribution.
24. *KL Divergence from Normal A*: KL Divergence of A from the normal distribution.
25. *KL Divergence from Normal B*: KL Divergence of B from the normal distribution.
26. *KL Divergence from Uniform A*: KL Divergence of A from the uniform distribution.
27. *KL Divergence from Uniform B*: KL Divergence of A from the uniform distribution.
28. *LiNGAM*: The LiNGHAM causality coefficient [8], implemented by the original author of this method.
29. *ICGI—Normal Integration*: IGCI Gaussian-Integration coefficient [6], implemented by the original authors of this method.
30. *ICGI—Uniform Integration*: IGCI Uniform-Integration coefficient, as above.

11.2.3 Classifier

Two Gradient Boosting Machines (GBM see [4]) have been used, with 3000 trees at each one. Each tree in each GBM has a maximum depth of 12 and a learning rate of approximately 0.0063640. The minimum samples required for each tree split is 5. The first GBM_1 is trained using only samples from the class 1 vs everything else, where everything else forms class 0). The other GBM_{-1} is trained using samples of class -1 vs everything else. To denote the probability of a sample belonging to a specific class P_{GBM} is used. the score of each sample is set to $S = P_{GBM_1}(1) - P_{GBM_{-1}}(-1)$. In other words the score attributed to each sample is the probability of having causal direction from A to B minus the probability of having causal direction B to A.

11.2.4 Hyperparameter Optimisation

A modified version of Stochastic Simultaneous Optimistic Optimisation [9] (StoSOO) was used to optimise the learning rate and the subsampling percentage (i.e. the samples to be used in a bagging-like procedure) for the two GBMs. StoSOO is a tree-like algorithm that samples the hyperparameter space by iteratively splitting it into smaller segments, which it then samples, until some cut-off point.

11.3   Experiments and Analysis

The resulting classifier and meta-optimisation technique is analysed in this section. Note that the AUC score of our classifier in the Kaggle's causality challenge test set is 0.79957. This gave us the third place in the competition out of 69 participants.

11.3.1   Hyperparameter Optimisation

A number of hyperparameters were optimized by a hyperparameters by a combination of hand-tuning and small runs of StoSOO. A sample run can be seen in Fig. 11.1, on a subset (10%) of the experimental data, 100 trees in our GBM and a maximum tree depth of 10. Notice StoSOO improving AUC using just a subset of the data. The AUC is obtained by doing threefold cross validation

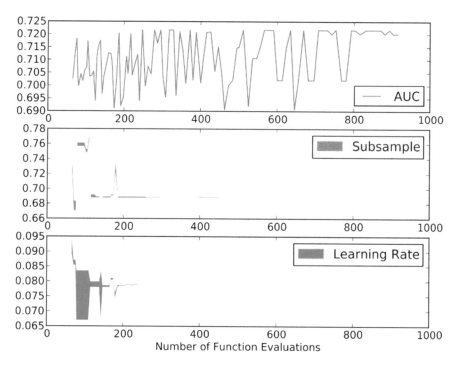

Fig. 11.1 Hyper-parameter Optimization Progress. Notice that both hyper-parameters affect regularization. Learning rate affects speed of convergence and sub-sample affects the portion of samples used at each iteration of each GBP learning cycle

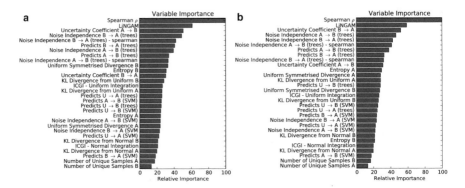

Fig. 11.2 Relative feature importance for each classifier. (**a**) Feature importances of GBM_1. (**b**) Feature importances of GBM_{-1}

over a random selected subset of that data (i.e. dataset splits are NOT fixed in every iteration). Notice the randomness of AUC score (within certain bounds), but the convergence of subsample and learning rate GBM attributes. Also notice the uncertainty concerning hyperparameter values early in the run.

11.3.2   Training and Classifier Analysis

In Fig. 11.2 one can see the relevant score of each variable plotted, with 100 being the most important variable. Feature importance signifies the average importance of each variable, as measured by how high in the tree the variable is (being higher in the tree means affecting more samples). In an ensemble of features produced by GPM the normalised average of these variables is what is plotted. From Fig. 11.2 one can see that the most important feature is Spear's correlation, presumably GBM is first throwing away cases that are uncorrelated. The least important feature involved (predictably) if the number of unique variables for variable B.

11.4   Conclusion

A method for detecting causality has been presented. Obvious improvements to the method include creating more curve fitting features and introducing more information theoretic features. One could, for example, add trees of different sizes, plus a number of SVMs with different kernels/kernel parameters. Fitting linear classifiers/regressors or higher level polynomials would be another option. Finally, at the beginning of this paper we emphasised the decision theoretic aspects of causality detection. It might be possible to directly tackle the problem using decision theoretic methods (e.g. standalone StoSOO or Monte Carlo Tree Search).

Acknowledgment This work was supported by EPSRC grant EP/H048588/1 entitled: "UCT for Games and Beyond".

Appendix: Causality Challenge

Title: Training Gradient Boosting Machines using Curve-fitting and Information theoretic features for Causal Direction Detection.
Participant name, address, email and website: Spyridon Samothrakis, Diego Perez, https://github.com/ssamot/causality.
Task(s) solved: Kaggle Competition.
Reference: This paper.
Method: A combination of feature extraction from the sample data, Gradient boosting machines and StoSOO meta-optimisation.

- Preprocessing: Exploit Symmetries.
- Causal discovery: Gradient Boosting Machine, Curve fitting/Information theoretic features.
- Feature selection: Feature Ranking.
- Classification: Gradient Boosting Machine
- Model selection/hyperparameter selection: Cross-validation, Stochastic Simultaneous Optimistic Optimisation.

Results (Table 11.1):

- quantitative advantages: The method and ideas behind our method are relatively simple. We advocate a feature extraction strategy based on curve fitting + information theoretic features.
- qualitative advantages: There are some elements of novelty, mostly in the ideas behind extracting features and doing hyper-parameter optimisation.

Code and installation instructions can be found here: https://github.com/ssamot/causality.

Table 11.1 Result table

Dataset/task	Score
Test set	0.79957

References

1. David Arthur and Sergei Vassilvitskii. k-means++: The advantages of careful seeding. In *Proceedings of the eighteenth annual ACM-SIAM symposium on Discrete algorithms*, pages 1027–1035. Society for Industrial and Applied Mathematics, 2007.
2. Andrea Falcon. Aristotle on causality. In Edward N. Zalta, editor, *The Stanford Encyclopedia of Philosophy*. Winter 2012 edition, 2012.
3. James George Frazer. *The Golden Bough: A Study in Magic and Religion. Vol. 13, Aftermath: a Supplement to the Golden Bough*. Macmillan, 1936.
4. Jerome H Friedman. Greedy function approximation: a gradient boosting machine. *Annals of Statistics*, pages 1189–1232, 2001.
5. Patrik O Hoyer, Dominik Janzing, Joris M Mooij, Jonas Peters, and Bernhard Schölkopf. Nonlinear causal discovery with additive noise models. 2009.
6. Dominik Janzing, Joris Mooij, Kun Zhang, Jan Lemeire, Jakob Zscheischler, Povilas Daniušis, Bastian Steudel, and Bernhard Schölkopf. Information-geometric approach to inferring causal directions. *Artificial Intelligence*, 182:1–31, 2012.
7. Judea Pearl. *Causality: models, reasoning and inference*, volume 29. Cambridge Univ Press, 2000.
8. Shohei Shimizu, Patrik O Hoyer, Aapo Hyvärinen, and Antti Kerminen. A linear non-Gaussian acyclic model for causal discovery. *The Journal of Machine Learning Research*, 7:2003–2030, 2006.
9. Michal Valko, Alexandra Carpentier, and Rémi Munos. Stochastic Simultaneous Optimistic Optimization. In *30th International Conference on Machine Learning*, Atlanta, États-Unis, February 2013. URL http://hal.inria.fr/hal-00789606.

Chapter 12
Conditional Distribution Variability Measures for Causality Detection

Josè A. R. Fonollosa

12.1 Introduction

There is no doubt that causality detection is a task of great practical interest. In a wide sense, attributing causes to effects guides all our efforts to understand our world and to solve any kind of real life problems. There is not, however, a simple and general definition of causality and the topic remains a staple in contemporary philosophy.

The development of analytical methods for detecting a cause-effect relationship in a set of ordered pairs of values also lacks of a universal formal definition of causality. From a pure statistical point of view any bivariate joint distribution can be expressed as the product of any of the two marginal distributions by the conditional distribution of the other variable given the first. And these two equivalent expressions can also be used to explain the generation process in both directions.

In order to be able to attack the causality detection problem we need to introduce one or more assumptions about the generation process or the shape of the joint distribution. Most of those assumptions come from the Occam's razor succinctness principle. We expect to have a simpler model in the correct direction that in the opposite, i.e. the algorithmic complexity or minimum description length of the generation process should be lower in the true causal direction than in the opposite direction. To be more precise, if the random variable X is the cause of the random variable Y we usually expect the conditional distribution $p(Y|X = x)$ to be unimodal or at least to have a similar shape for different given values x of X.

Several methods have been proposed in the literature as practical measures of the uncomputable Kolmogorov complexity of the generation model in the hypothetical

J. A. R. Fonollosa (✉)
Universitat Politècnica de Catalunya, Barcelona Tech. c/ Jordi Girona 1-3, Barcelona, Spain
e-mail: jose.fonollosa@upc.edu

© Springer Nature Switzerland AG 2019
I. Guyon et al. (eds.), *Cause Effect Pairs in Machine Learning*,
The Springer Series on Challenges in Machine Learning,
https://doi.org/10.1007/978-3-030-21810-2_12

causal direction. See [7] for a review of the usual assumptions and generation models. In this paper we develop new causality measures based on the assumption that the shape of the conditional distribution $p(Y|X = x)$ tends to be very similar for different values of x if the random variable X is the cause of Y. The main difference with respect to previous methods is that we do not impose a strict independence between the conditional distribution (or noise) and the cause. However we still expect the conditional distribution to have a similar shape or similar statistical characteristics for different values x of the cause.

The developed features are combined with standard statistical features following a machine learning approach: the selection of a good set of relevant features and of an adequate learning model.

12.2   Features

In this section we enumerate the features used by our model. All the measures are computed in both directions, i.e., exchanging the role of the two random variables X and Y, except if the measure is symmetric.

12.2.1   Preprocessing

Mean and Variance Normalization Numerical data is normalized to have zero mean and unit variance. All of our features are scale and mean invariant.

Discretization of Numerical Variables Discrete measures as the discrete entropy and discrete mutual information are also used as features of numerical date after a discretization or quantization process. The quantization uses $2 * maxdev * sfactor + 1$ equally spaced segments of $\sigma / sfactor$ length and truncates all absolute values above $maxdev * \sigma$. For almost all measures requiring a discretization of the input we selected $sfactor = 3$ and $maxdev = 3$ in our experiments, i.e., a quantization to 19 different values.

Relabeling of Categorical Variables The specific values assigned to categorical data are assumed to have no information by themselves. However, in some cases we considered the calculation of *numerical* measures (as skewness) for categorical variables. For these computations we assigned integer values to the categorical variables as a function of its probability. After the relabeling of variables with M different categories we have: $p(x = 0) \geq p(x = 1) \ldots \geq p(x = M - 1)$. This step let us obtain *numerical* features of categorical variables that do not depend on the labels but on the sorted probabilities.

12.2.2   Information-Theoretic Measures

In the baseline system we include the standard information-theoretic features as entropy and mutual information. Both the discrete and the continuous version of the entropy estimator are applied to numerical and categorical data after the preprocessing described above.

Discrete Entropy and Joint Entropy The entropy of a random variable is a information-theoretic measure that quantifies the uncertainty in a random variable. In the case of a discrete random variable X, the entropy of X is defined as:

$$H(X) = - \sum_x p(x) \log(p(x))$$

In our implementation of the discrete entropy estimator we added the simple [5] bias correction term to finally obtain

$$\hat{H}_m(X) = - \sum_x \frac{n_x}{N} \log(\frac{n_x}{N}) + \frac{M-1}{2N}$$

where M is the number of different values of the random variable X in the data set. We also considered the normalized version $\hat{H}_n(X) = \hat{H}_m(X)/\log(N)$ where $log(N)$ is the maximum entropy a discrete random variable with N different values. The definition and estimation of the entropy can be extended to a pair of variables replacing the counts n_x by the counts $n_{x,y}$ of the number of times the pair (x, y) appears in the sample set.

Discrete Conditional Entropy The conditional entropy quantifies the average amount of information needed to describe the outcome of a random variable Y given that the value of another random variable X is known. In our implementation, the discrete conditional entropy $H(Y|X)$ is computed as the difference between the discrete joint entropy $H(Y, X)$ and the marginal entropy $H(X)$.

Discrete Mutual Information The Mutual Information is the information-theoretic measure of the dependence of two random variables. It can be computed from the entropy of each of the variables and its joint entropy as $I(X; Y) = H(X) + H(Y) - H(X, Y)$. In addition to the above unnormalized version, we also included as features two normalized versions. The mutual information normalized by the joint entropy and the mutual information normalized by the minimum of the marginal entropies:

$$I_j(X; Y) = \frac{I(X; Y)}{H(X, Y)} \qquad I_h(X; Y) = \frac{I(X; Y)}{min(H(X), H(Y))}$$

Adjusted Mutual Information The Adjusted Mutual Information score is an adjustment of the Mutual Information measure. It corrects the effect of agreement solely due to chance, [8]. This feature is computed with the scikit-learn python package, [6].

Gaussian and Uniform Divergence These features are an estimation of the Kullback-Leibler divergence or *distance* of the distribution of the data with respect to a normalized Gaussian distribution and a uniform distribution respectively. After mean and variance normalization, the estimation of the Gaussian divergence is equivalent to the estimation of the differential entropy except for a constant factor.

$$D_g(X) = D(X||G) = H(X) - H(G) = H(X) - \frac{1}{2}\log(2\pi e)$$

An estimator of the differential entropy can also be used to compute the divergence respect an uniform distribution if the samples are first normalized in range:

$$X_u = \frac{X - min(X)}{max(X) - min(X)} \qquad D_u(X) = D(X_u||U) = H(X_u) - H(U) = H(X_u)$$

12.2.3 Conditional Distribution Variability Measures

In this section we define distribution variability measures that are used as tests of the spread of the conditional distribution $p(Y|X = x)$ for different values of x. If this variable is numerical we apply first the quantization process described in Sect. 12.2.1.

Standard Deviation of the Conditional Distributions This is a direct measure of the spread of the conditional distributions after normalization. If Y is a numerical variable, the conditional distribution $p(Y|X = x)$ is normalized for each value of x to have zero mean and then quantized as in Sect. 12.2.1. If Y is a categorical variable, the variability of the conditional distribution $p(Y|X = x)$ for different values of x is calculated after sorting these probabilities for each x. The standard deviation of the preprocessed conditional distributions is then computed as:

$$CDS(X, Y) = \sqrt{\frac{1}{M}\sum_{y=0}^{M-1} var_x(p_n(y|x))}$$

where $p_n(y|x)$ refers to the normalized conditional probability and var_x to the sample variance over x.

Standard Deviation of the Entropy, Skewness and Kurtosis These additional features use the standard deviation to quantify the spread of the entropy, variance and skewness of the conditional distributions for different values x of the hypothetical cause

$$HS(X, Y) = std_x(H(Y|X = x)) \qquad SS(X, Y) = std_x(skew(Y|X = x))$$

$$KS(X, Y) = std_x(kurtosis(Y|X = x))$$

Bayesian Error Probability This feature is an estimation of the average probability of error using the (discretized) conditional distributions. For each value of
x the probability of error is computed as one minus the probability of guessing y
given x if we choose for the prediction $\hat{y}$ the value that maximizes $p(Y|X = x)$.
$EP(X, Y) = E[p_e(x)]$ where $p_e(x) = 1 - max_y(p(Y|X = x))$.

12.2.4   Other Features

Number of Samples and Number of Unique Samples

Hilbert Schmidt Independence Criterion (HSIC) This standard independence
measure is computed using a python version of the MATLAB script provided by the
organizers.

Slope-Based Information Geometric Causal Inference (IGCI) The IGCI
approach for causality detection, Janzing et al. [3] proposes measures based on
the relative entropy and a *slope-based* measure that we also added to our set of
features.

Moments and Mixed Moments We included the skewness and kurtosis of each
of the variables as features, as well as the mixed moments $m_{1,2} = E[xy^2]$ and
$m_{1,3} = E[xy^3]$.

Pearson Correlation The *Pearson r* correlation coefficient computed by the *scipy*
python package, [4].

Polynomial Fit We propose two features based on a polynomial regression of order
2. The first feature is based on the absolute value of the second order coefficient. We
have observed that the causal direction usually requires a smaller coefficient. The
second feature measures the regression mean squared error or residual.

12.3   Classification Model Selection

We tested different learning methods for classification and regression. Gradient
Boosting, [2], significantly performed better that the rest of algorithms in our tenfold
cross-validation experiments on the training set after a manual hyperparameter
tuning. We used the scikit-learn implementation (GradientBoostingClassifier) with
500 boosting stages and individual regression estimators with a large depth (9).

The classification task of the ChaLearn cause-effect pair challenge is in fact a three-class problem. For each pair of variables A and B, we have a ternary truth value indicating whether A is a cause of B (+1), B is a cause of A (−1), or neither (0). The participants have to provide a single predicted value between $-\infty$ and $+\infty$, large positive values indicating that A is a cause of B with certainty, large negative values indicating that B is a cause of A with certainty, and middle range scores (near zero) indicate that neither A causes B nor B causes A. The official evaluation metric was the average of two Area Under the ROC curve (AUC) scores. The first AUC is computed associating the truth values 0 and −1 to the same class (the class 1 versus the rest), while the second AUC is computed grouping together the 1 and 0 classes (the class −1 versus the rest).

Note that the symmetry of the task allow us to *duplicate* the training sample pairs. Exchanging A with B in an example of class c provides a *new* example of the class $-c$.

To deal with this ternary classification problem we tested three different schemes:

1. A single ternary classification or regression model. The predicted value is computed in this case as $p_1 = p(1) - p(-1)$ where $p(1)$ and $p(-1)$ are the estimated probabilities assigned by the classifier to class 1 and class −1 respectively. Alternatively, we can use the output of any regression model. In the case of the selected Gradient Boosting model the classifier version with the *deviance* loss function gave better results than the regressor loss functions in our experiments.

2. A binary model for estimating the *direction* (class 1 versus class −1) and a binary model for *independence* classification (class 0 versus the rest). The first direction model is trained only with training sample pairs classified as 1 or −1, while the second independence model is trained with all the data after grouping class 1 and −1 in a single class. The predicted value is computed in this case as the product of the probabilities given by each of the models $p_2 = p_d(1)p_i(0)$ where $p_d(1)$ is the probability of class 1 given by the direction model and $p_i(0)$ is the independence probability provided by the second model.

3. A symmetric model based on two binary models. In this scheme we also have two binary models: a model for class 1 versus the rest and another model for class −1 versus the rest. In this sense, this configuration follows the same scheme of the evaluation metric. Both binary models are trained with all the training data after the corresponding relabeling of classes. The predicted value is then computed as the difference of the probability given by the first model to class 1 and the probability given by the second model to class −1, $p_3 = \frac{1}{2}p_{3,1}(1) - \frac{1}{2}p_{3,2}(-1)$.

Using the same set of selected features, the three schemes provide similar results as shown in Table 12.1. The proposed final model uses a equally weighted linear combination of the output of each of the three models to obtain an additional significant gain respect to the best performing scheme.

Table 12.1 Performance of the proposed schemes for the ternary model

Scheme	Score
1. Single ternary model	0.81223
2. Direction/independence models	0.81487
3. Symmetric models	0.81476
System combination	0.81960

Table 12.2 Results for different subset of the proposed features

Features	Score
Baseline(21)	0.742
Baseline(21) + Moment31(2)	0.750
Baseline(21) + Moment21(2)	0.757
Baseline(21) + Error probability(2)	0.749
Baseline(21) + Polyfit(2)	0.757
Baseline(21) + Polyfit error(2)	0.757
Baseline(21) + Skewness(2)	0.754
Baseline(21) + Kurtosis(2)	0.744
Baseline(21) + the above statistics set(14)	0.790
Baseline(21) + Standard deviation of conditional distributions(2)	0.779
Baseline(21) + Standard deviation of the skewness of conditional distributions(2)	0.765
Baseline(21) + Standard deviation of the kurtosis of conditional distributions(2)	0.759
Baseline(21) + Standard deviation of the entropy of conditional distributions(2)	0.759
Baseline(21) + Measures of variability of the conditional distribution(8)	0.789
Full set(43 features)	0.820

12.4 Results

The main training database includes hundreds of pairs of real variables with known causal relationships from diverse domains. The organizers of the challenge also intermixed those pairs with controls (pairs of independent variables and pairs of variables that are dependent but not causally related) and semi-artificial cause-effect pairs (real variables mixed in various ways to produce a given outcome). In addition, they also provided training datasets artificially generated.[1]

The results presented in this section correspond to the score of the test data given by the web submission system of the cause-effect pair challenge hosted by Kaggle. Previous cross-validation experiments on the training set provided similar results. Table 12.2 summarizes the results for different subsets of the proposed complete set of features. The baseline system includes 21 features: number of samples(1), number of unique samples(2), discrete entropy(2), normalized discrete entropy(2), discrete conditional entropy(2), discrete mutual information and the two

---

[1] http://www.causality.inf.ethz.ch/cause-effect.php?page=data.

normalized versions(3), adjusted mutual information(1), Gaussian divergence(2), uniform divergence(2), IGCI(2), HSIC(1), and Pearson R(1).

A more detailed analysis of the results of the proposed system and of other top ranking systems can be found in [1].

12.5   Conclusions

We have proposed several measures of the variability of conditional distributions as features to infer causal relationships in a given pair of variables. In particular, the proposed standard deviation of the normalized conditional distributions stands out as one of the best features in our results. The combination of the developed measures with standard information-theoretic and statistical measures provides a robust set of features to address the causality problem in the framework of the ChaLearn cause-effect pair challenge. In a test set with categorical, numerical and mixed pairs from diverse domains, the proposed method achieves an AUC score of 0.82.

Appendix: ChaLearn Cause-Effect Pair Challenge. Fact Sheet

Title: Conditional distribution variability measures for causality detection
Participant name, address, email and website: José A. R. Fonollosa, Universitat Politènica de Catalunya, c/Jordi Girona 1-3, Edifici D5, Barcelona 08034, SPAIN. jose.fonollosa@upc.edu, www.talp.upc.edu
Task solved: cause-effect pairs
Reference: José A. R. Fonollosa: Conditional distribution variability measures for causality detection. NIPS 2013 Workshop on Causality
Method:

- Preprocessing. Normalization of numerical variables. Relabeling of categorical variables
- Causal discovery. Standard features plus new measures base on variability measures of the conditional distributions $p(Y|X = x)$ for different values of x
- Feature selection. Greedy selection
- Classification. Gradient Boosting. Combination of three different multiclass schemes
- Model selection/hyperparameter selection. Manual hyperparameter selection

Results:

- quantitative advantages: the developed model is simple and very fast compared to other top ranking models

Table 12.3 Result table

Dataset/task	Official score	Post-deadline score
Final test	0.81052	0.81960

- qualitative advantages: it relaxes the noise independence assumption introducing less strict similarity measures for the conditional probability $p(Y|X = x)$.

The complete python code for training the model and reproducing the presented results (Table 12.3) is available at https://github.com/jarfo/cause-effect. The training time is about 45 min on a 4-core server, and computing the predictions for the test takes about 12 min.

References

1. Isabelle Guyon. Results and analysis of the 2013 chalearn cause-effect pair challenge. In *Proceedings of NIPS 2013 Workshop on Causality: Large-scale Experiment Design and Inference of Causal Mechanisms*, 2014.
2. Trevor Hastie, Robert Tibshirani, and Jerome Friedman. *The Elements of Statistical Learning*. Springer Series in Statistics. Springer New York Inc., New York, NY, USA, 2001.
3. Dominik Janzing, Joris Mooij, Kun Zhang, Jan Lemeire, Jakob Zscheischler, Povilas Daniušis, Bastian Steudel, and Bernhard Schölkopf. Information-geometric approach to inferring causal directions. *Artificial Intelligence*, 182:1–31, 2012.
4. Eric Jones, Travis Oliphant, Pearu Peterson, et al. SciPy: Open source scientific tools for Python, 2001–. URL http://www.scipy.org/.
5. G. A. Miller. Note on the bias of information estimates, 1955.
6. F. Pedregosa, G. Varoquaux, A. Gramfort, V. Michel, B. Thirion, O. Grisel, M. Blondel, P. Prettenhofer, R. Weiss, V. Dubourg, J. Vanderplas, A. Passos, D. Cournapeau, M. Brucher, M. Perrot, and E. Duchesnay. Scikit-learn: Machine learning in Python. *Journal of Machine Learning Research*, 12:2825–2830, 2011.
7. Alexander Statnikov, Mikael Henaff, Nikita Lytkin, and Constantin Aliferis. New methods for separating causes from effects in genomics data. *BMC Genomics*, 13(Suppl 8):S22, 2012. ISSN 1471-2164. doi: 10.1186/1471-2164-13-S8-S22. URL http://www.biomedcentral.com/1471-2164/13/S8/S22.
8. Nguyen Xuan Vinh, Julien Epps, and James Bailey. Information theoretic measures for clusterings comparison: is a correction for chance necessary? In *Proceedings of the 26th Annual International Conference on Machine Learning*, ICML '09, pages 1073–1080, New York, NY, USA, 2009. ACM. ISBN 978-1-60558-516-1. doi: 10.1145/1553374.1553511. URL http://doi.acm.org/10.1145/1553374.1553511.

Chapter 13
Feature Importance in Causal Inference for Numerical and Categorical Variables

Bram Minnaert

13.1 Introduction

Consider the following problem: we have a set of observations of (A, B) pairs. Without any context, can we give an estimate of the causal relationship between A and B? It is possible that A causes B (A → B), that B causes A (B → A), that they are independent (A | B) or that they have a common cause (C → A and C → B).

Recent years a number of very promising methods have been proposed to predict causal relationships [3, 8, 10, 12, 13, 15]. Most studies in the field of causal discovery require A and B to be numerical. This paper will concentrate on the differences between numerical and categorical data.

This paper will define some features and via machine learning techniques it will investigate the importances of these features and estimate the probability that A causes B:

$$P(A \rightarrow B) \in [0, 1]. \tag{13.1}$$

Section 13.2 will describe the model on a high level. Section 13.3 will zoom in on the different submodels. In Sect. 13.4 we look at the results of the model and we will focus on the importances of the features. We will focus on the differences between numerical and categorical data since only few studies have already been performed on categorical data [14]. At last, we will draw conclusions in Sect. 13.5.

B. Minnaert (✉)
ArcelorMittal, Ghent, Belgium

© Springer Nature Switzerland AG 2019
I. Guyon et al. (eds.), *Cause Effect Pairs in Machine Learning*,
The Springer Series on Challenges in Machine Learning,
https://doi.org/10.1007/978-3-030-21810-2_13

13.2 Model Description

Figure 13.1 shows the architecture of the model.

After some preprocessing steps, such as data normalisation, a list of features is extracted for every $A - B$ pair, for example the correlation coefficient. The preprocessing step and feature extraction is performed on a large number of $A - B$ pairs, which were provided in a training set. Because we know the correct solution for these $A - B$ pairs in the training set (the solution in the causal relationship, for example: A → B), we can apply supervised learning methods. Via the ensemble method *Random Forest* a large collection of classification trees is generated for the training set (features → causal relationship). After training we can use this trained model to predict new $A - B$ pairs with unknown causal relationship.

The model has been developed in Python and makes uses of the libraries Numpy, Pandas and SciPy [11]. The figures in this paper have been made using matplotlib [9].

In order to make this study replicable, the code has been made available on the following url: https://github.com/braincomic/CauseEffectChallenge.

13.3 Model Steps

13.3.1 Preprocessing

The following preprocessing steps are executed.

• Data normalisation if numerical (feature scaling). This is common in data processing. The range of A/B values can vary widely. Suppose that we would like to calculate the distances between two points. If we don't perform normalisation, this distance will be large if ranges of values are large and small if ranges of values are small.
• Reordering the categories from 0 to n if A/B is categorical in such a way that $E(B|A)$ is increasing in A. Figure 13.2 show examples. This will enable the numerical features to perform better on categorical data.

We have not performed outlier removal as preprocessing step because outliers can give an indication of a causal relationship.

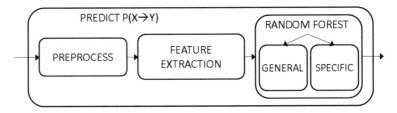

Fig. 13.1 Overview of the causal inference model

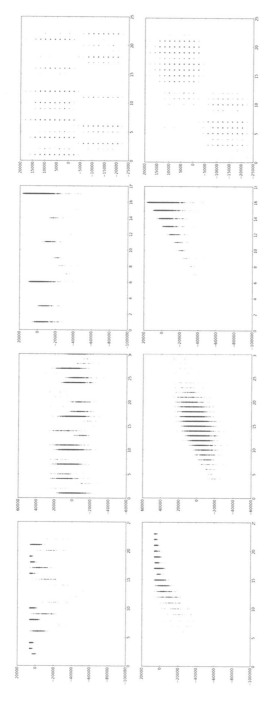

Fig. 13.2 Reordering of categorical values. The figures in the second row are the reordered versions of the corresponding figures of the first row

13.3.2 Features

In this step we extract 211 features. We will not describe the full list. Instead, we will describe groupings.

1. Number of samples: number of samples in the data set, number of unique samples, difference of unique samples A versus B, fraction of unique samples. These features serve mainly as control, we don't expect these features to matter.
2. Basic statistics: median, minimum, maximum, range, percentiles, skewness, curtosis and minimal precision.
3. Correlation: Pearson product-moment correlation coefficient, Spearman's rank correlation coefficient.
4. Polynomial regressions, as described in Hoyer et al. [8], ranging from degree 1 (linear regression) to degree 4. One feature will determine the best degree itself by splitting the sample into a training and test set, up to degree 9. Examples are shown in Fig. 13.3.
5. Logistic regression.
6. Moving average: quality of the moving average function
7. Uniformity and Normality.

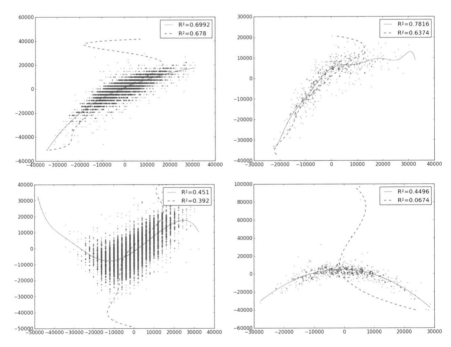

Fig. 13.3 In these figures the variable is the cause of the Y variable. We expect better regressions $Y=f(X)$, the green line, compared to regressions $X=f(Y)$, the red line. These figures are cherry picked to make the idea more clear, it is not always this obvious, unfortunately

8. Remainder test: first a regression is made (for example, regression with degree 4) and then the difference is made of the noisy data with the regression. The resulting distribution is tested for uniformity and normality.

9. Inversibility test: specific test to check if some polynomial regression is inversible or not.

10. Outlier detection.

11. Information theory features: Shannon entropy, conditional entropy, mutual information, homogeneity, completeness, v-measure and information gain. This is all calculated after binning. For each feature we used either fixed width or fixed frequency discretisation. We choose the method that obtained the best results on the training set. This also determined the number of bins.

12. IGCI: Information Geometric Causal Inference, both the entropy based and the integral-approximation based estimator, both for uniform and gaussian noise [10].

13. Clustering: quality of vector quantisation using k-means clustering.

13.3.3   Random Forest

We make use of a random forest regression [1]. This is an ensemble learning method that creates many classification trees when training the model.

Instead of using a random forest, we also tried gradient boosting [5, 6].

Even though gradient boosting scores slightly better than random forest in a comparison of 11 binary classification methods [2], random forest obtained better scores in the training set predictions, so we used random forest.

The training also showed that a random forest regression performed better than a random forest classification.

13.3.3.1   Training

We train the features using a random forest regression. In a random forest a number of features is randomly selected to train a classification tree. The training of this tree is not done on the entire training set, but only a random sample. This is done many time, so a lot of classification trees are generated, which we call a forest.

We do not only perform this training on the entire training set, but we train it on several subsets:

- Full training set.
- Numerical → Numerical.
- Categorical → Categorical.
- Categorical → Numerical.
- Numerical → Categorical.

In these subsets, binary variables are treated as Categorical.

13.3.3.2 Predicting

In the previous step we have trained our model via the ensemble method *random forest*, resulting into many classification trees. Now we can use this trained model to make predictions on new $A - B$ pairs. In the previous step we have not trained one model, we have trained five models. In order to predict a new $A - B$ pair, we need to take the weighted average of different predictions of different trained models.

1. Predict with the model trained with the full training set. We call this function

$$Pred_{\text{full}}(A, B) \tag{13.2}$$

2. Predict with the model trained with the specific training set for these types. We use T_A as the type of A (Numerical or Categorical) and T_B the type of B. For example, $Pred_{Categorical, Numerical}$.

$$Pred_{T_A, T_B}(A, B) \tag{13.3}$$

$$\text{with } T_A, T_B \in \{\text{``Numerical''}, \text{``Categorical''}\}$$

3. Take the weighted average of these two predictions. As we will see in Sect. 13.4, some models based on the specific training sets (types) achieve much better scores than others. Therefore the better models are given an extra benefit via a weight factor W that depend on the type of A and B. Normalisation is added: worst possible score is 0, best is 1.

$$P(A \to B) = \frac{W_{\text{full}, T_A, T_B} Pred_{\text{full}}(A, B) + W_{\text{spec}, T_A, T_B} Pred_{T_A, T_B}(A, B)}{\text{MAX}(W_{\text{full}, T_A, T_B} + W_{\text{spec}, T_A, T_B})} \tag{13.4}$$

If we would like to predict a ternary truth value $T(A, B)$ indicating whether A is a cause of B ($+1$), B is a cause of A (-1), or neither (0), we simply take the following difference.

$$T(A, B) = P(A \to B) - P(B \to A) \tag{13.5}$$

13.4 Results

13.4.1 AUC Score

We use the AUC (Area Under the ROC curve) as evaluation metric. The predictions of the full model are evaluated against a test set of 4050 A-B pairs. When we evaluate the ternary truth value T we use the average of the two AUC score related to $P(A \to B)$ and $P(B \to A)$

The following table summarizes the results. In the ChaLearn cause-effect pair challenge, hosted by Kaggle[4], this AUC score resulted in the fifth place from 267 competitors.

Subset	AUC score
Num → Num	0.818[a]
Cat → Cat	0.571[a]
Cat → Num	0.690[a]
Num → Cat	0.608[a]
Total	0.788

[a] As the detailed final results of the ChaLearn cause-effect pair challenge, hosted by Kaggle[4], has not yet been published, these lines contains the results on the cross validation set instead of the final test set. The total score on the other hand is based on the test set

We seem to have achieved the best job in predicting Numerical → Numerical. Categorical → Categorical on the other hand didn't work out well.

13.4.2 Feature Importances

Random forest regressions come with a very handy scoring of the features: the variable importance. For every feature we have calculated the sum of the variable importances and we have listed them in Fig. 13.4.

Feature category	SPECIFIC				FULL
	Num->Num	Cat-->Cat	Cat->Num	Num->Cat	
Number samples	0.2	0.5	0.4	0.7	0.3
Basic stats	1.5	11.7	4.4	16.2	1.8
Correlation	0.4	1.7	4.9	6.8	0.8
Polynomial regression	90.6	47.0	7.7	52.1	92.6
Logistic regression	0.0	2.0	0.2	0.7	0.0
Moving average	0.1	1.0	0.5	0.6	0.1
Uniformity and Normality test	4.7	5.7	0.9	3.1	1.9
Remainder test	0.5	1.2	0.5	1.0	0.3
Inversibility	0.1	0.4	0.1	0.2	0.0
Outlier detection	0.2	0.7	0.7	0.8	0.2
Information Theory	1.4	26.7	78.9	14.3	1.6
IGCI	0.1	0.3	0.4	0.5	0.1
Clustering	0.1	0.9	0.4	3.1	0.1
Total	100.0	100.0	100.0	100.0	100.0

Fig. 13.4 Importances of feature categories in the different submodels in sum of the percentages of the features in this category

Some features always perform badly:

- Logistic regression, even on the categorical data.
- Moving average
- Outlier detection. It seems we should have performed outlier removal in the preprocessing steps, or at least treated them separately.
- IGCI
- Clustering

13.4.2.1 Numerical → Numerical Feature Importance

Numerical to numerical is totally ruled by the polynomial regression features. The most important features are listed below.

- The most important feature is the R^2 value of a polynomial regression with variable degree. The degree is determined by splitting the data set into a training set to find the best polynomial regression and a cross-validation set to measure the quality of the regression. It's feature importance is 75.1%.
- The degree of this polynomial has feature importance 9.9%.

Interpretation: if A causes B, then the regression $B = f_1(A) + \epsilon_1$ will have a higher quality (better R^2) and will be simpler (lower degree) than the regression $A = f_2(B) + \epsilon_2$.

13.4.2.2 Categorical → Categorical Feature Importance

- Surprisingly the polynomial regressions do very well on categorical data. When we introduced reordering categories as described in Sect. 13.3.1, the variable importance of these features raised dramatically. All polynomial features sum up to 47.1%.
- Several features of information theory score pretty well. The best are the mutual information and correlated entropy, defined as the mutual information devised by the Shannon entropy. The corresponding feature importances are 12.6% and 7.5%.

13.4.2.3 Categorical → Numerical Feature Importance

- The features of information theory score very high. The best are the mutual information and the v-measure, having importances of 49.3% and 23.8%

13.4.2.4   Numerical → Categorical Feature Importance

- The polynomial regressions again have the highest importance, summing to 52.1%.
- From information theory, the mutual information has 9.1% importance.

13.5   Conclusion

When predicting causal relationships, the category of features that gives the most information heavily depends on the type of the variables: numerical or categorical. Thanks to category reordering the numerical features are still important to categorical data. The following table summarizes the most important categories of features.

Subset	Most important feature categories
Num → Num	Polynomial regression
Cat → Cat	Polynomial regression, information theory
Cat → Num	Information theory
Num → Cat	Polynomial regression, information theory
Total	Polynomial regression

Acknowledgements I would like to thank Kaggle and Chalearn to stir my interest into this topic [7] and I thank Isabelle Guyon and Mehreen Saeed for their assistance to make my source code portable.

References

1. Leo Breiman. Random forests. *Mach. Learn.*, 45(1):5–32, October 2001. ISSN 0885-6125. URL http://dx.doi.org/10.1023/A:1010933404324.
2. Rich Caruana and Alexandru Niculescu-Mizil. An empirical comparison of supervised learning algorithms. In *Proceedings of the 23rd International Conference on Machine Learning*, ICML '06, pages 161–168, New York, NY, USA, 2006. ACM. ISBN 1-59593-383-2. URL http://doi.acm.org/10.1145/1143844.1143865.
3. Povilas Daniušis, Dominik Janzing, Joris M. Mooij, Jakob Zscheischler, Bastian Steudel, Kun Zhang, and Bernhard Schölkopf. Inferring deterministic causal relations. In *Proceedings of the 26th Annual Conference on Uncertainty in Artificial Intelligence (UAI-10)*, 2010. URL http://event.cwi.nl/uai2010/papers/UAI2010_0121.pdf.
4. Isabelle Guyon et al. Results and analysis of the 2013 chalearn cause-effect pair challenge. 2014.
5. Jerome H. Friedman. Greedy function approximation: A gradient boosting machine. *Annals of Statistics*, 29:1189–1232, 2000.
6. Jerome H. Friedman. Stochastic gradient boosting. *Comput. Stat. Data Anal.*, 38(4):367–378, February 2002. ISSN 0167-9473. URL http://dx.doi.org/10.1016/S0167-9473(01)00065-2.

7. Isbelle Guyon. Cause-effect pairs challenge, 2013. Isabelle Guyon (ChaLearn) and Ben Hamner (Kaggle) and Alexander Statnikov (NYU) and Mikael Henaff (NYU) and Vincent Lemaire (Orange) and Bernhard Shoelkopf (MPI).

8. Patrik O. Hoyer, Dominik Janzing, Joris M. Mooij, Jonas Peters, and Bernhard Schölkopf. Nonlinear causal discovery with additive noise models. In D. Koller, D. Schuurmans, Y. Bengio, and L. Bottou, editors, *Advances in Neural Information Processing Systems 21 (NIPS*2008)*, pages 689–696, 2009.

9. J. D. Hunter. Matplotlib: A 2d graphics environment. *Computing In Science & Engineering*, 9(3):90–95, 2007.

10. Dominik Janzing, Joris Mooij, Kun Zhang, Jan Lemeire, Jakob Zscheischler, Povilas Daniušis, Bastian Steudel, and Bernhard Schölkopf. Information-geometric approach to inferring causal directions. *Artif. Intell.*, 182–183:1–31, May 2012. ISSN 0004-3702. URL http://dx.doi.org/10.1016/j.artint.2012.01.002.

11. Eric Jones, Travis Oliphant, Pearu Peterson, et al. SciPy: Open source scientific tools for Python, 2001–. URL http://www.scipy.org/.

12. Joris M. Mooij, Oliver Stegle, Dominik Janzing, Kun Zhang, and Bernhard Schölkopf. Probabilistic latent variable models for distinguishing between cause and effect. In J. Lafferty, C. K. I. Williams, J. Shawe-Taylor, R.S. Zemel, and A. Culotta, editors, *Advances in Neural Information Processing Systems 23 (NIPS*2010)*, pages 1687–1695, 2010. URL http://books.nips.cc/papers/files/nips23/NIPS2010_1270.pdf.

13. Shohei Shimizu, Patrik O. Hoyer, Aapo Hyvärinen, and Antti Kerminen. A linear non-gaussian acyclic model for causal discovery. *J. Mach. Learn. Res.*, 7:2003–2030, December 2006. ISSN 1532-4435. URL http://dl.acm.org/citation.cfm?id=1248547.1248619.

14. Xiaohai Sun, Dominik Janzing, and Bernhard Schölkopf. Causal inference by choosing graphs with most plausible Markov kernels. In *ISAIM*, 2006. URL http://dblp.uni-trier.de/db/conf/isaim/isaim2006.html#SunJS06.

15. K Zhang and A Hyvärinen. Distinguishing causes from effects using nonlinear acyclic causal models. In I Guyon, D Janzing, and B Schölkopf, editors, *JMLR Workshop and Conference Proceedings, Volume 6*, pages 157–164, Cambridge, MA, USA, 2010. MIT Press. URL http://www.is.tuebingen.mpg.defileadmin/user_upload/files/publications/2012/zhang-hyvärinen_2010.pdf.

Chapter 14
Markov Blanket Ranking Using Kernel-Based Conditional Dependence Measures

Eric V. Strobl and Shyam Visweswaran

14.1 Introduction

Causality refers to a relation between a variable and another variable such that the latter variable is understood to be a consequence of the former. Three groups of methods have been described in the literature to infer causality from observational data. The most popular group includes conditional independence test methods such as PC [14] and FCI [13] that attempt to construct a graph representing all causal relationships in a dataset. The second group takes a more local approach by identifying the Markov blanket, or those variables that are conditionally independent on a target given the remaining variables; examples include IAMB [16], HITON-MB [1], and MMMB [17]. The final group identifies pair-wise causal relationships by comparing the complexities of a forward and backward model such as LiNGAM [11] and additive noise models [5]). However, to remain tractable, all of these methods do not consider all possible multivariate interactions between variables. As a result, they may fail to identify subtle dependencies.

A number of kernel-based methods have recently been developed that perform multivariate conditional dependence measurements in reproducing kernel Hilbert space (RKHS; [2, 18]). In this paper, we take advantage of these methods by incorporating either one of two kernel-based conditional dependence measures (K-CDMs; [2, 18]) in a backward elimination algorithm to identify the Markov blanket in a fully multivariate fashion. The rest of this paper is structured as follows. We first provide background on Bayesian networks in Sect. 14.2 and then discuss related work in Sect. 14.3. In Sect. 14.4, we describe the new algorithm that identifies the

E. V. Strobl (✉) · S. Visweswaran
Department of Biomedical Informatics, University of Pittsburgh School of Medicine, Pittsburgh, PA, USA
e-mail: evs17@pitt.edu; shv3@pitt.edu

© Springer Nature Switzerland AG 2019
I. Guyon et al. (eds.), *Cause Effect Pairs in Machine Learning*,
The Springer Series on Challenges in Machine Learning,
https://doi.org/10.1007/978-3-030-21810-2_14

Markov blanket of a target by iteratively eliminating variables that minimize K-CDM. We finally provide results comparing the proposed algorithm with other feature ranking and subset selection methods in Sect. 14.5. Section 14.6 provides a brief conclusion.

14.2 Background

From here on, upper-case letters in italics will denote single variables, and upper-case letters in bold italics will denote sets of variables. A Bayesian network is a probabilistic model that combines a directed acyclic graph (DAG) with parameters to represent a joint probability distribution over a set of random variables. More specifically, the DAG contains a node for every variable in the dataset, and an edge between a pair of nodes $R - S$ is absent if R is independent of S given T for some T, and edge $R - S$ is present if R is dependent on S given T for all T [6]. The absence of edges in a DAG can be determined by performing tests of conditional independence. Two variables R and S are conditionally independent given a third variable T if and only if the value of R provides no information about the value of S and vice versa given the value of T. In mathematical notation, $R \perp\!\!\!\perp S|T$.

We now define Y as a target node, and $\mathbf{X}$ as the entire dataset without Y. The Markov blanket of Y ($\mathbf{MB}(Y)$) is a subset of $\mathbf{X}$ that includes the target's parent, child and spousal nodes. $\mathbf{MB}(Y)$ can be identified by showing that a target node is conditionally independent of all other nodes given its parents, children and spouses:

$$Y \perp\!\!\!\perp \{\mathbf{X}\backslash\mathbf{MB}(Y)\} \,|\mathbf{MB}(Y) \Leftrightarrow Y \perp\!\!\!\perp \mathbf{X}|\mathbf{MB}(Y). \tag{14.1}$$

In this paper, we assess conditional dependence between arbitrary distributions within reproducing kernel Hilbert spaces (RKHSs). Specifically, we map $\mathbf{X}$ and Y into RKHSs $\mathscr{F}$ and $\mathscr{G}$ respectively using two positive semidefinite kernels $K_{\mathbf{X}}$: $\mathscr{X} \times \mathscr{X} \to \mathbb{R}$ and K_Y : $\mathscr{Y} \times \mathscr{Y} \to \mathbb{R}$. There then exists a conditional cross-covariance operator $\Sigma_{YY|\mathbf{X}}$: $\mathscr{G} \to \mathscr{G}$ for any function $g \in \mathscr{G}$ as well as an inner product $\langle \cdot, \cdot \rangle_{\mathscr{G}}$ such that:

$$\langle g, \Sigma_{YY|\mathbf{X}}g \rangle_{\mathscr{G}} = \mathbb{E}_X \left[Var_{Y|\mathbf{X}} \left[g\left(Y\right) \mid \mathbf{X} \right] \right], \tag{14.2}$$

which represents the residual errors of predicting $g(Y)$ with $\mathbf{X}$ [2].

We now denote $\mathbf{X_s}$ as some subset of the variables in $\mathbf{X}$ such that $\mathbf{X_s} \subseteq \mathbf{X}$. Then, the conditional cross-covariance operator exhibits the following property: $\Sigma_{YY|\mathbf{X_s}} \geq \Sigma_{YY|\mathbf{X}}$, where the order is determined by the trace operator, and the equality holds when the subset $\mathbf{X_s}$ includes $\mathbf{MB}(Y)$ so that $Y \perp\!\!\!\perp \mathbf{X}|\mathbf{X_s}$.

Empirically, we can compute the kernel matrices $K_{\mathbf{X_s}}$ and K_Y from a sample size of n drawn i.i.d. from the distribution $P(\mathbf{X}, Y)$. The trace of the empirical conditional cross-covariance operator is then defined by:

$$M^1 = tr\left(G_Y(G_{\mathbf{X}_s} + n\varepsilon I_n)^{-1}\right), \tag{14.3}$$

where $G_{\mathbf{X}_s} = \left(I_n - \frac{1}{n}1_n1_n^T\right)K_{\mathbf{X}_s}\left(I_n - \frac{1}{n}1_n1_n^T\right)$ with n representing sample size, I_n an $n \times n$ identity matrix, and 1_n a vector of ones. The regularization term $\varepsilon \to 0$ is added for the inversion. A similar measure proposed by Zhang et al. [18] (Equation 12) is based on eigenvalue decompositions of centralized kernel matrices:

$$M^2 = tr\left(T_{\mathbf{X}_s}G_Y T_{\mathbf{X}_s}\right), \tag{14.4}$$

where $T_{X_S} = \varepsilon\left(G_{\mathbf{X}_s} + \varepsilon I_n\right)^{-1}$. Unlike M^1, this new measure was developed so that the authors could create a test of conditional independence using a statistic shown in their Equation 13 whose null distribution is approximated by a gamma distribution. Note that both Y and $\mathbf{X}_s$ can each be multivariate with either of the two K-CDMs. Moreover, both K-CDMs do not make assumptions about the data distributions of Y and $\mathbf{X}_s$ or their functional relationship.

14.3 Related Work

The original Hilbert Schmidt Independence Criterion (HSIC; [3]) is a sensitive measure of dependence between two kernels, where larger values denote a greater degree of dependence. Song et al. [12] developed an algorithm called BAHSIC that uses HSIC for feature selection by embedding the target in the first kernel and the remaining variables in the second kernel; the algorithm then uses backward elimination to remove variables from the second kernel that maximize HSIC. In practice, the algorithm can detect subtle dependencies and help increase classification accuracy to a greater extent than many other feature selection algorithms.

HSIC unfortunately can have difficulty in detecting all of the variables in $\mathbf{MB}(Y)$, since some of these variables may only show a weak association with the target. Measures of conditional dependence may instead be more useful in this regard. Nevertheless, correctly identifying the subset of variables to condition on can be difficult as the number of possible subsets grows exponentially with the number of variables [15]. Markov blanket discovery algorithms including IAMB, HITON-MB, and MMMB thus incorporate a forward selection phase, where variables are required to display an association to the target before being included in the conditioning set. For example, the HITON-MB algorithm relies on a univariate association between the tested variable R and the target Y. On the other hand, the IAMB and MMMB algorithms test the association between R and Y relative to a growing conditioning set of previously selected variables. In other words, both IAMB and MMMB initially rely on a univariate relationship with Y but gradually become more multivariate. These forward selection strategies can be suboptimal because some variables may reveal a relationship with the target only when all the other variables in $\mathbf{MB}(Y)$ are included in the conditioning set.

Several other limitations have been described in the literature. First, HITON-MB and MMMB may identify incorrect variables in the second step, since there are certain conditions under which variables *not* in $\mathbf{MB}(Y)$ can enter $\mathbf{MB}(Y)$ as described in Peña et al. [9]. Moreover, both these algorithms rely on HITON-PC and MMPC which also have shortcomings. The PC algorithms assume that if A is not a member of the set of variables which are parents and children of Y ($\mathbf{pc}(Y)$), then $Y \perp\!\!\!\perp A | \mathbf{B}$ for some $\mathbf{B} \subseteq \mathbf{pc}(Y)$, so any node *not* in $\mathbf{pc}(Y)$ is removed, which is not always true (an example of such a circumstance is in Table 2 of Peña et al. [9]). Second, Lou and Obradovic [7] highlight that conditional independence testing may become unreliable with small sample sizes. As a result, they have instead promoted algorithms that rely on sensitive dependence measurements such as HSIC as opposed to tests in order to discover $\mathbf{MB}(Y)$. However, in this paper, we will show that a new algorithm using Eqs. (14.3) or (14.4) can in fact perform very well by similarly avoiding statistical testing.

The main ideas used in this paper are motivated by the work of Fukumizu et al. [2], in which the authors introduced a method of kernel dimension reduction using Eq. (14.3). However, their method cannot be directly used to find $\mathbf{MB}(Y)$, since it finds orthogonal projections of $\mathbf{X}$ with respect to *kernel-induced feature* space. In this paper, we select variables with respect to *input* space to make the kernel-based conditional dimensionality reduction method more applicable to $\mathbf{MB}(Y)$ discovery.

14.4 The Algorithm

14.4.1 Main Idea

We discover $\mathbf{MB}(Y)$ using backward elimination. First, consider measuring the conditional dependence of Y and $\mathbf{X}$ given $\mathbf{X_s}$, where $\mathbf{X_s}$ is set to $\mathbf{X}$. Clearly, the conditional dependence measure is zero, since $\mathbf{X}$ cannot explain Y given itself. Next, consider removing a variable from the conditioning set $\mathbf{X_s}$. Since a target is completely shielded from the other variables given its $\mathbf{MB}(Y)$ by the definition of a Markov blanket, eliminating a variable in $\mathbf{MB}(Y)$ from $\mathbf{X_s}$ will cause the K-CDM to return a *larger* value (assuming enough sample size), since now $\mathbf{X}$ can better explain Y when $\mathbf{X_s}$ is missing a variable in $\mathbf{MB}(Y)$. In contrast, removing a variable *not* in $\mathbf{MB}(Y)$ will make *no difference*, since the conditional dependence measure is still zero if $\mathbf{X_s}$ contains $\mathbf{MB}(Y)$. This process of successively testing the removal of a variable in the conditioning set $\mathbf{X_s}$ and then permanently removing the variable that minimizes K-CDM is repeated until $\mathbf{X_s}$ is empty.

14.4.2 *Implementation*

The proposed method is a feature ranking algorithm that performs backward elimination using K-CDM. The pseudo-code for the method is shown in Algorithm 1, such that K-CDM is written as:

$$M^*(Y, \mathbf{X_s}, \sigma),$$

which denotes M^1 or M^2 evaluated with Y, $\mathbf{X_s}$, and σ such that σ is the set of kernel hyperparameters (if any).

The algorithm works as follows. It first computes K-CDM for every variable eliminated from the conditioning set $\mathbf{X_s}$ using appropriate kernel hyperparameters σ (if any) chosen with a user defined method Ξ. For example, the Gaussian sigma hyperparameter can be defined as the median distance between data points. The identified variable X which minimizes K-CDM when removed is then permanently removed from $\mathbf{X_s}$ and placed into $\mathbf{X}^\dagger$. The above procedure is repeated until $\mathbf{X_s}$ is empty. The underlying principle behind the algorithm is thus to find the variable combination that can best explain the dependence between Y and $\mathbf{X}$ by iteratively eliminating those variables that can least explain the dependence.

Note that the above procedure has some advantages over previous methods from the nature of directly performing backward elimination rather than first performing a forward selection step. First, the method considers *all* possible multivariate relationships in $\mathbf{MB}(Y)$, since all variables in $\mathbf{MB}(Y)$ are eliminated from $\mathbf{X_s}$ *after* the other variables assuming sufficient sample size to detect the relationships. Second, the proposed algorithm outputs a ranking of variables defined by the relative amounts of conditional dependence across the entire dataset. As a result, the ranking represents the relative importance of each of the variables in $\mathbf{MB}(Y)$.

Algorithm 1: Backward elimination

---

1. **Input**: Target feature Y, non-target features $\mathbf{X}$
2. **Output**: Non-target features in ascending order $\mathbf{X}^\dagger$
3. $\mathbf{X_s} \leftarrow \mathbf{X}$
4. $\mathbf{X}^\dagger \leftarrow \emptyset$
5. **repeat**
6. $X \leftarrow \min\limits_{X \in \mathbf{X_s}} M^*(Y, \{\mathbf{X_s} \backslash X\}, \sigma), \sigma \in \Xi$
7. $\mathbf{X_s} \leftarrow \mathbf{X_s} \backslash X$
8. $\mathbf{X}^\dagger \leftarrow \mathbf{X}^\dagger \cup X$
9. **until** $\mathbf{X_s} = \emptyset$

Algorithm 2: Forward selection

---
1. **Input**: Target feature Y, non-target features $\mathbf{X}$
2. **Output**: Non-target features in descending order $\mathbf{X}^{\dagger}$
3. $\mathbf{X_s} \leftarrow \mathbf{X}$
4. $\mathbf{X}^{\dagger} \leftarrow \emptyset$
5. **repeat**
6. $\qquad X \leftarrow \min_{X \in \mathbf{X_s}} M^*(Y, \{\mathbf{X}^{\dagger} \cup X\}, \sigma), \sigma \in \varXi$
7. $\qquad \mathbf{X_s} \leftarrow \mathbf{X_s} \backslash X$
8. $\qquad \mathbf{X}^{\dagger} \leftarrow \mathbf{X}^{\dagger} \cup X$
9. **until** $\mathbf{X_s} = \emptyset$

The forward selection procedure (Algorithm 2) is faster and can be implemented by including variables in $\mathbf{X}^{\dagger}$ in line 6 rather than removing variables from $\mathbf{X_s}$. However, this method underperforms backward elimination in practice and is *not* guaranteed to return $\mathbf{MB}(Y)$ in the infinite sample limit, since conditional dependence is not assessed within the context of the other variables in $\mathbf{X}$. Also note that the output is in descending order in $\mathbf{X}^{\dagger}$ instead of in ascending order.

14.4.3   Proof of Correctness

Theorem *The final variables in* $\mathbf{X}^{\dagger}$ *from Algorithm 1 will include* $\mathbf{MB}(Y)$ *under the assumptions that (1) K-CDM is defined by Eq. (14.3) or (14.4), and (2) the dataset* $\mathbf{X}$ *has an infinite sample size and is drawn i.i.d. from a joint probability distribution faithful to a DAG.*

Proof First, a lower value returned from Eq. (14.3) or (14.4) denotes a higher degree of conditional independence between Y and $\mathbf{X}$ given $\mathbf{X_s}$ than a higher value by design. Second, Y is conditionally independent of $\mathbf{X}$ given $\mathbf{MB}(Y)$ by the definition of a Markov blanket. As a result, K-CDM is guaranteed to return a higher value every time a variable in $\mathbf{MB}(Y)$ is tested for removal in line 6 compared to a variable *not* in $\mathbf{MB}(Y)$ assuming an infinite sample size, where the data points are drawn i.i.d. from a probability distribution faithful to a DAG. Then, if $\mathbf{X_s}$ contains variables in and not in $\mathbf{MB}(Y)$, a variable *not* in $\mathbf{MB}(Y)$ will be eliminated *earlier* from $\mathbf{X_s}$ in line 7. The variable eliminated from $\mathbf{X_s}$ will then be placed into $\mathbf{X}^{\dagger}$ in line 8. As a result, the final variables in $\mathbf{X}^{\dagger}$ will include $\mathbf{MB}(Y)$. ∎

14.4.4   Time Complexity

We assume that we remove $1 - \beta$ of $\mathbf{X_s}$ at every iteration. Then, the ith iteration of Algorithm 1 takes $O(\beta^{i-1}dn^3)$ where d represents the total number of variables and n^3 represents the inversion of the kernel when calculating K-CDM. Similarly, the ith iteration in Algorithm 2 has the same computational complexity if we iterate over every variable, but we can also stop the algorithm after obtaining t variables. In this case, the total number of iterations γ is $t = d\left[1 - (1 - \beta)^\gamma\right]$ which will require $\sum_{i=0}^{\gamma-1} d(1 - \beta)^i = d\left[1 - (1 - \beta)^\gamma\right]/\beta = t/\beta$ operations. Algorithm 2 thus takes $O(tn^3/\beta)$ time to discover t variables.

14.5   Experiments

14.5.1   Evaluation

We included two K-CDMs in Algorithm 1 by using Eq. (14.3) or 14.4, which we will now denote as Proposed-F and Proposed-Z respectively. We compared Proposed-F and Proposed-Z with four feature ranking methods including BAHSIC, Relief-F and SVM-RFE. Rankings were normalized to compare variables with different sized Markov blankets as follows. If the variables in $\mathbf{MB}(Y)$ were correctly identified back-to-back, then those variables were given the same rank. However, a break in the correct identification led to a higher rank. For example, if variables 2, 3 and 4 are in $\mathbf{MB}(Y)$ while 1, 5, and 6 are not, then an output of 6,3,5,4,2,1 in ascending order would be converted to the ranking 5,4,3,2,2,1. The algorithm which provides a lower mean rank of $\mathbf{MB}(Y)$ was then judged to perform better. In the example, the mean rank is 2.666, since the ranks of $\mathbf{MB}(Y)$ are 4,2,2.

Next, we used the following accuracy measure in order to compare Algorithm 1 with three conditional dependence-based feature subset selection methods including IAMB, HITON-MB and MMMB:

$$A\left(\mathbf{X}_c^\dagger, \mathbf{MB}(Y)\right) = \frac{\left|\mathbf{X}_c^\dagger \cap \mathbf{MB}(Y)\right|}{\left|\mathbf{X}_c^\dagger \cup \mathbf{MB}(Y)\right|} * 100, \qquad (14.5)$$

where $\mathbf{X}_c^\dagger$ is the subset output from the conditional dependence algorithms or, for Proposed-F and Z, $\mathbf{X}_c^\dagger$ is $\mathbf{X}^\dagger$ clipped to the size of $\mathbf{MB}(Y)$. For example, if variables 2, 3 and 4 are in $\mathbf{MB}(Y)$ while 1, 5, and 6 are not, then an output of 6,3,5,4,2,1 from Algorithm 1 would be converted 4,2,1. Also, $\left|\mathbf{X}_c^\dagger \cap \mathbf{MB}(Y)\right|$ is the cardinality of the intersection of the subset $\mathbf{X}_c^\dagger$ and the known $\mathbf{MB}(Y)$ and $\left|\mathbf{X}_c^\dagger \cup \mathbf{MB}(Y)\right|$ is the cardinality of the union. Note that score A is equal to 100 when the algorithm outputs the exact $\mathbf{MB}(Y)$. On the other hand, decreasing the cardinality of $\mathbf{X}_c^\dagger$ by failing to identify parts of the $\mathbf{MB}(Y)$ or increasing the cardinality of $\mathbf{X}_c^\dagger$ by random guessing both decrease A.

14.5.2 Synthetic Datasets

Due to the debate presented by Lou and Obradovic [7], we first evaluated the reliability of the dependence and conditional dependence measures in correctly identifying $\mathbf{MB}(Y)$ under multiple conditions by comparing BAHSIC to Proposed-F and Proposed-Z (Fig. 14.1). We compared these two algorithms because BAHSIC, Proposed-F and Proposed-Z have similar algorithmic structures but the former uses HSIC to measure dependence while the latter two use a K-CDM. We constructed synthetic Markov blankets containing six continuous variables (two parents, two children, two spouses) by (1) generating the data points of two parents and two spouses by drawing from a Gaussian distribution with a standard deviation of 1, (2) summing the two parents and adding Gaussian noise with a standard deviation of 1 to create the data points of Y, (3) similarly summing the spouses and Y and adding noise to create the data points of the two children. Thus, variables in $\mathbf{MB}(Y)$ were connected by linear weights of 1. We then equipped BAHSIC, Proposed-F and Proposed-Z with linear kernels. In Fig. 14.1, the solid lines represent the average ranking of $\mathbf{MB}(Y)$ with the corresponding 95% confidence intervals shown as two dashed lines of the same color.

For the first experiment, we introduced ten extraneous variables drawn from a Gaussian distribution with a standard deviation of 1 to the original seven variables (target plus six $\mathbf{MB}(Y)$ variables) and varied the number of data points from 1 to 500. We found that BAHSIC performed better in the small sample size range (<75) but was then overtaken by Proposed-F and Proposed-Z. In order to understand this phenomenon, recall that the parents and children display an association to the target in this case whereas the spouses do not. As a result, BAHSIC cannot detect the two spouses and saturates at an average rank of 3, whereas Proposed-F and Proposed-Z continue to improve. For the second experiment, we raised the noise level throughout the entire dataset from 0 to 5 standard deviations while keeping the sample size constant at 70 corresponding to 10 data points for the target and each of the six variables in $\mathbf{MB}(Y)$. Proposed-F and Proposed-Z performed better up to about a noise standard deviation of 1, suggesting that it may be more reliable to search for $\mathbf{MB}(Y)$ using dependence measures instead of conditional dependence measures in high noise situations. This is expected, since the spouses need a common child to be predictive [4], and thus their signal may be easily erased with noise.

Next, we re-connected the 17 variables with 1–100 edges, again with a sample size of 70. We also varied the number of extraneous variables from 1 to 128 with the same sample size. Finally, we changed the value of the linear weights from 0.1 to 2. Proposed-F and Proposed-Z outperformed BAHSIC in these last three experimental conditions across all values. Moreover, Proposed-F and Proposed-Z gave identical to near identical results in all of the five experiments; the difference was greatest in the extraneous variables experiment, but it was only by 2–3 ranks with 64 and 128 extraneous variables. These results suggest that both K-CDMs can perform better

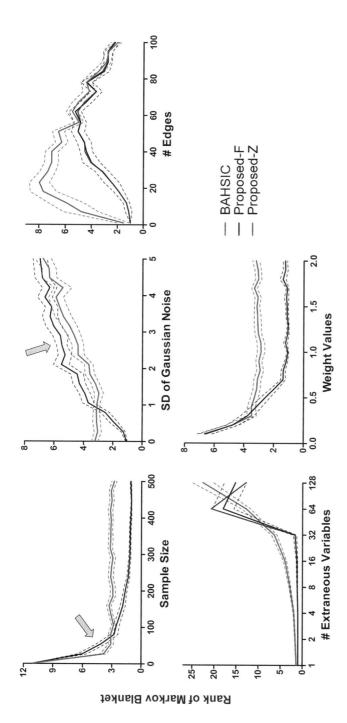

Fig. 14.1 Results from synthetic datasets assessing the accuracy of dependency and conditional dependency-based methods in detecting $\mathbf{MB}(Y)$ by comparing Proposed-F and Proposed-Z to BAHSIC. Solid lines represent the average rank of the Markov blanket and dotted lines represent the 95% confidence interval. Proposed-F and Proposed-Z outperform BAHSIC except in low sample size and high noise conditions as indicated by the arrows. Moreover, BAHSIC consistently fails to identify the spouses by saturating at a rank of 3, whereas the proposed algorithm does not

than dependence based methods in correctly identifying $\mathbf{MB}(Y)$ when the noise level is low enough and the sample size is large enough.

We compared Proposed-F and Proposed-Z to IAMB with Fisher's Z-test for the second set of synthetic experiments (Fig. 14.2). We wanted to compare the accuracy of directly performing backward elimination on the dataset using a K-CDM instead of first performing statistical testing with a forward selection step. The HITON-MB and MMMB algorithms were not included, since they are data efficient modifications of IAMB which do not help in better assessing the impact of the forward selection step; however, these two algorithms are included in the next section. We found that Proposed-F and Proposed-Z outperformed IAMB across all five experiments, since the forward selection step may prevent IAMB from considering all multivariate combinations when discovering $\mathbf{MB}(Y)$. Note that IAMB performs particularly poorly in the edges experiment as the Markov blanket size grows because statistical testing becomes unreliable with a fixed sample size. On the other hand, Proposed-F and Proposed-Z overcome this problem by not relying on statistical testing.

14.5.3 Expert-Designed Models and Real-World Datasets

We used three publicly available expert-designed Bayesian network models including Alarm (36 variables), Child (20), and Insurance (27) as well as two real-world datasets including CYTO (11; [10]) and the U.S. Linked Infant Birth and Death Dataset from 1991 (87; [8]). CYTO is a dataset of T-lymphocyte protein-protein interactions, and Infant is a dataset of clinical outcomes and decisions regarding infant births; in both of these, portions of $\mathbf{MB}(Y)$ have been experimentally verified and confirmed by experts. We appropriately incorporated RBF kernels with sigma set to the median distance between data points in all kernel methods to detect discrete non-linear patterns. The IAMB, HITON-MB, and MMMB algorithms were implemented with the G^2 test for discrete data. We iterated over all variables to obtain the mean rank and accuracy scores over different sample sizes. Results are shown in Figs. 14.3 and 14.4 for the expert-designed models and real-world datasets, respectively.

The results show that both Proposed-F and Proposed-Z outperform other feature ranking and subset selection methods in correctly identifying $\mathbf{MB}(Y)$ with larger sample sizes in the datasets of expert-designed models. Notice that the dependency based method BAHSIC plateaus at a relatively small sample size, but the proposed algorithm's performance continues to improve with larger sample sizes. These results held when using either the method from Fukumizu et al. [2] or Zhang et al. [18] as the K-CDM. For the real-world datasets, Proposed-F and Z outperformed all other conditional dependence-based algorithms. The results are less clear when comparing against the ranking algorithms in CYTO, since no algorithm consistently outperforms the others, but we observed that the proposed algorithm significantly outperforms Relief-F on occasion. For Infant, the proposed algorithm

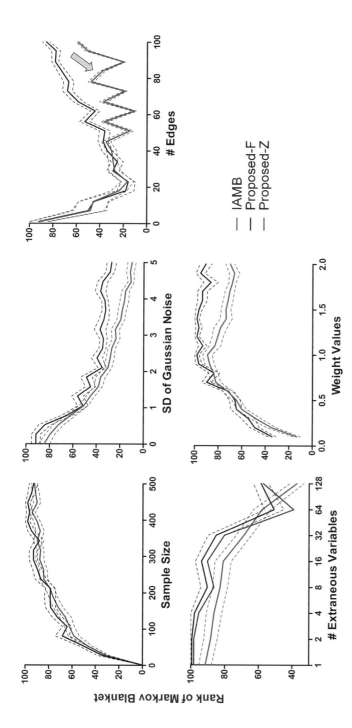

Fig. 14.2 Results from synthetic datasets assessing the impact of a forward selection step by comparing Proposed-F and Proposed-Z to IAMB. Solid lines and dotted lines represent the average value of the accuracy measure in Eq. (14.5) and 95% confidence intervals, respectively. Proposed-F and Proposed-Z outperform IAMB in all tested conditions. Notice that IAMB performs poorly in the edges experiment as indicated by the arrow, since statistical testing becomes unreliable with a growing $\mathbf{MB}(Y)$ size but fixed sample size

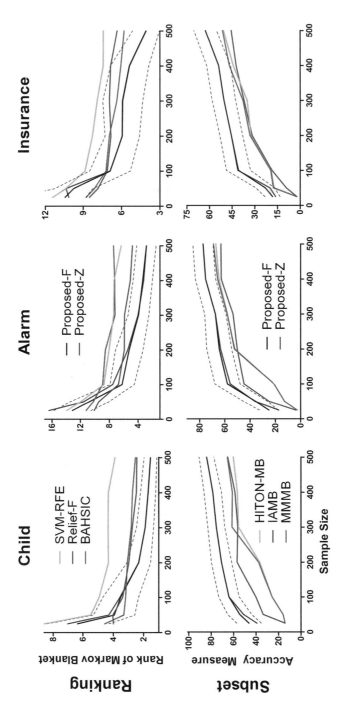

Fig. 14.3 Results from datasets created from expert-designed models. Solid lines and dotted lines again represent the average ranks of the Markov blanket or the average value of the accuracy measure in Eq. (14.5) and 95% confidence intervals, respectively. Proposed-F and Proposed-Z outperform all ranking methods across the larger sample sizes and subset selection methods across all of the sample sizes

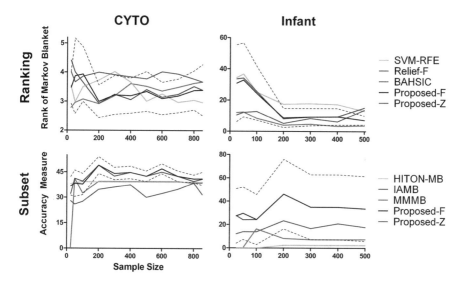

Fig. 14.4 Results from real-world datasets. Proposed-F and Proposed-Z outperform all subset selection methods across all of the sample sizes. However, both methods are consistently outperformed by BAHSIC in Infant

was outperformed by BAHSIC, since the Markov blankets in this dataset only contain parents and children; in this situation, kernel-based dependency methods may perform better, as we observed in the synthetic experiments.

14.6   Conclusion

We introduced a feature ranking algorithm that is useful for discovering **MB**(Y). The algorithm uses a K-CDM to eliminate variables using backward elimination. Overall, the method exhibits superior performance in synthetic data and in real datasets on average when compared to several feature ranking and subset selection methods.

Acknowledgements We thank Dr. Subramani Mani for providing the U.S. Linked Infant Birth and Death 1991 dataset. This research was funded by the National Library of Medicine grant T15 LM007059-24 to the University of Pittsburgh Biomedical Informatics Training Program and the National Institute of General Medical Sciences grant T32 GM008208 to the University of Pittsburgh Medical Scientist Training Program.

References

1. Constantin F Aliferis, Ioannis Tsamardinos, and Alexander Statnikov. Hiton: a novel markov blanket algorithm for optimal variable selection. In *AMIA Annual Symposium Proceedings*, volume 2003, page 21. American Medical Informatics Association, 2003.
2. Kenji Fukumizu, Francis R Bach, Michael I Jordan, et al. Kernel dimension reduction in regression. *The Annals of Statistics*, 37(4):1871–1905, 2009.
3. Arthur Gretton, Ralf Herbrich, Alexander Smola, Olivier Bousquet, and Bernhard Schölkopf. Kernel methods for measuring independence. *Journal of Machine Learning Research*, 6(Dec):2075–2129, 2005.
4. Isabelle Guyon, Constantin Aliferis, and André Elisseeff. Causal feature selection. In *Computational methods of feature selection*, pages 75–97. Chapman and Hall/CRC, 2007.
5. Patrik O Hoyer, Dominik Janzing, Joris M Mooij, Jonas Peters, and Bernhard Schölkopf. Nonlinear causal discovery with additive noise models. In *Advances in neural information processing systems*, pages 689–696, 2009.
6. Daphne Koller, Nir Friedman, and Francis Bach. *Probabilistic graphical models: principles and techniques*. MIT Press, 2009.
7. Qiang Lou and Zoran Obradovic. Feature selection by approximating the markov blanket in a kernel-induced space. In *ECAI:European Conference on Artificial Intelligence*, pages 797–802, 2010.
8. Subramani Mani and Gregory F Cooper. A study in causal discovery from population-based infant birth and death records. In *Proceedings of the AMIA Symposium*, page 315. American Medical Informatics Association, 1999.
9. Jose M Peña, Johan Björkegren, and Jesper Tegnér. Scalable, efficient and correct learning of markov boundaries under the faithfulness assumption. In *European Conference on Symbolic and Quantitative Approaches to Reasoning and Uncertainty*, pages 136–147. Springer, 2005.
10. Karen Sachs, Omar Perez, Dana Pe'er, Douglas A Lauffenburger, and Garry P Nolan. Causal protein-signaling networks derived from multiparameter single-cell data. *Science*, 308(5721):523–529, 2005.
11. Shohei Shimizu, Patrik O Hoyer, Aapo Hyvärinen, and Antti Kerminen. A linear non-gaussian acyclic model for causal discovery. *Journal of Machine Learning Research*, 7(Oct):2003–2030, 2006.
12. Le Song, Justin Bedo, Karsten M Borgwardt, Arthur Gretton, and Alex Smola. Gene selection via the bahsic family of algorithms. *Bioinformatics*, 23(13):i490–i498, 2007.
13. Peter Spirtes. An anytime algorithm for causal inference. In *AISTATS: Proceedings of the Eighth International Workshop on Artificial Intelligence and Statistics*, 2001.
14. Peter Spirtes, Clark N Glymour, Richard Scheines, David Heckerman, Christopher Meek, Gregory Cooper, and Thomas Richardson. *Causation, prediction, and search*. MIT Press, 2000.
15. Alexander Statnikov, Nikita I Lytkin, Jan Lemeire, and Constantin F Aliferis. Algorithms for discovery of multiple markov boundaries. *Journal of Machine Learning Research*, 14(Feb):499–566, 2013.
16. Ioannis Tsamardinos and Constantin F Aliferis. Towards principled feature selection: relevancy, filters and wrappers. In *AISTATS: Proceedings of the Ninth International Workshop on Artificial Intelligence and Statistics*, 2003.
17. Ioannis Tsamardinos, Laura E Brown, and Constantin F Aliferis. The max-min hill-climbing bayesian network structure learning algorithm. *Machine learning*, 65(1):31–78, 2006.
18. Kun Zhang, Jonas Peters, Dominik Janzing, and Bernhard Schölkopf. Kernel-based conditional independence test and application in causal discovery. In *Proceedings of the Twenty-Seventh Conference on Uncertainty in Artificial Intelligence*, pages 804–813. AUAI Press, 2011.

Printed in the United States
By Bookmasters